PRINCIPLES OF LEGAL RESEARCH

Third Edition

Kent C. Olson

Senior Research Librarian and Assistant Professor, General Faculty
University of Virginia School of Law

Aaron S. Kirschenfeld

Clinical Assistant Professor of Law and
Digital Initiatives Law Librarian
University of North Carolina School of Law

Ingrid Mattson

Interim Director of the Law Library and Lecturer in Law
Benjamin N. Cardozo School of Law

CONCISE HORNBOOK SERIES™

WEST
ACADEMIC
PUBLISHING

© 2009 Thomson Reuters
© 2015 LEG, Inc. d/b/a West Academic
© 2020 LEG, Inc. d/b/a West Academic
    444 Cedar Street, Suite 700
    St. Paul, MN 55101
    1-877-888-1330

Printed in the United States of America

ISBN: 978-1-64020-805-6

For my friends and coworkers at Rockfish Wildlife Sanctuary – KCO

For my parents, my teachers, my colleagues, and for Deb – ASK

For Kip, my children, and the Bunde family – IAM

Preface

This work is a guide for all legal researchers. It covers many more resources than a beginning law student needs but fewer than experienced legal researchers encounter in their careers. It teaches the principles of how legal institutions like legislatures, administrative agencies, and courts create legal information, and how that information is arranged by publishers into the resources a researcher must learn how to use. It is also a work that one can reference to refresh one's memory of how less-familiar resources function. Thus, the material is suitable for use in a legal research course, in practice, and at many points in between.

The book begins with an introduction to legal sources and to managing legal research problems. Secondary sources, often the easiest place to begin research, are discussed next, but to understand them you need to know something about the primary sources they analyze. The organization of primary sources is based on the treatment of the three branches of government identified in the Constitution. Following discussion of constitutional law, the legislature (Article I) is treated first, followed by the executive branch (Article II) and then the judiciary (Article III). Chapters on specialized materials for litigation and transactional practice follow, emphasizing the importance of understanding these valuable tools.

The final two chapters provide a brief treatment of international and foreign legal research, because no modern practice is untouched by globalization.

You will notice some changes in this edition of the book. First, two new voices have contributed insights and efforts to the whole of the work. Second, chapters have been added or significantly reorganized to respond to a changing legal research landscape. The chapters have also been arranged into five overarching parts that should make the book easier to navigate and reference. Third, online access to resources, when available, has been emphasized to help researchers access what they need when and where they need it.

Principles of Legal Research is the successor to *How to Find the Law*, a venerable work that was published in nine editions between 1931 and 1989. It still bears some genetic imprint of that work, but the world of legal research has of course changed dramatically. The primacy of printed materials in law libraries is long gone, microform has become a delivery vehicle of last resort, and subscription databases and government and academic websites take more responsibility for disseminating the primary and secondary sources of the law. Not everything, however, has been digitized or is available free online, and a thorough legal researcher needs to be familiar with both online and print materials as well as both free and subscription online resources. This book provides an overview of all of these resources. It includes a bit more historical background than some researchers may feel they need, but much of this material has been moved to the footnotes, which may provide a sense of the continuum from printed to electronic research as well as leads to further reading.

Legal research, like most areas at the intersection of law and technology, is in a state of flux. Lexis and Westlaw remain the preeminent platforms for legal research, but new publishers and products arrive on the scene regularly. Some become lasting research tools, others are acquired and integrated into existing platforms, and the rest fold or fade into obscurity. To the extent possible, we've included a wide range of these other online resources. Time will tell which ones remain for inclusion in future editions of this book.

Even though most researchers do the overwhelming majority of their research online, most of the illustrations are still based on PDFs or printed sources rather than screenshots, as platforms and their interfaces change rapidly. Browser windows also make for relatively poor book illustrations, as their information is unlocked by scrolling and by clicking from one site to another. A printed page still conveys more information in one image.

Any book is already becoming obsolete as soon as it is published, and this is certainly true of one with references to hundreds of websites. All links were current and active as of June 2020, but some will undoubtedly disappear or migrate. Some references have been archived with the Perma.cc service, and a regularly updated list of links to every site in this book is available through the University of Virginia Law Library website (libguides.law.virginia.edu/PLR).

In preparing this edition, we each benefited greatly from the help of many people, too numerous to name here. We have all appreciated the support of our colleagues and administrators throughout. In teaching our students, we have learned more than we could on our own. And in collaborating over the course of a year and a half, we have benefitted from each other despite the physical distance between us. Scholarly bibliography is vital to the survival and growth of our profession, and we genuinely hope that this work will be a valuable and lasting contribution. And while many have offered ideas and suggestions or have read draft chapters, any errors that remain are our own.

The first edition of *Principles of Legal Research* was dedicated to Morris Cohen, the retired librarian of the Yale Law School who was for many years the lead author of *How to Find the Law*. Kent, the lead author now, wrote then, "Morris is truly the godfather of legal bibliography, and legal research is just one aspect of his wide-ranging interests. In his ninth decade he still approaches life with more joy and curiosity than just about anyone I've met." The legal research community lost Morris in December 2010, but his voice still echoes in many passages of this book. For us, it continues to be an honor and a challenge to be his successor.

KENT C. OLSON
AARON S. KIRSCHENFELD
INGRID MATTSON

Charlottesville, Virginia
Chapel Hill, North Carolina
New York, New York
June 2020

Acknowledgments

Illustrations 2-1, 2-2, 2-3, 2-5, 3-3, 4-2, 4-3, 5-1, 5-3, 5-4, 5-6, 5-7, 5-8, 5-9, 5-12, 6-7, 8-6 10-2, 10-3, 11-3, 11-4, 11-7, 12-1, 12-2, 12-3, 12-6, 12-7, 12-8, 12-9, 12-10, 12-11, 12-12, 12-13, 13-1, 13-6, 13-7, 14-1, 14-2, 15-1, and 16-1 are reproduced with the permission of Thomson Reuters.

Illustration 2-4 from Restatement Third, Torts: Liability for Physical and Emotional Harm copyright © 2010 by The American Law Institute. Reproduced with permission. All rights reserved.

Illustration 3-1 is reprinted with the permission of Pace Law Review.

Illustration 3-2 is reprinted with the permission of the Minnesota State Bar Association.

Illustrations 3-4, 3-5, and 4-5 are reproduced with permission of HeinOnline.

Illustration 3-6 is reproduced with permission of EBSCO Information Services.

Illustration 3-7 is reproduced with permission of SSRN.

Illustrations 4-4, 5-2, 5-5, 5-13, 10-4, 11-5, 11-6, 12-4, 12-5, 12-14, 15-3, and 16-4 are reproduced with the permission of LexisNexis. Any further reproduction in any form without permission of LexisNexis is prohibited.

Illustration 5-14 is reprinted with the permission of Cheryl Nyberg.

The screen shots and their contents in Illustrations 6-5, 13-5, and 16-3 are published with permission of ProQuest LLC. Further reproduction is prohibited without permission. Inquiries may be made to: ProQuest LLC, 789 E. Eisenhower Pkwy, Ann Arbor, MI 48106-1346 USA. Telephone (734) 761-4700; E-mail: info@proquest.com; Web-page: www.proquest.com.

Illustration 6-8 is reproduced with permission of the copyright holder, the Michigan Legislative Council.

Illustration 9-3 is reproduced with permission of Municipal Code Corporation and Leon County, Florida, and Longmont, Colorado.

Illustration 11-8 is used with permission from the National Center for State Courts, Court Statistics Project, www.courtstatistics.org, 2014.

Illustrations 9-1 and 9-2 are reproduced with permission of the State of Montana.

Illustrations 13-2, 13-3, 15-2, and 16-5 are reproduced with permission from Bloomberg Law. Copyright (2020) by The Bureau of National Affairs, Inc. (800-372-1033) http://www.bloombergindustry.com.

Illustration 14-3 is reprinted with permission of the Florida Office of the State Courts Administrator.

Illustration 16-2 is reproduced with permission of Cardiff University.

Illustration 17-1 is reproduced with permission of Oxford University Press.

Illustrations 17-5 (from the United Nations Treaty Series) and 17-7 (from the Multilateral Treaties Deposited with the Secretary-General) are reprinted with the permission of the United Nations. © 1992 United Nations.

Illustration 17-6 is reproduced with permission of the copyright holder, the Institute of Advanced Legal Studies, School of Advanced Study, University of London.

Illustration 17-8 is used with permission of the International Court of Justice.

Illustrations 18-1 and 18-2 are reproduced by permission of RELX (UK) Limited, trading as LexisNexis.

Summary of Contents

Table of Contents

___

PART II. CONSTITUTIONS AND THE LEGISLATIVE BRANCH

PART III. THE EXECUTIVE BRANCH

PART IV. THE JUDICIARY

PART V. ADVANCED RESEARCH AREAS

PRINCIPLES OF LEGAL RESEARCH

Third Edition

Introduction

CONTEXT AND FRAMEWORK

The modern world is awash in information. Millions of published books have been supplemented by billions of web pages, many of which provide access to documents that would once have been nearly impossible to obtain. Navigating successfully through this sea of information is necessary for developing knowledge of a legal topic, and legal knowledge is an essential component of competent legal representation.[1]

Legal research is the ability to identify the rules that govern a situation and find resources that explain, analyze, or criticize those rules. These resources yield the knowledge necessary to provide accurate and insightful advice, to draft effective documents, or to defend a client's (or one's own) rights in court.

But you must know the landscape of available information to know where to begin and how to understand what you find. Most importantly, this foundation will help you know whether other relevant materials may yet be undiscovered—in print or online. With this knowledge comes confidence that the information you find is current, accurate, and complete, and that you're not missing anything that might affect or undermine the conclusions you reach or the arguments you make.

The major legal information vendors offer simple search boxes that make research appear easy and suggest everything you need is online in one place: their platform. Artificial-intelligence-powered search algorithms deliver predictive suggestions to expedite your research. These technological developments may direct you to resources you had not considered and may provide powerful new ways to understand information. Still, if you lack foundational knowledge of the U.S. legal system, the documents produced in the law-making process, and basic principles of organization for legal information, at best these tools will give you starting points to help you begin your research. At worst, they will give you the false sense that you have gathered everything you need to completely and accurately resolve a legal problem.

---

[1] Rule 1.1 of the Model Rules of Professional Conduct provides that a lawyer "shall provide competent representation to a client. Competent representation requires the legal knowledge, skill, thoroughness and preparation reasonably necessary for the representation."

1

Finding relevant information is only the first step towards competent representation. Analyzing that information, understanding its significance, and applying it to a new situation are essential components of the research process.[2] Legal research works hand-in-hand with the legal analysis skills learned in doctrinal law school classes like Torts and Constitutional Law. These classes teach you to evaluate factual situations and to determine the relevant fields of legal doctrine. Legal research skills give you the ability to identify the specific rules that apply to a particular situation.

Several aspects of the American legal system shape the process of legal research:

— The basic parameters are determined by the Constitution of the United States, which created a federal system with both national and state governments making laws.

— The federal and state constitutions all divide lawmaking power among legislative, executive, and judicial branches.

— The United States is part of the *common law* legal tradition, in which the law adapts and grows through the decisions of the courts as well as through the passage of statutes by legislatures.

— In both practice and scholarship, the law is divided into numerous doctrinal areas drawing from different sources of law. The boundaries between these areas can overlap, but each has its own distinct rules and literature.

Federalism. Instead of having a single government creating the laws enforced throughout the country, the United States is composed of fifty states (as well as territorial and tribal governments)[3] that

---

[2] " 'Legal research' is not merely a search for information; it is primarily a struggle for understanding. The need to think deeply about the information discovered is what makes legal research the task of a professional lawyer." Michael J. Lynch, *An Impossible Task but Everybody Has to Do It—Teaching Legal Research in Law Schools,* 89 LAW LIBR. J. 415, 415 (1997).

[3] On territorial law generally, see STANLEY K. LAUGHLIN, JR., THE LAW OF UNITED STATES TERRITORIES AND AFFILIATED TERRITORIES (1995), and Stanley K. Laughlin, Jr., *U.S. Territories and Affiliated Jurisdictions: Colonialism or Reasonable Choice for Small Societies?,* 37 OHIO N.U. L. REV. 429 (2011).

Native Americans have sovereign rights of self-government, including the power to pass laws and have court systems. Native American tribes are generally subject to federal law but not to state law, except under limited circumstances. COHEN'S HANDBOOK OF FEDERAL INDIAN LAW (Nell Jessup Newton ed., 2017, available on Lexis) is a foundational treatise. Reference resources include AMERICAN INDIAN LAW DESKBOOK (Conference of Western Attorneys General eds., 2018 ed., available on Westlaw), ENCYCLOPEDIA OF UNITED STATES INDIAN POLICY AND LAW (Paul Finkelman & Tim Alan Garrison eds., 2009), and MATTHEW L. M. FLETCHER, PRINCIPLES OF FEDERAL INDIAN LAW (2017). The University of Oklahoma College of Law's *American Indian Law Review* focuses on this topic, but relevant articles can be found in other law reviews as well. For more information, see Kelly Kunsch, *A Legal Practitioner's Guide to Indian and Tribal Law Research,* 5 AM. INDIAN L.J. 102 (2017).

create laws governing their citizens. The federal government has only the limited, specific powers granted to it under the Constitution, and the Tenth Amendment provides: "The powers not delegated to the United States by the Constitution, nor prohibited by it to the States, are reserved to the States respectively, or to the people." Many major areas of law, such as commercial law, criminal law, and family law, are governed primarily by state law and can differ dramatically between jurisdictions.

Federal law, of course, governs a wide range of activity under Article 1, Section 8 of the Constitution, such as the powers to collect taxes, to provide for the general welfare, and to regulate interstate commerce. Over the past century, federal legislation has come to encompass an ever-wider area of activity. Article VI, the Supremacy Clause, declares that the Constitution and laws made in pursuance thereof are the supreme law of the land, and that federal law governs in case of conflict between federal and state laws.

In legal research you must determine whether an issue is governed by federal or state law, but overlaps and conflicts in federal and state jurisdiction can make this a much more complicated question than it initially seems.

Three Branches of Government. Both federal and state governments are divided into legislative, executive, and judicial branches.

— The Legislature. As the elected voice of the citizens, the legislature is the primary lawmaking body of government. It raises and spends money, defines crimes, regulates commerce, and generally determines public policy by enacting statutes. Because statute drafters can rarely foresee all the situations to which their work may apply, the courts usually must interpret, clarify, and explain statutory language in the course of resolving legal controversies.

— The Executive. The executive branch consists of the President or governor, as well as most government agencies. The President's "executive power of the government" under Article II of the Constitution means that this branch is charged with enforcing the law. To do so fairly and predictably, it creates legally binding rules and standards in a variety of ways. The President and most governors issue executive orders, and administrative agencies provide detailed regulations governing activity within their areas of expertise. Agencies also act in a "quasi-judicial" capacity by conducting hearings and issuing decisions to resolve particular disputes. These *administrative law* sources are frequently less well publicized than statutes and court decisions, but they may be just as important in determining legal rights and responsibilities. Attorneys in heavily regulated areas such as securities law or telecommunications may work more frequently with agency pronouncements than with legislative enactments.

— **The Judiciary.** The judicial branch plays a complex role in this system. Judges apply the language of constitutions and statutes to court cases, which often involve circumstances that were not foreseen when the laws were enacted. These judicial interpretations can become as important as the text of the provisions they interpret. The courts have determined, for example, that sexual harassment is a form of employment discrimination under the Civil Rights Act of 1964 even though those words do not appear in the statute. Through the power of judicial review, asserted by Chief Justice John Marshall in the landmark case of *Marbury v. Madison*,[4] the courts also determine whether the acts of the legislative and executive branches are within the scope of their constitutional authority.

Each of these three branches of government has lawmaking power. Law school classes may emphasize court opinions, but many research issues are resolved more directly by statutes, regulations, and other administrative law sources.

The Common Law. In the common law system that the American colonists brought from Great Britain, the law is expressed in an evolving body of doctrine determined by judges in specific cases, rather than through the civil law paradigm of a group of codified abstract principles that is followed in many countries including most of mainland Europe and Latin America. As established rules are adapted to meet new situations, the common law grows and changes over time.[5]

An essential element of the common law is the doctrine of precedent, or *stare decisis* ("let the decision stand"). Under this doctrine, courts are bound to follow earlier decisions. These decisions guide later courts faced with similar cases, and aid in preventing further disputes. People can study earlier cases, evaluate the legal impact of planned conduct, and modify their behavior to conform to existing rules. Precedent is designed to provide both fairness and stability. People similarly situated are similarly dealt with, and judgments are consistent, rather than arbitrary, so that the consequences of contemplated conduct can be predicted by referring to the treatment afforded similar conduct in the past.

---

[4]   5 U.S. (1 Cranch) 137 (1803).

[5]   On the various meanings of "the common law," see Morris L. Cohen, *The Common Law in the American Legal System: The Challenge of Conceptual Research*, 81 LAW LIBR. J. 13 (1989), and the works it cites.

It is the role of judicial decisions as precedent that gives them such a vital place in American legal research. The precedential value of a decision is determined in large part by a court's place in the judicial hierarchy. Each jurisdiction, federal and state, has a system of trial and appellate courts, with a court of last resort (usually, but not always, called a supreme court) that creates rules that are binding on lower courts in the system. A central function of courts of last resort and other appellate courts is establishing rules of conduct for society, as well as simply determining the rights of the parties appearing before them.

Decisions from a higher court in a given jurisdiction are *binding* or *mandatory authority* and must be followed by a lower court in the same jurisdiction. Decisions from courts in other jurisdictions are not binding but may be very useful if a court in another state has considered a situation similar to that in issue. A decision that is not binding in a jurisdiction is called *persuasive authority*. A court may choose to follow its lead and reach a similar conclusion, or it may consider it inapplicable or poorly reasoned and arrive at a very different result.

When researching case law, pay attention to which court issued a decision to determine whether it is binding or persuasive authority for your situation.

Doctrinal Areas. Legal scholarship and the law school curriculum sort legal issues into distinct areas of doctrine such as contract, criminal law, property, and torts. Most legal problems also involve both substance (the rules governing the underlying activity) and procedure (the rules governing the ways in which legal proceedings are conducted). These classifications provide a framework for analyzing legal situations and applying a particular body of rules. Legal materials also follow this paradigm, and treatises and other resources often focus on specific fields such as torts or federal civil procedure. Being able to analyze a problem's doctrinal areas is key to knowing where to look for answers.

That said, it is necessary to learn how to classify an issue without pigeonholing it too narrowly. Analysis within a particular doctrinal field can clarify a specific issue, but most situations contain issues from a number of substantive and procedural areas. Analogous problems in other areas of law can also provide clarification and guidance in analyzing a novel or undecided legal issue.

As you develop experience in a particular area of law, your growing familiarity with its major statutes, cases, and regulations, and with the resources practitioners frequently use, will make you a more efficient and confident researcher.

Part I

STARTING POINTS

Chapter 1

RESEARCH METHODS
AND PROCESS

Table of Sections

Legal research is not a one-size-fits-all endeavor. No two research inquiries are alike. A wide range of knowledge and a diverse collection of resources are required for effective and thorough research. A major online platform such as Lexis or Westlaw is effective and sufficient for some projects but not all. For other research projects, you will need to consult a variety of books and online platforms with an almost limitless array of information.

There are, however, basic concepts that will enhance your work no matter what course it follows. This chapter outlines some of the baselines of research methodology, then provides a broad overview of how to approach a research project.

§ 1.1 THE FORMS OF LEGAL INFORMATION

While legal information bears similarities to literature in other disciplines, several key features distinguish research in the law. First, law is unique in that many historical sources from decades or centuries ago continue to have just as much validity as the latest material available online. Second, researchers must also understand

9

the crucial dichotomy in law between primary and secondary sources. Finally, even though researchers do most of their work online, legal research cannot be limited to digital platforms. Some content is still published only in print or has not yet been digitized.

(a) Current and Historical Information

The legal system is created over the course of time, and the law in force today is a combination of old and new enactments and decisions. The United States Constitution has been in force for over 230 years, and many judicial doctrines can be traced back even farther. Other laws are just days or weeks old, as legislatures, courts, and executive agencies continue to address issues of current concern.

These laws have been published as they were issued, and they retain their force and effect until they are expressly repealed or overruled. A medical text from the 18th century has little current value, but a judicial decision or statute from that period can still be binding law today. A large law library or a comprehensive online research platform has millions of documents dating back hundreds of years. The basic tools of legal research have been shaped by the need for coherent access to this vast body of information.

When researching statutes and regulations, for example, you are usually trying to identify the laws currently in effect. To facilitate this research, government agencies and publishers organize statutes and regulations in force by subject in codes, which are accessible online by keyword or in print through extensive indexes. Even laws that were repealed years ago, however, may still be important in resolving disputes. Interpreting a deed or will may require finding the statutes in force when it was drafted. Understanding a statute often involves examining documents from the time when specific language in issue was considered and enacted. To determine the law that governs a particular situation, you may need to examine a wide range of both current and historical sources.

Case research is even more complicated, because a court decision remains "the law" unless it has been reversed or overruled. A thorough search for relevant case law must cover decades or centuries of court decisions. The most widely used approach is keyword searching in databases containing the full text of thousands of opinions. More traditional means of access to court opinions, once limited to print format, have been adapted to make online research more focused and powerful. These include digests classifying summaries of points from cases; encyclopedias and treatises summarizing and comparing similar cases; and citators that can be used to trace doctrines forward in time.

Lawyers and others interested in the legal system also need to keep up with new developments, and numerous resources exist to provide current information. New statutes, regulations, and court decisions are issued by the government and by commercial publishers, both in print and online. Newsletters, legal journals, and blogs provide notice of and analyze these new developments. In addition, the codes and texts lawyers use are updated regularly to reflect changes. New documents can be incorporated into databases within minutes of their release. Many print publications are updated through the use of *pocket parts*, supplements that fit inside the back covers of bound volumes, while others are issued in looseleaf binders and updated with supplementary inserts or replacement pages. No matter what type of resource is used, electronic or print, it is essential to verify that it provides current information.

(b) Primary and Secondary Sources

Legal research makes an important distinction between *primary* and *secondary sources*. Primary sources, sometimes called *primary authorities*, are the official pronouncements of the governmental lawmakers: the court decisions, legislation, and regulations that form the basis of legal doctrine. Secondary sources are works that are not themselves law, but that discuss or analyze legal doctrine.[1] Whether a primary or secondary source, each document must be considered with a sense of its place in the hierarchy of authority.

Not all primary sources have the same force for all purposes. A decision from a state supreme court is binding authority in its jurisdiction and must be followed by the lower state courts. A state statute also must be followed within the state. Other primary sources are only *persuasive authority*; a court in one state may be influenced by decisions in other states faced with similar issues, but it is free to make up its own mind. A statute or regulation from one state is not even persuasive authority in another state.

Secondary sources include treatises, hornbooks, *Restatements*, practice manuals, and the academic journals known as law reviews. Secondary sources serve many important functions in legal research. Scholarly commentaries can have a persuasive influence on the law-making process by pointing out problems in current legal doctrine and suggesting solutions. More often, they serve to clarify the bewildering array of statutes and court decisions, or they provide current awareness about developing legal doctrines.

---

[1] This sense of the terms *primary* and *secondary* is different from that found in history and other disciplines, in which a "primary source" can be a letter or contemporary newspaper account and a "secondary source" is a later scholarly analysis.

A secondary source cannot be binding authority, but it may have more persuasive force than rulings of courts in other jurisdictions. Even primary and secondary sources that are not persuasive authority can be useful research resources, because their references can help analyze a problem and can provide fruitful research leads through references to both primary and other secondary sources.

Resources in disciplines other than law are also essential in legal research. In the 1800s and early 1900s, American judicial opinions typically cited only legal authorities in support of their conclusions. Many modern judicial opinions, however, articulate quite clearly the social, economic, political, and even psychological consequences with which they are concerned. Law has become an interdisciplinary study, and research in materials considered "nonlegal" is an inherent part of legal research.

(c) Print and Digital Sources

There was a time when all information necessary to resolve a legal question was available only in print. Today, however, almost all legal researchers begin their search online and move to print as needed.[2] Online research resources have several clear advantages over print resources. A variety of tasks that were once conducted with separate print sources, such as finding cases, checking the current validity of their holdings, and tracking down secondary commentary, can be integrated much more smoothly. An online resource can have much more current information than a print resource. Hyperlinks between documents allow you to follow lines of authority and reasoning, from a case to a secondary source, for example, and from there to another secondary source or statute. The ability to search full text makes it easy to find documents that address a specific confluence of factual and legal topics.

The fact that a great deal of primary and secondary material is now available online simply means that it is easier to access (once you know where to look and how online legal research databases function). It does not mean there is no need to be knowledgeable about the complete legal information landscape, including what is available only in print and why that might be the case.

---

[2] In 2012 the American Bar Association added Comment 8 to Model Rule of Professional Conduct 1.1, which pertains to an attorney's duty to maintain competence: "To maintain the requisite knowledge and skill, a lawyer should keep abreast of changes in the law and its practice, including the benefits and risks associated with relevant technology. . . ." As of 2020, thirty-eight states have formally adopted some version of Comment 8, the duty to require technological competence. *See* Robert Ambrogi, *Tech Competence*, LAWSITES (www.lawsitesblog.com/tech-competence) [https://perma.cc/9HV6-JK26].

Understanding the factors influencing the transition from predominantly print to digital formats provides a framework for knowing when to consult resources beyond those available on major legal information vendor platforms such as Westlaw and Lexis. Digital case law collections are fairly comprehensive; if it can be found in a print reporter, it can typically be found online in any of several databases. Online collections of other materials, however, have often been built by adding born-digital content as it was created, and by digitizing print content, often working from oldest to newest. Digitization of thousands of pages of print material takes time and money, and some vendors have prioritized adding older, rarer, more fragile material to their online collections. It is not uncommon to find gaps in coverage, often from the 1970s through the mid-1990s.

Also worth noting when considering what information is available online is the scope of library subscriptions and licensing agreements. Commercial databases can be quite expensive, and even if a collection has been fully digitized, coverage can be limited by the package available in your library. Coverage of copyrighted material can also vary dramatically between platforms. For example, Columbia Law Review Association, Inc. has entered into agreements allowing issues of the *Columbia Law Review* to be published and distributed online, but one platform has the full run of the *Columbia Law Review* online dating back to 1901; another has issues from 1951 to present; and a third goes back to October 1982. If you are attempting to find "every" law review article ever written on a particular topic, limiting your search to the latter databases would be a mistake.

The cost of digitization can also influence what is available online. For example, federal legislative history and pleadings in federal cases are often far more readily available online than the same content for states, which may be less able to prioritize funding for making this information accessible online.

As you can see, assuming everything is online is problematic. Develop a basic working knowledge of the factors that influence digital and print publication, and do not abandon common sense when trying to determine why you cannot find an answer in the place or format in which you think it should be found.

§ 1.2   RESEARCH METHODS

Legal research is not simply gathering information, but being able to analyze that information and grasp its significance. Applying rules of law to a specific set of facts, the process of legal research and analysis, requires determining the scope and meaning of various rules and how they pertain to a given situation. It is a process that requires a significant commitment of time and focus.[3]

Researchers forced to work only with an uncontrolled mass of electronic data can quickly find themselves drowning in unsorted information. Most online keyword searches can find only those documents that match their terms and will never discover related documents that use different wording (including terminology that changes over time) or involve slightly different facts. Some of the more sophisticated platforms use algorithms that can find some relevant documents even if they do not use the same terms, but relying on algorithms is a poor substitute for exercising your own judgment about the particular facts and issues of your case. Secondary sources such as treatises and encyclopedias, online or in print, are still invaluable starting points for understanding the terminology and parameters of an area of law.

No single process will work for all research situations. With experience comes an understanding of which resources to consult first in each situation, and how to use them most effectively.

(a) Finding Legal Information on the Internet

A quest for legal information often begins with a general search on the internet. Indeed, a web search can lead to a great deal of useful information, but it is important to know how to use the internet effectively and to understand its limitations. A search engine can point you in the general direction you need, but there are more focused ways to find answers and not all legal information is available free online. Just as a doctor must do more than a quick Google search before prescribing a course of treatment, a competent legal researcher needs to find the correct answers—not just some information. An online search can be a helpful starting point, but legal literature has a complex structure that is designed to lead you to the answers you need.

Free internet sites can be valuable sources of legal information. Sites provided by the federal and state governments are particularly useful and generally reliable. Statutes and regulations in force for most jurisdictions are available for free online, as is most case law. Among the most useful sites are those providing access to previously hard-to-find resources such as legislative documents, administrative agency materials, and court documents. What's missing from free

---

[3] *See, e.g., Williams v. Leeke,* 584 F.2d 1336, 1340 (4th Cir. 1978), *cert. denied,* 442 U.S. 911 (1979) ("We believe that meaningful legal research on most legal problems cannot be done in forty-five minute intervals."); *Glover v. Johnson,* 931 F. Supp. 1360, 1369 (E.D. Mich. 1996), *aff'd in part, rev'd in part,* 138 F.3d 229 (6th Cir. 1998) ("[O]rdinarily, meaningful legal research cannot be performed in time periods of less than two hours.") (quoting a Michigan Department of Corrections policy directive).

internet sites and apps are most of the major secondary sources and the structure tying together material such as statutes and cases.

When using information from free internet sites, always evaluate the currency and accuracy of the resource. Even government sites can present obsolete information without indicating that it is no longer current. Websites can also be biased or selective in coverage. Verifying that a website is current, accurate, and impartial leads to greater confidence in the information it contains.

Another problem with internet sites is *link rot*, the fact that material can be available one day but disappear the next.[4] URLs can change frequently, but a variety of strategies can be employed to locate "missing" webpages. Hunting around the site or running a site-specific search can often locate material that has been moved and assigned a different URL. Searching the original URL in Google and then clicking the upside-down triangle next to relevant search results and selecting "Cached" can give you a screenshot of what the page looked like the last time Google crawled it. The Internet Archive's Wayback Machine (archive.org) and other repositories provide some access to "obsolete" information. Specialized law-focused collections are available, including the End of Term Web Archive (eotarchive. cdlib.org/), the Federal Courts Web Archive (www.loc.gov/collections/federal-courts-web-archive/), and court websites' collections of archived links such as the Supreme Court's Online Sources Cited in Opinions (supremecourt.gov/opinions/cited_urls). Link rot remains an unsolved problem, although initiatives such as Perma.cc are now underway to provide permanent archives of webpages cited in journal articles and court opinions.[5]

Search Engines. Most people's first stop on the internet is a search engine, a service with a box in which to type keywords.[6] This

---

[4] A study in 2002 found that only thirty percent of URLs in law review citations still worked after four years. Mary Rumsey, *Runaway Train: Problems of Permanence, Accessibility, and Stability in the Use of Web Sources in Law Review Citations*, 94 LAW LIBR. J. 27 (2002). In a more recent study, almost one-third of internet citations in Supreme Court opinions no longer led to the information cited. Raizel Liebler & June Liebert, *Something Rotten in the State of Legal Citation: The Life Span of a United States Supreme Court Citation Containing an Internet Link (1996–2010)*, 15 YALE J.L. & TECH. 273 (2013). *See also* Laura Gordon-Murnane, *Linkrot + Content Drift = Reference Rot*, ONLINE SEARCHER, Nov./Dec. 2018, at 10; Adam Liptak, *In Supreme Court Opinions, Web Links to Nowhere*, N.Y. TIMES, Sept. 24, 2013, at A13.

[5] For more on Perma.cc, see Jonathan Zittrain et al., *Perma: Scoping and Addressing the Problem of Link Rot and Reference Rot in Legal Citations*, 127 HARV. L. REV. F. 176 (2014).

[6] "Now even the most traditional-minded scholar generally begins by consulting a search engine. As a cheerful editor at Cambridge University Press recently told me, 'Conservatively, ninety-five per cent of all scholarly inquiries start at Google.'" Anthony Grafton, *Future Reading: Digitization and its Discontents*, NEW YORKER, Nov. 5, 2007, at 50, 52.

is often a very sensible approach because a simple search can frequently lead directly to relevant information. This is particularly true if you are looking for specific facts or for the website of a particular institution or organization.

Internet searches are a place to start, but they rarely provide thorough and reliable answers to most legal questions. Sources of the law are too diverse and complex for a search engine to pick out authoritative documents from the mass of information available online. A search is ideal for finding specific documents, but legal research also requires familiarity with more specialized sites.

A number of search engines are available, each with features that are evolving over time. The market is currently dominated by Google (www.google.com), although several other major search engines such as Bing (www.bing.com) and DuckDuckGo (duckduck go.com) are also available. Search engines are designed to be simple, but you can achieve more relevant results with just a small amount of sophistication. Being an advanced web searcher requires five simple attributes:

— **Know the search engine's syntax.** Each search engine has its own rules for how it combines terms and searches the web. Your results can be more focused if you can understand and manipulate how words are connected to reach a result. Simply typing a string of words into a box may not retrieve the same result as a search that combines terms in a specific way. Google, for example, assumes an *and* between search terms, but you can search for synonyms by using *OR* (capitalized), and you can exclude a term by putting a minus sign directly in front of it. Most search engines have search tips or help screens with examples.

— **Use the Advanced Search screen.** Go beyond the basic search box and use advanced search options available from most search engines. Google's Advanced Search screen (www.google.com/ advanced_search) (available from the *Settings* menu on the main Google search screen) has very useful options such as searching only words in page titles, specifying documents in a particular format, or limiting retrieval to a particular domain or domain type. This makes it easy, for example, to search a specific agency's website or to retrieve only PDF documents from *.edu* domains. Like using search syntax correctly, the advanced search screen allows you to be more specific about the types of material for which you are searching.

— **Don't assume the search engine knows best.** Search engine algorithms attempt, by inference, to deliver results users really want, not just what they have entered in the search bar. That might be fine if you're looking for a good local restaurant, but not all searches are so simple. Legal researchers would be well served to evaluate search results and refine searches using more legally relevant terminology to produce more relevant results. Sometimes simply adding the word "law" can improve search results, and identifying the jurisdiction in your search may lead to more relevant websites.

    — Try more than one search engine. Despite the convenience of using a familiar search engine for most purposes, different search engines will return different results—and a second search engine may find sites or documents that the first one missed. Different search engines crawl and index webpages differently. For most purposes, the familiar favorite is probably fine. But for thorough research or for those times when your favorite isn't turning up what you need, be flexible and try another approach. Google and some other search engines personalize results based on your location and search history. Using a search engine that does not track your searches or anticipate your biases, such as DuckDuckGo, will produce different results.

    — If you encounter a paywall, try accessing the content through a library website. Search engine research can lead you to helpful newspaper and journal articles. Some publishers' websites require readers to pay a fee or subscribe to access their content. Before pulling out a credit card or beginning a trial subscription, try to find the content by going through your library's website or online catalog. Libraries—in particular academic libraries—subscribe to many databases that include newspaper and journal articles. In some instances (particularly if you are offsite), you will be prompted to log in to verify your affiliation with the library to access the articles at no cost.

    It is important to recognize that search engines don't cover everything on the internet, even everything available for free. Billions of pages of online information, known as the deep web or the invisible web, are beyond the reach of even the most powerful search engine because they are inside databases and do not have fixed URLs. It is estimated that search engines can locate several hundred billion pages of information, while the deep web covers many trillion pages.[7] Reaching this information requires familiarity with and access to the databases or other repositories where it is held.

    Guides and Other Resources. A search engine will not always lead you directly to the most useful sources of information. Sometimes a web research guide will have links to better sites than those that appear at the top of a list of search results. A guide is

---

    [7]   Marcus P. Zillman, *Deep Web Research and Discovery Resources* (deepweb.us).

particularly valuable if you want to learn what resources are available. If you search, for example, for "Illinois Supreme Court," you may go to one site that has the court's decisions but never learn that another site may offer deeper coverage or more extensive search options. But a guide to Illinois legal resources will list these various alternatives and provide for easy comparison of the sites. Working just with a computer and your choice of keywords, you can often find useful and relevant information. But turning to experts in the area through a web guide may turn up related information you didn't know to look for or didn't know was there.

The research guides available from most law school library websites, or directories listing sites by jurisdiction, such as the Library of Congress's Guide to Law Online (www.loc.gov/law/help/guide.php), can do the best job of selecting quality law-related sites. Sites such as these are prepared by experts and have links to sources for cases, statutes, journals, and many other materials.

This text examines legal research generally, but researchers should be aware that specialized areas of law have many idiosyncrasies. Numerous guides to these topics are available. Many law libraries have research guides to specialized areas on their websites, so a first approach may be to run a general search such as "environmental law research guide." More than 580,000 publicly available research guides across the library community can be searched at the LibGuides Community website (community.libguides.com). Guides have also been published in legal bibliography journals such as *Law Library Journal* and *Legal Reference Services Quarterly*, as well as in more general law reviews, and can be found through journal searches or periodical indexes. William S. Hein & Co. publishes a *Legal Research Guides* series of over sixty monographs on specific topics such as environmental justice or habeas corpus.

Other resources such as blogs and wikis can be useful in legal research, particularly early in the process when general information is needed. An article from Wikipedia (www.wikipedia.org) can quickly provide factual background information, although relying on such a source as authoritative may be problematic.[8]

---

[8] Wikipedia has been cited in many court opinions, but several decisions have expressed concern about this trend. *See, e.g., United States v. Lawson,* 677 F.3d 629, 650 (4th Cir. 2012) ("Given the open-access nature of Wikipedia, the danger in relying on a Wikipedia entry is obvious and real."); *Campbell v. Sec'y of Health and Human Servs.,* 69 Fed. Cl. 775, 781 (2006) ("A review of the Wikipedia website reveals a pervasive and, for our purposes, disturbing series of disclaimers. . . ."); *Rainey v. Grand Casinos, Inc.,* 47 So.3d 1199, 1204 (Miss. Ct. App. 2010) ("The articles written in Wikipedia are collaborative and authored anonymously; thus, any information found on Wikipedia may not be reliable and should be viewed with scepticism."). For an overview of these issues, see Jodi L. Wilson, *Proceed with Extreme Caution: Citation*

(b) Online Legal Research Platforms

Most academic law library websites feature a directory of online resources to which the library subscribes as well as some free online resources. Each new resource may require an initial learning curve to understand its features and search syntax, but this is time well spent. Familiarity with the resources available to you will broaden your research abilities well beyond many of your peers.

Two major commercial online platforms—Westlaw from Thomson Reuters (formerly West Publishing Company) and Lexis from LexisNexis—are widely used in law schools and in legal practice as comprehensive legal research tools. Law students generally have access to these resources through their school's subscriptions, but for other researchers these can be expensive tools.[9]

The Westlaw and Lexis research services were introduced in the 1970s as case research tools and have since grown to cover billions of pages of content including not only cases and statutes but also journal articles, books, news sources, and business information. Their current interfaces are called WestlawEdge and Lexis+.

While many law students limit their research to Westlaw or Lexis, numerous other online research platforms are needed for sophisticated and comprehensive research. HeinOnline is a major source for PDFs mirroring original printed sources (sometimes referred to as print equivalents), with a wide range of materials from law reviews to congressional documents to treaties. Bloomberg Law features resources in areas such as employment law and intellectual property, and is widely used in law schools for access to court dockets and filings. Wolters Kluwer's Cheetah offers curated primary and secondary sources in more than two dozen practice areas. Other platforms and databases are more specialized but just as essential. ProQuest Legislative Insight, for example, is limited to documents used to interpret congressional enactments.

Some commercial online research platforms focus on lower-cost access to primary sources. These generally have thorough access to case law and statutes, but they offer a smaller range of secondary sources and other features. Casemaker (www.casemaker.us) and Fastcase (www.fastcase.com) are perhaps the most important of these, because they are offered to lawyers as a free or low-cost benefit

---

to Wikipedia in Light of Contributor Demographics and Content Policies, 16 VAND. J. ENT. & TECH. L. 857 (2014).

[9] Much of the information in these services may be available to university faculty and students through Nexis Uni or Westlaw Campus Research.

of state bar membership.[10] A version of Casemaker, CasemakerX (www.casemakerx.com), is available free to law students. Fastcase is actively acquiring or developing more secondary source offerings and has a partnership with HeinOnline to search the law journal content on that platform.

Which platform to use for a particular research problem (if a choice is available) is a decision based in part on personal preference, in part on cost, and in part on the features and resources each platform offers. As we shall see over the course of this volume, each has some features and material not found in other platforms. Law students should learn to use more than one online platform, to take full advantage of each and to be prepared for whatever their employers offer once they enter practice.

Database Selection. After selecting a platform, one of the first choices you will confront is whether to search all databases offered at once, or only specific sources you select from a list or menu. Most online resources are designed so that you can begin with a search across most or all sources and then filter your results. It is tempting to begin all your research this way. But the search bar on a platform's homepage does not necessarily search everything contained on the site.[11] If you already know that you need a certain type of document (such as cases or law review articles), it is more efficient to start by searching in a more specific database. You need to know what types of documents you're looking for with either approach; the difference is whether you make that decision before or after your search. Thinking and choosing ahead of time can make your search more focused and reduce noise, and in some platforms it allows you to take advantage of advanced search features designed for specific types of documents.

You are also presented with an option of jurisdictions in which to search. You can search all state and federal materials, or you can limit to one or more specific jurisdictions. Whether to focus on a particular jurisdiction varies from project to project, depending on such factors as the purpose of the research and the value of information from other jurisdictions. Sometimes you are interested in information from around the country, but often you need to know the law in one specific jurisdiction.

---

[10] As of 2020, every state bar association provided member access to Fastcase, Casemaker, or both. For a state-by-state summary, see *Legal Research via State Bar Associations*, DUKE LAW (law.duke.edu/lib/statebarassociations/).

[11] This is particularly true with Westlaw, in which a "global" search does not include material designated on the homepage as "Specialty Areas" such as dockets, international material, and news. It also searches only the past two years of session laws, bills, and administrative registers.

Basic Searches. Online research platforms have sought to make research as simple as running an internet search. You enter your terms in a search box, and the platform's algorithms present you with a variety of relevant material sorted by document type (e.g., cases, statutes, secondary sources).

An algorithmic (or natural language) search allows you to enter a phrase, or a combination of words (e.g., *Is an owner without knowledge of her dog's vicious propensity liable for injuries?* or simply *vicious dog liability knowledge*). The computer assigns relative weights to the terms in a query, depending on how often they appear in the sources you are searching. It then retrieves the most relevant documents, giving greater weight to the less common terms. The system may also search for related terms you didn't enter, based on its glossaries and algorithms.

The people who create research algorithms try to achieve both high *precision* and high *recall*. High precision means that most of the search results reflect what the researcher was looking for, and high recall means that many or most of the multitudes of relevant results are included in the results list. High precision algorithms try to save the searcher time and work especially well for questions that have a concrete answer, such as the number of feet in a mile. High recall algorithms, on the other hand, will aim to return every document that might help a searcher answer their question, even if it means there will be some irrelevant results returned as well.

As you can see, the two goals of precision and recall are not always compatible. Some relevant documents are omitted from the search results, and many irrelevant documents are included. The documents listed first are often useful, because results are ranked by relevance, but it is often necessary to sift through a long list to ascertain which of the results best answers the search query.

Although research indicates that people are more likely to trust algorithms than human judgment,[12] it is important to remember that the algorithms used in research were created by humans and incorporate those humans' assumptions and biases. The exact same search entered in similar databases on two platforms, in fact, will usually retrieve very different results.[13] You cannot simply run one algorithmic search and trust that you have found the most relevant

---

[12] Jennifer M. Logg et al., *Algorithm Appreciation: People Prefer Algorithmic to Human Judgment*, 151 ORGANIZATIONAL BEHAV. & HUM. DECISION PROCESSES 90 (2019).

[13] Susan Nevelow Mart, *The Algorithm as a Human Artifact: Implications for Legal [Re]Search*, 109 LAW LIBR. J. 387 (2017).

material. It is usually necessary to try several different searches, or to try the same search in different platforms to compare results.

Advanced Searches. Legal research databases contain millions of documents. Your research projects will require you to cull the most relevant documents from those millions, a professional skill that often requires more than simple internet-type searches for keywords or phrases. Most legal research platforms permit much more powerful and focused searches, allowing the use of features such as synonyms, truncation, proximity connectors, and field restrictions for searching specific parts of documents. If you use these search techniques combined with knowledge of a subject area developed using a secondary source, rather than just relying on a legal research company's algorithms and relevancy rankings, you can be confident that you have identified the most relevant documents for your research.

An advanced search, also known as either a Boolean or "terms and connectors" search, requires learning a structured syntax, but it can provide greater precision and recall in retrieval. Specific terms or phrases are joined by logical connectors such as *and*, or by proximity connectors indicating the maximum number of words that can separate the search terms (e.g., */10* or *w/10*) or specifying that the words appear in the same sentence (*/s* or *w/sent*) or the same paragraph (*/p* or *w/para*).[14]

Connectors do not behave the same way across all platforms, so you should check a platform's help screens to learn its search syntax. In Westlaw, for example, an *or* connector is understood between two adjacent search terms so that the advanced search *dangerous dog* looks for documents containing either the word *dangerous* or the word *dog*. To search for a phrase such as "dangerous dog," you must place the words in quotation marks. Other platforms may require the use of *or* (sometimes capitalized, sometimes not) to find alternate terms and will search for a phrase without quotes.

Another aspect of advanced searching is the use of the truncation or expansion symbols *!* and ***. In most services, an exclamation point is used to find any word beginning with the specified letters. *Manufactur!*, for example, finds *manufacture, manufacturer, manufactured*, and *manufacturing*. Without the truncation symbol, only the word itself and its plural form are retrieved. *Manufacturer* retrieves *manufacturers*, but not *manufactured* or *manufacturing*. The asterisk, sometimes called a wildcard, is less frequently used, but usually represents a particular

---

[14] Rather than tracking sentence and paragraph breaks, Lexis calculates */s* as within 25 words and */p* as within 75 words.

character, a limited number of characters, or no character at all. *Legali*e* retrieves either the American *legalize* or the British *legalise*, and *hand*** retrieves *hand*, *handy*, or *handle* but not *handgun*. A search for *colo*r* retrieves results for *color* and *colour*.

Advanced searches also give you the opportunity to search within specific parts of a document, known as fields or segments, such as the title of an article or the name of the judge writing an opinion. Limiting a search to a particular field can produce much more focused results. A search in a case database for *bell* retrieves every decision mentioning the word *bell* anywhere in the opinion, but a search for *title(bell)* retrieves only those cases where one of the parties is named Bell.

On most platforms, including Westlaw and Lexis, the easiest way to construct an advanced search is to click on the "Advanced" or "Advanced Search" link, which leads to a screen that lists the available document fields and provides guidance on the available terms and connectors.

The list of document fields available on the Advanced Search screen depends on the particular type of content you've selected to search. For example, an advanced search in all Westlaw content only lists three fields: Date, Citation, and Name/Title. If you choose to search only cases, however, you have more than twenty document fields to choose from. You can easily retrieve a complete list of a judge's opinions by putting her name in the Judge field, or you can combine this request with other search terms to find her opinions on a particular topic. Advanced search screens sometimes include a sample document illustrating the scope of each field.

Why would you want to learn how to construct advanced searches when you can just enter your terms and get relevant documents? An advanced search puts you in charge, finding documents that more exactly match your requirements. You, not the algorithm, have made decisions and are in control.

The algorithmic and advanced search methods are best suited for different purposes. An algorithmic search is most useful as a starting point for finding a few highly relevant documents. Because documents are retrieved based mainly on how frequently search terms appear, it is also ideal for finding documents on issues involving frequently used terms such as "summary judgment." Many cases mention the standards for summary judgment, but the few decisions focusing on it in depth would be presented first as most relevant. Advanced searches, which require documents to match a request more exactly, are generally most effective when searching for a known item, a precise factual situation, or a specific relationship between concepts.

Results Display. Once you enter a search, the platforms generally display a list of results with snippets of text showing where your terms appear. Results are usually ranked by relevance, but you can opt instead to list the most recent documents first. Your results can be filtered by document type (if you have searched all content) and by other features such as jurisdiction, source, or date, depending on the type of material. Limiting a search by certain years, jurisdictions, or publication type can help you break your analysis of search results into more manageable chunks and give you a useful perspective on the effectiveness of your search query.

Most full-text documents include *star pagination*, which indicates the page breaks in the original printed sources. This allows you to cite to a particular passage in a case, law review article, or other document without having to track down the printed version.

Search Within Results. On some platforms, including Westlaw and Lexis, if a completed search retrieves a large number of documents you can narrow your inquiry by using a *Search Within Results* filter. This allows you to search within the retrieved set of documents for specific terms, even if those terms were not included in the initial request. This feature is particularly valuable if each new search costs money, because it does not generally incur an additional charge. This is also a good opportunity to search using specific facts once you have compiled a list of legally relevant search results.

History, Saved Searches, and Alerts. Several online platforms save your recent searches so that you can track your progress and return to earlier research results. They also give you the capability to collect and store documents and searches in folders or workspaces.

One of the most powerful features offered by many platforms is the ability to save a search and have it automatically run to check for new material on a daily or weekly basis. This alert feature is a convenient way to stay abreast of developments in a specific case or in an area of interest. Your legal research platform continues to check up on an issue while you move on to other matters.

Citators. Many documents, especially cases, have links not only to the resources they cite, but also to later sources that cite them. This is an invaluable way to find related materials and to bring research forward in time. This updating process is done through the citator features that are linked from the document display. These tools provide lists of cases, law review articles, court documents, and other sources that make some reference to the document being viewed. Citators play a particularly vital role in case research, where they are used to determine whether a decision is still "good law."

(c) Print Resources

Even though resources are rapidly being digitized, a great deal of legal information remains available only in printed form. Superseded code volumes provide information about the state of the law twenty or fifty years ago, and journal articles and treatises not available online may have valuable insights. Platforms such as Westlaw and Lexis provide the most current versions of secondary sources, while an older version may be accessible only in print.

Even for material that is available online, the print format can offer advantages. It is easier to browse from section to section in a book than online, and therefore to see related topics and to develop a sense of how a field of law is organized. Searching online may find individual documents matching the specific terms in a search, but it will not reveal analogies that might be discussed in related sections of a treatise or encyclopedia.

The computer plays an essential role in print-based research. The first step to researching in print material is usually to consult a library's online catalog, which tells you what the library has in print and where it is located.

Once you have found a relevant volume or set of volumes, peruse the table of contents at the front of the book or index at the back of the book or set of books to find a specific discussion. Indexes in legal publications can be lengthy and full of cross-references, but even the most thorough index cannot list every possible approach to a legal or factual issue. As with online research, you may need to rethink issues, reframe questions, check synonyms and alternate terms, and follow leads in cross-references. But the index provides related references that might be worth following, something keyword searches do not do.

Print-based research, of course, is not without limitations and problems. An online search can be the quickest way to find a precise point, and hyperlinks can quickly take you to related sources. Downloading material or requesting it by e-mail has several advantages over photocopying. But the ability to use printed resources is an important part of the skill set of any serious researcher.

§ 1.3   HANDLING A RESEARCH PROJECT

A research project generally involves answering a specific question by applying a general legal principle to a set of facts. It often requires two distinct steps: (1) coming up to speed in the law governing a situation, and (2) searching for the specific rules that apply. These are different tasks and require different approaches. It has been estimated that it takes eighty percent of a researcher's time to learn about an unfamiliar area, and just twenty percent to provide a specific answer.[15]

(a) First Steps

The first step in most research projects is to determine the legal issues in a factual situation. This is "thinking like a lawyer," as taught in law school, and it requires an understanding of basic doctrinal areas such as contract or tort law. The areas of law involved in a particular problem may determine the choice of resources.

Before looking anywhere, step back and study the problem. What are the material facts and issues that may be important in finding the relevant law? What is the relationship between the people involved? Are they, for example, employer/employee or parties to a contract? When did the significant events occur? If possible, determine whether the jurisdictional focus is federal or state. This may depend on where something occurred or on the area of law involved.

Determining material facts and issues is an important aspect of legal analysis, allowing you to assess documents for relevance to the situation you're researching. Some aspects of this research planning process you might consider making note of include:

(1) parties (e.g., physicians, children, or government agencies)

(2) objects or places (e.g., surgical knives, swimming pools, or airports)

(3) acts or omissions giving rise to a cause of action (e.g., malpractice, attractive nuisance, or discrimination)

(4) relief sought (e.g., money damages or injunctive relief)

(5) defenses (e.g., statute of limitations, assumption of risk, or sovereign immunity), or

(6) procedures (e.g., motion to exclude evidence, summary judgment).

---

[15] Thomas Keefe, *The 80/20 Rule of Legal Research*, 93 ILL. B.J. 258 (2005).

Which of these issues are significant in a specific situation depends on a variety of factors such as the nature of the case and the purpose of your research. Generally you are searching for cases, statutes, or other documents addressing similar or analogous factual or legal issues to determine how they apply to the specific facts of your case.

It's important to formulate tentative issues at the outset, but also to be prepared to revise your statement of the issues as research progresses and you learn more about the legal background. At its core, legal research involves taking similar steps over and over, adjusting for new information that you find. If the problem is complex, which it often is, then new questions will arise as you research. When they do, you'll begin the process again, seeking out new sources along the way.

The first step in most projects is to do some preliminary research to understand the context of the problem and to get some sense of the terminology and rules of an area of law. If you're unfamiliar with an area, start with some background reading to understand the significance of material found. Without knowing the parameters of a particular field, you cannot appreciate the nuances.

It is often best to begin research by going to a trustworthy secondary source, such as a legal treatise or a law review article. Primary sources such as statutes and cases can be confusing, ambiguously worded documents. Secondary sources try to explain the law and are usually more straightforward. They summarize the basic rules and the leading authorities and place them in context, allowing you to select the most promising primary sources to pursue.

A treatise explains the major issues and terminology, and provides a context in which related matters are raised or considered. If no treatise is available, a legal encyclopedia such as *American Jurisprudence 2d* or *Corpus Juris Secundum* can be a useful first step. Like a treatise, an encyclopedia outlines basic legal rules and has extensive references to court decisions. Even if it does not address a specific situation, a treatise or encyclopedia provides the general framework in which to place the situation.

Law review articles are particularly useful starting points when researching a new or developing area of law that may not be very well covered in treatises or encyclopedias. Sources such as bar journals, legal newspapers, newsletters, and blogs are even more current than law reviews and may provide helpful leads.

This early stage of the research process is also a good point at which to do some free internet research. At this point you are looking for background information and not definitive answers or citable authority, so free and readily accessible websites can be a real boon.

The internet can provide basic information, and sometimes it can lead to more in-depth resources.

The most difficult part of many research projects is finding the first piece of relevant information. Once one document is found, it often leads to a number of other sources. Cases cite earlier cases as authority; a statute's notes provide useful leads to decisions, legislative history documents, and secondary sources; and law review articles cite a wide variety of sources.

(b) In-Depth Research

Once you gain background knowledge of an area, you then must apply that knowledge to a specific set of facts. In some cases this is simple and straightforward, but it is often a process that requires time and concentration. Here is where your list of issues and material facts can be vital.

Several research tools are designed for in-depth research. Annotated codes have the texts of current statutes, and they also lead directly to most of the other relevant primary sources and perhaps even to secondary sources. Specialized services in areas such as securities or taxation often combine the statutory text with editorial explanatory notes. Key-number digests, whether used in print or on Westlaw, expand on keyword searches by grouping cases together by topic whether or not they use the same terminology. They are wonderful resources for finding analogous situations with different facts but similar legal issues.

Once you know the contours of a legal issue, you have the background necessary to talk to experts in the area. The most current information is not always available in print or online. Sometimes an e-mail or telephone call can uncover information that couldn't be found through ordinary research methods. Government agencies and professional associations are staffed with experts who can answer questions, provide invaluable references, or send essential documents. But do your homework first so you can ask knowledgeable questions, and make sure that the information isn't posted on the organization's website.

Your in-depth research must be sufficient to give you confidence that your work is based on information that is complete and accurate. The surest way to achieve this confidence is to try several different approaches to the research problem. If a review of several secondary sources, case law research, and examination of the underlying statutes all lead to the same sources and a single conclusion, chances are good that you have found all of the key pieces of information. If they turn up different sources or produce different conclusions, you need to keep researching.

Expect to be frustrated in a difficult research project. Try rephrasing the question and running searches using your new terminology. Taking a break from the project for a few hours or talking to colleagues may lead you to fresh insights.

(c) Having Current Information

An essential part of legal research is verifying that the information found is current, that new statutes have not been enacted, and that cases relied upon have not been reversed or overruled. You must verify that your sources are still in force and "good law." No research is complete unless you have checked the latest supplements, searched current-awareness sources for new developments, and determined the status of cases to be relied upon.

There are at least two distinct aspects to making sure that information is current. The major online platforms have citators that check the validity of precedent and find more current information. These services use signals indicating that the precedential value of cases might be affected by subsequent decisions or other developments, and they alert you to recent citing documents that might provide additional clarification or new perspectives.

The other aspect of having current information comes with experience in a particular subject area and is a result of monitoring new developments on a regular basis. When researching in an unfamiliar area, you may only learn about the effect of a new case or regulation by finding it in a keyword search. But keeping up with newsletters, trade magazines, and blogs allows you to anticipate change, ensures that you won't be blindsided by a new development, and enables you to be proactive in reaching out to clients to provide counsel on changes to the law.

(d) Completing a Project

Knowing when to stop researching can be just as difficult as knowing where to begin. In every research situation, however, there comes a time when it is necessary to synthesize the information found and produce the required memorandum, brief, or opinion letter.

Sometimes the limits to research are set by the nature of the project. An assignment may be limited to a specified number of hours or a certain amount of money. If so, the ability to find information quickly and accurately is essential.

If there is no preset limit to the amount of research to be done, it is up to you to determine when you are finished. The best gauge of this comes from having used several research approaches that lead to the same answers. Keyword searches, digests, and secondary sources may seem at first to provide distinct answers, but once they all fit together you can be more confident that you are not missing any key pieces of information.

You will have confidence in your research results if you have confidence in your research skills. Familiarity with legal resources and experience in their use will produce the assurance that your research is complete and accurate.

Chapter 2

ENCYCLOPEDIAS, *RESTATEMENTS*, AND TEXTS

Table of Sections

While primary sources of law such as legislative enactments and judicial decisions determine legal rights and govern procedures, codes and court reports can be notoriously difficult places to find answers. It is generally best to begin a research project by looking first for an overview and analysis written by a lawyer or legal scholar. This chapter and the next cover the major secondary source materials of American law—the encyclopedias, texts, and journal articles that provide background information and attempt to synthesize the mass of conflicting primary authorities into a coherent body of doctrine. Starting with secondary sources is a basic rule of successful legal research.

Law reviews, discussed in Chapter 3, are where much of academic legal theory is published. Most of the materials covered in this chapter serve the more straightforward purpose of explaining legal concepts, providing the context necessary to see how a particular issue relates to other concerns. They can serve as an introduction to a new area of law or refresh your recollection of a familiar area.

Another important feature of most secondary sources is that they include references to the primary sources that are the essential next step in most research. Texts and articles discuss relevant cases and statutes, with lengthy footnotes to these and other sources. These discussions can provide a more coherent and sophisticated

31

presentation of the primary sources than if you start with your own keyword search or a collection of headnotes in an annotated code or digest.

§ 2.1   OVERVIEWS AND INTERDISCIPLINARY WORKS

Even basic legal texts can be daunting to someone new to legal research generally or to a particular area of law. For a start in understanding and analyzing an issue, it may be helpful to begin with resources written for a more general audience.

There is nothing wrong with doing preliminary research with internet searches and free online resources such as Wikipedia (www. wikipedia.org), as long as you recognize that these are only starting points for background information. Further research in legal resources will be necessary to find the more sophisticated detail and supporting documentation required for legal analysis.

Several publications provide a broad outline of the American legal system, including *Fundamentals of American Law* (Alan B. Morrison ed., 1996), E. Allan Farnsworth, *An Introduction to the Legal System of the United States* (4th ed. 2010), and William Burnham, *Introduction to the Law and Legal System of the United States* (6th ed. 2016). These explain common legal concepts and procedures, survey doctrinal areas such as contract law, corporations, and labor law, and cite major cases and other sources. Farnsworth's book is quite short, but it includes "Suggested Readings" of basic texts in each area it discusses. Burnham's work is more of a textbook and is used in many courses for foreign attorneys looking to learn more about U.S. law.

Oxford Companion to American Law (Kermit L. Hall ed., 2002) is a one-volume work covering a broad range of major legal concepts, institutions, cases, and historical figures, with most articles accompanied by references for further reading. *The New Oxford Companion to Law* (Peter Cane & Joanne Conaghan eds., 2008) focuses primarily on British legal institutions, but it also covers American and general topics and contains a great deal of useful information on legal history and our common law heritage.

Encyclopedic works for a general audience such as the *Gale Encyclopedia of American Law* (3d ed. 2011) offer a basic introduction to legal issues. The *Gale Encyclopedia* has almost 5,000 entries, including articles on basic legal doctrines and terminology, major court decisions, government agencies, and influential jurists and lawyers. Most articles include brief bibliographies for further reading, but generally they are rather short with few research leads.

Greater depth is provided by interdisciplinary encyclopedias focusing on specific topics. These include several well-respected works with contributions from legal scholars as well as historians and political scientists. Constitutional law is particularly well represented, with major works such as *Encyclopedia of the American Constitution* (Leonard W. Levy & Kenneth L. Karst eds., 2d ed. 2000) and *The Oxford Companion to the Supreme Court of the United States* (Kermit L. Hall ed., 2d ed. 2005).

The fields of criminal law, criminology, and criminal justice have several encyclopedic works with overlapping coverage. *Encyclopedia of Crime and Justice* (Joshua Dressler ed., 2d ed. 2002), is one of the most wide-ranging and highly respected of these works, with extensive articles on both legal and behavioral aspects of criminal and law enforcement activity.[1]

Several multi-volume encyclopedias focus on other legal topics, providing an interdisciplinary perspective on issues that arise in legal practice and scholarship. Among the most frequently cited sources are *Encyclopedia of Bioethics* (Stephen G. Post ed., 3d ed. 2004), *New Palgrave Dictionary of Economics and the Law* (Peter Newman ed., 1998), and *Oxford International Encyclopedia of Legal History* (Stanley N. Katz ed., 2009).

Other interdisciplinary encyclopedias have more general perspectives of ethical or societal concerns. These works do not focus explicitly on law, but all contain extensive coverage of legal topics. Two of the most wide-ranging and highly respected works are *International Encyclopedia of the Social and Behavioral Sciences* (James D. Wright ed., 2d ed. 2015) and *International Encyclopedia of the Social Sciences* (William A. Darity, Jr. ed., 2d ed. 2008). These and other more specialized encyclopedias may be available through a university library in print or online.

Works such as these provide background information on legal issues and can place these issues in a broader social or historical context. They generally will not, however, answer specific questions about particular legal situations, and they contain relatively few references to the primary sources needed for thorough research. For more detailed coverage, we must turn to works designed specifically for lawyers and law students.

---

[1] The former Chief Justice of the Wisconsin Supreme Court noted in a review of the first edition that she "expected to find the articles . . . simplistic and unsatisfactory for the legal specialist," but ended up recommending the work to her clerks "for its value in providing an overview and a starting point for research." Shirley S. Abrahamson, *Some Enlightenment on Crime*, 83 MICH. L. REV. 1157, 1163 (1985) (reviewing ENCYCLOPEDIA OF CRIME AND JUSTICE (Sanford H. Kadish ed., 1983)).

§ 2.2   LEGAL ENCYCLOPEDIAS

"Legal encyclopedia" is a term with a very specific meaning. It is not simply a general encyclopedia about legal topics (such as the *Gale Encyclopedia of American Law*), but a work that attempts to systematically and exhaustively describe the entire body of a jurisdiction's legal doctrine. Two legal encyclopedias cover all of American law, while others focus on the jurisprudence of individual states.

Articles in a legal encyclopedia are arranged alphabetically. A typical legal encyclopedia has only about 400 articles, roughly mirroring the number of topics of the West Key Number System. Some articles cover very broad doctrinal areas such as corporations or evidence and are subdivided into hundreds or thousands of numbered sections. Articles are generally not on topics as specific as DNA evidence or adverse possession.

Legal encyclopedias are relatively easy to navigate and provide straightforward summaries of the law, but in most instances their perspective is quite limited. The articles tend to emphasize case law and neglect statutes and regulations, and they rarely examine the historical or public policy aspects of the rules they discuss. Unlike law review articles or scholarly treatises, they simply summarize legal doctrine without criticism or suggestions for improvement. Encyclopedias also tend to be relatively slow to reflect changes in the law or to cover significant trends in developing areas.

At one time legal encyclopedias were viewed as serious and reliable statements of law and were frequently cited by the courts. Today, however, they are generally not viewed as persuasive secondary authority but as introductory surveys of the law and, most helpfully to law students, as sources of references to judicial decisions.

(a)   *American Jurisprudence 2d* and *Corpus Juris Secundum*

Two national legal encyclopedias were once competing works but are now both published by Thomson Reuters: *American Jurisprudence 2d* (Am. Jur. 2d) and *Corpus Juris Secundum* (C.J.S.).[2] Each of these sets contains over 140 volumes, with

---

[2] *Am. Jur. 2d* began publication in 1962 and superseded *American Jurisprudence* (1936–60), which had in turn superseded *its* predecessor, *Ruling Case Law* (1914–31). *C.J.S.* began publication in 1936 and superseded *Corpus Juris* (1911–37). These older encyclopedias may still be of value in historical research, as may even earlier works such as *American and English Encyclopedia of Law* (1887–96). These sets are available online in libraries that subscribe to Westlaw's Rise of American Law

alphabetically arranged articles on topics from abandoned property to zoning. Each article is divided into numbered sections and begins with a section-by-section outline of its contents and an explanation of its scope.

Both *Am. Jur. 2d* and *C.J.S.* explain doctrinal concepts and provide references to cases and other sources. The two works are quite similar, but there are some differences. In *C.J.S.*, but not *Am. Jur. 2d*, each section or subsection begins with a concise "black letter" statement of the general legal principle. The discussion in *Am. Jur. 2d* tends to focus a bit more on federal law, while *C.J.S.* seeks to provide an overall synthesis of state law. *Am. Jur. 2d* is generally viewed as more accessible, while *C.J.S.* is a bit more comprehensive. Until the 1980s, in fact, *C.J.S.* claimed to represent "the entire American law as developed by all reported cases"; current volumes are more selective and are instead "a contemporary statement of American law as derived from reported cases and legislation."

Am. Jur. 2d and *C.J.S.* both include copious footnotes to illustrative cases from around the country. A cited decision from your jurisdiction is obviously the most useful, but almost any case can be used as a springboard to further research through its headnotes and citing references. Both encyclopedias include relevant West key numbers before each section, and these can be used to find cases on Westlaw or in West digests. *Am. Jur. 2d* also includes references to other sources, including *American Law Reports* (*ALR*) annotations describing cases in more detail. (Key numbers, digests, and *ALR* are discussed in Chapter 12 on case research.)

Westlaw has both encyclopedias, while *Am. Jur. 2d* is also available through Lexis. Each section is treated as a separate document, making it difficult at times to understand the scope of a specific discussion. Expanding the table of contents, however, makes it possible to see how a particular section fits in a broader context. You can begin by browsing through the table of contents, or you can search and then link from a retrieved section to the outline for its article.

Illustrations 2-1 and 2-2 show pages from the *Am. Jur. 2d* and *C.J.S.* "Animals" articles, discussing aspects of owners' liability for dog bites. Note that *C.J.S.* includes a summary in bold type at the beginning of its section, and that it has more footnotes than the *Am. Jur. 2d* example. Both works list relevant West key numbers.

---

database. The many superseded *Am. Jur. 2d* and *C.J.S.* volumes, on the other hand, are not online and must be accessed in print if needed.

a result, the horse's sudden rearing and jumping movements, because this is an inherent risk of horseback riding.[28] Moreover, under such a statute, cinching a rider's saddle too loosely is an inherent risk of horseback riding, for which the defendant will not be held liable where the plaintiff rider is injured as a result.[29]

c. Other Animals

§ 84 Liability for injury caused by cats

Research References

West's Key Number Digest, Animals ⟜66.6

Liability for injury inflicted by horse, dog, or other domestic animal exhibited at show, 68 A.L.R.5th 599

Liability for injuries caused by cat, 68 A.L.R.4th 823

Liability of owner or operator of business premises for injury to patron by dog or cat, 67 A.L.R.4th 976

Forms relating to injuries by cat, generally, see Am. Jur. Pleading and Practice Forms, Animals

Under the common law, the owner or keeper of a domesticated animal which is not naturally dangerous, such as a cat, is subject to liability for harm caused by the animal only if he or she knows or has reason to know that the particular animal is abnormally dangerous, and therefore, if a cat of a peaceable disposition suddenly and unexpectedly inflicts an injury, its owner or keeper is not liable under the common law to the person injured, assuming that the owner or keeper was exercising due care at the time of the incident.[1] In other words, an owner of a domestic cat is not liable for the unforeseeable actions of his or her cat.[2] However, when a cat has a propensity to attack other cats, knowledge of that propensity may render the owner liable for injuries to people that foreseeably result from such behavior.[3] Moreover, it is reasonably foreseeable that a person would attempt to protect his or her own cat from an attack by an abnormally aggressive cat and that the person could be injured by the abnormally aggressive cat, thereby giving rise to a duty of care in the owner to prevent such injuries.[4]

To recover in strict liability in tort for the injury, it is necessary to prove that the cat had vicious propensities and the defendants knew or

---

[28]Anthony v. Xanterra Parks and Resorts, Inc., 157 F. Supp. 3d 1184 (D. Wyo. 2015) (applying Wyoming law).

[29]Kovnat v. Xanterra Parks and Resorts, 770 F.3d 949 (10th Cir. 2014) (applying Wyoming law).

[Section 84]

[1]Amyotte ex rel. Amyotte v. Rolette

County Housing Authority, 2003 ND 48, 658 N.W.2d 324 (N.D. 2003).

[2]Jackson v. Mateus, 2003 UT 18, 70 P.3d 78 (Utah 2003).

[3]Allen v. Cox, 285 Conn. 603, 942 A.2d 296 (2008).

[4]Allen v. Cox, 285 Conn. 603, 942 A.2d 296 (2008).

Illustration 2-1. A page from *American Jurisprudence 2d*.

---

§ 332 Strict or absolute liability

Research References

West's Key Number Digest, Animals ⊕66.1, 66.2

> In some jurisdictions, an owner or possessor of an animal that the owner or possessor knows or has reason to know has dangerous tendencies abnormal for the animal's category is subject to strict liability for physical harm caused by the animal if the harm ensues from that dangerous tendency.

Under the Restatement view, an owner or possessor of an animal that the owner or possessor knows or has reason to know has dangerous tendencies abnormal for the animal's category is subject to strict liability for physical harm caused by the animal if the harm ensues from that dangerous tendency.[1] Thus, if the owner or possessor of the animal knows it is vicious and likely to cause injuries to others, the owner or possessor is strictly or absolutely liable.[2] It is then unnecessary to show negligence as to the manner of keeping the animal.[3] In addition, some statutory bases of strict liability render irrelevant the defendant's knowledge of the animal's viciousness,[4] as well as the defendant's negligence in keeping the animal.[5] Some jurisdictions completely reject ordinary negligence as a basis for the liability of a domestic animal owner whose animal causes injury, making strict liability the sole avenue for recovery on a showing of a known propensity for vicious behavior.[6]

Alternatively, in some jurisdictions, strict liability may be only one available theory of recovery, founded on the known vicious nature of the animal while an action in negligence remains available for the handling of a nonvicious animal.[7] Other authorities reject strict liability as a basis for liability for injuries caused by a domestic animal, requiring proof of

---

[Section 332]

[1]Restatement Third, Torts: Liability for Physical and Emotional Harm § 23.

[2]Cal.—Thomas v. Stenberg, 206 Cal. App. 4th 654, 142 Cal. Rptr. 3d 24 (1st Dist. 2012), review denied, (Aug. 15, 2012).

Kan.—Carr v. Vannoster, 48 Kan. App. 2d 19, 281 P.3d 1136 (2012).

Me.—Morgan v. Marquis, 2012 ME 106, 50 A.3d 1 (Me. 2012).

Mich.—Hiner v. Mojica, 271 Mich. App. 604, 722 N.W.2d 914 (2006).

Minn.—Anderson v. Christopherson, 816 N.W.2d 626 (Minn. 2012).

Mo.—Miles ex rel. Miles v. Rich, 347 S.W.3d 477 (Mo. Ct. App. E.D. 2011), reh'g and/or transfer denied, (July 12, 2011) and transfer denied, (Oct. 4, 2011).

N.Y.—Reil v. Chittenden, 96 A.D.3d 1273, 946 N.Y.S.2d 715 (3d Dep't 2012).

N.C.—Holcomb v. Colonial Associates, L.L.C., 358 N.C. 501, 597 S.E.2d 710 (2004).

Tex.—Labaj v. VanHouten, 322 S.W.3d 416 (Tex. App. Amarillo 2010), review denied, (Jan. 7, 2011).

[3]Kan.—Carr v. Vannoster, 48 Kan. App. 2d 19, 281 P.3d 1136 (2012).

N.Y.—Bloomer v. Shauger, 94 A.D.3d 1273, 942 N.Y.S.2d 277 (3d Dep't 2012), order aff'd, 21 N.Y.3d 917, 967 N.Y.S.2d 322, 989 N.E.2d 560 (2013).

N.C.—Patterson v. Reid, 10 N.C. App. 22, 178 S.E.2d 1 (1970).

Tex.—Wells v. Burns, 480 S.W.2d 31 (Tex. Civ. App. El Paso 1972).

[4]Conn.—Atkinson v. Santore, 135 Conn. App. 76, 41 A.3d 1095 (2012), certification denied, 305 Conn. 909, 44 A.3d 184 (2012).

La.—Pepper v. Triplet, 864 So. 2d 181 (La. 2004).

[5]Ohio—Beckett v. Warren, 124 Ohio St. 3d 256, 2010-Ohio-4, 921 N.E.2d 624 (2010).

As to other statutory bases of liability, see § 337.

[6]N.Y.—Gordon v. Davidson, 87 A.D.3d 769, 927 N.Y.S.2d 734 (3d Dep't 2011); Petrone v. Fernandez, 12 N.Y.3d 546, 883 N.Y.S.2d 164, 910 N.E.2d 993 (2009).

[7]Mich.—Hiner v. Mojica, 271 Mich. App. 604, 722 N.W.2d 914 (2006).

N.C.—Holcomb v. Colonial Associates, L.L.C., 358 N.C. 501, 597 S.E.2d 710 (2004).

Tex.—Bushnell v. Mott, 254 S.W.3d 451 (Tex. 2008).

As to negligence, see § 334.

Illustration 2-2. A page from *Corpus Juris Secundum.*

Although both *Am. Jur. 2d* and *C.J.S.* cite thousands of court decisions, neither work cites any state statutes. Even when expressly discussing state statutory provisions, the footnotes refer to cases that in turn cite these statutes. The focus is squarely on case law, although both works do cite federal statutes and uniform laws.

The print volumes in both sets are updated annually with pocket part supplements providing notes of new developments, and each encyclopedia publishes several revised volumes each year. In the instance of Illustrations 2-1 and 2-2, the *Am. Jur. 2d* volume was published in 2018 while the *C.J.S.* volume dates from 2013. In the online versions of these encyclopedias, Westlaw (but not Lexis) indicates in the document heading how recently the content has been updated. As with any legal resource you use, updating is essential to ensure that you are relying on current information. If you are using the print version, be sure to check the pocket part.

The basic means of access to the print encyclopedias are the multi-volume softcover indexes published annually for each set. The indexes are very detailed, but finding the right section can require patience and flexibility. You may need to rethink your search terms or follow cross-references to other headings. Each encyclopedia also includes a tables volume listing the federal statutes, regulations, court rules, and uniform laws it discusses.

Westlaw has searchable access to the indexes for both encyclopedias, and also allows you to restrict a keyword search to terms in section headings through an advanced search. You can use the field *PR* or *preliminary* for words in the titles of articles and subdivisions, and *TI* or *title* for words in individual section headings. On Lexis, you can choose to search only the table of contents and then link from the list of headings to the full text. Limiting a search to headings is often a productive way to zero in on the most relevant material.

You can also find relevant *Am. Jur. 2d* and *C.J.S.* sections through Westlaw Citing References, as both encyclopedias are listed as citing secondary sources for any case or federal statute they mention. Shepard's on Lexis covers other secondary sources, but not these national encyclopedias.

(b) Jurisdictional Encyclopedias

Several states have multi-volume encyclopedias specifically focusing on the law of their jurisdictions. While not generally viewed as authoritative, state encyclopedias can provide both a good general overview of state law and references to primary sources. Unlike *Am. Jur. 2d* and *C.J.S.*, they include citations to state statutes and often do a better job than the national encyclopedias of integrating treatment of statutory and case law. Their treatment of jurisdictionally specific concepts, such as community property or oil and gas law, can be particularly useful.

Only seventeen states have their own legal encyclopedias, but these include most of the more populous jurisdictions. Depending on its publisher, each state encyclopedia is available through Westlaw, Lexis, or both as well as in print:

California Jurisprudence 3d (Westlaw and Lexis)

Florida Jurisprudence 2d (Westlaw)

Illinois Law and Practice (Westlaw)

Indiana Law Encyclopedia (Westlaw)

Maryland Law and Practice (Westlaw)

Michigan Civil Jurisprudence (Westlaw and Lexis)

Michigan Law and Practice, 2d ed. (Lexis)

Dunnell Minnesota Digest (Lexis)

Encyclopedia of Mississippi Law (Westlaw)

New York Jurisprudence 2d (Westlaw and Lexis)

Strong's North Carolina Index 4th (Westlaw)

Ohio Jurisprudence 3d (Westlaw and Lexis)

Pennsylvania Law Encyclopedia (Lexis)

South Carolina Jurisprudence (Westlaw)

Tennessee Jurisprudence (Lexis)

Texas Jurisprudence 3d (Westlaw and Lexis)

Michie's Jurisprudence of Virginia and West Virginia (Lexis)

Some of these works are called *Encyclopedia*, while others are entitled *Jurisprudence*. To confuse matters further, Minnesota's encyclopedia is a *Digest* and North Carolina's is an *Index*. Despite these titles, each of these works is a comprehensive summary of its state's legal doctrine, organized like *Am. Jur. 2d* or *C.J.S.* into several hundred alphabetically arranged articles and regularly updated by annual supplements and revised volumes. Illustration 2-3 shows a page from *Strong's North Carolina Index 4th*, discussing strict liability under North Carolina law for injuries caused by dangerous dogs.

the punitive damages issue from the case.[4]

In an action to recover for personal injuries sustained when the minor plaintiff was bitten by the defendants' dog, the trial court erred in refusing to admit testimony that, approximately four weeks after the event in question, the defendants' dog again came onto the plaintiffs' premises, growled at the minor plaintiff and tried to jump at him.[5]

§ 11 Strict liability for injury or damage caused by dangerous dog; claim for injuries caused by dog

Research References

West's Key Number Digest, Animals ⊛66.5(2), 82

Liability, under 42 U.S.C.A. sec. 1983, for injury inflicted by dogs under control or direction of police, 102 A.L.R. Fed. 616

◆ **National Background:** As to liability for injuries caused by dogs, see Am. Jur. 2d, Animals §§ 75 to 79.

Statutes:

The owner of a dangerous dog is strictly liable in civil damages for any injuries or property damage the dog inflicts upon a person, that person's property, or another animal.[1]

A "dangerous dog" is a dog that: (1) without provocation has killed or inflicted severe injury on a person; or (2) is determined by the person or by the board designated by the county or municipal authority responsible for animal control to be potentially dangerous because the dog has engaged in one or more of the behaviors listed in the statute,[2] including (a) inflicting a bite on a person that resulted in broken bones or disfiguring lacerations or required cosmetic surgery or hospitalization; (b) killing or inflicting severe injury upon a domestic animal when not on the owner's real property; or (c) approaching a person when not on the owner's property in a vicious or terrorizing manner in an apparent attitude of

---

[4]Hunt v. Hunt, 86 N.C. App. 323, 357 S.E.2d 444 (1987), decision aff'd, 321 N.C. 294, 362 S.E.2d 161 (1987).

[5]Pharo v. Pearson, 28 N.C. App. 171, 220 S.E.2d 359 (1975).

[Section 11]

[1]N.C. Gen. Stat. § 67-4.4.

[2]N.C. Gen. Stat. § 67-4.1(a)(1).

Illustration 2-3. A page from a state legal encyclopedia.

Many states have other reference works with broad coverage of their law, although they are not encyclopedias with alphabetically arranged articles. Sets such as *Kentucky Jurisprudence* and *New Jersey Practice*, for example, contain separate volumes for doctrinal areas such as criminal procedure, domestic relations, and evidence. They may not cover all legal topics comprehensively, but they do address most major areas. Many of these resources, like the encyclopedias, are available on Westlaw or Lexis, and can be identified by browsing in secondary sources for a particular jurisdiction. A state research guide can also help you identify available publications.

Thomson Reuters also publishes an encyclopedia focusing specifically on federal law, *Federal Procedure, Lawyers' Edition* (available on Westlaw). It emphasizes procedural issues in civil, criminal, and administrative proceedings, but many of its eighty chapters also discuss matters of substantive federal law. Because it deals exclusively with federal law rather than attempting to generalize about fifty state jurisdictions, it is often more precise and useful than *C.J.S.* or *Am. Jur. 2d* and includes helpful pointers for federal practice.

§ 2.3   *RESTATEMENTS OF THE LAW*

Encyclopedias seek to summarize and define American legal doctrine. A series produced by the American Law Institute (ALI) known as *Restatements of the Law* has a similar purpose, but it is produced by leading scholars and is more highly regarded by the courts.

The ALI was founded in 1923. Its members include judges, lawyers, and law teachers. The organization's purposes, according to its certificate of incorporation, are "to promote the clarification and simplification of the law and its better adaptation to social needs" and "to secure the better administration of justice."[3] The primary vehicles for achieving these goals are the *Restatements*, a series that attempts to articulate the basic doctrines governing American law. The *Restatements* are useful both for students learning legal rules and for lawyers seeking to apply those rules to issues arising in practice.

---

[3] American Law Institute, Certificate of Incorporation of the American Law Institute, 1 *A.L.I. Proc.*, pt. II, 32, 33 (1923). The seven signatories included Charles Evans Hughes, Elihu Root, and William Howard Taft. On the history of the ALI, see G. Edward White, *The American Law Institute and the Triumph of Modernist Jurisprudence*, 15 LAW & HIST. REV. 1 (1997); G. Edward White, *From the Second Restatements to the Present: The ALI's Recent History and Current Challenges*, 16 GREEN BAG 2D 305 (2013).

Each *Restatement* covers a distinct area of law. The first series of *Restatements* was published between 1932 and 1944, and covered nine areas of law: *Agency, Conflict of Laws, Contracts, Judgments, Property, Restitution, Security, Torts,* and *Trusts.* An updated series of *Restatements of the Law (Second)* was issued between 1958 and 1992 for all the original topics except restitution and security, as well as *Foreign Relations Law.* The ALI began working on *Restatement of the Law (Third)* in 1978, and has published several volumes in this series: *Agency* (2006), *Foreign Relations Law* (1987), *The Law Governing Lawyers* (2000), *Property-Mortgages* (1997), *Property-Servitudes* (2000), *Property-Wills and Other Donative Transfers* (1999–2011), *Restitution and Unjust Enrichment* (2011), *Suretyship and Guaranty* (1996), *Torts-Apportionment of Liability* (2000), *Torts-Liability for Physical and Emotional Harm* (2012), *Torts-Products Liability* (1998), *Trusts* (2003–12), and *Unfair Competition* (1995). Other projects in the third series are still underway. *Restatement of the Law: Employment Law* was published in 2015, *Restatement (Fourth) of Foreign Relations Law: Selected Topics in Treaties, Jurisdiction, and Sovereign Immunity* in 2018, and *Restatement of the Law: Liability Insurance* in 2019.

The *Restatement* Format. A *Restatement* is divided into chapters, each examining a major aspect of the field. Most chapters are then divided into topics and titles, and finally into numbered sections, each of which deals with a general principle of law. A section contains a concise "black letter" statement of law, followed by explanatory comments and illustrations of the proposition. The comments and illustrations are in turn followed by Reporter's Notes with background information on the development of the section.[4]

The section numbering is continuous throughout each *Restatement,* so only the section number is included in a citation.[5] Illustration 2-4 shows a page from *Restatement (Third) of Torts: Liability for Physical and Emotional Harm* (2010) and its use of black-letter rule and comments.

---

[4] In the three earliest *Restatements* in the second series (*Agency, Torts,* and *Trusts*), the Reporter's Notes are not printed after each section but appear in separate appendix volumes.

[5] THE BLUEBOOK: A UNIFORM SYSTEM OF CITATION R. 12.9.4 (21st ed. 2020); ALWD GUIDE TO LEGAL CITATION R. 23.1(a) (6th ed. 2017).

Ch. 4   **STRICT LIABILITY**   **§ 23**

caused by a bear on the loose, the defendant is strictly liable. But under Comment *h*, if the fright is merely a response to the sight of a bear that itself is well controlled, strict liability is not available. The denial of strict liability in such a situation is supported by W. PAGE KEETON ET AL., PROSSER & KEETON ON THE LAW OF TORTS 561 (5th ed. 1984). This treatise cites 19th-century cases; there are no modern cases that might either confirm or dispute the Second Restatement's rejection of strict liability. The Second Restatement, in § 507, Comment *h*, leaves open the possibility of holding the defendant liable under negligence law—for having created an unreasonable risk. However, a finding of negligence would depend on an assessment of all relevant circumstances.

§ 23. Abnormally Dangerous Animals

An owner or possessor of an animal that the owner or possessor knows or has reason to know has dangerous tendencies abnormal for the animal's category is subject to strict liability for physical harm caused by the animal if the harm ensues from that dangerous tendency.

Comment:

a. Subject to strict liability. Even in cases covered by this Section, various limitations on liability apply and various defenses are available. The most pertinent of these are set forth in §§ 24, 25, and 29. Recovery for stand-alone emotional harm based on strict liability is addressed in § 47, Comment *k*, and § 48, Comment *m*.

b. Explanation and rationale. This Section supplements §§ 21 and 22. The premise of this Section is that, apart from animals that trespass (§ 21) and wild animals that pose an inherent risk of personal injury (§ 22), most animals normally are safe, or at least are not abnormally unsafe in a way that would justify the imposition of strict liability. In addition, such animals provide important benefits to those who own or maintain possession of them. Thus, livestock such as cows, horses, and pigs are of substantial economic value, while pets such as dogs and cats provide essential companionship for households and families. Indeed, dogs and cats are frequently regarded as members of the family. Furthermore, ownership of animals such as dogs and cats is widespread throughout the public; therefore, the limited risks entailed by ordinary dogs and cats are to a considerable extent reciprocal. Accordingly, the case on behalf of strict liability for physical or emotional harms that all such ordinary animals might cause is weak. However, even though animals in such categories generally entail only a modest level of danger, particular animals may present significant and abnormal dangers. Once the owner or possessor of such an animal knows or has reason to know of such a danger, strict liability, subject to limitations and defenses, becomes appropriate.

Illustration 2-4. A page from a *Restatement*.

The *Restatement* **Process.** *Restatements* go through an elaborate drafting procedure. Once a project has been chosen and approved by the Council, the ALI's governing body, the first step is the appointment of a Reporter, a leading scholar in the subject area. The Reporter prepares a *preliminary draft*, which is reviewed by a committee of fifteen to twenty appointed Advisors, also specialists in the area. A revised text, called the *council draft*, is then reviewed by the Council. The Council may decide that a draft is not yet ready for approval but would benefit from discussion at the ALI's annual meeting, and may circulate a *discussion draft* to the members. If the Council approves the draft, it is submitted as a *tentative draft* to all members of the ALI, considered, debated, and often further amended at the annual meeting. The text may be returned to the Reporter for revision or redrafting and may go through several tentative drafts before a *proposed final draft* is submitted for approval by the Council and membership. Once approved, the final text is published as a *Restatement*.[6]

These various drafts are often treated as a form of legislative history of the *Restatements*, and are frequently cited to explain or criticize particular *Restatement* rules. Transcripts of ALI discussions of drafts are printed in the *Proceedings* of the Institute. Like the drafts themselves, these provide insights into the rationale for the formulation of a *Restatement* as adopted.

Finding *Restatements*. The final, approved *Restatements* are published in bound volumes, available in most law libraries, and are also available on both Westlaw and Lexis.

The drafts are less widely available in print, but HeinOnline (home.heinonline.org) has a very thorough American Law Institute collection, with PDF versions of *Restatements* and any available drafts as well as other ALI materials such as annual reports and proceedings. Less comprehensive collections of recent drafts are available from Westlaw and Lexis.

The American Law Institute website (www.ali.org) has information on publications and pending projects, but it does not provide free access to the full text of its *Restatements*.

The Influence of the *Restatements*. The *Restatements* are not law, but they are perhaps more persuasive in the courts than any other secondary material.[7] Numerous court decisions and law review

---

[6] Harvey S. Perlman, *The Restatement Process*, 10 KAN. J.L. & PUB. POL'Y 2, 4–5 (2000).

[7] The *Restatements* were expressly adopted in the Virgin Islands and the Northern Mariana Islands, in statutes providing that the "rules of the common law, as expressed in the restatements of the law approved by the American Law Institute . . . shall be the rules of decision in the courts." V.I. CODE ANN. tit. 1, § 4 (1995); 7 N. MAR.

articles have analyzed *Restatement* doctrines and applied them to particular situations. These are very useful in determining the scope and value of *Restatement* principles.

The appendices for *Restatements* in the second and third series contain annotations of court decisions that have applied or interpreted each section. Westlaw includes these annotations after each section, arranged by jurisdiction. Cases and law review articles citing *Restatements* can also be found through Westlaw Citing References or Shepard's.

Other ALI Works. The ALI has produced or participated in several other influential publications, including suggested legislation such as the Model Penal Code and the Uniform Commercial Code. A comprehensive list of ALI projects is available on its website (www.ali.org/projects/).

In the 1990s the ALI launched a new series of works known as *Principles*. The difference between *Principles* and *Restatements* is that a *Restatement* is "firmly grounded in the existing case law [and] an effort to restate the governing rules in a coherent and systematic way," while *Principles* "make no pretense of being bound by existing law [and] are explicitly recommendations for change."[8]

Completed *Principles* projects include *Aggregate Litigation* (2010), *Corporate Governance* (1994), *Election Administration* (2019), *Family Dissolution* (2002), *Intellectual Property: Principles Governing Jurisdiction, Choice of Law, and Judgments in Transnational Disputes* (2008), and *Software Contracts* (2010). Several other projects are in the draft stages. *Principles* are published in a similar format to *Restatements*. As with the *Restatements*, HeinOnline offers full access to early drafts as well as the final text, and final versions and some drafts are available through Westlaw and Lexis.

I. CODE § 3401 (2011). The Supreme Court of the Virgin Islands has held, however, that it has the judicial power to "determine the common law without automatically and mechanistically following the Restatements." *Banks v. Int'l Renting & Leasing Corp.*, 55 V.I. 967, 979 (2011). *See* James L. Huffman, *A Common Law of and for the Virgin Islands*, 46 STETSON L. REV. 367 (2017).

On the influence of the *Restatements* generally, see, e.g., Kristen David Adams, *Blaming the Mirror: The Restatements and the Common Law*, 40 IND. L. REV. 205 (2007); Kristen David Adams, *The Folly of Uniformity? Lessons from the Restatement Movement*, 33 HOFSTRA L. REV. 423 (2004); and Harold G. Maier, *The Utilitarian Role of a Restatement of Conflicts in a Common Law System: How Much Judicial Deference Is Due to the Restaters or "Who Are These Guys, Anyway?"*, 75 IND. L.J. 541 (2000).

8   Perlman, *supra* note 6, at 4.

§ 2.4   TEXTS, TREATISES, AND MONOGRAPHS

Legal texts and treatises play a vital role in legal research. They analyze developing common law and contribute their own influence on its development. By synthesizing decisions and statutes, these works help to impose order on the chaos of individual precedents. Although they are less authoritative than *Restatements*, some are written by scholars of outstanding reputation and are well respected by the courts.

(a) Types of Legal Texts

Thousands of texts and treatises written by legal scholars and practitioners address topics of substantive and procedural law. These range from multi-volume specialized treatises and detailed surveys to short monographs on specific issues in particular jurisdictions. Some offer convenient practice checklists and sample forms. There is considerable overlap between types of texts, but they fit generally into several major genres:

— **Treatises.** These are scholarly surveys providing exhaustive coverage of particular fields of law. A treatise is like an encyclopedia in that it methodically outlines the basic aspects of legal doctrine, but its focus on a specific subject usually gives a treatise greater depth and insight.

The traditional treatise is a multi-volume work covering a broad area of legal doctrine such as contracts or trusts.[9] Modern treatises tend to focus on increasingly narrow areas of law, and many are just one or two volumes. Treatises are published in bound volumes or looseleaf binders, and are generally updated annually with either pocket parts or looseleaf supplements. Illustration 2-5 shows a page from Dan B. Dobbs et al., *The Law of Torts* (2d ed. 2011), a multi-volume treatise covering tort law in much greater detail than the encyclopedias or other more general sources.

---

[9]   The history of treatise publication is discussed in A.W.B. Simpson, *The Rise and Fall of the Legal Treatise: Legal Principles and the Forms of Legal Literature*, 48 U. CHI. L. REV. 632 (1981). For more current perspectives, see LAW BOOKS IN ACTION: ESSAYS ON THE ANGLO-AMERICAN LEGAL TREATISE (Angela Fernandez & Markus D. Dubber eds., 2012); and Richard A. Danner, *Oh, the Treatise!*, 111 MICH. L. REV. 421 (2013).

The dry and ponderous style of historical American treatises is succinctly summarized in LAWRENCE M. FRIEDMAN, A HISTORY OF AMERICAN LAW 608, 711 (4th ed. 2019): "Most nineteenth-century treatises were barren enough reading when they first appeared and would be sheer torture for the reader today. . . . [The early twentieth century] was the age of huge, elephantine treatises. Samuel Williston built a monumental structure (1920–1922) out of the law of contracts, volume after volume, closely knit, richly footnoted, and fully armored against the intrusion of any ethical, economic, or social ideas whatsoever. . . . [E]ach branch or field of law had at least one example of an arid and exhaustive treatise."

§ 439 Strict liability for abnormally dangerous domestic animals

Strict liability for personal injury caused by domestic animals. The common law rule already discussed made owners of livestock strictly liable for the trespasses of such animals, but that rule did not impose strict liability for personal injuries inflicted by livestock except as injury might be a direct result of trespass. Domestic animals like dogs and cats were treated differently; their owners or keepers[1] were not strictly liable for the animals' trespasses at all but under limited conditions could be strictly liable for personal injuries inflicted by such animals. And both owners-keepers and others could be liable for negligently failing to prevent harms inflicted by animals.[2] Apart from liability for negligence, strict liability is imposed only upon the owner or keeper and only then when he knows or has reason to know that his animal is abnormally dangerous in some way and injury results from that danger.[3]

For example, if a dog owner knows that his dog has an abnormal or vicious propensity to attack and bite,[4] or his horse to kick,[5] he is liable for the dog's biting and the horse's kicking. The owner would be liable for ordinary negligence or an intentional

---

[Section 439]

[1] A temporary caretaker such as a pet-sitter may not qualify as a keeper or possessor of the animal, but even such a person would be subject to liability for negligent failure to control. See Trager v. Thor, 445 Mich. 95, 516 N.W.2d 69 (1994). Similarly, an employer who merely permits an employee to bring his dog to a job site is not a keeper or harborer of the dog. Falby v. Zarembski, 221 Conn. 14, 602 A.2d 1 (1992).

[2] E.g., Allen v. Cox, 285 Conn. 603, 942 A.2d 296 (2008) (negligence liability for failing to control a cat known for a propensity to attach other cats); Holcomb v. Colonial Assocs., L.L.C., 358 N.C. 501, 597 S.E.2d 710 (2004); Strunk v. Zoltanski, 62 N.Y.2d 572, 468 N.E.2d 13, 479 N.Y.S.2d 175 (1984); contra, Smaxwell v. Bayard, 274 Wis.2d 278, 682 N.W.2d 923 (2004) (landlord who permitted wolf-dogs on the premises could not be liable for negligence because she was neither an owner nor a keeper of the dogs).

[3] Nutt v. Florio, 75 Mass. App. Ct. 482, 914 N.E.2d 963 (2009); Christensen v. Lundsten, 21 Misc.3d 651, 863 N.Y.S.2d 886 (2008); Jividen v. Law, 194 W.Va. 705, 461 S.E.2d 451 (1995); Marshall v. Ranne, 511 S.W.2d 255 (Tex. 1974); Restatement Second of Torts § 509 (1977); Restatement Third of Torts (Liability for Physical and Emotional Harm) § 23 (2010). Courts sometimes speak of mischievous or vicious propensities of the animal, but the dog's good faith is not an issue and the plaintiff need only show its dangerous tendency. See Restatement Second § 509 cmt. c.

[4] Moura v. Randall, 119 Md.App. 632, 705 A.2d 334 (1998); cf. Marshall v. Ranne, 511 S.W.2d 255 (Tex. 1974) (vicious hog biting plaintiff).

[5] Cf. Bauman v. Auch, 539 N.W.2d 320 (S.D. 1995) (horse rearing up when plaintiff attempted to mount). Because the question of an animal's vicious propensity is relevant both to strict liability and to negligence, decisions may permit the claim to go to

---

Illustration 2-5. A page from a multi-volume treatise on torts.

Treatises are the texts most likely to be available through one of the major online platforms, although some are still available only in print. When using a treatise in any format, you should be aware of how current it is and look for more recent authority as necessary. In print, check the date of the most recent edition or supplement; online, look for an information icon or "Currency" link.

Many treatises were originally written by leading scholars, such as James William Moore (*Moore's Federal Practice*) or John H. Wigmore (*Wigmore on Evidence*), but a number of titles are now produced by editorial staffs at publishing companies. These may have exhaustive commentaries and numerous references to primary sources, but they are generally not accorded the same level of deference as the work of a respected scholar. Some treatises, in fact, are now little more than collections of case references, useful for their research value but not as analysis.[10]

Most treatises are national in scope and analyze laws from various jurisdictions. Some works, however, focus specifically on federal law or on the law of an individual state. Smaller jurisdictions have very few treatises, but large states may have several multi-volume treatises. California, for example, has several treatises written by the late B.E. Witkin and members of the Witkin Legal Institute (www.witkin.com), including *California Criminal Law*, *California Evidence*, *California Procedure*, and *Summary of California Law*. All of these works are available on both Westlaw and Lexis.

— **Hornbooks.** These are straightforward one-volume statements of the law on a specific subject, such as *McCormick on Evidence* or *Wright on Federal Courts*. They are written primarily for law students but can be of value to anyone seeking an overview of a doctrinal area. There is no clear line distinguishing hornbooks from treatises, and some hornbooks (such as those by McCormick and Wright) have become influential sources of persuasive authority and are widely used by the bar. Some hornbooks are also published in two- or three-volume "practitioners' editions."

One distinction between hornbooks and treatises is that works designed for law students are less likely to be available online through the major services. Some law schools, however, have online subscriptions to study aids collections that include numerous hornbook titles.

---

[10] Gary E. O'Connor, *Restatement (First) of Statutory Interpretation*, 7 N.Y.U. J. LEGIS. & PUB. POL'Y 333, 343 (2004), noted that one such work was "less a coherent treatise than a stringing together of older and more recent citations under the relevant sections. That is, the updates appear to be more of a gradual process of citation accretion, rather than an effort to present a comprehensive, coherent view" of its field.

Hornbooks are distinct from the *casebooks* designed as teaching tools, which reprint case excerpts for discussion and tend to provide a less straightforward summary of legal doctrine. Many casebooks consist primarily of reprinted material and questions for classroom discussion, but some include explanations and references that can be useful for research purposes.

— **Practitioners' Handbooks and Manuals.** These works are somewhat similar to treatises but they tend to address practical concerns, and many include useful features designed to simplify routine aspects of law practice.[11] These are less useful for students looking for more than the leading cases on a topic but can be invaluable in real life. Handbooks often contain sample forms, checklists, and other documents offering practical guidance.

Handbooks and manuals are often published by organizations such as the Practising Law Institute (PLI) and bar associations, in many instances as course materials for continuing legal education programs. Some works provide a cohesive overview of an area of law, while others compile presentations by practitioners on a variety of developing topics.

Works focusing on a specific state can be particularly useful for quickly determining the laws in force and finding relevant primary sources. In smaller jurisdictions with few state-specific treatises, continuing legal education handbooks can be among the best available resources for summaries of state law.

Practitioner-focused works, in print and online, are discussed more fully in Chapter 14, Practice Materials, and Chapter 15, Transactional Law Research.

— **Scholarly Monographs.** These cover relatively narrow topics and differ from treatises in that they tend to focus heavily on the historical background, underlying causes and policies, and trends in areas of the law. Monographs tend to be more interdisciplinary in nature than other legal writings. They are often published by university presses or general-interest publishers, and are similar to scholarly works in other disciplines.

Monographs can help you understand the history or policy background of a particular area, but they are generally not exhaustive in their coverage of doctrinal issues and are rarely updated on a regular basis. As a result, they are usually not the best sources for current research leads. Many are published as e-books,

---

[11] Practice-oriented legal materials have a long history in American legal publishing. "With some exceptions, American legal literature was (and is) rigorously practical. Books were written for the practicing lawyer. The goal was to help him earn a living, not to slake his intellectual curiosity." FRIEDMAN, *supra* note 9, at 312.

but they are unlikely to be available online through platforms such as Westlaw or Lexis.

Doctoral dissertations are an extensive body of scholarly research that are often overlooked by law students and lawyers. A dissertation is usually the product of several years of research, and it often provides an exhaustive bibliography of published and manuscript sources. Reading a dissertation once required searching through an index and then borrowing or purchasing a print or microform copy. ProQuest Dissertations & Theses Global (www.proquest.com) now provides online access to most dissertations since 1997 as well as selected earlier works. (It also indexes dissertations back to 1743, including abstracts beginning in 1980.) In addition, many law schools and universities have begun collecting students' dissertations in their digital institutional repositories, and these collections are rapidly growing. Digital access has transformed dissertations from esoteric and hard-to-find items to readily available research tools.

— **Self-Help Publications.** These are written for the general public and often provide clear introductions to areas of law. One of the major publishers is Nolo (www.nolo.com) (e.g., *Patent It Yourself* and *Your Rights in the Workplace*). Books for nonlawyers can be useful introductions but they may oversimplify complex issues or fail to reflect variations in the law between jurisdictions. They also tend to have fewer leads to primary sources than works designed specifically for lawyers, making them less useful as starting points for further research. Very few self-help works are included in the major online platforms, but e-books or other online versions are widely available for purchase.

To be reliable for coverage of current legal issues, any publication, from treatise to self-help guide, must reflect changes in the law promptly and accurately. Some form of updating is usually essential to preserve a legal text's research value. An outdated text may be of historical or intellectual interest, but it cannot be relied upon for analysis of current law.

Part of the process of using a source for the first time is deciding whether it will assist you in your research. Even without extensive use and expertise in a subject area, you can ask several questions when encountering a new work:

— What is its purpose and intended audience? Is it written for experienced specialists or a more general readership?

— How is it organized, and what is its scope? Does it cover too broad an area for your purposes, or does it focus too narrowly on issues that don't concern you?

— What is the reputation of the author? Has she written other texts or articles in this area?

— How useful are such features as the work's footnotes, tables, bibliography, and index? Do they lead effectively to relevant passages in the work and to other resources?

— Is the work supplemented in an adequate and timely manner?

Ultimately the deciding factor in determining whether you will turn to a source a second time is: Did it help answer your question? Did it clarify matters and provide fruitful research leads? With growing familiarity in a particular area of law, you will develop a sense of which sources are useful for background information, for assistance in working through complicated legal issues, or for references to primary sources and other materials.

(b) Finding Texts

There are several ways to find relevant and useful texts and treatises, including online directories, your local law library's catalog, and guides and bibliographies. It is important not to limit yourself to materials available from the major online platforms if possible, as many important works still appear only in print. Nonetheless, we start with online resources as they are the most commonly used versions of most major treatises and texts.

Once you have found a relevant treatise section using a search in a major online platform, unless you are very familiar with the subject area or looking only for very specific information you should usually visit the table of contents to gain context and explore related material. If you read only the individual retrieved sections, you'll learn little about the contours in that area of law and may miss critical information.[12]

Online Platforms. Hundreds of treatises and other texts are available online. These versions are not necessarily more current than their print counterparts, but access is available from any laptop or mobile device and full-text searching allows means of access beyond browsing and subject indexes.

Secondary sources, including treatises, can be retrieved with general searches on the major legal research platforms, but you

---

[12] *See* Jasper L. Cummings, Jr., *Legal Research in Federal Taxation*, in TAX PLANNING FOR DOMESTIC & FOREIGN PARTNERSHIPS, LLCS, JOINT VENTURES & OTHER STRATEGIC ALLIANCES 2007, at 739, 761–62 (PLI Tax Law and Estate Planning Course Handbook Series, No. J–701, 2007) ("Reading an online source like a book is of oxygen-level importance to thorough and thoughtful online research. The point of doing this is to free yourself from the yoke of the search term, and allow you to go where the book leads you and to use its table of contents as a guide.").

should also browse to learn what resources are available as no single platform contains every treatise on a subject. This is in part because each has works from specific publishers and not others, and there is very little overlap in coverage. (This is roughly comparable to the differences in content on Hulu, Netflix, and Amazon's Prime Video.) A bit of exploring and familiarity with resources can pay dividends when you know where to turn in future research projects.

The Appendix in this volume, listing major treatises and hornbooks by subject, indicates the online platforms through which titles are available.

Westlaw has hundreds of treatises, including major works such as *McCarthy on Trademarks and Unfair Competition*, Rotunda & Nowak's *Treatise on Constitutional Law*, and Wright & Miller's *Federal Practice and Procedure*. After selecting "Secondary Sources" from the Westlaw home page, you can see a list of available titles by topic, and filter this list for works from a particular jurisdiction. You can search all the texts in a topical area, but if you click on a particular title you can also browse through its table of contents and get some sense of its scope and purpose. Clicking on the (i) icon next to a treatise's title will open a window explaining how recently the work has been updated.

Lexis has hundreds of Matthew Bender texts and treatises, including *Chisum on Patents*, *Collier on Bankruptcy*, *Immigration Law and Procedure*, and *Nimmer on Copyright*, as well as selected works from other publishers. To learn what's available, you can browse sources by practice area or industry. As with Westlaw, you can search or browse a work's table of contents and click on the (i) icon to learn about the scope of coverage.

Bloomberg Law has numerous practitioners' manuals and treatises. Of particular value are major Bloomberg BNA publications such as *Employment Discrimination Law* and *Supreme Court Practice*, as well as an online-only *Bloomberg Law: Bankruptcy Treatise*. The most effective way to see all of these works is to select Secondary Sources: Books & Treatises, which leads to listings by publisher. Treatises can also be found by subject within individual Practice Centers.

Other publishers also have online services providing access to treatises and texts they publish. The Practising Law Institute has a PLI Plus platform with access to more than 100 treatises it publishes, including older editions of the publications. Wolters Kluwer's Cheetah system includes numerous major treatises in antitrust, securities law, and other areas. Some Wolters Kluwer titles, such as *Wigmore on Evidence* and *The Law of Lawyering*, are also available through Fastcase, although these may not be included with all subscription plans.

Hornbooks and law student texts are generally not available through platforms such as Westlaw or Lexis, but each of the major publishers of law school materials has an e-book collection to which libraries or students can subscribe. One or more of these may be available from your law school library.

Library Collections. A basic starting place in looking for law books is your law library's online catalog. A title or keyword search can be used initially to find a few relevant works, but it is important to go beyond keywords and use the *subject headings* for more comprehensive research. If you search by keyword for "professional responsibility," you might miss relevant works using the phrase "legal ethics" in their titles. A subject search will catch relevant works regardless of their titles. In most online catalogs, each record's subject headings are standardized and hyperlinked to a list of other works on the same topic. The entry for one relevant text is a springboard to others.

Most online catalogs have an "advanced search" or "expanded search" screen that allows you to search for a combination of terms in specific fields. You can use this to find a particular work by a prolific author, for example, or to limit a search to a specific date range. Other catalogs let you filter results by date or library collection once a search is completed. These options can be particularly useful if a general keyword search turns up an unmanageably large number of publications.

Some catalogs include a work's format (e.g., electronic, print), and in some cases the catalog includes links to titles in many of the online research platforms to which the library subscribes. This is not always the case, however, so you can't expect to search a catalog and find a library's entire holdings.

In most libraries, books are shelved by subject using a call number classification system. One advantage of this system is that you can browse nearby books once you have located one relevant text. Most libraries use the Library of Congress (LC) classification system, in which United States law is assigned to numbers within the KF classification. The list of major treatises and hornbooks in the Appendix includes the LC classification ranges for several dozen major subject areas within American law.

Remember that you are not limited in your research to the holdings of one library. No law library has every possible text, and interlibrary loan is an invaluable resource for lawyers and scholars. Online catalogs from other libraries may be helpful in identifying resources available elsewhere. The catalogs for major research libraries such as Harvard University (hollis.harvard.edu) or the Library of Congress (catalog.loc.gov) can help in your research whether or not you plan to use these libraries' collections. Several websites, including Wikipedia, have lists of links to law school websites, from which other library catalogs can be reached.

WorldCat (www.worldcat.org) provides access to records for over two billion items in thousands of libraries worldwide. An Advanced Search screen allows you to combine keywords with words in the author, title, or subject fields and to limit results by date. Once a relevant text is found, its record lists libraries in which it is found and usually provides links to individual libraries' online catalogs.

Footnotes and Other References. Following research leads provided by other sources is usually a reliable way to identify useful works. Treatises are often cited in cases and law review articles, and these references are likely to lead to works that are considered well-reasoned and reputable. You can find highly esteemed treatises by searching the full text of case or journal databases (e.g., "leading w/2 treatise w/5 contracts") or simply noting the treatises that are cited repeatedly by judges or law professors.

Recommendations from lawyers, professors, or reference librarians can also be effective in identifying the most reliable and influential sources. If you receive an assignment in an unfamiliar area from a supervising attorney, consider asking what secondary sources she would use to begin the research. When talking to a partner or professor in her office, notice which works she keeps handy on her desktop or nearby shelves. Identifying the best tools is part of learning the tricks of the trade.

Guides to Treatises. As has already been noted, the Appendix in this volume lists major treatises and hornbooks in several dozen subject areas. Several other online and printed guides list legal texts by subject. Two of the most useful online guides are Legal Treatises by Subject, from the Harvard Law School Library (guides.library. harvard.edu/legaltreatises), and Treatise Finders, from the Georgetown Law Library (guides.ll.georgetown.edu/home/treatise-finders).

A very thorough list, annotated and updated annually, is found in Kendall Svengalis's *Legal Information Buyer's Guide and Reference Manual.* A chapter on treatises spans 500 pages and has annotated listings in more than sixty subject areas. The annotations provide useful summaries of the scope of the works listed, as well as the annual cost of maintaining subscriptions.

Treatises and practice materials focusing on the law of particular jurisdictions can be found in most state legal research guides. *State Practice Materials: Annotated Bibliographies* (Frank G. Houdek ed., 2002–date, available on HeinOnline) has descriptive listings of treatises by subject for almost forty states.

Historical Texts. Usually when searching for texts you are looking for current materials, as legal research usually involves determining the law now in effect. At times, however, you may also need information on legal developments occurring decades or centuries ago. The background of a court decision, statute, or constitutional provision can affect its current interpretation and is thus of more than historical or scholarly interest.

Classic texts such as William Blackstone's *Commentaries on the Laws of England* (1765–69) and Oliver Wendell Holmes, Jr.'s *The Common Law* (1881) are published in modern facsimile or scholarly editions, and the original works may be found in rare book collections in both general and law libraries.[13]

Historical texts are also widely available online in PDF. Three online subscription resources focus specifically on historical law books. The Making of Modern Law: Legal Treatises, 1800–1926 (www.gale.com) has over 22,000 American and British works from the nineteenth and early twentieth centuries, searchable by author, title, or subject as well as full text. HeinOnline's Legal Classics library has more than 10,000 titles, ranging in publication date from the 16th century through the early 21st century. Westlaw's Rise of American Law covers some 400 older encyclopedias and treatises from 1820 to 1970.

Legal materials are also included in more general online book collections. Early American Imprints (www.readex.com) focuses on American works and has over 70,000 books, pamphlets, and broadsides published between 1639 and 1819. Works before 1700 can be found in Early English Books Online (EEBO) (eebo.chadwyck.com), and English books from the 1700s are in Eighteenth Century Collections Online (ECCO) (www.gale.com). ECCO has some works published in the colonies, but it excludes many of the items covered in Early American Imprints.

Other more general digitization projects such as HathiTrust Digital Library (www.hathitrust.org), the Internet Archive's Text

---

[13] See ANN JORDAN LAEUCHLI, A BIBLIOGRAPHICAL CATALOG OF WILLIAM BLACKSTONE (2015) for a thorough treatment of the history of editions of the *Commentaries*, and Albert W. Alschuler, *Rediscovering Blackstone*, 145 U. PA. L. REV. 1, 3 n.4 (1996), for an explanation of how the work is cited. The *Bluebook* has a special rule for citing Blackstone: THE BLUEBOOK: A UNIFORM SYSTEM OF CITATION R. 15.8(b) (21st ed. 2020).

Archive (archive.org/details/texts), and Google Books (books.google. com) provide access to millions of books from major research libraries.[14] The full text is searchable, and PDF copies of books in the public domain (generally those published more than ninety-five years ago) are available.

Not all books have been digitized, and bibliographies of historical publications can still be useful in identifying relevant works. Morris L. Cohen, *Bibliography of Early American Law* (1998– 2003) is a comprehensive record of American law publishing up to 1860. In seven volumes, this magisterial work provides a descriptive listing of monographs, treatises, and other works by subject, with extensive indexing by author, title, jurisdiction, and year. Major guides to sources in English legal history are J. N. Adams & G. Averley, *A Bibliography of Eighteenth Century Legal Literature* (1982) and J. N. Adams & M. J. Davies, *A Bibliography of Nineteenth Century Legal Literature* (1992–96).[15]

---

[14] Google has an Advanced Book Search screen (books.google.com/advanced_book_search) that offers search boxes for author, title, and publication date, but it unfortunately does not link to this feature from its main search screen. HathiTrust includes much of the same content that was included in the Google Books project, and its interface remains quite robust and accessible.

[15] For more information on legal history resources, see JOHN B. NANN & MORRIS L. COHEN, THE YALE LAW SCHOOL GUIDE TO RESEARCH IN AMERICAN LEGAL HISTORY (2018); and Morris L. Cohen, *Researching Legal History in the Digital Age*, 99 LAW LIBR. J. 377 (2007).

Chapter 3

PERIODICALS

Table of Sections

Periodicals play a vital role in legal discourse, both as a leading repository of scholarship and as a source of information about new legislative, judicial, and regulatory developments. Researchers may look to texts for basic doctrine, but they more often turn to law reviews and journals to understand changes in the law.

Legal periodicals appear in a wide range of forms, from scholarly law reviews to blogs covering the most recent breaking news, and they serve a variety of research functions. Some law review articles have analyses and insights that merit study even decades after publication. Bar journals tend to highlight current practice trends, and legal newspapers, newsletters, and blogs offer current awareness of new developments. All of these resources can serve as springboards to further research.

Legal research also requires access to nonlegal periodicals. Scientific journal articles can provide information to underlie a tort claim. Contemporary coverage of business developments can be helpful in both litigation or transactional practice. Historical newspapers provide coverage of political and legal changes. These interdisciplinary and fact-finding resources can be just as valuable as the publications of lawyers and legal academics.

§ 3.1 TYPES OF LEGAL PERIODICALS

Journals play a central role in legal analysis. They often offer more intense and focused treatment of specific issues than treatises, and they cover new developments more quickly. Their voluminous footnotes can lead to a wealth of primary sources and other research leads.

Academic Law Reviews. Some of the most important scholarly commentary in American law appears in the academic legal journals known as law reviews. Since the late 19th century, academic law reviews have been an important intellectual force with thorough discussion of legal developments and analysis of decisions and statutes.[1] A number of influential articles have led directly to major changes in legal doctrine. Thousands of law review articles are published every year, so effective research requires precise searching and careful evaluation of articles found.[2]

The terms "law journal" and "law review" in periodical names do not have distinct meanings. Many legal newspapers are called "journals," as in the *National Law Journal* or the *New York Law Journal*, but the name is also used by prestigious academic law reviews such as the *Yale Law Journal*. Some journals, such as *Constitutional Commentary* or *Health Matrix*, use neither term in their titles but are nonetheless academic law reviews. It is a periodical's form and content that determine its nature, not its title.

The law review is a form of scholarly publication unknown to most disciplines. It is usually edited by law students rather than established scholars and serves as an educational tool for its editors as well as a forum for discussion of legal developments and theories. At most law reviews, law students exercise complete control over the acceptance and editing of articles submitted by law professors and practicing lawyers.[3] This system remains the norm despite frequent criticism over the years. Law reviews have been criticized for other

---

[1] For historical background, see Michael I. Swygert & Jon W. Bruce, *The Historical Origins, Founding, and Early Development of Student-Edited Law Reviews*, 36 HASTINGS L.J. 739 (1985). There is a vast literature on law reviews. For works up to the mid-1990s, see Mary Beth Beazley & Linda H. Edwards, *The Process and the Product: A Bibliography of Scholarship about Legal Scholarship*, 49 MERCER L. REV. 741 (1998).

[2] A study found that 43% of law review articles are never cited at all, and about 79% get ten or fewer citations. Thomas A. Smith, *The Web of Law*, 44 SAN DIEGO L. REV. 309, 335–36 (2007). "The large majority of law review articles quickly and irreversibly become completely obscure or 'dead,' and . . . are never or rarely cited." *Id.* at 346.

Several attempts have been made to rank the relative prestige of various law reviews. The most extensive ranking system is the Washington & Lee Law Library's *W&L Law Journal Rankings* (managementtools4.wlu.edu/LawJournals/), which offers several ways to rank more than 1,500 journals based on their citation in journal articles and cases.

[3] On the differences between student-edited law reviews and the peer-reviewed journals common in other disciplines, see Lawrence M. Friedman, *Law Reviews and Legal Scholarship: Some Comments*, 75 DENV. U. L. REV. 661 (1998); James Lindgren, *An Author's Manifesto*, 61 U. CHI. L. REV. 527, 535 (1994) ("In some other parts of the academy, legal journals are considered a joke. Scholars elsewhere frequently can't believe that, for almost all our major academic journals, we let students without advanced degrees select manuscripts."); and Gerald N. Rosenberg, *Across the Great Divide (Between Law and Political Science)*, 3 GREEN BAG 2D 267, 270–71 (2000).

reasons as well, including their irrelevancy to legal practice and their sheer proliferation.[4]

Most law reviews follow a fairly standard format, containing lengthy *articles* and shorter *essays* by professors and lawyers, as well as *comments* or *notes* by students. Articles and essays by established scholars are more influential, but the student contributions can also be very useful in research. Like articles, they usually begin with an introductory section providing a summary of the relevant legal doctrine and citing the key literature. This introduction can provide an excellent overview and a starting point for research.[5] The entire text is usually accompanied by footnotes citing cases, statutes, books, articles, websites, and other sources. An author and a team of law student editors may have worked months to gather citations and verify their accuracy, giving you a good head start in your research.

The terms *comment* and *note* are not quite interchangeable, but they have different meanings depending on the journal. In some, *comments* are similar in form to articles and provide extended analysis of legal issues while *notes*, or *casenotes*, are shorter examinations of specific cases. Other journals reverse this and have lengthy *notes* and short *case comments*. Student work was often published without author attribution or was identified only by the author's initials for much of the 20th century, but now almost every law review identifies the student authors of notes and comments. Student authors must be identified as such in citations to their work.[6] Their contributions are not less useful for research purposes than

---

[4] *See, e.g.*, Harry T. Edwards, *The Growing Disjunction Between Legal Education and the Legal Profession*, 91 MICH. L. REV. 34 (1992); Harry T. Edwards, *Another Look at Professor Rodell's* Goodbye to Law Reviews, 100 VA. L. REV. 1483 (2014); and Kenneth Lasson, *Scholarship Amok: Excesses in the Pursuit of Truth and Tenure*, 103 HARV. L. REV. 926 (1990).

The anti-law review literature has engendered a counter-literature in their defense. *See, e.g.*, Wendy J. Gordon, *Counter-Manifesto: Student-Edited Reviews and the Intellectual Properties of Scholarship*, 61 U. CHI. L. REV. 541 (1994); Cameron Stracher, *Reading, Writing, and Citing: In Praise of Law Reviews*, 52 N.Y. L. SCH. L. REV. 349 (2007/08).

Recent articles summarizing the various criticisms and defenses include John Doyle, *The Law Reviews: Do Their Paths of Glory Lead But to the Grave?*, 10 J. APP. PRAC. & PROCESS 179 (2009); Barry Friedman, *Fixing Law Reviews*, 67 DUKE L.J. (2018); and Richard A. Wise et al., *Do Law Reviews Need Reform? A Survey of Law Professors, Student Editors, Attorneys, and Judges*, 59 LOY. L. REV. 1, 7–32 (2013).

[5] *See* Gordon, *supra* note 4, at 547–48 ("[M]ost articles are expected to contain a lengthy introductory section where the author summarizes the relevant case law and literature from which her topic has arisen. . . . If I want to learn about a new area, I can do so by picking up virtually any article.")

[6] THE BLUEBOOK: A UNIFORM SYSTEM OF CITATION R. 16.7.1 (21st ed. 2020); ALWD GUIDE TO LEGAL CITATION R. 21.2(b) (6th ed. 2017). Student works are generally identified by indicating the type of piece (e.g., "Note" or "Comment") after the author's name.

articles by professors, but they are generally considered less persuasive as authority.

Illustration 3-1 shows a page from a recent law review article on safety issues involved in traveling with dogs.[7] The page shown is from the first part of the article, on empirical research explaining why dogs and humans enjoy riding together. Its footnotes do not cite any cases or statutes, but they do cite two books, a scientific journal article, and several internet sources.

Practically every law school accredited by the American Bar Association has a general law review that publishes articles on a wide range of topics, and most schools also have additional journals on specialized subjects. More than three dozen law reviews are published on issues in environmental law, for example, and about twenty on issues of gender, sexuality, or sexual orientation. Some larger law schools have ten or more specialized journals.

A few subject-specialized academic journals are edited by faculty rather than students. These include several highly respected journals such as *Constitutional Commentary* at the University of Minnesota, *Journal of Empirical Legal Studies* at Cornell, *Journal of Law, Economics and Organization* at Yale, *Law & Contemporary Problems* at Duke, *Tax Law Review* at New York University, and three titles— *Journal of Law and Economics*, *Journal of Legal Studies*, and *Supreme Court Review*—at the University of Chicago.[8]

Bar Journals. Specialized journals are also issued by bar associations and commercial publishers. Articles in these journals tend to be shorter and more practical than those found in academic law reviews, often focusing on current developments of interest to practicing lawyers. They are also more likely to feature articles written by practitioners than the general-interest law reviews.[9]

---

[7] Phyllis Coleman, *Keeping That Doggie in the (Car) Window Safe: Recommendations for Driving with Canine Companions*, 38 PACE L. REV. 338 (2018).

[8] On faculty editing or supervision of law reviews, see Christian C. Day, *The Case for Professionally-Edited Law Reviews*, 33 OHIO N.U. L. REV. 563 (2007); Neil Hamilton, *The Law Faculty's Ethical Failures Regarding Student-Edited Law Reviews*, 23:4 PROF. LAW. 34 (2016).

[9] *See* Robert M. Lawless & Ira David, *The General Role Played by Specialty Law Journals: Empirical Evidence from Bankruptcy Scholarship*, 80 AM. BANKR. L.J. 523, 542–43 (2006).

2018   *DOGGIE IN THE (CAR) WINDOW*   345

even catastrophic, misunderstandings."[22] Nevertheless, given what experts have learned about canines in the last decade or so since studying them became a serious profession, it is possible to theorize why pets get so enthusiastic when invited along on a ride.

As pack animals, dogs love to be with their families.[23] On a car trip, everyone is together on an exciting escapade, just as it would be in the wild. In addition, canines are typically interested in any adventure.[24] And one of the primary reasons a car trip is so stimulating to dogs is their super sensitivity to smells. Indeed, in using their noses to obtain information, they "are miles ahead of us humans,"[25] which means when traveling with access to an open window, they are experiencing a cornucopia of thousands of new odors every minute.[26] Turning to science,[27] it is easy to understand why a canine's sense of smell

---

22. JENNIFER ARNOLD, THROUGH A DOG'S EYES 106 (2010). Jennifer Arnold has trained service dogs for people with disabilities and special needs for more than two decades. *Our Founder*, CANINE ASSISTANTS, http://www.canine assistants.org/our-founder/ (last visited Apr. 30, 2018).

23. Indeed, renowned anthrozoologist (someone who studies interactions between human and nonhuman animals) and author Dr. John Bradshaw says "[m]any dogs — maybe as many as half the dogs in the West — that are kept in homes have a real problem with being left alone at some point in their lives . . . [a]nd the problem may last for weeks or years. . . . They crave the company of people." John Bradshaw, *The New Science of Understanding Dog Behavior*, NPR BOOKS (May 26, 2011, 11:30 AM), http://www.npr.org/2011/05/26/136497064/ the-new-science-of-understanding-dog-behavior.

24. *Why Dogs Love Car Rides*, TRIPSWITHPETS.COM [hereinafter *Why Dogs Love Car Rides*], https://www.tripswithpets.com/twp-blog/why-dogs-love-car-rides (last visited Apr. 30, 2018).

25. JOHN BRADSHAW, DOG SENSE: HOW THE NEW SCIENCE OF DOG BEHAVIOR CAN MAKE YOU A BETTER FRIEND TO YOUR PET 232 (2011). The author explains "[d]ogs live in a world that's dominated by their sense of smell – one that's quite unlike ours, which is constructed around what we see." *Id.* at 189, 225-28.

26. *Why Dogs Love Car Rides*, *supra* note 24.

27. Although a dog's strong sense of smell has been studied, repeatedly confirmed, and widely accepted for many years, a May 2017 article in *Science* challenges the common belief that, in this area, humans are comparatively deficient. John P. McGann, *Poor Human Olfaction is a 19th-Century Myth*, 356 SCIENCE 7263, 7263 (2017). Attributing "the idea that humans have tiny olfactory bulbs and a poor sense of smell" at least partially to religious politics of 19th-

Illustration 3-1. A page from a law review article.

Among the most respected of the specialized bar journals are several published by sections of the American Bar Association, such as *Administrative Law Review*, *Antitrust Law Journal*, and *Business Lawyer*. Some commercial publications such as *Tax Notes* or the *Journal of Passthrough Entities* are major vehicles for lawyers in specialized areas such as taxation to exchange ideas about current developments.

Most national and state bar associations publish monthly or quarterly magazines with shorter articles and more emphasis on graphics and readability. Even a glossy magazine, however, may contain valuable articles on topics of current interest in its jurisdiction. Because they are written for lawyers, even short articles generally have footnotes with references to cases, code provisions, and other sources.

Illustration 3-2 shows the first page of a recent state bar journal article on pet custody laws.[10] It's much shorter than a law review article (in this instance just two pages), but its notes lead to cases and statutes from several jurisdictions. The article shown is available on both Westlaw and HeinOnline.

Journals in Other Disciplines. Effective legal research, whether academic or practical, is not limited to the insular world of law journals. Several major interdisciplinary legal journals, such as *Law & Human Behavior* and *Law & Society Review*, contain articles with a broader perspective on legal issues, and journals in related disciplines such as economics, history, political science, and psychology can provide invaluable background and analysis. Thousands of scholarly journals are published, so a wealth of information is available to those who know how to tap into it.[11]

---

[10] Barbara J. Gislason, *Understanding Pet Custody Law: Trends in Animal Law Jurisprudence*, BENCH & B. MINN., Nov. 2019, at 22.

[11] Estimates of the number of scholarly journals vary. One report found that there were about 33,100 scholarly peer-reviewed English-language journals as of mid-2018. ROB JOHNSON ET AL., THE STM REPORT: AN OVERVIEW OF SCIENTIFIC AND SCHOLARLY JOURNAL PUBLISHING 5 (5th ed. 2018). The Elektronische Zeitschriftenbibliothek (EZB) (Electronic Journals Library) (ezb.uni-regensburg.de) has links to the homepages for more than 98,000 titles, of which more than two-thirds are available free online.

Understanding pet custody law

Trends in animal law jurisprudence

By Barbara J. Gislason

It is well-known that about 67 percent of U.S. households have pets, and expenditures on them exceed $72 billion per year.[1] Following Hurricane Katrina, according to one poll, 93 percent of pet owners claimed they would risk their lives for their pets.[2] Consider these developments against the backdrop of the 1897 landmark decision of *Sentell v. New Orleans Carrollton Railroad Co.*[3] According to *Sentell*, dogs, in particular, were "quasi-property" unless subdued or dead. Now that more than a century has passed and rabid dogs are rare, there are many indications that dogs are beginning to enter the family unit. This can be better understood by seeing how animal-related cases in unrelated subject matters, both within a state and across the country, affect each other. This is both a sophisticated and a complex analysis.

A predicate to the emerging view that animals are not merely property is the passage of animal cruelty laws. All states, as well as Washington D.C., Puerto Rico, and the Virgin Islands, have passed at least one type of animal cruelty felony law.[4] The earliest states to pass such laws were Massachusetts in 1804, Oklahoma in 1887, Rhode Island in 1896, and Michigan in 1931. The last state to enact a law of this type was South Dakota in 2014.[5] In a similar vein, a growing list of states have passed laws that enable a judge to include pets in orders for protection. According to the Animal Legal and Historical Center, 32 states had passed these laws as of 2017.[6]

At the turn of the last century, estate planning lawyers—aware that people could not bequeath their "property to property," and that this limitation was concerning for their clients—brought this problem to the attention of what is now called the Uniform Law Commission (ULC). The ULC created two types of uniform pet trust laws that served as the backbone for pet trust laws passed in all 50 states. These laws are indicative of the fact that companion animals, at the very least, are distinguishable from other types of property.

On another front, the seeds were planted for setting criteria that should be applied in pet custody disputes, including what negative behaviors the judiciary and legislators would tolerate.[7] Against all odds, dicta from an unpublished decision in Minnesota, *Pratt v. Pratt*,[8] gained national attention. In that decision, the appellate court, while declining to render its decision based upon the best interests of two St. Bernards, nevertheless speculated on what the court would do if mistreatment of a companion animal was involved. The court also pointed out that the trial court had broad discretion in rendering an award if there was an "acceptable basis in fact."[9]

Courts have wanted to take the best interests of animals into account as far back as 1944, when the seminal decision in *Akers v. Sellers*[10] was issued. In that often-cited case, the court complained that on appeal, it lacked an adequate record to decide whether the lower court had rendered a "just and wise decision." The court further stated, "Whether the interests and desires of the dog, in such a situation, should be the polar star pointing the way to a just and wise decision, or whether the matter should be determined on the brutal and unfeeling basis of legal title, is a problem concerning which we express no opinion." More so, the court went on to opine that it would be a tragedy to award the Boston Bull Terrier to one party when the affection and loyalty of the dog lay with another.

In a post-decree cat custody dispute, *Raymond v. Lachman*,[11] the New York court in 1999 issued a decision using best interest criteria for a cat named Lovey. There, the court recognized that not only could an owner love their cat, but that the cat could love them back. Ultimately, the court awarded Lovey to the party who had the house where Lovey had long lived, and where the cat prospered.

A case from New Jersey, *Houseman v. Dare*,[12] exemplifies how the courts, dealing with legal issues of first impression, have looked to a variety of well-reasoned animal law decisions across states as well as subject areas. Following their break-up, an unmarried couple effectively had shared custody of their Pug, Dexter, until one of them decided to keep the dog. The appellate court found that the underlying oral shared caregiving agreement into which the parties had entered following separation was enforceable. The higher court explored the contours of laws affecting companion animals and opened the door for the trial judge to render a joint physical custody decision, which the court effectively did.

Another influential case where the court undertook a sweeping analysis of national jurisprudence was New York's

Illustration 3-2. The first page of a bar journal article.

Open Access Scholarship. In recent years, law professors and other scholars have sought to escape the constraints of the law review system by finding new avenues for publishing their scholarship. Some authors post works on their own websites, and many use repositories of working papers and other current scholarship such as Law Commons (network.bepress.com/law) and Social Science Research Network (SSRN) (www.ssrn.com). In addition, many law schools and universities host institutional repositories providing free access to works published by their faculty and in their journals.[12]

§ 3.2 FULL-TEXT RESOURCES

You can find articles in periodicals and journals through a variety of means. The full-text databases in Westlaw and Lexis are among the most convenient and most frequently used resources, and PDF-based resources such as HeinOnline and JSTOR are particularly useful for historical and cross-disciplinary research. Indexes available online and in print can expand retrieval beyond full-text sources and focus it more accurately on a specific topic. You can also use citators to find articles discussing particular cases, statutes, or other authorities, including earlier articles.

Full-text searching has been the dominant means of finding journal articles for years, and digitization has made it a viable approach for both historical and current research. Several resources are available for this purpose.

Westlaw and Lexis. Both Westlaw and Lexis have databases containing articles from several hundred law reviews, with coverage extending back to the 1980s or early 1990s for most titles. (This means that neither platform has a complete run of most law reviews.) A general search can be filtered to focus on law review results, or you can opt for Secondary Sources (or Secondary Materials) and then Law Reviews & Journals. Law review coverage is also available through Nexis Uni (Lexis) and Campus Research (Westlaw) for university faculty and students.

---

[12] The clarion call of the open access movement for legal scholarship was Bernard J. Hibbitts, *Last Writes? Re-Assessing the Law Review in the Age of Cyberspace*, 71 N.Y.U. L. REV. 615 (1996). For more recent perspectives, see Richard A. Danner, *Open Access to Legal Scholarship: Dropping the Barriers to Discourse and Dialogue*, 7 J. INT'L COM. L. & TECH. 65 (2012); James M. Donovan et. al., *The Open Access Advantage for American Law Reviews*, 97 J. PAT. & TRADEMARK OFF. SOC'Y 4 (2015); Stephanie L. Plotin, *Legal Scholarship, Electronic Publishing, and Open Access: Transformation or Steadfast Stagnation?*, 101 LAW LIBR. J. 31 (2009); and Symposium, *Open Access Publishing and the Future of Legal Scholarship*, 10 LEWIS & CLARK L. REV. 733 (2006). On institutional repositories, see, e.g., Carol A. Parker, *Institutional Repositories and the Principle of Open Access: Changing the Way We Think about Legal Scholarship*, 37 N.M. L. REV. 431 (2007).

Search results are generally displayed by relevance, but this can be changed so that the most recent articles are listed first. When articles are listed by relevance rather than by date, be careful not to rely on outdated articles or miss important recent contributions. One way to make sure that your research is current once you find a relevant article is to click on its Citing References tab in Westlaw or its Shepardize link in Lexis. Even if the first article you find is several years old, these tools give you an easy way to find more recent articles that may be relevant to your topic. Illustration 3-3 shows the results of a law review search for *dog /10 car* in Westlaw.

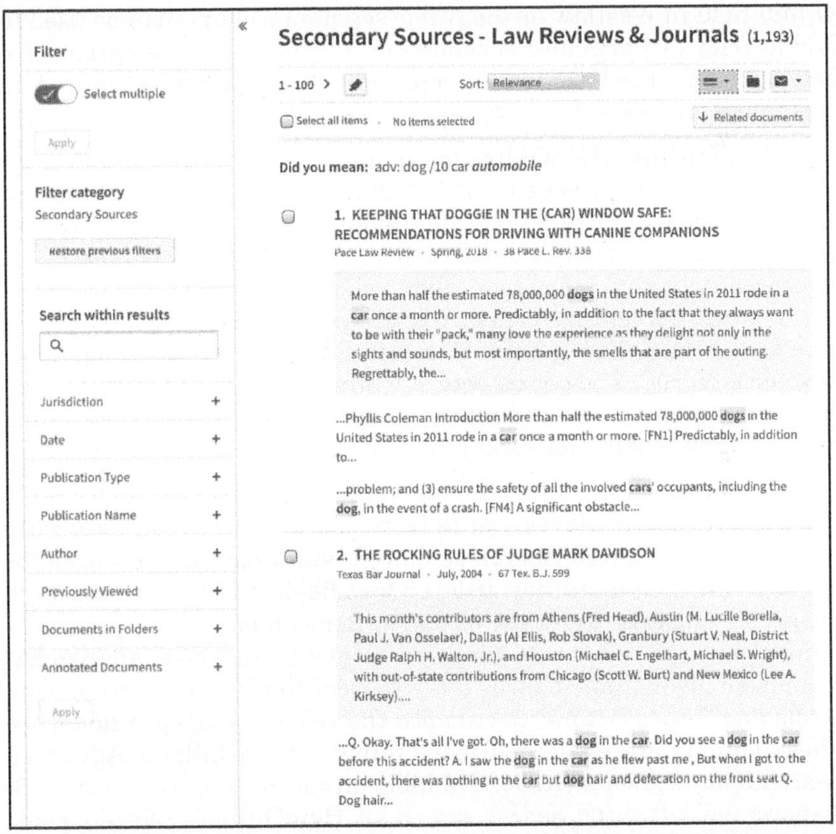

Illustration 3-3. Law review search results on Westlaw.

A law review search can pinpoint discussion or footnotes using any combination of words, including phrases, case names, or titles of other articles or books. Even an article that is not directly on point may have references to more relevant sources, including treatises or articles in journal volumes that are not themselves in the online database.

Because the online services have thousands of lengthy articles, a search limited to the *Title* field in Westlaw or Lexis may lead to a smaller but more relevant group of documents. You can also focus retrieval in terms and connectors searches by using proximity connectors and other features on advanced search screens. The *Author* field in Westlaw or the *Name* segment in Lexis can be used to find articles by particular scholars or lawyers, but these options are listed on advanced search screens only if a search is limited to secondary sources or law reviews.

HeinOnline. HeinOnline (heinonline.org) is an essential tool in law review research because it has digitized page images from the printed journals, including charts, tables, and other images, as well as the footnotes at the bottom of each page for convenient access. This is especially helpful when you need to check a citation as it appeared in the print source. In contrast, Westlaw and Lexis have the full text of articles, but they generally cannot display images and other graphic material. To see the text of footnotes requires hovering over or clicking on the note number, which can be a time-consuming process when looking for research leads.

HeinOnline offers full-text searching of its journals, and the Citation Navigator allows you to retrieve an article if you know its citation. An Advanced Search screen provides options to search for words or phrases in author, title, or text fields and to limit a search to specific subjects, journals, or dates. Boolean operators, proximity connectors, and wildcards can also be used, and new approaches include an algorithmic-based "fuzzy search" finding similarly spelled terms and "boost factors" to enhance the relevance of specific terms. These options are explained more fully in HeinOnline's Advanced Search Syntax User's Guide, available on its website. Illustration 3-4 shows the Advanced Search screen for HeinOnline's Law Journals Library.

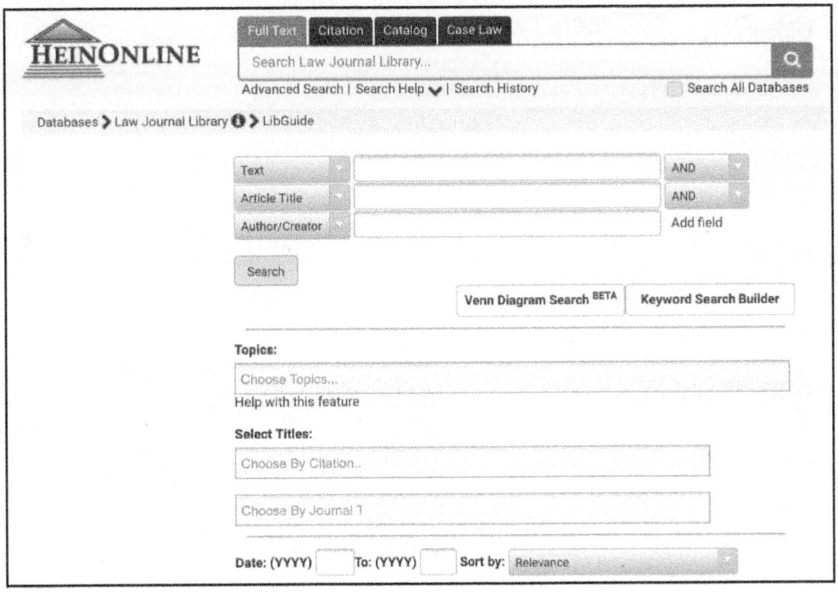

**Illustration 3-4. HeinOnline's Advanced Search
screen for law journals.**

Once a list of search results is displayed, text snippets show the context in which search terms appear and help you determine which articles to view in PDF. The display also indicates how many times each article is cited, with a direct link to the list of citing articles. You can sort results by relevance, date, or number of times cited.

Illustration 3-5 shows the law review article in Illustration 3-1 as it appears on HeinOnline, with buttons at the top for navigating through the document and downloading.

HeinOnline's coverage extends to the first volumes of most journals in its collection, making it particularly valuable in legal history research. It includes over 2,600 law reviews and law-related periodicals, and for most titles its coverage includes the most recently published issues. HeinOnline is generally considered most useful for historical research in articles not otherwise available online, or for retrieving PDF versions of articles identified through Westlaw or Lexis searches.

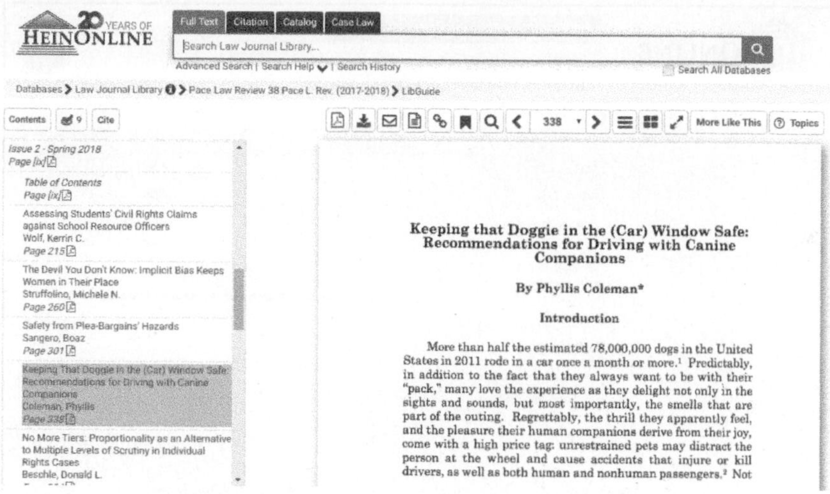

Illustration 3-5. A law review article as
displayed on HeinOnline.

Other Resources. Westlaw, Lexis, and HeinOnline are the most familiar collections of law review articles for most law students, but they are not the only available resources.

EBSCOhost Legal Source (www.ebscohost.com) has the full text of over 1,100 law journals, almost all in PDF images. Its coverage generally begins in the mid-1990s or later, but for some titles it is more current than HeinOnline. Search options include field searches (such as title, author, or subject terms) and basic Boolean connectors.

Illustration 3-6 shows the results of a subject search for articles about dogs and automobiles in Legal Source. Note that the entries include access to the full text of the articles in PDF, as well as ways to narrow retrieval by publication type and date.

Some libraries that do not subscribe to Legal Source may instead have Index to Legal Periodicals and Books Full Text (ILP) or Legal Collection, smaller collections of full text law journals from EBSCOhost. ILP has full text for almost 500 journals, and Legal Collection covers more than 350. All three products use the same interface, with the same search options.

Other sources have smaller collections of law reviews. The periodical index LegalTrac has the full text of about 200 titles.

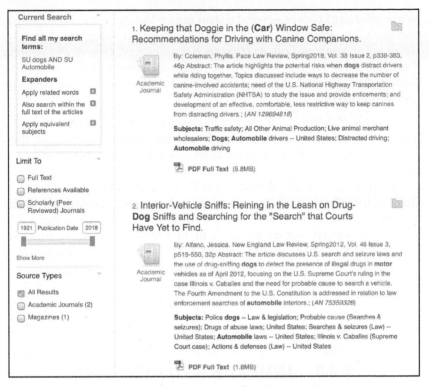

Illustration 3-6. Legal Source search results.

A growing number of law reviews now provide free access to recent articles on their websites, although some still feature only tables of contents or abstracts and many are not fully up to date. Some law schools also have institutional repositories that feature complete retrospective runs of their law journals in PDF form.

Several law review websites also feature shorter pieces available only electronically, in online supplements with titles like *Forum* or *Sidebar*.[13] A few law reviews, such as the *Virginia Journal of Law and Technology* (www.vjolt.org), are published only electronically.[14]

General Scholarly Journal Sites. Legal periodicals are also available through more general scholarly literature websites. JSTOR

---

[13] A list of these online supplements, with links, appears at *Law Review Companions*, LEGAL SCHOLARSHIP BLOG (legalscholarshipblog.com/law-review-companions/) [https://perma.cc/U39F-8FVM]. Bradley Scott Shannon, *Naming Online Law Review Supplements (Or Whatever They Are Called)*, 165 U. PA. L. REV. ONLINE 109 (2017), suggests several possible names for such supplements.

[14] A group of academic law library directors has called for an end to print publication of law journals, coupled with open access publication and permanent access to digital editions. *See* Richard A. Danner et al., *The Durham Statement Two Years Later: Open Access in the Law School Journal Environment*, 103 LAW LIBR. J. 39 (2011).

(www.jstor.org) covers several dozen major law reviews, for example, and includes some titles not available through Westlaw, Lexis, or HeinOnline such as *Law & Human Behavior* and *Law & Philosophy*. For some titles it does not have recent issues (generally from the past three to five years), but like HeinOnline it has retrospective coverage and is full-text searchable.

Google Scholar (scholar.google.com) provides full-text access to millions of articles, including those in law reviews and other legal journals. Access to some articles is free, but for others full-text access depends on whether your institution subscribes to services such as HeinOnline or JSTOR. Searching is through the familiar and simple Google interface, with some advanced search options available through the drop-down menu in the top left corner of the screen. The Advanced Search screen allows you to limit a search to words or phrases in the titles of articles and to specific publication dates. Search results include links to more recent works citing the listed article ("Cited by") and articles with similar terms ("Related articles"), providing opportunities to expand research. Google Scholar is free and can be a convenient place to begin research, although there is no way of learning the scope of its coverage and therefore no way of knowing whether important articles are omitted.[15]

§ 3.3   INDEXES AND CITATORS

Full-text searching is a powerful tool, but it does have limitations. Even with relevance ranking, keyword searches can retrieve many extraneous articles that use the search words but that are not relevant to your research. Limiting a search to keywords in the title field can help, but not all articles have very descriptive or informative titles.

An index is a way to narrow retrieval to articles more specifically on point. (In addition, thousands of articles remain available only in print and might never be found through full-text online searches.) Many libraries' online systems also offer "link resolvers" that lead

---

[15] *See, e.g.*, Péter Jacsó, *Google Scholar: The Pros and the Cons*, 29 ONLINE INFO. REV. 208, 209 (2005) ("The underlying problem with Google Scholar is that Google is as secretive about its coverage as the North Korean government about the famine in the country. There is no information about the publishers whose archive Google is allowed to search, let alone about the specific journals and the host sites covered by Google Scholar."). Google Scholar's lack of transparency remains unchanged. Christopher C. Brown, *Advisor Reviews—Standard Review: Google Scholar*, CHARLESTON ADVISOR, Oct. 2017, at 31, 31 ("Most vendors are forthcoming with journal title lists, dates of coverage, and full text availability. GS leaves it up to users to figure out what is or is not included in the indexing.").

Estimates of the size of the Google Scholar database vary. One recent article estimated that it contained 389 million records. Michael Greenbauer, *Google Scholar to Overshadow Them All? Comparing the Sizes of 12 Academic Search Engines and Bibliographic Databases*, 118 SCIENTOMETRICS 177 (2019).

directly from an index entry to the full text in HeinOnline or another service. This method combines the best of both research worlds: expert indexing to ensure that relevant articles are not missed, and immediate online access to the text.

ILP and LegalTrac. Two general indexes to English-language legal periodical literature are available online.[16] Index to Legal Periodicals and Books (ILP) is available from EBSCOhost (www. ebscohost.com), and to some subscribers through other online services. LegalTrac is available as part of Gale's InfoTrac service (www.gale.com), and is known as Legal Resource Index (LRI) on Westlaw and Lexis.

Each of these indexes covers more than 1,000 law reviews and periodicals, with coverage back to the early 1980s. As noted earlier, both include the full text of some of the more recent articles indexed. EBSCOhost also offers an Index to Legal Periodicals Retrospective database, cumulating entries from older index volumes from 1908 to 1981. The current and retrospective ILP products are incorporated into EBSCOhost's Legal Source platform.

Both LegalTrac and ILP offer keyword searching as well as subject indexing, making it easy to find articles on related topics. LegalTrac uses detailed Library of Congress subjects with subheadings and cross-references, while ILP generally has fewer, broader subjects. Each approach has advantages; sometimes your research may have a very specific focus, while at other times a broader survey is appropriate. Once you find one relevant article, clicking on its subject headings links you to other articles on related topics.

For research in legal history, the predecessor to the *Index to Legal Periodicals*, entitled *Index to Legal Periodical Literature*

---

[16] Printed versions of both periodical indexes have ceased publication, but they may be of occasional use in historical research. They have some idiosyncrasies of which users should be aware. *Index to Legal Periodicals (ILP)*, published from 1908 to 2012, indexed articles by subject and author, but in printed volumes before 1983 full bibliographic information appeared only under subject entries. The author entries consisted merely of subject heading cross-references, each followed by the first letter of the article's title. If you are looking for work by a specific author, you would need to turn to the appropriate subject heading and then scan its listings to find the title and location of the article.

The printed counterpart to LegalTrac, known as the *Current Law Index (CLI)*, was published from 1980 to 2016. Each annual index consisted of two volumes with separate author and subject sections. *CLI*'s scope was somewhat narrower than LegalTrac and Legal Resource Index because it omitted their coverage of legal newspapers and relevant articles in non-law periodicals.

(1888–1939, available on HeinOnline), may be of use. The first volume has retrospective coverage from 1770 to 1886.[17]

Citators. Resources such as Westlaw Citing References and Shepard's Citations serve two important purposes in periodical research. You can find articles that cite a primary source such as a case or statute, and you can track a law review article to find later sources in which *it* is cited. As noted above, HeinOnline also serves this latter function of tracking more recent citing articles.

You can also find references to a particular article in full-text databases on Westlaw, Lexis, or HeinOnline simply by using its title or citation as a search phrase. A full-text search can go beyond the scope of citator coverage and find references to *any* published work of interest—including articles in early or obscure law reviews, journal literature in other disciplines, treatises, or monographs.

General Periodical Indexes. Legal research is rarely confined to cases, statutes, and law review articles. You also need to be able to find information across a broad spectrum of disciplines. Several indexes to nonlegal periodical literature can supply valuable leads. Some of these are specialized indexes in particular disciplines, while others have comprehensive coverage of a wide range of sources. The online versions of many indexes link directly to full-text PDF versions of the articles they cover.

JSTOR was mentioned earlier as a source for retrospective coverage of several dozen legal journals; it also has full-text comprehensive coverage of over 2,000 other non-law scholarly journals. Online indexes from other disciplines such as ABI/INFORM (business and economics), America: History & Life (U.S. and Canadian history), EconLit (economics), PAIS Index (public policy), PsycINFO (psychology and related disciplines), or Sociological Abstracts may offer background information or interdisciplinary perspectives. A few indexes are available free, such as the National Library of Medicine's PubMed version of MEDLINE, the comprehensive index of biomedical journals (www.pubmed.gov). Most index databases are accessible only by subscription, but researchers in university or law school programs usually have access to several major resources. Most of these databases include searchable abstracts, which can be invaluable both in finding articles

---

[17] *Index to Legal Periodical Literature* is sometimes called the Jones-Chipman index after the names of its editors, Leonard A. Jones (vols. 1–2) and Frank E. Chipman (vols. 3–6). The development of legal periodical indexes is discussed in Richard A. Leiter, *A History of Legal Periodical Indexing*, LEGAL REFERENCE SERVICES Q., Spring 1987, at 35. KERMIT L. HALL, A COMPREHENSIVE BIBLIOGRAPHY OF AMERICAN CONSTITUTIONAL AND LEGAL HISTORY (1984–91) lists books and articles published between 1896 and 1987 and is another potentially useful source for legal historians.

and in identifying whether they would be of value, and some also include links to later works in which they are cited.

Major multidisciplinary indexes, one or more of which is usually available at an academic library, include Academic Search Complete (www.ebscohost.com), Academic OneFile (www.gale.com), and ProQuest Central (www.proquest.com). All of these platforms serve as one-stop shops for journal literature in the sciences, social sciences, and humanities. Two other subscription web databases with access to older journal articles from as far back as 1665 are Periodicals Archive Online (www.proquest.com) (full text of more than 700 journals) and Periodicals Index Online (www.proquest.com) (indexing over 6,000 other journals).

Scopus (www.scopus.com) and Web of Science (www.webof knowledge.com) are very broad indexes covering thousands of journals; either can be used to find articles by author or keyword, and they also link articles to later works in which they are cited. Ingenta Connect (www.ingentaconnect.com) also has comprehensive coverage of current journal literature, with tables of contents information from several thousand publications. Like Google Scholar, searching on Ingenta Connect is free to researchers unaffiliated with subscribing institutions. Most articles are available for fee-based download by nonsubscribers.

§ 3.4   CURRENT SCHOLARSHIP

The full-text databases and standard legal periodical indexes are valuable for subject searches, when you are trying to find articles on a particular topic. When you are looking for current scholarship in an area, you can use resources specifically designed to keep the scholarly community apprised of recent and forthcoming articles.

Current Index to Legal Periodicals (*CILP*), published weekly by William S. Hein & Co. on HeinOnline, reprints the tables of contents for new law review issues and indexes articles by subject. It covers almost 600 law reviews, indexing articles under approximately 100 subject headings. Subscribers can receive customized weekly e-mail "SmartCILP" updates focusing on particular subjects and journal titles.

Social Science Research Network (SSRN) and Law Commons (bepress) were mentioned earlier as alternatives to traditional law reviews for disseminating scholarship. Both are major repositories for working papers and pre-publication versions of law review articles, and new work is often available here long before it appears in print. Academic researchers, including law professors, may also make full-text drafts of their work available on bepress Expert Gallery profile pages or on law school repositories.

You can search SSRN's electronic library (papers.ssrn.com) by author or by keyword in titles and abstracts. The default display is by relevance, but you can focus on recent scholarship by sorting search results by date. Faculty and students at subscribing institutions can also sign up for weekly e-mail notification of abstracts of new articles in any of more than 100 legal subject-matter e-journals. The bepress Law Commons (network.bepress.com/law/) can also be searched by keyword, and articles can be browsed by subject to survey recent scholarship. Illustration 3-7 shows an SSRN search result, ranking retrieved articles by the number of times each has been downloaded.

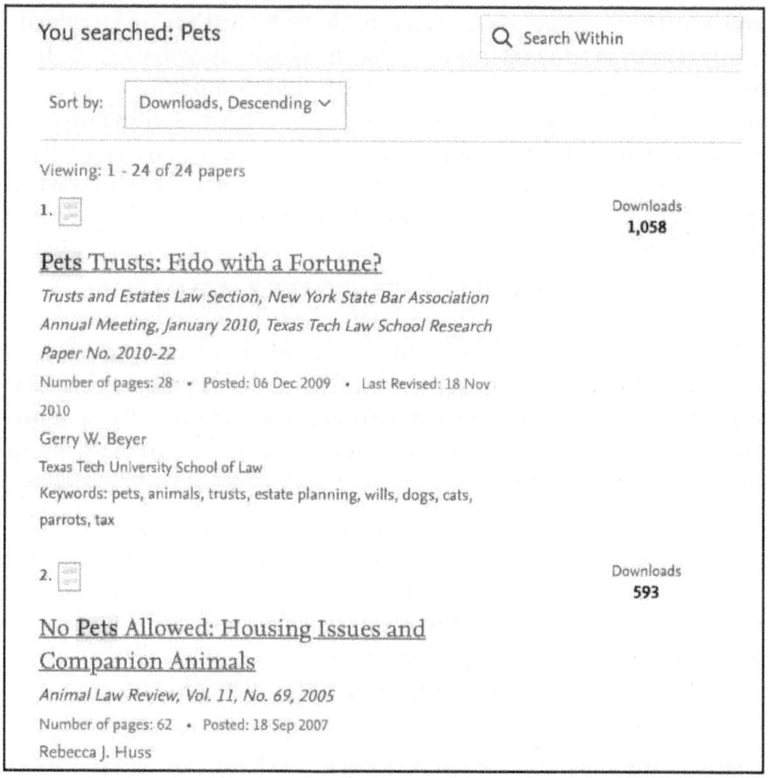

You searched: Pets

Search Within

Sort by: Downloads, Descending

Viewing: 1 - 24 of 24 papers

1\.

Downloads
1,058

Pets Trusts: Fido with a Fortune?

Trusts and Estates Law Section, New York State Bar Association Annual Meeting, January 2010, Texas Tech Law School Research Paper No. 2010-22

Number of pages: 28 • Posted: 06 Dec 2009 • Last Revised: 18 Nov 2010

Gerry W. Beyer

Texas Tech University School of Law

Keywords: pets, animals, trusts, estate planning, wills, dogs, cats, parrots, tax

2\.

Downloads
593

No Pets Allowed: Housing Issues and Companion Animals

Animal Law Review, Vol. 11, No. 69, 2005

Number of pages: 62 • Posted: 18 Sep 2007

Rebecca J. Huss

Illustration 3-7. Articles and working papers available from SSRN.

Part II

CONSTITUTIONS AND THE LEGISLATIVE BRANCH

Chapter 4

CONSTITUTIONAL LAW

Table of Sections

Constitutions are the basic law of states and nations, detailing the powers of the government and protecting individual liberties. They can take a variety of forms, ranging from relatively brief and general statements to lengthy documents of considerable specificity. The original United States Constitution was written on just four pages and remains one of the shortest of such documents in the world. The current Alabama constitution, in contrast, is over forty times its length.

Only a small part of constitutional law research relates to locating the relevant text. Most research problems focus on scholarly commentaries, judicial interpretations, and historical background. They involve research in case law and secondary sources, using resources and approaches to be discussed in later chapters. To a substantial extent, however, constitutional literature is a distinct research field with its own procedures and tools.

Most lawyers may not face constitutional law issues very often in their daily practice, but any time a client deals with the government there can be constitutional implications. Knowledge of the scope and meaning of the federal and state constitutions is also an asset to any informed citizen. The constitution of each jurisdiction determines the powers and structures of its government, while federal and state constitutions often overlap and work together in protecting rights.

This chapter first addresses sources for information on the federal constitution, and then has a shorter treatment of state constitutions.

§ 4.1   THE UNITED STATES CONSTITUTION

The Constitution of the United States is usually considered the oldest constitutional document in continuous force in the world today. Drafted in the summer of 1787 and ratified by the required nine states within a year, it entered into force in March 1789 and has been amended just twenty-seven times in more than two centuries. Among the most important of these amendments are the Bill of Rights, guaranteeing personal liberties, and the Fourteenth Amendment, applying these protections to the states.

The first step in constitutional research is often to find an overview or explanation of a doctrine; this is followed by more exhaustive case research applying a provision to specific facts, and in some instances by historical research into the background of the constitutional language. The following sections discuss sources for obtaining the text of the Constitution, interpreting its provisions, locating court decisions, and finding historical material on its framing and amendment.

(a) Text

The text of the Constitution can be found in a variety of sources. For most purposes, including citation form, any source will serve as well as another. Unlike most references to statutes, court decisions, or other authorities, a citation to a current state or federal constitution does not need to provide either a source or a date.[1]

The Constitution appears in many pamphlet editions, at the beginning of the first volume of the *United States Code*, in standard reference works such as *Black's Law Dictionary*, and in almost all state annotated codes. Its text is widely available on the internet and can be found with a simple search for "constitution." The Constitution

---

[1] THE BLUEBOOK: A UNIFORM SYSTEM OF CITATION R. 11 (21st ed. 2020); ALWD GUIDE TO LEGAL CITATION R. 13.2 (6th ed. 2017). Even obsolete provisions or outdated constitutions need only a date, not a source. This can sometimes make tracking them down a challenge, as the first step is to find a source for historical constitutions. These sources are discussed in § 4.2(c).

has not been amended since 1992, so just about any text you find will be current.[2]

(b) Reference Sources

The vast literature of constitutional law in such secondary sources as encyclopedias, treatises, and periodicals approaches the subject from both historical and contemporary viewpoints.

Encyclopedias and Handbooks. To get a sense of the nature of constitutional issues, it is often best to start with a broad overview. *The Oxford Handbook of the U.S. Constitution* (Mark Tushnet, Mark A. Graber & Sanford Levinson eds., 2015, also available online by subscription (www.oxfordhandbooks.com)) provides an introduction to the law and politics of the Constitution, with nearly fifty chapters covering a gamut of constitutional issues, such as the document's history, relations between branches of government and between the federal government and the states, specific rights protected by the Constitution, and general themes in constitutional interpretation. Each chapter includes footnotes and a brief bibliography.

Encyclopedia of the American Constitution (Leonard W. Levy & Kenneth L. Karst eds., 2d ed. 2000) is another comprehensive resource, still useful despite its age. This six-volume work contains over 2,000 articles, many by leading legal scholars, historians, and political scientists. More than half of the articles discuss doctrinal concepts of constitutional law, but others focus on specific people (including every Supreme Court justice up to Stephen Breyer), judicial decisions, statutes, and historical periods. Most articles include numerous cross-references and short bibliographies of further readings. The final volume has chronologies, a brief glossary, and indexes by case, name, and subject.

Coverage of constitutional issues can also be found in numerous other reference sources, particularly those dealing with the Supreme Court. Several of these are one-volume encyclopedias and reference handbooks. *The Oxford Companion to the Supreme Court of the United States* (Kermit L. Hall ed., 2d ed. 2005) covers constitutional principles as well as Supreme Court history and the American judicial system, with entries for major cases and Supreme Court justices. Robert L. Maddex, *The U.S. Constitution A to Z* (2d ed. 2008) is a shorter reference work for a general audience, with coverage of

---

[2] Capitalization and spelling may vary between versions, depending on which 1787 archetype is followed: the copy handwritten on parchment and signed by members of the constitutional convention, or the copy that was printed for the delegates. *See* Denys P. Myers, *History of the Printed Archetype*, in THE CONSTITUTION OF THE UNITED STATES, S. DOC. NO. 87–49, at 49 (1961), *reprinted in* 11 GREEN BAG 2D 217 (2008); Akhil Reed Amar, *Our Forgotten Constitution: A Bicentennial Comment*, 97 YALE L.J. 281 (1987).

the most significant cases and Supreme Court justices (excluding justices appointed after 2007).

A series of twenty smaller reference works, *Reference Guides to the United States Constitution*, was published between 2002 and 2013. Each volume focuses on a specific aspect of constitutional law, such as double jeopardy or freedom of speech, and includes a brief history of the topic, before and since its inclusion in the Constitution; a lengthy analysis of the state of the law in the area; and a bibliographical essay with annotated references to further readings.[3]

The Constitution of the United States of America: Analysis and Interpretation (Michael J. Garcia et al. eds., annual) (www. constitution.congress.gov) is an exhaustive, article-by-article commentary on the Constitution. This statutorily mandated work is prepared by the Congressional Research Service of the Library of Congress.[4] The constitutional text is accompanied by more than 2,100 pages of commentary, historical background, legal analysis, and summaries of judicial interpretation of each clause and amendment. The major constitutional decisions of the Supreme Court are discussed in detail, and footnotes include numerous citations to other relevant cases and scholarly interpretations. Illustration 4-1 shows the opening page of the discussion of the Nineteenth Amendment, with footnotes citing several court opinions and a scholarly monograph. The online version at Congress.gov includes links to the Supreme Court cases cited, but it does not include PDF images of the print publication. A PDF version is available on the Govinfo portal (www.govinfo.gov). The print volume and website both have tables of Acts of Congress, state constitutional and statutory provisions, and municipal ordinances that have been held unconstitutional by the Supreme Court; a list of Supreme Court decisions overruled by subsequent decisions is also included.[5]

---

[3] Titles in the series are CONSTITUTIONAL REMEDIES (2002), DOUBLE JEOPARDY (2004), FEDERALISM (2013), FREEDOM OF SPEECH (2004), FREEDOM OF THE PRESS (2004), THE FULL FAITH AND CREDIT CLAUSE (2005), JUDICIAL JURISDICTION (2007), LIMITS ON STATES (2005), THE POWER TO LEGISLATE (2006), POWERS RESERVED TO THE PEOPLE AND THE STATES (2006), PRIVILEGES AND IMMUNITIES (2003), PROCEDURAL DUE PROCESS (2004), PROHIBITED GOVERNMENT ACTS (2002), THE RELIGION GUARANTEES (2005), THE RIGHT TO A SPEEDY AND PUBLIC TRIAL (2006), THE RIGHT TO THE ASSISTANCE OF COUNSEL (2002), SEARCHES, SEIZURES, AND WARRANTS (2003), STATE SOVEREIGN IMMUNITY (2002), THE SUPREMACY CLAUSE (2004), and THE TAXING POWER (2005).

[4] 2 U.S.C. §§ 168–168d.

[5] As of 2017 the Supreme Court had invalidated 182 Acts of Congress and 1,332 state and local provisions, and it had overruled more than 300 of its earlier decisions.

WOMEN'S SUFFRAGE RIGHTS

NINETEENTH AMENDMENT

SECTIONS 1 AND 2. The right of the citizens of the United States to vote shall not be denied or abridged by the United States or by any State on account of sex.

Congress shall have power to enforce this article by appropriate legislation.

WOMEN'S SUFFRAGE

The Nineteenth Amendment was adopted after a long campaign by its advocates, who had largely despaired of attaining their goal through modification of individual state laws. Agitation in behalf of women's suffrage was recorded as early as the Jackson Administration, but the initial results were meager. Beginning in 1838, Kentucky authorized women to vote in school elections and its action was later copied by a number of other states. Kansas in 1887 granted women unlimited rights to vote in municipal elections. Not until 1869, however, when the Wyoming Territory accorded women suffrage rights on an equal basis with men and continued the practice following admission to statehood, did these advocates register a notable victory. Progress continued to be discouraging, only ten additional states having joined Wyoming by 1914, and, judicial efforts having failed.[1] A vigorous campaign brought congressional passage of a proposed Amendment in 1919 and the necessary state ratifications in 1920.[2]

Following the Supreme Court's interpretation of the Fifteenth Amendment, the state courts that passed on the effect of the Amendment ruled that it did not confer upon women the right to vote, but only the right not to be discriminated against on the basis of their sex in the setting of voting qualifications,[3] a formalistic distinction to be sure, but one that has restrained the possible applications of the Amendment. In only one case has the Supreme Court itself dealt with the Amendment's effect, holding that a Georgia poll

---

[1] Minor v. Happersett, 88 U.S. (21 Wall.) 162 (1875), a challenge under the Privileges or Immunities Clause of the Fourteenth Amendment.

[2] E. FLEXNER, CENTURY OF STRUGGLE: THE WOMAN'S RIGHTS MOVEMENT IN THE UNITED STATES (1959).

[3] State v. Mittle, 120 S.C. 526 (1922), *writ of error dismissed*, 260 U.S. 705 (1922); Graves v. Eubank, 205 Ala. 174 (1921); *In re* Cavelier, 287 N.Y.S. 739 (1936).

2293

Illustration 4-1. A page from *The Constitution of the United States of America: Analysis and Interpretation.*

Numerous scholarly monographs have been written on the U.S. Constitution. Akhil Reed Amar's *America's Constitution: A Biography* (2005) and Garrett Epps's *American Epic: Reading the U.S. Constitution* (2013) both survey the Constitution article-by-article, explaining the background and history of major provisions. Works such as Richard H. Fallon Jr., *The Dynamic Constitution: An Introduction to American Constitutional Law and Practice* (2d ed. 2013), Kent Greenawalt, *Interpreting the Constitution* (2015), and Mark A. Graber, *A New Introduction to American Constitutionalism* (2013) provide more general introductions to constitutional theory.[6] *The Cambridge Companion to the United States Constitution* (Karen Orren & John W. Compton eds., 2018) offers sixteen chapters on specific topics such as due process, federalism, and executive power.

Legal Treatises. Encyclopedias and other reference sources provide a broad perspective of constitutional history and theory. More detailed examination of constitutional issues from a doctrinal perspective is offered by several major treatises, which analyze the relevant case law in depth.

The most detailed work is Ronald D. Rotunda & John E. Nowak's *Treatise on Constitutional Law: Substance and Procedure* (5th ed. 2012–date), six volumes updated with annual pocket parts. Abridged one-volume versions are published as *Constitutional Law* (8th ed. 2010) and *Principles of Constitutional Law* (5th ed. 2016). The full treatise is available on Westlaw, and the abridged versions are in West Academic's Study Aids Subscription.

A one-volume work by Erwin Chemerinsky, *Constitutional Law: Principles and Policies* (5th ed. 2015), is less exhaustive but is cited more by scholars and courts than Rotunda and Nowak's treatise, and is available through Wolters Kluwer Law School Study Aids. Laurence H. Tribe, *American Constitutional Law* (2d & 3d eds. 1988–2000) was for years the most influential treatment of the subject and continues to be cited, although it is now considerably out of date.[7]

Journal Articles. Constitutional law is widely covered in many law reviews. In addition, several periodicals specialize in

---

[6] Older works can be found using SHELLEY L. DOWLING, THE JURISPRUDENCE OF UNITED STATES CONSTITUTIONAL INTERPRETATION: AN ANNOTATED BIBLIOGRAPHY (2d ed. 2010) and ROBERT J. JANOSIK, THE AMERICAN CONSTITUTION: AN ANNOTATED BIBLIOGRAPHY (1991).

[7] The author suspended revision of the work midway through the third edition. The first and second editions were single-volume works. Tribe published the first part of a two-volume third edition in 2000, but announced five years later in an "open letter to interested readers of American constitutional law" that the subject was in such a state of flux that he had decided not to complete the work. Laurence H. Tribe, *The Treatise Power*, 8 GREEN BAG 2D 291 (2005). The volume published in 2000 covers issues such as federalism and separation of powers but does not have much discussion of individual rights and liberties.

constitutional issues. *Constitutional Commentary* is a faculty-edited journal from the University of Minnesota with a preference for "shorter, less ponderous articles" than those found in most traditional law reviews.[8] Student-edited law reviews include *Duke Journal of Constitutional Law & Public Policy*, *First Amendment Law Review*, *Harvard Civil Rights-Civil Liberties Law Review*, *Hastings Constitutional Law Quarterly*, and *University of Pennsylvania Journal of Constitutional Law*. Journals focusing on the Supreme Court, such as the *Supreme Court Review* and the annual survey of the Court's term in the *Harvard Law Review*, also have thorough coverage of constitutional topics. All of these are generally available through Westlaw, Lexis, HeinOnline, and other sources for law reviews.

More than most areas of legal doctrine, constitutional topics are addressed widely by scholars outside the legal academy. Depending on the area of inquiry, journals in disciplines such as political science or history can have contributions every bit as important as those in law reviews. Searches in broad interdisciplinary resources such as JSTOR or Google Scholar can turn up valuable scholarship in academic journals and other sources.

(c) Court Decisions

The Constitution's provisions have been applied over the past two centuries to a wide array of situations which its drafters could not have foreseen. To interpret the language of the Constitution, it is essential to understand how it has been applied by the courts—particularly the Supreme Court, but also the lower federal courts and state courts. As Charles Evans Hughes said in a speech when he was governor of New York, "We are under a Constitution, but the Constitution is what the judges say it is."[9] Reference works and treatises highlight leading court decisions, but far more detailed coverage is available from two heavily annotated editions of the Constitution and other resources.

(1) Annotated Codes

Two of the most useful versions of the Constitution are published as part of the unofficial editions of federal statutes, *United States Code Annotated* (*USCA*) (on Westlaw and in print from Thomson Reuters) and *United States Code Service* (*USCS*) (on Lexis and in

---

[8]   *Preface*, 1 CONST. COMMENT. 181, 181 (1984).

[9]   *Speech before the Elmira Chamber of Commerce, May 3, 1907*, in ADDRESSES OF CHARLES EVANS HUGHES, 1906–1916, at 179, 185 (2d ed. 1916). The modern reader may think that Hughes was warning about the danger of judges' unchecked power, but he went on, "and the judiciary is the safeguard of our liberty and of our property under the Constitution."

print from LexisNexis). Both are annotated with notes of judicial decisions that have applied or interpreted each constitutional provision.

Each constitutional provision follows a standard format in *USCA* and *USCS*. The text of a section or amendment is broken down into individual clauses, each of which is followed by references to encyclopedias, annotations, and other texts; a list of law review articles; and then abstracts of cases arranged by subject. These abstracts may be divided into hundreds or even thousands of subject divisions. The Fourth Amendment in *USCA*, for example, has more than 4,000 classifications of notes on various aspects of search and seizure law, covering topics such as probable cause, exigent circumstances, electronic surveillance, and the exclusionary rule. Both *USCA* and *USCS* preface the annotations with a topical outline of the issues covered, followed by an alphabetical index listing specific note numbers. Without these research aids, finding relevant cases on heavily litigated provisions such as the First Amendment or the Equal Protection Clause of the Fourteenth Amendment could quickly become overwhelming.

Illustration 4-2 shows the page from the bound volume of *USCA* with the text of the Nineteenth Amendment, historical notes, and references to law review articles and research tools; Illustration 4-3 shows *USCA*'s case annotations, as they appear on Westlaw.

The online versions on Westlaw and Lexis make it possible to search the references and annotations by keyword and thus to find cases with very specific fact situations. But be careful—sometimes annotations will stretch over several separate documents. For this reason and others, there are times when the print volumes may be more productive to use than their online counterparts, especially early in the research process. Browsing through the annotations, which is more easily done in print, can provide a better research framework than simply pinpointing one or two cases by keyword.

Neither *USCA* nor *USCS*, in print or online, contains any explanatory text summarizing or linking the annotations, so these are not the places to find an overview of constitutional doctrine. Their exhaustive case abstracts, however, make them ideal for determining how the courts have applied the Constitution's broad principles to specific circumstances.

AMENDMENT XIX—WOMAN SUFFRAGE

The right of citizens of the United States to vote shall not be denied or abridged by the United States or by any State on account of sex.

Congress shall have power to enforce this article by appropriate legislation.

HISTORICAL NOTES

Proposal and Ratification

The nineteenth amendment to the Constitution of the United States was proposed to the legislatures of the several States by the Sixty-sixth Congress, on the 4th of June, 1919, and was declared, in a proclamation of the Secretary of State, dated the 26th of August, 1920, to have been ratified by the legislatures of 36 of the 48 States. The dates of ratification were: Illinois, June 10, 1919 (and that State readopted its resolution of ratification June 17, 1919); Michigan, June 10, 1919; Wisconsin, June 10, 1919; Kansas, June 16, 1919; New York, June 16, 1919; Ohio, June 16, 1919; Pennsylvania, June 24, 1919; Massachusetts, June 25, 1919; Texas, June 28, 1919; Iowa, July 2, 1919; Missouri, July 3, 1919; Arkansas, July 28, 1919; Montana, August 2, 1919; Nebraska, August 2, 1919; Minnesota, September 8, 1919; New Hampshire, September 10, 1919; Utah, October 2, 1919; California, November 1, 1919; Maine, November 5, 1919; North Dakota, December 1, 1919; South Dakota, December 4, 1919; Colorado, December 15, 1919; Kentucky, January 6, 1920; Rhode Island, January 6, 1920; Oregon, January 13, 1920; Indiana, January 16, 1920; Wyoming, January 27, 1920; Nevada, February 7, 1920; New Jersey, February 9, 1920;

Idaho, February 11, 1920; Arizona, February 12, 1920; New Mexico, February 21, 1920; Oklahoma, February 28, 1920; West Virginia, March 10, 1920; Washington, March 22, 1920; Tennessee, August 18, 1920.

Ratification was completed on August 18, 1920.

The amendment was subsequently ratified by Connecticut on September 14, 1920 (and that State reaffirmed on September 21, 1920); Vermont, February 8, 1921; Delaware, March 6, 1923 (after rejecting it on June 2, 1920); Maryland, March 29, 1941 (after rejecting it on February 24, 1920; ratification certified on February 25, 1958); Virginia, February 21, 1952 (after rejecting it on February 12, 1920); Alabama, September 8, 1953 (after rejecting it on September 22, 1919); Florida, May 13, 1969; South Carolina, July 1, 1969 (after rejecting it on January 28, 1920; ratification certified on August 22, 1973); Georgia, February 20, 1970 (after rejecting it on July 24, 1919); Louisiana, June 11, 1970 (after rejecting it on July 1, 1920); North Carolina, May 6, 1971; Mississippi, March 22, 1984 (after rejecting it on March 29, 1920).

LAW REVIEW AND JOURNAL COMMENTARIES

Expressive voting. Adam Winkler, 68 N.Y.U.L.Rev. 330 (1993).
The scope of national power vis-á-vis the states: The dispensability of judicial review. Jesse H. Choper, 86 Yale L.J. 1552 (1977).
Women and the constitution. Akhil Reed Amar, 18 Harv.J.L. & Pub.Pol'y 465 (1995).

LIBRARY REFERENCES

American Digest System
Elections ⊜13, 126(4).
Key Number System Topic No. 144.

Corpus Juris Secundum
CJS Elections § 14, Denial, Abridgment, or Discrimination on Account of Race or Sex.

Illustration 4-2. The Nineteenth Amendment in
United States Code Annotated.

Amendment XIX. Woman Suffrage
USCA CONST Amend. XIX · United States Code Annotated · Constitution of the United States (Approx. 1 page)

| Document | **Notes of Decisions (17)** | History (2) ▾ | Citing References (1,635) ▾ | Context & Analysis (29) ▾ |

Notes of Decisions (17)   Sort: Procedural Order   🔍 ✉ ▾

Filter	Hide

✓ Select multiple

Apply

Restore previous filters

Date	+
Jurisdiction	+
Key Number	+

Apply

Table of Contents   Hide

1. Generally

Except as to provisions of this amendment and Fifteenth Amendment, question of suffrage is left entirely to states.   Smith v. Blackwell, E.D.S.C.1940, 34 F.Supp. 989, affirmed 115 F.2d 186.   Election Law ⚬ 47

2. Constitutionality

There was nothing in the character of this amendment extending suffrage to women, which prevented its adoption in the exercise of the power of amendment conferred by the Constitution, even as against a state which refused to ratify it.   Leser v. Garnett, U.S.Md.1922, 42 S.Ct. 217, 258 U.S. 130, 66 L.Ed. 505.

3. Construction with other Constitutional provisions

County election workers' alleged act of refusing to permit voter whose voting machine had malfunctioned to cast another ballot amounted to negligence or incompetence, not willful conduct, precluding voter's § 1983 due process claim against county and county employees, absent showing of intent to cause deprivation of voter's right to vote, as opposed to mere intent to deny her another ballot.   Hill v. Gunn, S.D.N.Y.2005, 367 F.Supp.2d 532.   Constitutional Law ⚬ 4232; Election Law ⚬ 31; Public Employment ⚬ 913

4. Purpose

This amendment and Fifteenth Amendment were intended to bar federal government and states from denying right to vote on grounds of race and sex in presidential elections.   Williams v. Rhodes, U.S.Ohio 1968, 89 S.Ct. 5, 393 U.S. 23, 21 L.Ed.2d 24, 45 O.O.2d 236.   Constitutional Law ⚬ 1482; Election Law ⚬ 592; Election Law ⚬ 598

5. Prior law

Prior to the adoption of this amendment it was said that a state, in denying to women the right to vote, did not violate the letter or spirit of the Fifteenth Amendment, prohibiting the denial of the right to vote on account of race, color, or previous condition of servitude.   U.S. v. Anthony, C.C.N.Y.1873, 24 F.Cas. 829, 20 Pitts.L.J. 199, 5 Chi.Leg.N. 462, 5 Chi.Leg.N. 493, No. 14459.

6. Conferring right to vote

This amendment is in the precise terms of Fifteenth Amendment, with the substitution of the word "sex" for the words "race, color or previous condition of servitude."; it has been repeatedly held by the Supreme Court of the United States that the Fifteenth Amendment does not confer upon colored men the right of suffrage; it only forbids discrimination.   U.S. v. Reese, U.S.Ky.1875, 92 U.S. 214, 2 Otto 214, 23 L.Ed. 563.

Illustration 4-3. Notes of court decisions on the Nineteenth Amendment, on Westlaw.

There are some differences between the two sets. The annotations in *USCA* include relevant key numbers so that a search can easily continue by subject in a case digest or on Westlaw. *USCS* provides coverage of both federal and state cases, while *USCA* is limited to federal court decisions.

The printed *USCA* and *USCS* volumes are supplemented annually by pocket parts, and between pocket parts by quarterly pamphlets. On Westlaw and Lexis, new annotations are incorporated into the main listing—but coverage is no more current than the latest printed supplement. To find more recent decisions, you will need to search the case databases or use Westlaw's Citing References or Shepard's (as discussed below).

As noted earlier, the text of the U.S. Constitution also appears in the annotated code for nearly every state. Only a few of these state code publications, however, include case annotations for the federal constitution.[10] Those that do so provide a valuable service by allowing researchers to focus on how the Constitution's provisions have been interpreted in the context of a particular state's law. The annotations usually have abstracts of both state court decisions and federal cases arising in that state.

(2) Other Case-Finding Resources

References to court decisions applying and construing the provisions of the Constitution can also be found using Westlaw's Citing References or Shepard's Citations on Lexis. These services list citing cases, law review articles, and other secondary sources. They include references to far more documents than the selective coverage in *USCA* and *USCS*—well over 300,000 in the case of the Fourteenth Amendment, for example. Because the annotations in both the print and online versions of *USCA* and *USCS* do not include the most recent cases, the lists of citing references are also valuable for identifying decisions too new to be incorporated into the annotations.

For frequently cited constitutional provisions, the citators are most valuable if you narrow retrieval by searching within the citing documents for specific keywords. This allows you to narrow your research to very specific fact situations or legal issues mentioned in conjunction with a constitutional provision. "Search within results" only works, however, with 10,000 citing documents or fewer. For major constitutional provisions with tens of thousands of citing cases,

---

[10] The official state codes for Hawaii, Kansas, and New Mexico, and the LexisNexis annotated codes for Delaware, Georgia, Indiana, Massachusetts, Michigan, Mississippi, New Mexico, New York, Rhode Island, South Carolina, Tennessee, and Vermont all contain editions of the U.S. Constitution annotated with state cases. These versions of the federal constitution with notes from a specific state, however, are not available online from Lexis.

it is necessary first to restrict retrieval by document type or jurisdiction before limiting by keyword.

Standard case-finding tools can also be of value in finding court decisions under the Constitution. A search in Westlaw or Lexis can combine the citation of a constitutional section or amendment with relevant factual or legal terms, such as "first amendment" within the same paragraph as "commercial speech." West's "Constitutional Law" digest topic is arranged along general themes such as construction and interpretation of constitutions, governmental powers, and protection of individual liberties. These digest key numbers cover cases interpreting provisions of both the U.S. Constitution and state constitutions. These case research approaches are discussed more fully in Chapter 12.

(d) Historical Background

The events and discussions leading to the adoption of the Constitution and its amendments are recorded in a variety of reports, journals, and other documents. These materials continue to be important resources, as courts attempt to apply the terms of an 18th-century document to evolving modern circumstances. The significance of the framers' intent in interpreting the Constitution is a subject of considerable debate,[11] but for any researcher these proceedings and documents can provide valuable historical information.

(1) Drafting and Ratification

The constitutional convention that met in Philadelphia in the summer of 1787 has been the subject of numerous books, articles, and websites.[12] The convention met behind closed doors and kept no official record of its proceedings. The journal of proceedings was eventually edited by John Quincy Adams and published in 1819, more than thirty years later, but it contained only a simple record of questions presented and votes.[13] For more extensive background on

---

[11] There is a voluminous literature on the role of original intent in constitutional interpretation. An even-handed guide to the arguments and sources can be found in BRANDON J. MURRILL, CONG. RESEARCH SERV., R45129, MODES OF CONSTITUTIONAL INTERPRETATION (2018) (crsreports.congress.gov/product/pdf/R/R45129/3).

[12] The leading modern history of the convention is MICHAEL J. KLARMAN, THE FRAMERS' COUP: THE MAKING OF THE UNITED STATES CONSTITUTION (2016). JOHN R. VILE, THE CONSTITUTIONAL CONVENTION OF 1787: A COMPREHENSIVE ENCYCLOPEDIA OF AMERICA'S FOUNDING (2d ed. 2016) may be a convenient starting point for research on specific aspects of the convention. It has nearly 400 entries on the delegates, committee, and major issues, as well as charts, timetables, and references for further research.

[13] JOURNAL, ACTS AND PROCEEDINGS, OF THE CONVENTION . . . WHICH FORMED THE CONSTITUTION OF THE UNITED STATES (1819), available online from Google Books and HathiTrust. The volume was published pursuant to a congressional resolution,

the substance of the proposals and the debates, researchers must look to notes taken by James Madison and other delegates. Madison's notes were not published until 1840, four years after his death, and other notes were also published posthumously.[14]

The standard modern source for documentation of the convention is Max Farrand, *The Records of the Federal Convention of 1787* (1911; rev. ed. 1937; suppl. 1987, James H. Hutson ed.). This four-volume set includes the notes by major participants, arranged chronologically, and the texts of various alternative plans presented.[15] The Library of Congress website provides full-text access to the three volumes of the 1911 edition of Farrand's *Records* (memory.loc.gov/ammem/amlaw/lwfr.html), while Madison's notes are available from Yale Law School's Avalon Project (avalon.law.yale.edu). Both works are also available from HeinOnline, the former in World Constitutions Illustrated (first three volumes) and the latter in the Legal Classics Library.[16]

The cases for and against ratification were published at the time in the newspapers. The most famous series of articles in support of the Constitution, originally published under the pseudonym "Publius," was written by Alexander Hamilton, John Jay, and James Madison, and was published in collected form as *The Federalist: A Collection of Essays, Written in Favour of the New Constitution* (1788). The original edition is available on Google Books, HathiTrust, and HeinOnline. These essays remain an indispensable work for the study of the Constitution and have been published in numerous editions. Full texts of *The Federalist* are also available from the

---

Res. 8, 3 Stat. 475 (1818). For a discussion of the official journal's strengths and weaknesses, see Mary Sarah Bilder, *How Bad Were the Official Records of the Federal Convention?*, 80 GEO. WASH. L. REV. 1620 (2012).

[14] On the background and reliability of these sources, see Gregory E. Maggs, *A Concise Guide to the Records of the Federal Constitutional Convention of 1787 as a Source of the Original Meaning of the U.S. Constitution*, 80 GEO. WASH. L. REV. 1707 (2012), and James H. Hutson, *The Creation of the Constitution: The Integrity of the Documentary Record*, 65 TEX. L. REV. 1 (1986). MARY SARAH BILDER, MADISON'S HAND: REVISING THE CONSTITUTIONAL CONVENTION (2015) discusses changes Madison made in his notes as his views on constitutional issues evolved in later years.

[15] The fourth volume was added in a revised edition, published in 1937. This volume adds corrections to the three original 1911 volumes, additional materials, and an index.

[16] 1787: DRAFTING THE U.S. CONSTITUTION (Wilbourn E. Benton ed., 1986) reproduces excerpts from participants' notes, arranged by article and section. Earlier, officially published compilations of notes, letters, and other documents are DOCUMENTARY HISTORY OF THE CONSTITUTION OF THE UNITED STATES OF AMERICA, 1786–1870 (1894–1905), available from Google Books and HeinOnline, and DOCUMENTS ILLUSTRATIVE OF THE FORMATION OF THE UNION OF THE AMERICAN STATES, H.R. DOC. NO. 69–398 (1927).

Library of Congress (www.congress.gov/resources/) and the Avalon Project (avalon.law.yale.edu).[17]

The opponents of ratification, known generally as the Anti-Federalists, also presented their arguments in various newspapers and pamphlets. The most comprehensive collection of these writings is *The Complete Anti-Federalist* (Herbert J. Storing ed., 1981). The first volume has an analysis of Anti-Federalist thought; this is followed by the objections of non-signers of the Constitution, major series of pseudonymous essays published in contemporary newspapers (by writers such as Brutus, Cato, and the Federal Farmer), and materials from the state ratifying conventions. Jon L. Wakelyn, *Birth of the Bill of Rights: Encyclopedia of the Antifederalists* (2004) has biographies of 140 prominent Anti-Federalists, as well as major speeches and writings arranged by state.[18]

The Founders' Constitution (Philip B. Kurland & Ralph Lerner eds., 1987) (press-pubs.uchicago.edu/founders/) collects excerpts from the debates and articles, arranged by constitutional provision. It also reprints documents with which the founders would have been familiar (such as Blackstone's *Commentaries*, the Declaration of Independence, and early state constitutions) along with early post-Constitution court decisions and commentaries. The first volume is devoted to major themes such as republican government and separation of powers, the next three volumes cover the seven original articles of the Constitution, and volume five deals with the first twelve amendments.

Some consider the state convention debates concerning ratification of the federal Constitution to be more important as interpretive sources than the proceedings in the Philadelphia convention.[19] Historically the standard source for these has been

---

[17] For a more detailed discussion of the content and use of *The Federalist*, see Gregory E. Maggs, *A Concise Guide to the Federalist Papers as a Source of the Original Meaning of the United States Constitution*, 87 B.U. L. REV. 801 (2007).

[18] *See* Aaron Zelinsky, *Misunderstanding the Anti-Federalist Papers: The Dangers of Availability*, 63 ALA. L. REV. 1067 (2012), for a discussion of the major Anti-Federalist Papers and the Supreme Court's use and misuse of citations to these sources.

[19] In James Madison's view, "whatever veneration might be entertained for the body of men who formed our Constitution, the sense of that body could never be regarded as the oracular guide in expounding the Constitution. As the instrument came from them it was nothing more than the draft of a plan, nothing but a dead letter, until life and validity were breathed into it by the voice of the people, speaking through the several State Conventions. If we were to look, therefore, for the meaning of the instrument beyond the face of the instrument, we must look for it, not in the General Convention, which proposed, but in the State Conventions, which accepted and ratified the Constitution." 5 ANNALS OF CONG. 776 (1796). As he does with the convention records, the Articles of Confederation, and *The Federalist*, Gregory E. Maggs provides guidance on understanding and using the state ratification debates in *A Concise Guide*

Jonathan Elliot, *The Debates in the Several State Conventions on the Adoption of the Federal Constitution* (2d ed. 1836–45). Elliot's work is available from HeinOnline and from the Library of Congress website (memory.loc.gov/ammem/amlaw/lwed.html).

Elliot's *Debates* was riddled with errors,[20] and a much more comprehensive modern set originally edited by Merrill Jensen and now by John P. Kaminski et al., *The Documentary History of the Ratification of the Constitution* (1976–date) (digital.library.wisc.edu/1711.dl/History.Constitution), is considered more accurate and authoritative. It contains debates, commentaries, and other documents on the ratification process, gathered from a variety of sources, including convention journals, personal papers, contemporary newspapers and pamphlets, and secondary sources. Thirty-two volumes to date cover ratification debates in every state but North Carolina as well as commentaries in the contemporary press, personal papers, and other documents.[21]

(2) The Bill of Rights and Subsequent Amendments

Under the terms of Article V, amendments to the Constitution are proposed by Congress and presented to the states for ratification. The Constitution as originally ratified had no provisions for individual rights, in part because the framers felt that protections in state constitutions would be sufficient, but it was soon recognized that protection of rights on the national level was needed. The first ten amendments, the Bill of Rights, were proposed in 1789 and ratified in 1791. Although many other amendments have been suggested over the years, the Constitution has so far been amended only twenty-seven times.[22]

Constitutional amendments are discussed in reference sources such as *The Constitution of the United States of America: Analysis and Interpretation* and *Encyclopedia of the American Constitution.*

---

to the Records of the State Ratifying Conventions as a Source of the Original Meaning of the United States Constitution, 2009 U. ILL. L. REV. 457.

[20] *See* Hutson, *supra* note 14, at 13–21.

[21] Excerpts are also available in a shorter collection, THE DEBATE ON THE CONSTITUTION: FEDERALIST AND ANTIFEDERALIST SPEECHES, ARTICLES, AND LETTERS DURING THE STRUGGLE OVER RATIFICATION (Bernard Bailyn ed., 1993). Research in contemporary press coverage can be done through online services such as America's Historical Newspapers (www.readex.com), which includes full-text coverage of dozens of newspapers published at the time of the constitutional convention and ratification. Information about the North Carolina ratification convention may be found in THE RATIFICATION OF THE FEDERAL CONSTITUTION IN NORTH CAROLINA (Louise Irby Trenholme ed., 1932), also available from HeinOnline.

[22] PROPOSED AMENDMENTS TO THE U.S. CONSTITUTION, 1787–2001 (John R. Vile ed., 2003, with 2011 supplement covering 2001–10) reprints and updates several published reports analyzing and listing the more than 11,000 proposed amendments that have been introduced in Congress, with a comprehensive index.

Other reference works focus specifically on the amendments. *Constitutional Amendments* (Mark Grossman ed., 2d ed. 2017) addresses each amendment in order with a discussion of its proposal and ratification process, followed by excerpts from congressional debates and other documents. John R. Vile, *Encyclopedia of Constitutional Amendments, Proposed Amendments, and Amending Issues, 1789–2015* (4th ed. 2015) covers a broader range of topics, with over 500 short articles on the amendments and related issues.[23]

Documents on the Bill of Rights and other proposed or enacted amendments to the U.S. Constitution can be found in several sources. As noted above, *The Founders' Constitution* covers the first twelve amendments as well as the original seven articles. The texts of major documents relating to the Bill of Rights appear in Bernard Schwartz, *The Bill of Rights: A Documentary History* (1971) and *The Complete Bill of Rights: The Drafts, Debates, Sources, and Origins* (Neil H. Cogan ed., 2d ed. 2015). Schwartz's collection is arranged chronologically, while Cogan's work has excerpts from source documents arranged by amendment. Both include texts of proposals in Congress and from the state conventions; earlier and contemporaneous provisions on related issues; and discussion of the amendments in Congress, conventions, newspapers, and letters.

The most important amendments since the Bill of Rights have been the Reconstruction amendments, in particular the Fourteenth Amendment's Due Process and Equal Protection Clauses. The House and Senate debates on the amendments, originally published in the *Congressional Globe* and *Congressional Record*, are reprinted in *The Reconstruction Amendments' Debates: The Legislative and Contemporary Debates in Congress on the 13th, 14th, and 15th Amendments* (Alfred Avins ed., 1967), which includes a 30-page "Reader's Guide" explaining the context and significance of each document. Volume one of *Statutory History of the United States: Civil Rights* (Bernard Schwartz ed., 1970) also contains extensive excerpts from these debates.

§ 4.2   STATE CONSTITUTIONS

Each of the fifty states is governed by its own constitution, which establishes the structure of government and guarantees fundamental rights. These documents vary considerably in length and scope, and most address the day-to-day activities of government in a far more detailed manner than that of the U.S. Constitution. The federal

---

[23] Many resources offer more specific treatments of individual amendments. Introductory coverage is available from reference works such as ENCYCLOPEDIA OF AMERICAN CIVIL LIBERTIES (Paul Finkelman ed., 2006); ENCYCLOPEDIA OF THE FIRST AMENDMENT (John R. Vile et al. eds., 2009); and ENCYCLOPEDIA OF THE FOURTH AMENDMENT (John R. Vile & David L. Hudson eds., 2013).

constitution deals only with a limited number of specified powers, but state constitutions must deal with a broader range of institutions and government activity. In general, states also amend their constitutions far more frequently, with an average of more than 100 amendments per state.[24]

State constitutions can be a vital tool in ensuring citizens' rights, and many state constitutions have bills of rights that are broader and more detailed than their federal counterpart. Even where the words in a state document mirror those in the U.S. Constitution, the judiciary of each state can interpret the terms of its own fundamental law. A state constitution cannot deprive persons of federal constitutional rights, but it can guarantee additional protections not found in federal law. In an influential *Harvard Law Review* article in 1977, Justice William J. Brennan, Jr., urged the independent consideration and application of state constitutional rights.[25] This call for "judicial federalism" was followed by numerous similar articles by state court jurists in the 1980s, a scholarly backlash during the 1990s, and a continuing discussion in the literature.[26]

As with the federal constitution, a variety of online and print resources provide access to the constitutional texts as well as to notes of court decisions, commentary, and historical documents.

(a) Texts

The texts of state constitutions are easily located in several sources. Each state's statutory code contains the text of its current constitution, usually along with earlier constitutions and other fundamental documents, and virtually every state provides online access to its constitution through a government website. Several sites providing multistate access can be found by searching for "state constitutions."

Oxford Constitutions of the World (oxcon.ouplaw.com) is a comprehensive source for the texts of current state constitutions. The

---

[24] Christopher W. Hammons, *State Constitutional Reform: Is It Necessary?*, 64 ALB. L. REV. 1327, 1328–34 (2001).

[25] William J. Brennan, Jr., *State Constitutions and the Protection of Individual Rights*, 90 HARV. L. REV. 489 (1977).

[26] Recent contributions include NEW FRONTIERS OF STATE CONSTITUTIONAL LAW: DUAL ENFORCEMENT OF NORMS (James A. Gardner & Jim Rossi eds., 2010), and EMILY ZACKIN, LOOKING FOR RIGHTS IN ALL THE WRONG PLACES: WHY STATE CONSTITUTIONS CONTAIN AMERICA'S POSITIVE RIGHTS (2013). Sixth Circuit Judge Jeffrey S. Sutton has compared a lawyer who fails to invoke state constitutional rights when challenging a statute's validity to a basketball player who takes only one of two free throws with the game on the line. Jeffrey S. Sutton, *Why Teach—and Why Study—State Constitutional Law*, 34 OKLA. CITY U. L. REV. 165, 165–66 (2009). Judge Sutton has expanded on the importance of state constitutions in 51 IMPERFECT SOLUTIONS: STATES AND THE MAKING OF AMERICAN CONSTITUTIONAL LAW (2018).

documents are not accompanied by either case annotations or commentary, but this may nonetheless provide a convenient way to compare provisions between states. The state constitutions are also available in print as an eight-volume set, *Constitutions of the United States, National and State* (2d ed. 1974–date).[27]

(b) Cases and Secondary Sources

The most useful versions of state constitutions are those found in the annotated editions of the state codes, in which the text is accompanied by notes of court decisions and secondary sources. These are similar to the versions of the U.S. Constitution in *USCA* and *USCS*, and are the versions generally found on Westlaw or Lexis. Illustration 4-4 shows a section of the Utah Constitution, as it appears in the *Utah Code Annotated*. The text is followed by a brief historical note on its source, annotations of court decisions, and references to secondary sources.

Standard approaches to case-finding can also be used in researching state constitutional law. The state case law databases in Westlaw and Lexis allow you to search for documents by combining citations of constitutional provisions with specific keywords. The topic "Constitutional Law" is used in West's digests for issues arising under both federal and state constitutions, and many issues of state governmental powers are digested under the topic "States." Both Westlaw's Citing References and Shepard's on Lexis list citations to state constitutions, and for some provisions they include many more citing sources than the annotated code.

For research into a particular state's constitution, one of the best places to start may be that state's volume in the series *The Oxford Commentaries on the State Constitutions of the United States*, covering almost every state. Each volume, entitled *The ____ State Constitution*, includes a summary of the state's constitutional history, a detailed section-by-section analysis of the constitution with background information and discussion of judicial interpretations, and a brief bibliographical essay providing references for further research.[28]

---

[27] There is unfortunately no general index to the set, just two very dated topical indexes, "Fundamental Liberties and Rights: A 50-State Index" (1980), and "Laws, Legislature, Legislative Procedure: A Fifty State Index" (1982). The first (1915) and second (1959, with 1967 supplement) editions of INDEX DIGEST OF STATE CONSTITUTIONS may still be useful for historical coverage.

[28] As of 2020, the only states not yet covered are Missouri, Oregon, and Pennsylvania. The Oxford series replaced an earlier set from a different publisher, *Reference Guides to the State Constitutions of the United States*. Several volumes have now been published in a second edition, but the first Oxford editions in 2011 simply reprinted the earlier versions without any revisions or notes that the material was outdated.

Art. IV, § 1   CONSTITUTION OF UTAH

Section 1. [Equal political rights.]

The rights of citizens of the State of Utah to vote and hold office shall not be denied or abridged on account of sex. Both male and female citizens of this State shall enjoy equally all civil, political and religious rights and privileges.

History: Const. 1896.
Cross-References. — Statutory provisions concerning elections, Title 20.

NOTES TO DECISIONS

ANALYSIS

Age of majority.
Election contest.
Inheritance law.
Women's suffrage before adoption.

Age of majority.
Former law that prescribed a lower age of majority for females than for males was discriminatory and denied equal protection of the laws in the context of child support. Stanton v. Stanton, 421 U.S. 7, 95 S. Ct. 1373, 43 L. Ed. 2d 688 (1975).

Election contest.
This provision does not of itself confer jurisdiction on a court of equity to make inquiry into regularity of election contest, since the provisions of the election statutes must be strictly construed and followed. Ewing v. Harries, 68 Utah 452, 250 P. 1049 (1926).

Inheritance law.
Section 75-2-109, which permits a mother to inherit from her illegitimate child under all circumstances but requires a father to meet additional criteria by demonstrating that he has openly treated the child as his own and has not refused to support the child before he may inherit, does not violate constitutional due process and equal rights provisions. Scheller v. Pessetto, 783 P.2d 70 (Utah Ct. App. 1989).

Women's suffrage before adoption.
Portion of Election Law of 1878, which provided that all "male" voters should be taxpayers, without imposing same condition on "female" voters, was void. Lyman v. Martin, 2 Utah 136 (1877).
Women were without right to vote on question of ratification or rejection of Constitution. Anderson v. Tyree, 12 Utah 129, 42 P. 201 (1895).

COLLATERAL REFERENCES

Utah Law Review. — Recent Developments in Utah Law — Judicial Decisions — Family Law, 1987 Utah L. Rev. 200.

C.J.S. — 29 C.J.S. Elections § 30.
Key Numbers. — Elections ☞ 62; Officers ☞ 20.

Illustration 4-4. A section of a state constitution, accompanied by case annotations.

Robert L. Maddex, *State Constitutions of the United States* (2d ed. 2006) is useful for surveying constitutional provisions in several states. The volume has a brief summary of each state's constitutional history, followed by an article-by-article explanation of its current constitution. It also includes tables comparing issues such as governmental structure, number of amendments, and rights protected. *The Constitutionalism of American States* (George E. Connor & Christopher W. Hammons eds., 2008) also covers all fifty states, with a separate chapter on the constitutional history and theory of each state.

The first chapter of the Council of State Governments' annual *Book of the States* (knowledgecenter.csg.org/kc) focuses on constitutions. It has a narrative survey of current developments in state constitutional law, accompanied by tables on topics such as the length of each constitution, dates of adoption, and amendment procedures.

Guides to the study of state constitutions include G. Alan Tarr, *Understanding State Constitutions* (1998), discussing the nature and history of state constitutions since independence, and Robert F. Williams, *The Law of American State Constitutions* (2009), a reference guide to the functions and purposes of state constitutions. The three-volume set *State Constitutions for the Twenty-First Century* (G. Alan Tarr et al. eds., 2006) focuses on issues of constitutional reform and drafting. Law reviews feature symposia on state constitutions from time to time, and *Rutgers University Law Review* publishes an annual issue on state constitutional law.

The major treatise covering individual rights under state constitutions is Jennifer Friesen, *State Constitutional Law: Litigating Individual Rights, Claims, and Defenses* (4th ed. 2006– date). The first volume of this set discusses issues such as freedom of expression and civil actions for the violation of state constitutional rights; the second covers search and seizure, the rights of defendants, and punishment issues. This treatise is available as an e-book but is not accessible through the major legal research platforms.

(c) Historical Research

Unlike the venerable and rarely amended United States Constitution, state constitutions are subject to frequent amendment and revision. Many states have had several constitutional conventions and a number of complete revisions; Louisiana has had eleven constitutions in its history and Georgia has had ten. On the other hand, nineteen states still operate under amended versions of their original constitution, and the constitutions for Massachusetts, New Hampshire, and Vermont date back to the 18th century.

One of the most thorough sources for historical state constitutions is HeinOnline's State Constitutions Illustrated database. It contains the text of every constitution that has been in force for every state, as well as various pre-statehood documents such as colonial charters and territorial laws. Illustration 4-5 shows the list of documents available for New Jersey, including three constitutions dating back to 1776 and colonial ordinances and instructions.

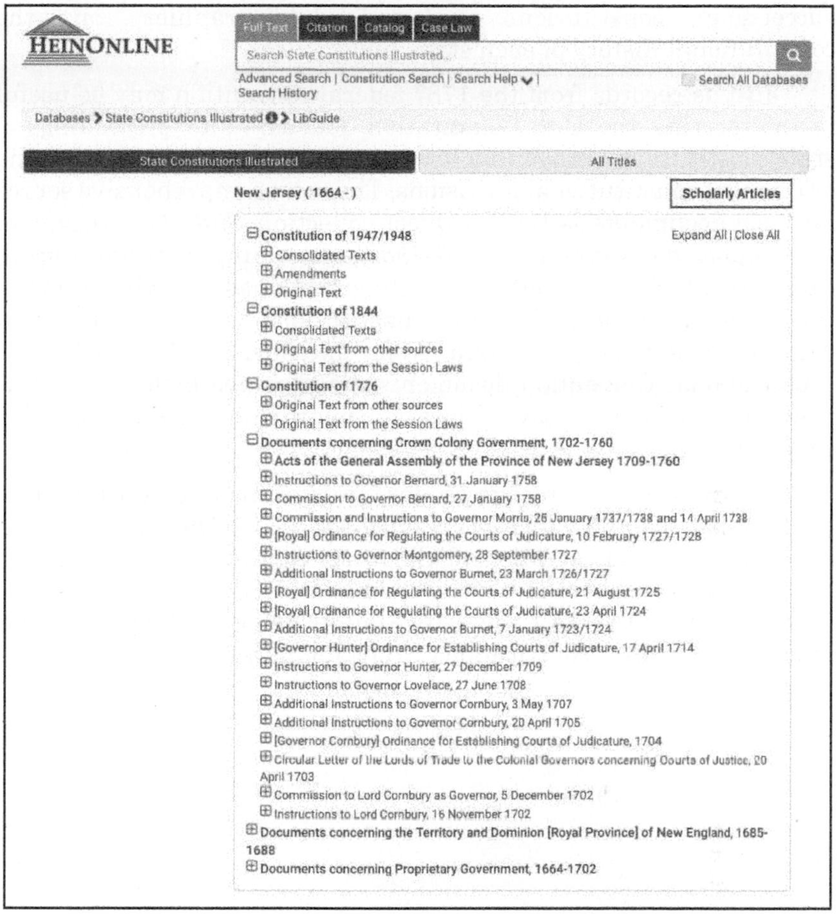

**Illustration 4-5. A list of documents in HeinOnline's
State Constitutions Illustrated.**

*Constitutional Documents of the United States of America 1776–
1860* (Horst Dippel ed., 2006–11) only covers the period before the
Civil War but it includes meticulously verified versions of all early
texts including failed constitutions and amendments. Later
constitutions can be found in the microfiche *Constitutions of the
World 1850 to the Present, Part 2: North and South America* (Horst
Dippel ed., 2007).

Constitutional documents through the mid-20th century are
available in *Sources and Documents of United States Constitutions*
(William F. Swindler ed., 1973–79). Enabling acts, acts of admission,
and constitutions are assembled in chronological order for each state,
with background notes, editorial comments on provisions of

succeeding   constitutions,   selected   bibliographies   on   the
constitutional history of each state, and indexes.[29]

Just as records from the 1787 federal convention may be useful
in interpreting the U.S. Constitution, journals and proceedings of
state constitutional conventions can provide insight into the meaning
or intent of constitutional provisions. The most comprehensive source
for such documents is the ProQuest collection *State Constitutional
Conventions on Microfiche (1776–1988),* containing material from all
fifty states.[30] LLMC Digital (www.llmc.com) has a fairly extensive
collection of historical state constitutions and constitutional
convention journals, digitized from microfiche. Many of these
constitutional convention documents are also available free online
from the Rutgers Law Library (njlaw.rutgers.edu/collections/
constitutions/).

Information on resources for territorial and initial state
constitutions can be found in *Prestatehood Legal Materials: A Fifty-
State Research Guide* (Michael Chiorazzi & Marguerite Most eds.,
2005). Links to modern materials and historical documents are listed
by state in the Indiana University Maurer School of Law's research
guide on state constitutions (law.indiana.libguides.com/state-
constitutions).

---

[29] The texts of the older documents in this set are mostly reprinted from two
government compilations that may still be valuable for historical research: THE
FEDERAL AND STATE CONSTITUTIONS, COLONIAL CHARTERS, AND OTHER ORGANIC
LAWS OF THE UNITED STATES (Benjamin Perley Poore ed., 2d ed. 1878); and THE
FEDERAL AND STATE CONSTITUTIONS, COLONIAL CHARTERS, AND OTHER ORGANIC
LAWS OF THE STATES, TERRITORIES AND COLONIES NOW OR HERETOFORE FORMING THE
UNITED STATES OF AMERICA, H.R. DOC. NO. 59–357 (Francis Newton Thorpe ed.,
1909), both available from HeinOnline. Commentators have noted, however, that these
sets contain numerous errors and omissions. *See, e.g.,* Horst Dippel, *The Trap of
Medium-Neutral Citations, or Why a Historical-Critical Edition of State Constitutions
Is Necessary,* 103 LAW LIBR. J. 219 (2011); W. F. Dodd, Book Review, 4 AM. POL. SCI.
REV. 135, 137–38 (1910).

[30] Access to the microfiche is provided by three guides: STATE CONSTITUTIONAL
CONVENTIONS FROM INDEPENDENCE TO THE COMPLETION OF THE PRESENT UNION,
1776–1959: A BIBLIOGRAPHY (Cynthia E. Browne comp., 1973), STATE
CONSTITUTIONAL CONVENTIONS, 1959–1978: AN ANNOTATED BIBLIOGRAPHY (1981),
and STATE CONSTITUTIONAL CONVENTIONS, COMMISSIONS & AMENDMENTS, 1979–
1988: AN ANNOTATED BIBLIOGRAPHY (1989).

Chapter 5

STATUTORY RESEARCH

Table of Sections

The role of statutory law in legal research is often underemphasized, in part because of the focus on appellate decisions in American legal education and the complexities of case research. In practice, however, statutes are central to most legal issues, and you should usually ascertain whether there is a governing statute before searching for judicial precedents. Indeed, the vast majority of appellate decisions today involve the application or interpretation of statutes rather than the consideration of purely common law principles.[1]

---

[1] Two influential series of lectures recognizing the importance of statutes in the judicial system are GUIDO CALABRESI, A COMMON LAW FOR THE AGE OF STATUTES (1982) and JAMES WILLARD HURST, DEALING WITH STATUTES (1982). The publication of these and other works led a leading scholar to refer to 1982 as the "annus mirabilis"

Statutory research is shaped by the doctrine of judicial review established in Chief Justice John Marshall's opinion in *Marbury v. Madison*, holding that the judicial branch has the power to review actions of the legislature and executive and to rule on their constitutionality.[2] In considering statutes, it is important to find not only the relevant text but also court decisions that interpret this text and define its terms. The most common research sources are *annotated codes*, which provide the text of the statutes in force accompanied by notes of court decisions.

The forms of statutory publication and research vary somewhat from jurisdiction to jurisdiction, although they share similar features. This chapter begins with an overview of the way statutes are published online and in print, discusses common research approaches and concerns, and then examines sources for federal and state statutes more closely. The scope of the chapter is limited to the sources and use of enacted legislation. The legislative process and research in pending bills are considered in Chapter 6.

§ 5.1   PATTERNS OF STATUTORY PUBLICATION

The texts of enacted legislation for the various jurisdictions of the United States are issued successively in a series of forms that follow a common pattern. Each of these forms of publication, whether used online or in print, may be needed in the research process. Although you will begin most statutory research with an annotated code, an understanding of the earlier forms of the statute is essential background.

Slip Laws. A new statute is first available as a slip law, a sheet or pamphlet containing the complete text of just one act. Slip laws are usually individually paginated, designated by a chapter or law number, and issued officially by the government.

Slip laws are not widely distributed in paper, but this is the form of law that is most frequently available in PDF from legislative websites. Some sites have only the *enrolled bill*, or the final form of the bill that was passed by the legislature and presented to the executive for approval, but most states and the federal government provide access to the legislation as approved and enacted into law. The enrolled bill and the slip law have the same text, but the former is identified by a bill number and the latter by an act or chapter number.

---

for the renaissance of interest in statutes. WILLIAM N. ESKRIDGE, JR., DYNAMIC STATUTORY INTERPRETATION 335 n.1 (1994).

   [2]   *Marbury v. Madison*, 5 U.S. (1 Cranch) 137 (1803).

Session Laws. At the end of a legislative session, the enacted laws are gathered and published together in chronological order in bound volumes. These generally include subject indexes and tables indicating which existing laws have been modified or repealed by newly enacted legislation. The titles of these publications vary between jurisdictions, but they are known by such names as *Statutes at Large, Laws, Session Laws, Acts*, or *Acts and Resolves*.

The slip laws and session laws print exactly the same legislation, unless typographical errors in the slip laws were found and corrected. The difference between these two sources is simply one of citation form: The session laws provide a page number by which the law can be cited. The session law source, with page numbers, is preferred over the slip law by *The Bluebook* and the *ALWD Guide to Legal Citation*.[3]

In most jurisdictions, the session laws constitute the *positive law* form of legislation—the authoritative, binding text of the laws, and the determinative language if discrepancies are found in subsequent printed versions such as codes. Codes are only *prima facie* evidence of the statutory language, unless they have been specifically designated as positive law by the legislature.

Many jurisdictions also have commercial services with prompt access to new laws as they are enacted. These services publish the texts of new laws in pamphlet form and are known as *advance legislative services* or *advance session law services*. They are also available through Westlaw and Lexis, and mirror the coverage of the slip laws on most official websites. The advance services generally do *not* have the same page numbers as the final session laws volumes, but they are *The Bluebook*'s preferred source for laws not yet printed in the code or the official session laws.[4]

Codes. Although session laws contain the official text of legislation, their chronological arrangement is of limited use in research. Lawyers usually need the laws currently in force, rather than those passed during a specific legislative term. They need to know about amendments and about other legislation on related topics. For this they turn to statutory compilations, known generally as codes, which collect current statutes of general and permanent application and reprint them by subject. Codes can be produced by governments or by commercial publishers.

In the strict sense of the word, a *code* is a broad, encompassing statement of general and systematic legal principles intended to cover all phases of human activity. This sort of comprehensive code

---

[3] THE BLUEBOOK: A UNIFORM SYSTEM OF CITATION R. 12.2 (21st ed. 2020); ALWD GUIDE TO LEGAL CITATION app. 1(B) (6th ed. 2017).

[4] THE BLUEBOOK: A UNIFORM SYSTEM OF CITATION R. 12.2.1(a) (21st ed. 2020).

is the basis of the legal system in civil law countries such as France and Germany. A *revision*, on the other hand, is a legislative redrafting and simplification of the various statutes previously enacted into law. A *compilation* is a subject arrangement without alteration of the statutes in force. In the past there was a clearer distinction between revision and compilation, but the two terms can generally be used interchangeably today.[5]

Only a few United States jurisdictions have codes in the civil law sense. The most well-known are the civil codes in California and Louisiana.[6] Most states actually have revisions or compilations, but in practice the word "code" is used to encompass all three types of statutory collections.

The statutes in a code are grouped into broad subject topics, usually called *titles*, and within each title they are divided into chapters and then numbered sections. The parts of a single legislative act may be printed together or may be scattered by subject through several different titles. In the process of rearranging the codified statutes, amendments are incorporated, repealed laws are deleted, and minor technical adjustments are sometimes made in the text of the laws to fit them into a functional and coherent compilation. Credits after each section provide session law citations for the statutory language, where you can see the original text of the legislative act in full, and in some codes revisor's notes explain the changes made by each law. A detailed index for the entire code provides access to the sections dealing with particular topics.

Almost every jurisdiction offers free online access to the text of its code, usually through the legislature's website. The free sites provide quick and convenient access to the statutes, but there are drawbacks. While all of the sites can be searched by keyword, only a few provide more sophisticated approaches such as natural language or proximity searching. Very few include notes of court decisions interpreting the statutes, and some do not even indicate the session law sources for code sections or amendments (vital information if you need to know when a law took effect). Many websites even include

---

[5] Revisions required reenactment by the legislature, but compilations were generally unofficially published without the requirement of legislative action. *See* John Bell Sanborn, *The Problem of Statutory Revision*, 4 PROC. AM. POL. SCI. ASS'N 113, 113–14 (1907).

[6] For histories of these two major codifications, see VERNON VALENTINE PALMER, THE LOUISIANA CIVILIAN EXPERIENCE: CRITIQUES OF CODIFICATION IN A MIXED JURISDICTION (2005), and Lewis Grossman, *Codification and the California Mentality*, 45 HASTINGS L.J. 617 (1994). For a broader survey of American codification efforts beginning in the 17th century, see Gunther A. Weiss, *The Enchantment of Codification in the Common-Law World*, 25 YALE J. INT'L L. 435, 498–527 (2000).

warnings that the online version is not official, and that the printed volumes must be consulted for the official text.

Some jurisdictions have official printed code publications containing the text of the statutes in force. In these jurisdictions, the official code is usually the authoritative text to which citation is expected in briefs and pleadings.[7] It is also the preferred source specified by *The Bluebook* and the *ALWD Guide*.[8] This can be somewhat problematic if you are conducting research outside a jurisdiction, because very few libraries in other states are likely to have copies of these official codes.

Whether online or in print, most official editions of codes have two major shortcomings. They may not be up to date and cannot be relied on for the most recent amendments. An outdated code may be good enough for a quick sense of the law, but serious research requires current information. Perhaps more significant for research purposes, the editorial material in most official codes is limited to a few notes about when a particular statute was enacted and amended. These are *unannotated codes*, which means that they do not provide citations to judicial decisions that have applied or construed the statutes. Finding relevant cases is such an important part of reading and interpreting statutes that unannotated codes are simply not adequate for most statutory research.[9]

Annotated Codes. An *annotated code* reproduces the text and arrangement of the official code. It incorporates new legislation, revisions, and amendments, as does the official code, but an annotated code does much more. After individual statutory sections, you will find a wealth of references to judicial and administrative decisions, as well as regulations, attorney general opinions, legislative history materials, law reviews, legal encyclopedias, and treatises.

The case references, called Case Notes or Notes of Decisions, are usually more than just lists of citations to relevant decisions, and most often take the form of short paragraphs summarizing specific points of law decided. These brief summaries allow you to browse or search the annotations to find relevant cases. Some statutory

---

[7] Some states have statutory presumptions about the official code's evidentiary value in that jurisdiction's courts. *See, e.g.,* N.C. GEN. STAT. § 164–11.1 (2017) (noting that "the General Statutes of North Carolina . . . are hereby constituted and declared to be prima facie evidence of the laws of North Carolina").

[8] THE BLUEBOOK: A UNIFORM SYSTEM OF CITATION R. 12.2.1(a) (21st ed. 2020); ALWD GUIDE TO LEGAL CITATION R. 14.1 (6th ed. 2017).

[9] "The annotations include descriptions of judicial decisions interpreting the statutes. Only a very bad lawyer would fail to consult them in determining the meaning of a statute." Adam Liptak, *Is It Legal to Post State Laws Online?*, N.Y. TIMES, May 14, 2019, at A14.

sections have been applied in thousands of court cases and are accompanied by dozens or hundreds of pages of case summaries. These are usually divided into subject classifications, making it easier to find cases fitting a particular research problem. Other sections may have no annotations at all if they are uncontroversial and have not led to litigation or are too new to have been considered in any published court decisions.

Most annotated codes are commercial publications and thus are not available on free internet sites. Westlaw and Lexis, however, have annotated codes for federal law and for all fifty states. These platforms are among the most thorough and up-to-date resources for statutory research, incorporating new legislation within days of enactment and providing a variety of research links that lead from a code section to related cases and secondary sources.

Bloomberg Law does not include editorial annotations, but it offers a feature called Smart Code that relies on computer automation to identify relevant sections of court opinions and rank these extracts by depth of discussion. Other subscription platforms such as Casemaker, Fastcase, and VersusLaw also have federal and state codes, although their versions are not annotated with notes of court decisions or other reference materials.

In print, most commercial annotated codes are supplemented by annual pocket parts and interim pamphlets over the course of the year. They are not as current as online sources but are usually much more up to date than official unannotated codes.

While annotated codes are the most useful resources in most statutory research, they are not the most authoritative sources of the text of statutes. If there is an official code, its language is controlling if there is any discrepancy between it and an annotated code. And, as mentioned earlier, the session laws generally control over the official code in case of discrepancies between those two sources.

Other Sources. Session laws and annotated codes are the major comprehensive sources for statutes, but in specialized areas other resources may be even more useful. Topical services provide the text of statutes in some areas, updated weekly in print and even more quickly online. Tax services such as the *Standard Federal Tax Reporter* (CCH, available on WoltersKluwer Cheetah) and the *United States Tax Reporter* (RIA, available on Thomson Reuters Checkpoint and Westlaw), for example, provide the complete text of the Internal Revenue Code with each section accompanied by related regulations, extensive excerpts from legislative history sources, and notes of cases and administrative decisions. These services are in effect very thorough annotated codes for their specific field of law.

§ 5.2   STATUTORY RESEARCH METHODS

Research in statutes usually begins by finding the relevant sections in an annotated code, either online or in print. Finding the statutory language, however, is just the first step of statutory research. Before relying on a statute as authority, you must verify that it is still in force and ascertain how it has been affected by subsequent legislation and judicial decisions. One reason that annotated codes are such effective research tools is that they provide regularly updated information on a statute's validity and treatment.

(a) Approaches to Online Research

Searching for statutes online is challenging in ways different from searching for case law or journal articles. Statutory provisions are often long, complicated documents with multiple subsections and sub-subsections, and it is necessary to be aware of how these different subsections relate to each other. An online source that does not indent subsections properly to indicate this hierarchy can make the task almost impossible. Reading a statute on the screen can also require extensive scrolling up and down to understand the scope of cross-references and provisos. Despite these difficulties, of course, online resources are now the most common starting points for statutory research.

This discussion of research procedures focuses primarily on Westlaw and Lexis, which provide access to the highly useful annotated versions of codes and which have the same search tools for statutes from all jurisdictions. Search approaches and features in other online resources for statutes may vary from state to state.

Both Westlaw and Lexis have a variety of resources to assist with statutory research. A Westlaw code display has tabs at the top of the screen with options to see Notes of Decisions, History (earlier versions and revisor's notes), Citing References, and Context & Analysis (commentary in law reviews, treatises, and other secondary sources). Lexis includes the case annotations below the statutory text, with a link to Shepard's citing references. Some of these features are shown in the displays in Illustrations 5-1 and 5-2.

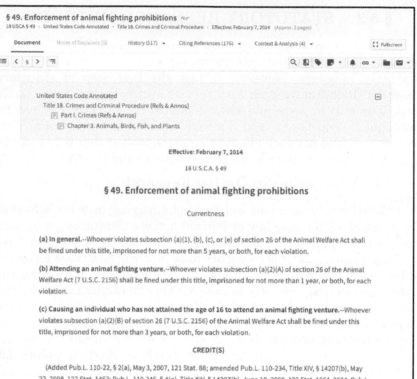

Illustration 5-1. A *U.S. Code Annotated* section as displayed on Westlaw.

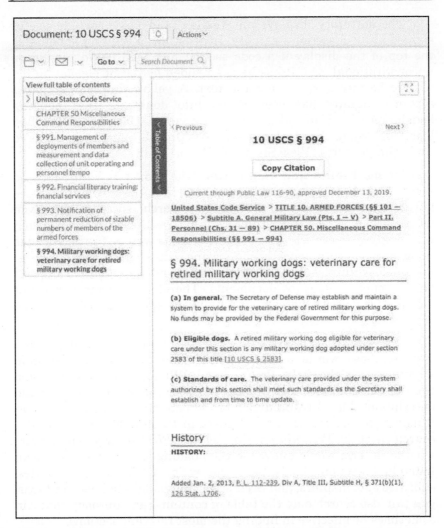

Illustration 5-2. A *U.S. Code Service* section as displayed on Lexis.

The statutory displays on Westlaw and Lexis include useful signals about a section's validity. In Westlaw, a red flag appears at the top of the display if a code section has been found invalid or unconstitutional, or if it has been amended by recent legislation too new to be incorporated into the text. A yellow flag shows that a section's validity has been called into doubt, or that pending legislation would amend a section if enacted. Clicking on the flag leads directly to these references. Lexis provides similar symbols to the right, next to a "View Shepard's Report" link.

Using Fields and Segments. The statutory databases on Westlaw and Lexis are rich resources, but their comprehensive nature can make them difficult to search successfully. Even sophisticated search algorithms ranking results by relevance find words appearing in the notes of decisions as well as in the statutes themselves. These notes summarizing cases often include legal terminology unrelated to the code section, and many searches return far too many irrelevant documents. Therefore, the most relevant sections for your purposes may not always appear at the top of the results list.

One way to focus retrieval is to search just the headings to a statute, those words used to identify the title and the section. Westlaw uses the field *Preliminary* (*PR*) for title, subtitle, and chapter designations, and *Caption* (*CA*) for the section number and description. The Advanced Search screen for statutes, shown in Illustration 5-3, provides easy access to these fields. You can also search in both (*Preliminary/Caption,* or *PR/CA*) if you're unsure whether a term would appear in the heading for a chapter or for an individual section. Lexis uses the segment *Heading* for titles, subtitles and chapters, and *Section* for individual sections. On Lexis, you can also search only the table of contents, an approach that can sometimes be effective in finding the most relevant sections.

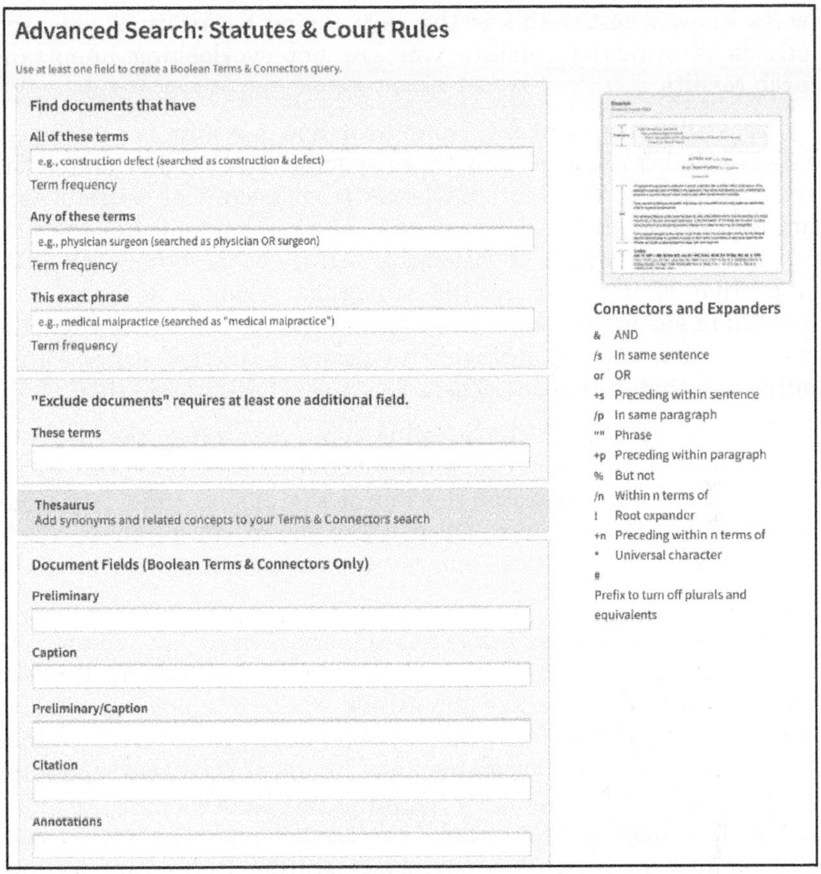

Advanced Search: Statutes & Court Rules

Use at least one field to create a Boolean Terms & Connectors query.

Find documents that have

All of these terms

e.g., construction defect (searched as construction & defect)

Term frequency

Any of these terms

e.g., physician surgeon (searched as physician OR surgeon)

Term frequency

This exact phrase

e.g., medical malpractice (searched as "medical malpractice")

Term frequency

"Exclude documents" requires at least one additional field.

These terms

Thesaurus
Add synonyms and related concepts to your Terms & Connectors search

Document Fields (Boolean Terms & Connectors Only)

Preliminary

Caption

Preliminary/Caption

Citation

Annotations

Connectors and Expanders

&   AND
/s   In same sentence
or   OR
+s   Preceding within sentence
/p   In same paragraph
""   Phrase
+p   Preceding within paragraph
%   But not
/n   Within n terms of
!   Root expander
+n   Preceding within n terms of
*   Universal character
#
Prefix to turn off plurals and
equivalents

**Illustration 5-3. Westlaw's Advanced Search
screen for statutes and court rules.**

You can also focus a Westlaw or Lexis search on just the statutory language, excluding the notes of decisions, by using the *Statutory Text (TE)* field or the *Text* segment. This field contains the headings, the text, and any official notes, but not the annotations.

In some instances, on the other hand, searching just the text of the statute may be underinclusive. Sometimes the language used in court decisions does not appear in the text of the law itself. A commonly cited example is federal employment discrimination law, which bars activities such as hostile work environment sexual harassment—without using any of those words in its text.[10] These words do, however, appear frequently in the annotations, so a full-text search retrieves the relevant code section. Because you do not

---

[10] 42 U.S.C. § 2000e–2(a)(1) prohibits discrimination "against any individual with respect to his compensation, terms, conditions, or privileges of employment, because of such individual's race, color, religion, sex, or national origin."

always know whether this is the case, using a variety of research methods is critical to ensure you are not overlooking important search results.

Establishing Context. No matter how a search is performed, be aware that it retrieves only those specific *sections* that match the particular query. Westlaw and Lexis treat each code section as a separate document. The online display of a section indicates the title and chapter in which it belongs, but there is otherwise little perspective of its place in the statutory scheme. Because it is essential in statutory research to understand the context of a specific provision, it is usually necessary to examine nearby sections after finding one that is on point. There are several ways to do this.

Both Westlaw and Lexis allow you to browse the sections immediately preceding and following the document on your screen. Westlaw has "< § >" links at the top of the display, and Lexis has "Previous" and "Next" links. These allow you to move from one code section to the next, rather than between documents matching the search query.

A more comprehensive way to grasp the context of a section is to see the table of contents for its chapter. Westlaw has a "Table of Contents" link at the top of the screen opening a pop-up window, while Lexis has a "Table of Contents" sidebar you can open. On either platform, you can also click on the linked names of the title or chapter above the text of the section. By scanning the list of sections, you may find sections labeled "Definitions" or "Exclusions" that have a very direct impact on whether a particular statute is relevant to your research. A word does not necessarily have as broad a meaning in a statute as it may in everyday language.[11]

Citing References. The notes of decisions in annotated codes, whether online or in print, do not contain references to *all* citing decisions. The annotations are selective, not comprehensive, and it can take months for new cases to be annotated in the code. Much

---

[11] In a case familiar to generations of law students, *Frigaliment Importing Co. v. B.N.S. Int'l Sales Corp.*, 190 F. Supp. 116, 117 (S.D.N.Y. 1960), Judge Henry Friendly posed the famous question "What is chicken?" The answer may depend on the jurisdiction and the context. A chicken is not an animal under the terms of the Nebraska Veterinary Medicine and Surgery Practice Act, which includes the following definition: "Animal means any animal other than man, and includes birds, fish, and reptiles, wild or domestic, living or dead, except domestic poultry." NEB. REV. STAT. § 38–3304 (2016). Other definitions of "animal" are even more restrictive. IOWA CODE § 717B.1 (2019) excludes livestock, game, fur-bearing animals, fish, reptiles, and amphibians from its definition, and N.Y. GEN. BUS. L. § 752(1) (McKinney 2012) says simply, " 'Animal' means a dog or a cat." The New York definition is so narrow because it applies only to a law covering the sale of dogs and cats. It is essential to understand the context when reading a code section.

more extensive and current research leads can be found by using citing references.

Westlaw Citing References include the cases summarized in code annotations but expand on these by listing other citing cases, articles, treatises, and other sources. Citing cases can be filtered to exclude those already seen in the Notes of Decisions, so that you can focus research on the most recent cases or ones you haven't already seen. A Westlaw Citing References display sorted with the newest decisions first is shown in Illustration 5-4.

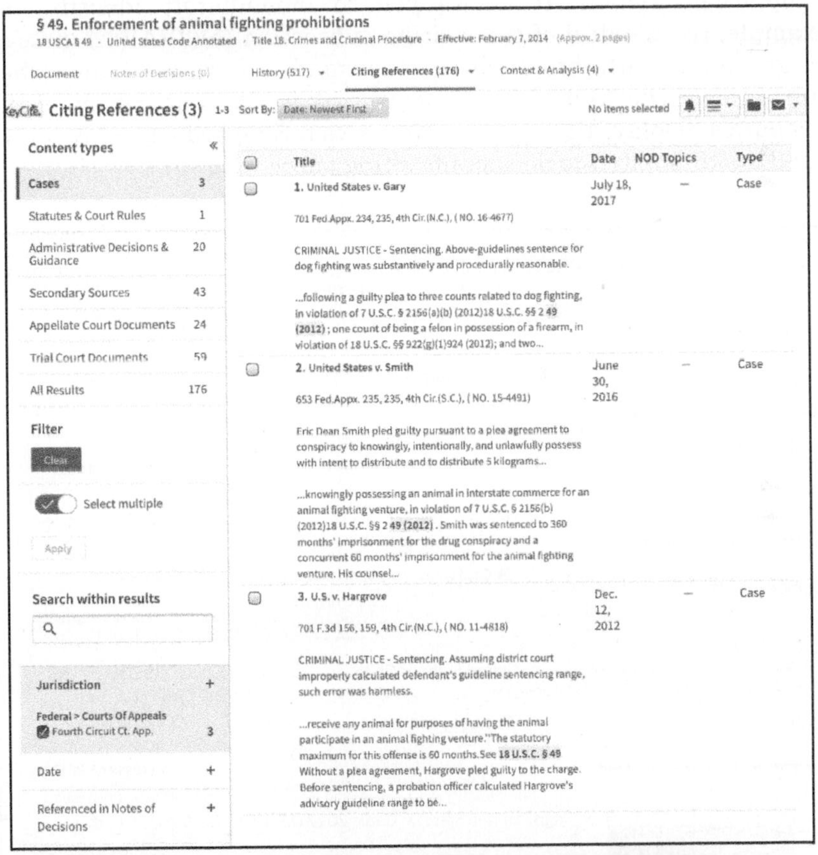

Illustration 5-4. Westlaw Citing References for 18 U.S.C. § 49, limited to cases from the U.S. Court of Appeals for the Fourth Circuit.

In Lexis, clicking on a "*Shepardize* this document" link provides information about pending legislation and citing decisions, secondary sources, and other documents. The Shepard's results can be narrowed in several ways, such as by jurisdiction or to focus on "Warning" documents with a potential negative impact on the section's validity.

Shepard's also has an important feature not found on Westlaw, "Subsection reports by specific court citation," which can focus on documents citing a specific subsection. This is particularly valuable when you are trying to interpret language that is part of a long, complicated section. It allows you to immediately identify, for example, the handful of cases citing subsection (b)(2)(A)(iii) instead of grappling with hundreds or thousands of cases citing other subsections. The "Subsection reports" link is found at the top of the Shepard's display. Illustration 5-5 shows a Shepard's display for 18 U.S.C. § 49, limited to documents citing subsection (a).

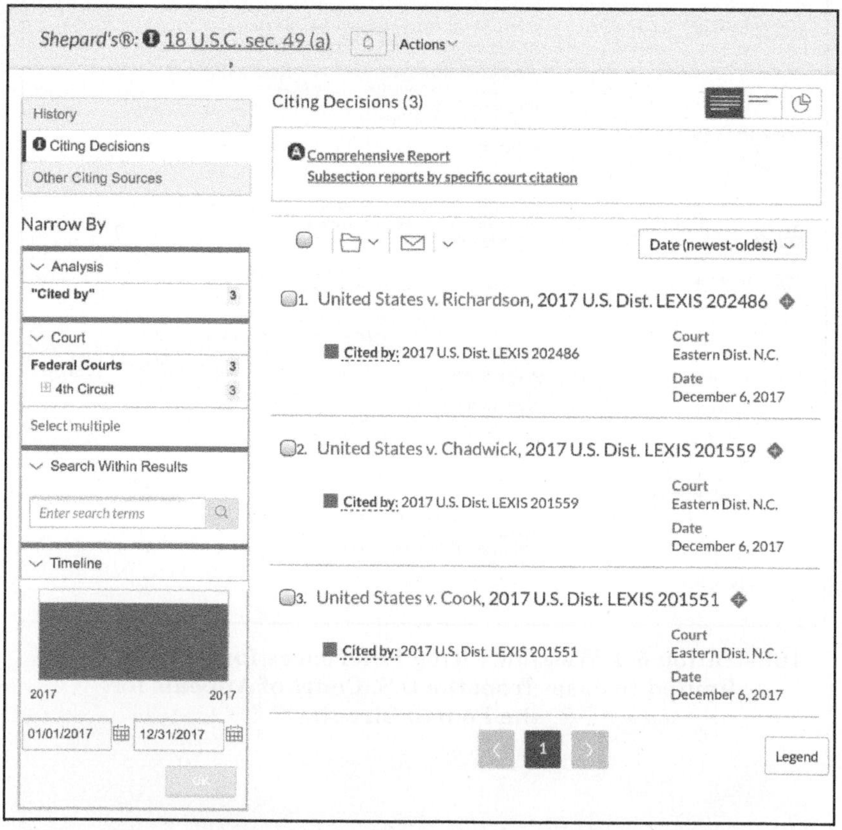

Illustration 5-5. Shepard's Citations for 18 U.S.C. § 49(a), using "Subsection reports by specific court citation."

One of the most powerful ways to use citing references is to limit retrieval to particular courts or to documents with specific keywords. These "Search within results" features allow you to narrow the group of cases citing a specific code section to those most relevant to your research.

The citing references in Westlaw and Shepard's also list any citing law review articles, encyclopedias, and other texts available through Westlaw or Lexis. In some instances these resources are also listed in the annotated codes, but codes vary widely between jurisdictions in the scope of their secondary source references. For some states, the citing references provide many more research leads than the annotated code.[12]

(b) Finding Older Versions of Statutes

In most research situations you are looking for the law currently in effect, but at times you need to see older statutes or determine when a particular change was made. Older versions of statutes may be needed for any number of reasons, not just historical research. The terms of a repealed section may still be of value in interpreting related provisions still in force, and older statutes are needed to determine the law in effect when a felony was committed or the meaning of terms when instruments such as wills or deeds were drafted. Tracing a law's language back in time can be a technical and difficult aspect of statutory research, in part because older versions of statutes may only be available in print.

Usually the keys to reconstructing an earlier version of a statute are found in the notes following the text of a code section. Parenthetical references provide leads to earlier codifications and to session laws that have amended the section. They may appear to be a hieroglyphic string of letters and numbers, but they have invaluable information. The notes after 18 U.S.C. § 49 in Illustration 5-1, for example, indicate that the section was added in 2007 and has been amended three times. For each enactment, the notes indicate the specific section of the Public Law, the date, and the *Statutes at Large* citation. Each of these four enactments might be the key to finding relevant information about specific language in the section.

Some codes merely present a list of citations, making it necessary to check the session laws to determine the changes. Worse yet, some codes indicate only recent changes or (particularly in the case of some free internet sites) have no notes at all. Many codes,

---

[12] In some libraries, *Shepard's Citations* is available in print as well as online. The current code is the only statutory source that can be checked online in either Westlaw or Lexis, but the printed versions of *Shepard's Citations* include citations to session laws and to older codifications as well as current code provisions.

however, make it easier to reconstruct past versions of a statute by including revisor's notes indicating the precise nature of each change. These notes explain exactly what language was added or removed with each amendment.

In addition to citations to session laws, the parenthetical references and revisor's notes may also indicate the location of the same or a comparable provision in an older codification. Many jurisdictions have recodified their statutes several times, so to find a related provision from fifty or a hundred years ago may require access to a set of superseded code volumes. These older sets can be found in many larger law libraries, and HeinOnline has "State Statutes: A Historical Archive" and "United States Code" collections with thousands of older code volumes back as far as the 18th century. LLMC Digital (llmc.com) also has an assortment of historical code volumes. Older codes, particularly those published before 1924 and in the public domain, may also be available from free websites such as Google Books (books.google.com), HathiTrust (www.hathitrust. org), and Internet Archive (archive.org).[13]

Access can be more complicated for sections printed in superseded volumes of the current set of the annotated code publication. These volumes are generally not available online, but they can often be found in major law libraries, particularly in the relevant jurisdiction.[14] William S. Hein & Co. publishes these volumes in microfiche by state in superseded state statutes collections.

For recent decades, earlier versions of statutes are generally available from the major commercial platforms. Westlaw and Lexis have statutes from most jurisdictions going back to the late 1980s or early 1990s, and their displays of a current code section have links to earlier versions of that section (in Westlaw under the History tab, and in Lexis as "Archived Code Versions").

Westlaw also makes the most recent changes even easier to identify with its Statutes Compare feature. Clicking on "Compare versions" on the display of a code section will show the section with deletions crossed out and added text highlighted. This feature for an amended section of the *U.S. Code* is shown in Illustration 5-6.

---

[13] Historic state codes may also be available online through local digital initiatives. The University of Georgia School of Law has added compilations and codes from 1799 through 1933 to its Digital Commons (digitalcommons.law.uga.edu/ga_code/), and the Minnesota Office of the Revisor of Statutes has a full archive back to 1851 (www.revisor.mn.gov/statutes/archive).

[14] For more information about how superseded statutes have been maintained by law libraries in the past, see Kaye V. Stoppel, *Superseded Material in the Law Library*, 78 LAW LIBR. J. 465 (1986).

Compare versions

Showing differences between versions effective [See Notes] to February 6, 2014 and February 7, 2014 [current]

<   Total: 7 differences   >   1 deletion · 6 additions   Key: deleted text added text   ⓘ   ◉◯   Highlights

18 U.S.C.A. § 49

§ 49. Enforcement of animal fighting prohibitions

(a) In general. -- Whoever violates subsection (a) (1), (b), (c), or (e) of section 26 of the Animal Welfare Act shall be fined under this title, imprisoned for not more than 5 years, or both, for each violation.

(b) Attending an animal fighting venture.--Whoever violates subsection (a)(2)(A) of section 26 of the Animal Welfare Act (7 U.S.C. 2156) shall be fined under this title, imprisoned for not more than 1 year, or both, for each violation.

(c) Causing an individual who has not attained the age of 16 to attend an animal fighting venture.-- Whoever violates subsection (a)(2)(B) of section 26 (7 U.S.C. 2156) of the Animal Welfare Act shall be fined under this title, imprisoned for not more than 3 years, or both, for each violation.

Credits

(Added Pub.L. 110-22, § 2(a), May 3, 2006 2007, 121 Stat. 88; amended Pub.L. 110-234, Title XIV, § 14207(b), May 22, 2008, 122 Stat. 1462; Pub.L. 110-246, § 4(a), Title XIV, § 14207(b), June 18, 2008, 122 Stat. 1664, 2224 ; Pub.L. 113-79, Title XII, § 12308(b)(2), Feb. 7, 2014, 128 Stat. 991 .)

18 U.S.C.A. § 49, 18 USCA § 49

Illustration 5-6. The "Compare versions" feature on Westlaw.

(c) Indexes and Tables

Even if you normally do all of your other work online, you might find it easier to begin statutory research with a printed code. To understand the scope of a specific section, it's usually necessary to see an entire code chapter or title. Scanning a few pages in a code volume can be easier (and more efficient) than going from document to document in an online platform. In addition, because the wording in statutes can be even more vague and technical than the language in other legal writing, the terms used in a code section may not be the ones that would occur to you in creating an online search. The indexes that accompany annotated codes can often provide quicker and more convenient access to relevant provisions than a keyword search or can jumpstart your thinking of new and relevant search terms.

Indexes. The index to a federal or state annotated code is a complex and lengthy document, occupying as many as six volumes. Statutory indexes usually include numerous cross-references, between related headings and from terms that are not used as subject headings. A researcher who looks in a code index under "Dogs," for example, may find nothing but an entry saying "See Animals" or "Animals, this index."

Statutory indexes, unfortunately, can sometimes be frustrating to use.[15] Indexers cannot foresee all possible terms a person might look up, so it sometimes is necessary to rethink search terms and reformulate a query in order to find references. An index may nonetheless allow you to zero in on statutes that are directly on point more quickly than a full-text keyword search.

Some statutory indexes are available online as well as in print. Westlaw has index databases for its federal and state codes, with links from the index to listed sections. The simplest way to get to a statutory index on Westlaw is to go to the statutory search page and click on the index link under "Tools & Resources." Lexis generally does not provide online indexes, and only a few free state code websites include access by means of subject indexes. Illustration 5-7 shows an excerpt from the index to the *United States Code Annotated* on Westlaw, with references to the code section shown in Illustration 5-1.

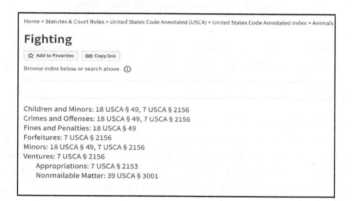

Home > Statutes & Court Rules > United States Code Annotated (USCA) > United States Code Annotated Index > Animals

Fighting

☆ Add to Favorites   ⊖⊖ Copy link

Browse index below or search above. ⓘ

Children and Minors: 18 USCA § 49, 7 USCA § 2156
Crimes and Offenses: 18 USCA § 49, 7 USCA § 2156
Fines and Penalties: 18 USCA § 49
Forfeitures: 7 USCA § 2156
Minors: 18 USCA § 49, 7 USCA § 2156
Ventures: 7 USCA § 2156
    Appropriations: 7 USCA § 2153
    Nonmailable Matter: 39 USCA § 3001

Illustration 5-7. Animal fighting references in the *United States Code Annotated* index on Westlaw.

---

[15] Few statutory index users are as admiring as this reviewer of an early 19th-century state code: "The index is very elaborate, copious and accurate, and presents a beautiful analysis of the whole volume. It may be called, to use the language of Bayle, the *soul* of the statutes. One may read them all, by passing his eyes over its fine type, so completely and analytically is the whole there displayed." *Revised Statutes of Massachusetts*, 15 AM. JURIST & L. MAG. 294, 319 (1836). Time and technology have not reduced the value of, or challenges associated with, creating a well-constructed legal index. *See* Kate Mertes, *Legal Indexing, in* INDEXING SPECIALTIES: SCHOLARLY BOOKS 15 (Margie Towery & Enid L. Zafran eds., 2005).

Popular Name Tables. At times you may have a reference to a law by its name, without a citation, and need to find the text of the statute. How do you find the Americans with Disabilities Act? You could run an online search or look in a subject index under "Disabilities," but another approach is to use a *popular name table*, which lists acts by name and provides references to citations in the session laws and code.

For older statutes, "popular name" often means a name with which a law has come to be associated over time, such as "Lanham Act" or "Mann Act." Most modern statutes, on the other hand, specify titles by which they may be cited. Some of these are short, some are technical, and some are rather tortured acronyms such as the Study of Underrepresented Classes Chasing Engineering and Science Success Act of 2018 (SUCCESS Act). Both types of names are listed in popular name tables. Illustration 5-8 shows an example of a popular name table in the *United States Code Annotated* on Westlaw, listing the Animal Fighting Prohibition Enforcement Act of 2007 that enacted the section illustrated in this chapter.

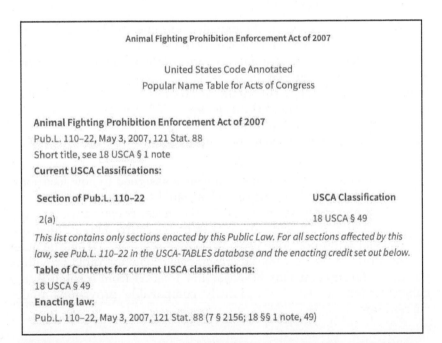

Illustration 5-8. An entry from a popular name table on Westlaw.

While popular name tables include the names by which acts are designated by Congress and state legislatures, they do not always encompass the terms by which laws are known in the media. "Title VII" and "Title IX" are familiar terms for antidiscrimination laws, but neither appears in the tables. In order to find citations from references such as these, the first step is to find more of the name (in these cases, Title VII of the Civil Rights Act of 1964 or Title IX of the Education Amendments of 1972). It may be simplest to do an online search for the phrase in order to identify the act. An internet search may turn up the full name of the act, and even better is a mention in a legal text or law review article that contains a footnote with the statute's code citation.

Parallel Reference Tables. At times you may have a citation to a statute, but not the one that provides immediate access in a code. Some references are to session law citations, while others are to outdated codifications. In either instance you will need to determine whether a law is currently in force and, if so, where it is codified. For this, most codes include *parallel reference tables* providing cross-references to the code sections.

The most extensive of the parallel reference tables are from the session laws to the code. These can occupy several volumes spanning more than 200 years of enactments. Most of these tables also indicate which sections of session laws have been repealed or were of a temporary nature. They thus make it possible to track the fate of an act as it was moved around the code, amended, and perhaps repealed in part. Illustration 5-9 shows an excerpt from a parallel reference table listing references from the federal session laws to the *United States Code*.

Not only are code sections sometimes assigned to new locations, but individual titles or entire codes can be reorganized under a revised numbering system. In such instances, tracking a statutory reference found in an older case or secondary source may require use of a parallel reference table providing cross-references from the older classification to the new one. If a code doesn't have a table providing parallel references, it may be necessary to start from scratch in the subject index or search to identify comparable provisions under current law.

TABLE 2. STATUTES AT LARGE

List of Abbreviations

P.L. 110-22, May 3, 2007

LAW	SECTION	STAT PAGE	USCA	STATUS
110-22	1	121 Stat. 88	18 s 1 nt	
110-22	2(a)	121 Stat. 88	18 s 49	
110-22	2(b)	121 Stat. 88	18 s prec. 41	
110-22	3(1)	121 Stat. 88	7 s 2156	
110-22	3(2)	121 Stat. 88	7 s 2156	

Illustration 5-9. A parallel reference table on Westlaw, showing codification of various sections of Pub. L. No. 110–22.

§ 5.3   STATUTORY INTERPRETATION

In finding a statute and obtaining current information on its validity, you have taken only the first steps in applying it to a real-life situation. Even though statutes generally are written in a way that tries to leave no room for confusion, lawyers are constantly able to find ambiguities. Several tools and methods are used to determine the purpose and meaning of the terms of a statute.

One major approach to statutory interpretation—the examination of legislative materials in order to determine the purpose or meaning of a statute—has its own research procedures and is a major focus of Chapter 6. Other methods include analyzing the plain meaning of a statute's words, examining the context in which a given provision was enacted, and applying canons of statutory construction.

These various methods of statutory interpretation are discussed in the treatise that dominates this field, Norman J. Singer & J. D. Shambie Singer, *Statutes and Statutory Construction* (7th/8th eds. 2007–date).[16] Known as *Sutherland Statutory Construction* from its

---

[16] The late Justice Antonin Scalia noted, "There is to my knowledge only one treatise on statutory interpretation that purports to treat the subject in a systematic and comprehensive fashion . . . . Despite the fact that statutory interpretation has increased enormously in importance, it is one of the few fields where we have a drought rather than a glut of treatises—fewer than we had fifty years ago, and many fewer than a century ago." ANTONIN SCALIA, A MATTER OF INTERPRETATION: FEDERAL

first author, J. G. Sutherland (1825–1902), and available on Westlaw, this work covers the topic in considerable depth and provides exhaustive references to federal and state cases.

William N. Eskridge, Jr., *Dynamic Statutory Interpretation* (1994) is one of the most frequently cited monographs in the field, and William D. Popkin, *Statutes in Court: The History and Theory of Statutory Interpretation* (1999) provides valuable historical background by surveying methods courts have used to interpret statutes over the past 200 years. Antonin Scalia & Brian A. Garner, *Reading Law: The Interpretation of Legal Texts* (2012) summarizes more than fifty major canons of statutory interpretation. Recent scholarly monographs include Frank B. Cross, *The Theory and Practice of Statutory Interpretation* (2009); Einer Elhauge, *Statutory Default Rules: How to Interpret Unclear Legislation* (2008); Kent Greenawalt, *Statutory and Common Law Interpretation* (2013); Robert A. Katzmann, *Judging Statutes* (2014); and William D. Popkin, *Statutory Interpretation: A Pragmatic Approach* (2018).

Introductory overviews of statutory interpretation are available in several texts, including William N. Eskridge, Jr., *Interpreting Law: A Primer on How to Read Statutes and the Constitution* (2016), and Linda Jellum, *Mastering Statutory Interpretation* (2d ed. 2013). Valerie C. Brannon, *Statutory Interpretation: Theories, Tools, and Trends* (2018) is a Congressional Research Service report (crs reports.congress.gov/product/pdf/R/R45153/2) with an overview similar to these other works, available free online. William D. Popkin, *A Dictionary of Statutory Interpretation* (2007) provides concise treatment of over 100 concepts.

The most authoritative interpretive guidelines are those mandated by the legislature, and every state code has provisions establishing the meaning of certain terms and clarifying topics such as the effect of amendments or repeals.[17] The Uniform Law Commission promulgated a Uniform Statute and Rule Construction Act in 1993, but it has been adopted in only one jurisdiction.[18] Commentators have also recommended that rules of statutory

---

COURTS AND THE LAW 15 (1997). The new 8th edition of *Sutherland* (2018–date) is replacing volumes in the 7th edition over a period of several years.

[17] These provisions in state codes are discussed and cited in Jacob Scott, *Codified Canons and the Common Law of Interpretation*, 98 GEO. L.J. 341 (2010). On state court approaches, see also Abbe R. Gluck, *The States as Laboratories of Statutory Interpretation: Methodological Consensus and the New Modified Textualism*, 119 YALE L.J. 1750 (2010).

[18] 14 U.L.A. 477 (2005); N.M. STAT. ANN. §§ 12–2A–1 to 12–2A–20 (West 2014). An earlier Model Statutory Construction Act (1965) was adopted in four states. 14 U.L.A. 709 (2005).

construction be adopted by Congress or drafted by the American Law Institute.[19]

§ 5.4   SOURCES FOR FEDERAL STATUTES

The United States Congress meets in two-year terms, consisting of two annual sessions, and enacts several hundred statutes each term. These statutes range from simple designations of commemorative days to complex trade bills or appropriations acts spanning hundreds of pages. Acts of Congress are introduced and passed as either *bills* or *joint resolutions*. There is no substantive distinction between these two forms, although joint resolutions are used primarily for limited or temporary matters. Other forms of congressional action, *simple resolutions* (adopted by only one chamber and either expressing its opinion or concerning internal procedures) and *concurrent resolutions* (adopted by both chambers but used to express "the sense of Congress"), do not become law.[20]

Each act is designated as either a *public law* or a *private law*, and assigned a number indicating the order in which it was passed.[21] The number, as in Public Law 110–22, identifies the Congress that enacted the law (in this case, the 110th Congress, which met in 2005–06) and the chronological sequence of its enactment (the 22nd public law enacted by that Congress).[22] Public laws are designed to be of general application, while private laws are passed for the benefit of a specific individual or small group.[23] Both types are passed in the same way and both appear in the session laws, but in separate numerical series. Only public laws, however, become part of the statutory code.

---

[19] *See, e.g.*, Gary E. O'Connor, *Restatement (First) of Statutory Interpretation*, 7 N.Y.U. J. LEGIS. & PUB. POL'Y 333 (2004); Nicholas Quinn Rosenkranz, *Federal Rules of Statutory Interpretation*, 115 HARV. L. REV. 2085 (2002); and Lawrence M. Solan, *Is It Time for a Restatement of Statutory Interpretation?*, 79 BROOK. L. REV. 733 (2014).

[20] For a discussion of resolutions without legal authority, see Jacob E. Gersen & Eric A. Posner, *Soft Law: Lessons from Congressional Practice*, 61 STAN. L. REV. 573 (2008).

[21] While most public laws contain one "act," some congressional enactments contain a combination of discrete "acts," each of which can be cited separately. There are 44 separately named acts within the Consolidated Appropriations Act, 2018, Pub. L. No. 115–141, 132 Stat. 348 (2018).

[22] Acts and joint resolutions were numbered in separate series (Public Laws and Public Resolutions) before 1941, but now they are both included among Public Laws.

[23] Most private laws in the modern era have concerned special relief for individuals under the immigration laws, but even these are now passed only once or twice per Congress. For more on the history of private laws and the rules and procedures by which they are enacted, see BERNADETTE MAGUIRE, IMMIGRATION: PUBLIC LEGISLATION AND PRIVATE BILLS (1997); Matthew Mantel, *Private Bills and Private Laws*, 99 LAW LIBR. J. 87 (2007).

(a) Slip Laws and Advance Session Law Services

The first official form of publication of a federal law is the *slip law,* a separately paginated pamphlet. Beginning with the 104th Congress in 1995, the United States Government Publishing Office's Govinfo service (www.govinfo.gov) provides PDF files of public laws. For current legislation this is one of the quickest and most useful sources. New laws are generally online in PDF within a few weeks of enactment, although lengthier acts may not be available for two or three months. You can either browse public laws by number or search for specific words or phrases. If a very recent enactment is not yet available from Govinfo, the legislative site Congress.gov (www.congress.gov) can provide the text of the enrolled bill, the version that was passed by both houses and sent to the President.

The form of the printing of slip laws is almost identical to that which appears in the bound session law publication, the *Statutes at Large,* and in fact the slip laws include *Statutes at Large* page references when they are first printed and posted on Govinfo. This makes it possible to cite to the official *Statutes at Large* as soon as a new public law is available.

Public laws are also available shortly after enactment from commercial resources, including Westlaw and Lexis. Westlaw's U.S. Public Laws collection (under Proposed & Enacted Legislation) has laws from the current and most recent terms of Congress, with older laws back to 1973 in a separate U.S. Public Laws-Historical database. The USCS-Public Laws database on Lexis has laws back to 1988. All of these databases include the *Statutes at Large* citations needed to cite acts of Congress.

In print, the next appearance of federal statutes after the slip laws is in the monthly advance session law services, Thomson Reuters's *United States Code Congressional and Administrative News* (*USCCAN*) and LexisNexis's *Advance* pamphlets to the *United States Code Service* (*USCS*). Like the slip laws, each page of text in both *USCCAN* and *USCS Advance* indicates the location at which it will eventually appear in the official *Statutes at Large.*[24]

---

[24] Availability of new laws on Govinfo has greatly diminished the need for *USCCAN* and *USCS Advance* in most research, but they do include some useful features. In addition to the text of newly enacted public laws, both services publish court rule amendments and presidential documents. Each pamphlet includes a cumulative index of the session's legislation and tables indicating the sections of the *United States Code* that have been affected by recent legislative, executive, or administrative actions. *USCCAN*, but not *USCS Advance*, also publishes selective legislative history materials such as House and Senate Reports. *Advance* pamphlets are designed only for temporary use until the new material is incorporated into *USCS*, but *USCCAN* pamphlets are cumulated at the end of each year into bound volumes to form a permanent record of session laws and legislative history.

(b) *Statutes at Large*

The official, permanent session law publication for federal laws is the *United States Statutes at Large* (abbreviated in legal citations as Stat.). The *Statutes at Large* is not the most convenient source for federal statutory research, but it maintains a vital role. It is needed to determine when a particular provision took effect or was repealed or to reconstruct the precise text as it was enacted. Sections of a public law may be scattered among several titles in the code, but the *Statutes at Large* provides each act of Congress in its entirety.

The *Statutes at Large* is the positive law form of statutes, and "legal evidence of laws . . . in all the Courts of the United States."[25] The *United States Code* is only *prima facie* evidence of the laws, except for those of its titles which have been reenacted by Congress as positive law.[26] If there is a discrepancy between what is in the *Statutes at Large* and what is in the *U.S. Code*, the former controls.[27]

At the end of each annual session of Congress, the enacted laws are published in chronological order, along with concurrent resolutions and presidential proclamations. In recent years, each session's compilation has comprised three to six volumes, with overall indexes by popular name and subject at the back of each volume.[28] A federal session law is cited by its Public Law number and the volume and page in which it appears in *Statutes at Large*.[29] The Animal Fighting Prohibition Enforcement Act of 2007, Pub. L. No. 110–22, 121 Stat. 88, shown in Illustration 5-10, begins on page 88 of volume 121 of the *Statutes at Large*.

---

[25] 1 U.S.C. § 112.

[26] 1 U.S.C. § 204.

[27] In *U.S. Nat'l Bank of Or. v. Indep. Ins. Agents of Am., Inc.*, 508 U.S. 439 (1993), the Supreme Court held that a statutory provision that had been omitted from the *U.S. Code* for more than forty years was still good law because it had never been repealed. As the leading treatise on statutory construction puts it, "[L]awyers still must rely upon the Statutes at Large as the primary source of federal law. No lawyer can afford to depend on the code as ultimate authority." 2 NORMAN J. SINGER & J. D. SHAMBIE SINGER, STATUTES AND STATUTORY CONSTRUCTION § 36A:10 (7th ed. 2009).

[28] The *Statutes at Large* indexes can be used to find laws passed in a particular year, but separate year-by-year coverage is not particularly useful for most research. Two retrospective indexes to federal law are also of occasional use in historical research: MIDDLETON G. BEAMAN & A. K. MCNAMARA, INDEX ANALYSIS OF THE FEDERAL STATUTES, 1789–1873 (1911), and WALTER H. MCCLENON & WILFRED C. GILBERT, INDEX TO THE FEDERAL STATUTES, 1874–1931 (1933).

[29] Before 1901, session laws were identified by chapter number rather than Public Law number. Public Law numbers have been assigned to acts of Congress since 1901, but chapter numbers remained the primary means of identification until they were discontinued at the end of the 1956 session. *The Bluebook* continues to follow this rule for statutes before 1957. THE BLUEBOOK: A UNIFORM SYSTEM OF CITATION tbl. T1.1 (21st ed. 2020). The *ALWD Guide* doesn't make this distinction and uses Public Law numbers for all federal session laws. ALWD GUIDE TO LEGAL CITATION R. 14.6 (6th ed. 2017).

121 STAT. 88   PUBLIC LAW 110–22—MAY 3, 2007

Public Law 110–22
110th Congress

An Act

May 3, 2007
[H.R. 137]

To amend title 18, United States Code, to strengthen prohibitions against animal
fighting, and for other purposes.

Be it enacted by the Senate and House of Representatives of
the United States of America in Congress assembled,

Animal Fighting
Prohibition
Enforcement Act
of 2007.
18 USC 1 note.

SECTION 1. SHORT TITLE.

This Act may be cited as the "Animal Fighting Prohibition
Enforcement Act of 2007".

SEC. 2. ENFORCEMENT OF ANIMAL FIGHTING PROHIBITIONS.

(a) IN GENERAL.—Chapter 3 of title 18, United States Code,
is amended by adding at the end the following:

"§ 49. Enforcement of animal fighting prohibitions

"Whoever violates subsection (a), (b), (c), or (e) of section 26
of the Animal Welfare Act shall be fined under this title, imprisoned
for not more than 3 years, or both, for each violation.".

(b) CLERICAL AMENDMENT.—The table of contents for such
chapter is amended by inserting after the item relating to section
48 the following:

"49. Enforcement of animal fighting prohibitions.".

SEC. 3. AMENDMENTS TO THE ANIMAL WELFARE ACT.

Section 26 of the Animal Welfare Act (7 U.S.C. 2156) is
amended—

(1) in subsection (c), by striking "interstate instrumentality"
and inserting "instrumentality of interstate commerce for
commercial speech";

(2) in subsection (d), by striking "such subsections" and
inserting "such subsection";

(3) by striking subsection (e) and inserting the following:

"(e) It shall be unlawful for any person to knowingly sell,
buy, transport, or deliver in interstate or foreign commerce a knife,
a gaff, or any other sharp instrument attached, or designed or
intended to be attached, to the leg of a bird for use in an animal
fighting venture.";

(4) in subsection (g)—

(A) in paragraph (1), by striking "or animals, such
as waterfowl, bird, raccoon, or fox hunting"; and

(B) by striking paragraph (3) and inserting the following:

"(3) the term 'instrumentality of interstate commerce'
means any written, wire, radio, television or other form of

Illustration 5-10. The first page of a public law in *Statutes at Large*.

The *Statutes at Large* was first published in 1846 and provides retrospective coverage back to 1789.[30] It contains all laws passed by Congress, including those that were already obsolete or had been repealed in 1846. The first five volumes of the *Statutes at Large* contain public laws from the 1st to the 28th Congresses (1789–1845), and volumes 6–8 have private laws, treaties with Indian tribes, and treaties with foreign countries respectively. (Treaties were included in the *Statutes at Large* until 1950, when they began being printed in a separate series. For an in-depth discussion of treaty resources, see Chapter 17.)

Bloomberg Law and HeinOnline have complete retrospective coverage of the *Statutes at Large* in PDF, with the text of all acts and treaties back to 1789 searchable by keyword or title. Westlaw also covers the *Statutes at Large* back to 1789, but full-text searching is available only from 1973 to date in the U.S. Public Laws-Historical database. Westlaw's United States Statutes at Large database has earlier acts as image-based PDFs, and only citations, dates, and summary information can be searched. Similarly, Lexis has a USCS-Public Laws database with full-text searching back to 1988, and a retrospective PDF-based United States Statutes at Large database in which only titles and synopses are searchable. If you know what law you are looking for, you can retrieve it by *Statutes at Large* citation on any of these platforms.

PDF copies of *Statutes at Large* are also available free through various government websites. The GPO's Govinfo portal includes access to *Statutes at Large* volumes beginning in 1951, with volume

---

[30] The first volumes of the *Statutes at Large*, edited by former Supreme Court reporter Richard Peters, were published pursuant to the Resolution of Mar. 3, 1845, no. 10, 5 Stat. 798, and they were declared to be competent evidence of the law by the Act of Aug. 8, 1846, ch. 100, § 2, 9 Stat. 75, 76. The new set had several predecessors. In its first session in 1789, Congress enacted a law ordering that the Secretary of State cause each of its acts "to be published in at least three of the public newspapers printed within the United States." Act of Sept. 15, 1789, ch. 14, § 2, 1 Stat. 68, 68. It did not take long to realize that a more permanent form of publication was necessary, and several chronological collections of federal laws with the title *Laws of the United States of America* were soon issued by private publishers under congressional authority. The first, authorized by the Resolution of Feb. 18, 1791, no. 1, 1 Stat. 224, was printed in 1791 by Andrew Brown and covered the three sessions of the First Congress. A more comprehensive set was authorized four years later by the Act of Mar. 3, 1795, ch. 50, 1 Stat. 443, this time with the specification that it include an index. Known as the Folwell edition from its printer, Richard Folwell, this set was published in 1796–97 in three volumes and covered the first four Congresses. Coverage was extended by eight supplementary volumes through the thirteenth Congress (1813–15), at which point Congress passed the Act of Apr. 18, 1814, ch. 69, 3 Stat. 129, authorizing a new edition to be published by John Bioren and W. John Duane. Additional volumes in this series covered acts through the twenty-eighth Congress (1843–45). For background on the history of federal statutory publication, see Ralph H. Dwan & Ernest R. Feidler, *The Federal Statutes—Their History and Use*, 22 MINN. L. REV. 1008 (1938), and Erwin C. Surrency, *The Publication of Federal Laws: A Short History*, 79 LAW LIBR. J. 469 (1987).

65. Volumes 1 to 81 (1789–1950) are available from the Library of Congress (www.loc.gov/law/help/statutes-at-large/).

The easiest way to find court decisions citing acts in the *Statutes at Large* is to do a full-text search for the citation in a case law database. Neither Westlaw Citing References nor Shepard's online covers citations to session laws, but the *United States Code Service* includes an "Annotations to Uncodified Laws and Treaties" volume with case summaries by *Statutes at Large* citation. This covers acts that have been repealed as well as those that were never codified.[31]

(c) Codification of Federal Statutes

The most useful sources of federal laws are arranged by subject, rather than chronologically like the *Statutes at Large*. The most important of these is the current *United States Code* in its various editions. But you may still need to reference its predecessor, an earlier codification called the *Revised Statutes*, which remains a source of positive law.

(1) Revised Statutes

Because of the difficulty of research in the numerous volumes of the *Statutes at Large* with their separate indexes, it became apparent by the 1860s that some form of codification or subject arrangement was needed. After much drafting and redrafting, the first and only complete revision of federal laws was enacted in 1874,[32] and published the following year as the *Revised Statutes of the United States*. The *Revised Statutes* was published as part one of 18 Stat. and contained the general and permanent statutes in force on December 1, 1873.

This first edition of the *Revised Statutes* confusingly goes by several titles: the "Revised Statutes of 1873" (for the cut-off date of the laws it includes), or "of 1874" (for the date of its enactment) or "of 1875" (for the date of its publication). In any case, the publication was more than just a topical arrangement of laws into seventy-four subject titles and 5,601 sections. (The numbering is continuous throughout the *Revised Statutes*, so a citation is simply to the section number, as in Rev. Stat. § 5601.) It was a reenactment as positive

---

[31] More citing references can be found using *Shepard's Citations* in print. *Shepard's Federal Statute Citations* covers citations in federal court decisions to acts in the *Statutes at Large* which have not been incorporated into the code. Citations to the *Statutes at Large* are among the few features in print *Shepard's* that are not available online.

[32] Act of June 22, 1874, 18 Stat. 1. The *Revised Statutes* were prepared pursuant to the Act of June 27, 1866, ch. 140, 14 Stat. 74. They were preceded by a few privately published subject collections of federal statutes, beginning with A DIGEST OF THE LAWS OF THE UNITED STATES OF AMERICA (Thomas Herty ed., 1800–02).

law of all the statutes it contained, and it expressly repealed their original *Statutes at Large* texts.[33] The *Revised Statutes* is the authoritative text for most laws predating its publication that remain in force, and it is still needed occasionally in modern research.

The discovery of several errors in the *Revised Statutes* led to the publication of a second edition in 1878, replacing the earlier version as 18 Stat. part 1.[34] The second edition was not enacted as positive law, but it is the edition most commonly found in sets of the *Statutes at Large*.

The *Revised Statutes* is online in PDF from several sources, as part of their coverage of the *Statutes at Large*. The Library of Congress provides free access to the 1878 second edition (lcweb2.loc. gov/ammem/amlaw/lwsl.html), while Lexis and Westlaw have the original, reenacted first edition. HeinOnline has both first and second editions in its U.S. Statutes at Large Library.

For the rare occasion when you have a reference to the *Revised Statutes* and need to determine whether a provision is still in force, all three versions of the *United States Code* have parallel reference tables listing Rev. Stat. sections and indicating where the modern counterpart appears in the current code or if a provision has been repealed. This table is also available online in Westlaw.

(2) United States Code

Almost fifty more years of publication of the *Statutes at Large* ensued before another effort at an official codification of federal laws was undertaken. The inconvenience in statutory research was somewhat alleviated by privately published subject compilations, but the need for an official code was apparent.[35] A new codification was

---

[33] The *Revised Statutes* repealed acts of Congress prior to December 1, 1873, but only if any portion of them was covered by a section of the revision. Any act in the *Statutes at Large* "no part of which [was] embraced in" the *Revised Statutes* was unaffected by its enactment and publication. Rev. Stat. § 5596. *Millsaps v. Thompson*, 259 F.3d 535, 542 n.3 (6th Cir. 2001), considered an 1872 enactment not included in the *Revised Statutes* or the *United States Code*, and held that it remained good law.

[34] Errors in the first edition were corrected by the Act of Feb. 18, 1875, ch. 80, 18 Stat. 316, and the Act of Feb. 27, 1877, ch. 69, 19 Stat. 240; and the second edition was published pursuant to the Act of Mar. 2, 1877, ch. 82, 19 Stat. 268. Despite the publication of *Revised Statutes* as part of the *Statutes at Large*, some libraries catalog and shelve copies of the *Revised Statutes* as a separate publication.

[35] Two supplements to the *Revised Statutes* were issued for the periods 1874–91 and 1892–1901, but these also did not have the status of positive law. They contained lists of *Revised Statutes* sections affected by subsequent legislation, but instead of title-by-title supplements these were just chronological arrangements of new laws. The first commercial subject compilation was COMPILED STATUTES OF THE UNITED STATES, 1901 (1902), and the first commercial version with extensive annotations similar to those used today was FEDERAL STATUTES ANNOTATED (1903–06). The legislative effort leading to the *United States Code* is recounted in William L. Burdick, *The Revision of the Federal Statutes*, 11 A.B.A. J. 178 (1925).

finally approved on June 30, 1926, and published as part 1 of 44 *Statutes at Large* under the title: *The Code of the Laws of the United States of America of a General and Permanent Nature, in Force December 7, 1925*. It has ever since been known as the *United States Code*.

Unlike the *Revised Statutes*, the new *U.S. Code* was not a positive law reenactment and did not repeal the prior session laws. It was *prima facie* evidence of the law, rebuttable by reference to the *Statutes at Large*. However, beginning in 1947 Congress has revised individual titles of the code and reenacted them into positive law. More than half of the titles have been reenacted so far, and are now legal evidence; for the rest the *Statutes at Large* remains legal evidence and the *U.S. Code* is *prima facie* evidence. A note following 1 U.S.C. § 204 indicates the titles that have been enacted into positive law.[36] Major code titles enacted as positive law include Title 11, Bankruptcy; Title 18, Crimes and Criminal Procedure; and Title 28, Judiciary and Judicial Procedure. For the purposes of conducting legal research, however, there is no difference in how you locate relevant statutory sections in a positive law or non-positive law title.

The *U.S. Code* is arranged in over fifty subject titles, generally in alphabetical order from Agriculture to War and National Defense. Titles are divided into parts and chapters and then into sections, with a continuous sequence of section numbers for each title. Citations to the code indicate the title, section number, and year. 18 U.S.C. § 49, for example, is in Title 18 (Crimes and Criminal Procedure), Part 1 (Crimes), Chapter 3 (Animals, Birds, Fish, and Plants), but the part and chapter number do not appear in the citation.

Following each statutory section in the *U.S. Code*, there is a parenthetical reference to its source in the *Statutes at Large*, including citations to any amendments. This reference enables you

---

[36] The Supreme Court has held more than once that the *Statutes at Large* controls even if a title has been reenacted as positive law, if the meanings differ and no substantive change was intended in the reenactment. *Cass v. United States*, 417 U.S. 72, 82 (1974) ("[T]he revisers expressly stated that changes in language resulting from the codification were to have no substantive effect."); *Fourco Glass Co. v. Transmirra Products Corp.*, 353 U.S. 222, 227 (1957) ("[N]o changes of law or policy are to be presumed from changes of language in the revision unless an intent to make such changes is clearly expressed.").

The distinction between positive law titles and *prima facie* titles has no effect on the validity of the laws, as litigants have learned if they attempt to argue that a title that has not been enacted into positive law has no legal force. *See, e.g., Ryan v. Bilby*, 764 F.2d 1325 (9th Cir. 1985) ("Congress's failure to enact a title into positive law has only evidentiary significance and does not render the underlying enactment invalid or unenforceable."); *United States v. Zuger*, 602 F. Supp. 889, 891–92 (D. Conn. 1984) ("[T]he failure of Congress to enact a title as such and in such form into positive law . . . in no way impugns the validity, effect, enforceability or constitutionality of the laws as contained and set forth in the title.").

to locate the original text, which may be the positive law form, and from there to find legislative history documents relating to the law's enactment. Illustration 5-11 shows 18 U.S.C. § 49 as it appears in the *United States Code*. The statutory text is followed by citations to the public laws in the *Statutes at Large* and by a history of changes made by amendments.

---

§ 49. Enforcement of animal fighting prohibitions

(a) IN GENERAL.—Whoever violates subsection (a)(1), (b), (c), or (e) of section 26 of the Animal Welfare Act shall be fined under this title, imprisoned for not more than 5 years, or both, for each violation.

(b) ATTENDING AN ANIMAL FIGHTING VENTURE.—Whoever violates subsection (a)(2)(A) of section 26 of the Animal Welfare Act (7 U.S.C. 2156) shall be fined under this title, imprisoned for not more than 1 year, or both, for each violation.

(c) CAUSING AN INDIVIDUAL WHO HAS NOT ATTAINED THE AGE OF 16 TO ATTEND AN ANIMAL FIGHTING VENTURE.—Whoever violates subsection (a)(2)(B) of section 26 (7 U.S.C. 2156) of the Animal Welfare Act shall be fined under this title, imprisoned for not more than 3 years, or both, for each violation.

(Added Pub. L. 110–22, §2(a), May 3, 2007, 121 Stat. 88; amended Pub. L. 110–234, title XIV, §14207(b), May 22, 2008, 122 Stat. 1462; Pub. L. 110–246, §4(a), title XIV, §14207(b), June 18, 2008, 122 Stat. 1664, 2224; Pub. L. 113–79, title XII, §12308(b)(2), Feb. 7, 2014, 128 Stat. 991.)

Illustration 5-11. A statute as it appears in the official *United States Code*.

Some titles of the *U.S. Code* have been revised and renumbered, but others retain the section numbering they were assigned in 1926. Because the basic structure is now almost 100 years old, several titles have grown unwieldy as new sections are shoehorned into their appropriate subject locations. Section numbers such as 15 U.S.C. § 78aaa and 42 U.S.C. § 2000e–2 are used to squeeze new material between existing sections. This doesn't mean that 2000e–2 is a subsection of 2000 or 2000e. Subsections are indicated with parentheses; 15 U.S.C. § 78(a) is a subsection, but 15 U.S.C. § 78a is a discrete section of the *United States Code*.

It is important to be aware that not every federal law is published as a section of the *United States Code*. The Office of the Law Revision Counsel of the House of Representatives, which is responsible for preparing the code, includes what it deems to be "general and permanent laws of the United States,"[37] but its determination does not have the force of law. Some laws appear only in the *Statutes at Large*, and others are published as notes following sections of the code. (Codification as a note happens most frequently if a public law is in the subject area of a positive law title, but Congress has failed to directly amend the *U.S. Code* language. The Office of the Law Revision Counsel cannot add sections in the text of positive law titles.) The validity of a statute is unaffected by whether it is published as a code section or a note, or is omitted entirely from the *United States Code*.[38]

The *United States Code* is published in a new edition every six years by the federal government and is updated between editions by annual bound supplements.[39] Each year's supplement incorporates material in preceding supplements, so that only the latest one need be consulted for changes since the last revision. Although the original 1926 edition and its 1934 successor were one-volume works, subsequent editions have grown into ever larger multi-volume publications. The 2012 edition was published in 41 volumes, and the 2018 edition when completed will be even larger.

The U.S. Code is available free online from several sources, including two government sites. The House of Representatives Office of the Law Revision Counsel (uscode.house.gov) has a searchable and regularly updated version, while Govinfo has a PDF version similar to the printed version.

The Office of the Law Revision Counsel site is the better source for most purposes, in that it is more current and easier to search than the Govinfo version. Its code sections are fully up to date; if changes in a very recent enactment have not yet been incorporated, affected sections have prominent warnings and links to the amending legislation. It provides search boxes for convenient access by title and

---

[37] 2 U.S.C. § 285b. Although the code contains laws of a "permanent" nature, Congress is increasingly enacting provisions of limited duration, often with express "sunset" clauses that set expiration dates. *See* Jacob E. Gersen, *Temporary Legislation*, 74 U. CHI. L. REV. 247 (2007). For a discussion of laws omitted from the *U.S. Code*, especially appropriations riders, see Will Tress, *Lost Laws: What We Can't Find in the United States Code*, 40 GOLDEN GATE U. L. REV. 129 (2010).

[38] On the validity of statutes published as notes in the *U.S. Code*, see Richard J. McKinney, *Authority of Statutes Placed in Section Notes of the United States Code*, LLSDC LEGISLATIVE SOURCE BOOK (www.llsdc.org/authority-statutes-in-section-notes-us-code) [https://perma.cc/DR73-6AKX], and Shawn G. Nevers & Julie Graves Krishnaswami, *The Shadow Code: Statutory Notes in the United States Code*, 112 LAW LIBR. J. ___ (2020).

[39] Properly citing the U.S. Code has, in the recent past, led to confusion because of this publication schedule, which is often staggered between print and online sources. *The Bluebook* changed its rule in the 21st edition, eliminating the need to reference a current section's year of publication. THE BLUEBOOK: A UNIFORM SYSTEM OF CITATION R. 12.3.2 (21st ed. 2020).

section number, and allows several search options including keywords using proximity connectors and truncation. The site also has options to search prior versions of the code back to 1994 and (under "Downloads") to access large PDF files for entire code titles, as well as bulk downloads in XML format.

Govinfo also has editions of the *U.S. Code* back to 1994, but it is only updated on an annual basis and its most recent version is only as current as the published edition. On both the Law Revision Counsel site and Govinfo, the PDF files incorporate material in the supplements to the printed edition of the code rather than presenting the supplements separately. This makes them more convenient than the printed version, which often requires flipping back and forth between two large volumes.

The *U.S. Code* in print and on the Law Revision Counsel site features several tables that can be useful in research, particularly if you are trying to track down a statute from its name or from an older citation. "Acts Cited by Popular Name" ("Popular Name Tool" online) lists laws alphabetically under either short titles assigned by Congress or popular names by which they have become known, and parallel conversion tables provide references from earlier revisions and between different forms of statutory publication. Online under "Other OLRC Tables and Tools," Table I covers *U.S. Code* titles that have been revised and renumbered since the original 1926 adoption of the code, showing where former sections of the title are incorporated into the current edition. Table II indicates the location and status of sections of the *Revised Statutes of 1878* within the code, and Table III lists the *Statutes at Large* in chronological order and indicates where each public law section is codified. Other tables cover executive orders, proclamations, reorganization plans, and internal cross-references within the code.

The Law Revision Counsel site also has a "Classification Tables" page (uscode.house.gov/classification/tables.shtml) containing regularly updated lists for each year of sections amended, enacted, omitted, repealed, or transferred. These are available sorted in Public Law order and by *U.S. Code* section. The tables are useful for completing a "codified at" reference for a recent enactment, or for identifying recent changes in a particular code title.

The print *U.S. Code* has a subject index spanning four volumes, an invaluable resource because keyword searches are not always the most effective way to find statutes. The index, unfortunately, is not available from either of the government's online versions.

Another online source for the *U.S. Code* is HeinOnline, which has every edition since 1926 in searchable PDF, including indexes, tables, and supplements.⁴⁰ The older editions can be useful for tracking the history of a provision and may be needed for a citation to a statute that is no longer in force.⁴¹

Although statutory provisions are often affected by court decisions, there is no indication or reflection of these decisions in the printed *U.S. Code* or in the versions available free on the internet. A statute can even be declared unconstitutional, but it remains in the text until Congress repeals or amends it. Before relying on a *U.S. Code* provision, you should use resources such as the annotated editions of the code to ascertain what judicial treatment may have occurred.

(3) Annotated Codes

Because the *United States Code* is not updated on a very timely basis and has no information about court decisions applying or interpreting code sections, most researchers turn to one of two commercial annotated editions of the code, *United States Code Annotated* (cited as U.S.C.A.), published by Thomson Reuters, or *United States Code Service* (cited as U.S.C.S.), published by LexisNexis.⁴² Each is available both as a print set of over 200 volumes and on its publisher's online platform. These annotated codes are more current and have much more extensive information than the official code.

The annotated codes provide the same research aids found in the official *U.S. Code,* such as authority references, historical notes, cross references, tables, and indexes. They also have references to such sources as the *Code of Federal Regulations*, law review articles, legal encyclopedias, *ALR* annotations, and major treatises. *USCA* adds references to legislative history materials in *U.S. Code Congressional and Administrative News* (*USCCAN*) and citations to digest topics and key numbers.

Following each code section that has been interpreted or applied judicially, *USCA* and *USCS* have "Notes of Decisions" or

---

⁴⁰ The Library of Congress also provides free access to digitized versions of the U.S. Code from 1926 through 1988, downloadable in PDF by chapter (www.loc.gov/law/help/us-code.php).

⁴¹ "Cite statutes no longer in force to the current official or unofficial code if they still appear therein. Otherwise, cite the last edition of the official or unofficial code in which the statute appeared, the session laws, or a secondary source—in that order of preference." THE BLUEBOOK: A UNIFORM SYSTEM OF CITATION R. 12.2.1(b) (21st ed. 2020). The *ALWD Guide* does not require a publication date for statutes no longer in force. ALWD GUIDE TO LEGAL CITATION R. 14.3(a) (6th ed. 2017).

⁴² *USCA* began publication in 1927, shortly after the 1926 creation of the *United States Code*. Its format is based on the publisher's earlier *United States Compiled Statutes Annotated* (1916–17). *USCS* succeeded an earlier compilation entitled *Federal Code Annotated*, first published in 1936.

"Interpretive Notes and Decisions" ("Case Notes" on Lexis), consisting of abstracts of cases dealing with the particular section. Unless there have been only a few cases, the annotations are arranged by topic into numbered sections. To assist in finding relevant cases, *USCA*'s annotations are preceded by an alphabetical subject index and *USCS*'s by a topical outline. Each has selective annotations of court decisions, and cases may be included in one but not the other. *USCA*'s annotations are generally more thorough, but some court decisions appear only in *USCS*. *USCS* is also the only source for references to administrative decisions, with notes covering several dozen agencies as well as court decisions. Illustration 5-12 shows notes of decisions on an animal welfare statute as printed in *USCA*.

Notes of Decisions

Constitutionality 1
Remand 4
Review 3
Standing 2

---

1. Constitutionality

Provision of the Animal Welfare Act prohibiting the knowing transportation of birds in interstate or foreign commerce for purposes of having the birds participate in a fighting venture was not unconstitutionally vague because it provided fair warning of what is proscribed. Slavin v. U.S., C.A.8 (Ark.) 2005, 403 F.3d 522. Constitutional Law ☞ 82(6.1)

2. Standing

Humane Society, in challenging United States Postal Service's (USPS) rejection of its petition to declare animal fighting periodical nonmailable under Animal Welfare Act, fell within zone of interests protected under Act's provisions on mailability of advertisement of animals or certain sharp instruments for use in animal fighting ventures, satisfying prudential standing requirements; Humane Society's reason for existence was to protect animals, and in practice could be expected to police interests protected by the Act. Humane Society of U.S. v. U.S. Postal Service, D.D.C.2009, 609 F.Supp.2d 85. Postal Service ☞ 14

Humane Society satisfied injury-in-fact standing criterion, as required to establish organizational standing under Article III in action challenging United States Postal Service's (USPS) rejection of its petition to declare animal fighting period-

ical nonmailable under Animal Welfare Act, despite fact that Humane Society was a volunteer organization and could not name an exact date or location of a raid on an illegal animal fight for which it would be called to assist animals; if the need to care for animals on an emergency basis was increased by USPS's circulation of animal fighting periodical, financial injury to Humane Society would be neither voluntary nor self-inflicted. Humane Society of U.S. v. U.S. Postal Service, D.D.C.2009, 609 F.Supp.2d 85. Associations ☞ 20(1)

3. Review

Letters from United States Postal Service (USPS) in response to Humane Society's requests to declare animal fighting periodical nonmailable under Animal Welfare Act unequivocally stating agency interpretation of the Act, was "final agency action," for purposes of determining whether Humane Society could seek judicial review of agency's determination. Humane Society of U.S. v. U.S. Postal Service, D.D.C.2009, 609 F.Supp.2d 85. Postal Service ☞ 14

4. Remand

Remand to the United States Postal Service (USPS) for further consideration of its mailability determination regarding animal fighting periodical was warranted, as Animal Welfare Act, which prohibited mailing advertisement of animals or certain sharp instruments for use in animal fighting ventures, had been amended since litigation began to clarify type of animal fighting material to be treated as nonmailable. Humane Society of U.S. v.

Illustration 5-12. Case annotations, as printed in
United States Code Annotated.

One minor difference between *USCA* and *USCS* is that *USCA* mirrors the language of the official *United States Code* and uses cross-references to other *USCA* sections, while *USCS* preserves the language of the original *Statutes at Large* text and uses parentheticals and notes for clarification. *USCA* may refer to "this chapter," while *USCS* uses the term "this Act" and prints cross-references as they appear in the original public law. There are sometimes differences in how the scope of a definition or exception is expressed, but these are not substantive changes.[43]

The online code databases in Westlaw and Lexis are updated to include laws from the current session of Congress, with a note accompanying each section indicating the most recent public law included in code coverage. Westlaw goes further by adding a red flag for sections with amendments that have not yet been incorporated in the text, so it generally provides notice of new amendments within a day or two of their enactment.

In print, *USCA* and *USCS* are kept up to date by annual pocket parts in the back of each volume that indicate changes in the statutory text and contain annotations to recent judicial decisions and other sources. Some volumes have so much new material that they are supplemented by separate softcover pamphlets rather than pocket parts.[44] Replacement volumes are published when supplements get too unwieldy. Some volumes in each set are several years old,[45] but every volume has an up-to-date supplement. Any time you use a *USCA* or *USCS* volume in print, you *must* check its supplement for current amendments or judicial developments.

Thorough research involving a particular statute may require checking both *USCA* and *USCS* due to the differences in annotations included. A person with access to both *USCA* and *USCS* usually develops a preference for one or the other but should be familiar with both. One edition can be used on a regular basis for most research needs, but the other may occasionally be needed for its editorial features or to ensure comprehensive coverage.

---

[43] Errors may also occasionally be found in one of the unofficial codes. In *United States v. Carroll*, 105 F.3d 740, 744 (1st Cir. 1997), the decision turned on a comma that was printed in the *Statutes at Large* and in the *United States Code*, but was omitted from *USCA*.

[44] Between annual pocket parts, legislative and judicial developments are noted in quarterly softcover pamphlets supplementing the entire set. Each pamphlet is arranged by code section and contains the text of new laws and notes of recent decisions. These are further updated by the monthly advance pamphlets of *USCCAN* and *USCS Advance*, which have the text of newly enacted statutes in chronological order and tables indicating the code sections affected by recent legislation.

[45] Title 27, Intoxicating Liquors, is the last of the original 1927 volumes in the current *USCA* set. It is still updated by a pocket part more than ninety years after its publication.

§ 5.5　　SOURCES FOR STATE STATUTES

Research in state statutory law is quite similar to the federal paradigm already outlined. State statutes also appear as slip laws, session laws, codes, and annotated codes. Current session laws and codes are available from government websites, and annotated codes are published on online commercial platforms and in print.

However, there are variations in statutory publication and research from state to state, and an online or print state legal research guide can provide valuable guidance in using a particular jurisdiction's code and session laws. These resources are particularly helpful for understanding sources for historical research in state statutes.

(a)　Slip Laws and Session Laws

Every state has a session law publication similar to the *U.S. Statutes at Large*, containing the laws enacted at each sitting of its legislature. The names of these publications vary from state to state (e.g., *Acts of Alabama*, *Statutes of California*, *Laws of Delaware*). In most states the session laws are the authoritative positive law text of the statutes, and they may be needed to examine legislative changes or to reconstruct the language in force on a particular date. These publications are listed in Table 1 of *The Bluebook* and Appendix 1 of the *ALWD Guide*.[46]

Slip laws from every state are available online in one form or another from state legislature websites. Most legislative websites permit browsing of recent slip laws, but in some states new laws are available only as enrolled bills and may even be mixed in with bills that are still pending or that did not become law. Only a few state websites include page numbers that would facilitate citation to the official session laws publication.[47]

Slip laws and session laws from all fifty states are also available from Westlaw and Lexis. These are found on Westlaw under the Proposed & Enacted Legislation heading, and are known on Lexis as Advance Legislative Services.[48] Bloomberg Law also has state session laws, back to the late 1990s for most jurisdictions.

---

[46] THE BLUEBOOK: A UNIFORM SYSTEM OF CITATION tbl. T1.3 (21st ed. 2020); ALWD GUIDE TO LEGAL CITATION app. 1 (6th ed. 2017).

[47] The discrepancies between states in the way session laws are published and designated have caused complaints for more than a century. *See Uniformity in the Preparation and Publication of Session Laws*, 11 AM. LAW. 144 (1903).

[48] The major difference between the two platforms is that Westlaw's Enacted Legislation database only covers the current legislative session, with a separate Historical Enacted Legislation for older session laws back to the late 1980s or early

In most states, commercially published advance session law services or legislative services publish new acts before they are printed in the bound session laws. These monthly or bimonthly pamphlets are generally issued as supplements to a state's annotated code and are like the *USCCAN* and *USCS Advance* pamphlets. They generally do not provide the pagination that will appear in the bound session laws volumes, but they are the preferred *Bluebook* source for laws not yet printed in the official volumes.[49]

HeinOnline's Session Laws Library has state session laws in PDF, with retrospective coverage from the first legislative session to the most recent volume. Some law libraries also have state session laws in microform, and individual older volumes may also be available online through sources such as Google Books.[50]

(b) State Codes

Publication of colonial and state law began early in the 17th century, with *For the Colony in Virginea Britannia: Lavves Diuine, Morall and Martiall, & c.* (1612), a short pamphlet containing mostly martial law provisions. The first revision of Virginia law was in 1632, although it was available only in manuscript form until 1809.[51] In 1648, the first printing press in the colonies published *The Book of the General Lawes and Libertyes*, a compilation of Massachusetts statutes arranged by subject.[52]

In the 18th and 19th centuries, the colonies and then the states issued a variety of compilations and codifications of their laws. The early publications were generally chronological collections of statutes in force, with subject-based collections becoming more prominent in the 19th century. Most publications were unofficial compilations, although from time to time most states had official revisions or

---

1990s. Lexis has just one database for each state combining current and archived sessions.

   [49] THE BLUEBOOK: A UNIFORM SYSTEM OF CITATION R. 12.2.1(a) (21st ed. 2020).

   [50] 2 PIMSLEUR'S CHECKLISTS OF BASIC AMERICAN LEGAL PUBLICATIONS (Marcia Singal Zubrow ed., 1962–date) provides a comprehensive listing of colonial, territorial, and state session law volumes. For information on the availability of state slip and session laws generally, see WILLIAM H. MANZ, GUIDE TO STATE LEGISLATION, LEGISLATIVE HISTORY, AND ADMINISTRATIVE MATERIALS (7th ed. 2008).

   [51] *A Grand Assembly Holden at James Citty the 4th Day of September, 1632*, 1 THE STATUTES AT LARGE, BEING A COLLECTION OF ALL THE LAWS OF VIRGINIA, FROM THE FIRST SESSION OF THE LEGISLATURE, IN THE YEAR 1619, at 178 (William Waller Hening ed., 1809). Hening's source for this revision was a manuscript owned by Thomas Jefferson.

   [52] Only one of 600 copies printed is known to exist, in the Huntington Library in San Marino, California. For more information on this collection of laws, see Mark D. Cahn, *Punishment, Discretion, and the Codification of Prescribed Penalties in Colonial Massachusetts*, 33 AM. J. LEGAL HIST. 107 (1989), and Thorp L. Wolford, *The Laws and Liberties of 1648: The First Code of Laws Enacted and Printed in English America*, 28 B.U. L. REV. 426 (1948).

codifications of their statutes akin to the federal *Revised Statutes of 1873.*[53]

Gradually compilations and codifications were published with increasingly extensive annotations of case law, by the early 20th century resulting in the now-familiar multi-volume annotated codes. All states now have subject compilations of their statutes similar to the *U.S. Code*, but the form and official status of these compilations vary from state to state. Some states have reenacted their codified statutes, while others rely on unofficial compilations.[54] Maryland, Pennsylvania, and Texas have for several years been in the lengthy process of completing official codifications.[55]

Every state makes its code available through its website. The easiest way to find an online code is to search for the state name and "statutes" or "code." These free online codes vary widely in their currency, official status, and features. For only five states (Colorado, Nebraska, New Mexico, Wisconsin, and Wyoming) they include annotations of court decisions, which are essential in evaluating the meaning and validity of statutory provisions.[56] Some online state

---

[53] Historical compilations and codifications for each state are listed in WILLIAM H. MANZ, GUIDE TO STATE LEGISLATION, LEGISLATIVE HISTORY, AND ADMINISTRATIVE MATERIALS (7th ed. 2008), and 1 PIMSLEUR'S CHECKLISTS OF BASIC AMERICAN LEGAL PUBLICATIONS (Marcia Singal Zubrow ed., 1962–date). On colonial codifications, see Erwin C. Surrency, *Revision of Colonial Laws*, 9 AM. J. LEGAL HIST. 189 (1965). Histories of state codifications appear in most state legal research guides. More detailed surveys of particular states include Joel Fishman, *The History of Statutory Compilations in Pennsylvania*, 86 LAW LIBR. J. 559 (1994); Robert W. Kerns Jr., *The History of the West Virginia Code*, 120 W. VA. L. REV. 165 (2017); Peggy Lewis & Nate Carr, *Understanding Colorado Statutory Source Notes*, COLO. LAW., Jan. 2013, at 39; and Kent C. Olson, *State Codes*, in VIRGINIA LAW BOOKS: ESSAYS AND BIBLIOGRAPHIES 1 (W. Hamilton Bryson ed., 2000).

[54] "Some states such as Alaska and Missouri have not enacted their code into positive law. The entire text is merely prima facie evidence of the law. Other states such as Arkansas enact their codes but with a 'rabbit hole' that allows writers to cite the session law instead if the code text is wrong. Still other states, such as Arizona, enact their codes but do not enact codified forms of the subsequent, amending session laws. Others such as Louisiana and Texas are in the codification process, and have a combination of completed codes and compilations. Finally, other states such as Alabama and California have enacted their entire codes and also enact codified amendments." Lynn Foster, *The Universal Legal Citation Project: A Draft User Guide to the AALL Universal Statutory Citation: Introduction*, 90 LAW LIBR. J. 91, 92 (1998) (citations omitted). For an in-depth look at the case of Arkansas' code, see Morell E. Mullins, *An Academic Perspective on Codification and the Arkansas Code of 1987 Annotated*, 11 U. ARK. LITTLE ROCK L.J. 285 (1988–89).

[55] Pennsylvania has been in the process of its first official revision, *Pennsylvania Consolidated Statutes*, since 1970; those subjects that have not yet been revised are cited to the unofficial compilation *Purdon's Pennsylvania Statutes Annotated. See* Peter J. Egler, *The Pennsylvania Statutory Codification Project—A Long and Winding Road*, 84 PA. B.A. Q. 86 (2013). Statutory revision in Texas has been ongoing since the mid-1960s. *See* Robert E. Freeman, *The Texas Legislative Council's Statutory Revision Program*, 29 TEX. B.J. 1021 (1966).

[56] In 2020 the Supreme Court affirmed that code annotations commissioned by a state government but prepared by a commercial publisher were not copyrightable.

codes bear prominent disclaimers that they are unofficial and for convenience only, and that it is necessary to consult the printed version for any official purpose. All of the codes, however, can be searched by keyword and browsed through tables of contents.

Some states publish in print an official, unannotated code, revised or supplemented on an annual or biennial basis. In states with regularly published official codes, these are usually the authoritative text to which citation is expected in briefs and pleadings, and according to the citation manuals. The manuals recognize, however, that very few libraries are likely to have copies of other states' unannotated codes and allow citation to other sources.[57]

Most researchers rely on codes annotated with summaries of relevant court decisions and other references, in most cases commercially published or accessed through Westlaw or Lexis. The authority of unofficial codes varies from state to state, but they are usually accepted as at least *prima facie* evidence of the statutory law.

Some annotated state codes are more thorough and comprehensive than others. Most codes are published by either Thomson Reuters or LexisNexis, and many states have competing codes from both publishers. A few states prepare and publish their own annotated codes. Most state codes consist of bound volumes supplemented by annual pocket parts, but a few are published instead in binders or in annual softcover editions. *The Bluebook* and the *ALWD Guide* have listings by state of the names and citations of current official and commercially published codes.[58]

In addition to noting state and federal cases applying or interpreting statutory provisions, most state codes include references to resources such as legal encyclopedias, law review articles, and *ALR* annotations. Illustration 5-13 shows a page from an annotated code for Rhode Island, published by LexisNexis.

Georgia v. Public.Resource.Org, Inc., 140 S. Ct. 1498 (2020). *See also* Leslie A. Street & David R. Hansen, *Who Owns the Law? Why We Must Restore Public Ownership of Legal Publishing*, 26 J. INTELL. PROP. L. 205 (2019), and David E. Shipley, *Code Revision Commission v. Public.Resource.Org and the Fight over Copyright Protection for Annotations and Commentary*, 54 GA. L. REV. 111 (2019).

[57] THE BLUEBOOK: A UNIFORM SYSTEM OF CITATION R. 12.2.1 (21st ed. 2020) ("If available, cite statutes currently in force to the current official code or its supplement."); ALWD GUIDE TO LEGAL CITATION R. 14.1 (6th ed. 2017) ("cite official versions of state statutes, if available").

[58] THE BLUEBOOK: A UNIFORM SYSTEM OF CITATION tbl. T1.3 (21st ed. 2020); ALWD GUIDE TO LEGAL CITATION app. 1 (6th ed. 2017).

549   DAMAGE BY ANIMALS   4-14-1

4-14-1. Animals at large — Civil liability — Penalty.

No horse, bull, boar, ram, or goat shall be permitted to run at large and if the owner or keeper of these, for any reason suffers any animals to do so he or she shall upon conviction be fined not in excess of one hundred dollars ($100) and be liable in addition for all damages done by the animal while so at large, although the animal escapes without the fault of the owner or keeper. The construction of any lawful fence shall not relieve the owner or keeper from liability for any damage committed by an animal of the enumerated class upon the enclosed premises of an adjoining owner.

History of Section.
  G.L. 1956, ch. 641, § 13; P.L. 1954, ch. 3317, § 1; G.L. 1956, § 4-14-1; P.L. 1974, ch. 231, § 1.

Cross References.
  Fences, § 34-10-1 et seq.

Liability for damages by dogs, § 4-13-16 et seq., § 4-13.1-7 et seq.

Comparative Legislation.
  Damages by animals:
  Conn. Gen. Stat. §§ 22-355 et seq., 47-55.
  Mass. Ann. Laws ch. 49, §§ 29 — 41.

NOTES TO DECISIONS

ANALYSIS

1. In general.
2. Liability.

1. In General.
  When an animal specified in R.I. Gen. Laws § 4-14-1 ceases to be "at large", a mixed question of law and fact is presented. Johnston v. Poulin, 844 A.2d 707, 2004 R.I. LEXIS 68 (R.I. 2004).
  For purposes of determining liability under R.I. Gen. Laws § 4-14-1, the distinguishing factor in determining whether an animal is "at large" is the presence or absence of control. If an animal is roaming at will and free to follow its own instincts, it may be said to be "at large;" however, if it is either physically restrained or subject to the moral authority of the person in charge, it is not "at large." Johnston v. Poulin, 844 A.2d 707, 2004 R.I. LEXIS 68 (R.I. 2004).

2. Liability.
  Whereas the strict liability of the dog-bite statute, R.I. Gen. Laws § 4-13-16, is predicated upon the location of the dog at the time of the injury, the strict liability of R.I. Gen. Laws § 4-14-1 is predicated upon the conduct of the horse at the time of injury, whether or not it was "at large" or unrestrained at the time of the injury. Johnston v. Poulin, 844 A.2d 707, 2004 R.I. LEXIS 68 (R.I. 2004).

Collateral References.
  Assault, land carrier's liability to passenger who becomes victim of third party's assault on or about carrier's vehicle or premises. 34 A.L.R.4th 1054.
  Automobiles: homeowner's insurance, construction and effect of provision excluding liability for automobile related injuries or damages from coverage of homeowner's or personal liability policy. 6 A.L.R.4th 555.
  Automobiles: small animals, liability of motorist for collision as affected by attempts to avoid dog or other small animal in road. 41 A.L.R.4th 1124.
  Bailments: damage to motor vehicle or injury to person riding therein resulting from collision with domestic animal at large in street or highway. 21 A.L.R.4th 132.
  Bankruptcy or insolvency: insurance company, validity, construction and effect of statute establishing compensation for claims not paid because of insurer's insolvency. 30 A.L.R.4th 1110.
  Bite: children, liability of parent for injury to unemancipated child caused by negligence — modern cases. 6 A.L.R.4th 1066.
  Bite: plastic surgery, cost of future cosmetic plastic surgery as element of damages. 88 A.L.R.4th 117.
  Bite: veterinarians, liability of owner of dog for dog's biting veterinarian or veterinarian's employee. 4 A.L.R.4th 349.
  Contributory negligence as a defense to a cause of action based upon violation of statute imposing duty upon keeper of animals. 10 A.L.R.2d 853.
  Damages, future disease or condition, or anxiety relating thereto, as element of recovery. 50 A.L.R.4th 13.
  Decedents' estates, liability of estate for tort

Illustration 5-13. Code section in *General Laws of Rhode Island* (LexisNexis), including history notes, cross references, notes of decisions, and collateral references.

The outline and arrangement of codes also vary from state to state. While most codes are divided into titles and sections, in a format like the *U.S. Code*, several states have individual codes designated by name rather than title number (e.g., commercial code, penal code, tax code). Louisiana has five subject codes (children's, civil, civil procedure, criminal procedure, and evidence) combined with numbered revised statutes. In the past, some states even had competing classification systems from different publishers.

State codes usually provide references to the original session laws in parenthetical notes following each section, but only a few include notes indicating the changes made by each amendment—making access to the session laws essential for reconstructing the language of an earlier version. Most codes also include tables with cross references from session law citations and earlier codifications to the current code, and each has a substantial index of one or more volumes.

Westlaw and Lexis provide access to codes from all fifty states, as well as the District of Columbia, Guam, Puerto Rico, and the Virgin Islands, including the case notes and other references from the annotated codes. Both platforms add notices to statutes that have been amended by slip laws but not yet incorporated into the code database. Lexis has a "Legislative Alert Service" with links to new acts, and the Westlaw display has a red flag linking to legislative action.

Westlaw Citing References and Shepard's Citations often provide references to cases and articles beyond those listed in the annotated code. Because codes publish selective annotations, a citator's coverage is usually more thorough than the code's. Citators are also updated continually, so they are considerably more current than the annotations. No matter how frequently a code is supplemented, it is necessary to use a citator for references to the latest developments. The disadvantage, of course, is that citators do not include summaries of the issues in the cases, unlike in Notes of Decisions or Case Notes.

The state attorneys general are often called upon to render opinions on statutory language of uncertain effect, and their opinions can be influential in statutory interpretation. The most thorough resource for finding these opinions is Westlaw Citing References. Only some annotated codes include references to attorney general opinions, and Shepard's covers these opinions for only a few states. Both Lexis and Westlaw have attorney general opinion databases for every state, however, and these can be searched for specific statutory citations. More information about these resources is available in Chapter 9.

(c) Multistate Research Sources

Most state statutory research requires finding the law in one particular state, for which that state's code is the primary research tool. Sometimes, however, it is necessary to compare statutory provisions among states or to survey legislation throughout the country. Conducting a multistate survey of state laws can be a time-consuming endeavor, in part because state codes do not always use the same terminology for similar issues. It may be necessary to search the index or full text of each state's code to complete a multistate survey.

Several resources make multistate statutory research a bit easier. Westlaw and Lexis can both search the codes of all fifty states at once. Even though statutory language differs from state to state, this is nonetheless a powerful tool for someone doing comparative statutory research or interested in finding how a particular word or phrase has been applied in other states.

Both Westlaw and Lexis also have compilations of state surveys on selected topics, listing citations with links to the full text databases. Westlaw's 50 State Statutory Surveys collection is available on the main "Secondary Sources" screen, and the surveys in Lexis can be browsed by choosing the source 50 State Surveys from the "Secondary Materials" screen or as a related resource on the "Statues & Legislation" screen. Each platform has surveys covering several hundred topics grouped by subject, providing state-by-state links to, and summaries of, relevant statutes. Some of the surveys on Westlaw are also available in print in Richard A. Leiter, *National Survey of State Laws* (8th ed. 2019). Westlaw offers customizable Jurisdictional Surveys (available on the Tools tab on the main page), which allow you to enter a citation, a keyword, or a Westlaw suggested topic (such as Consumer Law or Tax) and then be guided through suggested terms to create a list of statutory citations.

Bloomberg also offers customizable chart builders in the Practice Tools sections of several of its topical Practice Centers. You can, for example, create a table comparing the sales tax provisions on specific goods in all fifty states or in specific states you choose. If you save the table to your Workspace, the table will be automatically updated so you will not need to re-build it to ensure it is current.

Topical looseleaf and electronic services often collect state laws in their subject areas, providing a convenient way to compare state provisions in areas such as taxation or employment law. The *Blue Sky Law Reporter* (WoltersKluwer, on Cheetah) includes the text of state securities acts, for example, while Bloomberg Law's Labor & Employment Practice Center has summaries and texts of state statutes on topics such as wages and hours, fair employment practices, and individual employment rights. Bloomberg also publishes several topical state-by-state survey volumes covering major issues in employment law, under the auspices of the American Bar Association Section of Labor and Employment Law.

State laws on particular subjects are also collected or surveyed in a variety of other sources, such as treatises, websites, law review articles, and government publications. The website of an advocacy organization or lobbying group can be a good source, especially for developing areas of law. It is vital that any printed or online source summarizing state laws is regularly updated and that it provides the code citations necessary for verification and further research.

Various collections and lists of state statutes are described in a valuable bibliography prepared by Cheryl Rae Nyberg, *Subject Compilations of State Laws* (1981–date), available on HeinOnline as well as in annual print volumes. This work does not itself summarize or cite the statutes, but it provides annotated descriptions of sources that do so. Entries in *Subject Compilations* indicate whether sources include the code citations that are essential for verifying and updating their information. Illustration 5-14 shows a page from this publication, with entries for law review articles and a state government publication available online. The HeinOnline version of *Subject Compilations* is cumulative and has links to internet sites and to law review articles available in HeinOnline's database.

Animals

8089.01 Hillman, Claire M. "Capital Consequences: An Analysis of the U.S. Supreme Court's Decision to Uphold Oklahoma's Three-Drug Lethal Injection Protocol." *Washburn Law Journal* 55 (2016):503-28.

P. 523, fn. 157. Citations only. Cites to codes. Covers the twenty-six states that have laws banning neuromuscular blocking agents "in the euthanasia of animals."

8089.02 Hohmann, Kaci. "2016 State Legislative Review." *Animal Law* 23 (2017):521-38.

P. 530, fn. 71. Citations only. Cites to codes. Covers the seven states that have Good Samaritan laws permitting a person "to break into a vehicle to rescue an animal from a hot car." Includes California, Florida, Massachusetts, Ohio, Tennessee (referred to but not cited), Vermont, and Wisconsin.

8089.03 Huss, Rebecca J. "A Conundrum for Animal Activists: Can or Should the Current Legal Classification of Certain Animals Be Utilized to Improve the Lives of All Animals? The Intersection of Federal Disability Laws and Breed-Discriminatory Legislation." *Michigan State Law Review* 2015:1562-98.

Pp. 1594-95, fn. 160. Summaries. Cites to codes. Covers the thirty-one states that have laws requiring that a service animal trainer be accommodated like a disabled person using a service animal.

8089.04 Leduc, Janet Kaminski. *Misrepresentation of a Service Animal.* Hartford: Connecticut Office of Legislative Research, 2017. 7 pp. (OLR Research Report 2017-R-0255) OCLC 1012125865.

Pp. 2-7, "State Laws." Summaries. Cites to codes. Covers the nineteen states that have laws "making it unlawful to misrepresent an animal as a service animal or fraudulently represent oneself as having a right to be accompanied by a service animal." Dated Nov. 2017. Available at https://www.cga.ct.gov/2017/rpt/pdf/2017-R-0255.pdf. Archived at https://perma.cc/XST3-NJVP.

Illustration 5-14. Entries in *Subject Compilations of State Laws*.

(d) Uniform Laws and Model Acts

Multistate research usually requires finding a wide variety of legislative approaches to a particular topic. In a growing number of areas, however, states have adopted virtually identical acts, known as *uniform laws*, to reduce the confusion caused by conflicting state statutes.

The National Conference of Commissioners on Uniform State Laws, now generally known as the Uniform Law Commission (ULC), was formed in 1892 to promote state enactment of uniform laws. The ULC consists of representatives of each state, the District of Columbia, Puerto Rico, and the Virgin Islands, and meets annually to draft, promulgate, and promote uniform laws. States can then adopt uniform laws as proposed, modify them, or ignore them as they see fit, though the intent of the ULC is that states adopt uniform laws as written. Over 300 uniform laws have been approved by the ULC, of which more than half have been adopted by at least one state.[59]

The most widely known of the uniform laws is the Uniform Commercial Code (UCC), jointly sponsored by the Conference and the American Law Institute. The UCC was originally promulgated in 1951, but it has changed considerably over the years as individual articles have been revised and reissued.[60] The latest version is published annually in a paperback volume familiar to many law students, *Uniform Commercial Code: Official Text with Comments*. The UCC has a substantial literature, including its own series of court reports, *Uniform Commercial Code Reporting Service* (1964–date), and numerous treatises and hornbooks. James J. White et al., *Uniform Commercial Code* (6th ed. 2012–date), is widely considered to be the most authoritative of the treatises.

The UCC has been enacted by every state, but the law in force still varies from state to state depending on which revised articles have been adopted. A table listing the status of the UCC in each state requires twenty different footnotes indicating which articles are in force in each jurisdiction.[61]

Other, less well-known acts have been almost as widely adopted, such as the Uniform Act to Secure the Attendance of Witnesses from Without a State in Criminal Proceedings, which has been enacted in virtually every jurisdiction.[62] On the other hand, more than two dozen uniform acts have been adopted by just one or two states.

Uniform Laws Annotated, a multi-volume set published by Thomson Reuters and available on Westlaw, contains every uniform law approved by the ULC, tables of adopting states with code citations, commissioners' notes, and annotations to court decisions from any adopting jurisdiction. These annotations allow researchers

---

[59] For a history of the ULC and its proposed legislation, see James J. White, *Ex Proprio Vigore*, 89 MICH. L. REV. 2096, 2097–2105 (1991). For a more critical view of its lawmaking process, see Bruce H. Kobayashi & Larry E. Ribstein, *The Non-Uniformity of Uniform Laws*, 35 J. CORP. L. 327 (2009).

[60] Early drafts of the UCC have been published in the multi-volume sets UNIFORM COMMERCIAL CODE: DRAFTS (Elizabeth Slusser Kelly comp., 1984), and UNIFORM COMMERCIAL CODE: CONFIDENTIAL DRAFTS (Elizabeth Slusser Kelly & Ann Puckett comps., 1995). On the background, drafting and early history of the UCC, see two articles by Allen R. Kamp, *Uptown Act: A History of the Uniform Commercial Code, 1940–1949*, 51 SMU L. REV. 275 (1998), and *Downtown Code: A History of the Uniform Commercial Code, 1949–1954*, 49 BUFF. L. REV. 359 (2001).

[61] *Uniform Commercial Code: Tables of Jurisdictions Wherein Code has been Adopted*, 1 U.L.A. 1, 2–3 (2012). The *Uniform Commercial Code Reporting Service* includes a "State UCC Variations" volume indicating how each state varies from the official text.

[62] 11 U.L.A. 1 (2003).

in one state to study the case law developed in other states with the same uniform law. A decision from another state is not binding authority, but its interpretation of an identical or similar statute can be quite persuasive. The set is supplemented annually by pocket parts and by a softcover pamphlet, *Directory of Uniform Acts and Codes; Tables—Index*, which lists the acts alphabetically and includes a table of jurisdictions indicating the acts adopted in each state.

Lexis has a ULCLAW—Uniform Law Commission Model Acts collection of about 175 acts, with official commentary but no case annotations. The ULC website (www.uniformlaws.org) has the text of over 150 acts, as well as summaries of why states should adopt acts and information on enactments and pending legislation. The annual *Handbook of the National Conference of Commissioners on Uniform State Laws* contains minutes of proceedings, the text of uniform and model laws approved, and tables of state adoptions, but it is published after a delay of several years. The *Handbook* and other related publications are available in HeinOnline's Uniform Law Commission Library.

The text of a uniform law can also be found, of course, in the statutory code of each adopting state, accompanied by annotations from that state's courts. The state code contains the law as actually adopted and in force, rather than the text as proposed by the Commissioners.

Model acts are drafted for fields where individual states are expected to modify a proposed law to meet their needs, rather than adopt it *in toto*. Two of the most influential model acts are the Model Penal Code and the Model Business Corporation Act, both developed by the American Law Institute. Research resources for these acts include *Model Penal Code and Commentaries* (1980–85, online in HeinOnline's American Law Institute Library), and *Model Business Corporation Act Annotated* (4th ed. 2008–date, online from Bloomberg Law).[63]

The Council of State Governments (CSG) publishes an annual volume of *Shared State Legislation*. This reproduces statutes recently enacted in one jurisdiction and recommended for consideration in others, with each preceded by a brief explanation. The acts in each volume are printed alphabetically, but a cumulative subject index in each volume provides access to suggested legislation

---

[63] For more on model laws, see Mary Whisner, *There Oughta Be a Law—A Model Law*, 106 LAW LIBR. J. 125 (2014). Some have expressed concern that model laws are drafted by industry groups and other special interests. *See, e.g.*, Rob O'Dell & Nick Penzenstadler, *Who's Writing Your Laws? Not the Person You Elected*, ARIZ. REPUB., Apr. 7, 2019, at A9.

from the preceding twenty years or so. Recent volumes are available on the CSG website (www.csg.org/programs/policyprograms/SSL. aspx).

(e) Interstate Compacts

An interstate compact is an agreement between two or more states, which under the Constitution requires approval by Congress.[64] After the compact is agreed upon by the states, it goes to Congress for authorizing legislation. Each enacted compact is published in the *U.S. Statutes at Large* and in the session laws of the states which are parties to it. Most interstate compacts also appear in the annotated codes of the party states, and can usually be found in the indexes under "Compacts" or "Interstate Compacts" as well as by subject.

The website for the National Center for Interstate Compacts, a branch of the Council of State Governments (www.csg.org/ncic/), has a variety of useful resources on the subject, including background information and a searchable database of more than 1,500 compacts that indicates their citations in state codes. In some instances the text is also available.

Joseph F. Zimmerman, *Interstate Cooperation: Compacts and Administrative Agreements* (2d ed. 2012) discusses the compacting process, compact commissions, and formal and informal administrative agreements, and includes a lengthy bibliography of books, documents, and articles. Caroline N. Broun et al., *The Evolving Use and the Changing Role of Interstate Compacts: A Practitioner's Guide* (2006) also has background information as well as a survey of the contemporary uses of compacts, and an appendix lists and describes compacts with citations to the enabling federal and state legislation.

Statutory law plays a pivotal role in the legal system and in legal research. Most court decisions involve the application or interpretation of statutes, and the scope of judicial authority and jurisdiction is largely determined by legislative enactments. Administrative regulations, court rules, and local laws are all based on statutory delegations of power created by statute. All legal research must therefore include the question: Is there a statute on point?

---

[64] Article I, § 10 provides: "No state shall, without the Consent of Congress, . . . enter into any Agreement or Compact with another State . . . ."

In some ways statutory research is easier than case research because the major resources are more accessible and more regularly updated. In many situations an annotated code provides most of the necessary research leads. This convenience is undercut, however, by the ambiguity of statutory language. One of the major approaches to interpretation of ambiguous statutes is the study of legislative documents created during the drafting of the statutory text. This research in legislative history is the focus of the next chapter.

Chapter 6

LEGISLATIVE INFORMATION

Table of Sections

Legal researchers need legislative information in many contexts. Ambiguities are common in statutory language, and lawyers and scholars look to documents generated by the legislature before a law's passage to interpret the intended purpose of an act or the meaning of particular statutory terms. Congressional hearings and reports also provide background factual and legal information on a wide array of issues, from Supreme Court nominations to oversight of administrative agency actions. Because pending legislation may affect their clients' interests, lawyers also need to be able to determine the status of bills the legislature is considering.[1]

The use of legislative history documents in statutory construction is controversial, with strong disagreement within the Supreme Court and among commentators. Judges have traditionally

---

[1] For additional ways researching legislative documents may be relevant, see Mary Whisner, *Other Uses of Legislative History*, 105 LAW LIBR. J. 243 (2013).

used congressional materials to interpret ambiguous statutory language,[2] but textualist critics insist that meaning must be determined from the statutory language alone. Justice Antonin Scalia was well known for his opposition to the use of legislative history, while other justices rely on legislative history sources to correct drafting errors, to provide information on specialized meanings of terms, or to identify the purpose of a statutory phrase. In the words of Justice John Paul Stevens, they "see no reason why conscientious judges should not feel free to examine all public records that may shed light on the meaning of a statute."[3] Recent studies have shown that while federal courts have been relying on legislative history less than in the past, the practice is generally still used by judges across the ideological spectrum.[4]

Legislative information is one area in which there can be striking differences between federal and state research. Federal legislative history is thoroughly documented with numerous sources, while availability of state legislative history varies widely from state to state. This is an area in which the internet has made a significant contribution to the dissemination of information. Government websites make it easy to learn about the status of pending legislation and to obtain documents relating to recently passed acts. Resources on older state laws, on the other hand, may be found only on tape recordings or in archives at the state capitol, if they exist at all.

§ 6.1   THE FEDERAL LEGISLATIVE PROCESS

Consideration of legislative history begins with the legislative process itself—how a bill wends its way through Congress or a state legislature. The documents of legislative history must be understood

---

[2] For two classic articles offering history and context for the formerly uncontroversial use of legislative history by courts, written by a then-sitting judge on the U.S. Court of Appeals for the District of Columbia Circuit, see Patricia M. Wald, *Some Observations on the Use of Legislative History in the 1981 Supreme Court Term*, 68 IOWA L. REV. 195 (1983), and *The Sizzling Sleeper: The Use of Legislative History in Construing Statutes in the 1988–89 Term of the United States Supreme Court*, 39 AM. U. L. REV. 277 (1990).

[3] *Bank One Chicago, N.A. v. Midwest Bank & Trust Co.*, 516 U.S. 264, 278 (1996) (Stevens, J., concurring). Representative statements of the two positions from other Supreme Court justices are Stephen Breyer, *On the Uses of Legislative History in Interpreting Statutes*, 65 S. CAL. L. REV. 845 (1992), and ANTONIN SCALIA, A MATTER OF INTERPRETATION: FEDERAL COURTS AND THE LAW (1997). Articles summarizing the debate and providing references to earlier works include Paul E. McGreal, *A Constitutional Defense of Legislative History*, 13 WM. & MARY BILL RTS. J. 1267 (2005), and Lawrence M. Solan, *Private Language, Public Laws: The Central Role of Legislative Intent in Statutory Interpretation*, 93 GEO. L.J. 427 (2005).

[4] *See, e.g.*, James J. Brudney & Corey Ditslear, *The Decline and Fall of Legislative History? Patterns of Supreme Court Reliance in the Burger and Rehnquist Eras*, 89 JUDICATURE 220 (2006), and David Law & David Zaring, *Law Versus Ideology: The Supreme Court and the Use of Legislative History*, 51 WM. & MARY L. REV. 1653 (2010).

in the context of the parliamentary practices that produce them. The federal process is often long and complicated, beginning formally with the introduction of a bill and ending with passage by both houses of Congress of either an act or a joint resolution, and its approval by the President (or repassage over a presidential veto).[5]

Numerous brief overviews of the federal legislative process are available online, including explanations prepared by the House and Senate parliamentarians.[6] More extensive guides to congressional lawmaking procedures include Richard A. Arenberg, *Congressional Procedure: A Practical Guide to the Legislative Process in the U.S. Congress* (2018) and Walter J. Oleszek et al., *Congressional Procedures and the Policy Process* (11th ed. 2019). Explanations of legislative language are provided by Walter Kravitz, *Congressional Quarterly's American Congressional Dictionary* (3d ed. 2001), which defines hundreds of terms and phrases such as "continuing resolution" and "quorum call." Michael L. Koempel & Judy Schneider, *Congressional Deskbook* (6th ed. 2012) is a practical guide to congressional politics and procedures filled with illustrations, interesting facts, and research tips.

Background reference works for understanding Congress and its work in their historical and political contexts include the *CQ Press Guide to Congress* (7th ed. 2013). This two-volume set has a wide range of political, historical, and statistical information; Part III, Congressional Procedures, is particularly useful in understanding committee and floor action. One of the most thorough reference works is *The Encyclopedia of the United States Congress* (Donald C. Bacon et al. eds., 1995), which provides a broad historical and political science perspective on the institution. Sara L. Hagedorn & Michael C. LeMay, *The American Congress: A Reference Handbook* (2019) is a shorter work on the subject.

Because law firms in Washington, D.C., work closely with Congress and administrative agencies, they are particularly well known for their expertise in legislative history research. Several of the larger firms and agencies have librarians who specialize in this field. The Law Librarians' Society of Washington, D.C. (LLSDC) shares this expertise in its free online Legislative Source Book (www. llsdc.org/sourcebook), which includes insightful guides, historical information, and valuable lists and tables of printed and online resources.

---

[5] U.S. CONST., art. I, § 7, cl. 2.

[6] JOHN V. SULLIVAN, HOW OUR LAWS ARE MADE, H.R. DOC. NO. 110–49 (2007) (clerk.house.gov/legislative/legprocess.aspx); ROBERT B. DOVE, ENACTMENT OF A LAW (1997) (www.senate.gov/legislative/rules_procedure.htm) [https://perma.cc/5N4T-4T8Y].

Of the many types of documents issued by Congress, a few are particularly important for legislative history research. *Bills* are the major source for the texts of pending or unenacted legislation. *Committee reports* analyze and describe bills and are usually considered the most authoritative sources of congressional intent. *Floor debates* may contain a sponsor's interpretation of a bill or the only explanation of last-minute amendments. *Hearings* can provide useful background on the purpose of an act.

This section introduces these various documents, with a brief explanation of how they are published and their availability in electronic sources. Several major resources will be mentioned again and again. Two of these are free government websites: Congress.gov (www.congress.gov), the Library of Congress's website for legislative information, and the U.S. Government Publishing Office's Govinfo portal (www.govinfo.gov). The most comprehensive commercial site is ProQuest Congressional (congressional.proquest.com), which has a vast array of congressional documents back to the 18th century.

(a) Preliminary and Informal Consideration

Documents relating to particular enactments may exist even before a proposal is introduced as a bill. Hearings on a problem of legislative concern may be held prior to the introduction of specific bills to remedy that condition, even in an earlier term of Congress. Sometimes these hearings continue across several Congresses. Research into the legislative history of a particular law limited only to the term of its enactment may overlook relevant and important debates, hearings, or reports.

Many bills introduced in Congress stem from executive branch recommendations and may be accompanied by presidential messages or agency memoranda describing the purpose of the proposed legislation. The President's annual State of the Union message proposes various laws in general terms, and other presidential messages describe individual measures in greater detail and urge their introduction and passage.[7] Official messages to Congress are available in several sources, including the *Congressional Record* and the *Daily* or *Weekly Compilation of Presidential Documents*. Other presidential recommendations are published in a less formal manner, as press releases or fact sheets available on the White House website (www.whitehouse.gov).

---

[7] The President "shall from time to time give to the Congress Information of the State of the Union, and recommend to their Consideration such Measures as he shall judge necessary and expedient." U.S. CONST. art. II, § 3. For a discussion of the State of the Union and Recommendation Clauses, see Vasan Kesavan & J. Gregory Sidak, *The Legislator-in-Chief*, 44 WM. & MARY L. REV. 1 (2002).

Newspapers and services that cover Congress and politics are good sources on topics of possible congressional action, frequently containing information unavailable from official documentation. Even if no bill has been introduced or a bill appears to be stalled in committee, news stories and documents such as letters between members of Congress, press releases, and government agency reports can provide leads to what is happening behind the scenes. Several newspapers focus on developments in the federal government. *National Journal* (www.nationaljournal.com), *Roll Call* (www. rollcall.com), and *The Hill* (www.thehill.com) all provide free online access to at least some of their content. All three publications are also available through Westlaw and Lexis.

(b) Bills

An act of Congress begins its life as a bill.[8] The text of a bill can be helpful in interpreting an enacted law and in understanding pending or failed legislation. A bill may be amended at any stage of its legislative progress, in committee or on the floor, and some bills are amended many times. Comparing the different versions of a bill may lead to useful conclusions about the scope or meaning of the provisions that were ultimately enacted. If a provision you are studying was added after the bill was introduced, pinpointing the date of its insertion can help you determine the most pertinent legislative history sources.

Congressional bills are individually numbered in separate series for each chamber, either H.R. for House of Representatives or S. for Senate. Each bill is assigned a number when it is introduced and referred to a committee, and it retains its number through both of the annual sessions of each Congress. Pending bills lapse at the end of the two-year term of Congress, and a new bill on the topic must be introduced the following term if it is to be considered.

A citation to a bill includes the number of the Congress and the year in which the particular version was published, such as H.R. 137, 110th Cong. (2007).[9] Illustration 6-1 shows the first page of this House bill as introduced in January 2007.

---

[8] Some public laws arise from joint resolutions rather than bills. These usually, but not always, deal with matters of a limited or temporary nature. Joint resolutions and bills differ in form but have the same legal effect. Two other forms of resolution do not have the force of law: concurrent resolutions expressing the opinion of both chambers of Congress, and simple resolutions concerning the procedures or expressions of just one chamber. For more information about technical terminology and abbreviations related to a bill's progress through Congress, see "About Congressional Bills" (www.govinfo.gov/help/bills) [https://perma.cc/Q342-ZR8J].

[9] THE BLUEBOOK: A UNIFORM SYSTEM OF CITATION R. 13.2 (21st ed. 2020); ALWD GUIDE TO LEGAL CITATION R.15.1 (6th ed. 2017).

H. R. 137

To amend title 18, United States Code, to strengthen prohibitions against
animal fighting, and for other purposes.

IN THE HOUSE OF REPRESENTATIVES

JANUARY 4, 2007

Mr. GALLEGLY (for himself, Mr. BLUMENAUER, and Mr. BARTLETT of Maryland) introduced the following bill; which was referred to the Committee
on the Judiciary, and in addition to the Committee on Agriculture, for
a period to be subsequently determined by the Speaker, in each case for
consideration of such provisions as fall within the jurisdiction of the committee concerned

---

A BILL

To amend title 18, United States Code, to strengthen
prohibitions against animal fighting, and for other purposes.

1   *Be it enacted by the Senate and House of Representa-*

2 *tives of the United States of America in Congress assembled,*

3 **SECTION 1. SHORT TITLE.**

4   This Act may be cited as the "Animal Fighting Pro-

5 hibition Enforcement Act of 2007".

**Illustration 6-1. The first page of a House bill,
H.R. 137, 110th Cong. (2007).**

Often bills with similar or identical language, known as
companion bills, are introduced in both the House and Senate. A bill
that has passed only one house is known as an *engrossed bill*. If each
chamber passes its own bill, however, there is no single *enrolled bill*
that has passed both houses and can be presented to the President.
Congress frequently employs a procedure known as an *amendment
in the nature of a substitute*, which deletes everything after the
enacting clause (i.e., "Be it enacted by the Senate and House of

Representatives of the United States of America in Congress assembled")[10] and inserts new text in its place. Sometimes this is done simply because it is more convenient to replace an entire bill than to make specific changes, but it also permits the House and Senate to pass the same bill so that it can go to the President and become law. If the House passes H.R. 137 while the Senate passes S. 261, these are different bills even if their language is identical. Both must pass the same exact bill, with the same bill number. If the Senate amends H.R. 137 by substituting its language for the House language, the bill can then go back to the House for it to consider the Senate amendments. Both houses are then working with the same document, and if both pass an identical version it can be sent to the President.

The significance of this in research is that the number of the bill that becomes law may be different from the number of the version that was the subject of congressional hearings, committee reports, or perhaps even floor debates. The key language in an enacted law may have come from a bill with a different number and a different history. Sometimes you may need to compare the language in several similar bills. Tracing the development of particular statutory language can be like traveling up a river; you may need to determine which tributary to follow to get to a specific source.

Bills are available online from several sources. Congress.gov and Govinfo both have the text of recent bills, beginning with the 103rd Congress (1993–94). You can search the full text of bills in Congress.gov, and then refine a search using facets to focus on a specific Congress, subject, or sponsor. Early bills are available on the Library of Congress's "A Century of Lawmaking for a New Nation" Bills and Resolutions site (memory.loc.gov/ammem/amlaw/lwhbsb. html) (House bills from the 6th to 42nd Congresses, 1799–1873, and Senate bills from the 16th to 42nd Congresses, 1819–73). Commercial services also provide broad coverage of congressional bills, with the most extensive holdings in ProQuest Digital U.S. Bills and Resolutions, 1789–Present. A component of ProQuest Congressional, it has the text of every congressional bill accessible by number or through full-text searching.[11] Other sources have more limited coverage of recent bills. Lexis coverage begins in 1989, Bloomberg Law in 1993, and Westlaw in 1995.

Research platforms like Lexis, Westlaw, and Bloomberg Law have begun to develop products that attempt to predict whether

---

[10] This is the prescribed form for all congressional bills under 1 U.S.C. § 101.

[11] Many libraries also have microfiche collections of older bills, from the Government Publishing Office (96th–106th Congress, 1979–2000) and ProQuest Congressional (beginning with the 73rd Congress, 1933–34).

proposed legislation will eventually be enacted. These products track legislation and sometimes even assign a rough probability that a bill will be passed and signed into law. One product currently available on a wide scale is Legislative Outlook, which has been integrated into Lexis and has coverage of federal and state bills.

(c) Hearings

Hearings are held by standing and special committees of the House and Senate to investigate various issues of concern, and also to elicit views on proposed legislation from interested persons or groups, executive branch personnel, or other legislators. Hearings may be held to examine a controversial situation, to determine the need for new legislation, or to present information helpful to Congress's consideration of a pending bill. Hearings are not required for every bill, and legislation is frequently enacted without hearings in one or both houses.

Published hearings consist of prepared statements from government officials, scholars, interest group representatives, and other witnesses; the transcript of questions by the legislators and answers by witnesses; exhibits submitted by witnesses and others; and sometimes a copy of the bill under consideration.

Hearings provide useful background information, but they are not generally considered persuasive sources of legislative history on the meaning of an enacted bill. Their importance is limited because they focus more on the views of interest groups than on those of the lawmakers themselves. Statements and questions by legislators and testimony by agency officials who will be responsible for implementing legislation may, however, be helpful in determining the purpose and scope of a proposed statute.

Unlike other congressional materials such as bills and committee reports, published hearings are not cited in numbered series. They are generally identified by the title that appears on the cover, the bill number, the name of the subcommittee and committee, the term of Congress, and the year.[12] Illustration 6-2, for example, shows the first page of *Animal Fighting Prohibition Enforcement Act of 2005: Hearing on H.R. 817 Before the Subcomm. on Crime, Terrorism & Homeland Sec. of the H. Comm. on the Judiciary*, 109th Cong. (2006). This hearing was held a year before H.R. 137 was passed in the following Congress.

---

[12] THE BLUEBOOK: A UNIFORM SYSTEM OF CITATION R. 13.3 (21st ed. 2020); ALWD GUIDE TO LEGAL CITATION R. 15.5 (6th ed. 2017).

ANIMAL FIGHTING PROHIBITION
ENFORCEMENT ACT OF 2005

THURSDAY, MAY 18, 2006

HOUSE OF REPRESENTATIVES,
SUBCOMMITTEE ON CRIME, TERRORISM,
AND HOMELAND SECURITY
COMMITTEE ON THE JUDICIARY,
Washington, DC.

The Subcommittee met, pursuant to notice, at 11:31 a.m., in Room 2141, Rayburn House Office Building, the Honorable Howard Coble (Chairman of the Subcommittee) presiding.

Mr. COBLE. Good morning, ladies and gentlemen. We will convene the hearing. There will be a floor vote imminently, I am told, and we don't have a reporting quorum present, so Mr. Scott and I are going to give our opening statements, and then perhaps we'll be able to move along after that.

This hearing is to examine the issue of animal fighting in this country and whether Congress should take additional steps to address the issue. Animal fighting is not restricted to cockfighting, but also includes pitting dog against dog, or dogs against other animals, such as bears or wild hogs. Often small knives are attached to the animal for use in the fight.

In 1976 Congress passed a law to ban the sponsor or exhibit of animals that were moved to interstate or foreign commerce in an animal fighting venue. The law also made it illegal to transport an animal in interstate or foreign commerce for participation in an animal fighting venue.

On May 13th, 2002, Congress enacted amendments to the Animal Welfare Act. The changes made it a crime, regardless of State law, for exhibiting, sponsoring, selling, buying, transporting, delivering or receiving a bird or other animal in interstate or foreign commerce for the purpose of participation in an animal fighting venue such as cockfighting or dogfighting. For States where fighting among live birds is allowed under the law, the act only prohibited the sponsor or exhibit of a bird for fighting purposes if the person knew that that bird was moved in interstate or foreign commerce.

Currently dogfighting is prohibited in all 50 States and cockfighting is outlawed in most States under specific laws prohibiting it or general prohibitions against animal fighting. In a few States the practice is not specifically outlawed. However, general animal cruelty statutes may be interpreted to outlaw such activities. In two States cockfighting is legal. Dogfighting and cockfighting are legal in some United States territories. Although the possible fines

(1)

Illustration 6-2. Transcript of a House hearing on an
animal fighting prohibition bill.

Not every hearing is published, and they are also not systematically available online. Most committee websites have material from recent hearings. Some only provide the texts of prepared statements from legislators and witnesses, but others have the transcripts of the committee members' questions and witnesses' answers. Congress.gov provides a helpful directory of committee websites (www.congress.gov/committees), and LLSDC's Legislative Source Book has an annotated guide of "Quick Links to House and Senate Committee Hearings and Other Publications" (www.llsdc.org/hearings-quick-links) indicating the material available from each committee. Prepared testimony by government officials may also be available on their agencies' websites.

Congress.gov doesn't include hearings, but Govinfo coverage begins in 1995. The major retrospective online source is the ProQuest Congressional Hearings Digital Collection, with more than 120,000 hearings back to 1824.[13] The full text of the hearings is searchable, and witnesses can be found by name or affiliation. HeinOnline's U.S. Congressional Documents Library has over 60,000 hearings, almost all from the 1890s to date.

In libraries with hearings in print or microform, they are usually organized by committee under the Superintendent of Documents (SuDocs) classification system. The classification for the hearing shown in Illustration 6-2, for example, is Y 4.J 89/1:109–115. "J 89/1" is the designation used for hearings from the House Committee on the Judiciary.

Westlaw and Lexis both have transcripts of selected hearings, as well as prepared statements of witnesses. On Westlaw, the U.S. Political Transcripts database has entire hearings beginning in 1994, and the U.S. Congressional Testimony database has prepared statements back to 1993. Lexis has transcripts of hearings prepared by Federal News Service and statements from CQ Congressional Testimony, both found in the News section of search results.

Other services such as CQ Roll Call (cqrollcall.com) also provide hearing transcripts. Even if a hearing has not been transcribed, an

---

[13] This collection, a component of the ProQuest Congressional service, contains documents also available on microfiche and indexed in several ProQuest (formerly CIS) publications: CIS/INDEX (1970–date, covering contemporary hearings); CIS US CONGRESSIONAL COMMITTEE HEARINGS INDEX (1981–85, covering published hearings 1833–1969); CIS INDEX TO UNPUBLISHED US SENATE COMMITTEE HEARINGS (1986–2001, covering 1823–1980); and CIS INDEX TO UNPUBLISHED US HOUSE OF REPRESENTATIVES COMMITTEE HEARINGS (1988–2003, covering 1833–1972). These sources have abstracts of testimony, with indexing by subject, witness name, bill number, and hearing title. The Library of the United States Senate published another series of indexes to the hearings of both houses, CUMULATIVE INDEX OF CONGRESSIONAL COMMITTEE HEARINGS (1935–84, covering the 41st–96th Congresses, 1869–1980), but these have less detail and fewer points of access than the CIS indexes.

audio or video recording may be available from the committee's website or C-SPAN (www.c-span.org/congress).

(d) Committee Reports

The most important legislative history documents are generally considered to be the reports of the committees of each house, and those of conference committees held jointly by the two houses. House and Senate committees generally issue a report on each bill that is sent to the whole house for consideration, or "reported out of committee." These reports reflect the committee's proposal after a bill has been studied, hearings held, and amendments made.[14] They usually contain the revised text of the bill, an analysis of its content and purpose, and the committee's rationale for its recommendations. One of the most informative portions of a committee report is the section-by-section analysis of the bill, explaining the purpose and meaning of each provision. Sometimes the report also includes minority views, if there was disagreement among the committee members.

If different versions of a proposed enactment have been passed by each house, a conference committee is convened, including members from each house. The conference committee reconciles the differences and produces an agreed compromise for submission to both houses for final passage, as explained in its report. Conference committee reports are considered a very persuasive source for interpretation. Because they generally only consider points of difference between the two bills, however, conference committee reports do not discuss bill provisions as exhaustively as House or Senate committee reports.[15]

Committee reports and conference committee reports are generally given more weight than other legislative history documents because they are produced by those members of Congress who have worked most closely with the proposed legislation. In Justice John M.

---

[14] Committee reports may also be issued on investigations and issues not related to the consideration of a specific bill. Reports are issued, for example, on nominations to the executive and judicial branches.

[15] The politics and procedures of the conference process are discussed in ELIZABETH RYBICKI, CONG. RESEARCH SERV., 98–696, RESOLVING LEGISLATIVE DIFFERENCES IN CONGRESS: CONFERENCE COMMITTEES AND AMENDMENTS BETWEEN THE HOUSES (2019) (crsreports.congress.gov/product/pdf/RL/98-696). For an explanation of the content and use of conference committee reports, see Seth Grossman, *Tricameral Legislating: Statutory Interpretation in an Era of Conference Committee Ascendancy*, 9 N.Y.U. J. LEGIS. & PUB. POL'Y 251 (2005), and George A. Costello, *Average Voting Members and Other 'Benign Fictions': The Relative Reliability of Committee Reports, Floor Debates, and Other Sources of Legislative History*, 1990 DUKE L.J. 39, 47–50. For historical information on committee reports more generally, see Thomas F. Broden, *Congressional Committee Reports: Their Role and History*, 33 NOTRE DAME LAW. 209, 216–38 (1958).

Harlan's words, they are the "considered and collective understanding of those Congressmen involved in drafting and studying proposed legislation."[16]

Committee reports are published in numbered series for each two-year term, with conference committee reports included in the series of House reports. Their citations indicate the chamber, term of Congress, report number, and year, but do not include reference to the name of the originating committee. Illustration 6-3 shows a page from H.R. Rep. No. 110–27 (2007), reporting the House Committee on the Judiciary's views on the Animal Fighting Prohibition Enforcement Act of 2007. The page shown includes summaries of the background and need for the legislation and of committee consideration.

Committee reports are published by the Government Publishing Office and are available online through Congress.gov and Govinfo, going back to the 104th Congress (1995–96). Westlaw and Lexis both have all committee reports since 1990, as well as selected earlier reports, and Bloomberg Law coverage begins in 1995. In print, selected committee reports on major enactments are available in *U.S. Code Congressional and Administrative News,* and a few (usually just conference committee reports) appear also in the *Congressional Record.*

---

[16] *Zuber v. Allen,* 396 U.S. 168, 186 (1969). Justice Antonin Scalia repeatedly challenged the position that committee reports are the most reliable sources of legislative history, in part because they are prepared by staff members rather than members of Congress themselves. *See, e.g., Blanchard v. Bergeron,* 489 U.S. 87, 99 (1989) (Scalia, J., concurring) ("What a heady feeling it must be for a young staffer, to know that his or her citation of obscure district court cases can transform them into the law of the land, thereafter dutifully to be observed by the Supreme Court itself."). Others have argued that separation of powers principles demand that courts respect the way Congress chooses to organize its work and communicate its findings. *E.g.,* Wald, *The Sizzling Sleeper, supra* note 2, at 306–07.

THE AMENDMENT

The amendment (stated in terms of the page and line numbers of the introduced bill) is as follows:
Page 4, beginning in line 13, strike "or animals, such as waterfowl, bird, raccoon, or fox hunting".

PURPOSE AND SUMMARY

H.R. 137, the "Animal Fighting Prohibition Enforcement Act of 2007," strengthens the Federal prohibitions against animal fighting ventures. Under current law, animal fighting violations are misdemeanors under title 7 of the U.S. Code. H.R. 137 makes the buying, selling, or transporting of animals in interstate commerce for participation in animal fighting ventures felonies to be charged under title 18, with maximum prison sentences of 3 years, increased from 1 year under current law.

BACKGROUND AND NEED FOR THE LEGISLATION

Prohibitions against knowingly selling, buying, transporting, delivering, or receiving an animal in interstate or foreign commerce for the purposes of participation in an animal fighting venture were added to the Animal Welfare Act in 1976, with misdemeanor penalties of up to $5,000 in fines and up to 1 year in prison. Since then, Federal authorities have pursued fewer than a half dozen animal fighting cases, despite receiving numerous tips from informants and requests to assist with state and local prosecutions. The animal fighting industry continues to thrive within the United States, despite 50 State laws that ban dogfighting and 48 State laws that ban cockfighting. Numerous nationally circulated animal fighting magazines still promote these cruel practices, and advertise fighting animals and the accouterments of animal fighting. There are also several active websites for animal fighting enthusiasts, and paid lobbyists advocating animal fighters' interests.
In 2002, Congress amended these prohibitions to extend them more fully to live birds. Previously, none of the prohibitions had applied to live birds if the destination was a State in which their use in fighting was not a violation of that State's law.
While the 2002 amendments also increased penalties slightly, from a potential fine of $5,000 to one of $15,000, they were left at the misdemeanor level. By increasing penalties to the felony level, H.R. 137 will give prosecutors greater incentive to pursue cases against unlawful animal fighting ventures, and strengthen deterrence against them.

HEARINGS

The Subcommittee on Crime, Terrorism, and Homeland Security held a hearing on H.R. 137 on February 6, 2007. Testimony was received from two witnesses: Wayne Pacelle, President & CEO, The Humane Society of the United States, and Jerry Leber, President, United Gamefowl Breeders Association.

COMMITTEE CONSIDERATION

On February 6, 2007, the Subcommittee on Crime, Terrorism, and Homeland Security met in open session and ordered H.R. 137

Illustration 6-3. Excerpt from H.R. Rep. 110–27 on animal fighting prohibition.

Committee reports are also published as part of a bound series of volumes known as the *Serial Set*. The Serial Set includes such other publications as House and Senate documents, annual reports, and manuals of procedural rules and precedents.[17]

The ProQuest U.S. Serial Set Digital Collection has comprehensive retrospective coverage, with full text searching as well as access by subject or numerical designation (including report number, bill number, or public law number), and HeinOnline's U.S. Congressional Serial Set database is in the process of completing coverage. Other digitized sources for older Serial Set material include Readex's U.S. Congressional Serial Set (1817–1994) and the Library of Congress's "A Century of Lawmaking for a New Nation" (memory. loc.gov/ammem/amlaw/lwss.html) (which is free but has only selective coverage). Each of these resources also covers earlier publications collected and published under congressional authority in a set known as the *American State Papers* (1832–61).[18]

Other committee materials can be even more helpful than reports in interpreting statutory language. The process by which committees or subcommittees examine proposed legislation in detail and reach consensus is through *markup sessions*. The proceedings of these sessions are only rarely published, but transcripts or videos of some recent markup sessions are available through committee websites. Newspapers and wire services reporting on Capitol Hill matters frequently publish stories on markup sessions.

(e) Floor Debates

Floor debate in Congress on a pending bill can occur at almost any stage of its progress, but typically it takes place after the bill has been reported out by committee. During consideration of the bill, amendments may be proposed, discussed, and accepted or defeated.

---

[17] The Serial Set began with the 15th Congress in 1817, when Congress enacted legislation specifying standards for publishing and collecting its reports and documents. Resolution of Mar. 3, 1817, no. 3, 3 Stat. 400. Bound Serial Set volumes are not widely distributed after the 104th Congress (1995–96), but some libraries continue to bind their own sets of individual reports. For more information on the history and contents of the Serial Set, see Richard J. McKinney, *An Overview of the U.S. Congressional Serial Set* (www.llsdc.org/serial-set-volumes-guide#overview) [https://perma.cc/ZK93-7MZM].

[18] The most comprehensive bibliography of early congressional documents was published more than a century ago. A. W. GREELY, PUBLIC DOCUMENTS OF THE FIRST FOURTEEN CONGRESSES, 1789–1817: PAPERS RELATING TO EARLY CONGRESSIONAL DOCUMENTS, S. DOC. NO. 56–428 (1900). Greely noted that the publications of the early Congresses "were issued as the occasion required in all sorts of shapes and sizes, with separate or no pagination and without any serial numbering," and that "there exists neither a complete collection nor detailed list of the documents of the First to the Fourteenth Congresses, inclusive, 1789 to 1817." *Id.* at 5. General Greely was Chief Signal Officer of the U.S. Army, and devoted his leisure hours for five years to this project. *Id.* at 3.

Arguments for and against passage are made, and explanations of unclear or controversial provisions are offered.

Debates in the House and Senate are generally not as influential as committee reports as sources of statutory purpose. While reports represent the considered opinion of those legislators who have studied the bill most closely, floor statements are often political hyperbole and may even represent the calculated use of prepared colloquies designed to manufacture evidence of legislative intent. Nonetheless, floor debates can be of value. The most influential statements are those from a bill's sponsor or its floor managers (the committee members responsible for steering the bill through consideration).[19] These statements may even explain aspects of a bill not discussed in a committee report or correct errors in a report.

In some instances, floor debates are the best available legislative history source. If a bill is amended on the floor with language that was not considered in committee and thus was not discussed in a committee report, the record of floor debate may be the only explanation available of the intended purpose of the amendment.[20]

The essential source for the text of floor debates is the *Congressional Record*, which is published daily while either house is

---

[19] "Within the category of floor debate, some Members are more equal than others. Statements by sponsors and floor managers carry the most weight, statements by Members not associated with either formulation or committee consideration of the bill warrant little weight, and statements by bill opponents usually are not taken at face value." Costello, *supra* note 15, at 51. This paradigm is not always followed. Former representative (and judge) Abner Mikva described railing in hyperbolic terms against the excesses of Racketeer Influenced Corrupt Organizations (RICO) provisions, only to find his remarks later cited as evidence of the broad scope of RICO. Abner J. Mikva, *Reading and Writing Statutes*, 28 S. TEX. L. REV. 181, 185 (1986).

[20] The authoritative explanation of the Bankruptcy Reform Act of 1994, Pub. L. No. 103–394, 108 Stat. 4106, is considered to be a section-by-section review inserted in the *Congressional Record*, 140 CONG. REC. 27,691 (1994). The act "had an unusual history. It was passed by the Senate first, then the House waited until close to congressional recess to act on the bill. Since there was not enough time to pass a different bill and work out the differences with the Senate in conference, Senators and staffers interested in passage of the bill met with House members to work out differences before the bill passed the House. This was done. Thus, there is no conference report. This section-by-section review of the legislation was written after the compromise bill was agreed upon." Janet A. Flaccus, *A Potpourri of Bankruptcy Changes: 1994 Bankruptcy Amendments*, 47 ARK. L. REV. 817, 821 n. 30 (1994). This section-by-section review has been cited in more than 100 court decisions.

The most famous example of a significant change made on the floor with no supporting legislative history is the inclusion of sex discrimination in Title VII of the Civil Rights Act of 1964, Pub. L. No. 88–352, tit. VII, § 703, 78 Stat. 241, 255 (current version at 42 U.S.C. § 2000e–2). The traditional story is that "sex" was added at the last minute as a strategy to defeat the bill, although this version of events has been disputed. *See* Robert C. Bird, *More than a Congressional Joke: A Fresh Look at the Legislative History of Sex Discrimination of the 1964 Civil Rights Act*, 3 WM. & MARY J. WOMEN & L. 137 (1997). What is undisputed is that "[v]irtually no legislative history provides guidance to courts interpreting the prohibition of sex discrimination." *Ellison v. Brady*, 924 F.2d 872, 875 (9th Cir. 1991).

in session. The *Congressional Record* provides a more or less verbatim transcript of the legislative debates and proceedings, but legislators have the opportunity to revise their remarks and to insert material that was not actually spoken. Material that was not spoken is generally indicated in the Senate proceedings by the use of bullets, and in the House proceedings by a sans serif typeface.[21]

Each daily *Congressional Record* issue has separately paginated sections for Senate and House proceedings, with page number prefixed with either S or H. In addition, it includes an Extensions of Remarks section containing additional statements from members of the House of Representatives, tributes to constituents, reprints of newspaper articles, and whatever other material House members wish to have printed.

The *Congressional Record* never contains hearings and only rarely includes committee reports—although it does include the text of conference committee reports. Bills are sometimes read into the *Record*, particularly if they have been amended on the floor or in conference committee. The *Congressional Record*'s primary role, however, is as a report of debates and actions taken. An excerpt from the *Record*, showing House consideration of H.R. 137, is shown in Illustration 6-4.

Each issue of the *Congressional Record* contains a Daily Digest, which summarizes the day's proceedings, lists actions taken and enactments signed by the President that day, and provides useful committee information. Page references are included, making the Daily Digest a good starting place if only the date of congressional action is known.

---

[21] 44 U.S.C. § 901 provides that the *Record* "shall be substantially a verbatim report of proceedings." This language is unchanged since it was first enacted in 1895. Act of Jan. 12, 1895, c. 23, § 13, 28 Stat. 601, 603. On the history and practice of allowing legislators to revise their remarks and the use of symbols and typefaces, see MILDRED L. AMER, CONG. RESEARCH SERV., 93–60 GOV, THE *CONGRESSIONAL RECORD*: CONTENT, HISTORY AND ISSUES 14–21 (1993) (www.llsdc.org/assets/source book/crs-93-60.pdf); Howard N. Mantel, *The Congressional Record: Fact or Fiction of the Legislative Process*, 12 W. POL. Q. 981 (1959); and Michelle M. Springer, *The* Congressional Record: *"Substantially a Verbatim Report?"*, 13 GOV'T PUBLICATIONS REV. 371 (1986).

The typeface conventions are not always honored, particularly in the Senate, and some speeches that never occurred appear in the *Record* as if they had. In 2006, the Supreme Court rejected reliance on a colloquy between two senators that was inserted into the *Congressional Record* after the debate. *Hamdan v. Rumsfeld*, 548 U.S. 557, 580 n.10 (2006). *See also* 117 Cong. Rec. 36,506 (1971) (remarks of Rep. Hechler) ("I would like to indicate that I am not really speaking these words. . . . I do not want to kid anyone into thinking that I am now on my feet delivering a stirring oration. As a matter of fact, I am back in my office typing this out on my own hot little typewriter, far from the madding crowd, and somewhat removed from the House Chamber.").

7640   CONGRESSIONAL RECORD—HOUSE, Vol. 153, Pt. 6   *March 26, 2007*

A motion to reconsider was laid on the table.

RECESS

The SPEAKER pro tempore. Pursuant to clause 12(a) of rule I, the Chair declares the House in recess subject to the call of the Chair.

Accordingly (at 3 o'clock and 13 minutes p.m.), the House stood in recess subject to the call of the Chair.

□ 1700

AFTER RECESS

The recess having expired, the House was called to order by the Speaker pro tempore (Mr. SALAZAR) at 5 p.m.

ANIMAL FIGHTING PROHIBITION ENFORCEMENT ACT OF 2007

Mr. SCOTT of Virginia. Mr. Speaker, I move to suspend the rules and pass the bill (H.R. 137) to amend title 18, United States Code, to strengthen prohibitions against animal fighting, and for other purposes, as amended.

The Clerk read the title of the bill.

The text of the bill is as follows:

H.R. 137

Be it enacted by the Senate and House of Representatives of the United States of America in Congress assembled,

SECTION 1. SHORT TITLE.

This Act may be cited as the "Animal Fighting Prohibition Enforcement Act of 2007".

SEC. 2. ENFORCEMENT OF ANIMAL FIGHTING PROHIBITIONS.

(a) IN GENERAL.—Chapter 3 of title 18, United States Code, is amended by adding at the end the following:

"§ 49. Enforcement of animal fighting prohibitions

"Whoever violates subsection (a), (b), (c), or (e) of section 26 of the Animal Welfare Act shall be fined under this title, imprisoned for not more than 3 years, or both, for each violation.".

(b) CLERICAL AMENDMENT.—The table of contents for such chapter is amended by inserting after the item relating to section 48 the following:

"49. Enforcement of animal fighting prohibitions.".

SEC. 3. AMENDMENTS TO THE ANIMAL WELFARE ACT.

Section 26 of the Animal Welfare Act (7 U.S.C. 2156) is amended—

(1) in subsection (c), by striking "interstate instrumentality of interstate commerce for commercial speech";

(2) in subsection (d), by striking "such subsections" and inserting "such subsection";

(3) by striking subsection (e) and inserting the following:

"(e) It shall be unlawful for any person to knowingly sell, buy, transport, or deliver in interstate or foreign commerce a knife, a gaff, or any other sharp instrument attached, or designed or intended to be attached, to the leg of a bird for use in an animal fighting venture.";

(4) in subsection (g)—

(A) in paragraph (1), by striking "or animals, such as waterfowl, bird, raccoon, or fox hunting"; and

(B) by striking paragraph (3) and inserting the following:

"(3) the term 'instrumentality of interstate commerce' means any written, wire, radio, television or other form of communication in, or using a facility of, interstate commerce;"; and

(5) by adding at the end the following new subsection:

"(i) The criminal penalties for violations of subsection (a), (b), (c), or (e) are provided in section 49 of title 18, United States Code.".

The SPEAKER pro tempore. Pursuant to the rule, the gentleman from Virginia (Mr. SCOTT) and the gentleman from North Carolina (Mr. COBLE) each will control 20 minutes.

The Chair recognizes the gentleman from Virginia.

GENERAL LEAVE

Mr. SCOTT of Virginia. Mr. Speaker, I ask unanimous consent that all Members have 5 legislative days to revise and extend their remarks and include extraneous material on the bill under consideration.

The SPEAKER pro tempore. Is there objection to the request of the gentleman from Virginia?

There was no objection.

Mr. SCOTT of Virginia. Mr. Speaker, I yield myself such time as I may consume.

Mr. Speaker, H.R. 137 is a bipartisan effort by the Judiciary Committee, led by the gentleman from California (Mr. GALLEGLY) as the chief sponsor and the gentleman from Oregon (Mr. BLUMENAUER) as the lead Democratic sponsor. Both have worked long and hard on this issue. I would also like to express my appreciation to Chairman CONYERS, Ranking Member SMITH, and Subcommittee Ranking Member FORBES for their leadership and support in moving this matter forward, and also the former chairman of the committee, Mr. COBLE, who is with us today.

The Animal Fighting Prohibition Enforcement Act of 2007 addresses the growing problem of staged animal fighting in this country. It increases the penalties under the current Federal law for transporting animals in interstate commerce for the purpose of fighting and for interstate and foreign commerce in knives and gaffs designed for use in cockfighting.

Specifically, H.R. 137 makes violations of the law a felony punishable by up to 3 years in prison. Currently, these offenses are limited to misdemeanor treatment with the possibility of a fine and up to 1 year of imprisonment. Most States make all staged animal fighting illegal. Just one State currently allows cockfighting to occur legally.

The transport of game birds for the purpose of animal fighting and the implements of cockfighting are already prohibited by Federal law, though the current law only allows, as I have indicated, the misdemeanor treatment. In 1976 Congress amended title 7, U.S. Code, section 2156, the Animal Welfare Act, to make it illegal to knowingly sell, buy, transport, deliver, or receive a dog or other animal in interstate or foreign commerce for the purposes of participation in an animal fighting venture or knowingly sponsoring or exhibiting an animal in a fighting venture if any animal in the venture was moved in interstate or foreign commerce. Amendments to the Animal Welfare Act contained a loophole, however, that allowed shipments of birds across State lines for fighting purposes if the destination State allowed cockfighting.

While Congress did amend section 26 of the Animal Welfare Act to close this loophole in 2002, the penalty section and other provisions of the act have not been updated since their original enactment in 1976. This bill is designed to address those shortfalls to more effectively cover modern problems associated with animal fighting ventures.

As I have already mentioned, the legislation increases current penalties to provide a meaningful deterrent. One of the primary reasons for enacting the increased penalties under title 18 is the reluctance of U.S. Attorneys to pursue animal fighting cases under the current misdemeanor provisions because they view the penalties as ineffective against an animal fighting industry, which has continued unabated nationwide.

H.R. 137 further makes it a felony to transport cockfighting implements in interstate or foreign commerce. These implements take the form of razor-sharp knives, known as slashers; or gaffs, instruments shaped in the form of curved ice picks that are attached to birds' legs for fighting. Proponents of these implements within the game fowl community apparently contend that they inflict cleaner wounds upon the birds which are then quicker and easier to heal.

Since penalties against animal fighting were codified in 1976, Federal authorities have pursued less than half a dozen animal fighting cases, despite the fact that the USDA has received numerous tips from informants and requests to assist with State and local prosecutions.

In addition, despite the fact that all 50 States have banned dog fighting and all but one State has banned cockfighting, the animal fighting industry continues to thrive within the United States. Numerous nationally circulated animal fighting magazines advertise fighting animals, and paid lobbyists continue to advocate for animal fighters' interests. Thankfully, H.R. 137 will seek to bring an end to these practices.

Finally, Mr. Speaker, this bill affects matters within the jurisdiction of the

---

Illustration 6-4. A page from the *Congressional Record*, showing House consideration of H.R. 137.

An index to the *Congressional Record* and a History of Bills and Resolutions collection are available on Govinfo, with coverage back to 1983. These resources list page numbers in the *Congressional Record* daily edition but do not link directly to the relevant text. The index and History of Bills and Resolutions are also issued in print every two weeks, but the printed versions only cover recent developments and do not cumulate during a session. Online, the index and History of Bills are cumulative for each term of Congress.

The full text of the daily edition of the *Congressional Record* can be searched through several online sources. Coverage begins in 1995 on Congress.gov, and in 1994 on Govinfo. Westlaw and Lexis coverage extends back to 1985, and Bloomberg Law to 1989.

A bound permanent edition of the *Congressional Record* is published after the end of each session. There is generally a three- or four-year lag between a session and its coverage in bound volumes, but once the permanent edition is published it becomes the standard source to be cited for congressional debates.[22] The daily and permanent editions have the same volume numbers, but their page numbers are completely different. The separate S and H sections in the daily edition are merged in the permanent edition into one numerical sequence. (The page shown in Illustration 6-4 is from the permanent edition.)

Neither Westlaw nor Lexis has the permanent edition of the *Congressional Record*, but it is available from other online sources. The Govinfo portal has the entirety of the permanent edition. HeinOnline and ProQuest Congressional both have retrospective coverage back to the first volume in 1873. HeinOnline offers a "Congressional Record Daily to Bound Locator" tool providing cross-references from daily edition citations to permanent edition citations, with coverage back to 1980, easing what has in the past been an onerous process. Bloomberg Law has the permanent edition from 1933 to 1988.

The permanent edition also includes a comprehensive index to the session, a cumulative History of Bills and Resolutions table, and, since the 80th Congress (1947–48), a bound version of the Daily Digest. These versions of the index, table, and Daily Digest provide page numbers for the permanent edition. To convert a daily edition citation to the permanent edition without access to HeinOnline, you will usually need to start over in the index looking for references to the topic or speaker, or you can browse through the specific day's pages looking for the cited passage. HeinOnline coverage includes all

---

[22] THE BLUEBOOK: A UNIFORM SYSTEM OF CITATION R. 13.5 (21st ed. 2020); ALWD GUIDE TO LEGAL CITATION R. 15.10(a) (6th ed. 2017).

published indexes, history tables, and digests, and Govinfo has these features for volumes 1–144 (1873–1998).

The *Congressional Record* has been published by the government since the 43rd Congress (1873–74) and is the successor to three earlier series reporting debates of Congress.[23] The earliest sessions of Congress were not reported very thoroughly; the Senate even met behind closed doors until 1794. Decades later, newspaper accounts and other early sources covering the 1st Congress through the 18th Congress, 1st Session (1789–1824) were compiled and published as the *Annals of Congress* (also known as *The Debates and Proceedings in the Congress of the United States*) (1834–56).[24]

The period from 1824 to 1873 is covered by two overlapping private publications, the *Register of Debates* (1824–37) (18th Congress, 2d Session to 25th Congress, 1st Session) and the *Congressional Globe* (1833–73) (23rd to 42nd Congress). The *Register of Debates* and the early *Congressional Globe* volumes were summaries of statements rather than transcripts, but verbatim reporting became possible with improved shorthand techniques and by midcentury the *Globe*'s debates had taken on a form quite similar to the modern *Congressional Record*.

All of these earlier publications, as well as the *Congressional Record* for 1873–75, are available free online through the Library of Congress "A Century of Lawmaking for a New Nation" site (memory. loc.gov/ammem/amlaw/). The full text is not searchable, but indexes for each volume are available. Searchable versions of the *Record*'s predecessors are also included in the HeinOnline and ProQuest *Congressional Record* collections.

House and *Senate Journals* are also published, but unlike the *Congressional Record*, they do not include the verbatim debates. The journals merely record the proceedings, indicate whether there was debate, and report the resulting action and votes taken.[25] The *House*

---

[23] The standard reference on the early sources is Elizabeth Gregory McPherson, *Reporting the Debates of Congress*, 28 Q.J. SPEECH 141 (1942), an article based on the author's 1940 University of North Carolina dissertation, The History of Reporting the Debates and Proceedings of Congress. An excellent modern summary is provided by Richard J. McKinney, *An Overview of the Congressional Record and Its Predecessor Publications: A Research Guide* (www.llsdc.org/congressional-record-overview) [https://perma.cc/QH9L-NB3B].

[24] The first two volumes, published in 1834 and covering 1789–91, appear in two different printings with different pagination. One has the running title "History of Congress" at the top of each page while the other says "Gales & Seaton's History of Debates in Congress." The former is the version available on HeinOnline, while the Library of Congress and ProQuest have the latter. Most references unfortunately do not indicate which version was used, but you can find a cited passage by date or through a keyword search.

[25] The journals are the only publications required by Article I, § 5 of the Constitution: "Each House shall keep a Journal of its Proceedings, and from time to

Journal includes the texts of bills and amendments considered, and both journals have "History of Bills and Resolutions" tables. *House Journal* volumes back to 1992 are available through Govinfo.

(f) Presidential Approval or Veto

After a bill is passed by both houses of Congress, it goes to the President for approval. If the President approves a bill, it becomes law and generally goes into effect on the day of enactment, unless some other effective date is specified. If the President vetoes a bill, to become law it must be repassed by both houses by a two-thirds majority. The messages or statements issued when the President approves particular enactments, known as signing statements, can shed light on legislative history. Like other presidential messages to Congress, these documents appear in several places, including the *Congressional Record* and the *Daily* or *Weekly Compilation of Presidential Documents*.

While most presidential signing statements simply make general comments about a statute's purposes, a President sometimes uses signing statements to convey interpretations of ambiguous provisions. These statements have been included in *USCCAN*'s legislative history section beginning in 1986, although their importance in interpreting statutory language has been subject to dispute.[26]

§ 6.2 OTHER CONGRESSIONAL PUBLICATIONS

Congress also produces a variety of other publications that are less frequently consulted in legislative history research. These can be important sources of information, however, on statutes, legislative policies, and the workings of the federal government.

House and Senate Documents. Congress publishes many documents as required by law or by special request. These House and

---

time publish the same, excepting such Parts as may in their Judgment require Secrecy; and the Yeas and Nays of the Members of either House on any question shall, at the Desire of one fifth of those Present, be entered on the Journal."

[26] The American Presidency Project (www.presidency.ucsb.edu/signing statements.php) has collected significant signing statements back to 1929. For further background information on their use in recent administrations, see TODD GARVEY, CONG. RESEARCH SERV., RL33667, PRESIDENTIAL SIGNING STATEMENTS: CONSTITUTIONAL AND INSTITUTIONAL IMPLICATIONS (2012) (www.fas.org/sgp/crs/natsec/RL33667.pdf). *See also* John M. de Figueiredo & Edward H. Stiglitz, *Signing Statements and Presidentializing Legislative History*, 69 ADMIN. L. REV. 841 (2017); Joel Sievert & Ian Ostrander, *Constraining Presidential Ambition: Controversy and the Decline of Signing Statements*, 47 PRESIDENTIAL STUD. Q. 752 (2017); and Christopher S. Yoo, *Presidential Signing Statements: A New Perspective*, 164 U. PA. L. REV. 1801 (2016).

Senate Documents contain material such as the *Budget of the United States Government*, special studies and reports, reprints of presidential messages, executive agency reports and memoranda, reports of nongovernmental organizations, and a variety of papers ordered to be printed by either house of Congress. House and Senate Documents are usually unrelated to legislative history issues, but they may be of value in other research.

Documents are issued in numbered series for each Congress, similar to the way committee reports are identified. They are published, along with committee reports, in the Serial Set. Documents are available online back to the 104th Congress (1995–96) through Govinfo, with scattered coverage from 1975 to 1995, and in Bloomberg Law. Retrospective coverage is available in the ProQuest U.S. Serial Set Digital Collection and in Readex's U.S. Congressional Serial Set (1817–1994).

Senate Executive Reports and Treaty Documents. The Senate also issues two series of publications in connection with its responsibility for treaty ratification. Senate Treaty Documents contain the text of treaties sent to the Senate for its advice and consent, together with related messages or correspondence from the President and Secretary of State. Senate Executive Reports are issued by the Senate Foreign Relations Committee after its consideration of the treaty. These materials are discussed more fully in Chapter 17.

Committee Prints. Many congressional committees publish material prepared at their request, such as staff studies or compilations of legislative history documents. Some committee prints have statements by committee members on pending bills, and others can be useful analyses and compilations of laws under the jurisdiction of a committee. The House's *Green Book: Background Material and Data on Major Programs Within the Jurisdiction of the Committee on Ways and Means* is an example of a committee print with a wide range of useful information.

Committee prints are distributed by the Government Publishing Office, but they are not as widely available online as are reports or hearings. New committee prints are available on Congress.gov, and Govinfo and Bloomberg Law have a limited number of prints beginning in 1995. The most comprehensive source is the ProQuest Congressional Research Digital Collection, available as part of the ProQuest Congressional system. "Congressional Research" in the title means research performed for Congress, an apt description of the purpose of committee prints. This online collection includes tens of thousands of committee prints dating back to 1830, with PDF images of the original documents and search options including full text and indexed fields.[27]

Legislative Agency Publications. In addition to its own lawmaking and investigative functions, Congress also supervises three major investigative and research agencies that produce a range of important analyses and reports.

The Congressional Budget Office (www.cbo.gov) was created in 1974[28] and produces cost estimates for bills reported out of committee as well as a variety of budget reports, analytical studies, and background papers. The CBO website offers options to search its publications by subject area and by document type.

The Government Accountability Office (www.gao.gov) was created in 1921 as the General Accounting Office and given its present name in 2004.[29] It is charged with studying the programs and expenditures of the federal government. The GAO issues over 1,000 reports each year, and frequently recommends specific congressional actions. If legislation is enacted, these reports can have valuable background information on its purpose.

The GAO website provides extensive access to its reports, with publications available as far back as the 1930s. Older GAO reports (1994–2008) are available through Govinfo, while newer reports are available on the GAO website. Westlaw, Lexis, and Bloomberg Law also have coverage of GAO reports.

The third and most wide-ranging research arm of Congress is the Congressional Research Service, created in 1915 as the Legislative Drafting Bureau and Reference Division.[30] Each year it produces several thousand new or updated reports, including legal and policy analyses, economic studies, bibliographies, statistical reviews, and issue briefs that provide background information on

---

[27] ProQuest also publishes prints on microfiche, indexed in the CIS US CONGRESSIONAL COMMITTEE PRINTS INDEX (1980, covering 1830–1969), and CIS/INDEX (1970–date).

[28] Congressional Budget Act of 1974, Pub. L. No. 93–344, tit. 2, 88 Stat. 297, 302–05 (codified as amended at 2 U.S.C. §§ 601–612).

[29] The General Accounting Office was established by the Budget and Accounting Act of 1921, ch. 20, tit. 3, 42 Stat. 20, 23–27 (current version at 31 U.S.C. §§ 701–783). It was renamed the Government Accountability Office pursuant to the GAO Human Capital Reform Act of 2004, Pub. L. No. 108–271, § 8, 118 Stat. 811, 814. For the early history of the GAO, including its precursors, see ROGER R. TRASK, DEFENDER OF THE PUBLIC INTEREST: THE GENERAL ACCOUNTING OFFICE, 1921–1966 (1996).

[30] Act of Mar. 4, 1915, ch. 141, 38 Stat. 997, 1005. Thirty-one years later, the agency's mandate was expanded and it was named the Legislative Reference Service. Legislative Reorganization Act of 1946, ch. 753, § 203, 60 Stat. 812, 836. The present name was adopted and the Service's wide range of functions specified under the Legislative Reorganization Act of 1970, Pub. L. No. 91–510, § 321, 84 Stat. 1140, 1181–85 (codified as amended at 2 U.S.C. § 166).

major legislative issues. These reports are written exclusively for members of Congress and their staff, and until recently, were not officially published online or otherwise distributed to the public. Since 2018, however, most recently published CRS reports are now readily available (crsreports.congress.gov).[31]

For older CRS reports, several sites provide links to thousands of documents available free online. Two of the deepest collections are the University of North Texas Libraries' Congressional Research Service Reports site (digital.library.unt.edu/explore/collections/CRSR/) and EveryCRSReport.com.[32]

The most comprehensive subscription source for CRS reports back to 1916 is the ProQuest Congressional Research Digital Collection. As it does with committee prints, this service provides PDF images of the original documents and full-text searching. ProQuest also publishes a microform edition of reports since 1916 called *Major Studies and Issue Briefs of the Congressional Research Service*. Bloomberg Law has full coverage of CRS reports beginning in 2003, and other commercial suppliers include CQ Roll Call and Penny Hill Press (www.pennyhill.com).

§ 6.3   CONGRESSIONAL RESEARCH RESOURCES

Researchers are interested in Congress for numerous reasons, such as policy formation, voting patterns, and the influence of lobbyists on legislative behavior. This discussion, however, focuses on tools useful for two basic legal research tasks: investigating the meaning of enacted laws and tracking the status of pending legislation. A number of approaches can be used for these purposes. For recently enacted laws and pending legislation, a range of online resources provides current and thorough coverage. For older bills, the choices dwindle to a few tools that provide retrospective coverage.

Sometimes you may undertake legislative history research to get a general understanding of a law, but more often you will be looking for clues to interpret specific language in a code section. You will be looking for documentation as close as possible to the time when decisions were made to use the language you seek to interpret, such as the point at which it was added by amendment or the point at which it was voted on. You will be looking for statements by the

---

[31] *See* Consolidated Appropriations Act, 2018, § 154, Pub. L. No. 115–141, codified at 2 U.S.C. § 166a.

[32] LLSDC's Legislative Source Book includes a CRS page (www.llsdc.org/crs-report-links), with hundreds of reports on congressional procedures and links to several other free websites with CRS reports.

supporters of the language rather than its opponents, if there was a debate.[33]

Be warned that this can be a very frustrating endeavor. Even after finding all the relevant materials on a statute, you may learn that the legislature never explained or discussed the particular language you are researching. This is one reason that legislative history is just one of several tools used in statutory interpretation.

The increasing use of omnibus legislation and unorthodox procedures has also made legislative history research more difficult. Especially towards the end of a legislative session, numerous bills may be combined into mammoth enactments of several hundred pages. These can complicate the research process enormously, as materials addressing a provision within a huge omnibus bill can be much more difficult to locate than those on a bill with one discrete subject. Online keyword searches in lengthy committee reports and debates can pinpoint particular issues, but working with complex legislative histories is still an onerous task. In other instances a bill may bypass the committee process and go directly to the floor for consideration, meaning that there are no relevant committee reports to be found.[34]

With those caveats in mind, the key to finding congressional documents or tracing legislative action is usually the bill number. It appears on an enacted law both in its slip form and in the *Statutes at Large*. The first page of Pub. L. No. 110–22, the Animal Fighting Prohibition Enforcement Act of 2007, was shown in the last chapter in Illustration 5-10. The bill number (H.R. 137) is included in brackets in the left margin. Bill numbers have been included in *Statutes at Large* since 1903, but they unfortunately do not appear in the *United States Code* or in either of its annotated editions.[35]

Bill numbers lead easily to printed or electronic status tables, which indicate actions taken and provide references to relevant

---

[33] For more on these and related principles, see Victoria F. Nourse, *A Decision Theory of Statutory Interpretation: Legislative History by the Rules*, 122 YALE L.J. 70 (2012).

[34] For more information on omnibus bills and other changes in lawmaking procedures, see GLEN S. KRUTZ, HITCHING A RIDE: OMNIBUS LEGISLATING IN THE U.S. CONGRESS (2001), and BARBARA SINCLAIR, UNORTHODOX LAWMAKING: NEW LEGISLATIVE PROCESSES IN THE U.S. CONGRESS (5th ed. 2017). The authors of these works are political scientists, and they focus on institutional and public policy impacts rather than the effects of these changes on legislative history research.

[35] For laws before 1903, bill numbers can be found in EUGENE NABORS, LEGISLATIVE REFERENCE CHECKLIST: THE KEY TO LEGISLATIVE HISTORIES FROM 1789– 1903 (1982). Its tables provide references from public law numbers and *Statutes at Large* citations to bill numbers.

legislative documents. These tables can be used both for pending bill searches and for retrospective research on enacted laws.

A head start in legislative history research can come from the public law itself. At the end of each act, in either slip law or the *Statutes at Large*, there appears a brief legislative history summary with citations to committee reports, dates of consideration and passage in each house, and references to presidential statements. Summaries have appeared at the end of each law passed since 1975, and *Statutes at Large* volumes from 1963 to 1974 include separate "Guide to Legislative History" tables. The legislative history summaries in *Statutes at Large* are by no means complete, but they are conveniently published with the text of each act.

Numerous guides to legislative history are available on the internet. A particularly thorough and insightful resource, part of the LLSDC Legislative Source Book, is Richard J. McKinney & Ellen A. Sweet, "Federal Legislative History Research: A Practitioner's Guide to Compiling the Documents and Sifting for Legislative Intent" (www.llsdc.org/federal-legislative-history-guide). It even includes links to dozens of other online guides on the topic, and it is regularly updated.

The following sections describe several major legislative history research resources. Which of these to use in any particular circumstance depends on the date of the law you are researching and the scope of information needed. A compiled legislative history, if available, may have done most of your work for you. The most up-to-date information on current legislation is found in Congress.gov or one of the other online bill-tracking services. The most comprehensive coverage of documents is usually found in ProQuest materials. The handiest way to access the text of relevant committee reports may be to scan those reprinted in *USCCAN*. For legislative history information on some older laws, the only resource available may be the "History of Bills and Resolutions" in the *Congressional Record* index, which dates back to the 19th century.

(a) Compiled Legislative Histories

Identifying and gathering the documents that make up a legislative history can be a time-consuming process, and a resource that has already compiled these documents can make the research process much easier. Such resources, online and in print, are available for many federal acts.

The most exhaustive source of compiled legislative histories is ProQuest Legislative Insight (congressional.proquest.com/legislative insight), a subscription resource that covers more than 27,000 laws dating back to 1789. Its coverage is not yet complete, but for laws within its scope it has PDFs of all relevant bills, reports, hearings, floor debates, and other documents. Locating a compiled legislative history can be done by searching or by browsing a list of acts' popular names. Rather than limiting coverage to a single term of Congress, ProQuest Legislative Insight also collects relevant bills, reports, and hearings from prior terms. The documents for a complex and lengthy act can span several years and include hundreds of items. The full text of all documents for an enactment can be searched simultaneously for specific phrases or combinations of words. Documents that match the search request are indicated, but they must be downloaded and searched individually to see the context in which the terms appear. Illustration 6-5 shows the Legislative Insight summary for the Animal Fighting Prohibition Enforcement Act of 2007, with search boxes at the top and links to several version of bills.

Online compiled legislative histories are available on Lexis and Westlaw for several dozen major acts in areas such as bankruptcy, tax, and environmental law. Westlaw also has a U.S. GAO Federal Legislative Histories collection with several thousand legislative history compilations prepared by the Government Accountability Office. Coverage spans from 1921 to 1995. A keyword search retrieves a list of *Statutes at Large* citations; clicking on one of these citations retrieves a list of documents, including reports, *Congressional Record* excerpts, and hearings. The list highlights which documents contain the search terms, with links to the full text in PDF.

HeinOnline's U.S. Federal Legislative History Library has searchable PDFs of documents for several hundred acts, including major legislation in areas such as environmental law, immigration, intellectual property, labor law, and taxation. This collection is based on William S. Hein & Co.'s publications of compiled legislative histories, which has volumes covering individual acts as well as more extensive sets such as *Congress and the Courts: A Legislative History 1787–2010* and *Internal Revenue Acts of the United States, 1909–1950*. Printed legislative history compilations have also been issued by congressional committees, government agencies charged with the enforcement of particular acts, and interested groups such as trade associations.

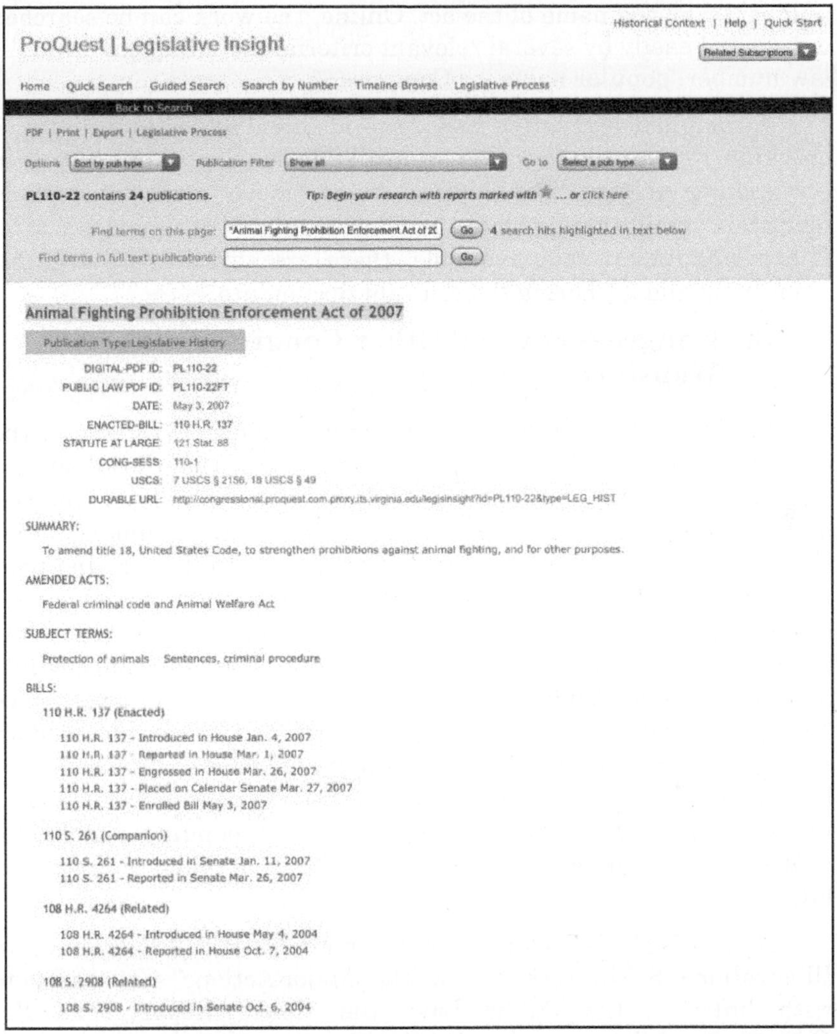

Historical Context | Help | Quick Start

ProQuest | Legislative Insight

Related Subscriptions

Home Quick Search Guided Search Search by Number Timeline Browse Legislative Process

Back to Search

PDF | Print | Export | Legislative Process

Options: Sort by pub type Publication Filter: Show all Go to: Select a pub type

PL110-22 contains 24 publications. Tip: Begin your research with reports marked with ... or click here

Find terms on this page: "Animal Fighting Prohibition Enforcement Act of 20 Go 4 search hits highlighted in text below

Find terms in full text publications: Go

Animal Fighting Prohibition Enforcement Act of 2007

Publication Type: Legislative History

DIGITAL-PDF ID: PL110-22
PUBLIC LAW PDF ID: PL110-22FT
DATE: May 3, 2007
ENACTED-BILL: 110 H.R. 137
STATUTE AT LARGE: 121 Stat. 88
CONG-SESS: 110-1
USCS: 7 USCS § 2156, 18 USCS § 49
DURABLE URL: http://congressional.proquest.com.proxy.its.virginia.edu/legisinsight?id=PL110-22&type=LEG_HIST

SUMMARY:

To amend title 18, United States Code, to strengthen prohibitions against animal fighting, and for other purposes.

AMENDED ACTS:

Federal criminal code and Animal Welfare Act

SUBJECT TERMS:

Protection of animals Sentences, criminal procedure

BILLS:

110 H.R. 137 (Enacted)

110 H.R. 137 - Introduced in House Jan. 4, 2007
110 H.R. 137 - Reported in House Mar. 1, 2007
110 H.R. 137 - Engrossed in House Mar. 26, 2007
110 H.R. 137 - Placed on Calendar Senate Mar. 27, 2007
110 H.R. 137 - Enrolled Bill May 3, 2007

110 S. 261 (Companion)

110 S. 261 - Introduced in Senate Jan. 11, 2007
110 S. 261 - Reported in Senate Mar. 26, 2007

108 H.R. 4264 (Related)

108 H.R. 4264 - Introduced in House May 4, 2004
108 H.R. 4264 - Reported in House Oct. 7, 2004

108 S. 2908 (Related)

108 S. 2908 - Introduced in Senate Oct. 6, 2004

Illustration 6-5. The ProQuest Legislative Insight summary of the Animal Fighting Prohibition Enforcement Act of 2007.

A basic tool for identifying and locating published and online compiled legislative histories is Ronald E. Wheeler & Jenna E. Fegreus, *Sources of Compiled Legislative Histories* (4th ed. 2018), which is also available as part of HeinOnline's U.S. Federal Legislative History Library. It covers not only compilations that reprint the legislative history documents in full, but also law review articles and other sources with references to the relevant documents. The print edition provides a checklist of available compiled legislative histories (other than Legislative Insight) for acts as far back as 1789, accessible chronologically by Congress and public law number or by the name of the act. Online, the work can be searched or browsed easily by several relevant criteria, including bill or public law number, popular name, or Congress.[36]

A compiled legislative history is an invaluable time-saver, so checking to see whether one is available is a vital first step in researching an act. The sources listed above may not provide identical compilations, so you should consult several if you are able. If a compilation is not available, there are several resources for identifying and gathering the relevant documents.

(b) Congress.gov and Other Congressional Websites

For current legislation or laws enacted since 1973, one of the easiest places to begin research is Congress.gov, the official site for legislative information. Congress.gov has the text of bills, summaries of their status, and legislative history documents, among other things. You can search by either keyword or bill number, and then filter search results by Congress, status, subject, or any of several other criteria. A bill's summary is accompanied by tabs linking to text versions, legislative actions, amendments, and related bills. While legislative history summaries are available for laws enacted since 1973, summaries for older laws lack some of the features included for more recent legislation. Links to the text of legislation are available beginning in 1989, and *Congressional Record* page references and links begin in 1993. For tracking currently pending legislation, Congress.gov offers e-mail alerts when action is taken on a specific bill.

A portion of the Congress.gov summary for H.R. 137 is shown in Illustration 6-6. This screen shows the "Major Actions" status section, with links to the Public Law, the House Report, and the *Congressional Record* page indicating Senate passage.

As noted earlier in the chapter, congressional documents are also available through the Government Publishing Office's Govinfo portal (www.govinfo.gov), but Govinfo has no links between documents and does not provide bill summaries or status information. The legislative branch resources on Govinfo include bills back to 1993, the *Congressional Record* daily edition beginning in 1994, committee reports and hearings from 1995, and selected

---

[36] Another source listing compilations is BERNARD D. REAMS, JR., FEDERAL LEGISLATIVE HISTORIES: AN ANNOTATED BIBLIOGRAPHY AND INDEX TO OFFICIALLY PUBLISHED SOURCES (1994). As the subtitle indicates, this volume covers only sources published by the federal government, such as a congressional committee or an agency. Coverage is thus not as broad as the Wheeler and Fegreus work, but the detailed annotations may be useful.

committee prints from 1992. Govinfo is the more comprehensive source for documents, but it does not summarize bills or collect related information the way Congress.gov does. All documents are full-text searchable, however, and they can be retrieved by citation or by browsing the list of available materials.

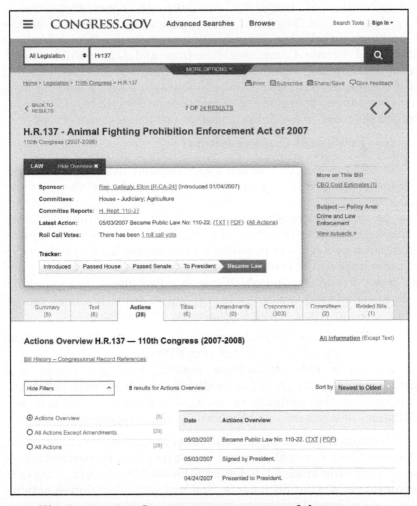

Illustration 6-6. Congress.gov summary of the same act.

While Congress.gov and Govinfo are the major comprehensive websites for congressional information, each house also maintains a website (www.senate.gov and www.house.gov) with information on its procedures and links to pages for individual members and committees. Most committee homepages have summaries of major pending legislation, background information, hearing statements, and schedules of upcoming meetings. In some instances, a "Legislation" link provides status tables for bills within the committee's jurisdiction. The LLSDC Source Book's "Quick Links to House and Senate Committee Hearings and Other Publications" (www.llsdc.org/hearings-quick-links) lists each House, Senate, and joint committee, with direct links to features such as hearing lists, news, schedules, testimony, and transcripts if available. Comments explain the scope of available resources on each committee's site.

(c) ProQuest Congressional

In 1970, a company called Congressional Information Service (CIS) began publishing a monthly service, *CIS/Index*, that provided indexing and abstracts of congressional publications. Its coverage was far more thorough and detailed than anything else then available.[37] For the first time, for example, one could track every appearance by a witness in published committee hearings. This CIS information is still the most comprehensive resource on Congress and is now available online through ProQuest Congressional (congressional.proquest.com), as well as in print in three annual volumes (*Abstracts*, *Legislative Histories*, and *Index*).

ProQuest Congressional now covers virtually all congressional publications since 1789, with full-text PDF copies available of most publications it lists. It indexes reports, hearings, prints, and documents by subject, title, and bill number, with abstracts summarizing the contents of these documents, the names and affiliations of witnesses, and the focus of their testimony.

In addition to abstracting individual congressional publications, ProQuest Congressional also has legislative history summaries for each enacted law since 1970, listing relevant bills, hearings, reports, debates, presidential documents, and any other legislative actions. Like the ProQuest Legislative Insight compiled legislative histories, these summaries do not limit coverage to a single term of Congress but include references to earlier hearings and other documents on related bills from prior congressional sessions. The difference

---

[37] For background on the situation before 1970 and the beginnings of CIS, see Sandra Peterson & Susan Tulis, *An Interview with James B. Adler and Esthy Adler, Founders, Congressional Information Service, Inc.*, 15 GOV'T PUBLICATIONS REV. 411 (1988).

between the two resources is that Legislative Insight collects the material so that it can all be searched together while Congressional merely lists (and provides links to) documents that must then be retrieved individually.

The easiest ways to focus a ProQuest Congressional search on legislative histories, rather than the thousands of congressional documents indexed, are to use the Advanced Search screen and limit by document type, or to use the Search by Number function and fill in the blanks with the Public Law number. Search results can be sorted in a number of ways, including by type of congressional document.

Acts before 1970 are not covered in ProQuest Congressional by legislative history summaries, but the thorough retrospective indexing means that reports and hearings on a particular bill are linked to that bill. You can search for documents associated with a bill by using the Search by Number feature. This is not always comprehensive, so it should be supplemented by keyword searching or other approaches.

Other features of ProQuest Congressional include bill-tracking summaries; full-text access to bills, reports, the *Congressional Record*, and other congressional documents beginning in the 1980s; transcripts of hearing testimony; and information on committees and legislators.

(d) *USCCAN* and Westlaw

United States Code Congressional and Administrative News (*USCCAN*) was mentioned in Chapter 5 as a source for the texts of enacted laws. For major acts it also reprints one or more committee reports, making it a convenient compilation for basic legislative history research. The scope of coverage varies, but *USCCAN* generally prints either a House or Senate report and, if one was issued, the conference committee report.

USCCAN is found in many smaller libraries that do not have very extensive collections of congressional materials. The need for a print source is minimized by expanded online coverage, but *The Bluebook* and the *ALWD Guide* mandate inclusion of a *USCCAN* citation for committee reports "when possible" or "if possible."[38]

The public laws and committee reports are published in separate "Laws" and "Legislative History" sections of *USCCAN*. Each section

---

[38] THE BLUEBOOK: A UNIFORM SYSTEM OF CITATION R. 13.4(a) (21st ed. 2020); ALWD GUIDE TO LEGAL CITATION R. 15.7(f) (6th ed. 2017).

prints material in order by public law number, and cross-references are provided between the laws and reports.

The Legislative History database on Westlaw includes the reports reprinted in *USCCAN* beginning in 1948, and from 1990 on it contains all congressional committee reports, including reports on bills that did not become law. Reports related to securities law are covered beginning in 1933.

USCCAN legislative histories are easy to find because references to them appear in the notes in the *United States Code Annotated*. A reference after a specific section, however, means only that legislative history on the act as a whole is available, not that pertinent material on that specific section will be found.

Because *USCCAN* in print has only selective coverage of committee reports, further research is often required. It omits references to hearings, prints, documents, or materials on related bills in previous Congresses, so anyone preparing a complete legislative history will need to use other resources. But it does provide a handy starting point, and the material in *USCCAN* may be sufficient if all you need is general background or a quick section-by-section analysis.

As noted earlier in the chapter, Westlaw also has resources such as bill texts, committee reports, and the *Congressional Record* for laws enacted since the 1990s. These are linked from *USCA* code sections under "Legislative History Materials" section of the History tab. As with the *USCCAN* references in the printed code, however, these links do not necessarily refer to the specific section. Illustration 6-7 shows Westlaw's list of documents related to Pub. L. No. 110–22, including links to the House Report and several *Congressional Record* pages.

§ 49. Enforcement of animal fighting prohibitions
18 USCA § 49 · United States Code Annotated · Title 18. Crimes and Criminal Procedure · Effective: February 7, 2014 (Approx. 2 pages)

Document   Notes of Decisions (0)   **History (517)** ▾   Citing References (176) ▾   Context & Analysis (4) ▾

Legislative History Materials (498)   KeyCite. 🔔 ✉ ▾

Pub.L. 110–22

Reports

460. Mar. 01, 2007, P.L. 110-22, ANIMAL FIGHTING PROHIBITION ENFORCEMENT ACT OF 2007, H.R. REP. 110–27(I)

Congressional Record

461. June 18, 2008, REPUBLICAN FILIBUSTERS, 154 Cong.Rec. S5708-01

462. Dec. 19, 2007, MISSED VOTES, 153 Cong.Rec. E2619-02

463. Aug. 04, 2007, HOUSE BILLS AND JOINT RESOLUTIONS APPROVED BY THE PRESIDENT, 153 Cong.Rec. H10014-05

464. May 16, 2007, HOUSE OF REPRESENTATIVES, 153 Cong.Rec. D691-01

465. May 04, 2007, NEW PUBLIC LAWS, 153 Cong.Rec. D622-03

466. Apr. 25, 2007, BILLS PRESENTED TO THE PRESIDENT, 153 Cong.Rec. H4173-03

467. Apr. 24, 2007, ENROLLED BILLS SIGNED, 153 Cong.Rec. S4917-01

468. Apr. 20, 2007, ENROLLED BILLS SIGNED, 153 Cong.Rec. S4809-03

469. Apr. 20, 2007, ENROLLED BILLS SIGNED, 153 Cong.Rec. H3721-09

470. Apr. 16, 2007, COMMUNICATION FROM THE CLERK OF THE HOUSE, 153 Cong.Rec. H3377-06

471. Apr. 10, 2007, SENATE, 153 Cong.Rec. D475-02

472. Apr. 10, 2007, ANIMAL FIGHTING PROHIBITION ENFORCEMENT ACT OF 2007, 153 Cong.Rec. S4317-02

Illustration 6-7. Legislative history documents on Westlaw.

(e) *CQ* and Tracking Services

Newspapers and services that cover Congress and politics are often good sources on congressional action, with information that may not be available from official documentation. Even if a bill appears to be stalled in committee, news stories and press releases can provide leads to what is happening behind the scenes.

CQ Roll Call, Inc., a news service focusing on political issues, publishes several resources with information on congressional activity. Its flagship publication is *CQ* (formerly *CQ Weekly*), which has information on pending legislation and news of current developments. *CQ* contains tables of House and Senate votes, a status table for major legislation, and a legislative history table for new public laws. It does not provide the texts of documents or comprehensive bill tracking, but it has valuable analysis and background discussion of laws and legislative issues.

An annual *CQ Almanac Plus* cumulates much of the information in the *Weekly* into a useful summary of the congressional session, and a series of multiyear *Congress and the Nation* volumes provides a broader perspective. For academic and public libraries, CQ Press Electronic Library (library.cqpress.com) has a subscription-based online version of *CQ* and related reference works. CQ also has its own online service, CQ Federal, designed for specialists needing current congressional information, offering a range of sophisticated tracking and bill-comparison features unavailable from free government sites and more general online services.

Govtrack.us (www.govtrack.us) is a popular, free resource for tracking current legislation. Bills can be searched by keyword, and the results show a bill's progress and link to its text. Registered users can sign up to receive updates about pending bills.

(f) Status Tables

Online resources have advantages of convenience and speed that are unmatched by printed resources. If online access is unavailable or does not cover earlier bills and laws, however, printed resources are still useful sources of information. There are several publications in which to find useful leads.

***Congressional Index* (Wolters Kluwer) (1937–date).** *Congressional Index* is a commercial looseleaf service issued in two volumes for each Congress, with weekly updates. Its coverage of pending legislation includes an index of bills by subject and author, a digest of each bill, and a status table of actions taken on each bill. This status table contains references to hearings, a feature lacking in some of the online resources.

The *Congressional Index* status table might not be your first choice when studying recent enactments, but older *Congressional Index* volumes back to the 75th Congress (1937–38) can be valuable sources of information on bills predating the coverage of modern bill-tracking services. Its subject index may even be a quicker and more thorough way to find bills than an online keyword search.

Congressional Index also provides a wide range of other information on Congress, including lists of members and committee assignments, an index of enactments and vetoes, lists of pending treaties and nominations, and a table of voting records.

Congressional Record and Earlier Status Tables (1789–date). As noted earlier, the *Congressional Record* index (to both the daily and permanent editions) includes a History of Bills and Resolutions table containing a brief summary of each measure, the name of the sponsor, the committee to which it has been referred, and references to debates, legislative actions, committee reports, amendments, and passage. Each entry also has references to the pages in the *Congressional Record* at which action is reported. This is one of the best sources of page citations for debates within the *Record*. It includes report and public law numbers, but no references to committee hearings or companion bills.

The History of Bills and Resolutions is one of the few sources of information available for older laws. These tables have been published annually since the 1867 volume of the *Congressional Globe*, long before the earliest coverage of most commercial publications. They are included in HeinOnline's version of the *Congressional Record* and *Globe*.

For even earlier acts, the House and Senate Journals all the way back to the First Congress (1789–91) include tables or lists of bills indicating which were reported, passed, or received other floor action. Most of these lists, usually found in the subject index under "Bills," are arranged by bill number, but some early volumes list bills without numbers by subject or by date of introduction. These early journals are all available online through the Library of Congress's "A Century of Lawmaking for a New Nation" site (memory.loc.gov/ammem/amlaw/).

Legislative Calendars (1919–date). Both houses and most committees issue calendars of pending business for the use of their members. These have current information on the status of pending bills and are particularly useful for information on hearings.

Perhaps the most valuable of these is *Calendars of the United States House of Representatives and History of Legislation*, which is issued daily. This includes a table, "History of Bills and Resolutions:

Numerical Order of Bills and Resolutions Which Have Been Reported to or Considered by Either or Both Houses," which cumulates legislative information for bills on which action has been taken. The table in the final *Calendars* issue at the end of each Congress cumulates major legislation from both sessions and is useful for retrospective reference. It provides report numbers and dates of consideration, but not *Congressional Record* page numbers. Govinfo has the current House and Senate calendars, as well as the final cumulative calendars beginning with the 104th Congress (1995–96).[39]

(g) Directories

One of the fastest ways to find out about the status of pending legislation is to contact congressional staff members responsible for drafting or monitoring the bill. They may be able to provide information or insights that would never appear in published status tables or reports.

The best source for detailed information on staff members is a commercial print and online directory, *Congressional Yellow Book* (www.leadershipconnect.io), which has addresses, telephone numbers, and (for some staff members) brief biographical information.

More general information about individuals, offices, and the organizational structure of Congress is also available in the *Official Congressional Directory*. It includes listings of committee assignments, staff for representatives and committees, and statistical data, as well as other information useful to representatives such as directories of the executive branch, foreign diplomatic offices in the United States, and the press galleries.

The *Official Congressional Directory* is available through Govinfo back to 1997. It began publication in 1866 during the 39th Congress, and older volumes have valuable information on members and committees in previous Congresses. These are available in HeinOnline's U.S. Congressional Documents collection.[40]

---

[39] Another resource of potential value for retrospective research, *Digest of Public General Bills and Resolutions* (1936–90), was published for more than fifty years by the Congressional Research Service. It summarized all bills and resolutions introduced and indicated major steps in the progress of enacted bills and all other measures reported out of committee, with indexes by sponsor and by subject. *Digest* volumes are available online through HathiTrust (catalog.hathitrust.org/Record/000520678).

[40] Committees and committee assignments in previous Congresses can also be found in a series of reference books, COMMITTEES IN THE U.S. CONGRESS, 1789–1946 (Charles Stewart III et al. eds., 2002); COMMITTEES IN THE U.S. CONGRESS, 1947–1992 (Garrison Nelson ed., 1993–94); and COMMITTEES IN THE U.S. CONGRESS, 1993–2010

A retrospective *Biographical Directory of the United States Congress, 1774–Present* (including coverage of the Continental Congress) is available online (bioguide.congress.gov), and has basic information on the more than 13,000 persons who have served in Congress. It is searchable by name, position, state, party, and year or Congress. Once a biography is displayed, clicking on "Research Collections" or "Bibliography" provides leads, if available, to manuscript collections and a list of books and articles by and about the person.

A printed version of the same resource, under the title *Biographical Directory of the American Congress, 1774–1996* (1997), covers the 1st through 104th Congresses. Although it is not as up to date as the online version, it includes valuable Congress-by-Congress directories of congressional leaders and state delegations. These lists fill over 500 pages, with footnotes indicating deaths, resignations, and other changes during the congressional term.

Two useful sources for background information on members of Congress, both published biennially, are National Journal's *Almanac of American Politics* (www.nationaljournal.com) and *CQ's Politics in America* (library.cqpress.com). These have in-depth biographical portraits with information on voting records and ratings from interest groups, as well as a brief narrative and statistical overview of each congressional district. ProQuest Congressional also includes member profiles, with information by term on bills sponsored and floor votes.

§ 6.4 STATE LEGISLATIVE INFORMATION

Legislative history on the state level is a research area of sharp contrasts. Information on current legislation is widely available online, but documents that might aid in the interpretation of enacted laws can be difficult or impossible to find. It's not that older materials have yet to be digitized, but that many states have never published resources such as committee reports or legislative debates.

Many legislative websites include an introductory guide to the state's lawmaking procedures, a useful starting point in state legislative history research. Even though state legislatures generally follow the federal paradigm, there can be significant differences from state to state.[41] An important first step in studying legislative action

---

(Garrison Nelson & Charles Stewart III eds., 2011). Each includes listings of committee rosters and indexes by representatives' names of committee assignments.

[41] This applies to differences in state courts' thoughts on statutory interpretation and the weight of legislative intent. West's topic number for statutes, 361, and key numbers 1061–1400 (in particular k1241–k1260) can be used to identify state cases addressing this topic. And several law review and bar journal articles illustrate states' approaches to the use of legislative history in statutory interpretation. *See, e.g.,* Abbe

in a particular state is to learn about its procedures and terminology. It may not be immediately apparent that "COW" in Arizona means "Committee of the Whole," or that a "truly agreed" version of a Missouri bill means one that has been passed by both houses of the legislature. Guides and other resources, such as glossaries and charts showing how bills become law, can save considerable time and confusion.[42]

A state guide to legislative research can also be invaluable. Most state legal research guides include discussion of available legislative history resources for their states, noting coverage dates for online resources and material available only in print. Law libraries in the jurisdiction you are researching, particularly the state legislative library, often have legislative history research guides on their websites. The Indiana University Maurer School of Law's "State Legislative History Research Guides Inventory" (law.indiana. libguides.com/state-legislative-history-guides) has links to guides from all fifty states, and law reviews and bar journals frequently publish articles on state legislative history research.[43] In addition to highlighting the various legislative materials available, these guides will often identify other, more comprehensive works on the topic for thornier research questions.

Two useful guides identify the legislative history resources available for each state. Lynn Hellebust's annual *State Legislative Sourcebook: A Resource Guide to Legislative Information in the Fifty States* has detailed information on the legislature and legislative process of each state, with references to available published and

---

R. Gluck, *Statutory Interpretation Methodology as "Law": Oregon's Path-Breaking Interpretive Framework and its Lessons for the Nation*, 47 WILLAMETTE L. REV. 539 (2011), and Adele Hedges & Garrett Gibson, *"Taking the Legislature at its Word": The Role of Legislative History in Statutory Construction in Texas*, ADVOCATE, Summer 2015, at 13.

[42] Chapter 3 of *The Book of the States* (knowledgecenter.csg.org/kc), "State Legislative Branch," has more than two dozen tables summarizing and comparing procedures in the fifty states.

[43] The January–June 2011 issue of *Legal Reference Services Quarterly* (30:1–2) was a special issue on state legislative history, with articles covering Alaska, California, Connecticut, Idaho, Louisiana, Michigan, Minnesota, New Jersey, North Carolina, North Dakota, and Oklahoma. Other relatively recent law review articles, alphabetically by state, include Susan Falk, *Introduction to Researching Alaska Legislative History Materials*, 28 ALASKA L. REV. 279 (2011); Kathryn C. Fitzhugh & Melissa M. Serfass, *Using Legislative History in Arkansas to Determine Legislative Intent: An Examination of Cases and Review of the Sources*, 32 U. ARK. LITTLE ROCK L. REV. 285 (2010); Peggy Lewis & Matt Dawkins, *Researching Legislative History*, 44 COLO. LAW. 33 (2015); Tom Gaylord, *Resources for Illinois Legislative History: The Seven-Year Itch*, 102 ILL. B.J. 450 (2014); Sean J. Kealy, *A Guide to Gathering and Using Legislative History in Massachusetts*, 97 MASS. L. REV. 46 (2016); Candice Spurlin, *The Basics of Legislative History in South Dakota*, 56 S.D. L. REV. 114 (2011); and Debora A. Person, *Legislative Histories and the Practice of Statutory Interpretation in Wyoming*, 10 WYO. L. REV. 559 (2010).

online sources. For each state there is a "best initial contact," as well as information on websites, introductory guides, telephone numbers for ascertaining bill status, bill tracking services, and legislative documents such as session laws and summaries of legislation. Also included are references to newspapers and services that cover political and legal developments in the state. William H. Manz, *Guide to State Legislation, Legislative History, and Administrative Materials* (7th ed. 2008, available on HeinOnline) lists printed and online sources for bills and for legislative history materials, if available, such as hearings, reports, floor debates, and journals.

Most state legislatures do excellent jobs of providing internet access to the current status and text of pending bills. The better websites have several means of searching for bills, and some offer e-mail notification services for when particular bills are acted upon. Some states have other features such as bill summaries, committee minutes, and staff analyses.[44] Illustration 6-8 shows a bill summary from the Michigan Legislature website (www.legislature.mi.gov), with links to major actions and explanatory documents on a bill involving animal fighting; Illustration 6-9 shows the first page of one of these documents, an explanation from the House Fiscal Agency.

Westlaw and Lexis have bill text and tracking databases that can monitor developments in legislatures throughout the country or in a specific state, with coverage in most states back to the early 1990s.[45] For thirty-six states and the District of Columbia, Westlaw also has legislative history documents such as reports, bill analyses, legislative journals, and committee reports back to the late 1990s or early 2000s, linked from state code sections. If a statute was enacted or amended by an act for which documents are available, Legislative History Materials appears as an option under the History tab. As with federal statutes, however, links to documents do not necessarily mean that there is relevant information on the particular statutory section.

---

[44] The National Conference of State Legislatures (www.ncsl.org) maintains a "Legislative Websites" page (linked at the bottom of its homepage) that allows you to go directly to a specific state page or to create a customized list of links for specific content (such as bill information or legislator biographies) from all states or a selected list of states. LLSDC's Legislative Source Book includes a "State Legislatures, State Laws, and State Regulations: Website Links and Telephone Numbers" page (www.llsdc.org/state-legislation), useful for quick links.

[45] Researchers in university and public libraries may have access to LexisNexis's bill-tracking and other legislative information through its State Net website (www.lexisnexis.com/en-us/products/state-net.page).

Senate Bill 0416 (2017) 🔖 rss?

Friendly Link: http://legislature.mi.gov/doc.aspx?2017-SB-0416
Public Act 461 of 2018 (Effective: 3/29/2019) Find this PA in the MCL

Sponsors
Tory Rocca (district 10)
Rick Jones, Ian Conyers, Steven Bieda, Curtis Hertel, Margaret O'Brien, Marty Knollenberg
(click name to see bills sponsored by that person)

Categories
Animals: animal shelters; Animals: dogs; Crimes: animals;

Animals; animal shelters; adoption of certain seized animals used in fighting operations; allow, and make other revisions.
Amends sec. 49 of 1931 PA 328 (MCL 750.49).

Bill Documents
Bill Document Formatting Information
[x]
The following bill formatting applies to the 2017-2018 session:
- New language in an amendatory bill will be shown in **BOLD AND UPPERCASE**.
- Language to be removed will be stricken.
- Amendments made by the House will be blue with square brackets, such as: [House amended text].
- Amendments made by the Senate will be red with double greater/lesser than symbols, such as: <<Senate amended text>>.
(gray icons indicate that the action did not occur or that the document is not available)

Documents

Senate Introduced Bill
Introduced bills appear as they were introduced and reflect no subsequent amendments or changes.

As Passed by the Senate
As Passed by the Senate is the bill, as introduced, that includes any adopted Senate amendments.

As Passed by the House
As Passed by the House is the bill, as received from the Senate, that includes any adopted House amendments.

Public Act
Public Act is a bill that has become law.

Bill Analysis
House Fiscal Agency Analysis
Summary as Reported From House Committee/Enacted Version (12/18/2018)
This document analyzes: SB416

Senate Fiscal Analysis
SUMMARY OF INTRODUCED BILL IN COMMITTEE (Date Completed: 6-5-17)
This document analyzes: SB0416

SUMMARY OF BILL REPORTED FROM COMMITTEE (Date Completed: 6-8-17)
This document analyzes: SB0416

ANALYSIS AS REPORTED FROM COMMITTEE (Date Completed: 9-12-17)
This document analyzes: SB0416

History
(House actions in lowercase, Senate actions in UPPERCASE)

Date ▲	Journal	Action
5/31/2017	SJ 53 Pg. 733	INTRODUCED BY SENATOR TORY ROCCA
5/31/2017	SJ 53 Pg. 733	REFERRED TO COMMITTEE ON JUDICIARY
6/8/2017	SJ 56 Pg. 778	REPORTED FAVORABLY WITHOUT AMENDMENT
6/8/2017	SJ 56 Pg. 778	COMMITTEE RECOMMENDED IMMEDIATE EFFECT
6/8/2017	SJ 56 Pg. 778	REFERRED TO COMMITTEE OF THE WHOLE
6/12/2018	SJ 60 Pg. 1496	REPORTED BY COMMITTEE OF THE WHOLE FAVORABLY WITHOUT AMENDMENT(S)
6/12/2018	SJ 60 Pg. 1496	PLACED ON ORDER OF THIRD READING
6/12/2018	SJ 60 Pg. 1514	RULES SUSPENDED
6/12/2018	SJ 60 Pg. 1514	PLACED ON IMMEDIATE PASSAGE
6/12/2018	SJ 60 Pg. 1520	PASSED ROLL CALL # 513 YEAS 36 NAYS 0 EXCUSED 1 NOT VOTING 0
6/12/2018	HJ 59 Pg. 1880	received on 06/12/2018

Illustration 6-8. A Michigan Legislature bill summary.

Legislative Analysis

ANIMAL FIGHTING

Mary Ann Cleary, Director
Phone: (517) 373-8080
http://www.house.mi.gov/hfa

Senate Bill 356 as passed by the Senate
Sponsor: Sen. Rick Jones

Senate Bill 357 as passed by the Senate
Sponsor: Sen. Bert Johnson

Senate Bill 358 as passed by the Senate
Sponsor: Sen. Steven Bieda

House Committee: Judiciary
Senate Committee: Judiciary

First Analysis (2-1-12)

BRIEF SUMMARY: Senate Bill 356 would subject the property of a person involved in animal fighting to forfeiture. Senate Bill 357 would declare a building, vehicle, boat, aircraft, or other place where animal fighting takes place to be a nuisance. Senate Bill 358 would include animal fighting as a predicate offense for racketeering.

FISCAL IMPACT: The bill would have an indeterminate fiscal impact on state and local units as discussed in more detail later in the analysis.

THE APPARENT PROBLEM:

Animal fighting (dog fighting, cockfighting, and dog-hog fighting, where dogs fight wild hogs) continues to be a growing problem in the state, with dog fighting particularly a problem in the greater Detroit area. Besides undue the cruelty and suffering inflicted on animals, studies show a relationship between cruelty to animals and perpetrating violent crimes against people. In one study conducted by the Chicago Police Department, as reported by the Humane Society of the United States, 65 percent of people charged with animal abuse crimes went on to commit violent crimes against people. In addition, children who witness animal cruelty often suffer emotional effects for a lifetime.

In an effort to stem the rise in animal fighting rings, some feel the state's laws need to be amended. For instance, current laws limit prosecution to a specific incident of animal fighting. In one Wayne County case, though there was evidence that a man had been conducting dog fights for years in the same house, law enforcement agencies were restricted by current laws to single incidents of dog fighting rather than being able to shut down the dog fighting enterprise.

In addition, much of animal fighting is related to illegal gambling and drugs. As such, some believe that those who run animal fighting rings should be prosecuted under the state's RICO laws, usually reserved for criminal enterprises such as gambling rings,

**Illustration 6-9. The first page of a Michigan
legislative history document.**

Govtrack.us (www.govtrack.us) is a free website that allows users to search and track pending legislation across all fifty states. The subscription site FiscalNote (www.fiscalnote.com) adds more sophisticated analysis tools.

Researchers needing to interpret statutes enacted before the late 1990s face a more difficult task. Bills from older sessions can be hard to locate. Almost every state has a legislative journal, but very few of these actually include transcripts of debates. Only a few states publish committee reports, and even fewer publish hearings.[46] The materials that are available vary widely from state to state. Sometimes they are not published either in print or online, and can be accessed only at the state capitol. Some states have "bill jackets" with legislative information, and some have microform records or tape recordings of sessions. In many instances, contemporary newspaper accounts may be the best available source of information about a sponsor's statements or proceedings. A few states have legislative history websites providing some retrospective coverage.[47] Official state agencies responsible for recommending and drafting new legislation, such as law revision commissions, judicial councils, and legislative councils, often publish annual or topical reports summarizing their work. For recommendations enacted into law, these reports may be valuable legislative history documentation. State legal research or legislative history guides are good sources of information on such agencies.

Contacting legislative staff members may be the quickest way to get information on current legislative activity, but state legislature websites vary in the extent of directory information they provide. Official state manuals (sometimes called *blue books*), published annually or biennially by most states, generally have information on state legislatures such as organization, members, committees, and staffs. These directories are listed in the *State Legislative Sourcebook* with other reference sources for each state.

---

[46] "As those who seek to determine the 'policy' informing significant state statutes continue to find, it is frequently impossible to determine the pertinent subjective intent of a state legislature from any source. Indifference to the documentation of legislative history at the state level has been, and continues to be to this day, a basic feature of American legal culture." Hans W. Baade, *"Original Intent" in Historical Perspective: Some Critical Glosses*, 69 TEX. L. REV. 1001, 1085 (1991) (footnote omitted).

[47] Pennsylvania (www.legis.state.pa.us), for example, has a "Legislation Enacted Since 1975" link to summaries for more than 30 years of acts, with copies of bill versions and references to remarks in the House and Senate Journal if any. Members of the Jenkins Law Library (www.jenkinslaw.org), a private library in Philadelphia, have access to a collection of compiled legislative histories for more than 2,500 Pennsylvania acts back as far as 1836.

The directory for a specific state is likely to have the most detailed information, but several multistate directories are also published. The Council of State Governments publishes an annual three-part *CSG State Directory*, covering legislatures in *Directory I: Elective Officials* and *Directory II: Legislative Leadership, Committees and Staff*. General multistate government directories such as Leadership Connect's *State Yellow Book* (www.leadershipconnect.io) also include coverage of the legislative branches, with information on members and committee assignments.

In twenty-four states, statutes or constitutional amendments can be not only introduced by the legislature but also submitted directly to voters through the initiative process. Twenty-three states permit popular referendums, or ballot measures to reject measures enacted by the legislature. Information on the enactment and intent of these measures may not appear in the standard legislative history sources. The Initiative & Referendum Institute at the University of Southern California (www.iandrinstitute.org) has state-by-state information on the history and procedures of popular ballot measures, with links to state-specific sites. M. Dane Waters, *Initiative and Referendum Almanac* (2003) has a comprehensive history as well as lists and charts tracking the use of these processes.[48] *Exploring Initiative and Referendum Law: Selected State Research Guides* (Beth Williams ed., 2007) explains the initiative processes and research procedures in twenty-three states.[49]

Legislative materials are essential tools both in interpreting statutes and in monitoring current legal developments, but legislative history documents are hardly the only resources of value in understanding statutes. Court decisions may provide authoritative judicial interpretations, and even secondary sources may be persuasive in determining the scope and meaning of an act. Many statutes are implemented by more detailed regulations and decisions from administrative agencies. These administrative materials, to be discussed in Part III, are key elements in understanding the application of the underlying statutes.

---

[48] For a briefer overview of these processes, see Frederick J. Boehmke & Joshua J. Dyck, *Initiative and Referendum, in* GUIDE TO STATE POLITICS AND POLICY 75–86 (Richard G. Niemi & Joshua J. Dyck eds., 2014).

[49] *Exploring Initiative and Referendum Law* was published both as a monograph and as 26 LEGAL REFERENCE SERVICES Q., nos. 3/4 (2007). California is omitted from its coverage but was the focus of Tobe Liebert, *Researching California Ballot Measures*, 90 LAW LIBR. J. 27 (1998).

Part III
THE EXECUTIVE BRANCH

Part III

Chapter 7

THE PRESIDENCY

Table of Sections

Under the American constitutional system, Congress has the power to enact laws. Enforcement of those laws, however, falls to the executive branch. The next three chapters address the lawmaking and enforcement powers of the executive branch, an area commonly known as administrative law. This chapter focuses on the President, Chapter 8 deals with the regulations and other legal documents of the federal executive departments and independent agencies, and Chapter 9 addresses administrative law at the state level.

Article II, section 1 of the Constitution begins simply: "The executive Power shall be vested in a President of the United States of America." Section 2 gives the President inherent powers as the nation's agent in foreign affairs and its military commander and provides that the President appoints judges, ambassadors, and numerous other government officials with the advice and consent of the Senate.[1]

These powers alone give the President a strong position from which to shape government policy, but the main source of presidential power is in section 3, specifying that the President "shall take Care that the Laws be faithfully executed." In fulfilling these various roles, the President issues executive orders, proclamations, and other documents of legal effect. In recent years, particularly during periods of congressional gridlock, the President's unilateral action has been the subject of numerous complaints about violation

---

[1] A 2012 Congressional Research Service report estimated that at least 1,200 government positions require Senate approval. MAEVE P. CAREY, CONG. RESEARCH SERV., R41872, PRESIDENTIAL APPOINTMENTS, THE SENATE'S CONFIRMATION PROCESS, AND CHANGES MADE IN THE 112TH CONGRESS (2012) (crsreports.congress.gov/product/pdf/R/R41872).

of constitutional norms.[2] Background information on the presidency is available in numerous sources. Two of the more comprehensive reference works are *Encyclopedia of the American Presidency* (Leonard W. Levy & Louis Fisher eds., 1993) and *Guide to the Presidency and the Executive Branch* (Michael Nelson ed., 5th ed. 2013). Both of these works cover a wide range of political and historical aspects of the presidency, and both include reference materials such as tables listing cabinet members and other presidential appointees. Presidential lawmaking powers more specifically are discussed in Louis Fisher, *The Law of the Executive Branch: Presidential Power* (2014), and Harold J. Krent, *Presidential Powers* (2005).[3]

§ 7.1   EXECUTIVE ORDERS AND PROCLAMATIONS

Two basic forms of executive fiat are used to perform presidential functions pursuant to statutory authority or inherent powers. *Executive orders* are issued to government officials and cover a wide range of topics, and *proclamations* are general announcements of policy issued to the nation as a whole. The two types of documents have substantially the same legal effect.

Executive orders are frequently used by presidents because they can effect change without the elaborate procedures required by legislation or regulations.[4] It was by executive order that the armed forces were desegregated in 1948, but executive orders were also used to send Japanese-Americans to internment camps during World War

---

[2]   *See, e.g.*, Ted Cruz, *The Obama Administration's Unprecedent Lawlessness*, 38 HARV. J.L. & PUB. POL'Y 63 (2015); David M. Driesen, *President Trump's Executive Orders and the Rule of Law*, 87 UMKC L. REV. 489 (2019).

[3]   The processes of sanctioning and removing the president under Article II, section 4, have been the subject of an extensive literature in recent years. *See, e.g.*, CHARLES L. BLACK, JR. & PHILIP BOBBITT, IMPEACHMENT: A HANDBOOK (2018); ANDREW COAN, PROSECUTING THE PRESIDENT: HOW SPECIAL PROSECUTORS HOLD PRESIDENTS ACCOUNTABLE AND PROTECT THE RULE OF LAW (2019); MICHAEL J. GERHARDT, IMPEACHMENT: WHAT EVERYONE NEEDS TO KNOW (2018); and LAURENCE TRIBE & JOSHUA MATZ, TO END A PRESIDENCY: THE POWER OF IMPEACHMENT (2018).

[4]   "In contrast to legislation or agency regulation, there are almost no legally enforceable procedural requirements that the president must satisfy before issuing (or repealing) an executive order or other presidential directive. That, no doubt, is central to their appeal to presidents." Kevin M. Stack, *The Statutory President*, 90 IOWA L. REV. 539, 552–53 (2005). Despite the lack of formal requirements, executive orders are usually issued after an extensive vetting process by the relevant executive departments. This process, however, has not always been followed. *See* W. Neil Eggleston & Amanda Elbogen, *The Trump Administration and the Breakdown of Intra-Executive Legal Process*, 127 YALE L.J.F. 825 (2018).

II and to prohibit citizens of several countries in 2017 from traveling to the United States.[5]

Proclamations are commonly associated with ceremonial occasions such as observance of National School Lunch Week, but some address substantive issues such as trade policy or the size of national monuments.

Executive orders and proclamations are published in the *Federal Register*, the U.S. government's official daily publication, as required by law.[6] They are numbered sequentially as they are issued, in separate series, and these numbers are the official and permanent means of identifying the documents. Illustration 7-1 shows the first page of an executive order establishing a task force to fight wildlife trafficking, Exec. Order No. 13,648, 78 Fed. Reg. 40,621 (July 1, 2013).

Presidential documents in the *Federal Register* since 1936 are available online from the Government Publishing Office's GovInfo portal (www.govinfo.gov), as well as in Lexis and Westlaw's Federal Register databases. Westlaw also has a Presidential Documents database with executive orders since 1936 and other presidential documents since 1984. On Westlaw, the display of proclamations and executive orders includes a Citing References tab, with links to amendments and citations in court decisions, secondary sources, administrative materials, and court documents.

---

[5] Presidential use of executive orders and other directives has been the focus of several recent books, including MICHELLE BELCO & BRANDON ROTTINGHAUS, THE DUAL EXECUTIVE: UNILATERAL ORDERS IN A SEPARATE AND SHARED POWER SYSTEM (2017); PHILLIP J. COOPER, BY ORDER OF THE PRESIDENT: THE USE AND ABUSE OF EXECUTIVE DIRECT ACTION (2d ed. 2014); and DANIEL P. GITTERMAN, CALLING THE SHOTS: THE PRESIDENT, EXECUTIVE ORDERS, AND PUBLIC POLICY (2017). Two Congressional Research Service publications also have background information. JOHN CONTRUBIS, CONG. RESEARCH SERV., 95-772A, EXECUTIVE ORDERS AND PROCLAMATIONS (1999) (fas.org/sgp/crs/misc/95-772.pdf) focuses on the two major types of documents, and HAROLD C. RELYEA, CONG. RESEARCH SERV., 98–611 GOV, PRESIDENTIAL DIRECTIVES: BACKGROUND AND OVERVIEW (2008) (fas.org/sgp/crs/misc/98-611.pdf) provides a broader overview of several presidential lawmaking instruments. On standards in judicial review of executive orders, see Lisa Manheim & Kathryn A. Watts, *Reviewing Presidential Orders*, 86 U. CHI. L. REV. 1743 (2019).

[6] 44 U.S.C. § 1505.

40621

Federal Register
Vol. 78, No. 129
Friday, July 5, 2013

Presidential Documents

Title 3—

The President

Executive Order 13648 of July 1, 2013

Combating Wildlife Trafficking

By the authority vested in me as President by the Constitution and the laws of the United States of America, and in order to address the significant effects of wildlife trafficking on the national interests of the United States, I hereby order as follows:

Section 1. *Policy.* The poaching of protected species and the illegal trade in wildlife and their derivative parts and products (together known as "wildlife trafficking") represent an international crisis that continues to escalate. Poaching operations have expanded beyond small-scale, opportunistic actions to coordinated slaughter commissioned by armed and organized criminal syndicates. The survival of protected wildlife species such as elephants, rhinos, great apes, tigers, sharks, tuna, and turtles has beneficial economic, social, and environmental impacts that are important to all nations. Wildlife trafficking reduces those benefits while generating billions of dollars in illicit revenues each year, contributing to the illegal economy, fueling instability, and undermining security. Also, the prevention of trafficking of live animals helps us control the spread of emerging infectious diseases. For these reasons, it is in the national interest of the United States to combat wildlife trafficking.

In order to enhance domestic efforts to combat wildlife trafficking, to assist foreign nations in building capacity to combat wildlife trafficking, and to assist in combating transnational organized crime, executive departments and agencies (agencies) shall take all appropriate actions within their authority, including the promulgation of rules and regulations and the provision of technical and financial assistance, to combat wildlife trafficking in accordance with the following objectives:

(a) in appropriate cases, the United States shall seek to assist those governments in anti-wildlife trafficking activities when requested by foreign nations experiencing trafficking of protected wildlife;

(b) the United States shall promote and encourage the development and enforcement by foreign nations of effective laws to prohibit the illegal taking of, and trade in, these species and to prosecute those who engage in wildlife trafficking, including by building capacity;

(c) in concert with the international community and partner organizations, the United States shall seek to combat wildlife trafficking: and

(d) the United States shall seek to reduce the demand for illegally traded wildlife, both at home and abroad, while allowing legal and legitimate commerce involving wildlife.

Sec. 2. *Establishment.* There is established a Presidential Task Force on Wildlife Trafficking (Task Force), to be co-chaired by the Secretary of State, Secretary of the Interior, and the Attorney General (Co-Chairs), or their designees, who shall report to the President through the National Security Advisor. The Task Force shall develop and implement a National Strategy for Combating Wildlife Trafficking in accordance with the objectives outlined in section 1 of this order, consistent with section 4 of this order.

Sec. 3. *Membership.* (a) In addition to the Co-Chairs, the Task Force shall include designated senior-level representatives from:

(i) the Department of the Treasury;

(ii) the Department of Defense;

**Illustration 7-1. An executive order as published
in the *Federal Register*.**

At the end of each year executive orders and proclamations are compiled and published as Title 3 of the *Code of Federal Regulations* (*CFR*), the annual codification of agency rules in force. This becomes the standard source for these documents.[7] Documents from the years 1936 to 1975 have been recompiled into multiyear hardcover editions, and all volumes since 1936 are available online as part of HeinOnline's U.S. Presidential Library.

The most comprehensive retrospective source for presidential documents is ProQuest Executive Orders and Presidential Proclamations 1789–Present, available in ProQuest Congressional. This collection includes PDFs of numerous historic orders, many of them unnumbered, before the beginning of *Federal Register* and *CFR* publication.

The American Presidency Project at the University of California, Santa Barbara (www.presidency.ucsb.edu) provides free online access to executive orders dating back to 1826 and proclamations back to 1789, as well as a wide range of other documents such as public papers, signing statements, inaugural addresses, and State of the Union messages.[8] It does not, however, include *Federal Register* or *CFR* citations.[9]

It is important to know whether an executive order is still in force.[10] The Office of the Federal Register website has a disposition table of all executive orders since 1937 (www.archives.gov/federal-register/executive-orders/), with information on their amendment, revocation, and current status. For executive orders since 1993, the site also includes subject indexes and links to the full text of documents.

Many executive orders are also reprinted in the notes following related sections of the *United States Code*. This is an important

---

[7] Both *The Bluebook* and the *ALWD Guide* require citation to the *CFR* if a document appears therein, or to the *Federal Register* if not. THE BLUEBOOK: A UNIFORM SYSTEM OF CITATION tbl. T1.2 (21st ed. 2020); ALWD GUIDE TO LEGAL CITATION R. 18.9(b) (6th ed. 2017).

[8] State of the Union messages through 1966 are available in print in the three-volume set THE STATE OF THE UNION MESSAGES OF THE PRESIDENTS, 1790–1966 (Fred L. Israel ed., 1966).

[9] Older documents can also be identified in the CIS INDEX TO PRESIDENTIAL EXECUTIVE ORDERS AND PROCLAMATIONS (1987) (covering 1787–1983) (catalog. hathitrust.org/Record/000402273), which is accompanied by a microfiche set of all documents indexed. HeinOnline provides access to two earlier guides edited by Clifford L. Lord, PRESIDENTIAL EXECUTIVE ORDERS (1944) and LIST AND INDEX OF PRESIDENTIAL EXECUTIVE ORDERS: UNNUMBERED SERIES (1789–1941) (1979).

[10] A short guide to modification or revocation of executive orders can be found in TODD GARVEY, CONG. RESEARCH SERV., RS20846, EXECUTIVE ORDERS: ISSUANCE, MODIFICATION, AND REVOCATION (2014) (crsreports.congress.gov/product/pdf/RS/RS 20846). *See also* Sharece Thrower, *To Revoke or Not Revoke? The Political Determinants of Executive Order Longevity*, 61 AM. J. POL. SCI. 642 (2017).

source, if only because *The Bluebook* requires a parallel U.S.C. citation "if also therein."[11] The Tables volumes in each version of the code list presidential documents by number and indicate where they can be found.

Executive orders and proclamations are also reprinted in *U.S. Code Congressional and Administrative News* and *USCS Advance*. USCCAN bound volumes have reprinted all orders and proclamations since 1943. Proclamations, but not executive orders, are also printed in *Statutes at Large* (with retrospective coverage back to 1791 in an appendix in volume eleven).

The National Archives website includes a *Codification of Presidential Proclamations and Executive Orders* (www.archives.gov/federal-register/codification/), which arranges proclamations and orders into fifty chapters by subject. It contains executive orders and proclamations of general applicability and continuing effect issued from April 13, 1945, to January 20, 1989, with amendments incorporated into the texts of documents.

§ 7.2   OTHER PRESIDENTIAL DOCUMENTS

While executive orders and proclamations are the most common forms of presidential directives, several other presidential documents have legal effect. The President issues administrative orders, transmits messages to Congress, and makes executive agreements with other countries.

Memoranda and Directives. A variety of other presidential documents are printed in the *Federal Register* along with executive orders and proclamations, but are not included in either numbered series. Many of these documents deal with foreign affairs and homeland security issues. They are reprinted in the annual cumulation of 3 C.F.R. (The President) in a separate section following executive orders.[12]

Some presidential directives relating to national security issues are not published at all in the *Federal Register* or *CFR*. The Federal Register Act requires only that proclamations and executive orders be published, so other documents can be used to advance presidential goals with less public scrutiny.[13] These have a variety of names such

---

[11] THE BLUEBOOK: A UNIFORM SYSTEM OF CITATION tbl. T1.2 (21st ed. 2020). The *ALWD Guide* says you "may include" a parallel citation. ALWD GUIDE TO LEGAL CITATION R. 18.9(e) (6th ed. 2017).

[12] Presidential memoranda are the focus of Kenneth S. Lowande, *After the Orders: Presidential Memoranda and Unilateral Action*, 44 PRES. STUD. Q. 724 (2014).

[13] "Presidents have learned since at least the Truman administration that, by using labels other than those specified in the Federal Register Act, they can avoid publication of statements issued with the formal authority of the presidency behind

as Homeland Security Presidential Directives or Presidential Policy Directives. These directives are often not easy to obtain, but a Federation of American Scientists website (www.fas.org/irp/offdocs/direct.htm) lists the designations and directives used by presidents since Truman and hosts digital copies of many of the documents. Directives and related documents are also available through the subscription Digital National Security Archive (www.proquest.com).[14]

Reorganization Plans. A reorganization plan consisting of a presidential proposal to transfer or abolish agency functions was a mechanism used from 1946 to 1979. Several major agencies, including the Environmental Protection Agency and the Department of Health, Education, and Welfare, were initially created by reorganization plans.

A reorganization plan became law automatically unless either chamber of Congress passed a resolution disapproving it, but in 1983 the Supreme Court found such one-house legislative vetoes to be unconstitutional.[15] The following year Congress enacted a law ratifying and affirming each reorganization plan implemented to that date, and providing that reorganization plans could only take effect if transmitted to Congress by the end of 1984.[16] Older reorganization plans, however, remain relevant in interpreting the scope of agency authority.

Reorganization plans were designated by year and plan number within that year, and were published in the *Federal Register,* Title 3 of the *CFR,* and the *Statutes at Large.*[17] Many are reprinted in all three versions of the *United States Code* (in appendices to Title 5 in the *U.S. Code* and *USCA,* and following 5 U.S.C.S. § 903). *USCA* and *USCS* include notes, presidential messages, and executive orders

---

them." Phillip J. Cooper, *Power Tools for an Effective and Responsible Presidency,* 29 ADMIN. & SOC'Y 529, 544 (1997).

[14] Some directives have been published in NATIONAL SECURITY DIRECTIVES OF THE REAGAN AND BUSH ADMINISTRATIONS: THE DECLASSIFIED HISTORY OF U.S. POLITICAL AND MILITARY POLICY, 1981–1991 (Christopher Simpson ed., 1995), and H. COMM. ON HOMELAND SECURITY, 110TH CONG., COMPILATION OF HOMELAND SECURITY PRESIDENTIAL DIRECTIVES (HPSD) (Comm. Print 2008).

[15] *Immigration and Naturalization Service v. Chadha,* 462 U.S. 919 (1983).

[16] Reorganization Act Amendments of 1984, Pub. L. No. 98–614, § 2(a), 98 Stat. 3192, 3193 (codified at 5 U.S.C. § 905(b)). A lone exception since 1984 is Reorganization Plan for the Department of Homeland Security, H.R. Doc. No. 108–16 (2003), which was mandated by the Homeland Security Act of 2002, Pub. L. No. 107–296, § 1502, 116 Stat. 2135, 2308. Congress expressly exempted this plan from § 905(b)'s prohibition.

[17] When submitted to Congress, reorganization plans were printed in the *Congressional Record* and in the House and Senate Documents series. These are the best sources for plans rejected by Congress.

relating to the plans, and are often the most useful research sources.[18]

Messages to Congress. Presidential messages to Congress may propose new legislation, explain vetoes, transmit reports or other documents, or convey information about the state of national affairs or some matter of concern. Messages are published in the *Congressional Record* and as House Documents. Messages proposing legislation may have some value in determining the intent of laws that are enacted as a result.

Presidential statements upon signing legislation into law have been discussed in the preceding chapter. These often provide the President's interpretation of ambiguous or disputed provisions. Their relevance in legislative history research is controversial, but they certainly provide guidance to executive agencies in how to carry out their duties under newly enacted legislation.

Executive Agreements. The President makes agreements with other countries, under the authority to conduct foreign affairs. Unlike treaties, executive agreements do not require the advice and consent of the Senate. In recent years, more and more diplomatic arrangements have been made through this more expeditious method. Because the purposes and publication methods of executive agreements are basically the same as treaties, the two forms of international agreements will be discussed together in Chapter 17.

Informal Communications. While official documents are the binding embodiments of legal action, increasingly presidents use other means to announce decisions to the public. President Trump used Twitter to announce major policy actions such as a ban of transgender persons from the military and a revocation of California's power to regulate emission standards.[19] Monitoring

---

[18] Reorganization plans that concern more than one agency now need congressional approval, but presidents continue to seek to restructure the federal government. Pursuant to Exec. Order No. 13,781, 3 C.F.R. 312 (2017), the Trump administration in 2018 released a plan that proposed to merge the Departments of Education and Labor and consolidate numerous other functions. EXECUTIVE OFFICE OF THE PRESIDENT, DELIVERING GOVERNMENT SOLUTIONS IN THE 21ST CENTURY: REFORM PLAN AND REORGANIZATION RECOMMENDATIONS (2018) (www.whitehouse. gov/wp-content/uploads/2018/06/Government-Reform-and-Reorg-Plan.pdf) [https:// perma.cc/H5NV-BG7E]. The report recognized that "[w]hile some of the recommendations identified in this volume can be achieved via Executive administrative action, more significant changes will require legislative action as well." *Id.* at 4.

[19] Trump used his Twitter account "to announce, describe, and defend his policies; to promote his Administration's legislative agenda; to announce official decisions; to engage with foreign political leaders; [and] to publicize state visits," among other purposes. "He uses the Account to announce 'matters related to official government business,' including high-level White House and cabinet-level staff changes as well as changes to major national policies." *Knight First Amendment Inst. v. Trump,* 928 F.3d 226, 231, 235–36 (2d Cir. 2019) (quoting Stipulation at 14, *Knight First Amendment*

presidential use of social media, or following news sources that report on such developments, is essential in maintaining current awareness of presidential action.

§ 7.3   COMPILATIONS OF PRESIDENTIAL PAPERS

The most comprehensive source for current presidential material is the *Daily Compilation of Presidential Documents*, which succeeded the *Weekly Compilation of Presidential Documents* in January 2009. The *Daily Compilation* includes nominations, announcements, and transcripts of speeches and press conferences, as well as orders, proclamations, signing statements, and other legally significant documents. Govinfo has *Daily Compilation* and *Weekly Compilation* issues back to 1993, and HeinOnline has comprehensive coverage back to the first *Weekly Compilation* volume in 1965.

Public Papers of the Presidents is an official publication cumulating the contents of the daily or weekly *Compilation of Presidential Documents*. Volumes are published twice a year and cover periods of approximately six months. Series of volumes have been published for Herbert Hoover and for all presidents after Franklin D. Roosevelt.[20] Govinfo and HeinOnline's U.S. Presidential Library both have the entire set of *Public Papers* volumes.[21]

While Franklin D. Roosevelt's papers have not been included in the official series and are not available on Govinfo, they were commercially published as *The Public Papers and Addresses of Franklin D. Roosevelt* (Samuel I. Rosenman ed., 1938–50, available in HeinOnline's U.S. Presidential Library). The papers of earlier presidents are available in various forms. A comprehensive official collection was published at the end of the 19th century, *A Compilation of the Messages and Papers of the Presidents, 1789–1897* (James D. Richardson ed., 1896–99); numerous later editions under the same title were commercially published, updating the set into the 1920s. Several editions are available on HeinOnline.

Institute v. Trump, 302 F. Supp. 3d 541 (S.D.N.Y. 2018) (No. 17–cv–5205). *See also* Kristina T. Bodnar, Note, *"Sheer Force of Tweet": Testing the Limits of Executive Power on Twitter*, 10 CASE W. RES. J.L. TECH. & INTERNET 1 (2019).

[20] The official set contains only annual indexes, but the commercially published CUMULATED INDEXES TO THE PUBLIC PAPERS OF THE PRESIDENTS OF THE UNITED STATES (1977–date) provides single-volume coverage of each administration.

[21] The American Presidency Project (www.presidency.ucsb.edu) also has a comprehensive collection, but without the volume and page references needed for legal citations.

Chapter 8

FEDERAL AGENCY LAW

Table of Sections

The executive is one of the three coordinate branches of government, but historically its lawmaking role was limited to orders and regulations needed to carry out the legislature's mandates. With the modern growth of government bureaucracy, however, the rules created by executive agencies have become legal sources with pervasive impact. In many aspects of modern society, administrative law plays a powerful role and can be more immediately relevant to day-to-day legal practice than either statutory or judge-made law.

Administrative law takes several forms, as agencies can act both somewhat like legislatures and somewhat like courts. They may promulgate regulations governing activities within their jurisdiction, or they may decide matters involving particular litigants on a case-by-case basis. Lawmaking approaches and available resources vary by agency and subject area. Part of becoming an expert in an area of law such as banking or immigration is learning about the idiosyncrasies of its administrative law materials.

Several major treatises are published on administrative law. They focus primarily on judicial review of agency decision-making, but most also cover topics such as historical developments, rulemaking and adjudication procedures, and access to government information. The most frequently cited work in the field is Richard J.

Pierce, Jr. & Kristin E. Hickman, *Administrative Law Treatise* (6th ed. 2018–date, available on Wolters Kluwer's Cheetah platform). The treatise's original author, Kenneth Culp Davis (1908–2003), is generally considered the founding father of administrative law.[1]

Two other multi-volume treatises are Charles H. Koch, Jr. & Richard Murphy, *Administrative Law and Practice* (3d ed. 2010–date), and Jacob A. Stein et al., *Administrative Law* (1977–date). The Koch & Murphy treatise is available on Westlaw, and the Stein treatise on Lexis. Single-volume texts written specifically for student use include Alfred C. Aman, Jr. & William T. Mayton, *Administrative Law* (3d ed. 2014) and Richard J. Pierce, Jr., Sidney A. Shapiro & Paul R. Verkuil, *Administrative Law and Process* (6th ed. 2014).

Two sets focus on procedural aspects of administrative practice. *West's Federal Administrative Practice* (3d & 4th eds. 1996–date) has chapters devoted to practice before specific federal agencies, and it includes forms as well as explanatory text. The voluminous *Federal Procedure, Lawyers Edition* (1981–date) provides guidance on practice before agencies and in court, and its accompanying set *Federal Procedural Forms, Lawyers Edition* (1975–date) includes numerous examples of official agency forms in addition to court documents. All three of these works are available on Westlaw.[2]

The leading specialized journal in the field is *Administrative Law Review*, published by American University in conjunction with the American Bar Association's Section of Administrative Law and Regulatory Practice. The ABA also publishes an annual *Developments in Administrative Law and Regulatory Practice*; all but the most recent volume are available in HeinOnline's Law Journal Library.

§ 8.1   AGENCY INFORMATION

Fifteen cabinet departments and dozens of independent agencies, boards, commissions, and advisory committees report to the

---

[1] On Davis's death, the chairman of the ABA administrative law section, William Funk, said that his "shadow falls over virtually all that administrative lawyers do. To say he was a giant in his field is like saying Mount Everest is a big mountain." Jack Williams, *Kenneth Culp Davis, 94; Pioneer in Administrative Law*, SAN DIEGO UNION-TRIBUNE, Sept. 19, 2003, at B-5.

[2] A short summary of administrative procedure from the ABA can be found in A BLACKLETTER STATEMENT OF FEDERAL ADMINISTRATIVE LAW (2d ed. 2013). FEDERAL ADMINISTRATIVE PROCEDURE SOURCEBOOK (sourcebook.acus.gov), an online resource published by the ABA and the Administrative Conference of the United States (ACUS), contains the texts of major statutes in the area, each accompanied by a brief overview, notes on legislative history, and a bibliography of government documents, books, and articles.

President.[3] Although executive agencies have existed in this country since its founding,[4] the expansion of administrative law began in the late 19th century as the government sought to deal with the increasingly complex problems of industrialized society. The creation of new independent regulatory commissions and the expansion of existing agencies provided the necessary expertise and specialization. The first of these new agencies was the Interstate Commerce Commission, created in 1887 to regulate railroads.

Other regulatory agencies, such as the Federal Reserve Board and the Federal Trade Commission, joined the ICC in the early 20th century. The real growth in administrative law, however, came in the 1930s as Congress created new entities to administer its New Deal programs. Major new agencies included the Federal Communications Commission, Federal Deposit Insurance Corporation, National Labor Relations Board, and Securities and Exchange Commission.

A third boom in administrative law occurred in the 1960s and 1970s, with the creation of new cabinet departments such as Housing and Urban Development and specialized agencies such as the Consumer Product Safety Commission and Environmental Protection Agency. The regulatory landscape continues to evolve. The Department of Homeland Security was created in 2002 and the Consumer Financial Protection Bureau in 2010.

When researching administrative law, it is important to determine what agency has jurisdiction and to develop a preliminary understanding of its structure and functions. In some situations the relevant agency is obvious, but in others it may require background analysis or a close reading of statutory and judicial sources to determine an agency's role. It is then important to develop an understanding of the agency's legal mandates, whether from specific statutes or from more general enabling legislation or executive action, to understand more fully the scope and purpose of the documents it produces.

---

[3] Cabinet departments and independent agencies operate under similar legal principles and create law in similar ways. The main distinction between the forms of organization is the degree of insulation from direct presidential supervision. For an overview, see Dominique Custos, *The Rulemaking Power of Independent Regulatory Agencies*, 54 AM. J. COMP. L. 615 (2006). On temporary advisory bodies, see LOUIS W. BOOKHEIM, REPORTS OF U.S. PRESIDENTIAL COMMISSIONS AND OTHER ADVISORY BODIES: A BIBLIOGRAPHICAL LISTING (2017), available on HeinOnline.

[4] The first cabinet departments were created by Congress in 1789. The Department of Foreign Affairs was created by the Act of July 27, 1789, ch. 4, 1 Stat. 28 (and renamed the Department of State less than three months later by the Act of Sept. 15, 1789, ch. 14, 1 Stat. 68); the Department of War by the Act of Aug. 5, 1789, ch. 7, 1 Stat. 49; and the Treasury Department by the Act of Sept. 2, 1789, ch. 12, 1 Stat. 65. The position of Attorney General was also created that year, as part of the Judiciary Act of 1789, § 35, 1 Stat. 73, 93.

(a) Government Websites

An agency's website is often a convenient source of information on its history and current activities. Here, depending on the agency, it is usually possible to find introductory overviews, organization charts, speeches, policy documents, directories, and other useful resources often unavailable in print.

One reason agency websites put regulatory information online is that they have been ordered to do so by Congress. The Electronic Freedom of Information Act Amendments of 1996 mandated that records available for inspection and copying under the Freedom of Information Act (FOIA) must be made accessible electronically.[5] Records to be available online include "statements of policy and interpretations that have been adopted by the agency and are not published in the *Federal Register*" as well as "administrative staff manuals and instructions to staff that affect a member of the public."[6]

Congress further defined the scope of agency websites in the E-Government Act of 2002.[7] This act mandates that each agency "ensure that a publicly accessible Federal Government website includes all information about that agency required to be published in the Federal Register," as well as information about the agency's organizational structure and descriptions of its mission and statutory authority.[8]

As a result of this legislation, an agency website is the first place to look for information on its history and current activities as well as documents such as regulations, decisions, and forms. Website organization and transparency, however, vary considerably from agency to agency. Some agencies have clearly marked "Laws and Regulations" links at the top of their homepages, with easy access to relevant statutes, regulations, administrative decisions, and other documents. Others may have significant documents only in an Electronic Reading Room accessible by clicking on a "FOIA" link at the foot of the page.

---

[5] Pub. L. No. 104–231, 110 Stat. 3048 (codified as amended at 5 U.S.C. § 552).

[6] 5 U.S.C. § 552(a)(2).

[7] Pub. L. No. 107–347, tit. II, 116 Stat. 2899, 2910 (codified at 44 U.S.C. § 3501 note).

[8] *Id.* at §§ 206(b), 207(f)(1), 116 Stat. at 2916, 2918. *But see* Michael Herz, *Law Lags Behind: FOIA and Affirmative Disclosure of Information*, 7 CARDOZO PUB. L. POL'Y & ETHICS J. 577, 595 (2009) ("In short, the E-Government Act is a classic example of Congress passing symbolic legislation and leading from behind, imposing a toothless mandate on agencies to do what they are already doing. Indeed, the very fact that these provisions have produced no decided cases and virtually no discussion of their drafting gibberish indicates how inconsequential they have been.").

Policies established under the E-Government Act of 2002 mandate that an agency's principal public website include a search function.[9] Some agency search engines work well, but others are rather rudimentary. Better results can often be achieved by using a general search engine such as Google, limited to a specific agency's URL. This can be done by using Google's Advanced Search page (www.google.com/advanced_search) and entering the URL in the "site or domain" field, or by using the *site* operator (e.g., site:fda.gov) as part of your search.

Most agency websites can be easily found through web searches or by using an acronym and the domain *.gov* as a URL. USA.gov (www.usa.gov), the federal government's public portal, provides an A–Z Index of U.S. Government Agencies with links to websites and other contact information.

(b) Guides and Directories

Reference guides to the federal government can be valuable resources for several purposes. They can help you identify which agency has jurisdiction over a particular subject area and provide background on its history and organization. Some directories also contain information unavailable from the agency's publications or website, such as contact information for specific personnel.

CQ Press's annual *Washington Information Directory* (library. cqpress.com) is a guide to federal agencies, congressional committees, and nongovernmental organizations, listed by subject in nearly 100 areas such as education, employment and labor, energy, and environment and natural resources. Its value is in identifying agencies and organizations you may not have known focused on a particular issue. Entries for agencies include brief descriptions, website addresses, and access information.

One of the most convenient sources for general information about agencies' structures, authority, and functions is the *United States Government Manual* (usgovernmentmanual.gov).[10] It has descriptive entries for each executive department and over fifty independent agencies and commissions, listing statutes under which the agencies operate and explaining their functions and major operating units. Sources of information (including publications, telephone numbers, and websites) are listed. A table, History of Agency Organizational Changes, lists executive agencies and

---

[9]   Office of Management and Budget, Policies for Federal Agency Public Websites (Dec. 17, 2004) (www.whitehouse.gov/sites/whitehouse.gov/files/omb/memoranda/ 2005/m05-04.pdf) [https://perma.cc/4ABB-VD77].

[10]   Older editions back to 1995 are available on Govinfo (www.govinfo.gov).

functions that have been abolished, transferred, or terminated since 1933.

The *United States Government Manual* provides an overview of the entire federal government, with relatively terse coverage for every department and agency. As a division of the Department of Health and Human Services, for example, the FDA merits just one short paragraph. Another guide with a more specific focus on major regulatory agencies is CQ Press's *Federal Regulatory Directory* (17th ed. 2016). Most of this directory focuses on twelve major agencies such as the Environmental Protection Agency, Federal Trade Commission, and Securities and Exchange Commission, with more summary treatment of nearly 100 other regulatory boards and agencies. The sections on major regulatory agencies include historical background and a discussion of current issues facing the agency, followed by listings of offices and contact persons, an annotated list of acts the agency enforces, and an explanation of its information sources.[11]

To learn about the status of a particular pending regulation or enforcement activity, you will often need to contact an agency directly by phone or e-mail. You should direct your inquiries as specifically as possible to the responsible division and official. Agency websites and resources such as the *U.S. Government Manual* and *Federal Regulatory Directory* have general information and the names of senior officials, but they are not particularly current and do not include very thorough listings of other personnel. Two commercial online products, GovSearch (www.govsearch.com) and Leadership Connect (www.leadershipconnect.io), have detailed information about specific offices and staff members, including telephone numbers and e-mail addresses.

§ 8.2   REGULATIONS

The major forms of agency lawmaking are regulations and adjudicative decisions. The Supreme Court has held that agencies have discretion to create policies through either of these methods.[12] The powers of early regulatory agencies were considered *quasi-judicial*, and they acted much like courts with lengthy trial-type

---

[11] Background information on executive departments and agencies can also be found in Part V of GUIDE TO THE PRESIDENCY AND THE EXECUTIVE BRANCH (Michael Nelson ed., 5th ed. 2013), and in A HISTORICAL GUIDE TO THE U.S. GOVERNMENT (George T. Kurian ed., 1998).

[12] *SEC v. Chenery Corp.*, 332 U.S. 194 (1947). For background on the choice between adjudication and rulemaking, see M. Elizabeth Magill, *Agency Choice of Policymaking Form*, 71 U. CHI. L. REV. 1383 (2004), and Reuel E. Schiller, *Rulemaking's Promise: Administrative Law and Legal Culture in the 1960s and 1970s*, 53 ADMIN. L. REV. 1139 (2001).

procedures. Gradually, however, rulemaking became the predominant form by which agency law was created. By the time the new agencies of the late 1960s and early 1970s were created, they were expressly charged by Congress to promulgate regulations in their subject areas.[13]

The *Federal Register* and the *Code of Federal Regulations (CFR)* are the two major resources in most federal administrative law research. Regulations are first published in the daily *Federal Register*, and the rules in force are arranged by agency and subject in the *CFR*. This publication of regulations, first chronologically and then by topic, mirrors the way statutes are published in the *Statutes at Large* and the *United States Code*.

Texts on rulemaking may help provide background and perspective. Jeffrey S. Lubbers, *A Guide to Federal Agency Rulemaking* (6th ed. 2018) has a concise overview of the rulemaking process, including chapters on the statutory framework of rulemaking and judicial review. Cornelius M. Kerwin & Scott R. Furlong, *Rulemaking: How Government Agencies Write Law and Make Policy* (5th ed. 2019) has a more political perspective on the substance and process of agency regulations, with chapters on topics such as public participation and congressional oversight.

(a) *Federal Register*

The executive branch has been issuing regulations since the beginning of the federal government. One of the acts passed during the first session of Congress in 1789 provided that pensions would be paid "under such regulations as the President of the United States may direct."[14] For almost 150 years, however, there was no standard procedure for publishing administrative regulations.[15]

---

[13] The terms "rule" and "regulation" are used interchangeably in administrative law and have the same meaning, according to the Administrative Committee of the Federal Register. 1 C.F.R. § 1.1 (2019).

[14] Act of Sept. 29, 1789, ch. 24, 1 Stat. 95, 95.

[15] The validity of unpublished administrative orders did not go unquestioned by courts and commentators. In 1873 the Supreme Court upheld the validity of an unpublished presidential proclamation, over Justice Ward Hunt's vigorous dissent. He wrote: "A proclamation may be published in the newspapers, or scattered by writing, or in any demonstrative manner, but it cannot be published by a deposit in a place to which the public have no access. . . . In the case before us no publicity was given to the paper. It was in no gazette, in no market-place, nor in the street. It was signed by the President and the Acting Secretary of State, and deposited in the Secretary's office. It does not appear that a single person besides the President and Secretary was aware of its existence. A deposit in the office of state is not notice or publicity." *Lapeyre v. United States*, 84 U.S. (17 Wall.) 191, 201–03 (1873) (Hunt, J., dissenting).

Decades passed, but little changed. A federal appellate court in 1906 voiced similar frustrations: "No department ever sends its compilation of regulations to the judges. They are frequently amended, and, without special information from the

New agencies created to deal with the effects of industrialization in the late 19th century and the extension of government control during World War I caused an increase in administrative regulation and demonstrated the need for a centralized system of publication. The government attempted to solve this problem in various ways but ultimately did not find a stable method of publicizing regulations until the mid-1930s.[16]

In 1935 the Federal Register Act initiated a daily gazette for the publication of regulations, notices, and other documents.[17] The first

---

department, no one can tell whether a particular regulation in some printed compilation was in force a year later. . . . It is a hopeless task for an appellate court to determine what such regulations were at any particular time. It must either accept counsel's statement, or itself make inquiry of the particular department; neither of which practices is to be commended." *Nagle v. United States*, 145 F. 302, 306 (2d Cir. 1906).

For guidance in identifying and finding 18th and 19th century regulations, see Michael VanderHejden, *How Little Is Known: Finding Regulations from the First 100 Years of the United States*, 37 LEGAL REFERENCE SERVS. Q. 257 (2019).

[16] During the First World War, a daily *Official U.S. Bulletin* included the texts of regulations and orders as well as war news and general government information, but publication ceased a few months after the Armistice. *See* John Walters, *The* Official Bulletin of the United States: *America's First Official Gazette*, 19 GOV'T PUB. REV. 243 (1992). A year after the *Official Bulletin* ceased, a scholar wrote: "In the matter of publication there is a maximum of variety and confusion. Not only is there no general system, but no department has developed a system for itself. Each bureau, and often each local office, has its own methods, or more often lack of method." John A. Fairlie, *Administrative Legislation*, 18 MICH. L. REV. 181, 199 (1920).

In the early years of the New Deal, thousands of regulations were issued with no regular method of publication, in many instances without even an attempt at public notice. In 1934 an American Bar Association committee advocated that regulations "should be made easily and readily available in some central office, and . . . should be subjected to certain requirements by way of registration and publication as prerequisite to their going into force and effect." *Report of the Special Committee on Administrative Law*, 59 A.B.A. REP. 539, 540 (1934). The issue was also the focus of an influential *Harvard Law Review* article later that year. Erwin N. Griswold, *Government in Ignorance of the Law—A Plea for Better Publication of Executive Legislation*, 48 HARV. L. REV. 198 (1934).

Public pressure for reform finally came to a head when two cases on New Deal regulation of the oil industry reached the Supreme Court, even though they were based on a provision that had been revoked before the lawsuits were filed. The cases proceeded through the courts with no one aware of the regulatory change, until finally the Solicitor General's office discovered the revocation and informed the parties and the Court. Newspapers reported on the "[c]austic criticism from the Supreme Court of the way in which the New Deal keeps its records" and "the tremendous eruption of administrative law." *NRA Made 10,269 Laws in Year, or 200 a Week*, N.Y. TIMES, Dec. 14, 1934, at 26. The resulting furor provided the final impetus for the enactment of remedial legislation the following year. For more on this background, see Lotte E. Feinberg, *Mr. Justice Brandeis and the Creation of the Federal Register*, 61 PUB. ADMIN. REV. 359 (2001).

[17] Ch. 417, 49 Stat. 500 (1935) (codified as amended at 44 U.S.C. §§ 1501–1511). Decades later Rep. Emanuel Celler, who introduced the bill, claimed that he conceived the idea for the *Federal Register* when Interior Secretary Harold Ickes appeared before his committee and pulled from his pocket an envelope on which a new departmental regulation had been scrawled. Richard L. Madden, *What Harding (and 8 Other Presidents) Told Manny Celler*, N.Y. TIMES, Oct. 5, 1972, at 49.

Federal Register issue was published on Saturday, March 14, 1936. Its statutory mandate is to publish "documents having general applicability and legal effect."[18] Publication in the *Federal Register* is deemed to provide any parties affected by a regulation with constructive notice of its contents.[19]

The *Federal Register* substantially improved access to regulations, but agencies were still free to use unclear or arbitrary decision-making procedures. In 1946, Congress passed the Administrative Procedure Act (APA) to create standards for agency actions.[20] The APA provides procedures for both formal and informal rulemaking, but formal rulemaking requiring trial-type hearings has been little used. For informal rulemaking, the APA requires that agencies publish notices in the *Federal Register* with "either the terms or substance of the proposed rule or a description of the subjects and issues involved," that individuals have the opportunity to comment on the proposed rules, and that the agency give a concise explanation of its basis for adopting the rule.[21]

The publication of proposed rules significantly expanded the scope of the *Federal Register*. In its first 1947 issue, the *Federal Register* inaugurated a new "Proposed Rule Making" section with proposed standards for grades of canned tangerine juice.[22] For years the agency explanations were cursory at best. Judicial decisions in the 1960s and 1970s, however, began taking a "hard look" at agency

---

[18] 44 U.S.C. § 1505(a). The Administrative Committee of the Federal Register has further defined "document having general applicability and legal effect" as "any document issued under proper authority prescribing a penalty or course of conduct, conferring a right, privilege, authority, or immunity, or imposing an obligation, and relevant or applicable to the general public, members of a class, or persons in a locality, as distinguished from named individuals or organizations." 1 C.F.R. § 1.1 (2019).

[19] 44 U.S.C. § 1507. Justice Jackson sharply criticized the effects of this constructive notice provision:

To my mind, it is an absurdity to hold that every farmer who insures his crops knows what the Federal Register contains or even knows that there is such a publication. If he were to peruse this voluminous and dull publication as it is issued from time to time in order to make sure whether anything has been promulgated that affects his rights, he would never need crop insurance, for he would never get time to plant any crops. Nor am I convinced that a reading of technically-worded regulations would enlighten him much in any event.

Federal Crop Ins. Corp. v. Merrill, 332 U.S. 380, 387 (1947) (Jackson, J., dissenting).

[20] Ch. 324, 60 Stat. 237 (codified as amended at 5 U.S.C. §§ 551–559, 701–706).

[21] 5 U.S.C. § 553. The APA does not provide the only rulemaking standards. Some rules are created under the Negotiated Rulemaking Act of 1990, Pub. L. No. 101–648, 104 Stat. 4969 (codified as amended at 5 U.S.C. §§ 561–570a), which permits interested parties to participate directly in rulemaking by meeting with agency personnel and negotiating the contents of rules under which they are affected.

[22] 12 Fed. Reg. 32 (Jan. 1, 1947).

regulations and overturning those seen as arbitrary or capricious.[23] This soon led agencies to supply fuller explanations of their actions and greater evidence of public involvement in the decision-making process. Within five years the number of pages in the *Federal Register* had tripled.[24]

Through 1972, explanations generally accompanied proposed rules but not final rules. Since 1973 agencies have been required to preface final rules with an explanatory preamble.[25] In 1976 the preamble to final rules was expanded to include summaries of the comments submitted and the agency's responses to these comments.[26]

As a result of these developments, most proposed and final rules in the *Federal Register* now include lengthy preambles describing the need for the regulatory changes and providing the required "concise general statement of . . . basis and purpose" of the rules.[27] These "concise" statements can be quite detailed, with extensive scientific and technical background information as well as responses to comments offered by interested parties.[28]

---

[23] This development is generally attributed to Judges David Bazelon and Harold Leventhal of the U.S. Court of Appeals for the District of Columbia Circuit. On this and other developments in judicial approaches to regulations, see Patricia M. Wald, *Judicial Review in Midpassage: The Uneasy Partnership between Courts and Agencies Plays On*, 32 TULSA L.J. 221 (1996), and Matthew Warren, Note, *Active Judging: Judicial Philosophy and the Hard Look Doctrine in the D.C. Circuit*, 90 GEO. L.J. 2599 (2002).

[24] Each year's output comprises a new volume of the *Federal Register*, with continuous pagination throughout the year. The first volume in 1936 contained 2,400 pages, while every year since 1991 has had more than 60,000 pages. Law Librarians' Society of Washington, D.C. (LLSDC), "Federal Register Pages Published Annually" (www.llsdc.org/assets/sourcebook/fed-reg-pages.pdf) [https://perma.cc/V2SL-R4VA].

The LLSDC website also has an informative and regularly updated guide to regulatory research. Richard J. McKinney, *A Research Guide to the Federal Register and the Code of Federal Regulations* (www.llsdc.org/fr-cfr-research-guide).

[25] The change was made by the Administrative Committee of the Federal Register in order to make the Register "a more meaningful and more useful publication." 41 Fed. Reg. 23,601, 23,602 (Nov. 4, 1972). The current version provides that the agency "prepare a preamble which will inform the reader, who is not an expert in the subject area, of the basis and purpose for the rule or proposal." 1 C.F.R. § 18.12(a) (2019). Additions to the contents of the *Federal Register* were also made in 1966 by the Freedom of Information Act (FOIA), mandating that agencies publish organizational descriptions and policy statements, and in 1976 by the Government in the Sunshine Act, requiring agencies to publish notices of most meetings.

[26] 41 Fed. Reg. 56,624 (Dec. 29, 1976) (codified as amended at 1 C.F.R. § 18.12(c) (2019)).

[27] 5 U.S.C. § 553(c).

[28] The FDA's final rule governing the marketing of cigarettes and tobacco products included a 220-page preamble, as well as a 700-page "annex" explaining the agency's basis for assuming jurisdiction over tobacco products. 61 Fed. Reg. 44,396 (Aug. 28, 1996). As one scholar has noted, "the modern statement of basis and purpose

The introductory preambles appear only in the *Federal Register* and are not reprinted with the text of regulations in the *Code of Federal Regulations*. A *Federal Register* preamble can be invaluable in interpreting the scope and meaning of a regulation, similar to the way that committee reports and other legislative materials help explain the purpose of a statute.[29]

Illustrations 8-1 and 8-2 show excerpts from an Animal and Plant Health Inspection Service rule on the importation of dogs, as published in the *Federal Register*. This rule was proposed in September 2011 and published as a final rule in August 2014, after thousands of comments were received. Illustration 8-1 shows the beginning of the preamble containing background information. Illustration 8-2 shows part of the text of the new rule as it appeared in the *Federal Register*.

The *Federal Register* has permanent reference value because it contains material that never appears in the *Code of Federal Regulations*. In addition to the agency preambles explaining regulatory actions, it also has any short-lived rule changes occurring between annual *CFR* revisions and is the only published source for proposed rules, agency policy statements, and other notices.

Access. The *Federal Register* is published in print, and most large academic and law libraries also have complete runs back to 1936 in microform. Most researchers, however, access the *Federal Register* online. The first stop for many is the *Register*'s own website (www.federalregister.gov), which has full-text issues back to volume 59 (1994). A search box at the top of each screen can be used for basic keyword searches and to retrieve material by citation, and an Advanced Search screen allows you to specify agency, type of document, and publication date. Each major agency has its own page on which you can browse recent documents and significant regulations. Illustration 8-3 shows the front page of the online *Federal Register* for the issue with the dog importation regulations in Illustration 8-2.

---

is often a monstrously long and complex document." GARY LAWSON, FEDERAL ADMINISTRATIVE LAW 428 (8th ed. 2019).

[29] "Although the preamble does not 'control' the meaning of the regulation, it may serve as a source of evidence concerning contemporaneous agency intent." *Wyoming Outdoor Council v. U.S. Forest Serv.*, 165 F.3d 43, 53 (D.C. Cir. 1999). For more on the use of preambles and other pre-promulgation sources in regulatory interpretation, see Lars Noah, *Divining Regulatory Intent: The Place for a 'Legislative History' of Agency Rules*, 51 HASTINGS L.J. 255 (2000); Kevin M. Stack, *Interpreting Regulations*, 111 MICH. L. REV. 355 (2012); and Kevin M. Stack, *Preambles as Guidance*, 84 GEO. WASH. L. REV. 1252 (2016).

48653

Federal Register

Vol. 79, No. 159

Monday, August 18, 2014

Rules and Regulations

DEPARTMENT OF AGRICULTURE

Animal and Plant Health Inspection Service

9 CFR Part 2

[Docket No. APHIS–2009–0053]

RIN 0579–AD23

Animal Welfare; Importation of Live Dogs

AGENCY: Animal and Plant Health Inspection Service, USDA.

ACTION: Final rule.

SUMMARY: We are amending the regulations to implement an amendment to the Animal Welfare Act (AWA). The Food, Conservation, and Energy Act of 2008 added a new section to the AWA to restrict the importation of certain live dogs. Consistent with this amendment, this rule prohibits the importation of dogs, with limited exceptions, from any part of the world into the continental United States or Hawaii for purposes of resale, research, or veterinary treatment, unless the dogs are in good health, have received all necessary vaccinations, and are at least 6 months of age. This action is necessary to implement the amendment to the AWA and will help to ensure the welfare of imported dogs.

DATES: *Effective date:* November 17, 2014.

FOR FURTHER INFORMATION CONTACT: Dr. Gerald Rushin, Veterinary Medical Officer, Animal Care, APHIS, 4700 River Road Unit 84, Riverdale, MD 20737–1236; (301) 851–3740.

SUPPLEMENTARY INFORMATION:

Background

Under the Animal Welfare Act (AWA or the Act, 7 U.S.C. 2131 *et seq.*), the Secretary of Agriculture is authorized to promulgate standards and other requirements governing the humane handling, care, treatment, and transportation of certain animals by dealers, research facilities, exhibitors, operators of auction sales, and carriers and intermediate handlers. The Secretary has delegated responsibility for administering the AWA to the Administrator of U.S. Department of Agriculture's (USDA) Animal and Plant Health Inspection Service (APHIS). Within APHIS, the responsibility for administering the AWA has been delegated to the Deputy Administrator for Animal Care (AC). Regulations and standards are established under the AWA and are contained in the Code of Federal Regulations (CFR) in 9 CFR parts 1, 2, and 3 (referred to below as the regulations). Part 2 provides administrative requirements and sets forth institutional responsibilities for regulated parties.

The Food, Conservation, and Energy Act of 2008 (Pub. L. 110–246, signed into law on June 18, 2008) added a new section 18 to the Animal Welfare Act (7 U.S.C. 2148) to restrict the importation of certain live dogs. As amended, the AWA now prohibits the importation of dogs into the United States for resale purposes, unless the Secretary determines that the dogs are in good health, have received all necessary vaccinations, and are at least 6 months of age. Section 18 of the AWA includes a scoping definition for the term "resale." When read in context of the requirements of that section, the term "resale" includes, but is not limited to, any transfer of ownership or control of imported dogs to another person, for more than *de minimis* consideration. The AWA further provides that the Secretary, by regulation, must provide an exception to these requirements in any case in which a dog is imported for research purposes or veterinary treatment. The AWA also provides an exception to the at least 6-month age requirement for dogs that are lawfully imported into Hawaii from the British Isles, Australia, Guam, or New Zealand in compliance with the applicable regulations of Hawaii, provided the dogs are not transported out of Hawaii for purposes of resale at less than 6 months of age.

The AWA provides that any importer who fails to comply with these provisions is subject to penalties under 7 U.S.C. 2149 and must provide for the care (including appropriate veterinary care), forfeiture, and adoption of each applicable dog, at his or her expense.

On September 1, 2011, we published in the **Federal Register** (76 FR 54392–54397, Docket No. APHIS–2009–0053) a proposed rule [1] to add requirements concerning the importation of certain live dogs as required by the Food, Conservation, and Energy Act of 2008.

We proposed, with limited exceptions, to prohibit the importation of any dog for resale, veterinary treatment, or research [2] unless the dog is in good health; has received vaccinations for rabies and distemper, hepatitis, leptospirosis, parvovirus, and parainfluenza virus (DHLPP); and is at least 6 months of age. We proposed to require that the dog be accompanied by an import permit issued by APHIS and a health certificate and rabies vaccination certificate issued by a veterinarian with a valid license to practice veterinary medicine in the country of export. We proposed to allow exceptions to health, vaccination, and age requirements for dogs imported for veterinary treatment that cannot be obtained in the exporting country and for dogs imported for use in research, tests, or experiments if the requirement would interfere with a research protocol approved by the research facility's Institutional Animal Care and Use Committee (IACUC). Additionally, we proposed that dogs less than 6 months old could be lawfully imported into Hawaii from the British Isles, Australia, Guam, or New Zealand as long as the dog was not transported from Hawaii for resale purposes at less than 6 months of age.

We solicited comments for 60 days ending October 31, 2011. We received a total of 74,218 comments. These included 382 unique comments from animal welfare associations, private breeders, veterinarians, foreign exporters, domestic importers, and other individuals. Two animal welfare associations mailed an additional 73,836 comments that had been

---

[1] To view the proposed rule and the comments we received, go to *http://www.regulations.gov/#!docketDetail;D=APHIS-2009-0053.*

[2] Under the AWA, as amended, dogs imported for resale include dogs imported for the purpose of transferring ownership or control to a research facility or to a veterinarian for veterinary treatment. However, because research and veterinary treatment are not commonly considered resale purposes, we separately identify each of these activities as context requires.

Illustration 8-1. The beginning of a regulation as published in the *Federal Register*.

Federal Register/Vol. 79, No. 159/Monday, August 18, 2014/Rules and Regulations 48659

We believe that the benefits of this rule, including the unquantifiable enhancement of animal welfare, justify the costs. Benefits of the rule include promoting the humane treatment of covered imported dogs in keeping with the requirements of the Animal Welfare Act and with standard health practices for dogs in the United States. The rule could also yield benefits in preventing the spread of communicable diseases by unvaccinated, imported dogs to other dogs or humans in the United States.

Executive Order 12988

This final rule has been reviewed under Executive Order 12988, Civil Justice Reform. It is not intended to have retroactive effect. The Act does not provide administrative procedures which must be exhausted prior to a judicial challenge to the provisions of this rule.

Paperwork Reduction Act

In accordance with section 3507(d) of the Paperwork Reduction Act of 1995 (44 U.S.C. 3501 *et seq.*), the information collection or recordkeeping requirements included in this final rule, which were filed under 0579–0379, have been submitted for approval to the Office of Management and Budget (OMB). When OMB notifies us of its decision, if approval is denied, we will publish a document in the **Federal Register** providing notice of what action we plan to take.

E-Government Act Compliance

The Animal and Plant Health Inspection Service is committed to compliance with the E-Government Act to promote the use of the Internet and other information technologies, to provide increased opportunities for citizen access to Government information and services, and for other purposes. For information pertinent to E-Government Act compliance related to this rule, please contact Mrs. Celeste Sickles, APHIS' Information Collection Coordinator, at (301) 851–2908.

List of Subjects in 9 CFR Part 2

Animal welfare, Pets, Reporting and recordkeeping requirements, Research.

Accordingly, we are amending 9 CFR part 2 as follows:

PART 2—REGULATIONS

■ 1. The authority citation for part 2 continues to read as follows:

Authority: 7 U.S.C. 2131–2159; 7 CFR 2.22, 2.80, and 371.7.

■ 2. Subpart J, consisting of §§ 2.150 through 2.153, is added to read as follows:

Subpart J—Importation of Live Dogs

Sec.
2.150   Import permit.
2.151   Certifications.
2.152   Notification of arrival.
2.153   Dogs refused entry.

Subpart J—Importation of Live Dogs

§ 2.150   Import permit.

(a) No person shall import a live dog from any part of the world into the continental United States or Hawaii for purposes of resale, research, or veterinary treatment unless the dog is accompanied by an import permit issued by APHIS and is imported into the continental United States or Hawaii within 30 days after the proposed date of arrival stated in the import permit.

(b) An application for an import permit must be submitted to the Animal and Plant Health Inspection Service, Animal Care, 4700 River Road Unit 84, Riverdale, MD 20737–1234 or though Animal Care's Web site (*http://www.aphis.usda.gov/animal_welfare/*). Application forms for import permits may be obtained from Animal Care at the address listed above.

(c) The completed application must include the following information:

(1) The name and address of the person intending to export the dog(s) to the continental United States or Hawaii;

(2) The name and address of the person intending to import the dog(s) into the continental United States or Hawaii;

(3) The number of dogs to be imported and the breed, sex, age, color, markings, and other identifying information of each dog;

(4) The purpose of the importation;

(5) The port of embarkation and the mode of transportation;

(6) The port of entry in the United States;

(7) The proposed date of arrival in the continental United States or Hawaii; and

(8) The name and address of the person to whom the dog(s) will be delivered in the continental United States or Hawaii and, if the dog(s) is or are imported for research purposes, the USDA registration number of the research facility where the dog will be used for research, tests, or experiments.

(d) After receipt and review of the application by APHIS, an import permit indicating the applicable conditions for importation under this subpart may be issued for the importation of the dog(s) described in the application if such dog(s) appears to be eligible to be imported. Even though an import permit has been issued for the importation of a dog, the dog may only be imported if all applicable requirements of this subpart and any other applicable regulations of this subchapter and any other statute or regulation of any State or of the United States are met.

(Approved by the Office of Management and Budget under control number 0579–0379)

§ 2.151   Certifications.

(a) *Required certificates.* Except as provided in paragraph (b) of this section, no person shall import a live dog from any part of the world into the continental United States or Hawaii for purposes of resale, research, or veterinary treatment unless the following conditions are met:

(1) *Health certificate.* Each dog is accompanied by an original health certificate issued in English by a licensed veterinarian with a valid license to practice veterinary medicine in the country of export that:

(i) Specifies the name and address of the person intending to import the dog into the continental United States or Hawaii;

(ii) Identifies the dog on the basis of breed, sex, age, color, markings, and other identifying information;

(iii) States that the dog is at least 6 months of age;

(iv) States that the dog was vaccinated, not more than 12 months before the date of arrival at the U.S. port, for distemper, hepatitis, leptospirosis, parvovirus, and parainfluenza virus (DHLPP) at a frequency that provides continuous protection of the dog from those diseases and is in accordance with currently accepted practices as cited in veterinary medicine reference guides;

(v) States that the dog is in good health (i.e., free of any infectious disease or physical abnormality which would endanger the dog or other animals or endanger public health, including, but not limited to, parasitic infection, emaciation, lesions of the skin, nervous system disturbances, jaundice, or diarrhea); and

(vi) Bears the signature and the license number of the veterinarian issuing the certificate.

(2) *Rabies vaccination certificate.* Each dog is accompanied by a valid rabies vaccination certificate[6] that was issued in English by a licensed veterinarian with a valid license to practice veterinary medicine in the country of export for the dog not less

---

[6] Alternatively, this requirement can be met by providing an exact copy of the rabies vaccination certificate if so required under the Public Health Service regulations in 42 CFR 71.51.

Illustration 8-2. New regulations as published in the *Federal Register*.

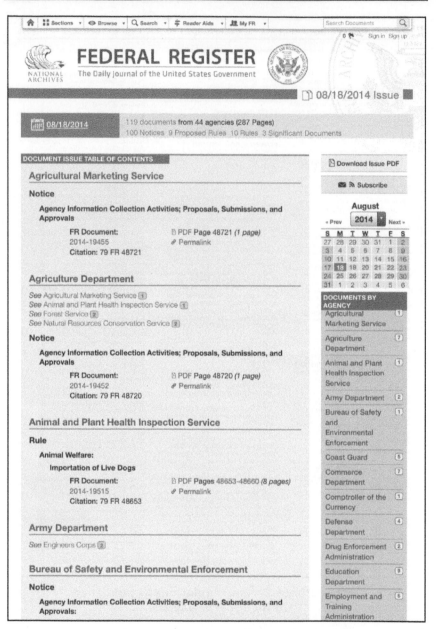

Illustration 8-3. A daily *Federal Register*
issue on Federalregister.gov.

The text of regulations and other material on FederalRegister.gov is unofficial, but each document includes a link to the official PDF version replicating the printed *Federal Register*. This is housed on Govinfo (www.govinfo.gov), which can also be accessed directly but is less user-friendly than FederalRegister.gov. Govinfo contains PDFs of every issue of the *Federal Register* ever published, dating back to 1936.

Scanning the *Federal Register* for developments affecting clients is part of many lawyers' daily routine, and from FederalRegister.gov you can sign up to have the table of contents delivered each morning by e-mail or subscribe to documents from a particular agency. The site also has a Public Inspection page providing advance access to documents that are scheduled for publication in upcoming *Federal Register* issues.

The *Federal Register* is also available online through several commercial platforms. Westlaw, Lexis, and Bloomberg Law all have current issues the day they are published, with coverage back to the first *Federal Register* issue in 1936. Older issues may be available only in PDF, but all documents arc full-text searchable.

HeinOnline is another commercial retrospective source for all *Federal Register* issues. Its searchable PDF collection extends from 1936 to current issues. For issues before 1995 a HeinOnline search result retrieves an entire issue rather than a specific regulatory document, so it may take a few moments to determine the context and scope of the regulation or other document found.

Pending Regulations. Lawyers whose clients are subject to federal regulation need to know more than the rules currently in force. They also need to anticipate rule changes and to track developments in pending regulations. A notice of proposed rule making (NPRM) can be just as significant as a newly adopted regulation. Several tools are available for monitoring the development of regulations that have not yet come into force.

The Unified Agenda of Federal Regulatory and Deregulatory Actions, from the Office of Management and Budget's Office of Information and Regulatory Affairs (www.reginfo.gov), is a useful resource to track the development of regulations. It lists and summarizes regulatory actions under development and provides information on their projected dates of completion, although those dates are subject to revision. This can also be a way to learn about areas of agency activity that have not even reached the proposed rulemaking stage. An abridged Unified Agenda of significant rulemaking actions is published twice a year in the *Federal Register*.

Dockets of recent and current regulatory decision-making are also available online, providing access to agency analyses, public comments, and other documents involved in the rulemaking process. Regulations.gov (www.regulations.gov) is a centralized site for commenting on proposed regulations and viewing submitted comments. Illustration 8-4 shows the Regulations.gov page for the dog importation rulemaking process, including links to agency documents and comments.

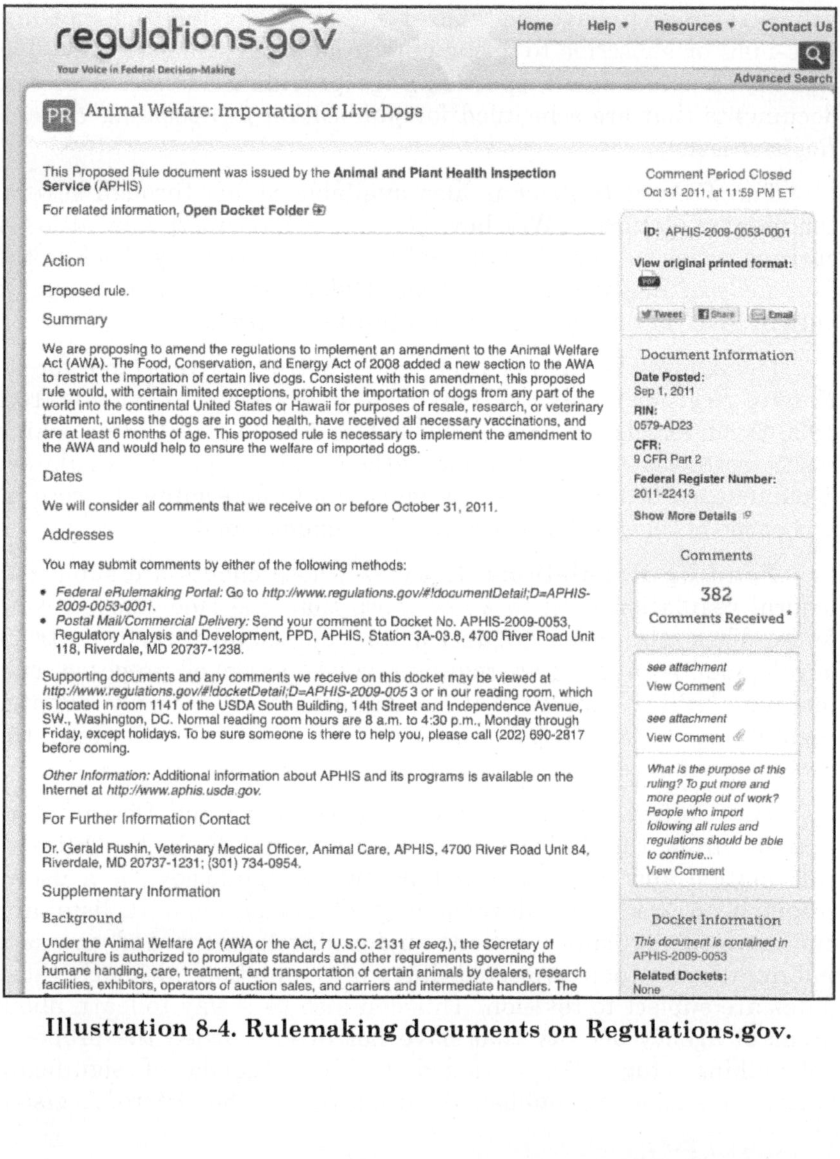

regulations.gov
Your Voice in Federal Decision-Making

Home Help Resources Contact Us
Advanced Search

PR Animal Welfare: Importation of Live Dogs

This Proposed Rule document was issued by the **Animal and Plant Health Inspection Service** (APHIS)

For related information, **Open Docket Folder**

Comment Period Closed
Oct 31 2011, at 11:59 PM ET

ID: APHIS-2009-0053-0001

View original printed format:

Tweet Share Email

Action

Proposed rule.

Summary

We are proposing to amend the regulations to implement an amendment to the Animal Welfare Act (AWA). The Food, Conservation, and Energy Act of 2008 added a new section to the AWA to restrict the importation of certain live dogs. Consistent with this amendment, this proposed rule would, with certain limited exceptions, prohibit the importation of dogs from any part of the world into the continental United States or Hawaii for purposes of resale, research, or veterinary treatment, unless the dogs are in good health, have received all necessary vaccinations, and are at least 6 months of age. This proposed rule is necessary to implement the amendment to the AWA and would help to ensure the welfare of imported dogs.

Dates

We will consider all comments that we receive on or before October 31, 2011.

Addresses

You may submit comments by either of the following methods:

- *Federal eRulemaking Portal:* Go to *http://www.regulations.gov/#!documentDetail;D=APHIS-2009-0053-0001.*
- *Postal Mail/Commercial Delivery:* Send your comment to Docket No. APHIS-2009-0053, Regulatory Analysis and Development, PPD, APHIS, Station 3A-03.8, 4700 River Road Unit 118, Riverdale, MD 20737-1238.

Supporting documents and any comments we receive on this docket may be viewed at *http://www.regulations.gov/#!docketDetail;D=APHIS-2009-005* 3 or in our reading room, which is located in room 1141 of the USDA South Building, 14th Street and Independence Avenue, SW., Washington, DC. Normal reading room hours are 8 a.m. to 4:30 p.m., Monday through Friday, except holidays. To be sure someone is there to help you, please call (202) 690-2817 before coming.

Other Information: Additional information about APHIS and its programs is available on the Internet at *http://www.aphis.usda.gov.*

For Further Information Contact

Dr. Gerald Rushin, Veterinary Medical Officer, Animal Care, APHIS, 4700 River Road Unit 84, Riverdale, MD 20737-1231; (301) 734-0954.

Supplementary Information

Background

Under the Animal Welfare Act (AWA or the Act, 7 U.S.C. 2131 *et seq.*), the Secretary of Agriculture is authorized to promulgate standards and other requirements governing the humane handling, care, treatment, and transportation of certain animals by dealers, research facilities, exhibitors, operators of auction sales, and carriers and intermediate handlers. The

Document Information

Date Posted:
Sep 1, 2011

RIN:
0579-AD23

CFR:
9 CFR Part 2

Federal Register Number:
2011-22413

Show More Details

Comments

382
Comments Received*

see attachment
View Comment

see attachment
View Comment

What is the purpose of this ruling? To put more and more people out of work? People who import following all rules and regulations should be able to continue...
View Comment

Docket Information

This document is contained in APHIS-2009-0053

Related Dockets:
None

Illustration 8-4. Rulemaking documents on Regulations.gov.

(b) *Code of Federal Regulations*

In 1935, when Congress finally sought to control the tremendous mass of federal regulations, it understood the need for subject access to regulations in force. The Federal Register Act required each agency to compile and publish in the *Register* its then-current body of regulations.[30] An amendment in 1937 established a regular form of codification, the *Code of Federal Regulations (CFR)*.[31] The first edition was published in 1939 and contained regulations in force as of June 1, 1938.

The *CFR* contains "complete codifications of the documents of each agency of the Government having general applicability and legal effect [that] are relied upon by the agency as authority for, or are invoked or used by it in the discharge of, its activities or functions."[32] The regulations are codified in a subject arrangement of fifty titles somewhat similar to that used for federal statutes in the *United States Code*. In the back of every *CFR* volume there is an alphabetical list of federal agencies indicating the location of each agency's regulations.

CFR titles are divided into *chapters*, each of which is devoted to the regulations of a particular agency. The regulations in a chapter are divided into *subchapters*, each covering a general subject area, and *parts*, each of which consists of a body of regulations on a particular topic or agency function. Parts are sometimes divided further into *subparts*, and finally into *sections*, the basic unit of the code. The citation identifying a *CFR* section shows the title, the part, and the section (but not the chapter or subchapter), so that 9 C.F.R. § 2.1 is title 9 (Animals and Animal Products), chapter I (Animal and Plant Health Inspection Service), subchapter A (Animal Welfare), part 2 (Regulations), subpart A (Licensing), section 1 (Requirements and application). Illustration 8-5 shows the beginning of 9 *CFR* Part

---

[30] Ch. 417, § 11, 49 Stat. 500, 503 (1935). The only pre-*CFR* compilation of rules was a one-volume collection, *Federal Rules and Regulations*, privately published in 1918 and never supplemented. *See* Nicholas Triffin & Penny Hazelton, *Questions and Answers*, 76 LAW LIBR. J. 684, 685 (1983).

[31] Act of June 19, 1937, ch. 369, 50 Stat. 304 (codified as amended at 44 U.S.C. § 1510).

[32] 44 U.S.C. § 1510(a). Recent years have seen an increasing use of incorporation by reference (IBR) of technical standards created by industry organizations. This has created concerns about legal rules that are only available to the public at considerable cost. *See, e.g.,* Emily S. Bremer, *Incorporation by Reference in an Open-Government Age*, 36 HARV. J.L. & PUB. POL'Y 131 (2013); Peter L. Strauss, *Private Standards Organizations and Public Law*, 22 WM. & MARY BILL RTS. J. 497 (2013). Following a petition by a group of law professors, the Office of the Federal Register in 2014 required that agencies add more information in *Federal Register* preambles about the content and accessibility of IBR materials. Incorporation by Reference, 79 Fed. Reg. 66,267 (Nov. 7, 2014) (codified at 1 C.F.R. pt. 51).

2, in which the dog importation regulations seen in the earlier *Federal Register* illustrations have been codified.

Animal and Plant Health Inspection Service, USDA   **§2.1**

EFFECTIVE DATE NOTE: At 64 FR 15920, Apr. 2, 1999, the definitions of *buffer area, interactive area, interactive session, sanctuary area,* and *swim-with-the-dolphin (SWTD) program* were suspended, effective Apr. 2, 1999.

PART 2—REGULATIONS

Subpart A—Licensing

Sec.
2.1   Requirements and application.
2.2   Acknowledgement of regulations and standards.
2.3   Demonstration of compliance with standards and regulations.
2.4   Non-interference with APHIS officials.
2.5   Duration of license and termination of license.
2.6   Annual license fees.
2.7   Annual report by licensees.
2.8   Notification of change of name, address, control, or ownership of business.
2.9   Officers, agents, and employees of licensees whose licenses have been suspended or revoked.
2.10 Licensees whose licenses have been suspended or revoked.
2.11 Denial of initial license application.
2.12 Termination of a license.

Subpart B—Registration

2.25 Requirements and procedures.
2.26 Acknowledgement of regulations and standards.
2.27 Notification of change of operation.

Subpart C—Research Facilities

2.30 Registration.
2.31 Institutional Animal Care and Use Committee (IACUC).
2.32 Personnel qualifications.
2.33 Attending veterinarian and adequate veterinary care.
2.34 [Reserved]
2.35 Recordkeeping requirements.
2.36 Annual report.
2.37 Federal research facilities.
2.38 Miscellaneous.

Subpart D—Attending Veterinarian and Adequate Veterinary Care

2.40 Attending veterinarian and adequate veterinary care (dealers and exhibitors).

Subpart E—Identification of Animals

2.50 Time and method of identification.
2.51 Form of official tag.
2.52 How to obtain tags.
2.53 Use of tags.
2.54 Lost tags.
2.55 Removal and disposal of tags.

Subpart F—Stolen Animals

2.60 Prohibition on the purchase, sale, use, or transportation of stolen animals.

Subpart G—Records

2.75 Records: Dealers and exhibitors.
2.76 Records: Operators of auction sales and brokers.
2.77 Records: Carriers and intermediate handlers.
2.78 Health certification and identification.
2.79 C.O.D. shipments.
2.80 Records, disposition.

Subpart H—Compliance With Standards and Holding Period

2.100 Compliance with standards.
2.101 Holding period.
2.102 Holding facility.

Subpart I—Miscellaneous

2.125 Information as to business; furnishing of same by dealers, exhibitors, operators of auction sales, intermediate handlers, and carriers.
2.126 Access and inspection of records and property; submission of itineraries.
2.127 Publication of names of persons subject to the provisions of this part.
2.128 Inspection for missing animals.
2.129 Confiscation and destruction of animals.
2.130 Minimum age requirements.
2.131 Handling of animals.
2.132 Procurement of dogs, cats, and other animals; dealers.
2.133 Certification for random source dogs and cats.
2.134 Contingency planning.

Subpart J—Importation of Live Dogs

2.150 Import permit.
2.151 Certifications.
2.152 Notification of arrival.
2.153 Dogs refused entry.

AUTHORITY: 7 U.S.C. 2131–2159; 7 CFR 2.22, 2.80, and 371.7.

SOURCE: 54 FR 36147, Aug. 31, 1989, unless otherwise noted.

Subpart A—Licensing

§2.1   Requirements and application.

(a)(1) Any person operating or intending to operate as a dealer, exhibitor, or operator of an auction sale, except persons who are exempted from the licensing requirements under paragraph (a)(3) of this section, must have a valid license. A person must be 18 years of

---

Illustration 8-5. Animal welfare regulations in the *Code of Federal Regulations*.

At the beginning of each *CFR* part or subpart is an *authority note* showing the statutory or executive authority under which the regulations have been issued. Some of these are statutes directly related to the topic of the regulation, while others are more general grants of rulemaking authority to the agency. After this note is a *source note* providing the citation and date of the *Federal Register* in which the regulations were most recently published. This reference is the key to finding the preamble with background information explaining the regulations. If an individual section has been added or amended more recently than the other sections in a part, it is followed by a separate source note. In Illustration 8-5, the source of "54 FR 36147, Aug. 31, 1989, unless otherwise noted" is indicated near the end of the second column.

The current *CFR* consists of more than 230 volumes, which are revised and reissued on a quarterly basis. Titles 1–16 contain regulations in force as of January 1 of the cover year; titles 17–27 as of April 1; titles 28–41 as of July 1; and titles 42–50 as of October 1. The date of the latest annual edition can be an important detail to note because it is the source that must be cited in most *CFR* references.[33] One year's volumes gradually supplant the previous year's, and a current *CFR* set almost always consists of volumes of two annual editions. The colors of the volume covers change each year, so annual editions can be readily distinguished from each other.

The *CFR* is available in several online formats. Govinfo has a PDF mirroring the printed edition and containing the official text needed for citations. A much more current *Electronic Code of Federal Regulations*, or *e-CFR* (www.ecfr.gov), incorporates new amendments from the *Federal Register* within two business days and is one of the handiest available sources for up-to-date regulatory information. The *e-CFR*, though managed by the Office of the Federal Register and the GPO, is an "unofficial" edition of the code subject to correction in the annual revision. Either version can be accessed by browsing or through keyword searches, and the *e-CFR* includes a hyperlinked Agency List leading to each agency's regulations.

Current versions of the *CFR* are also available online from all of the major subscription services. Like the *e-CFR*, these resources are updated on an ongoing basis to reflect changes published in the *Federal Register* and incorporate amendments within days. Westlaw's *CFR* provides notice of even newer developments because

---

[33] *The Bluebook* mandates citation to the official, annually revised edition of the *CFR*. THE BLUEBOOK: A UNIFORM SYSTEM OF CITATION R. 14.2 (21st ed. 2020). The *ALWD Guide* permits citation to an online service, if the source is noted parenthetically. ALWD GUIDE TO LEGAL CITATION R. 18.1(c) (6th ed. 2017).

it includes red flags indicating "Regulatory Action" and links to *Federal Register* documents the same day they are published.

Older editions of the *CFR* are sometimes needed to trace a regulation's history and to determine the regulations in force on a specific date. Govinfo retains older editions as new versions are added, with coverage starting in mid-1996. Westlaw and Lexis offer deeper historical access, with retrospective coverage extending back to the early 1980s. HeinOnline has the most comprehensive online historical collection, with all versions back to the original 1938 edition.[34] Older editions are also available in retrospective microform collections in most large law libraries.

(c) Regulatory Research

Research in federal regulations involves several distinct steps, from finding relevant regulations to searching for documents that might affect their validity. It is always important to verify that regulations are current and to look for cases in which they are applied and interpreted. It may also be necessary to track changes over time by reading older editions of the *Federal Register* or *CFR*.

Finding Regulations. You can find federal regulations through several methods. The *Federal Register* and the *Code of Federal Regulations* have indexes, and both publications can be searched through Govinfo or other platforms including Westlaw and Lexis. You can also start your research in an annotated edition of the *U.S. Code* or an agency website, and references are often found in cases, texts, and articles.

Most research into the regulations of a federal agency begins with the *Code of Federal Regulations*, rather than the daily *Federal Register*. The *CFR* includes an annually revised *Index and Finding Aids* volume providing access by agency name and subject. This index is far less detailed than most statutory indexes, listing parts rather than specific sections.[35] Much more detailed subject access is

---

[34] The first edition of the *CFR* consisted of seventeen volumes kept up-to-date through cumbersome bound supplements. For the second edition, delayed by World War II until 1949, a different method of supplementation was instituted: pocket parts, with republication of volumes as necessary. Gradually this approach became unworkable, as an increasing number of volumes required annual republication. In 1967 the code changed to paperbound volumes published annually.

[35] The *Index and Finding Aids* volume was first published in 1979, after an attorney sued to compel the government to publish an analytical subject index to the set. *Cervase v. Office of the Federal Register*, 580 F.2d 1166 (3d Cir. 1978). It was a marked improvement over earlier indexes, and the plaintiff agreed to dismissal of his suit upon its publication. Howard A. Hood, *Indexing and the Law*, 8 INT'L J.L. LIBR. 61 (1980).

FederalRegister.gov has a regularly updated index to the *Register*, with entries listed by agency rather than by subject. Older annual indexes back to 1994 are

provided in the annual four-volume *West's Code of Federal Regulations General Index*, which indexes specific *CFR* sections rather than entire parts. This index is available on Westlaw as a link from the *CFR* search page.

Online keyword searches can also be an effective way to find regulations, although the *CFR* is so voluminous and wide-ranging that you should search within a particular title or chapter when possible. Another approach is to check an agency's website. Most agency sites have their current body of regulations and information on proposed rules, as well as the texts of the statutes under which they operate.

If you have a statute and need to find related regulations promulgated under its authority, the simplest method is to check the *U.S. Code Annotated* (in print or on Westlaw) or *U.S. Code Service* (in print or on Lexis). Cross-references to relevant *CFR* parts or sections often accompany individual sections in both codes. The online versions have links from the statutes to the regulations, under the Context & Analysis tab on Westlaw and in the Research References & Practice Aids section after the annotations on Lexis.[36]

ProQuest Regulatory Insight (regulatoryinsight.proquest.com) collects the *Federal Register* and *CFR* documents related to Public Laws since 1936, allowing you to examine how a statutory mandate was implemented by federal agencies. Documents are searchable and include both proposed and final rules, and links lead to related material in ProQuest's Legislative Insight and Supreme Court Insight products.

For some agencies, regulations are reprinted in treatises and topical services covering their subject area. Services such as the *Federal Securities Law Reporter* (Wolters Kluwer, available on Cheetah) and the *United States Tax Reporter* (RIA, available on Thomson Reuters Checkpoint and Westlaw) have regularly updated and well-annotated texts of both statutes and regulations. These services are discussed more fully in Chapter 15.

Updating and Tracking Changes. Making sure that you have the current language of a regulation is a relatively simple task for users of the *e-CFR*, commercial services, or looseleaf services, because the versions of *CFR* available through these sources are regularly updated. For researchers using the *CFR* in its print format

---

available on the National Archives website (www.archives.gov/federal-register/the-federal-register/indexes.html), and back to 1936 on HeinOnline.

[36] The *CFR's Index and Finding Aids* volume has a Parallel Table of Authorities and Rules that lists every statute and presidential document cited by an agency as authority for its rules. The table is available as a "Related Resources" link on the Govinfo and *e-CFR* websites.

or in its official version on Govinfo, it is necessary to update a regulation from the most recent annual *CFR* edition. The simplest course is to check a section in the *e-CFR* or a commercial service to see if it lists among its sources any *Federal Register* issues more recent than the latest annual *CFR* revision.

Another tool for updating regulations is a monthly pamphlet accompanying the *CFR* entitled *LSA: List of CFR Sections Affected* (also available through Govinfo), which lists the *Federal Register* pages of any rule changes affecting *CFR* sections since the most recent annual revision. *LSA* brings a search for current regulations up to date within a month or so, and more recent changes can then be found by using a cumulative "List of CFR Parts Affected" in the latest *Federal Register* issue (and perhaps the last issue of the previous month). This cumbersome procedure is often no longer necessary, but *LSA* can still be a convenient resource for scanning an entire *CFR* chapter or part to identify any recent regulatory changes.

While *LSA*'s value in current regulatory research has diminished, older issues remain important resources in tracking regulatory history. Because regulations change frequently, you may occasionally hit a dead end when trying to find a *CFR* reference cited in a case or article. The regulation may have been repealed, or it may have been transferred to another *CFR* location. Tables tracing regulatory changes for the most recent five years are published in the back of each *CFR* volume (in print and on Govinfo), listing all sections in that volume that have been repealed, transferred, revised, or otherwise affected. To trace a section beyond these five years, you would need to check each year's cumulative *LSA* issue. Govinfo's *LSA* page has coverage from 1986, and HeinOnline's *CFR* and *Federal Register* collections have *LSA* issues back to 1949.

Interpreting Regulations. A court may invalidate a regulation or provide an important interpretation of key provisions, making identifying relevant cases an essential part of regulatory research. The official *CFR*, whether used in print or online (including the *e-CFR*), contains no annotations of court decisions like those in the *United States Code Annotated* or *United States Code Service*.

The most convenient way to find court decisions is to use the *CFR* on either Westlaw or Lexis, as both platforms include notes of decisions similar to those in annotated statutory codes, as well as citing references in agency decisions, statutes, and secondary sources. These can provide a springboard from the text to a wide range of research references. Symbols such as red flags (on Westlaw) and exclamation points (on Lexis) warn that a section may have been amended, repealed, or adversely affected by a court decision. Illustration 8-6 shows the Context & Analysis tab for the Westlaw version of 9 C.F.R. § 2.1, including links to law review articles and *United States Code Annotated* sections.

On Lexis, the Shepard's link offers a "Subsection reports by specific court citation" option that lists references under the particular subsection cited. Some *CFR* sections run for dozens of pages with multiple subsections, and this can be a great time saver if you are looking for references to a specific provision within a lengthy and complex *CFR* section. "Subsection reports by specific court citation" is a link at the top of the Shepard's display.

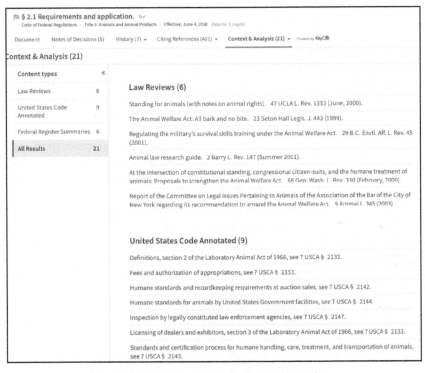

**Illustration 8-6. Context & Analysis for a
CFR section on Westlaw.**

§ 8.3   OTHER SOURCES OF AGENCY LAW

Federal agencies have methods of making law outside of the traditional notice-and-comment rulemaking, albeit to a somewhat less authoritative effect. These methods, such as the issuance of guidance documents and agency adjudications, may produce information that is widely applicable to industry, government, and the public generally. Thorough research on a legal issue involving a federal agency requires familiarity with the types of materials discussed in this section.

(a) Guidance Documents

Regulations published in the *Federal Register* and *CFR* are the most authoritative sources of agency law, but over the years the creation of regulations has become increasingly time-consuming and complicated, as agencies must solicit and consider comments from interested parties. As a result of this "ossification" of the rulemaking process, agencies now are just as likely to create policy through documents that do not require the notice-and-comment procedures mandated by the Administrative Procedure Act. These guidance documents include a wide range of agency pronouncements and publications, such as handbooks, policy statements, interpretive rules, circulars, fact sheets, bulletins, and private advice letters. Guidance documents do not have the same binding force as regulations, but they can be important indications of how an agency perceives its mandate and how it will respond in a specific situation.[37] Illustration 8-7 shows a guidance document from the Animal and Plant Health Inspection Service, answering questions about its dog importation regulations.

---

[37] The leading article on the ossification of rulemaking is Thomas O. McGarity, *Some Thoughts on "Deossifying" the Rulemaking Process*, 41 DUKE L.J. 1385 (1992). On the difference between legislative rules (which must follow APA requirements) and interpretive rules (which need not), see, e.g., David L. Franklin, *Legislative Rules, Nonlegislative Rules, and the Perils of the Short Cut*, 120 YALE L.J. 276, 282–89 (2010), and William Funk, *A Primer on Nonlegislative Rules*, 53 ADMIN. L. REV. 1321 (2001). It is not always clear whether a rule is legislative or interpretive. *See* Kristin E. Hickman, *Coloring Outside the Lines: Examining Treasury's (Lack of) Compliance with Administrative Procedure Act Rulemaking Requirements*, 82 NOTRE DAME L. REV. 1727 (2007). Whether a rule is legislative or not also may make no difference to those subject to the rule. *See* Nicholas R. Parrillo, *Federal Agency Guidance and the Power to Bind: An Empirical Study of Agencies and Industries*, 36 YALE J. ON REG. 165 (2019).

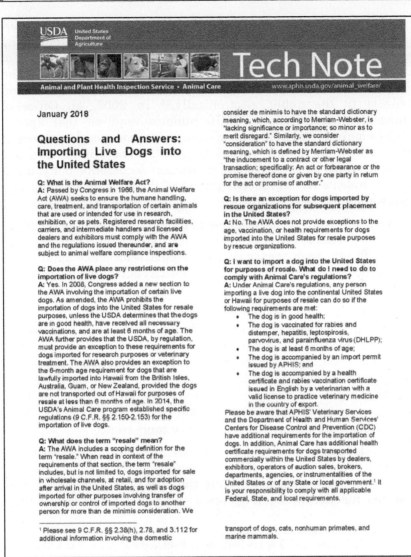

USDA United States Department of Agriculture

Tech Note

Animal and Plant Health Inspection Service • Animal Care   www.aphis.usda.gov/animal_welfare/

January 2018

Questions and Answers: Importing Live Dogs into the United States

Q: What is the Animal Welfare Act?
A: Passed by Congress in 1966, the Animal Welfare Act (AWA) seeks to ensure the humane handling, care, treatment, and transportation of certain animals that are used or intended for use in research, exhibition, or as pets. Registered research facilities, carriers, and intermediate handlers and licensed dealers and exhibitors must comply with the AWA and the regulations issued thereunder, and are subject to animal welfare compliance inspections.

Q: Does the AWA place any restrictions on the importation of live dogs?
A: Yes. In 2008, Congress added a new section to the AWA involving the importation of certain live dogs. As amended, the AWA prohibits the importation of dogs into the United States for resale purposes, unless the USDA determines that the dogs are in good health, have received all necessary vaccinations, and are at least 6 months of age. The AWA further provides that the USDA, by regulation, must provide an exception to these requirements for dogs imported for research purposes or veterinary treatment. The AWA also provides an exception to the 6-month age requirement for dogs that are lawfully imported into Hawaii from the British Isles, Australia, Guam, or New Zealand, provided the dogs are not transported out of Hawaii for purposes of resale at less than 6 months of age. In 2014, the USDA's Animal Care program established specific regulations (9 C.F.R. §§ 2.150-2.153) for the importation of live dogs.

Q: What does the term "resale" mean?
A: The AWA includes a scoping definition for the term "resale." When read in context of the requirements of that section, the term "resale" includes, but is not limited to, dogs imported for sale in wholesale channels, at retail, and for adoption after arrival in the United States, as well as dogs imported for other purposes involving transfer of ownership or control of imported dogs to another person for more than de minimis consideration. We

consider de minimis to have the standard dictionary meaning, which, according to Merriam-Webster, is "lacking significance or importance; so minor as to merit disregard." Similarly, we consider "consideration" to have the standard dictionary meaning, which is defined by Merriam-Webster as "the inducement to a contract or other legal transaction; specifically: An act or forbearance or the promise thereof done or given by one party in return for the act or promise of another."

Q: Is there an exception for dogs imported by rescue organizations for subsequent placement in the United States?
A: No. The AWA does not provide exceptions to the age, vaccination, or health requirements for dogs imported into the United States for resale purposes by rescue organizations.

Q: I want to import a dog into the United States for purposes of resale. What do I need to do to comply with Animal Care's regulations?
A: Under Animal Care's regulations, any person importing a live dog into the continental United States or Hawaii for purposes of resale can do so if the following requirements are met:
- The dog is in good health;
- The dog is vaccinated for rabies and distemper, hepatitis, leptospirosis, parvovirus, and parainfluenza virus (DHLPP);
- The dog is at least 6 months of age;
- The dog is accompanied by an import permit issued by APHIS; and
- The dog is accompanied by a health certificate and rabies vaccination certificate issued in English by a veterinarian with a valid license to practice veterinary medicine in the country of export.

Please be aware that APHIS' Veterinary Services and the Department of Health and Human Services' Centers for Disease Control and Prevention (CDC) have additional requirements for the importation of dogs. In addition, Animal Care has additional health certificate requirements for dogs transported commercially within the United States by dealers, exhibitors, operators of auction sales, brokers, departments, agencies, or instrumentalities of the United States or of any State or local government.[1] It is your responsibility to comply with all applicable Federal, State, and local requirements.

[1] Please see 9 C.F.R. §§ 2.38(h), 2.78, and 3.112 for additional information involving the domestic transport of dogs, cats, nonhuman primates, and marine mammals.

Illustration 8-7. A guidance document from the Animal and Plant Health Inspection Service.

Most guidance documents do not appear in the *Federal Register*, the *CFR*, or any other widely available published source, but many are available through agency websites. The Electronic Freedom of Information Act Amendments of 1996 mandates that agencies make policy statements, manuals, and frequently requested information available to the public electronically.[38] In 2007, an Office of Management and Budget (OMB) bulletin required that agency websites maintain current lists of significant guidance documents in effect, with links to each document listed.[39] There is no standard format in which agencies display significant documents, but you can search a website for "significant guidance" if a relevant link is not as readily apparent as it should be.

This uncertain status of access to guidance documents is subject to change, under an executive order issued in October 2019 mandating that each agency create a single, searchable database of its guidance documents and issue regulations governing its guidance practices.[40]

Currently, only a few agencies have issued regulations articulating their perspectives on guidance documents. The Food and Drug Administration, for example, has stated that guidance documents "do not establish legally enforceable rights or responsibilities" and "do not legally bind the public or the FDA," but that "they represent the agency's current thinking. Therefore, FDA employees may depart from guidance documents only with appropriate justification and supervisory concurrence."[41]

Developments may change access to and interpretation of guidance documents, but they will undoubtedly remain essential statements of agency policy despite the lack of consistency in their form and function between agencies and judicial criticism of their

---

[38] Pub. L. No. 104–231, § 4, 110 Stat. 3048, 3049 (codified at 5 U.S.C. § 552(a)(2)).

[39] Final Bulletin for Agency Good Guidance Practices, 72 Fed. Reg. 3432, 3440 (Jan. 25, 2007). The bulletin's preamble explains that the lists should be maintained "in a quickly and easily identifiable manner (e.g., as part of or in close visual proximity to the agency's list of regulations and proposed regulations)." *Id.* at 3437. The Administrative Conference of the United States has issued guidance documents building on the OMB bulletin. Recommendation 2017–5, Agency Guidance Through Policy Statements, 82 Fed. Reg. 61,734 (Dec. 14, 2017); Recommendation 2019–3, Public Availability of Agency Guidance Documents, 84 Fed. Reg. 38,931 (Aug. 8, 2019).

[40] Exec. Order No. 13,891, 84 Fed. Reg. 55,235 (Oct. 9, 2019). A second order the same day mandated that guidance documents could not be used to impose new standards of conduct beyond applicable statutes and regulations. Exec. Order No, 13,892, 84 Fed. Reg. 55,239 (Oct. 9, 2019). Unlike some other recent executive action, these executive orders have been met with bipartisan support. *See, e.g.,* Cass R. Sunstein, *Trump's New Executive Orders Deserve Praise,* BLOOMBERG OPINION, Oct. 15, 2019.

[41] 21 C.F.R. § 10.115(d)(1)–(3) (2019).

validity.[42] Regulations take basically the same form from all agencies and are published in the *Federal Register* and *CFR*, but an understanding of guidance documents requires a familiarity with an agency's website and the ways in which the agency informs interested parties of its policies and interpretations.

(b) Decisions and Rulings

While regulations and guidance documents are the primary means by which most agencies create legal rules and standards within their areas of expertise, administrative agencies also have quasi-judicial functions in which they hold hearings and issue decisions concerning specific parties. These adjudications usually involve a fact-finding process and the application of agency regulations to particular situations or problems. The procedures and precedential value of these decisions vary among agencies.

Formal Adjudications. In most agencies, adjudicatory hearings are only used when imposing a sanction on an individual or organization. In many instances they are not binding on other parties or on the agency in future adjudications. Some agencies such as the Federal Trade Commission and National Labor Relations Board, however, rely on adjudication to establish legal rules. In effect they use the case-by-case adjudication process to create a common law in their subject fields.[43]

Agency hearings are usually conducted by an administrative law judge, who has a role very similar to that of a trial judge and issues the initial decision of the agency.[44] That decision can be appealed to

---

[42] In *Appalachian Power Co. v. E.P.A.*, 208 F.3d 1015 (D.C. Cir. 2000), the court set aside a guidance document in its entirety as improperly promulgated without complying with rulemaking procedures. Its opinion explained:

> The phenomenon we see in this case is familiar. Congress passes a broadly worded statute. The agency follows with regulations containing broad language, open-ended phrases, ambiguous standards and the like. Then as years pass, the agency issues circulars or guidance or memoranda, explaining, interpreting, defining and often expanding the commands in the regulations. One guidance document may yield another and then another and so on. Several words in a regulation may spawn hundreds of pages of text as the agency offers more and more detail regarding what its regulations demand of regulated entities. Law is made, without notice and comment, without public participation, and without publication in the Federal Register or the Code of Federal Regulations.

Id. at 1020. For discussion of the judicial treatment of guidance documents, see Ronald M. Levin, *Rulemaking and the Guidance Exemption*, 70 ADMIN. L. REV. 263 (2018), and Mark Seidenfeld, *Substituting Substantive for Procedural Review of Guidance Documents*, 90 TEX. L. REV. 331 (2011).

[43] *See* Charles H. Koch, Jr., *Policymaking by the Administrative Judiciary*, 56 ALA. L. REV. 693 (2005). *See also* Daniel J. Solove & Woodrow Hartzog, *The FTC and the New Common Law of Privacy*, 114 COLUM. L. REV. 583 (2014) (outlining how one agency, the FTC, uses adjudications to regulate).

[44] Agency adjudications are subject to procedural requirements mandated by §§ 5–8 of the Administrative Procedure Act, 5 U.S.C. §§ 554–557. For an overview of

a higher administrative authority, such as the secretary of the department or a review commission, and appeals of final agency decisions can generally be brought in federal court. The statutes governing judicial review of decisions by many major agencies provide that review is by the U.S. Court of Appeals rather than at the U.S. District Court level.

Most federal agencies write formal opinions to justify or explain their decisions. An agency decision can be an important document in interpreting a regulation or statute, or in applying regulations to particular facts. Although most agencies do not consider themselves strictly bound by their prior decisions under the doctrine of *stare decisis*, the decisions do have considerable precedential value for attorneys practicing before an agency or appealing an agency decision. Illustration 8-8 shows the beginning of a Department of Agriculture decision under the Animal Welfare Act, as published in *Agriculture Decisions*.

About fifteen federal agencies and regulatory commissions publish official reports of their decisions, in a form very similar to official court reports. According to *The Bluebook* and the *ALWD Guide to Legal Citation*, these reports are the source to which decisions should be cited if they appear therein.[45] Recent decisions are also available from agency websites, but there is little consistency in how agencies provide access to these documents. Even once a site with decisions is found, its search engine may be ineffective and it may lack retrospective coverage.[46] This makes collections of federal agency decisions available from commercial online platforms particularly valuable. The decisions of more than seventy agencies are available through both Westlaw and Lexis. In many instances, coverage is retrospective to the first published decisions. Westlaw and Lexis coverage includes many administrative decisions not published in official reports, and generally extends much earlier than official websites. Bloomberg Law also has decisions and other documents from numerous agencies, with coverage for some sources that is broader than what is available on the official websites.

---

hearing procedures, see Morell E. Mullins, *Manual for Administrative Law Judges*, 23 J. NAT'L ASS'N ADMIN. L. JUDGES (Special Issue 2004).

[45] THE BLUEBOOK: A UNIFORM SYSTEM OF CITATION R. 14.3.2(a) (21st ed. 2020); ALWD GUIDE TO LEGAL CITATION R. 18.5(b) (6th ed. 2017). Major series of agency reports are listed in both citation guides. THE BLUEBOOK tbl. T1.2; ALWD GUIDE TO LEGAL CITATION app. 7(a).

[46] For an examination of the problem, see Daniel J. Sheffner, *Access to Adjudication Materials on Federal Agency Websites*, 51 AKRON L. REV. 447 (2018).

Stearns Zoological Rescue & Rehab Center, Inc.
76 Agric. Dec. 45

In re: STEARNS ZOOLOGICAL RESCUE & REHAB CENTER, INC., a Florida corporation d/b/a DADE CITY WILD THINGS.
Docket No. 15-0146.
Decision and Order.
Filed February 15, 2017.

AWA.

Samuel D. Jockel, Esq., for Complainant.
William J. Cook, Esq., for Respondent.
Initial Decision and Order entered by Bobbie J. McCartney, Chief Administrative Law Judge.

DECISION AND ORDER

The Animal Welfare Act (7 U.S.C. §§ 2131 *et seq.*) (AWA or Act) regulates the commercial exhibition, transportation, purchase, sale, housing, care, handling, and treatment of "animals," as that term is defined in the Act and in the regulations issued under the Act (9 C.F.R. Part 1, *et seq.*) (Regulations). Congress delegated to the Secretary of Agriculture (USDA) authority to enforce the Act.

On July 17, 2015, Complainant filed a complaint alleging that respondent Stearns Zoological Rescue & Rehab Center, Inc., violated the AWA and the Regulations on multiple occasions between July 27, 2011 and November 21, 2013. On August 5, 2015, Stearns Zoo filed an answer admitting the jurisdictional allegations and denying the material allegations of the complaint. An oral hearing was held before me, Chief Administrative Law Judge Bobbie J. McCartney, on June 27, 28, 29, and 30, 2016 in Tampa, Florida.

I. Identification of Animals

The Regulations provide:

> A class "C" exhibitor shall identify all live dogs and cats under his or her control or on his or her premises, whether held, purchased, or otherwise acquired:

Illustration 8-8. An administrative decision as published in *Agriculture Decisions*.

Retrospective collections of published reports are also offered by both HeinOnline and LLMC Digital (www.llmc.com). Each covers decisions from several dozen administrative agencies, with PDF copies of the original printed reports.

Many administrative decisions are also published, along with other documents such as statutes, regulations, and court decisions, in topical looseleaf and online services.

Researchers working in an unfamiliar area can have a difficult time identifying and finding decisions of relevant agencies. *United States Code Service* (in print or on Lexis) provides a convenient way to learn of administrative decisions, because its annotations include notes of decisions from more than fifty commissions and boards. *United States Code Annotated* does not have annotations of administrative decisions, but Westlaw does list them as citing references under "Administrative Decisions & Guidance." Shepard's on Lexis does not cover citations in administrative decisions.

Advice Letters and Other Rulings. Agencies also provide advice to individuals or businesses seeking clarification of their policies or regulations as applied to particular factual situations. This advice is usually accompanied by a disclaimer that the reply has no precedential value in future instances, but it is nonetheless a strong indication of how an agency interprets its mandate.

Internal Revenue Service private letter rulings and Securities and Exchange Commission no-action letters are leading examples of this sort of decision. These documents were originally sent only to the recipients and not made public, but changing views of the value of informal rulings led to their availability first in print and now online.[47]

---

[47] The SEC decided in 1970 to release its no-action letters for public availability. Procedures Regarding Public Availability of Requests for No-Action and Interpretative Letters and Responses, Release Nos. 33–5098, 34–9006, 35–16875, 39–281, IC–6220, IAA–274, 35 Fed. Reg. 17,779 (Oct. 29, 1970) (codified as amended at 17 C.F.R. § 200.81 (2019)). A lawsuit was required, however, for the IRS to begin releasing its private letter rulings. *Tax Analysts and Advocates v. IRS*, 362 F. Supp. 1298 (D.D.C. 1973), *modified*, 505 F.2d 350 (D.C. Cir. 1974). The dispute was finally settled in 1976. *Protagonists Reach Agreement on IRS Rulings Disclosure*, TAX NOTES, Mar. 15, 1976, at 3.

SEC regulations explain its official perspective on informal advice by its staff:

While opinions expressed by members of the staff do not constitute an official expression of the Commission's views, they represent the views of persons who are continuously working with the provisions of the statute involved. And any statement by the director, associate director, assistant director, chief accountant, chief counsel, or chief financial analyst of a division can be relied upon as representing the views of that division.

17 C.F.R. § 202.1(d) (2019). On the reception by the courts of no-action letters and private letter rulings, see Donna M. Nagy, *Judicial Reliance on Regulatory Interpretations in SEC No-Action Letters: Current Problems and a Proposed*

Materials like private letter rulings and no-action letters are available from agency websites and in topical services, as well as from major commercial platforms such as Westlaw and Lexis. These platforms generally offer the most sophisticated search options, and their databases combine these materials with related statutes, regulations, and court decisions.

The difficult first step is identifying what informal documentation is available from a particular agency. You can do this by perusing its website, by noting the sources cited in the case law and secondary literature, or by studying a guide to the resources in a particular area of law.[48] The learning curve may take some time, as many agencies are notorious for having idiosyncratic processes governed as much by unwritten "lore" as by statutes and regulations.[49]

Attorney General Opinions. Somewhat different from other agency decisions are the opinions of the Attorney General of the United States and the Department of Justice's Office of Legal Counsel (OLC). As the federal government's law firm, the Department of Justice provides legal advice to the President and to other departments.[50] These are advisory opinions and are not binding, but they are nonetheless usually given some persuasive authority.[51]

Between 1791 and 1982, opinions were signed by the U.S. Attorney General and published in a series entitled *Opinions of the Attorneys General of the United States.* The opinion function has now

---

Framework, 83 CORNELL L. REV. 921 (1998); Dale F. Rubin, *Private Letter and Revenue Rulings: Remedy or Ruse?*, 28 N. KY. L. REV. 50 (2001).

[48] SPECIALIZED LEGAL RESEARCH (Penny Hazelton ed., new ed. 2014–date) covers administrative and other resources in several major areas including securities regulation, federal income taxation, copyright law, federal labor and employment law, environmental law, admiralty and maritime law, immigration law, banking law, patent and trademark law, government contracts, and customs law.

[49] *See, e.g.*, GARY M. BROWN, SECURITIES LAW AND PRACTICE DESKBOOK § 1:3, at 1–11 (6th ed. 2012) ("There is one other item that must be considered—what securities lawyers sometimes call 'lore.' Much of the knowledge it takes to deal with the Commission, and otherwise practice in the field, is not the subject of an official pronouncement. If, for example, a lawyer were to prepare and file a Securities Act registration statement following only the statute, rules, and registration statement form, the Commission would likely reject it on the basis that it is so far afield that the staff does not know how to deal with it."); Stanley M. Gorinson et al., *Competition Advocacy before Regulatory Agencies*, ANTITRUST, Summer 1991, at 24, 24 ("Regulatory agencies have their own unique law and lore. Lawyers acclimated to the courtroom can be astounded by the 'oddities' that are the heart of regulatory practice.").

[50] 28 U.S.C. §§ 511–512. This responsibility of the Attorney General dates back to the Judiciary Act of 1789, ch. 20, § 35, 1 Stat. 73, 93.

[51] *See* Sonia Mittal, *OLC's Day in Court: Judicial Deference to the Office of Legal Counsel*, 9 HARV. L. & POL'Y REV. 211 (2015).

been delegated to the OLC.[52] The opinions of this office are available on the DOJ website (www.justice.gov/olc/), and were published in the print series *Opinions of the Office of Legal Counsel* (1977–2008). Opinions of the Attorney General and OLC are also available online through the major commercial platforms, and HeinOnline's U.S. Federal Agency Documents, Decisions, and Appeals library contains opinions back to 1791.

(c) Other Publications

Regulations, guidance documents, and agency decisions are among the most legally significant of federal government publications, but they constitute only a small fraction of the information available. Agencies also issue other materials containing a great deal of information relating to their legal business and the areas they regulate. These include annual reports, monographs, and websites and pamphlets providing information for the public or regulated industries.

Annual reports can be important information sources about the work of an agency. They may describe important litigation and include statistics concerning cases handled, prosecutions, settlements, and dispositions. They often discuss enforcement policies and interpret agency statutes or proposed amendments. Almost every agency also produces material explaining its structure and operation, varying from short, popular descriptions to detailed administrative handbooks. Many agencies publish general periodicals in their field of activity, such as the *Federal Reserve Bulletin* and *Monthly Labor Review,* as well as technical journals and newsletters. Agencies and commissions have also issued special studies, reports, and monographs on major problems.[53]

Recently published reports and documents are generally available on agency websites, but finding older material may require some hunting in a government depository library. The Government Publishing Office distributes materials at no cost to libraries around the country. A selected number of libraries, usually one per state, are known as "regional depositories" and receive everything GPO publishes for distribution. Many law libraries are "selective

---

[52] 28 C.F.R. § 0.25(a) (2019). *See generally* Arthur H. Garrison, *The Opinions by the Attorney General and the Office of Legal Counsel: How and Why They Are Significant,* 76 ALB. L. REV. 217 (2012/2013); Symposium, *Attorney General's Opinion Function and the Office of Legal Counsel,* 15 CARDOZO L. REV. 337 (1993).

[53] POPULAR NAMES OF U.S. GOVERNMENT REPORTS (4th ed. 1984, available on HeinOnline) provides help in identifying older reports known by short or unofficial titles, such as the subject or the name of a commission chairperson.

depositories" and collect many significant law-related GPO publications.[54]

Material distributed by the GPO can be found through its online and print catalogs. The online catalog (catalog.gpo.gov) lists publications since 1976 and is expanding its coverage of older material, which can also be found using the printed *Monthly Catalog of United States Government Publications* (1895–2004).[55] These resources are useful not only in determining what the government publishes, but they also provide the Superintendent of Documents (SuDocs) classification numbers used to shelve government documents in most large libraries.[56] This is important because many libraries' online catalogs do not include all of their extensive holdings of older federal documents.

Not all documents produced by the federal government are published by GPO and made available to depository libraries. Thousands of "fugitive documents" are published internally by agencies or made available temporarily online, with no system for permanent archiving or preservation. Some information formerly available on agency websites has disappeared when policies have changed or agencies have terminated or been eliminated.[57] Two major sources for online material no longer available from the

---

[54] 44 U.S.C. § 1912. The GPO website has a map with information about each federal depository library (www.fdlp.gov/about-the-fdlp/federal-depository-libraries).

[55] Several hundred thousand older publications from the executive departments and independent agencies are available online in ProQuest Executive Branch Documents 1789–1932, an add-on module to ProQuest Congressional. In some libraries they are available in microfiche and indexed in CIS INDEX TO EXECUTIVE BRANCH DOCUMENTS 1789–1909 (1990–97) and CIS INDEX TO EXECUTIVE BRANCH DOCUMENTS 1910–1932 (1996–2002). The earlier content is based on CHECKLIST OF UNITED STATES PUBLIC DOCUMENTS: 1789–1909 (1911).

[56] The SuDocs system is also the basis of GUIDE TO U.S. GOVERNMENT PUBLICATIONS (Donna Andriot ed.), an annual publication that lists the published series and periodicals for all agencies, both current and defunct. It includes indexes by agency, title, and subject keyword, and is a good first place to learn what reports and documents a particular agency has published over the years.

CASSANDRA J. HARTNETT ET AL., FUNDAMENTALS OF GOVERNMENT INFORMATION: MINING, FINDING, EVALUATING, AND USING GOVERNMENT RESOURCES (2d ed. 2016) and BETHANY LATHAM, FINDING AND USING U.S. GOVERNMENT INFORMATION: A PRACTICAL GUIDE FOR LIBRARIANS (2018) provide further information on the SuDocs system and access to federal government information generally. For more on the origins of this system, see Gail K. Nelson & John V. Richardson, Jr., *Adelaide Hasse and the Early History of the U.S. Superintendent of Documents Classification Scheme*, 13 GOV'T PUBLICATIONS REV. 79 (1986).

[57] *See* Robert Pear, *In Digital Age, Federal Files Blip Into Oblivion*, N.Y. TIMES, Sept. 13, 2008, at 1. Changes in presidential administration can lead to wholesale revisions or removal of information on agency websites. Finding information from a previous administration may require consulting resources such as the Internet Archive (archive.org). Some resources, such as the Website Monitoring project of the Environmental Data & Governance Alliance (envirodatagov.org/website-monitoring/), track changes in websites over time.

government are CyberCemetery (govinfo.library.unt.edu), which has archived websites for more than eighty defunct commissions, boards, and other entities from 1995 to 2013, and the Internet Archive's Wayback Machine (archive.org), which captures periodic snapshots of government and other websites.

(d) Unpublished Information

Even though agency websites have greatly increased access to government information, the government also has a vast store of additional documentation that it does not publish, such as internal records, data collected on individuals, and staff studies. The Freedom of Information Act (FOIA) dramatically expands the public's access to government files by enabling individuals to request copies of most documents, although it may take weeks, months, or years to receive a reply let alone copies of the documents requested. There are broad exceptions of material that agencies need not disclose, such as classified documents, internal personnel material, trade secrets, and law enforcement information.[58]

The first place to check for information-request policies and procedures is the specific department or agency's website, which should have a Freedom of Information or FOIA link on its front page. This link leads to frequently requested documents made available online under e-FOIA and to instructions for filing requests with the agency. For some agencies, you can use the federal government's central FOIA website (www.foia.gov) for placing and tracking requests, as well as for searching past FOIA requests and responses.

More general resources are also available for assistance in filing FOIA requests. The Reporters Committee for Freedom of the Press has a useful iFOIA website (www.ifoia.org), which includes a template for filing FOIA requests. The House Committee on Government Reform has published a handbook with sample request forms, *A Citizen's Guide on Using the Freedom of Information Act and the Privacy Act of 1974 to Request Government Records,* H.R. Rep. 112–689 (2012).

Several books provide lengthier treatment of the history and interpretation of FOIA, including procedures and sample forms for filing requests and suing to compel disclosure. P. Stephen Gidiere III, *The Federal Information Manual: How the Government Collects, Manages, and Discloses Information Under FOIA and Other Statutes*

---

[58] 5 U.S.C. § 552(b). *But see* Lotte E. Feinberg, *FOIA, Federal Information Policy, and Information Availability in a Post-9/11 World,* 21 GOV'T INFO. Q. 439 (2004) (noting that access to government records "is increasingly shifting to a nether world" of new categories of records protected from disclosure but not governed by FOIA exemptions).

(2d ed. 2013) includes a chapter on "The Elements of a Successful FOIA Request." More comprehensive treatises include Cornish F. Hitchcock, *Guidebook to the Freedom of Information and Privacy Acts* (annual), and James T. O'Reilly, *Federal Information Disclosure* (semiannual). All three of these works are available on Westlaw.

Chapter 9

STATE ADMINISTRATIVE LAW AND LOCAL LAW

Table of Sections

Federal administrative law is so dominant in American legal discourse that it is sometimes easy to forget that state governments can affect their citizens no less profoundly than does the federal bureaucracy. State agencies set and enforce public health and housing standards, fix and regulate utility rates and practices, and govern labor and business activities. Governors issue executive orders establishing commissions and declaring emergencies, and state attorneys general play important roles in enforcing and interpreting state law.

This chapter also covers local law, the charters and ordinances of counties and cities. Although the powers of local governments vary from state to state, they play an important role in regulating commerce, health and safety, and other activities within their jurisdictions.

§ 9.1   STATE ADMINISTRATIVE LAW

To a significant extent, research in state administrative law follows the federal paradigm. It is necessary to identify relevant agencies, track regulations as promulgated and codified, and find relevant administrative and judicial decisions. Many of these resources are available online, but in most states publication of agency rules and decisions is less systematic and thorough than it is on the federal level.

(a) Background and Framework

Treatises covering state administrative law generally are not easy to find, as many texts and treatises in this field focus exclusively on federal law. One exception is Charles H. Koch, Jr. & Richard Murphy, *Administrative Law and Practice* (3d ed. 2010–date, available on Westlaw), in which each chapter concludes with several sections on state law, highlighting decisions of state courts on these issues. The legal encyclopedia *American Jurisprudence 2d* (available on both Lexis and Westlaw) also incorporates discussion of state law into its Administrative Law article.

A treatise focusing on a specific area subject to regulation or on an individual state is often a better starting point. Most subject treatises cover both federal and state law, and a few, such as Daniel P. Selmi & Kenneth A. Manaster, *State Environmental Law* (1989–date, available on Westlaw), focus specifically on state-level issues.

A text or treatise dedicated to a specific state can incorporate discussion of state administrative law issues in a way that more general works cannot. These state-specific works can be identified from library website guides or from state legal research guides.

Every state has statutes mandating the procedures that its agencies must follow in creating law, and an annotated state code can be an invaluable resource for interpreting these provisions. In over half of the states, the relevant statutes are based on the Model State Administrative Procedure Act (1961) drafted by the Uniform Law Commission (ULC). The ULC has also drafted two revisions of this act, in 1981 and 2010.[1] All three acts are in volumes 15 and 15A of *Uniform Laws Annotated* (available on Westlaw), accompanied by comments and notes of court decisions from adopting jurisdictions. In a state with a law based on the Model Act, decisions from other jurisdictions may be helpful persuasive authority on issues the state's own courts have not yet addressed.

(b) Websites and Guides

As is true on the federal level, it is important that lawyers become familiar with state administrative agencies that may affect their clients. State websites are often the best starting point to determine the jurisdiction of relevant agencies and their publications. If a search engine does not quickly lead you to the state

---

[1] The 1981 act has been adopted in just three jurisdictions and no state has yet adopted the 2010 act. For a background and discussion of all three acts, see John Gedid, *Administrative Procedure for the Twenty-First Century: An Introduction to the 2010 Model State Administrative Procedure Act*, 44 ST. MARY'S L.J. 241 (2012). *See also* Symposium, *Modernizing Agency Practice: The 2010 Model State Administrative Procedure Act*, 20 WIDENER L.J. 697 (2011).

government homepage, USA.gov (www.usa.gov/states-and-territories) has links for each state, including links to major state administrative agencies.

Most states publish official manuals, or "blue books," paralleling the *United States Government Manual* and providing basic information about government agencies and officials. Some of these manuals describe state agency functions and publications, while others simply serve as government phone directories. The American Library Association's Government Documents Round Table has a State Blue Books and Encyclopedias page (godort.libguides.com/bluebooks) that lists most of these resources and links to versions available online. The annual *State Legislative Sourcebook* also lists directories and manuals for each state, as well as websites, statistical abstracts, and other reference sources. A thorough legal research guide for a specific state will discuss relevant resources and explain any idiosyncrasies of that state's administrative law processes and publications.

When working with a state agency, it often helps to develop a broader understanding of the issues that concern state governments. Numerous national organizations of government officials publish policy documents and analyses of current developments on these issues. The Council of State Governments (www.csg.org) studies policy trends in a broad range of areas, and dozens of more specific organizations represent officials in areas ranging from bank supervisors to fish and wildlife agencies. If there is a state agency in a particular field, there is likely a national organization that provides news, analysis, and links to agencies in other states. These organizations can be valuable information resources and can be found with internet searches such as "state [subject] agencies association."

Often the best way to obtain information is to contact the agency directly. State and multistate websites may include lists of officials' names and numbers, but these are generally less thorough and specific than two commercial online resources, GovSearch (www.govsearch.com) and Leadership Connect (www.leadershipconnect.io). These generally have the most detailed listings and contact information for state administrative personnel.

If you need statistical or survey data, the Council of State Governments' annual *Book of the States* (knowledgecenter.csg.org) summarizes recent developments and has more than 170 tables presenting a broad range of legal, political, and statistical information on government operations in each of the fifty states. Chapter 4 of *Book of the States* focuses on state executive branches, with tables summarizing the powers and duties of governors, lieutenant governors, secretaries of state, attorneys general, and other officials.

(c) Regulations and Executive Orders

Almost every state issues a subject compilation of its administrative regulations, and a weekly, biweekly, or monthly register of new and proposed regulations, executive orders, and notices. These resources are listed in the *Bluebook* and *ALWD Guide*'s lists of the major primary sources for each state.

Regulations. In promulgating regulations, states generally follow the paradigm established by the federal government, although explanations of rulemaking actions are rarely as thorough as those found in *Federal Register* preambles. In many states, new regulations are simply published with no explanation whatsoever.

State administrative law is an area in which most research is done online.[2] Law libraries within a state generally have print copies of its administrative code and register, but very few libraries have administrative law resources for other states. As with statutory research, you can do basic work with free government websites but more thorough information is often available from the major commercial legal research platforms.

Links to official online versions of codes and registers are available from the National Association of Secretaries of State's Administrative Codes and Registers section (www.administrative rules.org). As with state statutes, unfortunately, some state sites carry prominent warnings that the online version is unofficial and that the only official source is the (rarely available) printed version.

Illustration 9-1 shows a section of *Administrative Rules of Montana*, the codification of Montana regulations, on the capture and transportation of prairie dogs. Note at the bottom that it gives references to the *Montana Code Annotated* and to the initial publication of this rule in the *Montana Administrative Register*. This publication is shown in Illustration 9-2. Unlike new rules published in the *Federal Register*, it does not include a lengthy preamble explaining the scope and purpose of the new rule.

---

[2] For historical research, however, sometimes print or microformat is your only option. A helpful state administrative law research guide can provide guidance on when this might be the case, including noting, for example, when a state's regulations were codified and how you might track down versions produced by agencies before they were compiled in a code.

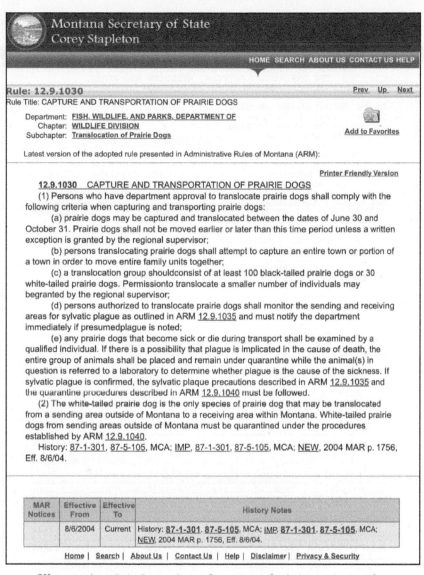

Illustration 9-1. A section of a state administrative code.

-1756-

BEFORE THE FISH, WILDLIFE AND PARKS COMMISSION AND
THE DEPARTMENT OF FISH, WILDLIFE AND PARKS
OF THE STATE OF MONTANA

In the matter of the adoption)
of new rules I through XI)   NOTICE OF ADOPTION
pertaining to translocation)
of prairie dogs   )

    TO: All Concerned Persons

    1.   On February 26, 2004, the Fish, Wildlife and Parks
Commission (commission) and the Department of Fish, Wildlife and
Parks (department) published notice of the proposed adoption of
new rules I through XI pertaining to translocation of prairie
dogs at page 370 of the 2004 Montana Administrative Register,
Issue Number 4.

    2.   The   commission   and   department   have   adopted   the
following new rules exactly as proposed:

        Rule III   (ARM 12.9.1010)
        Rule IV   (ARM 12.9.1015)
        Rule V   (ARM 12.9.1020)
        Rule IX   (ARM 12.9.1040)
        Rule X   (ARM 12.9.1045)
        Rule XI   (ARM 12.9.1050)

    3.   The   commission   and   department   have   adopted   the
following new rules with the following changes, stricken matter
interlined, new matter underlined:

        Rule I   (ARM 12.9.1001)
        Rule II   (ARM 12.9.1005)
        Rule VI   (ARM 12.9.1025)
        Rule VII   (ARM 12.9.1030)
        Rule VIII (ARM 12.9.1035)

    NEW RULE I (ARM 12.9.1001) DEFINITIONS (1) "Confirmed
sylvatic plague" means the presence of plague-positive fleas,
prairie dogs or other mammals has been documented.
    (2)   "Historically   occupied   range"   means   the   area
encompassed by the outer limits of the historic distribution of
a species.   The historic range of the black-tailed prairie dogs
is depicted on page 12 of the "Conservation Plan for Black-
tailed and White-Tailed Prairie Dogs in Montana" published in
2002.   This   document   is   posted   on   the   department   webpage
http://fwp.state.mt.us.
    (3)   "Presumed   sylvatic   plague"   means   that   visual
observation indicates evidence of numerical declines in prairie
dog numbers in the absence of poisoning or other known sources
of prairie dog mortality.
    (1) through (3) remain as proposed, but are renumbered (4)
through (6).

15-8/5/04   Montana Administrative Register

Illustration 9-2. Announcement of a new rule in a state register.

Westlaw, Lexis, and Bloomberg Law all have administrative codes from every state and the District of Columbia. On any of these platforms you can search an individual state's regulations or all state regulations at once. Westlaw also has archived Historical Regulations files of earlier versions of administrative codes back generally to the early 2000s, a Regulations Compare feature allowing you to see red-lined changes between two versions (if at least two versions exist in Westlaw), Regulation Tracking databases for information on proposed and recently adopted regulations, and 50 State Regulatory Surveys with citations and links for each state's administrative code provisions on several hundred topics.

CAL INFO Guide to the Administrative Regulations of the States & Territories is an annual publication that reprints the tables of contents for each administrative code. This information can make it easier to identify relevant regulations from state to state, to know which title or code is needed. CAL INFO's website has links to state administrative codes and registers (www.calinfo.net/links.htm).

Executive Orders. Like the President of the United States, a state governor can exercise authority through the issuance of executive orders or similar legal pronouncements.[3] These are usually included in the state registers containing new regulations, and most governors include the text of executive orders on their websites. USA.gov maintains links to gubernatorial websites (www.usa.gov/state-governor). The National Governors Association (www.nga.org) covers issues of concern to governors nationwide.

(d) Decisions, Rulings, and Other Documents

Some state agencies hold adjudicative hearings, like their federal counterparts, and publish official reports of their decisions.[4] The most common are the reports of commissions governing banking, insurance, taxation, and utilities. Many state administrative decisions are included on the online platforms and on agency websites, and a few topical services and reporters also include state agency decisions. Two rather dated guides, William H. Manz, *Guide to State Legislation, Legislative History, and Administrative Materials* (7th ed. 2008) and Cheryl Rae Nyberg, *State Administrative Law Bibliography: Print and Electronic Sources* (2000), may still be useful for tracking down agency rulings, decisions, and orders.

---

[3] For a discussion of the history and modern scope of gubernatorial authority, see Miriam Seifter, *Gubernatorial Administration*, 131 HARV. L. REV. 480 (2017).

[4] On the independence of state agencies and their relationship to the other branches of state government, see Miriam Seifter, *Understanding State Agency Independence*, 117 MICH. L. REV. 1537 (2019).

The opinions of state attorneys general, written in response to questions from government officials, can have considerable significance in legal research. Although attorney general opinions are advisory in nature and do not have binding authority, courts generally give them considerable weight in interpreting statutes and regulations.[5] Most states publish attorney general opinions in bound volumes, and recent opinions are available on the attorneys general's websites. Opinions are also available online in Lexis and Westlaw, for most states beginning in 1977 or earlier. Some attorney general opinions are included in the annotations in state codes, but coverage varies from state to state. Westlaw also includes attorney general opinions as citing sources in its coverage of cases, statutes, and other resources. If you are working from an attorney general opinion, however, citing references are not listed so you would need to search by keyword to track its treatment in cases and articles.

As with federal agencies, guidance documents and other publications from agencies can also be important in interpreting state law. Materials such as guidelines and manuals are increasingly available from agency websites.[6]

Like the federal government, each state has open records laws under which unpublished information can be obtained upon request. Information on each state's laws and procedures is available from the National Freedom of Information Coalition (www.nfoic.org/organizations/state-foi-resources) and the Reporters Committee for Freedom of the Press's Open Government Guide (rcfp.org/open-government-guide).

§ 9.2   THE LAW OF COUNTIES AND CITIES

Legal problems and issues are governed not only by federal and state law, but also by the laws of counties, cities, and other local authorities. Education, housing, social welfare, transportation, and zoning are all heavily regulated at the local level of government.

---

[5] See Ian Eppler, *The Opinion Power of the Attorney General and the Attorney General as a Public Actor*, 29 B.U. PUB. INT. L.J. 111 (2019), for a fifty-state survey of attorney general opinions' nature and structure.

[6] The role of guidance documents in state administrative law is examined in Michael Asimow, *Guidance Documents in the States: Toward a Safe Harbor*, 54 ADMIN. L. REV. 631 (2002), and in a more specific context in Samuel J. McKim, III, *The Sometimes Dubious Efficacy of Michigan Department of Treasury "Rules," "Revenue Administrative Bulletins," "Letter Rulings," "Questions and Answers," and Other Publications*, 60 TAX LAW. 1019 (2007).

One way to identify available documents, online or in print, is to check a state's periodic list of publications. Older state documents in print can be hard to identify and even harder to locate, but the *Monthly Checklist of State Publications*, published by the Library of Congress from 1910 to 1994, may provide leads.

Counties and cities are administrative units of the states, with lawmaking powers determined by state constitution or by legislative delegation of authority. There is a distinction between counties—which generally administer state functions—and municipal corporations such as cities, towns, and the like. Indeed, the types of local governments and their responsibilities and powers vary greatly from state to state and from region to region. The scope of local government authority also varies considerably from state to state. Basically, states either follow Dillon's Rule, under which local government only has powers expressly delegated by the state, or Home Rule, through which localities have inherent lawmaking powers in some areas.[7]

Local governments create a variety of legal documents that can be important in legal research. A local government's *charter* is its organic law, similar in purpose to a federal or state constitution. An *ordinance* is a measure passed by its council or governing body to regulate local matters. Many localities also have administrative agencies that issue rules or decisions.

Most cities and counties publish or otherwise make available collections of their charters and ordinances on their websites and sometimes in print. As with other units of government, USA.gov has links to local websites (www.usa.gov/local-governments).

Several publishers specialize in publication of local ordinances and have free code libraries on their websites. The largest of these is Municipal Code Corporation (Municode) (library.municode.com), which publishes codes for about 3,500 local governments, including over half of the country's fifty largest cities. For most jurisdictions, you can also opt to search archived versions of codes back to 2011 or 2012. Illustration 9-3 shows a Longmont, Colorado, ordinance on prairie dogs, from the Municode Library.

---

[7] DALE KRANE ET AL., HOME RULE IN AMERICA: A FIFTY-STATE HANDBOOK (2001) has a state-by-state survey of the relationship between state governments and their counties and cities. For a historical introduction to the two forms, see Hugh Spitzer, *"Home Rule" vs. "Dillon's Rule" for Washington Cities*, 38 SEATTLE U. L. REV. 809, 813–24 (2015). *See also* Steve M. Wise et al., *The Power of Municipalities to Enact Legislation Granting Legal Rights to Nonhuman Animals Pursuant to Home Rule*, 67 SYRACUSE L. REV. 31 (2017) (illustrating a detailed application of home rule).

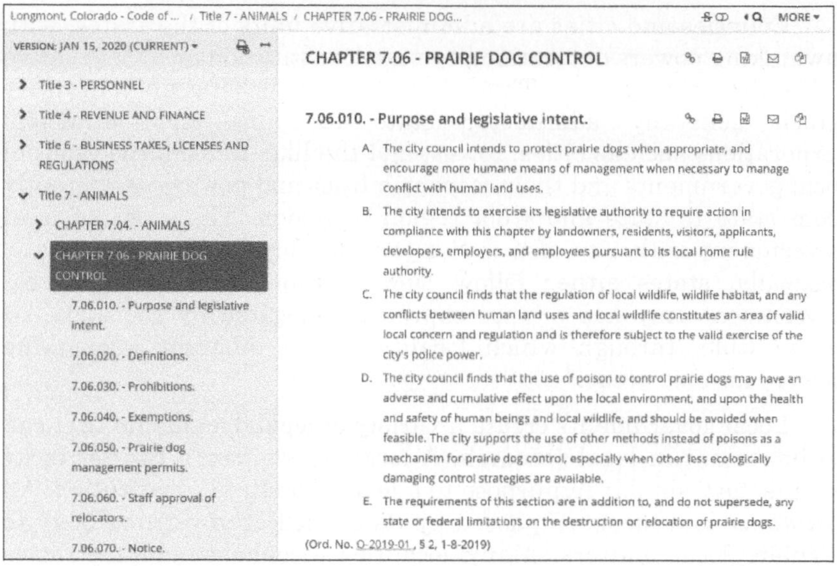
Longmont, Colorado - Code of... / Title 7 - ANIMALS / CHAPTER 7.06 - PRAIRIE DOG... MORE

VERSION: JAN 15, 2020 (CURRENT)

Title 3 - PERSONNEL
Title 4 - REVENUE AND FINANCE
Title 6 - BUSINESS TAXES, LICENSES AND REGULATIONS
Title 7 - ANIMALS
CHAPTER 7.04. - ANIMALS
CHAPTER 7.06 - PRAIRIE DOG CONTROL
7.06.010. - Purpose and legislative intent.
7.06.020. - Definitions.
7.06.030. - Prohibitions.
7.06.040. - Exemptions.
7.06.050. - Prairie dog management permits.
7.06.060. - Staff approval of relocators.
7.06.070. - Notice.

CHAPTER 7.06 - PRAIRIE DOG CONTROL

7.06.010. - Purpose and legislative intent.

A. The city council intends to protect prairie dogs when appropriate, and encourage more humane means of management when necessary to manage conflict with human land uses.

B. The city intends to exercise its legislative authority to require action in compliance with this chapter by landowners, residents, visitors, applicants, developers, employers, and employees pursuant to its local home rule authority.

C. The city council finds that the regulation of local wildlife, wildlife habitat, and any conflicts between human land uses and local wildlife constitutes an area of valid local concern and regulation and is therefore subject to the valid exercise of the city's police power.

D. The city council finds that the use of poison to control prairie dogs may have an adverse and cumulative effect upon the local environment, and upon the health and safety of human beings and local wildlife, and should be avoided when feasible. The city supports the use of other methods instead of poisons as a mechanism for prairie dog control, especially when other less ecologically damaging control strategies are available.

E. The requirements of this section are in addition to, and do not supersede, any state or federal limitations on the destruction or relocation of prairie dogs.

(Ord. No. O-2019-01, § 2, 1-8-2019)

Illustration 9-3. A city ordinance on Municode.com.

American Legal Publishing Corporation (www.amlegal.com/code-library) is another major publisher of local codes, with close to 1,500 jurisdictions including Los Angeles and New York City. General Code LLC (www.generalcode.com/resources/ecode360-library/) has about 2,500 jurisdictions, including several hundred towns and villages in New York. Smaller publishers include Code Publishing Company (www.codebook.com/listing/) and Sterling Codifiers (www.sterlingcodifiers.com), each with about 500 jurisdictions, and Quality Code Publishing (www.qcode.us/codes.html) with about 150 localities, mostly in California. Each of these publishers makes the codes it publishes available free online.

Lexis provides access to almost all of Municode's county and city codes within its Statutes & Legislation collection. In Lexis you cannot choose to search one particular locality's code, but this collection does allow multistate searches for ordinances on particular topics. Westlaw has far fewer local codes, but New York City materials are available both there and on Lexis.

State and local law often incorporates industry codes on areas such as construction and fire safety. The International Code Council (www.iccsafe.org) publishes a series of model codes on building and construction standards. The current model codes are available on Westlaw, and older versions of many codes adopted by states and localities are available free from Public.Resource.org (law.resource.org/pub/us/code/safety.html).

Works of national scope that might be of help in a local law problem include the leading treatise in the area, Eugene McQuillin et al., *The Law of Municipal Corporations* (3d ed. 1949–date), and *Ordinance Law Annotations* (1969–date), which has abstracts of court decisions on local law issues, arranged by subject. Both are available on Westlaw. Other treatises include Sandra M. Stevenson, *Antieau on Local Government Law* (2d ed. 1998–date, available on Lexis) and John C. Martinez, *Local Government Law* (2d ed. 2012–date, available on Westlaw).

Because much local law information is not available in print or online, direct contact with officials by telephone or e-mail may be essential. As with state government agencies, more detailed information than is available on city or county websites may be available from the commercial resources GovSearch and Leadership Connect.

Part IV

THE JUDICIARY

Chapter 10

COURT SYSTEMS AND CASE LAW

Table of Sections

The legislative branch makes law by enacting statutes, and the executive branch enforces these laws through regulations and other administrative action. The judicial branch decides disputes, but in doing so it creates law and determines how statutes and regulations will be interpreted. The judiciary has a vital place in the American legal system, and reports of judicial decisions are among the most important sources of legal authority in the common law system.

The next four chapters concentrate on the judicial branch. This chapter introduces judicial decisions and provides some historical background on case publication. Chapters 11 and 12 explain where to find these decisions and several of the major methods used for case law research. Chapter 13 discusses several other aspects of judicial and case information that are important resources in legal research, such as court rules and briefs.

§ 10.1 THE NATURE OF CASE LAW

"Case law" generally refers to the written opinions of appellate courts on specific issues raised in litigated disputes. Understanding case law's role in the common law system requires a familiarity with the hierarchical structure of court systems and the nature of judicial decisions.

(a) Court Systems

Each jurisdiction, federal and state, has a system of trial and appellate courts, with a *court of last resort* that creates rules binding on the lower courts in the system. A central function of courts of last resort and other appellate courts is to establish rules of conduct for society, as well as simply determining the rights of the parties appearing before them.[1]

Trial Courts. The *trial court* is where litigation usually begins. The jurisdiction of these courts may be based on geography (the U.S. District Courts in the federal system, or county courts in many states) or subject (the U.S. Tax Court, or state family courts and probate courts). In the trial court, *issues of fact* (such as which of two cars entered an intersection first) are decided by the fact finder, either the judge or a jury. These findings are binding on the parties and cannot be appealed. *Issues of law* (such as whether a witness's statement is admissible at trial) are decided by the judge, and a party who disagrees with these rulings can appeal them to a higher court.

Appellate Courts. Appeals from trial court decisions are generally taken to an intermediate appellate court (the U.S. Courts of Appeals and similar state tribunals). An appellate court usually consists of a panel of three or more judges, who typically confer and vote on the issues after considering written briefs and oral argument for each side. One judge writes an opinion summarizing the question and stating the court's holding. Dissenting judges may write separate opinions outlining their views.

Courts of Last Resort. The court of last resort in each jurisdiction (called the Supreme Court in the federal system and in most states) consists of five, seven, or nine judges who sit *en banc* (together) rather than in panels. Courts of last resort usually review cases from the intermediate appellate courts, but they may take appeals directly from trial courts. Unlike other appellate courts, most courts of last resort have discretion in deciding which cases they will hear.[2] Their role in the judicial system is not to resolve every individual dispute, but rather to establish rules, review the validity of legislative and administrative acts, and resolve differences among intermediate appellate courts. A court of last resort's decisions on issues of law are binding on all courts within its jurisdiction.

---

[1] Numerous works discuss the role of judges in deciding cases and creating legal doctrine. Useful introductory works include LAWRENCE BAUM, AMERICAN COURTS: PROCESS AND POLICY (7th ed. 2013), ROBERT A. CARP ET AL., JUDICIAL PROCESS IN AMERICA (11th ed. 2020), and GREGORY MITCHELL & DAVID KLEIN, AMERICAN COURTS EXPLAINED (2016).

[2] Most courts of last resort can simply reject an appeal from a lower court. When the Supreme Court of the United States refuses to hear a case, its action is known as *denying a petition for writ of certiorari,* or "denying cert." The Supreme Court has repeatedly stressed that a denial of certiorari has no precedential value. *See, e.g., Brown v. Allen,* 344 U.S. 443, 488–97 (1953) (opinion of Frankfurter, J.). Nonetheless, a court of last resort may determine the outcome of a case by refusing to hear an appeal and thereby letting a lower court decision stand. This is frequently reported in the press as a "decision," even though no opinion is issued.

(b) The Doctrine of Precedent

An essential element of the common law is the doctrine of precedent, or *stare decisis* ("let the decision stand"), under which courts are bound to follow earlier decisions. These decisions provide guidelines to later courts faced with similar cases and aid in preventing further disputes by helping attorneys assess the potential outcome of a case before pursuing it in court. Although the law changes with time, precedent is designed to provide both fairness and stability. People similarly situated are similarly dealt with, and judgments are consistent rather than arbitrary.

The precedential value of a decision is determined in large part by a court's place in the judicial hierarchy. Decisions from a higher court in a jurisdiction are *binding* or *mandatory authority* and must be followed by a lower court in the same jurisdiction. Decisions from courts in other jurisdictions are not binding, but a court in another state may have considered a situation similar to that at issue; those decisions may provide *persuasive authority* if there is no binding authority available. A court may be convinced to follow the persuasive authority and reach a similar conclusion, or may consider it poorly reasoned or inapplicable and arrive at a very different result.[3]

Under the doctrine of *stare decisis,* a case's holding will govern other cases in its jurisdiction presenting the same or substantially similar facts and issues. The holding, or *ratio decidendi,* of a case can usually be summed up in a succinct sentence or two. In theory, only the holding of the court is authoritative and binding under the doctrine of precedent. The holding is limited to the resolution of the issues in dispute and the significant or material facts upon which the court necessarily relied in arriving at its determination.

Everything else in the court's opinion is *dictum,* something "said by the way."[4] A judge may comment in an opinion on extraneous

---

[3] What *binding, mandatory, persuasive,* and *authority* mean has been explored in legal scholarship. *See, e.g.,* Chad Flanders, *Toward a Theory of Persuasive Authority* 62 OKLA. L. REV. 55 (2009), and Frederick Schauer, *Authority and Authorities,* 94 VA. L. REV. 1931 (2008). *See also* 5 AM. JUR. 2D *Appellate Review* §§ 516–21 (2018).

[4] There is more than one type of dicta. Judicial dicta are comments by the court on matters on which it was briefed but about which it is not making any findings or issuing holdings. *Obiter dicta* are the court's comments on issues that were not raised by the parties at all. *See* Note, *Dictum Revisited,* 4 STAN. L. REV. 509 (1952). For a review of how courts can confuse dicta and holdings, and potential dangers to the integrity of the judicial process from the perspective of a federal appellate judge, see Pierre N. Leval, *Judging Under the Constitution: Dicta About Dicta,* 81 N.Y.U. L. REV. 1249 (2006). *But see* David Klein & Neal Devins, *Dicta Schmicta: Theory Versus Practice in Lower Court Decision Making,* 54 WM. & MARY L. REV. 2021 (2013) (arguing that there is no practical difference between dicta and holdings based on an empirical study of federal court decisions).

issues or speculate about possibilities not at issue in the immediate controversy.[5] These portions of an opinion are dicta and therefore not binding. Dictum in an opinion can explain a decision and signal the court's intention regarding the narrowness or breadth of its holding, so the entire opinion is important and none of it can be ignored. A later court, however, is free to disagree with dictum, which should be identified as such if cited.[6]

§ 10.2   FORMS OF COURT DECISIONS

Most court reports, both online and in print, consist of the decisions of courts of last resort and intermediate appellate courts on issues of law. Trial court decisions on issues of fact have no precedential effect and usually do not even result in written judicial opinions. A jury verdict at the end of a trial, for example, produces no published decision unless the judge rules on a motion challenging the verdict on legal grounds. Some trial court decisions on issues of law are published, especially from the U.S. District Courts, but these are generally less important than appellate court decisions.

Whether online or in print, most judicial decisions are published in two formats. Their first appearance contains only the text of the court's opinion, but then editorial features such as headnotes are added to help readers understand the case and to use it as a vehicle for finding other documents. These editorial enhancements are found in the versions of cases in most reporter volumes and on the major online platforms Westlaw and Lexis. These editorial enhancements are not the law and should not be cited as such.

Slip Opinions. A new decision first appears as the official *slip opinion*, usually available in PDF from the court's website. Slip opinions are individually paginated documents containing the full text of the court's decision, but they have two major drawbacks for research purposes. They rarely provide material that would facilitate research, such as a summary of the court's decision, and because their page numbering is not final they are cited by docket number and date rather than to a permanent published source.[7] Illustration

---

[5] A useful description of this kind of *dictum* is that it serves as an aside not essential to the case's holding. Michael C. Dorf, *Dicta and Article III*, 142 U. PA. L. REV. 1997, 2007 (1994). *See also* Andrew C. Michaels, *The Holding-Dictum Spectrum*, 70 ARK. L. REV. 661, 663 (2017) (distinguishing asides from overly broad statements of law that may be *dicta* and arguing against a strict dichotomy between the concepts of *dictum* and holding).

[6] THE BLUEBOOK: A UNIFORM SYSTEM OF CITATION R. 10.6.1(a) (21st ed. 2020) ("When a case is cited for a proposition that is not the single, clear holding of a majority of the court (e.g., alternative holding; by implication; dictum; dissenting opinion; plurality opinion; holding unclear), indicate that fact parenthetically.").

[7] THE BLUEBOOK: A UNIFORM SYSTEM OF CITATION R. 10.8.1(b) (21st ed. 2020); ALWD GUIDE TO LEGAL CITATION R. 12.15 (6th ed. 2017).

10-1 shows a slip opinion as issued by the North Carolina Court of Appeals.

DOROTHY HARRIS, Plaintiff, v. CLARENCE BAREFOOT, LUCIA CASTALDO, and RICHARD CLYDE, jointly and severally, Defendants.

NO. COA09-1313

(Filed 3 August 2010)

Negligence - dog attacks - knowledge of vicious propensities - summary judgment

    The trial court did not err by granting summary judgment in favor of defendants in a negligence case arising out of an attack by two dogs on plaintiff postal worker. Plaintiff failed to show defendant dog owners knew or should have known of the vicious propensities of their dogs.

Appeal by plaintiff from judgments entered 22 June 2009 by Judge E. Lynn Johnson in Cumberland County Superior Court. Heard in the Court of Appeals 11 March 2010.

    Washington & Pitts, P.L.L.C., by Marshall B. Pitts, Jr., for plaintiff.

    Hedrick, Gardner, Kincheloe & Garofalo, L.L.P., by Thomas M. Buckley and Suzanne R. Walker, for defendant Castaldo.

    Pope & Tart, by P. Tilghman Pope, for defendant Barefoot.

ELMORE, Judge.

    On 5 July 2005, Dorothy Harris (plaintiff) was delivering mail for the United States Postal Service at 3362 Meadowlark Road in Harnett County when she was attacked by two dogs.

    Per her deposition, plaintiff relates the events of the incident as follows: plaintiff had delivered a package to 3362 Meadowlark Road, which was located directly across the street from the home of Clarence Barefoot (defendant Barefoot). She then walked back up the driveway toward the road and saw two dogs barking at her from across the street near the Barefoot home.

Illustration 10-1. A slip opinion from the
North Carolina Court of Appeals.

The slip opinion shown in Illustration 10-1 would be cited as *Harris v. Barefoot*, No. COA09–1313 (N.C. Ct. App. Aug. 3, 2010). The major platforms provide access to slip opinions as soon as they are available, and add their own online citations, as in 2010 WL 3001399 or 2010 N.C. App. LEXIS 1436. If a case is then published in a reporter volume, its online citation is generally replaced by a citation to the reporter volume and page number: *Harris v. Barefoot*, 704 S.E.2d 282 (N.C. Ct. App. 2010).

Court Reports. The next form of court reports provides the editorial enhancements and page citations absent in slip opinions. Some courts publish official reports, which are the versions that should be cited in court documents filed in that jurisdiction. The *United States Reports*, for example, are the official reports of the Supreme Court of the United States. *Harris v. Barefoot* appears in the *North Carolina Court of Appeals Reports*, with the citation 206 N.C. App. 308 (2010).

Cases from federal and state courts are also published by Thomson Reuters in a set called the National Reporter System. In these volumes and on Westlaw, each case is prefaced with a brief summary of its holding, called a *synopsis*, and with numbered editorial abstracts, or *headnotes*, of the specific legal issues. Each headnote is assigned a legal topic and a number indicating a particular section within that topic. This classification plan, known as the Key Number System, consists of over 400 broad topics with tens of thousands of sections. The headnotes are reprinted by subject in *digests*, case-finding resources that will be discussed in Chapter 12. Illustrations 10-2 and 10-3 show *Harris v. Barefoot* as it appears in the printed *South Eastern Reporter*, with five numbered headnotes, in the Judgment, Negligence, and Animal topics, and on Westlaw.

Lexis also replaces the initial slip opinion with a version that adds editorial material, including a case summary, a list of computer-generated *core terms*, and headnotes. Illustration 10-4 shows the Lexis version of *Harris v. Barefoot*, including subsequent history, core terms, and the beginning of the case summary.

In print several cases are issued together in weekly or biweekly pamphlets known as *advance sheets*, some published by the courts and some by commercial publishers. The cases in advance sheets are published with volume and page numbers, and are eventually reissued with revisions and corrections in permanent bound volumes that consolidate the contents of several advance sheets. These volumes are numbered consecutively, often in more than one successive series.

282 N. C.   **704 SOUTH EASTERN REPORTER, 2d SERIES**

Dorothy HARRIS, Plaintiff,

v.

Clarence BAREFOOT, Lucia Castaldo, and Richard Clyde, jointly and severally, Defendants.

No. COA09–1313.

Court of Appeals of North Carolina.

Aug. 3, 2010.

Background: Mail carrier brought negligence action against dog owners arising out of dog attack and bites. The Superior Court, Cumberland County, E. Lynn Johnson, J., granted owners' motions for summary judgment, and mail carrier appealed.

Holdings: The Court of Appeals, Elmore, J., held that:

(1) owner of part-Rottweiler dog was not liable absent evidence that dog had a vicious propensity and that owner knew or should have known that dog posed a danger to others, and

(2) owner of Australian Heeler/Border Collie mix was not liable absent evidence that dog had a vicious propensity and that owner knew or should have known that dog posed a danger to others.

Affirmed.

1. Judgment ⬤=185.3(21)

Negligence ⬤=202

For a plaintiff's negligence action to survive a defendant's motion for summary judgment, a plaintiff must set forth a prima facie case (1) that defendant failed to exercise proper care in the performance of a duty owed plaintiff, (2) the negligent breach of that duty was a proximate cause of plaintiff's injury, and (3) a person of ordinary prudence should have foreseen that plaintiff's injury was probable under the circumstances.

2. Animals ⬤=66.2

If the plaintiff establishes that an animal is in fact vicious, the plaintiff must then demonstrate that the owner knew or should have known of the animal's dangerous propensities.

3. Animals ⬤=66.2

The test of liability of the owner of a vicious animal does not contemplate the intentions of the animal but whether the owner should know from past conduct that the animal is likely, if not restrained, to do an act in which the owner could foresee injury to person or property.

4. Animals ⬤=66.5(2)

Owner of part-Rottweiler dog was not liable for mail carrier's dog bite injuries absent evidence that dog had a vicious propensity and that owner knew or should have known that dog posed a danger to others.

5. Animals ⬤=66.5(2)

Owner of Australian Heeler/Border Collie mix dog was not liable for mail carrier's dog bite injuries absent evidence that dog had a vicious propensity and that owner knew or should have known that dog posed a danger to others.

———

Appeal by plaintiff from judgments entered 22 June 2009 by Judge E. Lynn Johnson in Cumberland County Superior Court. Heard in the Court of Appeals 11 March 2010.

Washington & Pitts, P.L.L.C., by Marshall B. Pitts, Jr., for plaintiff.

Hedrick, Gardner, Kincheloe & Garofalo, L.L.P., by Thomas M. Buckley and Suzanne R. Walker, for defendant Castaldo.

Pope & Tart, by P. Tilghman Pope, for defendant Barefoot.

ELMORE, Judge.

On 5 July 2005, Dorothy Harris (plaintiff) was delivering mail for the United States Postal Service at 3362 Meadowlark Road in Harnett County when she was attacked by two dogs.

Per her deposition, plaintiff relates the events of the incident as follows: plaintiff had delivered a package to 3362 Meadowlark Road, which was located directly across the

Illustration 10-2. The case as published in a Thomson Reuters regional reporter.

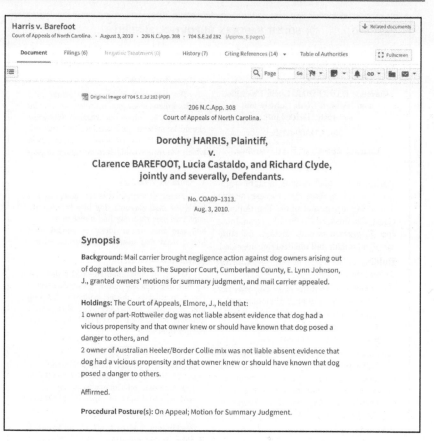

Illustration 10-3. The same case as it appears on Westlaw.

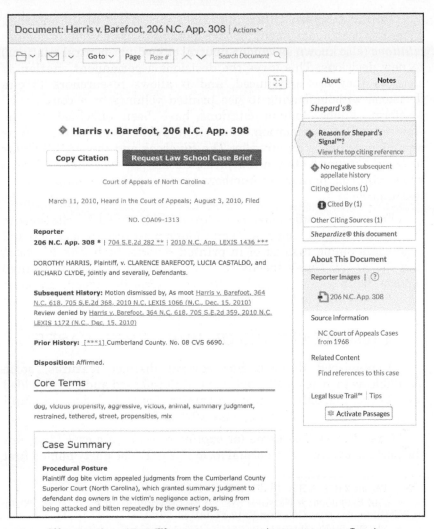

Illustration 10-4. The same case as it appears on Lexis.

Public Domain Citations. Since the advent of the internet, there has been a movement for jurisdictions to assign *public domain citations* (also known as vendor-neutral or medium-neutral citations) to new decisions. This gives the decisions a permanent citation as soon as they are announced, and it allows researchers to cite decisions without having to use printed volumes or a commercial platform. Public domain citations have been endorsed by the American Bar Association,[8] and if a public domain citation is available its use is required by *The Bluebook* and the *ALWD Guide to Legal Citation*.[9] Only a few jurisdictions, however, have adopted rules requiring paragraph numbers or other public domain citation features.[10]

For most jurisdictions, cases are still identified by citations to the published print volumes. Even though most researchers find and read cases online instead of in printed reports, both *The Bluebook* and the *ALWD Guide* specify that cases should be cited to printed reports if they are published in that form.[11] Indeed, in most jurisdictions the published version is the official text in case of any discrepancies between it and an online version.[12]

§ 10.3 FEATURES OF PUBLISHED CASES

A published decision has several distinct features, some available as soon as the slip opinion is first released and others added later to the final online or printed version. Several of these standard features are shown in Illustrations 10-1 to 10-4.

Case Name. The name (or *caption* or *style*) of a case identifies the parties involved. The normal form is *X v. Y*. The party named first

---

[8]   121 no. 2 REP. A.B.A. 16–19, 427–52 (1996).

[9]   THE BLUEBOOK: A UNIFORM SYSTEM OF CITATION R. 10.3.1 (21st ed. 2020); ALWD GUIDE TO LEGAL CITATION R. 12.17 (6th ed. 2017).

[10]   *The Bluebook*'s table of United States jurisdictions indicates which states have public domain citation formats. THE BLUEBOOK: A UNIFORM SYSTEM OF CITATION tbl. T1.3 (21st ed. 2020). *ALWD* includes this information in Appendix 2 and directs readers to each jurisdiction's specific rule. ALWD GUIDE TO LEGAL CITATION app. (6th ed. 2017). The American Association of Law Libraries has issued a UNIVERSAL CITATION GUIDE (3d ed. 2014) providing rules for a uniform public domain format. *See* Jamie Pamela Rasmussen, *Horseless Carriages with Buggy-Whip Holders: The Failure of Legal Citation Reform in the 1990s*, 110 LAW LIBR. J. 221 (2018) (providing background on the public domain citation movement).

[11]   THE BLUEBOOK: A UNIFORM SYSTEM OF CITATION R. 10.3.1 (21st ed. 2020); ALWD GUIDE TO LEGAL CITATION R. 12.3 (6th ed. 2017).

[12]   Discrepancies are rare but do indeed occur. For several years the Westlaw version of *Diffenderfer v. Diffenderfer*, 491 So.2d 265 (Fla. 1986), contained a typographical error changing the phrase "her interest in the pension" to "his interest in the pension," causing some citing courts to misapply its holding. Sixteen years later, *Acker v. Acker*, 821 So.2d 1088, 1091 (Fla. Dist. Ct. App. 2002), *aff'd*, 904 So. 2d 384 (Fla. 2005), held that the version of the case published in the bound reporter was authoritative.

is usually the plaintiff, i.e., the party bringing suit, and the second party the defendant. In appellate cases the first party is often the appellant or petitioner (i.e., the party that filed the appeal) and the second party the appellee or respondent, no matter which was the original plaintiff. In *Harris v. Barefoot*, for example, Dorothy Harris was the appellant and Clarence Barefoot the first of three defendants. In some cases, a procedural phrase such as *Ex parte* or *In re* is used instead, followed by the name of one party or a description of the property that is the subject of the action.

Docket Number. The docket number, or record number, is assigned by the court clerk to the case when it is filed initially for the court's consideration. It is the number the court uses to keep track of the documents and briefs filed in the case. As noted earlier, the docket number in the case shown in Illustrations 10-1 to 10-4 is No. COA09–1313. Cases are generally cited by docket number only if they are not available in a published reporter. The docket number is useful for following the status of a pending case and for finding the parties' briefs and joint appendices.

Citation. While slip opinions are generally cited by docket number, published opinions are cited by the reporter volume in which they appear, the abbreviated reporter name, and the page number on which the caption appears (and by public domain citation in those jurisdictions that have adopted such systems). A full case citation also identifies the deciding court, if not obvious from the reporter abbreviation, and includes the year of decision.[13] These are both essential pieces of information for determining the importance of a case and its weight as precedent.

Many cases have more than one reporter citation, particularly if they are published in both official and commercial sources. Two citations to the same case are known as *parallel citations*. Which citation, or citations, to use is determined by the rules being followed—such as local court rules, *The Bluebook*, or the *ALWD Guide*. Westlaw, Lexis, and most other online sources provide all print citations for cases. Many printed reporters also include the parallel citation if it is available when the volume is issued.

Official Syllabus and Headnotes. Below the docket number in many official reporters is the *syllabus,* a summary of the case's facts and the court's holding. Many actions contain more than one question of law, and a court may dispose of several individual legal questions in a single opinion. Some official reports provide separate headnotes describing the various points decided by the court.

---

[13] THE BLUEBOOK: A UNIFORM SYSTEM OF CITATION R. 10.4–10.5 (21st ed. 2020); ALWD GUIDE TO LEGAL CITATION R. 12.3–12.5 and 12.7 (6th ed. 2017).

In the official reports of some jurisdictions, the syllabus is written by the court itself.[14] Generally, however, the syllabus and headnotes are prepared by a reporter and are not an official statement of the holding.[15] The syllabus and headnotes serve as useful guides to what is discussed in the case, but the holding is found in the words of the opinion itself. If a syllabus or headnote is inconsistent with the court's opinion, the opinion governs.[16] Not all cases include official syllabi or headnotes. The U.S. Supreme Court has lengthy syllabi, but there are none for decisions of the lower federal courts.

Commercial Summaries and Headnotes. The official syllabus and headnotes are preceded or followed in some sources, such as Westlaw, Lexis, and Thomson Reuters reporters, by summaries and headnotes prepared by the publisher's editorial staff.

Westlaw and Thomson Reuters reporters include a synopsis, similar to but generally more concise than an official syllabus. The synopsis for cases since 2003 is divided into separate sections for "Background," explaining the facts and procedure of the case, and "Holdings," itemizing the matters decided by the court. Older cases have a shorter one-paragraph synopsis.

The Thomson Reuters synopsis is followed by numbered headnotes, which are assigned topics and key numbers to identify the subject matter. The online headnotes are hyperlinked to the portion of the opinion from which they are drawn, and bracketed bold numbers in the text of the opinion (online and in print) indicate the corresponding headnote. The use of key numbers in case research is discussed in greater depth in Chapter 12.

---

[14] Though not the norm, this happens often enough that Westlaw has a topic and key number on point: *106k109* (Courts, Syllabi).

[15] The syllabus is prepared by the court in three states. KAN. STAT. ANN. § 20–111 (2007); OHIO REV. CODE ANN. § 2503.20 (LexisNexis 2016); W. VA. CONST. art. 8, § 4. For an explanation of the significance of court-written syllabi and their relation to opinions, see *State v. McKinley*, 764 S.E.2d 303, 309 (W. Va. 2014). In other jurisdictions, justices may review syllabi prepared by the reporter. Justice Ruth Bader Ginsburg described Supreme Court practices in a published speech: "The syllabus is drafted by the Reporter of Decisions, but the justice who wrote the opinion may edit it closely and sometimes rewrite passages, as I more than occasionally do, mindful that busy lawyers and judges may not read more." Ruth Bader Ginsburg, *Informing the Public About the U.S. Supreme Court's Work*, 29 LOYOLA U. CHI. L.J. 275, 275–76 (1998). For the story of an extended dispute among Supreme Court justices and their reporter about the wording of a headnote, see Alan F. Westin, *Stephen J. Field and the Headnote to* O'Neil v. Vermont: *A Snapshot of the Fuller Court at Work*, 67 YALE L.J. 363 (1958).

[16] Every U.S. Supreme Court slip opinion carries a warning that the syllabus "constitutes no part of the opinion of the Court and has been prepared by the Reporter of Decisions for the convenience of the reader," citing *United States v. Detroit Timber & Lumber Co.*, 200 U.S. 321, 337 (1906).

Lexis cases generally begin with a case summary divided into three sections: procedural posture, overview (summarizing the issues), and outcome. Lexis also provides headnotes, drawn directly from the language of the opinion. As in Westlaw, the headnotes are hyperlinked to the corresponding location in the text.

The Westlaw and Lexis synopses or case summaries and headnotes are not prepared by the court and should not be cited or relied upon as authoritative. Many headnotes cover topics discussed in dictum, sometimes even dictum in footnotes, rather than the case's holding. It is necessary to read the opinion to determine the court's holding, and then to rely on and cite the text in the opinion rather than an editorial summary.[17]

Names of Counsel. In most sources, the names of the lawyers who represented the parties usually appear after the headnotes and before the opinion of the court. At one time, court reports regularly carried excerpts or summaries of the arguments of counsel. These summaries are no longer provided in most reports, but resources such as Westlaw and Lexis frequently provide links from opinions to the full texts of the briefs.

Opinion(s). Finally we get to the work of the court, the opinion. A *majority opinion*, representing the opinion of the court, almost always appears first. It is usually signed by an individual judge, but in some cases a *per curiam* opinion is issued, one which represents the court without authorship attributed to any individual judge. *Per curiam* opinions are generally short, and either cover points of law the court feels are too obvious to merit elaboration or represent sensitive issues the court does not want to treat at length.[18] They do, however, carry the weight of precedent. It can be assumed that all other judges subscribe to the first opinion, unless they have written or expressly joined in either a concurring or dissenting opinion.

Occasionally there is no line of reasoning agreed upon by a majority, and a *plurality opinion* is printed first. This announces the judgment of the court, but its reasoning is not binding authority in subsequent cases.

A *concurring opinion* is written when a judge agrees with the result reached by the majority of the court, but either does not fully

---

[17] It is not unheard of for judges to chide counsel for quoting from the syllabus or headnotes rather than the text of opinions. *See, e.g., Lindgren v. United States*, No. 92 C 8038, 1993 WL 141790, at *2 n.1 (N.D. Ill. Apr. 30, 1993); *Meadows v. Commonwealth*, No. 2010–CA–001155–DG, 2012 WL 410259, at *4 n.7 (Ky. Ct. App. Feb. 10, 2012).

[18] For a criticism of the use of *per curiam* opinions, see Ira P. Robbins, *Hiding Behind the Cloak of Invisibility: The Supreme Court and Per Curiam Opinions*, 86 TUL. L. REV. 1197 (2012).

agree with the reasoning used to reach that result or feels the need to add something further. In some decisions, there is more than one concurring opinion.

Following the majority opinion and any concurrences, there may be one or more *dissenting opinions*. These reflect the views of judges who do not agree with the result reached by the majority of the court. Some cases, particularly from the U.S. Supreme Court, feature a dizzying array of concurrences and dissents, with some judges concurring in part and dissenting in part and others joining an opinion except for a particular section or even a footnote.[19]

Although dissenting opinions carry no precedential force, they may have persuasive authority and can be cited if clearly labeled as dissents. A well-reasoned dissent may eventually lead to changes in the law. Dissents by justices such as John Marshall Harlan and Oliver Wendell Holmes, Jr. are among the most influential opinions in the Supreme Court's history.[20]

§ 10.4 A BRIEF HISTORY OF CASE PUBLICATION

A knowledge of the history of court reports can help in understanding case law. Decisions are usually found online, but they are still cited to printed sources. A case citation communicates information about the scope and nature of a decision's precedential value. A familiarity with cited sources and their background can place a decision in context and provide a quicker understanding of its importance.[21]

From its earliest beginnings in antiquity, the reporting of cases helped to achieve certainty in the law by providing written records for later tribunals faced with similar issues, thereby reducing further disputes. The earliest evidence of recorded judicial decisions in England dates from the 11th century. Two hundred years later a

---

[19] A great variety of permutations is possible. In *Kisor v. Wilkie*, 139 S. Ct. 2400 (2019), for example, "KAGAN, J., announced the judgment of the Court and delivered the opinion of the Court with respect to Parts I, II-B, III-B, and IV, in which ROBERTS, C. J., and GINSBURG, BREYER, and SOTOMAYOR, JJ., joined, and an opinion with respect to Parts II-A and III-A, in which GINSBURG, BREYER, and SOTOMAYOR, JJ. joined. ROBERTS, C. J., filed an opinion concurring in part. GORSUCH, J., filed an opinion concurring in the judgment, in which THOMAS, J., joined, in which KAVANAUGH, J., joined as to Parts I, II, III, IV, and V, and in which ALITO, J., joined as to Parts I, II, and III. KAVANAUGH, J., filed an opinion concurring in the judgment, in which ALITO, J., joined."

[20] *See, e.g., Plessy v. Ferguson*, 163 U.S. 537, 552 (1896) (Harlan, J., dissenting); *Lochner v. New York*, 198 U.S. 45, 74 (1905) (Holmes, J., dissenting).

[21] Well-crafted citations can artfully illustrate the authority of a decision and its impact on a legal argument. Alexa Z. Chew, *Stylish Legal Citation*, 71 ARK. L. REV. 823 (2018).

series known as the Year Books began providing notes of debates between judges and counsel on the points in issue in cases. While not containing the texts of decisions, the Year Books were used as guidance in subsequent cases. Manuscripts of reported cases exist from as early as the 13th century, the first printed versions appeared in about 1481, and the Year Books continued until 1535.[22]

The Year Books were followed by *nominative* reports, that is, reports named for the person who recorded or edited them. The first volume of nominative reports was prepared by Edmund Plowden and published in 1571. It was followed by numerous series by dozens of jurists and lawyers, of varying accuracy and authority.[23] The development of printed reports changed the nature of legal practice dramatically, from a reliance on general principles to an increasing use of case citations as authority.[24]

More than 270 series of nominative reports were cumulated into *The English Reports* (1900–32), covering cases from 1220 to 1865 in 176 volumes. This is now the standard source for older English cases, many of which have been incorporated as part of American common law.[25] *The English Reports* is available from several subscription

---

[22] On the period before the Year Books, see Paul Brand, *The Beginnings of English Law Reporting*, in LAW REPORTING IN BRITAIN 1 (Chantal Stebbings ed., 1995); on the Year Books, see PERCY H. WINFIELD, THE CHIEF SOURCES OF ENGLISH LEGAL HISTORY 158–83 (1925).

Many of the Year Books have been translated from Law French into English and published by the Selden Society. An eleven-volume set of Year Books published from 1678 to 1680, known as the Vulgate edition, was reissued in 2007 with introductory tables and notes by David J. Seipp, who has also prepared an online index, bibliography, and searchable database (www.bu.edu/law/seipp/). The Vulgate edition and the Selden Society volumes are available online from HeinOnline. Anyone interested in deciphering the original texts should probably start with J.H. BAKER, MANUAL OF LAW FRENCH (2d ed. 1990).

[23] L. W. ABBOTT, LAW REPORTING IN ENGLAND 1485–1585 (1973) is an excellent history of early English reports, and JOHN WILLIAM WALLACE, THE REPORTERS, ARRANGED AND CHARACTERIZED WITH INCIDENTAL REMARKS (4th ed. 1882) has a lengthier discussion of each reporter. Among the less reliable reporters Wallace discusses were Joseph Keble (1632–1710) ("Mr. Justice Park burned his copy, thinking it not worth while to lumber his library with trash.") and Thomas Barnardiston (1706–52) (quoting the 19th century jurist Lord Lyndhurst telling a lawyer that it was said that Barnardiston "was accustomed to slumber over his note-book, and the wags in the rear took the opportunity of scribbling nonsense in it."). *Id.* at 315, 424.

[24] By 1600 lawyers could already complain about "such an ocean of reportes, and such a perplexed confusion of opinions." WILLIAM FULBECK, A DIRECTION, OR PREPARATIVE TO THE STUDY OF THE LAWE 5b (London: T. Wight 1600). On the changing nature of precedent during this period, see Peter M. Tiersma, *The Textualization of Precedent*, 82 NOTRE DAME L. REV. 1187 (2007).

[25] The "reception" statutes passed by many early state legislatures accepted English common law limited to cases that were not repugnant to the law of the newly independent state, and often further limited to cases decided before the date of independence or the founding of the first English colony. These statutes are conveniently listed and summarized in Joseph Fred Benson, *Reception of the Common*

online sources, including Westlaw and HeinOnline. The Commonwealth Legal Information Institute has free access to the set (www.commonlii.org/uk/cases/EngR/).[26]

The American colonies inherited the English legal system and its common law tradition. The decisions of American courts were not published at all during the colonial period and the early years of independence, and American lawyers and judges relied for precedent on the decisions of the English courts. The first volumes of American court decisions were not published until 1789 when Ephraim Kirby's *Reports of Cases Adjudged in the Superior Court of the State of Connecticut* and Francis Hopkinson's *Judgements in the Admiralty of Pennsylvania* both appeared.[27] In a preface Kirby discusses the concerns that led to the publication of his reports, including the inapplicability of English law in the new country and the need to create a permanent body of American common law.

Reports from other states and from the new federal courts soon followed, although the courts of some states operated for decades without published decisions. Official series of court reports (published pursuant to statutory direction or court authorization) began in several states in the early 1800s. Many of these early publications were nominative reports, cited, like their English predecessors, by the names of their reporters.

Gradually the nominative reports gave way to officially published sets of sequentially numbered reports. Some states subsequently renumbered their early reports, incorporating the nominative volumes as the first numbered volumes in the official set, but other states have nominative volumes that are not part of an

---

Law in Missouri: Section 1.010 as Interpreted by the Supreme Court of Missouri, 67 MO. L. REV. 595, 607–11 (2002).

[26] Two other compilations of older English cases, including some not found in *The English Reports*, are the *Revised Reports* and the *All England Law Reports Reprint, 1558–1935*. Decisions in some criminal cases appear in the nominative reports and *The English Reports*, but the source for accounts of major trials for treason and related offenses is *A Complete Collection of State Trials* (William Cobbett & Thomas Bayly Howell eds., 1809–28), available in HeinOnline's World Trials Library. Less lofty criminal proceedings are represented in The Proceedings of the Old Bailey, 1674–1913 (www.oldbaileyonline.org), which has synopses of nearly 200,000 trials at London's infamous central criminal court.

[27] The decisions in Kirby's reports followed a 1784 Connecticut statute requiring that judges provide written opinions to be kept on file in order that "a Foundation be laid for a more perfect and permanent System of common Law in this State." An Act Establishing the Wages of the Judges of the Superior Court, 1784 Conn. Acts & Laws 268. For more on Kirby, see Alan V. Briceland, *Ephraim Kirby: Pioneer of American Law Reporting, 1789*, 16 AM. J. LEGAL HIST. 297 (1972). Although Kirby and Hopkinson's reports were the first to be published, their cases were not the earliest reported. Thomas Jefferson, for example, compiled a collection of Virginia General Court cases dating back to 1730, but these weren't published until 1829, three years after his death.

overall numbering sequence. If a reporter abbreviation (such as Blackf. or D. Chip., sources respectively for opinions of the Indiana and Vermont supreme courts) doesn't identify the jurisdiction and deciding court, you need to include this information in parentheses as part of the citation.

As the country grew in the 19th century, the number of reported decisions increased dramatically, and official reporting systems began to lag further and further behind.[28] The need for timely access to cases was met by commercial publishers. In 1876, John B. West began publishing selected decisions of the Minnesota Supreme Court in a weekly leaflet, the *Syllabi*. Three years later he launched the *North Western Reporter*, covering Minnesota and five surrounding states.

Other publishers also began their own series of regional reporters, with the result that some states were covered by two or three rival publications.[29] West, however, established a national system, publishing all the states' decisions in seven regional reporters as well as reporters covering the Supreme Court and the lower federal courts. By 1887 the competitors had folded and West's National Reporter System had become the dominant commercial source for court opinions.[30] One of the most significant aspects of West's reporters as they developed over the following decades was that each case was accompanied by the classified key number headnotes that allowed comprehensive and uniform subject access to the cases of different jurisdictions.

The next major development in American case reporting was electronic access, as exemplified initially by the competing commercial platforms Lexis and Westlaw. The Ohio State Bar Association began work in 1966 on the product that became Lexis, and it was introduced in 1973, providing access to the decisions of all fifty states and the federal system. West Publishing Company's Westlaw began in 1975, initially with only the headnotes to its

---

[28] As a journal article in the 1870s noted, "Seventy-five years ago, in this country, there were but eight volumes of indigenous reports; to-day there are about 2,700, and the number is increasing about ninety volumes yearly." *Reports, Reporters, and Reporting*, 5 S. L. REV. (N.S.) 53, 53 (1879).

[29] "This rivalry is really to be regretted. These enterprising houses have started out to do a very important work for the legal profession, and each of them ought to reap the reward of its enterprise in reasonable profits. But this competition will have the effect of dividing up the patronage among them, so that it will prove a losing enterprise for all." *The New "Reporters"*, 19 AM. L. REV. 930, 932 (1885). It turned out, of course, to be a losing enterprise for all but one.

[30] For more on the history of West (now Thomson Reuters), see Robert M. Jarvis, *John B. West: Founder of the West Publishing Company*, 50 AM. J. LEGAL HIST. 1 (2008–2010), and Thomas A. Woxland, *"Forever Associated with the Practice of Law": The Early Years of the West Publishing Company*, LEGAL REFERENCE SERVICES Q., Spring 1985, at 115.

published decisions, but full-text retrieval was added in 1979.[31] At first coverage in some states extended back a few decades, but both platforms now have comprehensive retrospective coverage back to the earliest reported decisions.

Westlaw and Lexis dominated electronic case publishing until the rise of the internet in the 1990s. Both services adapted to web-based interfaces and continue to be the most comprehensive sources for opinions, but they have been joined by a number of other subscription and free websites.

Other subscription platforms generally provide thorough coverage of modern opinions but lack the editorial summaries and headnotes found in Westlaw and Lexis. Free use of some commercial platforms, such as Casemaker and Fastcase, is available as a benefit of state or local bar membership.[32]

The burgeoning "free law movement" has meant more cases are available for free online, though the scope of coverage can vary widely, particularly on court websites. A few state supreme courts have complete retrospective coverage of their opinions, while others are limited to only the most recent slip opinions. Google Scholar (scholar.google.com) has all U.S. Supreme Court cases, other federal appellate cases back to 1923, and state appellate cases back to at least 1950. In most instances, the free online opinions also lack the editorial enhancements that can make research more efficient, and they often provide no indication of whether the cases you are reading are still good law.

Nonprofit organizations and academic institutions are also making case law more widely available on the internet. CourtListener (www.courtlistener.com), part of the Free Law Project, is an extensive database of opinions as well as oral arguments, judicial information, and federal filings. The Caselaw Access Project (case.law), based at Harvard Law School's Library Innovation Lab, is a recent effort to digitize official reports of federal and state courts, and its data can be searched in a variety of ways.

With an ever-increasing volume of cases available online, one of the leading issues of case publication in recent years has been how and whether to limit the significance of some of those cases. For several decades, many courts have followed policies of selective publication to shape precedent and to cut down on the glut of reported cases. The online platforms and the internet, however, have made the

---

[31] For a survey of these early developments, see William G. Harrington, *A Brief History of Computer-Assisted Legal Research*, 77 LAW LIBR. J. 543 (1985).

[32] For a state-by-state summary, see *Legal Research via State Bar Associations*, DUKE LAW (law.duke.edu/lib/statebarassociations/).

"unpublished" cases more widely accessible. As we will see in the next chapter, courts and judges are still debating how to deal with this increased access to their decisions.

Chapter 11

CASE LAW SOURCES

Table of Sections

This chapter discusses the courts one encounters in working with American case law, as well as the online and print sources in which court decisions appear. Even if most research is done electronically, it is still important to learn about the reporters to which case law is cited, and it may even be necessary to consult an official printed source.

Because of the preeminent role of the United States Supreme Court, in both practical and jurisprudential terms, its decisions are discussed first and in some detail. Treatment of the lower federal courts, state courts, and other jurisdictions follow in subsequent sections.

§ 11.1 SUPREME COURT OF THE UNITED STATES

The Supreme Court of the United States stands at the head of the judicial branch of the federal government and provides the definitive interpretation of the U.S. Constitution and federal statutes. Its decisions are studied not only by lawyers but also by political scientists, historians, and citizens interested in the development of social and legal policy.

The Supreme Court is the court of last resort in the federal system. It also has the final word on federal issues raised in state courts, and it hears cases arising between states. The Court exercises tight control over its docket and has wide discretion to decline review. It usually accepts for consideration only those cases that raise significant legal or policy issues. In recent years it has issued opinions in fewer than eighty cases during its annual term, which begins on the first Monday of October and ends in late June.[1]

(a) Reference Resources

Numerous reference works explain the history and role of the Supreme Court in the American political and legal system. Three standard sources are *Encyclopedia of the American Constitution* (Leonard W. Levy et al. eds., 2d ed. 2000); *Encyclopedia of the Supreme Court of the United States* (David S. Tanenhaus ed. 2008); and *The Oxford Companion to the Supreme Court of the United States* (Kermit L. Hall ed., 2d ed. 2005), each of which include articles on historical developments, doctrinal areas, and individual justices. They also have articles on several hundred cases, providing quick synopses of the background and impact of major decisions.[2]

David G. Savage, *Guide to the U.S. Supreme Court* (5th ed. 2010) is arranged thematically rather than alphabetically, but it too explains major doctrines and discusses the history, politics, and procedures of the Court. An appendix provides a chronology of major decisions, with concise summaries of more than 600 cases from 1793 to 2010.

The most practical reference work about the Supreme Court is Stephen M. Shapiro et al., *Supreme Court Practice* (11th ed. 2019, available on Bloomberg Law), a guide for lawyers bringing cases before the Court. In addition to procedural matters and case-preparation tips, it also explains the Supreme Court's jurisdiction, discusses factors affecting the decision whether to grant review, and

---

[1] On the size of the Court's docket, see, e.g., Randy J. Kozel & Jeffrey A. Pojanowski, *Discretionary Dockets*, 31 CONST. COMMENT. 221 (2016); Ryan J. Owens & David A. Simon, *Explaining the Supreme Court's Shrinking Docket*, 53 WM. & MARY L. REV. 1219 (2012).

[2] The *Oxford Companion*'s articles on cases are also available in THE OXFORD GUIDE TO UNITED STATES SUPREME COURT DECISIONS (Kermit L. Hall & James W. Ely, Jr. eds., 2d ed. 2009).

covers specialized topics such as the Court's original jurisdiction, extraordinary writs, and capital cases.[3]

Numerous texts have been devoted to the history and decisions of the Supreme Court. Among the many historical treatments of the Court, the most ambitious is the Oliver Wendell Holmes Devise *History of the Supreme Court of the United States* (1971–date), under the general editorship of Paul A. Freund (succeeded first by Stanley N. Katz and currently by Maeva Marcus). This multi-volume, detailed history is still incomplete, with only ten of thirteen projected volumes issued so far.[4]

Among the many law review articles covering the Supreme Court, two sources merit special mention. The *Supreme Court Review,* a faculty-edited journal published by the University of Chicago, is an annual volume of articles by leading scholars on important, recent U.S. Supreme Court decisions. The first issue of each *Harvard Law Review* volume contains a thorough analysis by its student editors of the activity of the Supreme Court in the preceding term. The survey is prefaced each year by introductory articles written by noted scholars (a lengthy "Foreword" and somewhat briefer "Comments" on more specific issues).

---

[3] The first edition of the treatise, published in 1950, was written by Robert L. Stern and Eugene Gressman. Some practitioners may still identify it as "Stern & Gressman."

For advocates arguing before the Court and others needing to say, rather than write, the names of cases, Yale Law School offers a Pronouncing Dictionary of the Supreme Court of the United States (documents.law.yale.edu/pronouncing-dictionary) with audio clips of the correct pronunciations of more than 500 potentially difficult names in cases between 1793 and 2013.

[4] Each volume covers the major constitutional issues and decisions in its respective period:

JULIUS GOEBEL, ANTECEDENTS AND BEGINNINGS TO 1801 (1971)

GEORGE LEE HASKINS & HERBERT A. JOHNSON, FOUNDATIONS OF POWER: JOHN MARSHALL, 1801–15 (1981)

G. EDWARD WHITE, THE MARSHALL COURT AND CULTURAL CHANGE, 1815–35 (1988)

CARL B. SWISHER, THE TANEY PERIOD, 1836–64 (1974)

CHARLES FAIRMAN, RECONSTRUCTION AND REUNION 1864–88 (2 vols., 1971–87); FIVE JUSTICES AND THE ELECTORAL COMMISSION OF 1877 (1988)

OWEN M. FISS, TROUBLED BEGINNINGS OF THE MODERN STATE, 1888–1910 (1993)

ALEXANDER M. BICKEL & BENNO C. SCHMIDT, THE JUDICIARY AND RESPONSIBLE GOVERNMENT, 1910–21 (1984)

WILLIAM WIECEK, THE BIRTH OF THE MODERN CONSTITUTION: THE UNITED STATES SUPREME COURT, 1941–1953 (2006)

Three volumes are yet to be published, covering 1921–30, 1930–41, and 1953–76. For a brief history of the series, see Stanley N. Katz, *Official History: The Holmes Devise History of the Supreme Court,* 141 PROC. AM. PHIL. SOC'Y 297 (1997).

Many news sources have information about current proceedings and new opinions from the Court. Two worth noting are SCOTUSblog (www.scotusblog.com), which often has the first reports of new decisions and developments in pending cases, and Bloomberg Law's *The United States Law Week: Supreme Court Today*, which summarizes pending cases and tracks developments on the docket.

The Supreme Court Compendium: Data, Decisions, and Developments (Lee Epstein et al. eds., 6th ed. 2015) has a wide range of statistical and historical information, including information on the Court's caseload, voting alignments, litigants, and public opinion. Other sources for statistics on recent terms include the annual Supreme Court issue of the *Harvard Law Review* and "Stat Packs" on SCOTUSblog.

(b) Sources for Current Opinions

Reference sources are useful for historical and general background, but they are no substitute for reading the opinions of the Supreme Court. The Court makes law through its decisions in individual cases. These decisions can be retrieved through several free internet sites and commercial platforms, and they are published in three permanent bound reporters. Maintaining current awareness of new decisions is essential.

The Supreme Court announces its decisions on an irregular basis at its 10 a.m. sessions, beginning in October or November and reaching a peak when the most contentious cases of the term are decided in late June. The first official appearance of a new decision is as a *bench opinion*, a pamphlet version available at the Court and distributed electronically to several publishers. The major platforms generally make the opinion available online within minutes.

The bench opinion is superseded, usually within an hour, by the official *slip opinion*, which is posted in PDF format on the Supreme Court website (www.supremecourt.gov). The bench opinion and slip opinion are usually identical, but it is possible that the slip opinion may contain corrections not found in the bench opinion. The slip opinion text controls if there is any discrepancy between the two.

The quickest source for new slip opinions is usually SCOTUSblog, which also provides some of the earliest commentary and analysis of new decisions. Cornell Law School's Legal Information Institute (LII) (www.law.cornell.edu/supct/) also provides free access to slip opinions, and has a free e-mail Supreme Court Bulletin that delivers the syllabi of new opinions with links to the full text.

Slip opinions contain the text of the Supreme Court's opinions, in a format very similar to the final published version, but they are individual pamphlets and lack the volume and page references necessary for citation. For that purpose, and also because the final published version may contain corrections to the slip opinion, you should rely instead on the permanent official reports of the Court's opinions if available.

(c) *United States Reports*

Begun in 1790 as a private venture, the *United States Reports* (cited as U.S.) became the official edition of United States Supreme Court decisions in 1817 and continues in this capacity today.[5] Two to four volumes of the *U.S. Reports* are published each year. The slip opinions are only cumulated after more than four years, into an official advance sheet (called the "preliminary print") that contains the pagination that will appear in the final bound volume.[6] The bound volume is published about two years later and is the authoritative text of the Court's decisions.[7]

The early volumes of Supreme Court decisions are now numbered sequentially as part of the *U.S. Reports* series, but for many years they were cited only by the names of the individual reporters. *Bluebook* and *ALWD* citations to these early cases include a parenthetical reference to the nominative reporter volume, as in

---

[5]   Act of Mar. 3, 1817, ch. 63, 3 Stat. 376. The act was limited to three years, but it was renewed periodically until finally made permanent in 1842. Act of Aug. 29, 1842, ch. 264, 5 Stat. 545.

[6]   This delay creates a problem for judges and litigants wishing to cite recent Supreme Court cases to the official reports, as is the norm in opinions and briefs. Citations cannot be made to a particular page number until one is assigned. A case from 2019, such as *Franchise Tax Bd. of California v. Hyatt*, will be cited as 587 U.S. ____ (2019) until it receives a page number in the preliminary print. This may also be a problem for future readers of cases who need to find decisions referred to by these incomplete citations.

[7]   The Court's website warns: "In case of discrepancies between the print and electronic versions of these bound volume materials, the print versions control. Only the bound volumes of the United States Reports contain the final, official text of the opinions of the Supreme Court." SUPREME COURT OF THE UNITED STATES, *Information about Opinions* (www.supremecourt.gov/opinions/info_opinions.aspx) [https://perma.cc/S7LZ-B4VP].

Justices can revise their opinions after they are initially issued, leading to confusion when different versions appear in different sources. *See* Richard J. Lazarus, *The (Non)Finality of Supreme Court Opinions*, 128 HARV. L. REV. 540 (2014); Adam Liptak, *Final Word on U.S. Law Isn't: Supreme Court Keeps Editing*, N.Y. TIMES, May 25, 2014, at A1. Opinions can be revised even after the bound volume is published, and errata lists regularly appear at the beginning of *U.S. Reports* volumes. In 2006, at 565 U.S. ii, the Court corrected a word in *Conrad, Rubin & Lesser v. Pender*, 289 U.S. 472 (1933). More than a decade later Westlaw's version had made the change, but most other resources, including Lexis and Bloomberg Law, had not.

Marbury v. Madison, 5 U.S. (1 Cranch) 137 (1803).[8] Older cases and articles tended to cite only the nominative reports, a practice continued by some of the current Supreme Court justices, so a familiarity with the early reporters' names and their periods of coverage makes it easier to read and understand these citations:

1–4 Dall. (Alexander Dallas)	1–4 U.S. (1790–1800)
1–9 Cranch (William Cranch)	5–13 U.S. (1801–15)
1–12 Wheat. (Henry Wheaton)	14–25 U.S. (1816–27)
1–16 Pet. (Richard Peters)	26–41 U.S. (1828–42)
1–24 How. (Benjamin C. Howard)	42–65 U.S. (1843–61)
1–2 Black (Jeremiah S. Black)	66–67 U.S. (1861–63)
1–23 Wall. (John W. Wallace)	68–90 U.S. (1863–75)

The earliest volumes were somewhat haphazard.[9] Alexander Dallas's first volume of the *United States Reports* contains only Pennsylvania decisions, and none from the U.S. Supreme Court. His second and third volumes contain cases from both Pennsylvania and the U.S. Supreme Court, and his fourth volume adds decisions from

---

[8] THE BLUEBOOK: A UNIFORM SYSTEM OF CITATION R. 10.3.2 (21st ed. 2020); ALWD GUIDE TO LEGAL CITATION R. 12.4(b)(4) (6th ed. 2017).

[9] The early reporters, though immortalized through nominative citations, were not all highly esteemed. "Delay, expense, omission and inaccuracy . . . were among the hallmarks of Dallas' work." Craig Joyce, *The Rise of the Supreme Court Reporter: An Institutional Perspective on Marshall Court Ascendancy*, 83 MICH. L. REV. 1291, 1305 (1985). Justice Joseph Story complained that William Cranch's work was "particularly & painfully erroneous." *Id.* at 1309–10 (quoting a letter from Joseph Story to Richard Peters, Jr., Dec. 10, 1829). Henry Wheaton was an exception, and "brought to his duties a scholarly aptitude and zeal unique in the history of the reportership." *Id.* at 1388. He was succeeded, however, by Richard Peters, who "apparently not burdened by the weight of an overpowering intellect." *Id.* at 1389.

Another commentator wrote that "the head-notes of the sixteen volumes of Peters were abominable. . . . It is hard to understand how a court of that dignity, sensitive of its reputation, could have kept such a stick in such an office for so many years." Seymour D. Thompson, *The Reporter's Head-Note*, 2 GREEN BAG 215, 218 (1890). An unnamed reviewer (probably Thompson again, based on his choice of epithets) wrote of Peters' successor, Benjamin Howard: "Howard was not a good reporter. . . . It remains a wonder to the profession how the court could get along for so many years with such a stick for a reporter of its decisions." *Book Review*, 18 AM. L. REV. 708, 708 (1884).

MORRIS L. COHEN & SHARON HAMBY O'CONNOR, A GUIDE TO THE EARLY REPORTS OF THE SUPREME COURT OF THE UNITED STATES (1995) contains biographical sketches of the first seven reporters. Two of the early reporters made a significant contribution to American jurisprudence when Richard Peters, the fourth reporter, decided to publish a new condensed edition of his three predecessors' volumes. He was sued by Henry Wheaton, who asserted copyright in his reports, and the resulting Supreme Court decision held that United States copyright was governed by federal statute, not common law, and that the reporter had no copyright in the text of the decisions. *Wheaton v. Peters*, 33 U.S. (8 Pet.) 591 (1834).

Delaware and New Hampshire. His reports contained numerous errors and did not even include all the Court's cases from the period.[10]

Beginning with volume 91 (October Term 1875), *U.S. Reports* volumes are cited only by number and not by the name of the reporter. The opening pages of *United States v. Olson*, 546 U.S. 43 (2005), appear in Illustrations 11-1 and 11-2. The Court's reporter of decisions prefaces the text of each decision with a syllabus. The syllabus in U.S. Supreme Court opinions is not a statement of the law. It merely summarizes the case and the Court's holding. Following the syllabus, Illustration 11-2 indicates that the opinion was unanimous, identifies the attorneys in the case, and shows the beginning of the opinion of the Court by Justice Stephen Breyer.

---

[10] For researchers interested in the early Supreme Court, DOCUMENTARY HISTORY OF THE SUPREME COURT OF THE UNITED STATES, 1789–1800 (Maeva Marcus ed., 1985–2007, available on LLMC) includes three volumes focusing on the early cases, containing notes, opinion drafts, correspondence, and other documents. Other volumes in the series cover the early appointments and proceedings, the circuit court duties of the justices, the legislation creating and organizing the federal judiciary, and suits against states.

Dallas was hardly the only reporter to omit cases. Henry Wheaton noted in a preface to his first volume that "discretion has been exercised in omitting to report cases turning on mere questions of fact, and from which no important principle, or general rule, could be extracted." 14 U.S. (1 Wheat.) iv (1816). More than 100 cases omitted from earlier reports were collected and printed by J. C. Bancroft Davis, the second of the Court's "post-nominative" reporters. Appendix, 131 U.S. lxiv (1889). Davis printed another 200 omitted cases four years later, noting "It was assumed that it was not worth while to occupy the space necessary to report these cases in full. The fact that two or three of them have been referred to in opinions of the court, since rendered, shows that this assumption was not well founded, and calls upon the reporter to print them in full." Appendix, 154 U.S. 531 (1893).

Even the modern reports omit opinions of individual justices on emergency applications from the lower federal courts. These opinions from 1926 to 2010 have been collected and printed in A COLLECTION OF IN CHAMBERS OPINIONS BY THE JUSTICES OF THE SUPREME COURT OF THE UNITED STATES (Cynthia Rapp comp., 2004–11). The Court now publishes in-chambers opinions on its website (www.supremecourt.gov/opinions/in-chambers.aspx). For more context, a reprinting of Rapp's original collections, and a continuation of the series, see JOURNAL OF IN-CHAMBERS PRACTICE (journaloflaw.us/10%20JICP/JICP_home.html) [https://perma.cc/645T-AHJ3].

Syllabus

UNITED STATES *v.* OLSON ET AL.

CERTIORARI TO THE UNITED STATES COURT OF APPEALS FOR THE NINTH CIRCUIT

No. 04–759. Argued October 12, 2005—Decided November 8, 2005

Claiming that federal mine inspectors' negligence helped cause a mine accident, two injured workers (and a spouse) sued the United States under the Federal Tort Claims Act (Act), which authorizes private tort actions against the Government "under circumstances where the United States, if a private person, would be liable to the claimant in accordance with the law of the place where the act or omission occurred," 28 U. S. C. § 1346(b)(1). The District Court dismissed in part on the ground that the allegations did not show that Arizona law would impose liability upon a private person in similar circumstances. The Ninth Circuit reversed, reasoning from two premises: (1) Where unique governmental functions are at issue, the Act waives sovereign immunity if a state or municipal entity would be held liable under the law where the activity occurred, and (2) federal mine inspections are such unique governmental functions since there is no private-sector analogue for mine inspections. Because Arizona law would make a state or municipal entity liable in the circumstances alleged, the Circuit concluded that the United States' sovereign immunity was waived.

Held: Under § 1346(b)(1), the United States waives sovereign immunity only where local law would make a "private person" liable in tort, not where local law would make "a state or municipal entity" liable. Pp. 45–48.

   (a) The Ninth Circuit's first premise is too broad, reading into the Act something that is not there. Section 1346(b)(1) says that it waives sovereign immunity "under circumstances where the United States, if a *private person,*" not "the United States, if a state or municipal entity," would be liable. (Emphasis added.) This Court has consistently adhered to this "private person" standard, even when uniquely governmental functions are at issue. *Indian Towing Co.* v. *United States,* 350 U. S. 61, 64; *Rayonier Inc.* v. *United States,* 352 U. S. 315, 318. Even though both these cases involved Government efforts to *escape* liability by pointing to the *absence* of municipal entity liability, there is no reason for treating differently a plaintiff's effort to *base* liability solely upon the fact that a State would impose liability upon a state governmental entity. Nothing in the Act's context, history, or objectives or in this Court's opinions suggests otherwise. Pp. 45–46.

Illustration 11-1. The first page of an opinion in the *United States Reports*.

44   UNITED STATES *v.* OLSON

                              Opinion of the Court

(b) The Ninth Circuit's second premise reads the Act too narrowly. Section 2674 makes the United States liable "in the same manner and to the same extent as a private individual under *like circumstances.*" (Emphasis added.) The words "like circumstances" do not restrict a court's inquiry to the *same circumstances,* but require it to look further afield. See, *e. g., Indian Towing, supra,* at 64. The Government in effect concedes, and other Courts of Appeals' decisions applying *Indian Towing*'s logic suggest, that private person analogies exist for the federal mine inspectors' conduct at issue. The Ninth Circuit should have looked for such an analogy. Pp. 46–47.

(c) The lower courts should decide in the first instance precisely which Arizona tort law doctrine applies here. P. 48.

362 F. 3d 1236, vacated and remanded.

BREYER, J., delivered the opinion for a unanimous Court.

Deanne E. Maynard argued the cause for the United States. With her on the briefs were *Solicitor General Clement, Assistant Attorney General Keisler, Deputy Solicitor General Kneedler, Mark B. Stern,* and *Dana J. Martin.*

Thomas G. Cotter argued the cause and filed a brief for respondents.

JUSTICE BREYER delivered the opinion of the Court.

The Federal Tort Claims Act (FTCA or Act) authorizes private tort actions against the United States "under circumstances where the United States, if a private person, would be liable to the claimant in accordance with the law of the place where the act or omission occurred." 28 U. S. C. § 1346(b)(1). We here interpret these words to mean what they say, namely, that the United States waives sovereign immunity "under circumstances" where local law would make a *"private person"* liable in tort. (Emphasis added.) And we reverse a line of Ninth Circuit precedent permitting courts in certain circumstances to base a waiver simply upon a finding that local law would make a "state or municipal entit[y]" liable. See, *e. g., Hines* v. *United States,* 60 F. 3d 1442, 1448 (1995); *Cimo* v. *INS,* 16 F. 3d 1039, 1041 (1994); *Cameron* v. *Janssen Bros. Nurseries, Ltd.,* 7 F. 3d 821, 825

**Illustration 11-2. *U.S. Reports* continued, showing the
beginning of the Court's opinion.**

The official *U.S. Reports* versions of Supreme Court decisions are available online in PDF from three major sources. The Supreme Court website, under the heading "Opinions—Bound Volumes" (www.supremecourt.gov/opinions/boundvolumes.aspx) has files containing the bound volumes of *U.S. Reports* beginning with volume 502 (October Term 1991).[11] HeinOnline (home.heinonline.org) has more thorough and convenient coverage, with page images of the *U.S. Reports* all the way from volume one through the preliminary prints to the most recent slip opinions. HeinOnline's Supreme Court Library also includes numerous historic texts and several journals focusing on the history and decisions of the Court.[12] LLMC Digital (www.llmc.com) has coverage back to volume one but does not have the most recent volumes.

(d) *Supreme Court Reporter* and *Lawyers' Edition*

Supreme Court opinions are also printed in two commercially published series, Thomson Reuters's *Supreme Court Reporter* (cited as S. Ct.) and LexisNexis's *United States Supreme Court Reports, Lawyers' Edition* (known simply as *Lawyers' Edition*, and cited as L. Ed.). These reporters contain editorial features not available in the official *U.S. Reports*, and they are the versions found in Westlaw and Lexis respectively.

Because the *U.S. Reports* are published so slowly, *The Bluebook* and the *ALWD Guide to Legal Citation* specify that a recent opinion that does not yet have a *U.S.* citation should be cited to the *Supreme Court Reporter* or *Lawyers' Edition*, in that order of preference.[13] Cases are published in both of these sources in paperback advance sheets within a few weeks of decision, and the citations are available online before then. The permanent bound volumes of the commercial editions are not published until the cases appear in the *U.S. Reports* volumes, so that they can incorporate any corrections and include star pagination with references to where each page in the official *U.S.*

---

[11] Before volume 545 (2005), the page numbers of the PDF documents include the prefatory matter in the volume and therefore do not match the printed page numbers. Page 1 of a volume, for example, could be page 95 or page 203 of the PDF file. The text is searchable, however, so the quickest way to find a particular case is often to retrieve its volume and search for its name. Cases in more recent volumes can be found by page number.

[12] The Library of Congress also offers access to cases in volumes 1–542 (1789–2004) of the *United States Reports* (www.loc.gov/collections/united-states-reports/). This is a rather cumbersome interface, but the text of the opinions is searchable.

[13] THE BLUEBOOK: A UNIFORM SYSTEM OF CITATION tbl. T1.1 (21st ed. 2020); ALWD GUIDE TO LEGAL CITATION R. 12.4(b)(3) (6th ed. 2017). *The Bluebook* goes on to specify citation to *The United States Law Week* for very recent decisions not yet in the commercial reporters, but that newsletter ceased print publication in 2018.

Reports begins. Both Westlaw and Lexis use asterisks to indicate the beginnings of new pages in the printed reporters.

The *Supreme Court Reporter* began in 1882, with cases from volume 106 of the *U.S. Reports*. As a component of West's National Reporter System encompassing federal courts and state appellate courts, it includes the publisher's editorial synopses and headnotes. The opening page of *United States v. Olson* as it appears in the *Supreme Court Reporter* at 126 S. Ct. 510 is shown in Illustration 11-3, including the synopsis, the West headnotes, and the beginning of the syllabus.

Westlaw provides the text of cases as they appear in the *Supreme Court Reporter*, as well as complete historical coverage of the Court's decisions since 1790 and new decisions immediately upon release. For cases since 1882 that have been published in bound *Supreme Court Reporter* volumes, Westlaw provides the option to view and print a PDF of the printed version. Illustration 11-4 shows the beginning of *United States v. Olson*, as it appears on Westlaw.

Lawyers' Edition also began publication in 1882, but it contains all Supreme Court decisions since the Court's inception in 1790. For the earlier cases, its editors worked from the opinions on file in the clerk's office, correcting errors in the official reports and even printing some opinions that had been omitted.[14] For some cases *Lawyers' Edition* includes information not found in the official reports, such as the exact date of decision.[15] In 1956 *Lawyers' Edition* began a second series after reaching 100 volumes, and its version of *Olson* is cited as 163 L. Ed. 2d 306 (2005). The first page of the decision is shown in Illustration 11-5.

Lawyers' Edition 2d also includes a *Quick Case Table with Annotation References*, a set of supplementary pamphlets that contain corrections, and a "Citator Service" providing summaries of later Supreme Court cases citing each decision.

---

[14] Book Review, 18 AM. L. REV. 1067, 1068 (1884); Book Review, 29 AM. L. REV. 477, 477 (1895).

[15] Dates of argument and decision for cases from 1791 to 1882 can also be found in a table prepared by Anne Ashmore of the Supreme Court Library and available on the Court's website (www.supremecourt.gov/opinions/datesofdecisions.pdf) [https://perma.cc/CGN3-VCV7].

546 U.S. 43, 163 L.Ed.2d 306

UNITED STATES, Petitioner,

v.

Joseph OLSON, et al.

No. 04–759.

Argued Oct. 12, 2005.

Decided Nov. 8, 2005.

Background: Injured miners sued the Mine Safety and Health Administration (MSHA) pursuant to the Federal Tort Claims Act (FTCA), alleging negligence by federal mine inspectors. The United States District Court for the District of Arizona, William D. Browning, J., granted MSHA's motion to dismiss, and miners appealed. The United States Court of Appeals for the Ninth Circuit, 362 F.3d 1236, reversed and remanded. Certiorari was granted.

Holding: The Supreme Court, Justice Breyer, held that FTCA waives federal government's sovereign immunity only where local law would make private person liable in tort, not where local law would make state or municipal entity liable, even where uniquely governmental functions are at issue; abrogating *Hines v. United States*, 60 F.3d 1442; *Cimo v. INS*, 16 F.3d 1039; *Cameron v. Janssen Bros. Nurseries, Ltd.*, 7 F.3d 821; *Aguilar v. United States*, 920 F.2d 1475; *Doggett v. United States*, 875 F.2d 684.

Vacated and remanded.

1. United States ☞78(3, 14)

Federal Tort Claims Act (FTCA) waives federal government's sovereign immunity only where local law would make private person liable in tort, not where local law would make state or municipal entity liable, even where uniquely governmental functions are at issue; abrogating

Hines v. United States, 60 F.3d 1442; *Cimo v. INS*, 16 F.3d 1039; *Cameron v. Janssen Bros. Nurseries, Ltd.*, 7 F.3d 821; *Aguilar v. United States*, 920 F.2d 1475; *Doggett v. United States*, 875 F.2d 684. 28 U.S.C.A. § 1346(b)(1).

2. United States ☞78(3)

Provision of Federal Tort Claims Act imposing liability in same manner and to same extent as private individual under "like circumstances" does not restrict court's inquiry to same circumstances; rather, it is required to look further afield. 28 U.S.C.A. § 2674.

↓₂*Syllabus* *

Claiming that federal mine inspectors' negligence helped cause a mine accident, two injured workers (and a spouse) sued the United States under the Federal Tort Claims Act (Act), which authorizes private tort actions against the Government "under circumstances where the United States, if a private person, would be liable to the claimant in accordance with the law of the place where the act or omission occurred," 28 U.S.C. § 1346(b)(1). The District Court dismissed in part on the ground that the allegations did not show that Arizona law would impose liability upon a private person in similar circumstances. The Ninth Circuit reversed, reasoning from two premises: (1) Where unique governmental functions are at issue, the Act waives sovereign immunity if a state or municipal entity would be held liable under the law where the activity occurred, and (2) federal mine inspections are such unique governmental functions since there is no private-sector analogue for mine inspections. Because Arizona law would make a state or municipal entity

---

* The syllabus constitutes no part of the opinion of the Court but has been prepared by the Reporter of Decisions for the convenience of

the reader. See *United States v. Detroit Timber & Lumber Co.*, 200 U.S. 321, 337, 26 S.Ct. 282, 50 L.Ed. 499.

Illustration 11-3. A Supreme Court case as published in *Supreme Court Reporter*.

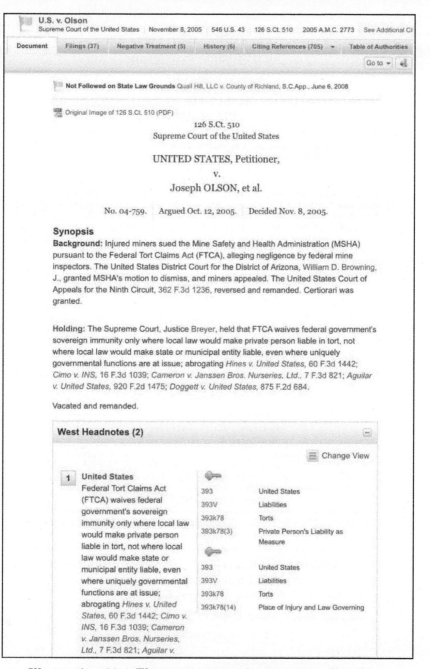

Illustration 11-4. The same case as it appears on Westlaw.

[546 U.S. 43]

UNITED STATES, Petitioner

v

JOSEPH OLSON, et al.

546 U.S. 43, 126 S. Ct. 510, 163 L. Ed. 2d 306

[No. 04-759]

Argued October 12, 2005. Decided November 8, 2005.

Decision: United States held to waive sovereign immunity under Federal Tort Claims Act provision (28 U.S.C.S. § 1346(b)(1)) only where local law would make "private person" liable in tort.

SUMMARY

Workers who had been injured in a mine accident in Arizona brought, against the United States on the basis of federal mine inspectors' alleged negligence, a suit under the Federal Tort Claims Act (FTCA) (28 U.S.C.S. §§ 1346, 2671 et seq.), which in 28 U.S.C.S. § 1346(b)(1), authorized private tort actions against the United States "under circumstances where the United States, if a private person, would be liable to the claimant in accordance with the law of the place where the act or omission occurred."

The United States District Court for the District of Arizona dismissed the lawsuit in part on the ground that the allegations were insufficient to show that Arizona law would impose liability on a private person in similar circumstances.

The United States Court of Appeals reversed, as the Court of Appeals (1) reasoned that (a) where unique governmental functions were at issue, the FTCA waived sovereign immunity if a state or municipal entity would have been subject to liability under the law where the activity occurred, (b) federal mine inspections were unique governmental functions, since they had no private-sector analogue; and (2) held that the FTCA waived sovereign immunity in the instant case, since Arizona law would have made state or municipal entities liable in the circumstances alleged (362 F. 3d 1236).

SUBJECT OF ANNOTATION

Beginning on page 1223, infra

Supreme Court's construction and application of Federal Tort Claims Act (FTCA) provisions (in 28 U.S.C.S. §§ 1346(b)(1) and 2674, and similar predecessors) concerning "private person" and "private individual under like circumstances" standards for liability of United States

---

Summaries of Briefs; Names of Participating Attorneys, p 1154, infra.

306

Illustration 11-5. A Supreme Court case as published in
LexisNexis's *United States Supreme Court
Reports, Lawyers' Edition.*

Lexis has Supreme Court cases since the Court's inception in 1790, with new decisions as soon as they are announced. The online cases have an array of editorial additions; they include the *Lawyers' Edition* summaries and headnotes and the official syllabus, but these are preceded by a separate case summary and Lexis headnotes in the same style as other Lexis cases. Illustration 11-6 shows the beginning of *United States v. Olson* in Lexis.[16]

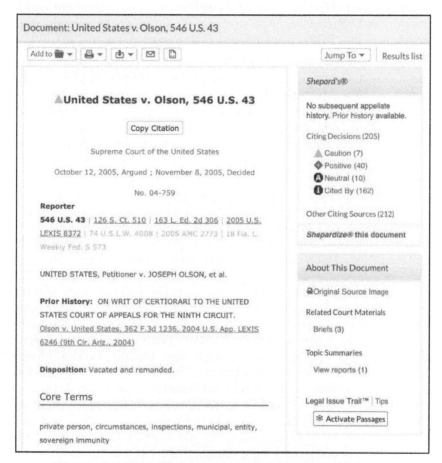

Illustration 11-6. The same case as it appears on Lexis.

---

[16] Lexis also provides links to PDFs of cases as they appear in the official *U.S. Reports* volumes. After 1921 the syllabi and other editorial matter are redacted due to potential copyright concerns.

(e) Other Electronic Sources

Researchers without Westlaw or Lexis access can find Supreme Court opinions at several free internet sites, in addition to the Court's own website and Cornell's Legal Information Institute. Sites providing free access to the entire retrospective Supreme Court collection back to 1790 include Google Scholar (scholar.google.com) and Justia (justia.com). Both of these sites have hypertext links to other cases cited in the opinions, as well as star pagination indicating the precise *U.S. Reports* location of specific language from an opinion. Justia also has PDFs of the official *U.S. Reports* back to 1991.

Subscription sites such as Bloomberg Law (www.bloomberglaw. com), Casemaker (www.casemaker.us), Casetext (casetext.com), and Fastcase (www.fastcase.com) also have complete retrospective coverage, and VersusLaw (www.versuslaw.com) has Supreme Court cases back to 1882. ProQuest Supreme Court Insight has a complete collection of opinions (as well as dockets, amicus briefs, petitions for certiorari, and oral arguments) back to 1975, and will grow over time as earlier material is added.

§ 11.2 THE LOWER FEDERAL COURTS

Congress has power to create the lower federal courts under Article III of the Constitution, which vests the judicial power of the United States "in one supreme Court, and in such inferior Courts as the Congress may from time to time ordain and establish." The Judiciary Act of 1789, which established the federal court system, created thirteen District Courts, one for each of the eleven states that had ratified the Constitution as well as for the Districts of Kentucky and Maine, and three Circuit Courts.[17] Both District and Circuit Courts served as trial courts, with the Circuit Courts having appellate jurisdiction in limited areas. The federal court system has grown considerably from this original structure, with one of the most significant changes occurring in 1891 when Congress created the Circuit Courts of Appeals to serve as intermediate appellate courts.[18] Twenty years later it abolished the old Circuit Courts,[19] and the Circuit Courts of Appeals were renamed the United States Courts of Appeals in 1948.[20]

---

[17] Judiciary Act of 1789, ch. 20, §§ 2–4, 1 Stat. 73, 73–75.

[18] Act of Mar. 3, 1891, ch. 517, 26 Stat. 826, sometimes known as the Evarts Act after its principal sponsor, Sen. William M. Evarts of New York.

[19] Act of Mar. 3, 1911, ch. 231, § 289, 36 Stat. 1087, 1167.

[20] Act of June 25, 1948, ch. 646, § 2(b), 62 Stat. 869, 985. The growth and development of the federal court system are detailed in PETER CHARLES HOFFER ET AL., THE FEDERAL COURTS: AN ESSENTIAL HISTORY (2016) and ERWIN C. SURRENCY, HISTORY OF THE FEDERAL COURTS (2d ed. 2002). Historical documents are reprinted in DEBATES ON THE FEDERAL JUDICIARY: A DOCUMENTARY HISTORY (Bruce A.

The 1891 act created nine numbered circuits, each covering several states. The Tenth Circuit was added in 1929, and the Fifth Circuit was divided to create the Eleventh Circuit in 1980. As part of the 1948 codification of the Judiciary Act, the U.S. Court of Appeals for the District of Columbia was renamed the U.S. Court of Appeals for the District of Columbia Circuit. Each of these twelve Courts of Appeals hears cases from the trial courts within its circuit, and its decisions have binding authority over those trial courts. Cases are generally decided by three-judge panels, but litigants can petition for a rehearing en banc by all of the circuit judges (or a panel of eleven judges in the Ninth Circuit, by far the largest circuit).[21]

Every Court of Appeals has its own website, usually with recent opinions, information on pending cases, rules, forms, and other information. These sites can be found with simple internet searches, or through links on the U.S. Courts website (www.uscourts.gov/about-federal-courts/federal-courts-public/court-website-links).

A thirteenth circuit, the Federal Circuit (www.cafc.uscourts. gov), was created in 1982 with specialized subject matter jurisdiction to hear appeals from throughout the country on such matters as patents, trademarks, international trade, and government contracts.[22] It is the successor to the U.S. Court of Customs and Patent Appeals (1910–82) and to the appellate division of the U.S. Court of Claims (1855–1982).

The federal court system also includes two other appellate courts with specialized jurisdictions:

— The United States Court of Appeals for the Armed Forces (www.armfor.uscourts.gov) hears cases from the Courts of Criminal Appeals for individual branches of the

---

Ragsdale ed., 2013), available online from the Federal Judicial Center (www. fjc.gov/history).

[21] FED R. APP. P. 35; 9TH CIR. R. 35–3. Only about one of every thousand cases is reheard en banc. Table B-10—U.S. Courts of Appeals Judicial Business (Sept. 30, 2018), U.S. COURTS (www.uscourts.gov/statistics/table/b-10/judicial-business/2018/09/30) [https://perma.cc/52FL-4CBJ]. On en banc review generally, see Tracey E. George, *The Dynamics and Determinants of the Decision to Grant En Banc Review*, 74 WASH. L. REV. 213 (1999); Stephen L. Wasby, *Why Sit En Banc?*, 63 HASTINGS L.J. 747 (2012). Most circuits have developed informal procedures to circumvent formal en banc review. *See* Amy E. Sloan, *The Dog That Didn't Bark: Stealth Procedures and the Erosion of Stare Decisis in the Federal Courts of Appeals*, 78 FORDHAM L. REV. 713 (2009).

[22] Federal Court Improvement Act of 1982, Pub. L. No. 97–164, 96 Stat. 25. The jurisdiction of the Federal Circuit is determined by 28 U.S.C. § 1295. For more on the court's history and practice, see BRUCE D. ABRAMSON, THE SECRET CIRCUIT: THE LITTLE-KNOWN COURT WHERE THE RULES OF THE INFORMATION AGE UNFOLD (2007), and STEVEN FLANDERS, THE FEDERAL CIRCUIT—A JUDICIAL INNOVATION: ESTABLISHING A US COURT OF APPEALS (2010).

service, and its decisions are reviewable by the Supreme
Court.

— The United States Court of Appeals for Veterans
Claims (www.uscourts.cavc.gov) reviews decisions of the
Board of Veterans Appeals, and its decisions can in turn be
appealed to the Court of Appeals for the Federal Circuit.

The general trial courts, the United States District Courts, are
divided into ninety-four geographic districts, with one or more in each
state. California, New York, and Texas are each divided into four
districts, while twenty-six of the states have just one district apiece.
Each district has a specified number of judges, from two in several
districts to twenty-eight in the Southern District of New York.[23] The
map in Illustration 11-7 shows the boundaries of the circuits and
districts.

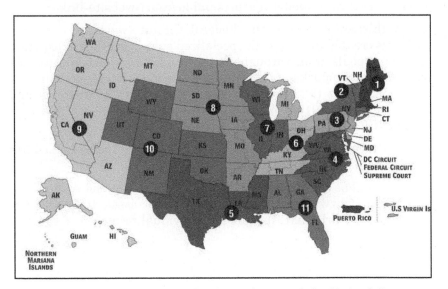

**Illustration 11-7. Geographic boundaries of the United States
Courts of Appeals and United States District Courts.**

---

[23] 28 U.S.C. § 133. The districts with two judges are Idaho, the Northern District
of Iowa, North Dakota, the Eastern District of Oklahoma, Vermont, and the Western
District of Wisconsin. The history of each state's federal courts is recounted in *Sketches
of the Establishment of the Federal Courts by States [Jurisdiction] and Their Judges*,
212 F.R.D. 611 (2003). A majority of the districts are further subdivided into
"divisions," which can be helpful to know about in planning for litigation. *See* Alex
Botoman, Note, *Divisional Judge-Shopping*, COLUM. HUM. RTS. L. REV., Winter 2018,
at 297.

Each District Court has a website with case information, local rules, forms, contact information, and other documents for attorneys, litigants, and jurors. These too are on the U.S. Courts list of website links.

In addition, the federal court system has several trial courts with specialized jurisdictions:

— United States Bankruptcy Courts are located in each district as adjuncts to the District Courts, with specialized jurisdiction over bankruptcy matters. The system of separate bankruptcy courts was created in the 1978 revision of the Bankruptcy Code.[24]

— The United States Court of Federal Claims (www. uscfc.uscourts.gov) has jurisdiction over federal contract disputes and most other claims for money damages against the United States. It was created at the same time as the Federal Circuit and is the successor to the trial division of the U.S. Court of Claims (1855–1982). The new court was originally called the U.S. Claims Court but was renamed in 1992.[25]

— The United States Court of International Trade (www.cit.uscourts.gov) hears cases involving customs law and other aspects of international trade. Its decisions are appealed to the Federal Circuit. The Court of International Trade was created in 1980 to replace the U.S. Customs Court (1890–1980).[26]

— The United States Tax Court (www.ustaxcourt.gov) shares jurisdiction with the District Courts in disputes about federal income taxation. A decision is reviewable by the U.S. Court of Appeals for the circuit in which the petitioner resides or has its principal office. The Tax Court was created in 1942 as the successor to the Board of Tax Appeals (1924–42).[27]

The jurisdiction and procedures of the federal courts are the subject of challenging law school classes and have spawned a voluminous literature. The leading hornbooks in the field are Charles

---

[24] Bankruptcy Reform Act of 1978, Pub. L. No. 95–598, § 201, 92 Stat. 2549, 2657 (current version at 28 U.S.C. §§ 151–159).

[25] Federal Court Administration Act of 1992, Pub. L. No. 102–572, tit. IX, 106 Stat. 4506, 4516. The provisions governing the Court of Federal Claims are at 28 U.S.C. §§ 171–180.

[26] Customs Court Act of 1980, Pub. L. No. 96–417, 94 Stat. 1727 (current version at 28 U.S.C. §§ 251–258).

[27] Revenue Act of 1942, § 504, ch. 619, 56 Stat. 798, 957. The provisions governing the Tax Court are at 26 U.S.C. §§ 7441–7479.

Alan Wright & Mary Kay Kane, *Law of Federal Courts* (8th ed. 2017) and Erwin Chemerinsky, *Federal Jurisdiction* (7th ed. 2016).

Two comprehensive treatises by distinguished scholars in the fields of federal courts and procedure are *Federal Practice and Procedure* and *Moore's Federal Practice*. *Federal Practice and Procedure* (1st–4th eds. 1969–date, available on Westlaw) is an exhaustive treatment of federal procedural and jurisdictional issues. The entire set is commonly referred to as "Wright & Miller," after its original authors, Charles Alan Wright and Arthur R. Miller, although they have been joined on specific volumes by more than a dozen coauthors. *Moore's Federal Practice* (3d ed. 1997–date, available on Lexis), the other major treatise, is named after the primary author of the first two editions, James William Moore. The current edition is written by a team of over forty authors. *Moore's* has volumes focusing on matters such as court rules, jurisdiction, Supreme Court practice, admiralty practice, and the federal law of attorney conduct. *Moore's* has been cited in over 45,000 federal cases, and Wright & Miller in nearly twice that number.

Another multi-volume treatment of federal practice, the encyclopedic *Federal Procedure, Lawyers' Edition* (1982–date, available on Westlaw), is more practical and far less frequently cited. Some of its eighty chapters focus on procedural issues (Access to District Courts, New Trial), and some on topical areas of federal law (Atomic Energy, Job Discrimination). The work deals with civil, criminal, and administrative practice, and includes checklists, synopses of law review articles, and texts of relevant statutes.

Federal Appellate Practice (Philip Allen Lacovara ed., 2d ed. 2013, available on Bloomberg Law), has a more focused treatment of procedures in the U.S. Courts of Appeals. Of the many guides to federal trial practice, one of the most thorough is *Business & Commercial Litigation in Federal Courts* (Robert L. Haig ed., 4th ed. 2016–date, available on Westlaw).

(a) Online Resources

There is no counterpart to the *U.S. Reports* for the decisions of the U.S. Courts of Appeals and District Courts. The only officially published sources are the individual slip decisions that the courts issue and post on their websites. The Court of Appeals sites generally only include cases since the mid-1990s or early 2000s and provide rudimentary searching options. District Court sites are even more widely varied; some require login to the PACER case management system and have no full-text search capabilities.[28] PACER charges a

---

[28] Federal law requires that each court maintain a website with "[a]ccess to the substance of all written opinions issued by the court, regardless of whether such

per-page fee to view pleadings and other documents but provides free access to many opinions.

Govinfo.gov has a United States Courts Opinions collection, a collaborative effort of the Government Publishing Office and the Administrative Office of the U.S. Courts. Decisions from all of the Courts of Appeals are represented, but materials from only 60–65% of District and Bankruptcy Courts are included. The collection has cases back to the early 2000s, but dates of coverage vary by court.

The deepest coverage of federal court decisions is in commercially published reports and electronic sources. The most comprehensive sources are the databases of Westlaw, Lexis, and Bloomberg Law, which have complete coverage from the beginning of the court system in 1789 and generally have new decisions within hours or days. These services include thousands of decisions not available in any other form, except as slip opinions.

Other online sources have extensive collections, if not quite as comprehensive. Subscription services such as Casemaker, Casetext, Fastcase, and VersusLaw all have more than sixty years of Court of Appeals and District Court decisions. This coverage may not be as useful for exhaustive historical research, but it is sufficient for almost any modern legal inquiry.

While opinions at court websites are generally limited to the most recent decade or two, other free websites have broader coverage. Google Scholar and Justia both cover Court of Appeals and District Court decisions since 1924.

(b) Case Reporters

Despite the widespread online availability of lower federal court decisions, *The Bluebook* and the *ALWD Guide* require that cases be cited to published reporters if available in print.[29] It is worth developing a familiarity with reporter citations, even if you do all your research online, because the citations provide quick information about the source and precedential value of cases. The most

---

opinions are to be published in the official court reporter, in a text searchable format." E-Government Act of 2002, § 205(a)(5), Pub. L. No. 107–347, 116 Stat. 2899, 2913 (codified at 44 U.S.C. § 3501 note). *But see* Peter W. Martin, *District Court Opinions That Remain Hidden Despite a Long-Standing Congressional Mandate of Transparency—The Result of Judicial Autonomy and Systemic Indifference*, 110 LAW LIBR. J. 305 (2018).

[29] THE BLUEBOOK: A UNIFORM SYSTEM OF CITATION R. 18.2 (21st ed. 2020) ("*The Bluebook* requires the use and citation of traditional printed sources when available, unless there is a digital copy of the source available that is authenticated, official, or an exact copy of the printed source. . . ."); ALWD GUIDE TO LEGAL CITATION R. 30.1 (6th ed. 2017) ("In general, if a source appears both in print and electronic versions, cite the print version if it is readily available to most readers.").

comprehensive printed sources for lower federal court decisions are West reporters published by Thomson Reuters. Like the *Supreme Court Reporter*, these contain editorial synopses and headnotes with key numbers, allowing researchers to find cases through the West digest system online or in print. (The digest system is discussed in more detail in the next chapter.)

United States Courts of Appeals. In 1880 West's *Federal Reporter* began covering decisions of both the district and circuit courts, as well as the new Circuit Courts of Appeals following the reorganization of the federal judiciary system in 1891. Since 1932 it has covered only the Courts of Appeals, and after more than 2,200 volumes it is now in its third series (cited as F.3d).[30]

As in the *Supreme Court Reporter*, each decision is prefaced with a concise synopsis summarizing the issues and the holding, and with headnotes paraphrasing specific points of law in the case. The headnotes are arranged by topic and key number in the West series of digests, and the synopses and headnotes are included in Westlaw's version of the case. Westlaw provides page images of the *Federal Reporter* version, from the earliest cases through the most recently published bound volume. Lexis also has *Federal Reporter* page images, but with the synopses and headnotes redacted.

Because the *Federal Reporter* covers many different courts (unlike the *U.S. Reports*), citations must identify the specific circuit in parentheses.[31] The lower court's ruling in the *Olson* case (the Supreme Court decision shown in Illustrations 11-1 to 11-6), for example, is cited as *Olson v. United States*, 362 F.3d 1236 (9th Cir. 2004). Knowing the jurisdiction is vital in evaluating the scope and precedential value of a decision, but beginning researchers often omit this information (as does Westlaw, unfortunately, in the headers at the top of its case downloads).

Despite publishing over thirty volumes each year, the *Federal Reporter* contains only a small percentage of the decisions of the U.S. Courts of Appeals. It is limited to those opinions that the courts have designated as "published" and therefore as precedential. Since the 1970s, each circuit has had rules limiting publication to decisions meeting specific criteria. Generally a decision is published if it lays down a new rule of law or alters an existing rule, criticizes existing

---

[30] The *Federal Reporter* has also contained decisions of various specialized courts created by Congress, including the U.S. Commerce Court (1910–13); Court of Customs and Patent Appeals (1929–82), U.S. Court of Claims (1930–32, 1960–82) (Court of Claims coverage was moved to the *Federal Supplement* from 1932 to 1960), Emergency Court of Appeals (1942–61), and Temporary Emergency Court of Appeals (1972–92).

[31] THE BLUEBOOK: A UNIFORM SYSTEM OF CITATION R. 10.4 (21st ed. 2020); ALWD GUIDE TO LEGAL CITATION R. 12.6(c) (6th ed. 2017). This practice is also a simple, powerful tool for attorneys to convey the weight of their arguments more fully.

law, resolves an apparent conflict of authority, or involves a legal issue of continuing public interest.[32] As a result fewer than twelve percent of Court of Appeals cases are terminated with a published opinion.[33]

From the beginning of the "nonpublication" era, commentators argued that the development of an unpublished body of decisions reduced judicial accountability, hindered the operation of stare decisis, and exacerbated inequities between frequent litigants such as government agencies (who would see numerous unpublished decisions and could predict how a court would rule) and infrequent litigants such as social security claimants.[34] Even if they could not be cited as precedent, these cases could provide useful guidance of how a court would treat a similar subsequent claim.

Until 2006, unpublished decisions could not even be cited as persuasive authority under most circuits' rules. This prohibition, however, did not quell the demand for unpublished cases. Thousands of these decisions were accessible online and the controversy grew about whether they should be considered as precedent. The issue reached a crisis point in 2000, when a panel of the Eight Circuit ruled in *Anastasoff v. United States* that the ban on citing unpublished opinions was an unconstitutional violation of Article III.[35] This decision was vacated on other grounds within a few months, but the battle had been joined and the early 2000s saw a flurry of commentary on the issue.[36]

---

[32] *See, e.g.*, D.C. CIR. R. 36(c)(2). The criteria for each circuit are summarized in LAURAL HOOPER ET AL., CASE MANAGEMENT PROCEDURES IN THE FEDERAL COURTS OF APPEALS tbl. 10, at 33–34 (2d ed. 2011), which is available from the Federal Judicial Center website (www.fjc.gov) and also includes a general overview of each circuit's rules.

[33] Table B-12—U.S. Courts of Appeals Judicial Business (Sept. 30, 2018), U. S. COURTS (www.uscourts.gov/statistics/table/b-12/judicial-business/2018/09/30) [https://perma.cc/2HX7-CC52].

[34] *See, e.g.*, William L. Reynolds & William M. Richman, *An Evaluation of Limited Publication in the United States Courts of Appeals: The Price of Reform*, 48 U. CHI. L. REV. 573 (1981); William L. Reynolds & William M. Richman, *The Non-Precedential Precedent—Limited Publication and No-Citation Rules in the United States Courts of Appeals*, 78 COLUM. L. REV. 1167 (1978); Lauren K. Robel, *The Myth of the Disposable Opinion: Unpublished Opinions and Government Litigants in the United States Courts of Appeals*, 87 MICH. L. REV. 940 (1989).

[35] 223 F.3d 898 (8th Cir.), *vacated as moot*, 235 F.3d 1054 (8th Cir. 2000) (en banc).

[36] *See, e.g.*, Stephen R. Barnett, *No-Citation Rules under Siege: A Battlefield Report and Analysis*, 5 J. APP. PRAC. & PROCESS 473 (2003); Penelope Pether, *Inequitable Injunctions: The Scandal of Private Judging in the U.S. Courts*, 56 STAN. L. REV. 1435 (2004); Lauren Robel, *The Practice of Precedent:* Anastasoff, *Noncitation Rules, and the Meaning of Precedent in an Interpretive Community*, 35 IND. L. REV. 399 (2002). Symposium, *Have We Ceased to Be a Common Law Country?: A Conversation on Unpublished, Depublished, Withdrawn and Per Curiam Opinions*, 62 WASH. & LEE L. REV. 1429 (2005), has nearly a dozen articles on the topic. Elizabeth

In the wake of the *Anastasoff* decision, West began publishing the *Federal Appendix* in 2001, a series limited to Court of Appeals decisions "not selected for publication in the *Federal Reporter*." These decisions are published with synopses and headnotes and are indexed in the West digests, but it remains necessary to determine for each circuit to what extent they can be cited as precedent. Westlaw does not have PDFs of *Federal Appendix* opinions.

A new Federal Rule of Appellate Procedure was adopted in 2006 that permits "unpublished" or "non-precedential" decisions to be cited as persuasive authority. Rule 32.1 provides that courts cannot prohibit or restrict the citation of such opinions, but it is limited to decisions issued after January 1, 2007. The rule takes no position on how earlier decisions should be handled, and policies vary from circuit to circuit. Some circuits have declared by rule that unpublished opinions are not precedent, while others say that unpublished cases are not binding but can be cited for persuasive value.[37]

United States District Courts. In 1932, with the increasing volume of litigation in the federal courts, West began another reporter series called *Federal Supplement* (F. Supp.) for selected U.S. District Court decisions (leaving the *Federal Reporter* to cover the U.S. Courts of Appeals). *Federal Supplement* is now in its third series (F. Supp. 3d), and also includes decisions of the U.S. Court of International Trade and rulings from the Judicial Panel on Multidistrict Litigation.[38]

Very few U.S. District Court cases are represented by opinions published in the *Federal Supplement*. More decisions are available from the online platforms and through PACER or Govinfo, but many District Court cases do not even result in written opinions. Unlike appellate cases in which a panel of judges resolve specific legal issues, trial court litigation can be tried to a jury verdict or settled before trial with no resulting court opinion. District Court cases may have a number of rulings on issues such as the exclusion of evidence or the

---

Y. McCuskey, *Submerged Precedent*, 16 NEV. L.J. 515 (2016), provides a more current perspective on case law unavailable to most litigants.

[37] The circuits' approaches are summarized in David R. Cleveland, *Local Rules in the Wake of Federal Rule of Appellate Procedure 32.1*, 11 J. APP. PRAC. & PROCESS 19 (2010). For criticism of these rules, see, e.g., Penelope Pether, *Constitutional Solipsism: Toward a Thick Doctrine of Article III Duty; or Why the Federal Circuits' Nonprecedential Status Rules Are Profoundly Unconstitutional*, 17 WM. & MARY BILL RTS. J. 955 (2009). For a study of the availability of non-precedential decisions, see Michael Kagan et al., *Invisible Adjudication in the U.S. Court of Appeals*, 106 GEO. L.J. 683 (2018).

[38] The *Federal Supplement* has also included decisions of the U.S. Court of Claims (1932–60), the U.S. Customs Court (1956–80), and the Special Court under the Regional Rail Reorganization Act of 1973 (1974–97).

qualification of expert witnesses, and some of these are published or available online, but only a few cases have a final written "decision" in the same sense as an appellate proceeding. The Westlaw and Lexis cases databases vary considerably in terms of which District Court materials are available on each platform.

Another West series, *Federal Rules Decisions* (F.R.D.), began publication in 1940 and contains a limited number of U.S. District Court decisions dealing with procedural issues under the Federal Rules of Civil Procedure and the Federal Rules of Criminal Procedure. *Federal Rules Decisions* does not contain all District Court procedural decisions; some cases involving interpretation of court rules continue to appear in *Federal Supplement,* and many others are available only online. *Federal Rules Decisions* also includes judicial conference proceedings and occasional speeches or articles dealing with procedural law in the federal courts.

Westlaw has PDF images of cases published in both *Federal Supplement* and *Federal Rules Decisions*.

Specialized Courts. As Congress has periodically restructured the federal judiciary to create specialized courts over the years, West (now Thomson Reuters) has at times added their coverage to the *Federal Reporter* or *Federal Supplement.* It has also created several new topical reporters to cover some of these courts. Each of these reporters includes West synopses and headnotes so that cases can be found through key number searches in West digests or on Westlaw (which also has PDFs of the printed versions of these cases).

Two West reporters began publication in the early 1980s for the decisions of newly created courts. *West's Bankruptcy Reporter* (1980– date) covers decisions of the Bankruptcy Courts, as well as some District Court opinions on bankruptcy issues. The *United States Claims Court Reporter* began in 1982 to cover the United States Claims Court and became the *Federal Claims Reporter* when the court was renamed the Court of Federal Claims in 1992.[39]

Since 1978 *West's Military Justice Reporter* has published the decisions of the U.S. Court of Appeals for the Armed Forces (formerly the U.S. Court of Military Appeals) and selected decisions of the Courts of Criminal Appeals for each military branch. Decisions of the U.S. Court of Appeals for Veterans Claims are published in *Veterans Appeals Reporter* (1991–date).

West's National Reporter System does not include decisions from the U.S. Tax Court. These are published by the government in

---

[39] Both reporters also include appellate opinions from the Supreme Court and Courts of Appeals, but these are simply reprinted from the *Supreme Court Reporter* and *Federal Reporter* with their original page numbers.

Reports of the United States Tax Court (1942–date), and by the major commercial tax publishers in *American Federal Tax Reports* (RIA) and *U.S. Tax Cases* (CCH). Tax Court memorandum opinions, issued in cases that do not involve novel legal issues, are not published in the official reports but they can be cited as precedent. These opinions are available online and are published in *TC Memorandum Decisions* (RIA) and *Tax Court Memorandum Decisions* (CCH).

Topical Reporters. Federal court decisions are also available in print and online from a variety of other sources, including commercial topical reporters published for practitioners in specialized subject areas. Some cases appearing in these sources are not printed in the *Federal Reporter* or *Federal Supplement*, but most are generally available from the major online services.

In addition to *Federal Rules Decisions*, Thomson Reuters publishes two other series of cases on procedural issues. These are *not* part of its National Reporter System but are preferred over online sources in citations. These series, *Federal Rules Service* (1939–date) and *Federal Rules of Evidence Service* (1979–date), duplicate some coverage with the National Reporter System volumes but also contain cases not found there.

Cases also appear in several dozen specialized reporters. Most of these series also include reports of agency adjudications and state court decisions as well.

(c) Historical Sources

During the 19th century, a number of individual nominative reporters published decisions of the lower federal courts. Over sixty separate reporters, most covering just a single court, published cases of the circuit and district courts, and scattered decisions appeared in over 100 other publications.

In the 1890s, West collected the decisions from these various reporters and compiled them in a set entitled *Federal Cases* (cited as F. Cas.). More than 18,000 cases are arranged in alphabetical order by case name and numbered. The thirty-volume set contains all available lower federal court case law up to 1880. These are cited by name, citation, and case number, e.g. *In re Zug*, 30 F. Cas. 947 (C.C.W.D. Pa. 1877) (No. 18,222). The first volume includes lists of the nominative reporters and other publications from which cases were drawn, as well as lists of all federal judges up to 1894 by jurisdiction and alphabetically, and the final volume reprints judicial tributes from the original reporters and has brief biographical notes on the judges.

Westlaw, Lexis, and Bloomberg Law all have complete retrospective coverage of the early federal cases, often with citations to both the original nominative sources and *Federal Cases*. Westlaw does not provide PDFs of these early decisions, but the page images are available in HeinOnline's Early American Case Law collection and from LLMC Digital.

§ 11.3 STATE COURTS

Although federal law governs an increasing range of activities, state courts have a vital lawmaking role on many issues, including important areas such as family law, contracts, insurance, many kinds of torts, and substantive criminal law. A state's court of last resort has the final say in interpreting the state's constitution and statutes.

The structure of most state court systems roughly follows the federal paradigm, with various trial courts, intermediate appellate courts, and a court of last resort. There are, however, wide variations. A few states have no intermediate appellate courts, with appeals going directly from the trial court to the state supreme court. Other states have more complicated systems, with more than one appellate court for different subject areas. Oklahoma and Texas, for instance, have separate courts of last resort for civil and criminal matters.[40]

The National Center for State Courts (NCSC) publishes charts showing the structure of each state's court system, indicating the jurisdiction of the various courts and the routes of appeal within the court hierarchy. These Court Structure Charts are available through the NCSC's Court Statistics Project website (www.courtstatistics. org), along with a broad range of other information on the caseloads and work of state courts. The Maryland chart in Illustration 11-8, for example, shows that the Court of Appeals is the state's court of last resort, and that probate cases are handled in the Orphans' Court.[41]

More detailed information can usually be found on state court system websites and in state legal research guides. The NCSC maintains a comprehensive listing of state judicial branch and court websites (www.ncsc.org/information-and-resources/state-court-websites).

---

[40] For a brief overview, see Paul Brace, *Organization and Structure of State Courts*, in GUIDE TO STATE POLITICS AND POLICY 259–74 (Richard G. Niemi & Joshua J. Dyck eds., 2014).

[41] The court structure charts are reprinted in several reference volumes, including BNA's *Directory of State and Federal Courts, Judges, and Clerks*, Leadership Connect's *Federal-State Court Directory*, and the *Legal Researcher's Desk Reference*.

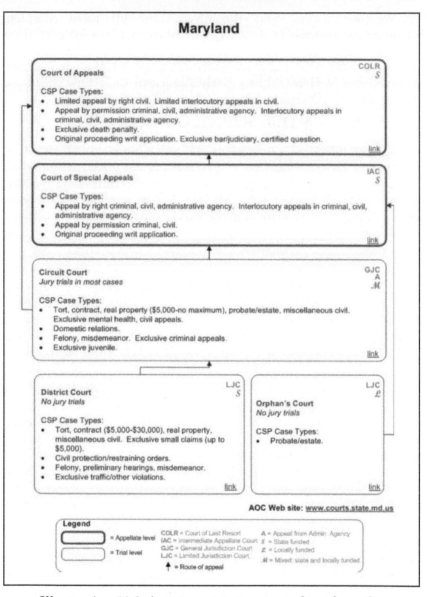

Maryland

Court of Appeals   COLR
                                                                        S

CSP Case Types:
- Limited appeal by right civil. Limited interlocutory appeals in civil.
- Appeal by permission criminal, civil, administrative agency. Interlocutory appeals in criminal, civil, administrative agency.
- Exclusive death penalty.
- Original proceeding writ application. Exclusive bar/judiciary, certified question.

                                                                        link

Court of Special Appeals   IAC
                                                                        S

CSP Case Types:
- Appeal by right criminal, civil, administrative agency. Interlocutory appeals in criminal, civil, administrative agency.
- Appeal by permission criminal, civil.
- Original proceeding writ application.

                                                                        link

Circuit Court   GJC
Jury trials in most cases   A
                                                                        M

CSP Case Types:
- Tort, contract, real property ($5,000-no maximum), probate/estate, miscellaneous civil. Exclusive mental health, civil appeals.
- Domestic relations.
- Felony, misdemeanor. Exclusive criminal appeals.
- Exclusive juvenile.

                                                                        link

District Court   LJC   **Orphan's Court**   LJC
No jury trials   S   *No jury trials*   £

CSP Case Types: CSP Case Types:
- Tort, contract ($5,000-$30,000), real   - Probate/estate.
  property, miscellaneous civil. Exclusive
  small claims (up to $5,000).
- Civil protection/restraining orders.
- Felony, preliminary hearings, misdemeanor.
- Exclusive traffic/other violations.

                                    link   link

AOC Web site: www.courts.state.md.us

Legend

☐ = Appellate level   COLR = Court of Last Resort   A = Appeal from Admin. Agency
☐ = Trial level   IAC = Intermediate Appellate Court S = State funded
                           GJC = General Jurisdiction Court   £ = Locally funded
                           LJC = Limited Jurisdiction Court   M = Mixed: state and locally funded
                           ↑ = Route of appeal

Illustration 11-8. A state court structure chart from the
National Center for State Courts.

Decisions from state courts are available in sources like those from the federal courts, with comprehensive access to appellate decisions in online commercial services, coverage of modern cases on the free internet, and published reporter volumes. Appellate decisions are widely available, but very few state trial court decisions are published either in print or in online case databases.

(a) Online Resources

Westlaw and Lexis are virtually comprehensive sources for state appellate court decisions, including, for some states, numerous opinions that are not published in the official reports. All decisions of courts of last resort are generally published, but publication of decisions by intermediate appellate courts may be sharply limited. As in the federal system, many states limit the citation or precedential value of unpublished opinions.[42]

Coverage of state trial court decisions on Westlaw and Lexis has until recently been sparse, with the case databases generally including decisions from only a handful of states.[43] Westlaw has recent rulings by trial court judges, but these are found in separate "Trial Court Orders" collections. In a global search from the main Westlaw screen, it may be necessary to filter by both Cases and Trial Court Orders to find all relevant judicial decisions. Lexis also has selected trial court orders, included in its state case law databases.

In addition to Westlaw and Lexis, other commercial online services also provide access to state court decisions at the intermediate appellate level and higher; Bloomberg Law extends back well into the 19th century, and sources such as Casemaker, Casetext, Fastcase, and VersusLaw generally have coverage back to the mid-20th century or earlier. Although these services may not be sufficient for comprehensive historical research, any of them would provide more than adequate coverage for most contemporary case law research.

Free resources are also available. Google Scholar covers all state appellate courts back to at least 1950 and permits combined searching of all state jurisdictions. State cases published in official

---

[42] For a lead on state rules on unpublished opinions, see David R. Cleveland, *Appellate Court Rules Governing Publication, Citation, and Precedential Value of Opinions: An Update*, 16 J. APP. PRAC. & PROCESS 257 (2015). Jason B. Binimow, Annotation, *Precedential Effect of Unpublished Opinions*, 105 A.L.R.5th 499 (2003), summarizes cases on this topic from more than forty states as well as federal circuits.

[43] Selected decisions are included from general-jurisdiction trial courts in Connecticut, Delaware, Massachusetts, New Jersey, New York, Ohio, Pennsylvania, and Virginia. The databases also cover tax courts and other courts with specialized jurisdictions in several states.

reporters in some jurisdictions are available from the Caselaw Access Project (case.law) as well.

Most state court websites provide access to court decisions beginning in the mid- to late-1990s, although some states maintain only very recent decisions on their official websites. A few states lead the way with much more extensive databases; Arkansas (opinions. arcourts.gov) and Oklahoma (www.oscn.net) have complete retrospective collections of their states' appellate case law.

(b) West's National Reporter System

Just as Supreme Court decisions are published both in the official *U.S. Reports* and in commercial reporters, so decisions from state appellate courts are traditionally published both in official reports, issued by or under the auspices of the courts themselves, and by Thomson Reuters in the West series of National Reporter System volumes.

West's National Reporter System includes a series of regional reporters publishing the decisions of the appellate courts of the fifty states and the District of Columbia. The National Reporter System divides the country into seven regions and publishes the decisions of the appellate courts of the states in each region together in one series of volumes.

The regions were assigned in the 1880s and make little sense from a modern geographical perspective:

Atlantic Reporter: Connecticut, Delaware, the District of Columbia, Maine, Maryland, New Hampshire, New Jersey, Pennsylvania, Rhode Island, Vermont

North Eastern Reporter: Illinois, Indiana, Massachusetts, New York, Ohio

North Western Reporter: Iowa, Michigan, Minnesota, Nebraska, North Dakota, South Dakota, Wisconsin

Pacific Reporter: Alaska, Arizona, California, Colorado, Hawai'i, Idaho, Kansas, Montana, Nevada, New Mexico, Oklahoma, Oregon, Utah, Washington, Wyoming

South Eastern Reporter: Georgia, North Carolina, South Carolina, Virginia, West Virginia

South Western Reporter: Arkansas, Kentucky, Missouri, Tennessee, Texas

Southern Reporter: Alabama, Florida, Louisiana, Mississippi

Two of these sets are now in their second series (*North Western* (N.W.2d) and *South Eastern* (S.E.2d)), and five have started their third series (*Atlantic* (A.3d), *North Eastern* (N.E.3d), *Pacific* (P.3d), *South Western* (S.W.3d), and *Southern* (So. 3d)).

These sets are supplemented by separate reporters for California and New York, *California Reporter* (Cal. Rptr. 3d) and *New York Supplement* (N.Y.S.3d). Cases from the highest courts of California and New York appear in both the regional and the state reporter, while lower court cases are not published in the *Pacific* or *North Eastern Reporter*. These nine reporters, together with the West federal court reporters, are all tied together by the key number headnote and digest system.

Illustration 10-2 showed the first page of *Harris v. Barefoot*, an opinion of the North Carolina Court of Appeals, as printed in West's *South Eastern Reporter*. The opinion is prefaced, as in other West reporters, by an introductory synopsis and numbered headnotes. The *South Eastern Reporter* version includes bracketed numbers indicating where headnoted topics are discussed in the opinion.

Regional reporter citations are the sources used in most law review references to state court decisions, especially from states that have not instituted public domain citation systems.[44] The title of a regional reporter does not identify the deciding court, so remember to include this information in a citation: *Harris v. Barefoot*, 704 S.E.2d 282 (N.C. Ct. App. 2010).

Citations, including pinpoint cites to quoted material from opinions, can generally be found through the major online platforms without consulting the printed volumes. Most online versions include star pagination indicating page breaks in the text, and Westlaw also has PDFs back to the beginning of the National Reporter System.

(c) Official Reports

Like the *U.S. Reports*, state official reports are the authoritative version of a court's decisions and must be cited in briefs before that court. Official reports are generally less widely available than commercial reporters, which are usually published more quickly and are more useful in research. As lawyers came to rely increasingly on National Reporter System volumes in the 20th century, twenty states

---

[44] THE BLUEBOOK: A UNIFORM SYSTEM OF CITATION R. 10.3.1(b) (21st ed. 2020); ALWD GUIDE TO LEGAL CITATION R. 12.4(b)(5) (6th ed. 2017). *But see* Gil Grantmore, *True Blue*, 20 CONST. COMMENT. 5, 8–9 (2003) (discussing *The Bluebook* 17th ed. 2000) ("If a state goes to the trouble of paying for its own official reporter and requiring its lawyers and judges to cite that reporter, law journals should respect that choice (however frivolous it may seem in an age of electronic publishing and public domain citations).").

decided to discontinue their official reports and to designate the West reporter as the authoritative source of state case law. Florida was the first to make this move, in 1948.[45] These states have been joined more recently by Arkansas, Illinois, Nebraska, and New Mexico, all of which have since 2009 discontinued their printed reports and made online versions official.[46]

In most states, however, cases appear in both official and unofficial editions. Tables in both *The Bluebook* and the *ALWD Guide to Legal Citation* have information on the current status of the published reports in each state. Forms of publication vary from state to state. Some states publish just one series of reports, containing decisions of the state supreme court and in some instances of intermediate appellate courts as well. More than a dozen states issue two or more series of reports, with separate series for the court of last resort, for intermediate appellate courts, and in a few states for selected decisions of trial courts. New York, for example, has three official series: *New York Reports*, covering the Court of Appeals, the state's court of last resort; *Appellate Division Reports*, covering the Appellate Divisions of the Supreme Court; and *Miscellaneous Reports*, with decisions of various lower courts. Some states, but not all, publish official slip decisions and advance sheets as well as bound volumes. Illustration 10-1 showed the official slip opinion of *Harris v. Barefoot*; instead of numbered headnotes, it has an introductory paragraph summarizing the decision.

Even though official reports do not generally include links to a comprehensive digest system like West's, they can still provide a valuable perspective on a state's appellate court decisions. Summaries or headnotes written by court staff or by lawyers practicing in that state may be more attuned to local judicial developments than headnotes written by commercial editors.[47] Some

---

[45] *See* George A. Dietz, Legislative Note, *Sketch of the Evolution of Florida Law*, 3 U. FLA. L. REV. 74, 80–81 (1950) ("Gone at last are the tedious waiting for the official reports, the inevitable discrepancies between the earlier unofficial reports and the much later official ones, the needless duplication in printing resulting in higher cost per copy, the tremendous waste [of] time involved in checking what should be—but all too frequently is not—the same phraseology in two sets of books, and the squandering of space for citations on two references when one serves the purpose equally as well.").

[46] *See* Tom Gaylord, *The New, Online-Only Illinois Reports*, 99 ILL. B.J. 477 (2011); Peter W. Martin, *Abandoning Law Reports for Official Digital Case Law*, 12 J. APP. PRAC. & PROCESS 25 (2011); Robert A. Mead, *A Eulogy for New Mexico Reports: The Evolution of Appellate Publication from 1846 to 2012*, 42 N.M. L. REV. 417 (2012).

[47] *See* Richard F. Jones, *The Role of Official Headnotes in Legal Research*, 59 LAW LIBR. J. 277, 279 (1966) ("[T]he official reporter is not only an expert on the law of his jurisdiction, but he is also a specialist in dealing with the opinions of one particular court. He is personally acquainted with the authors of the opinions he headnotes, and familiar with their methods of expressing themselves."). State reports may also include syllabi, which, like headnotes, are generally unofficial editorial additions. One

official reports include research leads not found in the West reporters, and others have their own classification and digest systems. Although official reports are less widely used than West's, in some states they maintain a valuable research role.[48]

For cases before the beginning of the National Reporter System in the 1880s, the official state reports are the only and authoritative source. Most of these early volumes are available digitally in HeinOnline's State Reports: A Historical Archive and from LLMC Digital. Lexis also includes PDFs of state reporter cases, although the headnotes are redacted in cases after 1921.

As with the early *U.S. Reports* volumes, the early reports of several states were once published and cited as nominative reports (identified by the names of their reporters). Many of these volumes have now been incorporated into the numbered series, but some early nominative citations are still used. You can usually retrieve a case by citation online even if you don't know what the citation stands for, but it may at times be necessary to use an abbreviations dictionary or other reference work to identify and find an older case.

In states with official reports, as noted earlier, those reports are the authoritative source for the decisions and must be cited in briefs and other court papers. *Bluebook* and *ALWD* rules dictate, however, that the more widely available regional reporter is the preferred source for most citations. If you have a citation to only one report of a case and need the other, there are several ways to find its parallel citation. The simplest is usually to retrieve the case in a commercial online platform, which will generally provide both citations. In printed reporters, the parallel citation is sometimes, but not always, provided at the beginning of the case.

Remember that not all cases have parallel citations. Only the official citations exist for cases before the National Reporter System, and only West reporter citations are available for recent cases in states that have discontinued their official reports and that do not have public domain citation systems. Even if official reports are published, they are generally issued more slowly than the regional reporters and the unofficial citation is frequently the only one available for very recent cases.

---

exception, however, is Ohio, in which the syllabus is an official statement of the law. *See Akers v. Serv-A-Portion, Inc.,* 508 N.E.2d 964, 964 n.1 (Ohio 1987).

[48] In most states, however, any local perspective of official reports has been abandoned. Besides the states without official reports at all, several states have continued the state's numbered report series but simply reprint the same editorial synopsis and headnotes that appear in the West regional reporter or on Westlaw. *See* Martin, *supra* note 46, at 32–33.

(d) Topical Reporters and Other Sources

Numerous looseleaf services and topical reporters also contain state court decisions. Some areas, such as insurance or utilities regulation, are determined largely by state law, so reporters in these areas have predominantly state court decisions. Reporters in areas such as commercial law or employment rights have a mix of federal and state cases. Even legal issues that are distinctly federal can arise in state court, so some state cases appear in admiralty, federal tax, and patent services.

A few of the legal newspapers published in large cities report lower court decisions that do not appear in the standard state court reports or the regional reporters. These elusive opinions can be hard to locate, even online, especially if they are treated as newspaper articles rather than court decisions and are found only in news databases.

Older cases, particularly from the colonial period, can also be found in a variety of other sources. Many early court cases were preserved in manuscript collections but were never published as court reports, and some of these have been printed during the modern era in historical collections or journal articles. *Prestatehood Legal Materials: A Fifty-State Research Guide* (Michael Chiorazzi & Marguerite Most eds., 2005) has a state-by-state overview of available resources from colonial and territorial courts. Other early decisions may be collected in topical compilations such as *Judicial Cases Concerning American Slavery and the Negro* (Helen Tunnicliff Catterall ed., 1926–37). These cases are still of significant historical value, even if they may not be very useful as modern-day precedent.

§ 11.4 TERRITORIAL AND TRIBAL COURTS

The United States has a number of appellate courts that are not represented at all in West's National Reporter System, and may even be hard to find in online sources. These are the courts of the territories and the Indian nations.

The District of Columbia Court of Appeals is included in the *Atlantic Reporter* with state court cases, but the supreme courts of Guam, Northern Mariana Islands, Puerto Rico, and the Virgin Islands can only be found in official reports (in some instances) or online through the commercial platforms or court websites. These territories also have U.S. District Courts, with decisions included in the federal case databases (and selectively in the *Federal Supplement*) and appealed to the First (Puerto Rico), Third (Virgin Islands), and Ninth (Guam and Northern Mariana Islands) Circuits.

Tribal court decisions have traditionally been even harder to find, with very few cases available in reporters or from the major online platforms. *West's American Tribal Law Reporter* has coverage back to 1997 of decisions from more than twenty tribal courts. These decisions are also available on Westlaw to some subscribers. Lexis has a database called All Tribal, which contains opinions from over forty tribal courts, though coverage varies between courts. The most extensive coverage of tribal courts is offered by Casemaker, with cases from over sixty jurisdictions. The Tribal Court Clearinghouse (www.tribal-institute.org) has links to tribal websites that post some or all of their court opinions. Since 1983, selected cases from some tribal courts have also been published in *Indian Law Reporter*.[49]

This chapter has focused on the court systems of the American governments and sources for their decisions, both in print and through a variety of electronic means. Using these sources to find case law relevant to a particular research problem is the topic of the next chapter.

---

[49] For sources of decisions from specific courts, see the University of Washington Law Library's guide Tribal Court Decisions: Sources (guides.lib.uw.edu/law/Indian-tribal/tribal-decisions). There are no published decisions, however, for a majority of the federally recognized tribes in the United States. *See* Bonnic Shucha, *"Whatever Tribal Precedent There May Be": The (Un)availability of Tribal Law*, 106 LAW LIBR. J. 199 (2014).

On tribal courts generally, see, e.g., NAVIGATING TRIBAL LAW: LEADING LAWYERS ON UNDERSTANDING THE UNIQUE PROCEDURES, INTRICACIES, AND CHALLENGES INVOLVED WITH TRIBAL CASES (2012); Frank Pommersheim, *Tribal Court Jurisprudence: A Snapshot from the Field*, 21 VT. L. REV. 7 (1996); and Michael Taylor, *Modern Practice in the Indian Courts*, 10 U. PUGET SOUND L. REV. 231 (1987).

Chapter 12

CASE RESEARCH

Table of Sections

For the doctrine of precedent to operate effectively, lawyers must be able to find cases that control or influence a court's decision-making. This requires locating "cases on point," earlier decisions with factual and legal issues similar to a dispute at hand. It is then necessary to determine whether these decisions are valid law and have not been reversed, overruled, or otherwise discredited.

This chapter discusses several major case research tools, but it is not exhaustive. Several resources discussed in other chapters—such as legal encyclopedias and treatises (Chapter 2), law review articles (Chapter 3), and annotated codes (Chapter 5)—are also valuable in case research.

Generally you conduct case research to find decisions from courts that create binding or persuasive authority in your jurisdiction, on topics related to the issues in your case. As explained in Chapter 1, a case could be relevant because it involves similar parties, objects or places, acts or omissions, relief sought, defenses, or procedures. You are searching for cases addressing factual or legal issues like yours, to determine how their holdings apply to the specific facts of your case.

To make sure you locate all the most relevant cases, you must use several different research techniques. This discussion starts with an overview of online case research, the approach most widely used in legal practice today. It then introduces editorial case-finding tools such as West digests and *ALR* annotations.

It is vital in case research not to rely exclusively on keyword searches. If the facts and holding of a decision do not precisely match your keywords or the computer's algorithms, that decision will remain undiscovered unless other research methods are also used. These types of searches are valuable (and sometimes feel easiest to novice researchers who are not yet comfortable identifying legal relevance), but they are most effective as part of a research strategy that integrates other tools and approaches.

Resources such as digests and *ALR* annotations are the works of experienced editors who have analyzed cases and classified them according to the legal principles they address. They can help you get to important results, insights, and analogies that you might never find using only keyword searches. Using several different approaches will ensure that you're not missing anything and will give you confidence in your results.

§ 12.1   ONLINE CASE RESEARCH

Chapter 1 provided a brief overview of basic online research techniques. This section begins with a more in-depth analysis of searching on legal platforms, focusing more specifically on effective case research. It discusses Westlaw and Lexis in detail, because those platforms add important editorial features such as synopses and headnotes that can guide you to the most relevant cases more quickly than general keyword searches. It also addresses the nature of computer-assisted legal research and the impact of algorithms on the case research process.[1] For researchers without access to Westlaw and Lexis, other subscription and free platforms that cover a great deal of case law with a range of search capabilities are also described.

No matter which platform or website you use, case research can be a complicated business requiring multiple searches or other research tactics. An initial search can find one or two relevant cases, which will provide additional terms or citations that can be used in refining and expanding a search.

---

[1]   *See* Robert C. Berring, *Legal Research and the World of Thinkable Thoughts*, 2 J. APP. PRAC. & PROCESS 305 (2000).

(a) General Principles

You may recall from Chapter 1 that major online research platforms offer two basic approaches to finding documents: algorithmic searches using natural language and Boolean searches using terms and connectors. Each approach has its strengths and its appropriate uses.

Legal research platforms are complex, yet they are designed to feel simple, safe, and effective for finding just the answers to your legal research questions. However, the same natural language search across different research platforms can produce very different results. The algorithmic tools designed to help you avoid the pitfalls of a poor keyword search are also subject to producing widely varying results lists of "relevant" cases.[2]

Three Steps of Search. It can be helpful to think of case searching as a process consisting of three steps. Researchers cannot know precisely how complex legal platforms work, but it is possible to trace the contours of how all contemporary systems function as you enter terms into an empty search bar.[3]

The first step of the search process concerns the way that you, as a searcher, craft a query that best represents what you'd like to find in the database. Regardless of whether you use Boolean searches or natural language searches, this first step also includes some degree of intervention by the search platform, generally known as "query processing." That means that the platform is adding to or otherwise changing the text that you have entered before submitting a revised query into its system.

The second step concerns how your now-revised query is matched with documents in the platform's databases. Here, you must understand that each database contains a slightly (or sometimes more than slightly) different set of documents that can be searched. While Westlaw, Lexis, and other search providers offer rough information about the coverage their platforms provide, no single platform can be considered comprehensive, meaning your query may not return the results you expect because some cases are simply not included as part of the platform you are searching.

---

[2] Susan Nevelow Mart, *The Algorithm as a Human Artifact: Implications for Legal (Re)Search*, 109 LAW LIBR. J. 387 (2017), ran the same searches on six research platforms and found that each platform had an average of 40% unique cases in the top ten results, with little overlap among the remaining cases.

[3] Susan Nevelow Mart et al., *Inside the Black Box of Search Algorithms*, AALL SPECTRUM, Nov.–Dec. 2019, at 10. This short article provides some general information about searching and brief statements from Lexis, Westlaw, Bloomberg Law, and Fastcase specific to those platforms' search operations.

The third step of the search process is the ranking of the results returned by the platform. By default, results are presented based on their responsiveness to the query entered, a concept known as "relevance." A variety of factors are weighted to determine relevance, and therefore the order in which the results appear. Factors include how many times query terms appear in the returned documents, how close together those terms are, the recency of those documents, and how often those documents are cited by other relevant documents.

Searching for Cases Consciously. Based on what we know about how search works in general, it is possible to identify tactics that should offer you more control over the research process. After narrowing down the database you are searching to "Cases," you can take steps that will increase the likelihood that you find case law that will be relevant to the question you are trying to answer.

First, it is possible to exert greater or lesser control over the search terms you enter. Boolean searches allow you to specify the importance of, or relationship between, the terms by using search operators (i.e., connectors). Natural language searches, on the other hand, are more heavily influenced by algorithms, which infer the relative importance of the search terms or the relationship among those terms. In both types of searches, algorithms are at work expanding or excluding terms and suggesting keywords from a pre-existing glossary built into the platform. With natural language searches, the algorithms add related legally significant terms as well. Algorithms are also often designed to change in response to search queries typed in by researchers. These algorithms are proprietary, so it is impossible to know everything about their function and how they impact search results. That said, well-crafted Boolean searches still offer the greatest opportunity to retain control over how the system interprets your query.

Second, while it is not possible to audit a legal research platform's coverage of cases, it is possible to recognize that different platforms contain slightly different sets of cases.[4] For this reason and the others discussed in this section, using multiple platforms to conduct a range of searches is your best bet for ensuring complete, accurate case law research.[5]

---

[4] For a discussion of how inconsistencies in courts' publication practices cause differences in legal research platforms' collection of case law documents, see Peter W. Martin, *District Court Opinions That Remain Hidden Despite a Long-Standing Congressional Mandate of Transparency—The Result of Judicial Autonomy and Systemic Indifference*, 110 LAW LIBR. J. 305, 310 (2018).

[5] Mart, *supra* note 2, at 390 ("Legal research has always required redundancy in searching; one resource does not usually provide a full answer, just as one search does not provide every necessary result. . . . [T]his need for redundancy has not faded with

Third, the difference in how results are ranked and presented is another opportunity for regaining control over your case research. While viewing cases in the default relevance order can be helpful with an unfamiliar topic or area of law, Westlaw and Lexis provide other ways of manually sorting results. Lexis offers you the options of sorting results by court, jurisdiction, date, or alphabetically by title in addition to sorting by relevance. If you select Ravel View on Lexis, you can also see a visual depiction of which cases have been cited most often. Westlaw offers the options of sorting by court, date, number of times cited, and term frequency.

In sum, researchers must develop facility with evaluating their search results and assessing algorithms' impact on those results. Though you may not be able to know the specific way algorithms function, you should be aware of how they work in general and how they impact your search results.

Other Case Research Tactics. On the major research platforms, you can either run a broad search and then filter your results to a specific jurisdiction or choose a jurisdiction at the outset. With either approach, you need to determine whether you should limit your research to a specific jurisdiction or read cases from other courts as well. For some research questions, cases from other jurisdictions can be persuasive authority or may provide useful analysis. For most issues, however, the most relevant cases are those from a particular state or within a narrow doctrinal area. Decisions from courts in other states matter little and only add unnecessary clutter to search results.

For most research questions on state law, your best approach may be to begin by limiting a search to a specific state and related federal cases. Federal courts often are required to interpret state laws; even though federal decisions interpreting state law have less precedential value than decisions of the state appellate courts, they may consider issues the state courts have not addressed.

Case research is not like a general internet search because ultimately you need to make sure that you are finding not just *some* cases but *all* relevant cases. Taking advantage of more powerful search features such as proximity connectors, truncation or expansion, and document fields will help you make sure you're not missing anything. But beware: just because a document contains your search terms doesn't mean that they reflect its holding. The terms may be nowhere near each other, or they may appear in a peripheral discussion unrelated to the holding. Using advanced

the rise of the algorithm. . . . [R]esearchers who want full results need to mine multiple resources with multiple searches.").

search features increases the chances that a case is indeed relevant. In any event, researchers must read retrieved cases in full to understand their holdings and their relevance to the research.

Most research platforms provide convenient tools to determine when the cases you retrieve are cited in later cases. These tools are vital for determining the current validity of the cases, but the citing references serve a broader purpose in case research. They are another way to broaden retrieval beyond the cases that match your keywords. A decision may not use your search terms, but if it cites a case you already know to be relevant it may address the issues you are researching. The other cases *it* cites may then lead you to new research avenues. This process of using citing references and verifying that the cases you have found are "good law" is discussed more fully in § 12.4.

One aspect of case research that technological advances has made possible takes place long after initial searches have been completed. Several research platforms offer brief analyzers, which allow you to upload a document to discover other potentially relevant cases that it *doesn't* cite. This approach was pioneered by CARA, a free feature of Casetext (casetext.com), but other platforms including Bloomberg Law, Lexis, and Westlaw now or will soon feature similar tools.

(b) Westlaw

As discussed in the preceding chapter, Westlaw is a comprehensive source for federal and state case law dating back to the earliest reported decisions. This means that it offers more than nine million searchable cases. Finding one's way effectively through such a mass of documents requires considerable skill.

As noted in Chapter 1, Westlaw permits you to run a search from the main screen without first selecting a particular kind of authority, such as cases. And as mentioned earlier, limiting a search to a Cases database allows you to take advantage of some of the more powerful research tools that Westlaw offers.

Westlaw's WestSearch Plus[6] technology allows you to create a simple, natural-language search, much as you would in Google or another general search engine. This suite of technologies finds cases

---

[6] Westlaw introduced WestSearch when it launched WestlawNext in 2010. WestSearch Plus is the search engine behind Westlaw's newest iteration, Westlaw Edge. WestSearch was billed as "the world's most advanced legal search engine" with its primary feature being the introduction of the all-in-one search box as the primary access point into Westlaw databases. WestSearch Plus, the "legal research engine of tomorrow, today" offers a similar all-in-one search box with more results suggestions for researchers based on predictive analytics (meaning that it suggests search results based on results that other researchers have previously selected).

based on the words you use as well as other factors such as alternate terms, key numbers, and usage patterns by other researchers. This can be an excellent way to find a few relevant cases, especially in an area of law unfamiliar to you.

Searching Synopses and Headnotes. While searching the full text of opinions can usually find some relevant cases, the most effective and reliable Westlaw searches take advantage of the editorial synopsis and headnotes that precede each case. The synopsis is the introductory summary of the case's facts and holdings, prepared by West's editors. The synopsis is followed by headnotes describing the subjects of specific points of law in the case, which are also tied into the West digest system, discussed in § 12.2 below. Limiting a search to terms appearing in the synopses and headnotes focuses retrieval on cases that turn on the specific research issues, rather than any and all cases that simply use the terms in passing.

The simplest way to search synopses and headnotes is to use the Advanced Search screen, which (once you have limited a search to Cases) lists these and more than twenty other Document Fields. (You get a mere three Document Fields—Date, Citation, and Name/Title—if you do not limit your search to Cases.) When you type words in the Synopsis or Digest box, note that Westlaw puts your terms in parentheses after the two-letter abbreviation SY or DI.[7] Once you are familiar with abbreviations such as these, you can type them in the search box yourself rather than using the Advanced Search screen. Illustration 12-1 shows some of the fields available on the Advanced Search screen for cases.

Often the strongest search is one that encompasses the synopsis and digest by using both fields at once, using either the Synopsis/Digest box on the Advanced Search screen or the abbreviation SY,DI. A search for *SY,DI(animal /s cruelty)* will retrieve a smaller body of cases more precisely on point than a full-text search for *cruelty to animals* or *animal /s cruelty*.

---

[7] In cases added to Westlaw since December 2003, the synopsis is divided into Background (BG) and Holding (HG) fields, as shown in Illustrations 10-2 and 11-3. In earlier cases, the synopsis is just one paragraph. The background and holding can also be searched separately, but this finds only cases from 2003 to date. The Synopsis (SY) field combines the two and searches older cases as well.

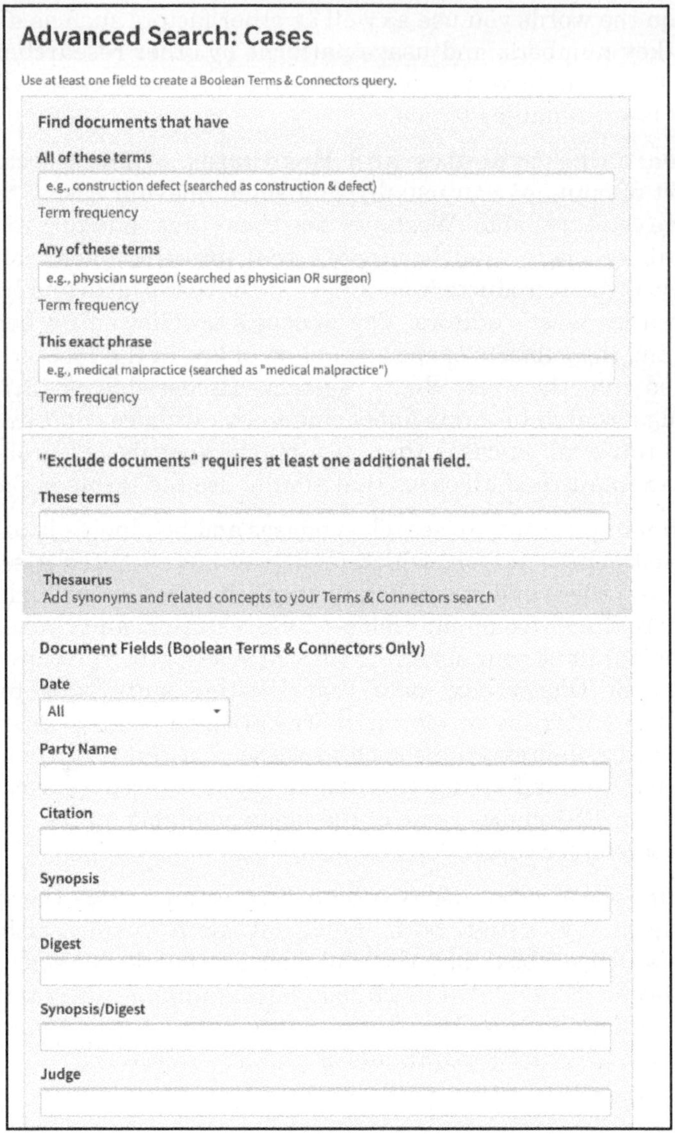

Advanced Search: Cases

Use at least one field to create a Boolean Terms & Connectors query.

Find documents that have

All of these terms

e.g., construction defect (searched as construction & defect)

Term frequency

Any of these terms

e.g., physician surgeon (searched as physician OR surgeon)

Term frequency

This exact phrase

e.g., medical malpractice (searched as "medical malpractice")

Term frequency

"Exclude documents" requires at least one additional field.

These terms

Thesaurus
Add synonyms and related concepts to your Terms & Connectors search

Document Fields (Boolean Terms & Connectors Only)

Date

All ▾

Party Name

Citation

Synopsis

Digest

Synopsis/Digest

Judge

Illustration 12-1. Westlaw's Advanced Search screen for cases.

The Synopsis and Digest fields are powerful tools for focusing on the most relevant cases, but for comprehensive research they must be supplemented by full-text keyword searches and other approaches. Westlaw has cases for which it does not provide editorial material, including many unreported decisions. Because these cases have no synopses or headnotes, a search limited to these fields would miss them entirely.

In addition to the Synopsis and Digest, other fields can be used to search particular parts of case documents. Thus searches can be limited to the names of the parties (*TI* or *Title*), the judge writing the opinion (*JU* or *Judge*), or a particular court (*CO* or *Court*). The easiest way to use these fields in Westlaw is to enter terms on the Advanced Search screen, but remember that these fields are listed only if you have chosen to search Cases.

Using Key Numbers. The headnotes preceding most Westlaw cases are valuable in case research, not only because they can be the focus of an advanced search. Each headnote is assigned a classification identifying its point of law within the West digest system. This classification consists of over 400 topics, arranged alphabetically from Abandoned and Lost Property to Zoning and Planning. Each topic is then divided into numbered sections, called *key numbers*, designating specific points of law for that topic. This classification system serves the same purpose for legal topics that call numbers do for library books, in that it allows related items to be classed together whether or not they use the same keywords. Similar legal issues may arise, for example, in cases involving dogs and cats, but it may not occur to you to include both terms in your search. The key numbers provide a way to find related cases that might otherwise be missed.

A separate numbering sequence is used for each topic, so a particular point of law is known by a combination of its topic name and its key number within that topic. Some of the larger and more complex topics have thousands of key numbers, while smaller topics have only a few. West uses the same topics and key numbers in every jurisdiction, so the same key number search can be used to find similar decisions throughout the federal and state courts.

As an example, *Harris v. Barefoot*, 704 S.E.2d 282 (N.C. Ct. App. 2010), the beginning of which was shown in Illustration 10-2, has five headnotes, assigned to various key numbers in the topics Judgment, Negligence, and Animals. The second headnote, on the standard of owner liability for an animal's vicious propensities, is assigned to the Animals topic, ☞ 66.2, Injuries to Persons/Vicious Propensities and Knowledge Thereof.

Westlaw offers two ways to view headnotes, a List View that simply shows the topic and specific subject (e.g., Animals—Vicious propensities and knowledge thereof), and a Grid View that shows the full key number hierarchy and facilitates research by helping you place the issue in context. The *Harris v. Barefoot* headnote as it appears in Grid View is shown in Illustration 12-2.

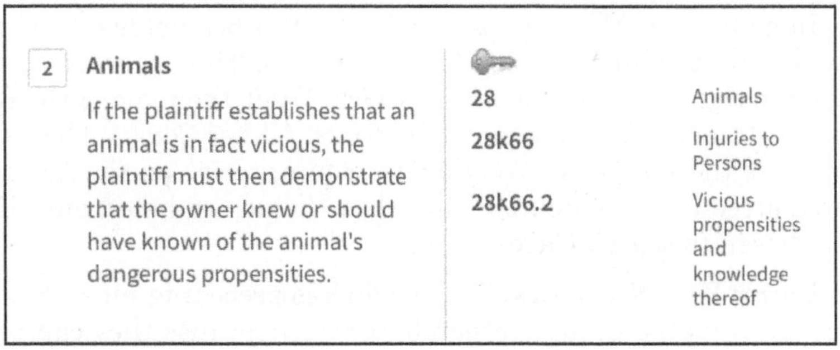

2	Animals			
	If the plaintiff establishes that an animal is in fact vicious, the plaintiff must then demonstrate that the owner knew or should have known of the animal's dangerous propensities.	28		Animals
		28k66		Injuries to Persons
		28k66.2		Vicious propensities and knowledge thereof

Illustration 12-2. A headnote as it appears on Westlaw.

For use in Westlaw, each topic has been assigned a designation between 1 and 450. Animals is topic 28, for example, and a search for the topic and key number pair Animals ⟶ 66.2 is *28k66.2*. This key number can be used in combination with other terms to create a very precise and effective search.

Obviously you are not going to begin a research project with a search like *28k66.2*. You can, however, assess the headnotes in the cases you retrieve through keyword searches; if a headnote is particularly relevant, you can use its key number to find other cases that may be on point. One way to do this is to click on the headnote's hyperlinked key number, which leads you to a list of other cases under this number. You can then search within these results for cases that meet your specific facts or legal issues. Illustration 12-3 shows the results when clicking from the *Harris v. Barefoot* key number. Note that the default display is limited to North Carolina state and federal cases, but this can be changed at the top of the screen to find cases from all or selected other jurisdictions.

⌐66.2 —Vicious propensities and knowledge thereof (571) ①
Jurisdiction: All States Change

1 - 100 >   Sort: Topic then Most Cited   ⊝ ■ ± ▾

☐ Select all items · No items selected

28 ANIMALS (Up to 10,000)
  — 28 ⌐ 66 Injuries to Persons 8,284
    — 28 ⌐ 66.2 Vicious propensities and knowledge thereof. 571

☐ ⚑ **1. Bard v. Jahnke**
Court of Appeals of New York. · May 2, 2006 · 6 N.Y.3d 592

Headnote: Once owner's knowledge of domestic animal's vicious propensities is established, the owner faces strict liability.   Restatement (Second) of Torts § 509.
71 Cases that cite this legal issue
Document Preview: TORTS - Animals. Owner was not strictly liable for injuries caused by unrestrained dairy bull.

☐ ⚑ **2. Collier v. Zambito**
Court of Appeals of New York. · February 17, 2004 · 1 N.Y.3d 444

Headnote: "Vicious propensities" of a domestic animal, which will result in the animal owner's liability if the animal causes harm as a result of those propensities, include the propensity to do any act that might endanger the safety of the persons and property of others in a given situation.
62 Cases that cite this legal issue
Document Preview: TORTS - Animals. Dog owners had no knowledge of its alleged vicious propensities, and thus were not liable for bitten guest's injuries.

☐ ⚑ **3. Petrone v. Fernandez**
Court of Appeals of New York. · June 9, 2009 · 12 N.Y.3d 546

Headnote: When harm is caused by a domestic animal, its owner's liability is determined solely by application of the rule of strict liability for harm caused by a domestic animal whose owner knows or should have known of the animal's vicious propensities.
57 Cases that cite this legal issue
Document Preview: TORTS - Animals. Violation of local leash law did not provide basis for imposing strict liability in mail carrier's personal injury action.

☐ ⚑ **4. Collier v. Zambito**
Court of Appeals of New York. · February 17, 2004 · 1 N.Y.3d 444

Headnote: The owner of a domestic animal who either knows or should have known of that animal's vicious propensities will be held liable for the harm the animal causes as a result of those propensities.   Restatement (Second) of Torts § 509.
46 Cases that cite this legal issue
Document Preview: TORTS - Animals. Dog owners had no knowledge of its alleged vicious propensities, and thus were not liable for bitten guest's injuries.

**Illustration 12-3. Westlaw digest entries, linked
from the headnote in Illustration 12-2.**

The West Key Number System can also be clicked on from the main page on Westlaw (where it simply reads "Key Numbers"). From this screen you can browse through the classifications or search for terms appearing in key number descriptions. Clicking on a specific key number brings up a list of its headnotes, from which you can link to the full text of cases. If a key number has too many cases to read through, you can limit results to a specific jurisdiction or do a keyword search within the headnotes. You can also locate relevant key numbers by typing terms into the search bar and looking at the search suggestions, an example of one kind of query processing done by Westlaw before you click the search button.

There are distinct advantages to using this case finding method to complement natural language, Boolean, and field searches. First, relying simply on citing references from other cases or from other tools like annotated codes, secondary sources, or citators may be overinclusive, giving you every case that cites a helpful case you've found whether for your legal issue or not; the headnote and key number approach returns just those cases that include the legal point you're interested in. Second, the helpful case you choose to start with may be so new there are not many cases that cite it yet. Key numbers return cases from all available years.

Working with Search Results. Once a search is entered, Westlaw displays a list of cases, with a snapshot view of where the search terms appear. Remember, the default order of the list is relevance, based generally on the frequency of your search terms in the returned documents; it is often helpful in case research to change the sort order to date to more quickly develop a sense of the law as it currently stands.

Some cases have a red or yellow flag to the left of their names, providing an indication that they may no longer be good law in some way (although you need to read the citing case to determine the significance of the flag). When displayed in full, each case is accompanied by tabs at the top linking to available briefs and other filings, negative treatment, case history, and citing references.

(c) Lexis

Lexis is a leading resource for case law because it has comprehensive coverage and includes editorial material that can help focus a search. Cases on Lexis have case summaries and headnotes, accompanied by computer-generated "core terms" listing major keywords found in the opinion. Illustrations 12-4 and 12-5 show the case summary and headnotes in the Lexis display of *Harris v. Barefoot*.

Case Summary

Procedural Posture
Plaintiff dog bite victim appealed judgments from the Cumberland County
Superior Court (North Carolina), which granted summary judgment to
defendant dog owners in the victim's negligence action, arising from
being attacked and bitten repeatedly by the owners' dogs.

Overview
The victim was delivering mail to a house when she was attacked by two
dogs who were at a house directly across the street. They knocked her to
the ground and bit her repeatedly. She filed suit against the dog owners,
alleging negligence. The trial court granted summary judgment to the dog
owners. On appeal, the court agreed with the trial court's summary
judgment ruling. It held that the victim failed to provide evidence to show
that the dogs possessed a vicious propensity and that the owners knew or
should have known of this propensity. Rather, the victim failed to present
evidence to support her claim as to the type of breed and weight of one
dog. She failed to show competent evidence that the other breed of dog
was generally known to have a vicious propensity. And her claim that
tethering a dog for long periods of time indicated that the owner knew
the dog needed restraint, and that it enhanced the dog's dangerousness
was also not supported by proper evidence. Accordingly, she failed to
show the necessary elements in order to avoid summary judgment.

Outcome
The court affirmed the judgments of the trial court.

Illustration 12-4. A case summary on Lexis.

Like Westlaw, Lexis allows you to start with a general search
and then filter your results to find cases or to focus a search on cases
at the outset. It also lets you search all case law or limit a search to
decisions from a particular jurisdiction, with the option to include
related federal content.

Lexis headnotes do not employ a numerical classification system
like West's key numbers, but they can also be useful in case research.
Once a relevant case is found, its headnotes can be used as a
springboard to further research by clicking on the heading to get
other cases on similar issues. Lexis's classifications are usually
somewhat broader than West's key numbers.

The Lexis counterparts to Westlaw's Document Fields are called
Document Segments/Fields. You can use the Summary segment/field
to focus in on the most relevant cases, and the Headnotes
segment/field to find discussion of particular points of law. Other
useful segments/fields in case research include *Name* for a particular
party and *Writtenby* for opinions by a particular judge.

Illustration 12-5. Lexis headnotes.

Lexis has several innovative ways to visualize and organize search results. It offers a Graphical View (also known as a Search Term Map) that features a "term visualization bar" that highlights each word in your keyword search in a different color, spread out across a bar at the top of your case to make it simpler to see how often each term appears and to navigate to them. A blue star indicates the "best" excerpt from the case—a determination based on a proprietary algorithm.

Lexis's Ravel View[8] presents not just search results but also an interactive map of circles showing how the most significant cases are linked together, with circle size indicating the number of times a case

---

[8] Ravel View is named after the company that created it, Ravel Law, which was acquired by Lexis in 2017. *See* Robert Ambrogi, *Exclusive First Look: Ravel Law's Integration with Lexis Advance*, LAWSITES (Feb. 2, 2018) (lawsitesblog.com/2018/02/exclusive-first-look-ravel-laws-integration-lexis-advance.html) [https://perma.cc/M2 UF-CQ8P].

has been cited and lines connecting each case to the cases it cites and those that cite it.

The Lexis case display also includes graphic indicators of a case's validity as precedent (such as red stop signs and yellow "caution" triangles), and a summary of citations in subsequent cases. A "Shepardize this document" link leads to further information, as will be discussed in § 12.4.

(d) Other Resources

Bloomberg Law's strength is its integration of legal and business information, but it also provides comprehensive access to federal and state case law. Instead of summaries and headnotes, it offers a feature called Points of Law. These are highlighted portions of case opinion text that are used in at least five other opinions. Clicking on the highlighted text will lead to a list of relevant cases, as well as the option to view related Points of Law. Bloomberg Points of Law are algorithmically created, relying at least in part on term or phrase frequency in judicial opinions.

Several lower-cost platforms include thorough coverage of case law, and many college and university libraries subscribe to Nexis Uni, which incorporates some of Lexis's features. These platforms provide access to most of the same cases as Westlaw and Lexis, but they generally have no or limited introductory summaries or headnotes to provide research springboards to other cases. Despite the absence of editorial material, subscription-based platforms are providing increasingly sophisticated approaches to searching case law. Most allow truncation, proximity connectors, and searching particular document fields; some have natural language search options. Also, just as Westlaw and Lexis's algorithms evolve and their platforms are redesigned, so too should a researcher expect other platforms to change and evolve.

Many lawyers have access to either Casemaker (www.case maker.us) or Fastcase (www.fastcase.com) as a benefit of bar membership, making them cost-effective research tools. Both platforms offer a variety of search approaches, with general searches that can be filtered by jurisdiction, features such as proximity connectors and truncation, and tools for finding later citing cases and determining whether your case is still good law.

Fastcase offers several innovative features, including an Interactive Timeline feature and Forecite, a tool designed to give you legally relevant cases even if they do not contain your search terms. On its newest interface, Fastcase also offers a suite of advanced search tools that allows you to adjust the factors weighed by the platform's algorithm before your results are returned. Another feature is the visual display of cases in search results.

Free access to case law is available from Google Scholar (scholar. google.com), which has coverage of U.S. Supreme Court cases since 1791, federal cases since 1923, and state appellate cases since at least 1950. You can search all case law or limit a search to one or more specific jurisdictions. Results can be sorted by relevance or date. A "How cited" link shows excerpts from later decisions citing the displayed case and lists all citing documents. Complex searches can also be run across the case collections at CourtListener (www. courtlistener.com) and the Caselaw Access Project (case.law).

Websites for individual courts or jurisdictions also offer opinions, but some sites are much more accessible and more comprehensive than others. Some state court sites simply provide chronological access to opinions with no full text searching, while others have searchable retrospective collections of appellate court decisions. Except for a very few exemplary sites, court websites are not the best place to do case research but can be useful for obtaining copies of new decisions and monitoring recent developments.[9]

§ 12.2   WEST KEY NUMBER DIGESTS

In the previous section's discussion of Westlaw, we looked at the importance of headnote classifications in finding relevant cases. The West Key Number System covers every case in the publisher's National Reporter System, and subject access can frequently find relevant cases that a keyword search would miss. Editorial analysis and classification can identify cases that use different words but decide analogous issues.

Although online research has become the primary case-finding method for most researchers, the digest, a tool that reprints in a subject arrangement the headnote summaries of each case's points of law, continues to be a valuable resource for finding cases by topic. A digest functions in a manner similar to an index; instead of simple one-line entries, however, it consists of paragraphs describing the legal principles decided in cases, with citations to the full text of the cases.

Printed digests are now used far less frequently than online research,[10] but not all researchers have ready access to expensive

---

[9]   The difficulties in searching official court websites are discussed in Andrew T. Solomon, *Making Unpublished Opinions Precedential: A Recipe for Ethical Problems & Legal Malpractice?*, 26 MISS. C. L. REV. 185, 208–10 (2007). Unfortunately, not much has changed in the years since this article's publication.

[10]   *See, e.g.,* Ellie Margolis, *Authority Without Borders: The World Wide Web and the Delegalization of Law,* 41 SETON HALL L. REV. 909, 929–32 (2011); Lee F. Peoples,

online platforms. Even if electronic resources are available, browsing through a collection of headnotes on related topics can at times be more cost-effective and productive than searching online.[11]

English precursors to modern American digests began with *Statham's Abridgment,* published about 1490, which consisted of summaries of case law grouped under alphabetically arranged subject headings. This, and its many successors, employed relatively few subjects, broad in scope and lacking the detailed subdivisions of modern digests.[12] The first comprehensive American digest, covering both federal and state courts, began publication in 1848 as the *United States Digest.*

The West Publishing Company (now Thomson Reuters) acquired the property rights to this work and its classification scheme in 1887 and began publication of a new annual *American Digest.* West began assigning numbered headnotes to the cases in its reporters, adding section numbers in 1908 and designating these as "key numbers" in 1915.[13] For many decades, the West digest system was the preeminent case-finding method, and it exercised an enormous intellectual impact on American jurisprudence.[14]

The first appearance of a new case in a printed digest is in the front of each West paperback advance sheet, where the headnotes for the cases published are arranged by topic and key number. These headnotes are cumulated in the back of each bound reporter volume, and then reprinted in multi-volume digest series to provide subject access to the cases in hundreds of reporter volumes. Illustration 12-6 shows an excerpt from a West digest with headnotes under Animals 🗝 66.2 from *Harris v. Barefoot,* as well as headnotes from other cases dating back as far as 1825.

The Death of the Digest and the Pitfalls of Electronic Research: What Is the Modern Legal Researcher to Do?, 97 LAW LIBR. J. 661 (2005).

[11] "By skimming scores (or hundreds) of relevant headnotes or descriptions, you will refine your sense for this area of the law. . . . Only then, after you know the location, size, and shape of the haystack, are you able to search intelligently for the needle." MARK HERRMANN, THE CURMUDGEON'S GUIDE TO PRACTICING LAW 24 (2d ed. 2019).

[12] For an informative and entertaining look at the authors of the early abridgments, see David J. Seipp, *Year Book Men,* in ENGLISH LEGAL HISTORY AND ITS SOURCES: ESSAYS IN HONOUR OF SIR JOHN BAKER 3 (David Ibbetson et al. eds., 2019).

[13] For a recent history of West's digest system, see Michael O. Eshleman, *A History of the Digests,* 110 LAW LIBR. J., 235, 247–57 (2018).

[14] For a discussion of the influence of West's digest system on legal thinking, see Robert C. Berring, *Legal Research and Legal Concepts: Where Form Molds Substance,* 75 CAL. L. REV. 15 (1987), and Richard A. Danner, *Influences of the Digest Classification System: What Can We Know?,* 33 LEGAL REFERENCE SERVICES Q. 117 (2014).

⊂⊃46 ANIMALS 1A N C D 2d—34

N.C. 1850. A. sold a slave, that owned a horse, to B., and the horse was taken to B.'s plantation, and he objecting to keeping the horse, it was given to the slave's son, who belonged to C., and after remaining awhile on C.'s plantation, without any claim of title by C., the horse was sold. Held, that B. could not maintain trover against C. for the value of the horse.—Francis v. Welch, 33 N.C. 215, 11 Ired. 215.

N.C. 1825. Where A. turned cattle into the woods, and B., thinking one of them to be his, took possession of it, after which A., ignorant of B.'s possession, sold it to C., who was also ignorant of it, it was held that C. might sue B. in his own name.—Morgan v. Bradley, 10 N.C. 559, 3 Hawks 559.

⊂⊃49. —— Statutory regulations in general.

N.C. 1961. The 1959 Act prohibiting cattle from running at large along the outer banks and authorizing and directing the sheriff of Carteret County without judicial inquiry to dispose of all cattle in the particular area is invalid as a local act relating to abatement of a public nuisance. Laws 1959, c. 782, § 1 et seq.; Const. art. 2, § 29. —Chadwick v. Salter, 119 S.E.2d 158, 254 N.C. 389.

⊂⊃50(1). In general.

N.C. 1916. Pub.Loc.Laws 1915, c. 116, relating to elections to determine whether the stock law or the fence law should control, and chapter 505, relating to the taxes to be imposed should a fence be required, are in pari materia, and must be construed together as one and the same law, especially as the latter statute refers to the former.—Keith v. Lockhart, 88 S.E. 640, 171 N.C. 451, Am.Ann.Cas. 1918D,916.

N.C. 1908. One who has violated the stock law (Revisal 1905, § 1684) after its adoption in the county of his residence, by permitting his stock to run at large on the property of his neighbors within the county, cannot attack the constitutionality of the law and its adoption on the sole ground that an adjoining county has not adopted the law, and that his property is subject to incursions from animals straying across the county line from such other county.—State v. Mathis, 63 S.E. 99, 149 N.C. 546.

foot v. City of Fayetteville, 28 S.E. 515, 121 N.C. 418, 61 Am.St.Rep. 668, 39 L.R.A. 245.

⊂⊃66.2. —— Vicious propensities and knowledge thereof.

N.C.App. 2010. If the plaintiff establishes that an animal is in fact vicious, the plaintiff must then demonstrate that the owner knew or should have known of the animal's dangerous propensities.—Harris v. Barefoot, 704 S.E.2d 282, 206 N.C.App. 308, review denied 705 S.E.2d 359, 364 N.C. 618.

The test of liability of the owner of a vicious animal does not contemplate the intentions of the animal but whether the owner should know from past conduct that the animal is likely, if not restrained, to do an act in which the owner could foresee injury to person or property.—Id.

⊂⊃66.5(2). Vicious propensities and knowledge thereof.

N.C.App. 2010. Owner of part-Rottweiler dog was not liable for mail carrier's dog bite injuries absent evidence that dog had a vicious propensity and that owner knew or should have known that dog posed a danger to others.—Harris v. Barefoot, 704 S.E.2d 282, 206 N.C.App. 308, review denied 705 S.E.2d 359, 364 N.C. 618.

Owner of Australian Heeler/Border Collie mix dog was not liable for mail carrier's dog bite injuries absent evidence that dog had a vicious propensity and that owner knew or should have known that dog posed a danger to others.—Id.

⊂⊃66.5(8). Landlords.

N.C.App. 2014. It is not mere generalized control of leased property that establishes landlord liability for a dog attack, but rather specific control of a known dangerous animal.—Stephens v. Covington, 754 S.E.2d 253.

A third party victim who is seeking to recover damages from a landlord for an attack by a dog owned by a tenant must specifically establish both: (1) that the landlord had knowledge that a tenant's dog posed a danger; and (2) that the landlord had control over the dangerous dog's presence on the property in order to be held liable for the dog attacking a third party.—Id.

Illustration 12-6. West digest entries.

The same key number system covers all federal and state jurisdictions, so it can be used to find cases from throughout the country. This means, however, that the classification system sometimes fails to recognize significant differences between states in approaches to jurisprudential issues.

Whether online or in print, digests are valuable case-finders but have several shortcomings. They consist simply of case headnotes, with no text to explain which decisions are more important or how they fit together. A textual discussion of an area of law, such as in a treatise, encyclopedia, or a law review article, usually offers a clearer and more selective introduction to relevant case law.[15] Finding a case

[15] As early as 1945, it was recognized that digests were "not usually the best starting point in research. The reason is obvious. In the digests there is neither fusion nor assimilation. . . . Each 'pin-point' is an isolated speck of light; its relationship, if any, to the specks around it is of no concern of the digester." Paul M. Dwyer, *Approach*

in a digest depends on an editor's subjective decision in assigning a key number to a headnote, and different editors can read cases differently.[16]

Scanning headnotes in a digest is never a substitute for reading the full text of cases. Headnotes may reflect dicta, rather than holdings, and may even misstate points of law in the cases they abstract. Not every point of law in every case is headnoted, and if there is no headnote then there is no digest entry for that point.

Digests also generally do not indicate that a case may no longer be good law, unless it was directly reversed or modified on appeal. An overruled case continues to be listed in the digest, with no notes on its validity. After reading the cases themselves to find those that are actually pertinent, you must use a citator to verify their current status.

(a) Finding Cases in Digests

Using a digest requires identifying the topic and key number relevant to a specific issue. The simplest way to do this is to use the headnotes of a case you already know to be on point. If you know of one relevant case, you can find it on Westlaw or in a West reporter volume, scan its headnotes for relevant issues, and then use the key numbers accompanying those headnotes to search the digest. This approach, of course, requires that you find at least one initial case through other means, such as a full-text search or a reference in a treatise or journal article.

Without a case already in hand, the basic entry point into a printed digest is the Descriptive-Word Index shelved at the beginning or end of each digest set. This multi-volume index lists thousands of factual and legal terms, with references to key numbers. You can look up legal issues, such as causes of action, defenses, or relief sought, or factual elements in an action, such as parties, places, or objects involved. It is generally more productive to search for specific relevant facts rather than for general legal theories, but success may require rethinking issues and checking synonyms and cross-

---

to *Legal Research: A Study in Sources and Methods*, 21 NOTRE DAME LAW. 92, 95 (1945).

[16] Dwyer also noted that "digesters are quite human, and what Digester A regards today as the proper pigeon-hole may not at all be the same as what Digester B will choose ten years later." *Id.* at 96. This was made very apparent when a U.S. District Court case, *McGinnis v. United Screw & Bolt Corp.*, was somehow published in both *Federal Supplement* and *Federal Rules Decisions*. The two versions, at 637 F. Supp. 9 and 109 F.R.D. 532 (E.D. Pa. 1985), received different treatment by West editors; even though the text was the same, the F. Supp. version has four headnotes in the Workers' Compensation topic while the F.R.D. version has two headnotes under Federal Civil Procedure. (The F.R.D. version also corrected three minor errors not caught by the F. Supp. editors.)

references. Illustration 12-7 shows an excerpt from a Descriptive-Word Index, including references to "Knowledge of Vicious Propensities" of dogs.[17]

```
DOGS—Cont'd

HUMANE societies, Anim ☞ 3.5(11)

IMPUTED knowledge of vicious
    propensities,
  Personal injuries caused by dog, Anim
      ☞ 66.5(2)

INJURIES,
  Caused by dog, Anim ☞ 53
    Assumption of risks, Anim ☞ 66.5(6)
    Constructive knowledge of vicious
        propensities, Anim ☞ 66.5(2)
    Contributory and comparative
        negligence, Anim ☞ 66.5(4)
    Defenses in general, Anim ☞ 66.5(3)
    Duties in general, Anim ☞ 66.5(1)
    Firefighter's rule, Anim ☞ 66.5(6)
    Harm's way defense, Anim ☞ 66.5(6)
    Imputed knowledge of vicious
        propensities, Anim ☞ 66.5(2)
    Knowledge of vicious propensities, Anim
        ☞ 66.5(2)
    Landlords, liability of, Anim ☞ 66.5(8)
    Liabilities in general, Anim ☞ 66.5(1)
    Notice of vicious propensities, Anim
        ☞ 66.5(2)
    Persons liable,
        Generally, Anim ☞ 66.5(7)
        Landlords, Anim ☞ 66.5(8)
    Policeman's rule, Anim ☞ 66.5(6)
    Provocation, Anim ☞ 66.5(5)
    Running at large, Anim ☞ 53
    To other animals, Anim ☞ 81
    Trespasser defense, Anim ☞ 66.5(3)
    Vicious propensities, Anim ☞ 66.5(2)
    Warning signs as defense, Anim
        ☞ 66.5(3)
  To dog, damages, Damag ☞ 39, 113, 139

KNOWLEDGE of vicious propensities,
  Personal injuries caused by dog, Anim
      ☞ 66.5(2)

LANDLORDS, liability of,
  Personal injuries caused by dog, Anim
      ☞ 66.5(8)
```

Illustration 12-7. An excerpt from a West Descriptive-Word Index.

[17] Digests also include case tables that can be used to find decisions by name. Most of these tables list cases under both plaintiffs' and defendants' names. In addition to reporter citations, they provide a list of key numbers under which each case's headnotes are digested.

When turning from the index to a volume of digest abstracts, it is often helpful to look first at the outline of the topic to verify that the legal context is indeed appropriate. You may be looking for cases on substantive negligence issues, for example, but find that a key number that appeared relevant actually deals with some other issue such as the standard of review for summary judgment. Illustration 12-8 contains part of the outline for the Animals topic, showing how 66.2 fits with other related issues.

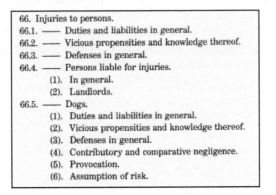

```
66. Injuries to persons.
66.1.  —— Duties and liabilities in general.
66.2.  —— Vicious propensities and knowledge thereof.
66.3.  —— Defenses in general.
66.4.  —— Persons liable for injuries.
        (1). In general.
        (2). Landlords.
66.5.  —— Dogs.
        (1). Duties and liabilities in general.
        (2). Vicious propensities and knowledge thereof.
        (3). Defenses in general.
        (4). Contributory and comparative negligence.
        (5). Provocation.
        (6). Assumption of risk.
```

Illustration 12-8. An excerpt from the outline of the Animals digest topic.

The key number system has been in use for more than a century, but the law of course has not remained static in that time. Old doctrines have faded in significance and new areas of law have developed. West attempts to reflect new developments by revising and expanding old topics and by establishing new topics. The first sex discrimination cases, for example, were classified under "Rights protected by civil rights laws in general" because there were not yet any key numbers dealing with a more specific topic. The Civil Rights topic has since been revised several times, and there are now over thirty key numbers covering various aspects of sex discrimination and sexual harassment.

When new or revised topics are introduced, West editors reclassify the headnotes in thousands of older relevant cases. On Westlaw, the numbers assigned to older cases are updated when the key number system is revised, and the current classification can be used to find relevant cases of any age. The new classifications are also used when digest volumes are recompiled. Until the recompilation, new or revised topics are accompanied by tables converting older topics and key numbers to those newly adopted and vice versa.

The digest changes slowly, however, and it may take several years for new areas of legal doctrine to be recognized and to receive adequate coverage. Because cases in newly developing areas of the law are often assigned to general key numbers, digest research may not be the best way to find these kinds of cases.

(b) Jurisdictional and Regional Digests

West digests are available for the entire country, for some of the regional reporters, and for most individual states. Choosing the right digest depends on the scope of your inquiry. For most research you want to find cases from a specific jurisdiction, but for some projects you may be interested in developments throughout the country. A more focused digest is usually easier to use.

Thomson Reuters publishes West digests for every state but Delaware, Nevada, and Utah, as well as for the decisions in four of the regional reporter series (*Atlantic, North Western, Pacific,* and *South Eastern*). (Cases from Delaware, Nevada, and Utah are covered in the *Atlantic* and *Pacific Digest.*) The state digests include references to all the cases in West reporters from the state's courts, as well as federal cases arising from the U.S. District Courts in that state. Federal courts often interpret and apply state law, sometimes addressing issues with which the state courts have not yet dealt.[18]

Thomson Reuters also publishes a separate series of digests for federal court decisions, containing headnotes reprinted from the *Supreme Court Reporter, Federal Reporter, Federal Appendix, Federal Supplement, Federal Rules Decisions,* and the reporters for specialized federal courts. The current set, *West's Federal Practice Digest 5th,* has coverage beginning in 2003 in almost 400 volumes. Earlier cases are covered by five previous sets.[19]

---

[18] State digests are kept up to date by annual pocket parts in the back of each volume, by pamphlets between annual supplements, and by occasional replacement volumes incorporating the newer material. A single volume can thus contain headnotes of decisions from the earliest nominative reporters through a few months ago. For about a dozen states, the current digest only provides coverage of cases from recent decades. An earlier digest set must be consulted for complete retrospective coverage of the older court decisions, but most research requires consulting only the current set for modern cases on point.

[19] The current volumes are supplemented by annual pocket parts, with further updates in bimonthly pamphlets. The earlier federal digests are *Federal Digest* (1754–1939), *Modern Federal Practice Digest* (1939–61), *Federal Practice Digest 2d* (1961–75), *Federal Practice Digest 3d* (1975 to mid-1980s), and *Federal Practice Digest 4th* (mid-1980s to mid-2000s).

The decisions of the Supreme Court of the United States are also covered by a West digest devoted solely to its decisions, the *United States Supreme Court Digest.* Other digests for specialized federal courts include *West's Bankruptcy Digest, West's Military Justice Digest, United States Federal Claims Digest,* and *West's Veterans*

(c) *General* and *Decennial Digests*

The most comprehensive series of digests is known as the American Digest System. This covers cases in all of the West federal and state reporters, and is therefore a massive and rather unwieldy finding tool. Its most current component, the *General Digest*, compiles headnotes from the advance sheets for about twenty West reporter volumes. A *General Digest* volume is published about every three weeks and covers the entire range of over 400 digest topics.[20]

Every few years, Thomson Reuters recompiles the headnotes from the *General Digest* and publishes them in a multi-volume set called a *Decennial Digest*. The name *Decennial* comes from the fact that these sets used to be published every ten years, but Thomson Reuters now compiles these digests after every fifty volumes of the *General Digest*. The *Twelfth Decennial Digest, Part 4* is the most recent set, covering 2016–18.

One challenge in using *Decennial Digests* is that older volumes are not revised to reflect changes in topics and classifications. Cases on Westlaw are updated with new key numbers and jurisdictional digest volumes are revised and reissued, but *Decennial Digest* users must use conversion tables indicating corresponding key numbers in older and newer classifications.

The first unit of the American Digest System, called the *Century Digest*, covers early cases from 1658 to 1896. It was followed by a *First Decennial Digest* for 1897 to 1906, and subsequent *Decennials* for each decade since. *Decennial Digests* are little used these days, but they can be found in most large law libraries. For researchers without Westlaw access, they remain the most comprehensive collection of case headnotes available.[21]

Appeals Digest. References to these cases all appear as well in the *Federal Practice Digest* series.

[20] The entries in the *General Digest* do not cumulate, so you may have to look through several dozen volumes to search for recent cases. This search is eased somewhat by tables listing the key numbers found in each volume. These tables cumulate every tenth volume. If twenty-seven *General Digest* volumes have been published, for example, you would need to check the tables in volumes 10, 20, and 27 to see which volumes contain cases classified under a specific key number. Even with this short cut, checking the *General Digest* can be a rather time-consuming process.

[21] The West Key Number System is not the only digest classification used in legal research. Many specialized topical reporters provide subject access to their cases through digests, usually including references to administrative agency decisions as well as court decisions. Some of these digests are organized on an alphabetical basis like West's system, but with topics designed for a specialized area of law. Others use a classified numerical framework or are arranged by code or rule section (making them like the notes in annotated codes). Lawyers specializing in particular fields often swear by these topical digests. Because they focus on one specific area of law, they can be

(d) *Words and Phrases*

Thomson Reuters reprints some headnote abstracts in a separate multi-volume set, *Words and Phrases*. Headnotes are included in *Words and Phrases* if a court defines or interprets a legally significant term. *Words and Phrases* is arranged alphabetically rather than by key number, and it can be a useful tool when the meaning of a specific term is at issue. Illustration 12-9 shows an excerpt from *Words and Phrases* including headnotes from cases defining terms such "vicious dog," "vicious nature," and "vicious propensities."

The *Words and Phrases* set covers the entire National Reporter System. Shorter "Words and Phrases" lists also appear in many West digests and in West reporters. Judicial definitions from *Words and Phrases* can also be found on Westlaw by searching the Words & Phrases (WP) field or by using the Words and Phrases Content Page (listed in "Tools & Resources" on the Cases page). For example, a search for *WP(vicious)* will retrieve the cases shown in Illustration 12-9.

---

more finely tuned to developments in that area and quicker to adjust to changes in the law than the much more general key number system.

VICIOUS PROPENSITIES

sioning domestic broils.—Shutt v. Shutt, 17 A. 1024, 71 Md. 193, 17 Am.St.Rep. 519.

VICIOUS DISPOSITION

Del.Super. 1899. A horse is of "vicious disposition" when it is possessed of those habits and propensities which are dangerous in their character to persons coming in contact with it.—Brown v. Green, 42 A. 991, 17 Del. 535, 1 Penne. 535.

VICIOUS DOG

Mont. 1998. Hunting dog, which had never bitten or attempted to bite a human being, was not a "vicious dog," within meaning of county ordinance prohibiting keeping, harboring, or maintaining a vicious dog in county unless dog is securely and adequately confined upon its owner's property, even though dog was bred to hunt mountain lions.—Vennes for Vennes v. Miller, 954 P.2d 736, 287 Mont. 263, 1998 MT 23.—Anim 3.5(4).

Ohio App. 10 Dist. 1991. Statute defining "vicious dog," for purposes of provision prohibiting the failure to restrain a vicious dog, allows defendant to rebut state's prima facie showing that dog is vicious because it is a "pit bull dog"; however, statute conclusively deems the dog vicious if the dog has without provocation killed or injured a person, killed another dog, or caused injury to another person, and does not allow rebuttal of prima facie showing that dog is "vicious" by merely showing that dog has not killed or injured a person or killed a dog. R.C. § 955.11(A)(4)(a), (A)(4)(a)(i-iii).—State v. Ferguson, 603 N.E.2d 345, 76 Ohio App.3d 747.—Anim 57.

VICIOUS NATURE

N.Y.Sup. 2000. A "vicious nature," for purposes of presumption of negligence attaching to person who keeps dog with knowledge of its vicious nature and fails to prevent dog from injuring others, includes biting, jumping on people, and running at large in a roadway.—Ayala v. Hagemann, 714 N.Y.S.2d 633, 186 Misc.2d 122.—Anim 66.5(2), 74(3).

VICIOUS OR DANGEROUS PROPENSITY

La. 1966. Whether the kicking by a colt was playful mischievousness or viciousness, it endangered safety of others and was therefore a "vicious or dangerous propensity" within rule making owner responsible for actions of his animal which is known to have a vicious or dangerous propensity. LSA–C.C. art. 2321.—Tamburello v. Jaeger, 184 So.2d 544, 249 La. 25.—Anim 66.7.

VICIOUS PROPENSITIES

Hawai'i 1977. The terms "vicious propensities" and "dangerous propensities" have been defined as any propensity on part of dog, which is likely to cause injury under circumstances in which person controlling the dog placed it, and a vicious propensity does not mean only the type of malignancy exhibited by a biting dog, that is, a propensity to attack human beings; it includes as well a natural fierceness or disposition to mischief as might occasionally lead him to attack human beings without provocation.—Farrior v. Payton, 562 P.2d 779, 57 Haw. 620.—Anim 66.5(2).

Mo.App. E.D. 1993. In cases involving injuries caused by dogs, dog's "vicious propensities," are not established by evidence of dog's barking, running loose, jumping, and lunging, since these are activities in which all dogs engage.—Brouk v. Brueggeate, 849 S.W.2d 699.—Anim 66.5(2).

Mo.App. 1974. Terms "vicious propensities" and "dangerous propensities" in a dog bite case generally refer to tendency of dog to injure persons, whether dog acted out of anger, viciousness, or playfulness and such terms are not confined to a disposition on part of dog to attack every person he might meet but includes as well a natural fierceness or disposition to mischief as might occasionally lead dog to attack human beings without provocation.—Frazier v. Stone, 515 S.W.2d 766.—Anim 66.5(2).

Mo.App. 1962. "Vicious" and "dangerous", within dog bite case instruction which referred both to "vicious propensities" and "dangerous propensities", connoted quality of dog which could or would

Illustration 12-9. An excerpt from *Words and Phrases*.

§ 12.3 *AMERICAN LAW REPORTS* ANNOTATIONS

At the same time that West was developing its National Reporter System in the late 19th century, other publishers were attempting a different approach to case reporting. They selected "leading cases" for full-text publication, and added commentaries, or *annotations*, which surveyed other decisions on the subject of the selected case. Selective publication was not a successful alternative to comprehensive reporting, but the annotations have remained valuable case research tools.

Among the early sets of annotated reporters were *American Reports* (1871–88), *American Decisions* (1878–88), *American State Reports* (1888–1911), *Lawyers Reports Annotated* (1888–1918), and *American and English Annotated Cases* (1901–18). These were succeeded in 1919 by *American Law Reports* (*ALR*), which is now published as *ALR7th* for general and state legal issues and *ALR Federal 3d* for issues of federal law. (Another series, *ALR International*, focuses on treatment of international law issues by U.S. and foreign courts, and will be discussed in Chapter 17.)

An *ALR* annotation provides a comprehensive summary of the case law on a specific topic. *ALR* does not cover all research issues, but an annotation directly on point can save considerable research time. It does the initial time-consuming work of finding relevant cases and arranges them according to specific fact patterns and holdings. Because it synthesizes the cases into a narrative discussion and compares decisions that have reached conflicting results, rather than simply offering a collection of headnotes, an annotation is usually easier to understand than a digest.

Annotations differ significantly from other narrative resources such as treatises and law review articles. Their purpose is to present in a systematic way the varied judicial decisions from around the country. They generally do not criticize these decisions or analyze legal problems, nor do they attempt to integrate case law into a broader societal perspective. Courts occasionally cite annotations, but as convenient compilations of prevailing judicial doctrine rather than as secondary sources with their own persuasive authority.

ALR annotations are available on Westlaw, where coverage goes back to the earliest annotations from 1919, and Lexis, which picks up with *ALR2d* in 1948 and also has *Lawyers' Edition* annotations focusing on Supreme Court cases. In either platform, a general search in secondary sources can quickly be filtered to highlight *ALR* results.

(a) Format and Content

ALR annotations are written in a standard form. Each begins with a table of contents, a detailed subject index, and a table listing the jurisdictions of the cases discussed. In annotations since 1992 (the beginning of *ALR5th*), this introductory material has also included a Research References section with leads to encyclopedias, practice aids, digests, and other sources, as well as West key numbers and sample online search queries. Research References on Westlaw and in recent volumes also include lists of related *ALR* annotations; in earlier printed volumes, these are listed in § 1[b] of the annotation itself.

The first two sections of an annotation are an introduction describing its scope and a summary providing a general overview and giving practice pointers. The annotation then summarizes cases from around the country, arranged according to their facts and holdings. Illustrations 12-10 and 12-11 show pages from an *ALR5th* annotation on whether a dog can be considered a deadly or dangerous weapon. Illustration 12-10 shows the table of contents, organizing the annotation's sections according to specific issues and criminal statutes. Illustration 12-11 shows an excerpt from the discussion of cases.

No matter when an annotation was originally published, annual supplements cover more recent cases. The annotation in Illustrations 12-10 and 12-11 was originally published in 2004, but its pocket part or online supplement provides references to new developments.[22]

---

[22] Online annotations are updated with "Cumulative Supplement" or "Cumulative Cases" notes after each section. In print, *ALR3d–7th* and *ALR Fed-Fed 3d* are updated with annual pocket parts in each volume. Many of the annotations in *ALR1st* and *ALR2d* continue to be updated, but these older series use other methods instead of pocket parts in each volume. *ALR2d* has a separate set of blue *Later Case Service* volumes, which have their own pocket parts; and *ALR1st* has an accompanying set, *ALR1st Blue Book of Supplemental Decisions*, that lists relevant case citations.

TABLE OF CONTENTS

Research References
Index
Jurisdictional Table of Cited Statutes and Cases

ARTICLE OUTLINE

I. PRELIMINARY MATTERS

§ 1. Introduction
  [a] Scope
  [b] Related annotations

§ 2. Background, summary, and comment
  [a] Generally
  [b] Practice pointers

II. IN GENERAL

§ 3. Dog as deadly weapon
  [a] View that dog can be deadly weapon
  [b] View that dog cannot be deadly weapon

§ 4. Dog as dangerous weapon
§ 5. Dog as dangerous instrument
§ 6. Dog as offensive weapon

III. SUFFICIENCY OF EVIDENCE IN PARTICULAR PROSECUTIONS

§ 7. Dog as deadly weapon
  [a] Prosecution under assault and battery statute
  [b] Prosecution under resisting arrest statute

§ 8. Dog as dangerous weapon
  [a] Prosecution under robbery statute
  [b] Prosecution under sexual offense statute
  [c] Prosecution under weapons offense statute

§ 9. Dog as dangerous instrument
§ 10. Dog as offensive weapon

Illustration 12-10. The table of contents of an *ALR* annotation.

124 ALR5th DOG—DEADLY OR DANGEROUS WEAPON § 4
124 ALR5th 657

[b] View that dog cannot be deadly weapon

The following authority expressed the view that a dog cannot be a deadly weapon as that term is defined by a particular criminal statute.

In dismissing a count in an indictment charging the defendant with criminal possession of a deadly weapon in the fourth degree, to wit, a German shepherd dog, the court in People v. Torrez, 86 Misc. 2d 369, 382 **N.Y.S.2d** 233 (Sup 1976), ruled that a German shepherd dog cannot be a "deadly weapon" as defined in New York Penal Law, although the court held that the dog can be a "dangerous instrument."[22] The applicable statute, N.Y. Penal Law § 10.00(12), defines deadly weapon as any loaded weapon from which a shot, readily capable of producing death or serious bodily injury, may be discharged, or a switchblade knife, gravity knife, dagger, billy, blackjack, or metal knuckles. The court reasoned that the listing of specific weapons qualified the general term "weapon," and concluded that no matter how serious may be the physical injury the dog could do to another on command of its master, the dog did not fit into the statutory definition of a deadly weapon.

§ 4. Dog as dangerous weapon

The courts in the following cases expressed the view, either expressly or implicitly, that a dog may be a dangerous weapon for purposes of a criminal statute aggravating an offense committed with a dangerous weapon.

La.—State v. Michels, 726 So. 2d 449 (La. Ct. App. 5th Cir. 1999).

Mass.—Com. v. Tarrant, 367 Mass. 411, 326 N.E.2d 710 (1975); Com. v. Davis, 10 Mass. App. Ct. 190, 406 N.E.2d 417, 8 A.L.R.4th 1259 (1980) (recognizing rule).

Mich.—People v. Kay, 121 Mich. App. 438, 328 N.W.2d 424 (1982); People v. Malkowski, 198 Mich. App. 610, 499 N.W.2d 450 (1993) (recognizing rule).

Wis.—State v. Sinks, 168 Wis. 2d 245, 483 N.W.2d 286 (Ct. App. 1992); State v. Bodoh, 226 Wis. 2d 718, 595 N.W.2d 330 (1999).

Illustration 12-11. An excerpt from an *ALR* annotation.

If later cases substantially change the law on a subject covered by an annotation, a new annotation may either supplement or completely supersede the older annotation. Online, a notice with a link to the newer annotation simply replaces the older work. In print, the older volume's pocket part or other supplement alerts you to the existence of the newer treatment (another good reason to *always* check the pocket part for new developments). Superseded and supplemented annotations are also listed in an "Annotation History Table" in the back of each volume of the *ALR Index*.

(b) Finding Annotations

The online versions of *ALR* annotations are searchable by keyword, just like cases or other documents. Because annotations summarize the facts of the cases discussed, including aspects unrelated to the topic under discussion, a full-text search may turn up numerous annotations on irrelevant topics. It is often best to limit a search to the titles of annotations by using the Title field in Lexis or Westlaw. Relevance ranking should also increase the likelihood that the most useful annotations appear early in a list of search results.

The basic tool for subject access to the printed version of *ALR* is the nine-volume *ALR Index*. A less comprehensive *ALR Quick Index* covering only *ALR3d–7th* is published annually, and a separate *ALR Federal Quick Index* is limited to *ALR Fed* and *ALR Fed 2d–3d* annotations. Illustration 12-12 shows an excerpt from the *ALR Index*, including two references under "Dogs" to the annotation shown.[23] The *ALR Index* is also available on Westlaw.

Remember that each *ALR* annotation includes a list of other annotations on related topics. If an online search or a check of the index does not turn up an annotation directly on point but does lead to one on a related issue, the most productive next step may be to read through that annotation's list of related annotations. This could bring up analogies or concepts you may not have thought to search for initially. The list for the annotation on animal cruelty, for example, includes references to annotations on topics such as the liability of dog owners and the malpractice liability of veterinarians.

---

[23] Another means of access to annotations is through the *ALR Digest*, a multi-volume set classifying ALR's annotations and cases in West's Key Number System. With a key number in hand, a researcher can find relevant ALR annotations on that subject. Older digests using a different classification system may be found in some libraries, but these are no longer being updated.

ALR INDEX

DOGS—Cont'd
Constitutional law—Cont'd
  constitutionality of dog laws, **49 ALR 847**
  destruction of property as violation of Fourth Amendment, **98 ALR5th 305, § 3(d), 7, 9(b), 13, 15, 18**
  due process, in this topic
  federal cases, use of trained dog to detect narcotics or drugs as unreasonable search in violation of Fourth Amendment, **150 ALR Fed 399**
  mail, warrantless detention of mail for investigative purposes as violative of Fourth Amendment, **115 ALR Fed 439, § 3, 4(b, c)**
  schools, search conducted by school official or teacher as violation of Fourth Amendment or equivalent state constitutional provision, **31 ALR5th 229, § 6, 14, 29(b), 31(b), 40, 64, 69**
  state cases, use of trained dog to detect narcotics or drugs as unreasonable search in violation of state constitutions, **117 ALR5th 407**
Contributory negligence or assumption of risk
  business patron, liability of owner or operator of business premises for injury to patron by dog or cat, **67 ALR4th 976**
  exhibition, liability for injury inflicted by horse, dog, or other domestic

DOGS—Cont'd
Criminal law—Cont'd
  trailing, evidence of trailing by dogs in criminal cases, **81 ALR5th 563**
Cruelty
  experiments or tests, applicability of state animal cruelty statute to medical or scientific experimentation employing animals, **42 ALR4th 860**
  liability for statement or publication charging plaintiff with killing of, cruelty to, or inhumane treatment of animals, **69 ALR5th 645, § 3, 4(a, c), 6(b), 11, 12**
  what constitutes offense of cruelty to animals, **6 ALR5th 733**
Damages
  emotional distress, recovery of damages for emotional distress due to treatment of pets and animals, **91 ALR5th 545**
  killing or injuring dog, **61 ALR5th 635**
Deadly or dangerous weapon, dog as deadly or dangerous weapon for purposes of statutes aggravating offenses such as assault and robbery, **124 ALR5th 657**
Death. Destruction or killing of animal, in this topic
Defense of person or property, dog as deadly or dangerous weapon for purposes of statutes aggravating offenses such as assault and robbery, **124 ALR5th 657**

Illustration 12-12. An excerpt from the *ALR Index*.

You can also find leads to relevant annotations from cases or statutes. Westlaw Citing References includes citing annotations in its coverage of cases and statutes, although Shepard's on Lexis does not. Online or in print, many annotated codes and encyclopedias also have references to relevant *ALR* annotations.

Because each annotation is written about a specific topic, coverage in the series is not comprehensive and there are many issues for which no annotation can be found. But if you locate an annotation on a point you are researching, then you can benefit from the author's work examining the issue and collecting almost every relevant case.

§ 12.4 CITATORS

The nature of case law is referential. Cases decided today will cite earlier cases, relying on binding precedent extracted from their holdings or from persuasive arguments of other judges. Cases decided in the future, likewise, may rely on cases decided at any earlier point, including cases decided today. Specialized research tools called citators can help you keep track of these citation networks in two primary ways: (1) by locating other relevant legal authorities, namely other cases or secondary sources, citing your case and (2) by determining the validity of your case.

Almost all citator research takes place online through one of the major research platforms. The main general-purpose citators are Westlaw Citing References (also known as KeyCite) and Shepard's Citations on Lexis. Several other citation analysis resources such as Authority Check (Fastcase), BCite (Bloomberg Law), or CaseCheck (Casemaker) are also available, but tend to be more limited in the types of resources they cover.

(a) Locating Additional Authorities

Citators serve as powerful links from one case to others addressing similar issues, providing one of the most effective ways to find sources for further research. You can use citators to shape your research and to focus on specific aspects of relevant cases. Even the absence of citing references can provide important information about a case; if a decision has remained uncited for decades, it may indicate that it is a neglected backwater that might not be accorded much weight by a current court.[24]

Citing references can be limited in various ways, by document type, headnote number, jurisdiction, or keyword. Searching for keywords within citator results is particularly effective, because the cases you're searching are likely to be highly relevant if they contain your search terms. This approach (called "Search Within Results" on Westlaw and Lexis, and "Search These Documents" on Bloomberg Law) can focus immediately on those documents applying a precedent to a particular set of facts. Some citators also sort citing decisions by the extent to which they discuss the cited case, so you can focus quickly on what are likely to be the most relevant and informative decisions.

---

[24] A citation study of more than four million published federal and state cases found that about 400,000 cases had never been cited and another 773,000 had been cited only once. Thomas A. Smith, *The Web of Law*, 44 SAN DIEGO L. REV. 309, 324–28 (2007).

Illustrations 12-13 and 12-14 show Westlaw Citing References and Shepard's Citations results for *Hill v. Williams*, a case that was discussed in the *Harris v. Barefoot* case. Both displays have been limited to the cases citing *Hill v. Williams* on issues in relevant headnotes.

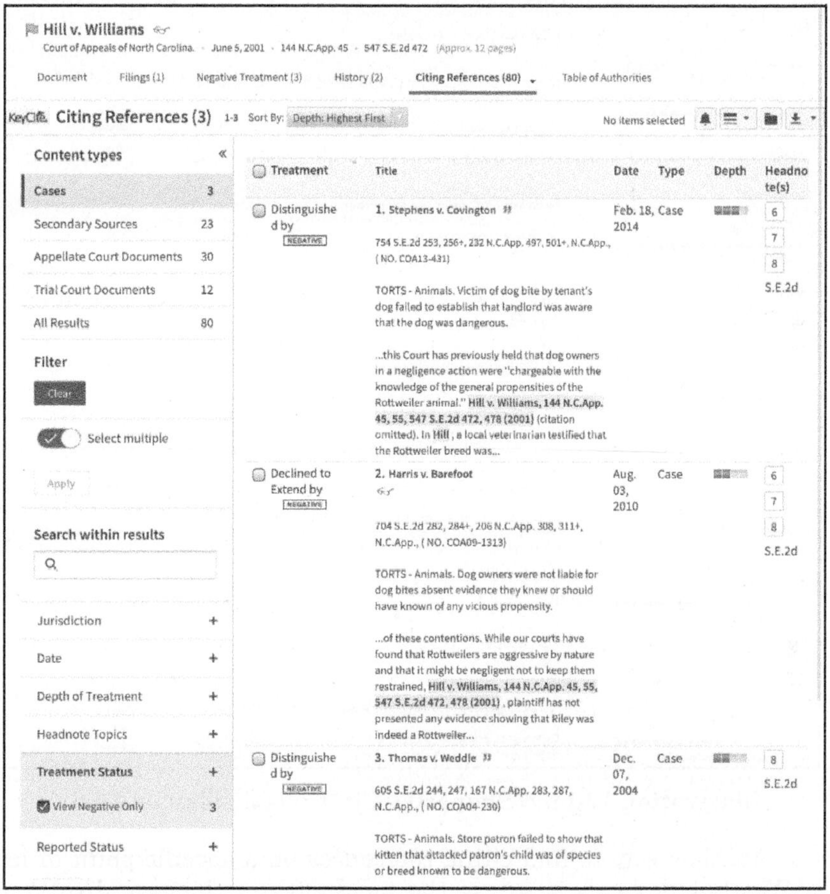

Illustration 12-13. A Westlaw Citing References display.

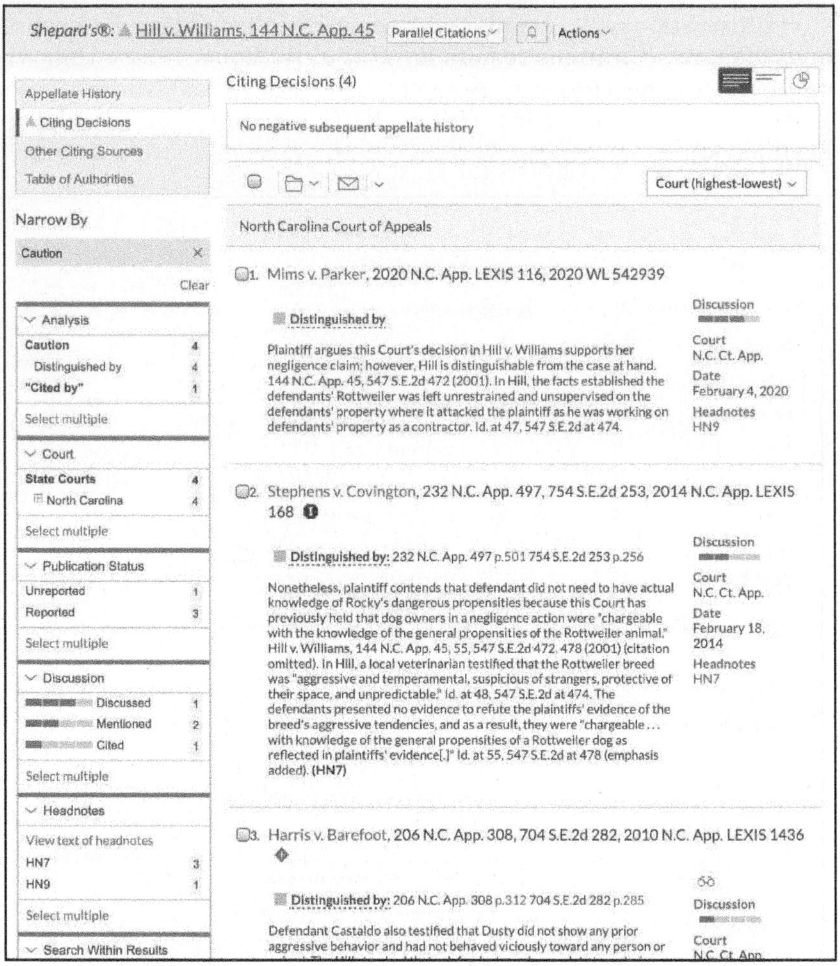

Illustration 12-14. A Shepard's Citations display on Lexis.

Another way to find citing references on a specific point of law in Westlaw or Lexis is to use the headnotes in the case display to pinpoint a legal issue and then click on the *[Number] Cases that cite this headnote* or *Shepardize—Narrow by this Headnote* link. This should take you immediately to the most relevant cases, but be aware that not all relevant cases may be linked to a specific headnote.[25] Lexis has a "Legal Issue Trail" feature that allows you to highlight specific passages in an opinion. Clicking on one of these passages connects you to cases citing the opinion on that point of law, as well as to the cases your opinion cites.

---

[25] *See* Susan Nevelow Mart, *Research Strategies Using Headnotes: Citators and Relevance*, 44 COLO. LAW. 123 (2015).

Another feature that sets Westlaw and Lexis apart is that their citators list not only subsequent cases but also citing treatises and law review articles. These references can be enormously helpful in putting your case in a broader context and leading to other relevant primary authority. If you're interested in coverage of secondary sources, you should check both Westlaw Citing References and Shepard's. Both have similar references to law reviews, but otherwise each focuses on materials available on its platform. Thus Westlaw includes *ALR* annotations and Thomson Reuters treatises, while Lexis includes treatises and encyclopedias published by LexisNexis or Matthew Bender.

Other case resources can provide some of the benefits of citator services. Google Scholar, for instance, includes a "How cited" link that lists citing cases, indicating the extent to which the cited case is discussed, and provides excerpts from these cases.

(b) Determining Case Validity

Under the doctrine of precedent, the holdings of governing cases determine the resolution of issues in subsequent controversies. A precedential decision continues to have binding effect regardless of its age, but its authority can be affected by either sudden change or gradual erosion. A decision might be reversed on appeal to a higher court or overruled years later by a decision of the same court. Later cases may also criticize or question the reasoning of a decision, or limit its holding to a specific factual situation. Any of these circumstances can diminish or negate the authority of a case.

Before relying on any case, it is necessary to verify its current validity. The need for such information was first met by an 1821 publication by Simon Greenleaf, *A Collection of Cases Overruled, Denied, Doubted, or Limited in Their Application*, and a variety of successor publications in the 19th century. In 1875 Frank Shepard began printing lists of citations to Illinois Supreme Court cases on gummed paper for attorneys to stick in the margins of their bound reporters. Before long he was publishing his citation lists in book form, and coverage expanded gradually to include every state and the federal courts. As a result of the importance of these *Shepard's Citations* volumes, this process of updating cases became known as *Shepardizing*.[26] While *Shepard's Citations* is still published in

---

[26] For a history of Shepard's and its predecessors, see Patti Ogden, *"Mastering the Lawless Science of Our Law": A Story of Legal Citation Indexes*, 85 LAW LIBR. J. 1 (1993). For the more recent history of online citators, see Laura C. Dabney, *Citators: Past, Present, and Future*, 27 LEGAL REFERENCE SERVICES Q. 165 (2008).

print,[27] these days the bulk of case validation work is done in one of the online citators mentioned above.

Citators perform two major case validation functions. They provide parallel citations and references to other proceedings in the same case, allowing you to trace a case's judicial history, and they indicate if subsequent cases have overruled, limited, or otherwise diminished a case's precedent, enabling you to determine whether it is still good law.

Case History. Seeing other decisions in the same litigation allows you to follow the proceeding through the court system, to clarify facts, and perhaps to determine whether your case has been affirmed or reversed on appeal. Westlaw uses a History tab at the top of the case, while Lexis and Bloomberg Law indicate to the right of the display that there are case history documents. Be aware, however, that this is not a complete history and that only decisions also available on the platform are listed. For many cases there is no indication of what happened before or after the decision, because no other opinions from the litigation are online.

Case Validity. The major platforms all include symbols next to case names as notices about their validity. Red flags or stop signs indicate that a case's precedential value has been seriously affected. Other symbols, such as yellow flags or caution symbols, indicate that a holding may have been questioned or distinguished in subsequent cases. Clicking on this symbol, or on a link to the right of the case display, takes you to a list of the more recent and potentially problematic decisions.

In addition to the flags or symbols, Westlaw has a "Negative Treatment" tab at the top of the case display while Lexis and Bloomberg Law include tables to the right of case displays listing analysis symbols such as "Caution" or "Distinguished" and the number of citing cases for each.

These signals and symbols are just tools for your use, not authoritative statements of the law.[28] Relying on a red flag or a stop sign is no substitute for reading a citing document and determining

---

[27] Information on using *Shepard's Citations* in print is available in the first edition of *Principles of Legal Research* and earlier works.

[28] This admonition is more significant with the increase in legal publishers' efforts to show relationships between cases in an effort to expedite the legal research process. Publishers' classification of cases' relationships can result in citator signals being changed simply through a reassessment of citing case law, and may leave you feeling as though the helpful signals do not really tell you as much as you'd like (or as much as they promise).

for yourself its scope and effect.[29] A case that has been overruled on one point may still be good law on other issues, but learning this requires reading the overruling case itself and perhaps examining *its* subsequent history. Note that Illustrations 12-13 and 12-14 show that Westlaw says that *Harris v. Barefoot* "declined to extend" the holding of *Hill*, while Shepard's says that *Harris* "distinguished" its holding.

In addition, terms such as "negative" are broadly defined.[30] A lower court decision that declines to extend a Supreme Court precedent beyond its intended scope is listed as "distinguishing" its holding. This is considered negative treatment, even though it has no impact on the Supreme Court decision's precedent.[31] Again, you need to read the citing cases to determine their impact.

Despite these caveats, the ability to confirm whether a case is not bad law is what distinguishes a true citator from a simple algorithm that finds subsequent references to a citation. Not every overruling case uses that explicit terminology, and the editorial work of analyzing new decisions and gauging the impact on older cases is a vital contribution to the research process.

Alerts. Most platforms also offer alert services that can monitor developments in a case's history or citing references and send you e-mail notices of new citing references. Some can be tailored to references meeting specific criteria such as cited headnote number or jurisdiction. Westlaw's KeyCite Alert, for example, can be set up to send notices for any case history developments, for just negative history, or for any and all citing references. It can also limit citing references by headnote, jurisdiction, keywords, or depth of treatment, providing an easy way to learn of new cases meeting very specific citing criteria. One could, for example, receive KeyCite Alert notifications for any North Carolina cases affecting *Harris v. Barefoot*'s value as precedent on the specific issue summarized in its second headnote.

---

[29] *See* Aaron S. Kirschenfeld, *Yellow Flag Fever: Describing Negative Legal Precedent in Citators*, 108 LAW LIBR. J. 77 (2016), which suggests that citators do not apply symbols or descriptions of negative treatment consistently.

[30] Occasionally, different citators disagree about whether a given citation is negative at all. *See* Paul Hellyer, *Evaluating Shepard's, KeyCite, and BCite for Case Validation Accuracy*, 110 LAW LIBR. J. 449 (2018).

[31] A study several years ago found that more than half of one term's Supreme Court cases were assigned "negative history" symbols by both Westlaw and Shepard's before the start of the next term. They were still good law, but lower courts had distinguished or declined to extend their holdings. Kent C. Olson, *Waiving a Red Flag: Teaching Counterintuitiveness in Citator Use*, 9 PERSPECTIVES 58, 60 (2001).

Each research method discussed in this chapter can lead you to cases that the other methods might not discover. We have concentrated on tools such as online searches, digests, and annotations that are designed expressly for finding cases. Resources discussed in other chapters can also serve as case-finding tools. Annotated statutory codes, for example, include notes of relevant cases applying or interpreting the terms of each code section, and secondary sources such as treatises, encyclopedias, and law review articles provide extensive footnote citations to cases. Using a combination of approaches—even if online platforms market their services to suggest that one search will do the trick—provides greater confidence that you have not missed any significant precedent.

Chapter 13

OTHER COURT INFORMATION

Table of Sections

While much legal literature focuses on substantive rights, the processes under which parties come before courts to settle disputes play a vital role in determining the scope and exercise of these rights. A lawyer must be familiar with governing rules and procedures to avoid compromising clients' interests.[1]

For centuries the rules governing court proceedings developed piecemeal through case law, eventually creating the arcane and formalistic pleading rituals of the Court of Chancery in Charles Dickens's *Bleak House*. Reforms within the past century have made court procedures simpler and more flexible, but there are still unforeseen complexities and differences of interpretation. Rules that seem straightforward must be applied in light of the large body of case law that has developed. Annotated sets of rules and an extensive secondary literature help to guide litigants through the intricate maze of court proceedings.

This chapter also covers resources dealing with court proceedings, including dockets, briefs, and oral arguments, which

---

[1]   As Justice Hugo Black noted many years ago, "Judicial statistics would show, I fear, an unfortunately large number of meritorious cases lost due to inadvertent failure of lawyers to conform to procedural prescriptions having little if any relevancy to substantial justice." Order Adopting Revised Rules of the Supreme Court of the United States, 346 U.S. 945, 946 (1954) (Black, J., dissenting).

contain background information on decided cases or pending lawsuits. A developing suite of tools lets you research how judges tend to rule when confronted with particular legal questions or proceedings, and directories provide practical assistance for anyone who needs to contact courts.

§ 13.1 COURT RULES

Court rules are designed to guide and regulate the conduct of judicial business. They range from procedural details, such as the format to be followed in preparing a brief, to matters of substantial importance, such as the grounds for appeal, time limitations, or the types of motions and appeals that a court will hear. Court rules may specify or limit available remedies and thus can affect rights in significant ways. Rules regulating court proceedings have the force of law, to the extent that they do not supersede or conflict with statutes.

Most jurisdictions have sets of rules governing trial and appellate procedure, as well as rules for specialized tribunals or for particular actions such as admiralty or habeas corpus. Each jurisdiction has its own requirements and procedures for creating these rules. Some involve action by special conferences of judges, and others require approval by the jurisdiction's highest court. Courts traditionally have inherent power to control the conduct of their affairs, but rules are generally promulgated under authority granted by the legislature. Some court rules require a combination of judicial action and legislative approval, while others are statutory and are created by legislatures. Knowing how rules are created in a jurisdiction can inform where you begin your research.[2]

(a) Federal Rules

There are four sets of federal rules that govern the business of federal courts: the Federal Rules of Civil Procedure, the Federal Rules of Criminal Procedure, the Federal Rules of Appellate Procedure, and the Federal Rules of Evidence. The Rules of Civil Procedure have been in development the longest, though they were thoroughly modernized in the late 1930s.[3] Work on the Federal Rules

---

[2] Zachary D. Clopton, *Making State Civil Procedure*, 104 CORNELL L. REV. 1 (2018), explains that forty-one states have court-based rulemaking, while nine states (California, Connecticut, Georgia, Illinois, Kansas, Louisiana, New York, North Carolina, and Oklahoma) rely primarily on the legislature to promulgate rules. The article includes a detailed appendix table outlining the rulemaking mechanism in each state.

[3] In 1789 the first Congress expressly gave the new federal courts the power "to make and establish all necessary rules for the orderly conducting business in the said courts, provided such rules are not repugnant to the laws of the United States." Judiciary Act of 1789, ch. 20, § 17, 1 Stat. 73, 83. An act three years later vested rule-

of Criminal Procedure dates from about that time as well.[4] The
Federal Rules of Appellate Procedure followed three decades later.[5]
And the Federal Rules of Evidence were the last of the group to be
promulgated in their contemporary form.[6]

---

making power more specifically in the Supreme Court, providing that courts follow
state procedures "subject . . . to such regulations as the supreme court of the United
States shall think proper from time to time by rule to prescribe to any circuit or district
court." Act of May 8, 1792, ch. 36, § 2, 1 Stat. 275, 276. In 1822 the Supreme Court
promulgated its first set of rules for procedures in equity, 20 U.S. (7 Wheat.) v (1822),
but it did not issue general rules for actions at law for more than another century.

In 1934, Congress gave the Court authority to combine equity and law into one
federal civil procedure and to make and publish rules governing federal actions as long
as they did not "abridge, enlarge, nor modify the substantive rights of any litigant."
Rules Enabling Act, ch. 651, § 1, 48 Stat. 1064, 1064 (1934) (current version at 28
U.S.C. § 2072). On the history and interpretation of the act, see Stephen B. Burbank,
The Rules Enabling Act of 1934, 130 U. PA. L. REV. 1015 (1982), and Martin H. Redish
& Uma M. Amuluru, *The Supreme Court, the Rules Enabling Act, and the
Politicization of the Federal Rules: Constitutional and Statutory Implications*, 90
MINN. L. REV. 1303 (2006). The resulting Federal Rules of Civil Procedure were
prepared by a judicial Advisory Committee, adopted by the Supreme Court in
December 1937, and became effective September 16, 1938.

The new rules were a widely acclaimed success in modernizing federal civil
practice. One enthusiastic lawyer wrote that the rules were "one of the greatest
contributions to the free and unhampered administration of law and justice ever
struck off by any group of men since the dawn of civilized law." B. H. Carey, *In Favor
of Uniformity*, 18 TEMP. U. L.Q. 146, 146 (1943). For more background on the adoption
of the rules, see Paul V. Niemeyer, *Revisiting the 1938 Rules Experiment*, 71 WASH. &
LEE L. REV. 2157 (2014), and Stephen N. Subrin, *How Equity Conquered Common
Law: The Federal Rules of Civil Procedure in Historical Perspective*, 135 U. PA. L. REV.
909 (1987).

[4] Congress gave the Supreme Court authority to promulgate rules governing
criminal appeals in 1933, and in 1940 the Court was also empowered to make rules
with respect to criminal trial court proceedings. Act of Feb. 24, 1933, ch. 119, 47 Stat.
904, as amended by Act of Mar. 8, 1934, ch. 49, 48 Stat. 399; Act of June 29, 1940, ch.
445, 54 Stat. 688. *See* Max Minzner, *The Criminal Rules Enabling Act*, 46 U. RICH. L.
REV. 1047 (2012). In his 1940 report, Attorney General Robert H. Jackson stressed the
need for reform, writing that criminal procedure "still remains largely in a chaotic and
archaic state. Many technicalities dating back a century or two are still in full vigor in
the Federal courts." ANNUAL REPORT OF THE ATTORNEY GENERAL OF THE UNITED
STATES, H.R. DOC. NO. 77–9, at 5 (1940). The Federal Rules of Criminal Procedure
went through several drafts before finally becoming effective March 21, 1946.
DRAFTING HISTORY OF THE FEDERAL RULES OF CRIMINAL PROCEDURE (Madeleine J.
Wilken & Nicholas Triffin eds. 1991) is a comprehensive, seven-volume work that
includes a brief history, letters, comments, Supreme Court memoranda, and drafts of
the rules. It is available on HeinOnline.

[5] The original criminal rules governed post-conviction and appellate
proceedings, but appeals in civil cases continued to be handled differently in each
circuit. In 1966 Congress finally empowered the Supreme Court to prescribe rules for
the Courts of Appeals in civil actions. Act of Nov. 6, 1966, Pub. L. No. 89–773, 80 Stat.
1323. The Federal Rules of Appellate Procedure, governing both civil and criminal
proceedings, took effect July 1, 1968.

[6] In 1972 the Supreme Court submitted proposed Federal Rules of Evidence to
Congress, which passed a law preventing the rules from taking effect until expressly
approved. Act of Mar. 30, 1973, Pub. L. No. 93–12, 87 Stat. 9. To some critics, the
proposed rules covering evidentiary privileges were seen as substantive rather than
procedural in nature, and were thus beyond the scope of the Court's rulemaking
authority. Congress enacted its own amended version of the rules, which became law

In addition to the sets of rules applying to the federal courts in general, there are also rules governing specialized procedures and particular courts. Rules governing bankruptcy proceedings were first promulgated in 1898,[7] and the current rules were adopted in 1983 for proceedings in the new Bankruptcy Courts created in the 1978 revision of the Bankruptcy Code.[8]

These various sets of federal procedural rules have all been amended numerous times in the years since their initial adoption. Standing Advisory Committees for each set of rules recommend changes to the Judicial Conference, the principal policy-making body for administration of the federal court system. If the Judicial Conference approves the changes, it submits them to the Supreme Court for its approval. The Court in turn transmits the proposed amendments to Congress, which has at least seven months to enact legislation to reject, modify, or defer the changes. The rule amendments take effect if Congress declines to act. On several occasions Congress has also passed legislation that directly amends federal rules.

The major source for information on pending and recent amendments to federal rules is the "Rules & Policies" section of the U.S. Courts website (www.uscourts.gov/rules-policies). This site provides the text of pending and proposed rule changes, background information on the rulemaking process, and Advisory Committee reports and minutes of committee meetings back as far as the 1930s.[9]

The commentary by the Advisory Committee usually consists of a few paragraphs for each rule, discussing procedure under prior law and the purpose of the new rule or amendment. These notes can be an invaluable starting point in interpreting a rule provision.[10]

---

on July 1, 1975, and gave the Supreme Court authority to make amendments other than those creating, abolishing, or modifying privileges. Act of Jan. 2, 1975, § 2(a)(1), Pub. L. No. 93–595, 88 Stat. 1926, 1948 (current version at 28 U.S.C. § 2074(b)). For a history of the proposed rules and their rejection in Congress, see Kenneth S. Broun, *Giving Codification a Second Chance—Testimonial Privileges and the Federal Rules of Evidence*, 53 HASTINGS L.J. 769, 772–78 (2002).

[7] General Orders and Forms in Bankruptcy, 172 U.S. 653 (1898), promulgated pursuant to the Bankruptcy Act of 1898, § 30, ch. 541, 30 Stat. 544, 554.

[8] *See* Lawrence P. King, *The History and Development of the Bankruptcy Rules*, 70 AM. BANKR. L.J. 217 (1996).

[9] Rule amendments are also printed as House Documents and reprinted in *United States Code Congressional and Administrative News, United States Code Service Advance,* and advance sheets for West's federal reporters. Legislative history documents on congressional action involving the rules and the federal courts generally are available in HeinOnline's Congress and the Courts collection.

[10] "In interpreting the federal rules, the Advisory Committee Notes are a very important source of information and direction and should be given considerable weight. Although these Notes are not conclusive, they provide something akin to a 'legislative history' of the rules, and carry, in addition, the great prestige that the

Sources. The various rules governing federal court proceedings can be found in a wide array of online and print sources, some unannotated and some accompanied by Advisory Committee Notes, summaries of judicial decisions, and practice commentaries.

The "Rules & Policies" section of the U.S. Courts website contains regularly updated versions of the Federal Rules of Appellate Procedure, Bankruptcy Procedure, Civil Procedure, Criminal Procedure, and Evidence, published by the House Committee on the Judiciary as committee prints. The Legal Information Institute at Cornell Law School (www.law.cornell.edu/rules) has searchable versions of all of these rules, accompanied by Advisory Committee Notes.

Federal court rules are also available from the online platforms and in a variety of pamphlets and reference publications. The major sets of rules, with Advisory Committee comments, are printed in the *U.S. Code*.[11] *United States Code Annotated* (available on Westlaw) and *United States Code Service* (available on Lexis) contain not only Advisory Committee notes but also headnotes of cases applying and interpreting the rules, as well as other research aids such as references to treatises, law review articles, and legal encyclopedias. These annotations can be quite thorough; the Federal Rules of Civil Procedure, for example, occupy 21 volumes in *USCA*.[12] Illustration

---

individual members of the successive Advisory Committees, and the Committees themselves, have enjoyed as authorities on procedure." 4 CHARLES ALAN WRIGHT ET AL., FEDERAL PRACTICE AND PROCEDURE § 1029, at 173–74 (4th ed. 2015) (footnotes omitted). *But see* Laurens Walker, *Writings on the Margin of American Law: Committee Notes, Comments, and Commentary*, 29 GA. L. REV. 993 (1995) (arguing that courts should give little, if any, weight to committee notes).

[11] An appendix to Title 28, Judiciary and Judicial Procedure, contains the Federal Rules of Civil Procedure, Appellate Procedure, and Evidence, as well as rules governing proceedings in the Supreme Court and specialized courts. The Federal Rules of Criminal Procedure appear in an appendix to Title 18, Crimes and Criminal Procedure, and Bankruptcy Rules and Official Forms are in an appendix to Title 11, Bankruptcy.

[12] *USCA* includes the rules at the same places they appear in the *U.S. Code*, following the code titles to which they are most closely related. *USCS* has most of the rules in unnumbered "Court Rules" volumes shelved at the end of the set. The one exception is the Federal Rules of Evidence; because they were enacted by Congress, *USCS* publishes them as an appendix to Title 28.

A somewhat less overwhelming source of annotated federal rules is the *United States Supreme Court Digest, Lawyers' Edition*. Several volumes of this set include the text of the major sets of rules, as well as rules for specialized federal courts, accompanied by Advisory Committee comments, commentaries by National Institute for Trial Advocacy professors, and annotations of Supreme Court cases. While this is a less comprehensive source, it may be a useful starting point for someone seeking significant judicial interpretations of the rules.

The texts of the major rules are also published in paperback desktop editions. Thomson Reuters' *Federal Procedure Rules Service National* (annual) contains the text and Advisory Committee notes for all the major rules except the Federal Rules of

13-1 shows just a few of the annotations for Rule 6, as they appear on Westlaw.

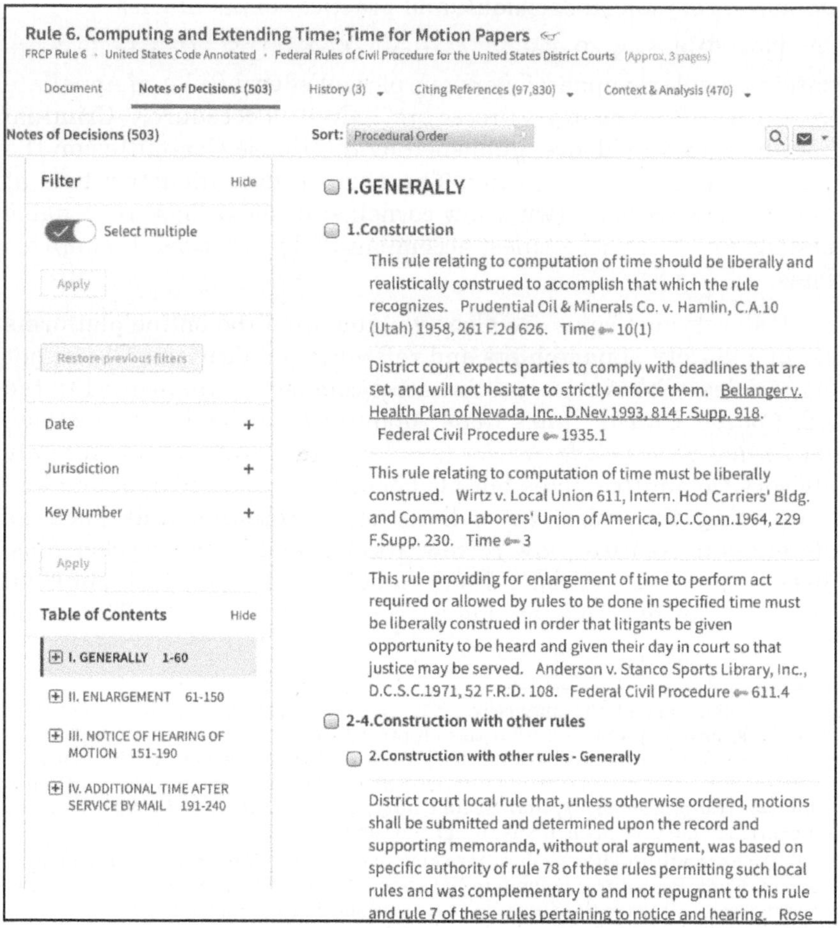

Illustration 13-1. Notes of Decisions for
a federal court rule on Westlaw.

Treatises. The technical nature of the rules and their importance in legal practice have led to the development of a number of excellent commentaries. The comprehensive treatises on federal practice, *Federal Practice and Procedure* and *Moore's Federal Practice*, both cover the rules in depth. *Federal Practice and Procedure* (1st–4th eds. 1969–date, available on Westlaw), often known by the names of its original authors, Wright & Miller, covers the Federal Rules of Civil Procedure, Criminal Procedure, Appellate

---

Bankruptcy Procedure, and a variety of other annual pamphlet editions are published for practitioners or as casebook supplements.

Procedure, and Evidence, discussing each rule's history, purpose, and application with copious footnotes to cases and other materials. It devotes 27 volumes just to the Rules of Civil Procedure. *Moore's Federal Practice* (3d ed. 1997–date, available on Lexis), devotes several volumes to rule-by-rule analyses of the Federal Rules of Civil Procedure, Criminal Procedure, and Appellate Procedure.

Other secondary sources cover specific subject areas and may be helpful for detailed research. For example, Mark S. Rhodes et al., *Orfield's Criminal Procedure Under the Federal Rules* (2d ed. 1985–date, available on Westlaw) is a multivolume treatise limited to federal criminal practice. It discusses the history of each rule's drafting, the law prior to its adoption, and judicial developments.

A number of works focus on the Federal Rules of Evidence, explaining the intent and application of each provision. The most frequently cited treatise is *Weinstein's Federal Evidence* (2d ed. 1997–date, available on Lexis). The first edition was written by Judge Jack B. Weinstein, one of the principal drafters of the rules, and Margaret A. Berger. Other multi-volume rule-by-rule analyses available in print and online include Michael H. Graham, *Handbook of Federal Evidence* (8th ed. 2016–date, available on Westlaw); Christopher B. Mueller & Laird C. Kirkpatrick, *Federal Evidence* (4th ed. 2013–date, available on Westlaw); and Stephen A. Saltzburg et al., *Federal Rules of Evidence Manual* (12th ed. 2019–date, available on Lexis).

Local Rules. Individual federal courts also have their own rules to supplement the national sets of rules. The Federal Rules of Civil Procedure and each of the other sets of national rules (except the Federal Rules of Evidence) provide that any federal court can establish rules for the conduct of its business, as long as they are not inconsistent with Acts of Congress or rules prescribed by the Supreme Court.[13]

Local court rules often detail procedural matters such as the time allowed to file papers, the format of documents, and the fees for filing various documents. Over the years, however, they have proliferated into an array of local requirements that commentators have called "byzantine" and that have resulted in a "balkanization" of federal procedure.[14] In addition to rules for specific districts, some

---

[13] FED. R. CIV. P. 83; FED. R. CRIM. P. 57; FED. R. APP. P. 47; FED. R. BANKR. P. 9029.

[14] *See, e.g.*, Gregory C. Sisk, *The Balkanization of Appellate Justice: The Proliferation of Local Rules in the Federal Circuits*, 68 U. COLO. L. REV. 1 (1997); Carl Tobias, *Local Federal Civil Procedure for the Twenty-First Century*, 77 NOTRE DAME L. REV. 533 (2002). Local rules have, however, been defended as "attractive—if not quite heroic." Samuel P. Jordan, *Local Rules and the Limits of Trans-Territorial Procedure*, 52 WM. & MARY L. REV. 415, 415 (2010).

individual judges also promulgate guidelines, in the form of standing orders, for the cases they hear. What this means in practical terms is that lawyers must be every bit as aware of local and judge-specific rules as they are of more general rules.

Federal law requires that each court's website provide access to local court rules and individual judges' rules.[15] Many court websites also include answers to frequently asked questions about filing requirements and trial procedures. Local court homepages are easily located by search, but links are also available through the U.S. Courts website (www.uscourts.gov).

The Supreme Court's rules, in addition to being available online from the Court (www.supremecourt.gov/filingandrules/), are also included in the *U.S. Code, USCA,* and *USCS,* in print and online.[16]

The local rules of the lower federal courts are also available from the major online platforms. In Lexis and Westlaw's directories, Court of Appeals rules are found with other federal materials while rules of U.S. District and Bankruptcy Courts are more likely to be located with state resources. The easiest way to find these rules on Westlaw is to type "Federal Local Court Rules" in the search box and choose from the list of states displayed. On either Lexis or Westlaw, typing "[State] court rules" in the search box will take you to the federal and state rules for the jurisdiction.

The rules for each of the Courts of Appeals are also published in *USCA, USCS,* and several other sources including court rules pamphlets published for individual states within each circuit, in some instances with annotations of court decisions applying the rules. Local U.S. District Court rules are also available in these pamphlets. Court of Appeals and District Court rules and standing orders from the entire country are published, unannotated, in a ten-volume looseleaf set, *Federal Local Court Rules* (4th ed. 2013–date, available on Westlaw). Rules and standing orders of individual judges are published in the three-volume *Directory of Federal Court Guidelines* (1996–date, also on Westlaw).

Citing references to federal court rules in Westlaw and Shepard's are similar to those for statutes, providing many more

---

[15] E-Government Act of 2002, § 205(a)(2)–(3), Pub. L. No. 107–347, 116 Stat. 2899, 2913 (codified at 44 U.S.C. § 3501 note).

[16] HeinOnline's U.S. Supreme Court Library has a bibliography of 45 pamphlets published between 1850 and 2019 that contain the *Rules of the Supreme Court of the United States,* as found in the holdings of the Library of the U.S. Supreme Court. This bibliography is described as "probably not complete, especially for the early years," but it provides a good starting point for researching the development of the rules and is accompanied by links to all rule adoptions and changes as published in the *United States Reports.*

references than the annotations. Both resources cover local rules as well as the national sets.

Sentencing Guidelines. The Federal Sentencing Guidelines are not court rules, but they occupy a similar position in the hierarchy of legal authorities. They were originally promulgated in 1987 by the U.S. Sentencing Commission, which was created by Congress as an independent agency within the judicial branch. Like court rules, guidelines take effect unless Congress expressly disapproves them. The sentencing guidelines are not published with the official *U.S. Code*, but the Commission (www.ussc.gov) publishes an annual *Guidelines Manual* in print and online.

Both *USCA* and *USCS* include the sentencing guidelines, accompanied by notes of court decisions and other references. Westlaw and Lexis add citing references to the annotations.

Federal Practice and Procedure and *Moore's Federal Practice* do not cover sentencing guidelines, but shorter works such as *Practice Under the Federal Sentencing Guidelines* (David Debold ed., 6th ed. 2019–date), and Thomas W. Hutchison et al., *Federal Sentencing Law and Practice* (annual), provide similar treatment, with extensive commentary and notes of court decisions applying the guidelines. Both of these are available on Westlaw. Professor Douglas A. Berman's blog Sentencing Law and Policy (sentencing.typepad.com) is an excellent free resource for current developments in this area.

(b) State Rules

There are significant differences in rules and procedures from state to state. These distinctions have decreased in recent decades as many states have adopted provisions modeled on the federal rules, particularly the Federal Rules of Evidence. If you know the relevant evidence rule in federal court, it is usually easy to find the comparable state provision.[17] Federal procedural rules are less likely than evidence rules to be mirrored in state court practice, though there are still significant similarities.[18]

Procedures in state courts are generally governed by a combination of statutory provisions and court rules. The rules are

---

[17] Rule-by-rule comparisons of federal and state evidence provisions are available in "Table of State and Military Adaptations of Federal Rules of Evidence," 6 WEINSTEIN'S FEDERAL EVIDENCE T-1 (2015, available on Lexis).

[18] John B. Oakley, *A Fresh Look at the Federal Rules in State Courts*, 3 NEV. L.J. 354 (2003). The author had surveyed the impact of the Federal Rules of Civil Procedure on state court procedures in the 1980s, in John B. Oakley & Arthur F. Coon, *The Federal Rules in State Courts: A Survey of State Court Systems of Civil Procedure*, 61 WASH. L. REV. 1367 (1986). Upon revisiting the issue, he found that the Federal Rules were "less influential in state courts than at anytime in the past quarter-century." 3 NEV. L.J. at 355.

usually included in the annotated state codes, accompanied by notes of relevant cases. The versions on Westlaw and Lexis include citing references as well. As in the federal courts, there may also be local and judge-specific rules on court websites.

Most states also have annual paperback volumes with rules and procedural statutes. Many of these publications are unannotated, but some contain useful case notes and comments by scholars or drafting committees. State court rules can also be found in annotated codes and in state-specific court rules pamphlets. More elaborate treatises on civil and criminal practice are also published in many jurisdictions. Like *Federal Practice and Procedure* or *Moore's Federal Practice*, the best of these provide a scholarly commentary on the rules and extensive analysis of relevant case law. Depending on the publisher, these works may be available on either Westlaw or Lexis.

State court websites generally have convenient access to rules and other procedural information. The National Center for State Courts' listing of court web sites (www.ncsc.org/information-and-resources/state-court-websites) is a convenient source for finding both appellate and trial state courts on the internet.

§ 13.2 CASE RECORDS

As soon as a case is initiated, the parties' lawyers and the court begin to submit documents, known as filings. Some of these filings are substantive, such as pretrial motions, supporting affidavits, and orders, while others are administrative in nature, such as scheduling notices for hearings or oral argument or trial dates. The initial access point for information about a case is its docket sheet, which lists these proceedings and documents in chronological order as they are filed.

For appellate cases, two types of documents are particularly informative for the purposes of legal research. Briefs are the written arguments by the attorneys for the parties on appeal, which contain citations to many relevant authorities. Records are documents from the lower court proceeding submitted as an appendix to the briefs, and which can include pleadings, motions, trial transcripts, and judgments. You can also learn a great deal about a case by reading oral argument transcripts, which are becoming easier to find for many jurisdictions.

(a) Dockets

Judicial opinions reflect just a fraction of the activity surrounding cases when it comes to the overall volume of litigation. Though some cases result in judges' opinions, such as a decision granting a motion for summary judgment, many matters are decided without a written opinion. Cases can be decided by jury verdict, summary disposition, or settlement agreement and voluntary dismissal. Some cases produce dozens of memoranda or briefs submitted to support or oppose motions before, during, and after trial, while others go to trial without any written submissions on points of law. A trial transcript, if available, can be an essential source of information. This complete record of activity can be found in a case's docket sheet.

In either trial or appellate court, a case generally begins with an initial filing such as a complaint or appeal. The court clerk assigns a case number or docket number, which is used to identify the case and its documents. The docket number usually appears at the beginning of a published decision and is the key to finding case documents. Docket numbers typically include the year the case was initially filed and often include letters indicating the type of case filed (e.g., CV for civil or CR for criminal).

There are a growing number of online sources for docket sheets, although you will not always be able to obtain every document listed on a docket. Federal dockets and case documents are generally easier to find online than state dockets and documents; very few dockets for cases before the 1990s are online (except for significant jurisdictions like the United States Supreme Court); and appellate dockets and their case documents are easier to track down online than sources from the trial level, particularly for state cases.

Supreme Court. The Supreme Court's website has docket information for current and recent cases since the beginning of the 2001 term (www.supremecourt.gov/docket/). The docket provides a chronological listing of documents filed and actions taken as well as contact information for the parties' attorneys. It includes links to the full text of briefs or other documents for more recent cases.

Information on the Supreme Court's docket is also available through *The United States Law Week: Supreme Court Today*, a newsletter on Bloomberg Law that publishes a record of proceedings and reports on arguments and other developments.[19]

Federal Courts. For recent cases in federal court, access to docket sheet information is generally available electronically. The federal courts' PACER (Public Access to Court Electronic Records) service covers the U.S. Courts of Appeals, District Courts, and

---

[19] *The United States Law Week* was published in print from 1933 to 2018 and included an annual Case Status Report listing cases by docket number and providing references to developments. These tables may still be useful sources of information for older cases.

Bankruptcy Courts.[20] The service has a central registration site (www.pacer.gov). This site includes a PACER Case Locator, an index-like tool that gives you some ability to search courts nationwide, but it does not include all data from court sites and has somewhat limited functionality. Each court has its own CM/ECF (Case Management/ Electronic Case Files) site. For the most accurate results, search each court's system separately.

With electronic filing of case documents now the norm in federal courts, most pleadings, motions, and orders in recent cases are available through PACER sites along with docket information. Cases can be found by docket number or by parties' or attorneys' names. Registration is required, and there is a per-page charge to view docket sheets or documents other than opinions.[21]

There are alternatives to PACER dockets and documents that are easier to navigate and more flexible than the official interface. Several are standalone databases. PacerPro (www.pacerpro.com) is one of the original alternative gateways to PACER with a more modern interface and improved searching options, but new competitors continue to join in providing this service, among them DocketBird (www.docketbird.com), Docket Alarm from Fastcase (www.docketalarm.com), and CourtDrive (www.courtdrive.com).

Other alternatives to PACER are part of larger platforms. Bloomberg Law, Lexis, and Westlaw all allow you to search PACER's information and to retrieve documents. When viewing a docket on Bloomberg Law, click on the "Update Docket" link to ensure you have the most current information from PACER. The full text of documents that have been downloaded through Bloomberg are searchable, making it easy to search for particular motions or arguments. If a document has not been downloaded into Bloomberg's

---

[20] The Federal Judicial Center launched PACER as a pilot program in 1989 in a few bankruptcy and district courts. Coverage expanded to additional bankruptcy and district courts in 1992. The CM/ECF system was introduced in 1998 and adopted by individual courts over the next few years. Coverage in PACER today still reflects this gradual implementation across jurisdictions.

[21] Fees not exceeding $30.00 per quarter are waived. Open-government activists have been working to make federal court records available online for free, through a browser extension called RECAP that archives documents that people download from PACER (free.law/recap). For a history of PACER fees, see Michael Lissner, *A Complete Chronology of PACER Fees and Policies*, FREE LAW PROJECT (Apr. 13, 2017) (free.law/ 2017/04/13/a-complete-chronology-of-pacer-fees-and-policies/) [https://perma.cc/S78T-WVXF].

PACER fees have long been the focus of discontent, and are the subject of litigation pending in the federal courts. *Nat'l Veterans Legal Servs. Program v. United States*, 291 F. Supp. 3d 123 (D.D.C. 2018), appeal pending, No. 19–1081 (Fed. Circ. 2018). Bipartisan bills have been introduced in both houses of Congress to eliminate fees for PACER records. *See, e.g.*, Electronic Court Records Reform Act of 2019, H.R. 1164 and S. 2064, 116th Cong. (2019).

system, you are limited to searching terms that appear on the docket sheet. Documents that have not already been downloaded, however, are available on request by any user for a fee, which is waived for most researchers using a law school subscription. Any document available online on PACER can be added to Bloomberg and will then become full-text searchable.

Illustration 13-2 shows the docket search screen on Bloomberg Law, including options to search by keyword, docket number, party name, filing type (e.g. complaint or motion to dismiss), and nature of suit (subject matter). Illustration 13-3 shows a docket on Bloomberg Law, listing the parties and attorneys and linking to each docket entry.

Westlaw and Lexis also have docket information drawn from PACER, with the major difference from Bloomberg Law currently being that law school users cannot request documents that have not already been requested by commercial subscribers. On Westlaw, docket sheets and other documents are available under the Filings tab accompanying many court opinions. Like Bloomberg Law, Westlaw dockets have "Update" links to retrieve the most current information from the official court systems. A separate Westlaw service, Court Express (courtexpress.westlaw.com), enhances coverage by giving subscribers the option to order retrieval of documents that are not available online.

Lexis added its formerly standalone product, CourtLink, to its main platform in 2019. CourtLink, accessed via the grid on the top left side of the homepage, allows you to search docket descriptions or documents themselves using terms and connectors. If you want to search docket descriptions and documents simultaneously, you are limited to natural language searching. CourtLink can be searched by keyword, docket number, party name, judge, attorney or firm, or case status. Docket updates can be requested by commercial subscribers, but law school users do not have the option to request updates.

Dockets can occasionally be found online for cases predating PACER and the CM/ECF systems introduced in the 1990s, but the documents that comprise the case are less frequently available, particularly for district courts. You must identify and locate the documents in print (their original format). The National Archives holds these records, which are stored at Federal Records Centers around the country. A listing of the location of case records is on the National Archives' court records pages (www.archives.gov/research/court-records).

Illustration 13-2. Bloomberg Law's docket search screen.

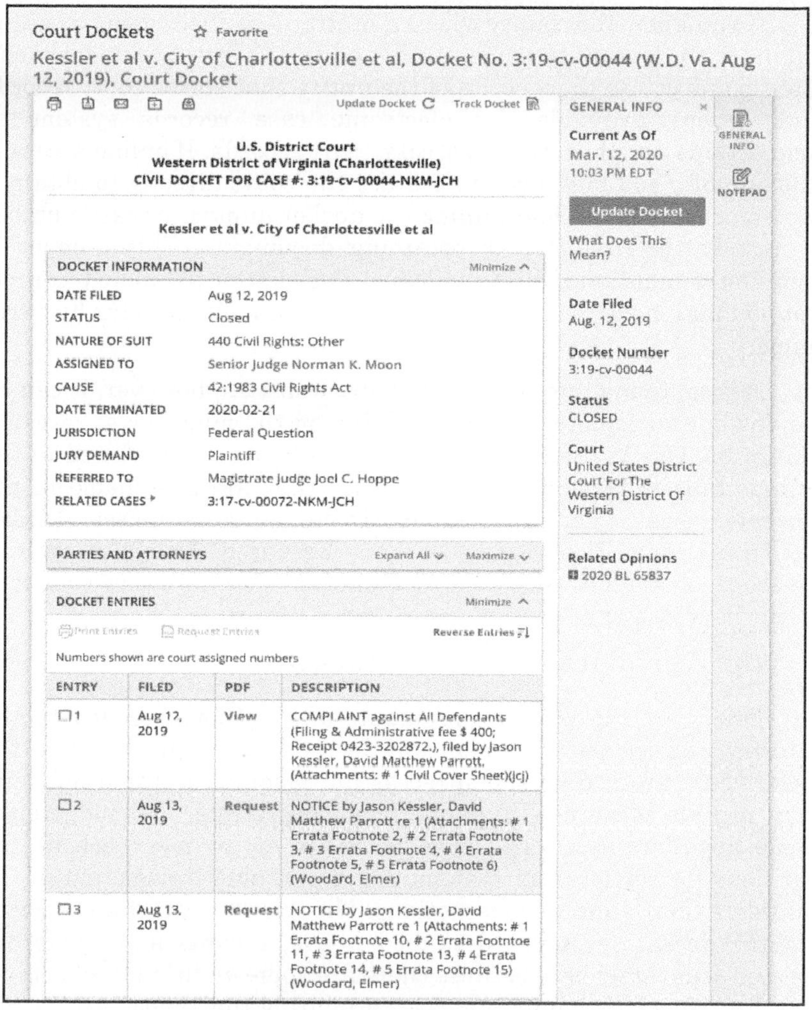

Court Dockets ☆ Favorite

Kessler et al v. City of Charlottesville et al, Docket No. 3:19-cv-00044 (W.D. Va. Aug 12, 2019), Court Docket

Update Docket Track Docket

U.S. District Court
Western District of Virginia (Charlottesville)
CIVIL DOCKET FOR CASE #: 3:19-cv-00044-NKM-JCH

Kessler et al v. City of Charlottesville et al

DOCKET INFORMATION Minimize

DATE FILED	Aug 12, 2019
STATUS	Closed
NATURE OF SUIT	440 Civil Rights: Other
ASSIGNED TO	Senior Judge Norman K. Moon
CAUSE	42:1983 Civil Rights Act
DATE TERMINATED	2020-02-21
JURISDICTION	Federal Question
JURY DEMAND	Plaintiff
REFERRED TO	Magistrate Judge Joel C. Hoppe
RELATED CASES	3:17-cv-00072-NKM-JCH

PARTIES AND ATTORNEYS Expand All Maximize

DOCKET ENTRIES Minimize

Print Entries Request Entries Reverse Entries

Numbers shown are court assigned numbers

ENTRY	FILED	PDF	DESCRIPTION
1	Aug 12, 2019	View	COMPLAINT against All Defendants (Filing & Administrative fee $ 400; Receipt 0423-3202872.), filed by Jason Kessler, David Matthew Parrott. (Attachments: # 1 Civil Cover Sheet)(jcj)
2	Aug 13, 2019	Request	NOTICE by Jason Kessler, David Matthew Parrott re 1 (Attachments: # 1 Errata Footnote 2, # 2 Errata Footnote 3, # 3 Errata Footnote 4, # 4 Errata Footnote 5, # 5 Errata Footnote 6) (Woodard, Elmer)
3	Aug 13, 2019	Request	NOTICE by Jason Kessler, David Matthew Parrott re 1 (Attachments: # 1 Errata Footnote 10, # 2 Errata Footntoe 11, # 3 Errata Footnote 13, # 4 Errata Footnote 14, # 5 Errata Footnote 15) (Woodard, Elmer)

GENERAL INFO

Current As Of
Mar. 12, 2020
10:03 PM EDT

Update Docket

What Does This Mean?

Date Filed
Aug. 12, 2019

Docket Number
3:19-cv-00044

Status
CLOSED

Court
United States District Court For The Western District Of Virginia

Related Opinions
2020 BL 65837

GENERAL INFO
NOTEPAD

Illustration 13-3. A U.S. District Court docket as displayed on Bloomberg Law.

State Courts. Dockets in state courts are less widely available than federal court dockets, and the documents comprising a case can be even more difficult to find. Many states do not have a centralized case management or electronic filing system across all counties. The National Center for State Courts (www.ncsc.org) maintains a Privacy/Public Access to Court Records site that has state-by-state links to sites, with brief annotations of contents.[22]

[22] For a discussion of problems in access to state court docket information, see Peter W. Martin, *Online Access to Court Records—From Documents to Data, Particulars to Patterns*, 53 VILL. L. REV. 855, 871–84 (2008).

If you know the county where a matter was filed, using a search engine with the county name, state, and the phrase "court clerk" can often point you to the website of the entity that stores court records and, where available, its electronic case records system or instructions on other ways to access court records. If online access is unavailable, you may need to contact the court directly to obtain a copy of a document. Determining the docket number or case number is usually the first step in obtaining documents. This number is sometimes mentioned in a published decision or secondary source, but you may have to ask the court clerk to consult an index by party name.

Before diving into individual court websites, however, it can be worthwhile to explore what is available on the major legal research platforms. On Westlaw, dockets and documents can be found in the Filings tab for appellate decisions, and they are searchable in the Dockets, Briefs, and Trial Court Documents databases. Lexis's CourtLink and Bloomberg's Dockets Research Tool also include coverage of state dockets and documents. For an elusive case, it might be worthwhile to compare all three resources.

(b) Appellate Briefs and Records

Briefs are the written arguments and authorities cited by the attorneys for the parties on appeal. Records are documents from the lower court proceeding submitted as an appendix to the briefs, and may include pleadings, motions, trial transcripts, and judgments. Some appellate cases also have petitions for review (such as the petitions for certiorari or statements of probable jurisdiction in the Supreme Court) and various motions. Though they can often be found via the docket resources described above, records and briefs are treated separately here because there are some additional collections that are especially helpful for cases predating the 1990s.

Supreme Court Briefs. As you might expect, briefs from United States Supreme Court cases are the most widely available. They are often the most voluminous as well. In addition to petitions for certiorari, oppositions to petitions, and the parties' briefs on the merits, many cases also have numerous filings by *amici curiae* ("friends of the court") supporting one side or the other.

In its first decade the Supreme Court adopted a rule requiring that counsel submit "a statement of the material points of the Case."[23] Very few briefs survive from the Court's early cases, even

---

[23] "Ordered, That the Gentlemen of the Bar be notified, that the Court will hereafter expect to be furnished with a statement of the material points of the Case, from the Counsel on each side of a Cause." Rules, Supreme Court of the United States, February Term, 1795, 3 U.S. (3 Dall.) 120, 120 (1795).

after the rule was strengthened in 1821 to require "a printed brief or abstract of the cause, containing . . . the points of law and fact intended to be presented at the argument."[24]

Some early briefs are available in the Court's case files at the National Archives, but for most cases none are available.[25] A microfilm collection, *Appellate Case Files of the Supreme Court of the United States, 1792–1831*, contains various handwritten and printed documents such as lower court judgments, exhibits, motions, correspondence, and other documents. Finding the correct reel for a specific case can be done using *Index to the Appellate Case Files of the Supreme Court of the United States, 1792–1908* (archive.org/details/scotusindexcards/), a digitized microfilm collection of 59,000 index cards providing file numbers.

Beginning in 1832, the availability of briefs gradually increases. Retrospective online coverage is offered by Gale's The Making of Modern Law: U.S. Supreme Court Records and Briefs, 1832–1978 (www.gale.com). This searchable collection contains over 200,000 documents, including appendices and other filings as well as petitions and briefs.[26] Illustration 13-4 shows the Advanced Search screen, with options to search by case name, date, or citation.

ProQuest Supreme Court Insight (supremecourt.proquest.com) covers more recent cases from 1975 through 2016. It includes dockets, certiorari petitions, amicus briefs, and joint appendices. In addition to options to search by case name, date, citation, and attorney, indexing allows you to search by subject, court of origin, or organization (allowing you to identify all amicus briefs filed by a specific interest group). ProQuest also offers a module allowing you to search denied petitions for certiorari from 1997 through the 2017–

---

[24] Rule XXX, General Rules, February Term, 1821, 19 U.S. (6 Wheat.) v, v (1821).

[25] Michael McReynolds, *Documentary Sources for the Study of U.S. Supreme Court Litigation: Part III—Materials in the National Archives*, 69 LAW LIBR. J. 448, 449 (1976). Another problem with early Supreme Court records is that the clerk's office had five fires in the 19th century, culminating in an 1898 gas explosion that destroyed many of the Court's original documents. James R. Browning & Bess Glenn, *The Supreme Court Collection at the National Archives*, 4 AM. J. LEGAL HIST. 241, 243 (1960). For more information on the use of briefs in the early Supreme Court, see R. Kirkland Cozine, *The Emergence of Written Appellate Briefs in the Nineteenth-Century United States*, 38 AM. J. LEGAL HIST. 482 (1994).

[26] The Gale collection is a valuable resource, but particularly for older cases the individual documents are not always well identified. Something listed as a 300-page Transcript of Record may actually be a 100-page record followed by the parties' briefs. You may need to download or page through the documents to be sure what's included.

Most large law libraries also have records and briefs back to 1832 in microform, and a few libraries around the country even have print collections. Libraries with Supreme Court records and briefs in paper or microform are listed geographically in MICHAEL WHITEMAN & PETER SCOTT CAMPBELL, A UNION LIST OF APPELLATE COURT RECORDS AND BRIEFS: FEDERAL AND STATE (2d ed. 2017).

18 term. Illustration 13-5 shows some of the documents available on ProQuest Supreme Court Insight for *United States v. Olson*, the case shown in illustrations at the beginning of Chapter 11.

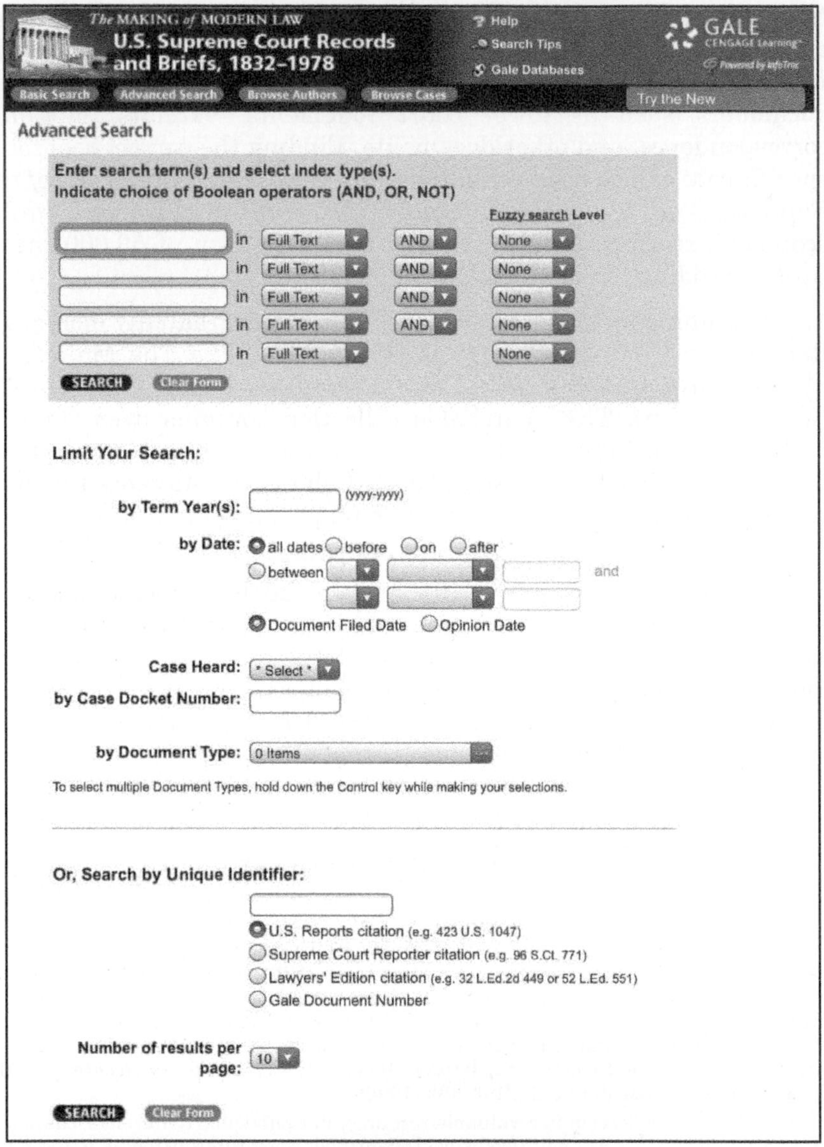

Illustration 13-4. The Advanced Search screen for The Making of Modern Law: U.S. Supreme Court Records and Briefs, 1832–1978.

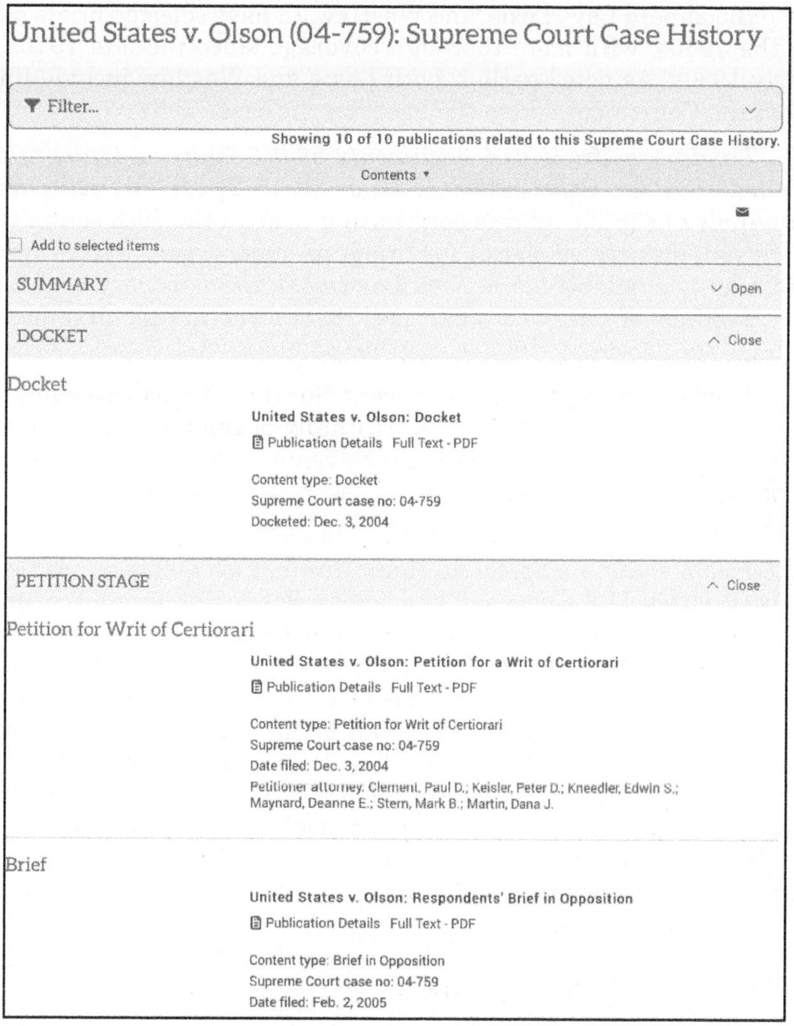

United States v. Olson (04-759): Supreme Court Case History

▼ Filter...   ⌄

Showing 10 of 10 publications related to this Supreme Court Case History.

Contents ▾

✉

☐ Add to selected items

SUMMARY   ⌄ Open

DOCKET   ⌃ Close

Docket

United States v. Olson: Docket
📄 Publication Details Full Text - PDF

Content type: Docket
Supreme Court case no: 04-759
Docketed: Dec. 3, 2004

PETITION STAGE   ⌃ Close

Petition for Writ of Certiorari

United States v. Olson: Petition for a Writ of Certiorari
📄 Publication Details Full Text - PDF

Content type: Petition for Writ of Certiorari
Supreme Court case no: 04-759
Date filed: Dec. 3, 2004
Petitioner attorney: Clement, Paul D.; Keisler, Peter D.; Kneedler, Edwin S.;
Maynard, Deanne E.; Stern, Mark B.; Martin, Dana J.

Brief

United States v. Olson: Respondents' Brief in Opposition
📄 Publication Details Full Text - PDF

Content type: Brief in Opposition
Supreme Court case no: 04-759
Date filed: Feb. 2, 2005

**Illustration 13-5. The record for a Supreme Court case on
ProQuest Supreme Court Insight.**

Bloomberg Law, Lexis, and Westlaw all have selected briefs back to the 1930s, with more thorough coverage since the late 1970s or early 1980s. As noted earlier, both Lexis and Westlaw include links from the Court's opinion to the briefs in the case.

Landmark Briefs and Arguments of the Supreme Court of the United States: Constitutional Law (1975–2011), which covers hundreds of significant decisions dating back to the 19th century, is a convenient printed source for briefs in major cases. Recent briefs are readily available online, but *Landmark Briefs* is very useful for its coverage of cases through the 1973 term in the first eighty volumes of the set.

Briefs in current and very recent Supreme Court cases are the easiest to access, because the Court finally began putting briefs and other filings online beginning in November 2017. These are not separately searchable but are linked from the docket entries.[27]

Other Appellate Courts. Records and briefs of the U.S. Courts of Appeals and state appellate courts are not as widely available as those from the U.S. Supreme Court, but recent cases are well covered. Westlaw has nationwide coverage of federal and state appellate courts, although the scope of its holdings varies by jurisdiction. Briefs as far back as the 1970s for some federal circuits are available, while for state courts the starting date can be as late as 2007. Lexis also has briefs as part of its "Briefs, Pleadings and Motions" collection. Coverage generally begins in 2000 but is not comprehensive. Illustration 13-6 shows the briefs and trial court pleadings available on Westlaw for *Harris v. Barefoot,* the North Carolina Court of Appeals case shown in Chapter 10.

---

[27] Some briefs are also available on non-court websites. Parties or amici curiae may post their briefs in major cases, and high-profile documents are often available from news websites. The Office of the Solicitor General's website (www.justice.gov/osg) has selected coverage of its briefs back to 1982.

Harris v. Barefoot

Court of Appeals of North Carolina. · August 3, 2010 · 206 N.C.App. 308 · 704 S.E.2d 282 (Approx. 6 pages)

| Document | **Filings (6)** | Negative Treatment (0) | History (7) | Citing References (14) | Table of Authorities |

Filings (6)   1-6   No items selected

Content types »

Appellate Court Documents	2
Trial Court Documents	4
All Results	6

Filter

Search within results

Title	PDF	Court	Date	Type
1. Defendant-Appellees' Brief	📄	N.C.App.	Jan. 20, 2010	Brief
Dorothy HARRIS, Plaintiff-Appellant, v. Clarence BAREFOOT, Lucia Castaldo, and Richard Clyde, Jr., Jointly and Severally, Defendants-Appellees. 2010 WL 371448				
2. Plaintiff-Appellant's Brief	📄	N.C.App.	Dec. 15, 2009	Brief
Dorothy HARRIS, Plaintiff-Appellant, v. Clarence BAREFOOT, Lucia Castaldo, and Richard Clyde, jointly and severally, Defendants-Appellees. 2009 WL 5128999				
3. Answer and Crossclaim	📄	N.C.Super.	Oct. 13, 2008	Pleading
Dorothy HARRIS, Plaintiff, v. Clarence BAREFOOT, Lucia Castado, and Richard Clyde, Jr., jointly and severally, Defendants. 2008 WL 8183529				
4. Complaint	📄	N.C.Super.	July 02, 2008	Pleading
Dorothy HARRIS, Plaintiff, v. Clarence BAREFOOT, Lucia Castado, and Richard Clyde, Jr., jointly and severally, Defendant. 2008 WL 8183528				
5. Memorandum of Law in Support of Defendant Castaldo's Motion for Summary Judgment	📄	N.C.Super.	May 15, 2009	Motion
Dorothy HARRIS, Plaintiff, v. Clarence BAREFOOT, Lucia Castaldo, and Richard Clyde, Jr., Jointly and Severally, Defendants. 2009 WL 7234624				

Illustration 13-6. Briefs and trial court pleadings on Westlaw.

Some court websites also provide access to recent briefs. As already noted, PACER has federal court briefs and other documents as well as docket information. Briefs in recent cases for some state appellate courts are available online from the court or from a law school within the jurisdiction.[28] For most courts, print appellate records and briefs can also be found in local law libraries within the circuit or state. In some instances, however, it may be necessary to contact the court or a judicial records center to obtain copies.[29]

---

[28] Sites for briefs are listed in Michael Whiteman, *Free and Fee-Based Appellate Court Briefs Online* (iti.bz/os111213), an online supplement to Carol Ebbinghouse, *Nontraditional Legal Research: Appellate Briefs*, ONLINE SEARCHER, Nov./Dec. 2013, at 38.

[29] WHITEMAN & CAMPBELL, *supra* note 26, has information on the scope and format of each library's holdings and its lending policy, as well as contact information for libraries and court clerks.

Trial Courts. Westlaw's Trial Court Documents database and Lexis's Briefs, Pleadings and Motions database provide extensive collections of court filings. Coverage is quite thorough after 2000 or so, with selected older documents also available. You can search pleadings, motions, and other filings from all available courts, or focus in on individual courts, specific types of filings, and particular subject areas.

(c) Oral Arguments and Transcripts of Proceedings

While documents such as motions and briefs provide much insight into court proceedings, not everything transpires on paper. The examination of witnesses and the discussion of legal topics between lawyers and judges can also be valuable sources of information. On the appellate level, oral arguments are fairly standard: lawyers present their cases and answer questions from judges. Trial courts have a much more diverse range of proceedings from arguments on motions through cross-examination to closing arguments.

Transcripts of arguments in the U.S. Supreme Court are relatively straightforward to find, but it can be more difficult for other courts. For cases since around 2000, video or audio recordings of proceedings may be available. Those seeking transcripts for lower level courts may have to purchase a copy from the court reporter if a recording or transcript is not available online.

Supreme Court. Oral argument in the Supreme Court predates the filing of written briefs. Arguments were summarized by the reporters in the early volumes of the *United States Reports*, and arguments in a case could last for days.[30] Today argument is generally limited by rule to thirty minutes per side.[31]

Transcripts of Supreme Court oral arguments have been officially prepared on a regular basis since 1968, and earlier transcripts for some cases back to 1935 were prepared privately by shorthand reporters. The Supreme Court website has transcripts of arguments the same day that cases are heard, with older arguments beginning with the 2000 term. Microform collections begin with the 1953 term, and online coverage starts in 1979 (Lexis) and 1990 (Westlaw).[32] Arguments in major cases, if transcribed, are available

---

[30] Arguments in *The Telephone Cases*, 126 U.S. 1 (1888), stretched over twelve days from January 24 to February 8, 1887.

[31] SUP. CT. R. 28.

[32] More than 100 pre-1953 transcripts are held by the Supreme Court Library. Alice I. Youmans et al., *Questions and Answers*, 78 LAW LIBR. J. 203, 206 (1986).

in *Landmark Briefs and Arguments of the Supreme Court of the United States: Constitutional Law.*[33]

The National Archives has audio records of oral arguments back to 1955, although some of its tapes have deteriorated and are not available to the public.[34] Oyez (www.oyez.org) has recorded arguments in several hundred of these older cases. It continues to provide audio recordings of current cases, along with case summaries and other Supreme Court resources.

When full Supreme Court argument transcripts are unavailable, excerpts can often be found in contemporary newspaper accounts. One of the most thorough sources for information on arguments back to the 1930s is the discontinued print version of *The United States Law Week*, which covered about two dozen arguments in depth each term.

Other Courts. Audio files of oral arguments for U.S. Courts of Appeals can generally be found on each court's website. The Third and Ninth Circuits both have coverage back to 2000, but most of the circuits' collections start in the late 2000s. Westlaw includes transcripts of oral arguments for the Seventh, Eighth, and Ninth Circuits (back to 2000 or 2001) in its database of Trial Transcripts and Oral Arguments.

State court oral arguments are rarely transcribed, but most states' appellate courts have audio or video recordings of proceedings. An increasing number of courts are making these recordings available on their websites. LexisNexis's Courtroom Cast (courtroom cast.lexisnexis.com) allows subscribers to watch trial and appellate proceedings. You can browse by case name, jurisdiction, judge, practice area, industry, law firm, lawyer, or party.

(d) Jury Verdicts and Settlements

As noted earlier, the vast majority of all court proceedings do not result in written opinions nor have extensive files of motions and briefs from which to glean information. Some cases proceed to trial and are decided by jury verdicts, while others are settled out of court.

---

[33] One frustration with older oral argument transcripts is that justices were traditionally not identified by name but only by the word "Question." Some lawyers who frequently argued before the Court made a point of prefacing their answer with the name of the justice, but in many instances the identity of the speaker is unclear from the transcript. This changed in September 2004 when the Court decided that transcripts would begin finally to identify justices by name.

[34] "About the Audio," OYEZ, www.oyez.org/about-audio/ [https://perma.cc/GGM4-4EXH].

Very little information on these cases may be available, sometimes to the public's detriment.[35]

For some cases, however, sources exist. Information on trial verdicts and damage awards, primarily for various types of tort litigation, is available in services known as *verdict reporters*. These generally provide a brief summary of the case's facts and claims, list attorneys and expert witnesses for each side, and report the resulting verdict. The account of a case rarely provides much detail, but in the absence of any published opinions it may be the best available record of a case's background and outcome. Several verdict reporters are published for specific states, and national services such as VerdictSearch (verdictsearch.com) are available. Westlaw and Lexis both have Jury Verdict and Settlements collections, which can be searched generally or limited to specific jurisdictions.

§ 13.3 INFORMATION ON COURTS AND JUDGES

At the trial stage of litigation, no single person is more important to the outcome than the judge (with the exception, perhaps, of the court clerk). Unlike in intermediate appeals, where the identity of judges on a panel will likely not be known in advance, trial matters are assigned to a judge or magistrate soon after the pleadings are filed. In federal courts, judges are appointed to life terms, which means those judges generally serve for a long time and a good deal of information about their rulings can accumulate. Newer commercial tools offering automated analysis of this aggregated data and more traditional, time-tested tools like biographical directories seek to equip lawyers with the information about judges they may need to craft the strongest and most targeted arguments on behalf of their clients. That said, a thorough understanding of procedural and substantive law as it applies to the specific facts of a case remains, and likely will remain, the best "tool" available to any advocate.

(a) Analytics

New technologies can provide detailed information about the practices of specific judges. Several of these resources are available from the major online platforms, but smaller companies are developing them as well. These tools are still in their early stages, and each is only as good as the quality and sample size of data from which it draws. As analytics tools develop across legal practice—

---

[35] *See, e.g.*, Lori E. Andrus, *Rein In Secret Settlements*, TRIAL, Oct. 2018, at 40; Laurie Kratky Doré, *Secrecy by Consent: The Use and Limits of Confidentiality in the Pursuit of Settlement*, 74 NOTRE DAME L. REV. 283 (1999); Rhonda Wasserman, *Secret Class Action Settlements*, 31 REV. LITIG. 889 (2012).

including in transactional law or practice management contexts—the ways in which they are marketed, sold, and used may change significantly.[36]

Resources such as Judicial Analytics (Bloomberg Law), Legal Analytics and Lex Machina (Lexis), Litigation Analytics (Westlaw), Monitor Suite (Thomson Reuters), Docket Alarm (Fastcase), and Docket Navigator offer reports on judges' litigation history, such as how they have ruled on particular motions and the percentage of their decisions that have been affirmed or reversed. All of these resources use data from PACER, the federal courts' electronic filing system, so most of them are limited to federal court judges. Differences in the software used for each product and inaccurate data from PACER mean that no two products will produce identical reports.[37]

Two other tools, Westlaw's Precedent Analytics and Lexis's Context, analyze the language in judicial opinions and produce reports identifying the opinions, jurisdictions, courts, and judges most cited by a given judge. Searching by judge and narrowing by topic or motion type are your best approach for using these tools. Precedent Analytics can be accessed as one tab of Westlaw's Litigation Analytics tool. Context is available to law school subscribers through Lexis or to other subscribers as a standalone product. Because these tools do not rely on PACER data, they can be used to analyze most state appellate-level judges as well as federal judges.

These analytics tools are frequently touted as revealing judges' hidden biases and providing concrete data that can back up an attorney's impression regarding judges' decision-making. Remember, however, the framework within which these resources operate. First, each resource identifies patterns based on the data available in the particular system. That data may be flawed, which will naturally result in some errors in the analytical tools' output. Second, *stare decisis* dictates in large part which courts and opinions are binding and therefore must be cited by a lower court. Rather than revealing

---

[36] "Legal analytics" as a term can have a broad set of meanings, and legal technology companies market many types of products using it. While this section introduces tools designed with the need of litigators or researchers in need of case information in mind, you should be aware that other uses of analytics—essentially, software designed to make probabilistic inferences from datasets—are becoming widespread in legal practice and law firm management.

[37] For an overview of the variations among the leading tools, see Bob Ambrogi, *Legal Analytics Products Deliver Widely Divergent Results, Study Shows*, LAWSITES (Nov. 25, 2019), (www.lawsitesblog.com/2019/11/legal-analytics-products-deliver-widely-divergent-results-study-shows.html) [https://perma.cc/GCK9-RY3H].

judicial bias, then, the resources may simply be providing a visualization of precedent.

Illustration 13-7 shows Westlaw's analytics report for the Hon. Richard A. Elmore, the North Carolina Court of Appeals judge who wrote the opinion in *Harris v. Barefoot*. Charts in the illustration show the percentage of times Judge Elmore admitted challenged expert testimony and the percentage of times his opinions were affirmed on appeal.

Illustration 13-7. Judicial analytics information on Westlaw.

(b) Directories

Court directories provide contact information for clerks' offices, and some include judges' biographical data. This can be useful for litigants appearing before a particular judge or panel, and for law students applying for clerkships after graduation.[38]

Court websites, accessible through portals such as the directories on the U.S. Courts and National Center for State Courts websites, usually include judges' names and contact data as well as some brief biographical information.

Court sites, however, often have less information than is available through unofficial directories. *Almanac of the Federal Judiciary* (almanacofthefederaljudiciary.com), also available on Westlaw, has detailed biographical information on federal judges, including annotated listings of noteworthy rulings, summaries of media coverage, and anonymous quotations by lawyers evaluating judges' abilities and temperaments. In the print looseleaf version, updated three times a year, volume 1 covers district, magistrate, and bankruptcy judges, and volume 2 covers Supreme Court justices and circuit judges.

The American Bench is the most comprehensive biographical source, covering almost every federal and state judge in the United States. It includes an alphabetical index of all judges listed. Leadership Connect's *Judicial Yellow Book* (www.leadershipconnect.io) has basic biographical information for federal judges and state appellate judges, as well as listings of court personnel such as clerks and staff attorneys. Basic contact information for judges, clerks, and other court personnel is available in *BNA's Directory of State and Federal Courts, Judges, and Clerks* (available on Bloomberg Law), *Federal-State Court Directory*, and *Directory of State Court Clerks & County Courthouses*.

Contact information for tribal courts is available in April Schwartz & Mary Jo B. Hunter, *United States Tribal Courts Directory* (4th ed. 2011), and online through the Tribal Court Clearinghouse (www.tribal-institute.org). The American Bar Association's *Directory of Minority Judges of the United States* (4th ed. 2008) also includes tribal judges, as well as African-American, Asian/Pacific Island, Hispanic, and Native American judges.

Sometimes information is needed about a judge who was involved in an older case or who sat on a particular court. If only the

---

[38] For students seeking clerkships with new judges, and for others monitoring the judicial appointment process, Leadership Connect has a website (www.leadership connect.io/judicial-nominations/) with information on recent nominations and confirmations.

last name at the head of an opinion is known, the first step may be to determine a judge's full name. This can be found in tables in the front of most reporter volumes. Since 1882, for example, the *Federal Reporter* has listed the sitting federal judges, with footnotes indicating any deaths, retirements, or appointments since the previous volume. Similar listings appear in each of the West regional reporters and in most official state reporters.

Biographies of many appellate judges can be found in standard sources such as *American National Biography* (1999, with 2002 and 2005 supps.) (www.anb.org), *The African American National Biography* (2008, with 2013 supp.), or *Who Was Who in America* (1943–date). The Federal Judicial Center (www.fjc.gov/history/judges) maintains a Biographical Directory of Federal Judges, with information on all life-tenured federal judges since 1789. Entries include links to information about manuscript sources and lists of more extensive biographical sources, if available. The website also has histories of individual circuit and district courts, listing all judges chronologically. A print version, *Biographical Directory of the Federal Judiciary, 1789–2000*, was published in 2001 and also includes information on the history of each circuit and district court.[39]

---

[39] Biographical information on former judges can often be found in tributes published in reporter volumes upon their retirement or death. For tributes to federal judges published through 2000, see Barbara L. Fritschel, *An Index to Special Court Sessions in West's Federal Reporters*, 93 LAW LIBR. J. 109 (2001).

Part V

ADVANCED RESEARCH AREAS

Chapter 14

PRACTICE MATERIALS

Table of Sections

Thus far, we have discussed secondary sources, which provide commentary on the law, and primary authorities, which are the law. Nearly every legal research problem can be thoroughly investigated using these types of sources and the strategies associated with them. But there is another category of useful legal resources, practice materials, which can make your work more efficient. Practice materials focus in greater depth on specific areas of law and the tasks that lawyers practicing in those areas regularly perform. This chapter and the next describe a range of resources for litigators and transactional lawyers.

This chapter begins with a discussion of topical services, sometimes called looseleafs, and their modern iteration: practice centers (which are also addressed more fully in Chapter 15). Topical services combine primary and secondary authorities, including recent developments, into convenient one-stop resources in heavily regulated practice areas. We then describe practice manuals and handbooks, which are available in a wider array of practice areas and can be used as a quick reference or as an initial step in your research.

Forms and pattern jury instructions, materials that all lawyers should be familiar with because they take some of the guesswork out of completing repetitive lawyering tasks, are discussed next. Finally, we cover how to research your ethical obligations as a lawyer. Resources specifically relating to transaction-oriented practice areas are discussed in Chapter 15.

§ 14.1 TOPICAL SERVICES AND CURRENT AWARENESS

Researching developments in heavily regulated areas of law using the resources discussed to this point can be cumbersome both because of the volume of information available and the frequency with which it is updated. It can require consulting secondary sources, statutes, regulations, agency websites, and judicial decisions. Legal publishers recognize the amount of effort that this multifaceted research can demand. Publishers also recognize that in legal practice, time is money, and that lawyers are willing to spend a good deal of money on products that make their research easier and less time-consuming. Topical services are publishers' answer to this demand.

(a) Topical Services

A *topical service*, also known as a looseleaf, is a frequently updated resource that compiles the statutes, regulations, administrative decisions, court decisions, and other materials in a focused area of law, and presents them in a cohesive manner accompanied by commentary or analysis. The term "looseleaf" comes from the traditional manner of print publication and supplementation in binders, but most modern looseleaf services are available online as well as in print. In this section, we use the terms "looseleaf service" and "topical service" interchangeably, though looseleafs generally refer to print publications and topical services to their online counterparts.

Looseleaf services have long been major research tools for specialists in areas such as securities regulation or tax law, because they coordinate and explain such a broad range of resources. They continue to have value for researchers trying to make sense of complex areas of practice. Not all looseleaf services cover topics with extensive administrative law sources, but those services that provide convenient access to regulations and administrative decisions are particularly valuable because they integrate the resources in ways that official websites cannot.

The first looseleaf services were issued shortly before World War I to facilitate research in the new federal income tax law. By the 1930s other services had developed in public law areas where government regulation was the central focus of legal development, such as antitrust, labor law, and securities regulation. Services are now also published in numerous other heavily regulated areas such as banking, environmental protection, health care, and product safety.[1]

There are several ways to determine whether there is a looseleaf service for a particular area of law. Lawyers or professors specializing in a field can provide helpful advice, and references to services may appear in law review articles and cases. The annual directory *Legal Looseleafs: Electronic and Print* (www.infosourcespub.com) lists over 3,000 publications, with notes of online availability and a subject index. In addition to regularly updated services, however, it also includes numerous other publications that are supplemented annually or not at all. In this volume, the Appendix includes selected coverage of looseleaf and topical services in fields of major interest.

Print services are the format most likely to be available to public law library patrons, but many lawyers and other researchers rely on online topical services. Keyword searching provides more flexibility than indexes, and hypertext links allow you to move conveniently back and forth between documents. Major platforms for topical services include Bloomberg Law (www.bloomberglaw.com), Thomson Reuters Checkpoint (checkpoint.riag.com), and Wolters Kluwer Cheetah (wkcheetah.com).

Topical services cover a wide range of subjects, and the methods of access and organization vary according to the nature of the primary sources and the characteristics of the legal field. In areas where a major set of statutes dominates the legal order, services are usually arranged by code section. In the major tax services, for example, each section of the Internal Revenue Code is followed by excerpts from legislative history documents, regulations, and references to court decisions and Internal Revenue Service documents. Other services are organized more broadly by subject.

Most print looseleaf services are updated by adding and replacing individual pages throughout the set, so that the text is kept current without the need for separate supplements. To help identify specific references as page numbers change, many services assign *paragraph numbers* to each section of material, a practice that is carried over to online topical services. A "paragraph" in this sense can vary in length from a few sentences to several pages. Each court decision, for example, is assigned one paragraph number and retains this number no matter how many new pages are added to the service. Paragraph numbers are generally used in indexes and cross-

---

[1] For a history of the looseleaf form of publication and the administrative state and technological innovations leading to its ascendancy in legal research, see Howard T. Senzel, *Looseleafing the Flow: An Anecdotal History of One Technology for Updating*, 44 AM. J. LEGAL HIST. 115 (2000).

references, and they are the designations by which most looseleaf services are cited.[2]

A typical service includes several types of indexes. The general or *topical index* provides detailed subject access. *Finding lists* provide direct references to statutes, regulations, or cases by their citations. These can be particularly useful in searching for numerically designated agency materials, such as IRS rulings or SEC releases.[3]

Detailed instructions, often entitled "How to Use This Reporter" or "About This Publication," are frequently provided at the beginning of the first volume of a print looseleaf service or near the top of the table of contents online. A few moments of orientation in these instructions can save you considerable time and frustration, as a service may include features that appear confusing at first but are very useful to the experienced researcher.

Many specialized looseleaf and topical services provide subject access to their cases through digests of some sort. These digests usually include references to administrative agency decisions as well as court decisions. Some of these digests use numerical frameworks, similar to West's Key Number System but focusing on one area of law, while others are arranged by code or rule section.

While using looseleafs in print or online can be challenging for a novice researcher, learning the value of resources in a specialized area of law is one part of achieving expertise in that area. Moreover, developing experience with these resources will ultimately make your research more efficient.

(b) Practice Centers

The primary way that legal publishers have adapted their practice materials to online research is not through the creation of more topical services, but through the organization of resources (including topical services) into *practice centers*. Practice centers tend to be more approachable and broader in coverage than online topical services.

Platforms like Bloomberg Law and Wolters Kluwer's Cheetah use practice centers as the primary means of organizing certain resources. Bloomberg Law has practice centers for health law, technology and telecommunications law, and privacy and data

---

[2] THE BLUEBOOK: A UNIFORM SYSTEM OF CITATION R. 19.1(c) (21st ed. 2020); ALWD GUIDE TO LEGAL CITATION R. 24.1(e) (6th ed. 2017).

[3] Another device used in some services is the *cumulative index*. This is not a subject index but a tool providing cross-references from the main body of the service to current material. Under listings by paragraph number, cumulative indexes update each topic with leads to new materials that have not yet been incorporated into the main discussion.

security law, among many other more traditional transactional areas. Cheetah has practice centers addressing human resources law, the law governing pensions, and products liability, along with ones devoted to more traditional transactional areas as well.

The value of a practice center is that it tends to gather a platform's resources on a particular legal practice area, including its topical services and practice manuals, alongside links to primary law. Bloomberg Law's Environmental & Safety practice center contains links to various secondary sources, including manuals and news sources, and to agency documents. Cheetah's Energy & Environment practice center likewise contains a variety of secondary and primary authorities relevant to a practitioner working in those areas. When topical services exist, they are included within the practice center covering their topic.[4]

(c) Legal News Sources

Practicing lawyers must keep aware of developments in their areas of practice.[5] They must maintain current knowledge of new court decisions, pending legislation, and agency announcements, as well as changes in the political, financial, or business world.

Current awareness also serves another purpose. Individual research assignments can build your expertise on specific questions, but they don't give you a broad overview of an area of law. Only by reading about new developments on a regular basis will you develop the confidence that you're seeing the big picture and that your knowledge has no significant gaps. If you are new to a practice area, find out what senior attorneys read on a daily or weekly basis and sign up to receive these publications. If you will be working with a particular industry, reading its trade or professional journals will

---

[4] Lexis and Westlaw also have groupings of material by practice area or subject matter. These groupings have various labels designating them as collections of helpful resources on particular topics or focused on particular practice areas. While they are like the practice centers described in this section, they tend to be more generalized collections of resources rather than attempts to mirror the ways looseleaf services have evolved over the years.

[5] *See* MODEL RULES OF PROF'L CONDUCT R. 1.1 cmt. 8 (2020) ("To maintain the requisite knowledge and skill, a lawyer should keep abreast of changes in the law and its practice, including the benefits and risks associated with relevant technology, engage in continuing study and education and comply with all continuing legal education requirements to which the lawyer is subject.").

Current awareness demands can undoubtedly be stressful. *See* Steven Keeva, *The Joy of Not Knowing*, LAW PRAC. MGMT., Jan./Feb. 2000, at 46, 46 ("The amount of law the average lawyer is required to know these days seems to proliferate like some mutant culture spilling from legislative and judicial petri dishes. And keeping up with clients' businesses in today's nanosecond environment demands constant vigilance. Each day there's more to know, and feeling responsible for knowing it all creates anxiety and a sense of depletion.").

help you communicate with your clients and anticipate their concerns.

There are several approaches to keeping on top of current activities and new developments in the law, including legal and general-interest newspapers, newsletters, and blogs. Using features like WestClip and Lexis Alerts, you can set up automated searches that will run regularly and notify you by e-mail if a search retrieves new documents matching your criteria. Similarly, you can use the free alerting features of major search engines like Google Alerts (www.google.com/alerts) to automatically search the web for specific terms. Many law firms use subscription resources such as Manzama (www.manzama.com) or Vable (www.vable.com) to create customized current awareness content for their attorneys.

News about the legal profession is available from a number of daily or weekly newspapers. Legal newspapers often cover developing topics and decisions of lower courts that may not be reported elsewhere. They also contain court calendars and legal announcements that are required by statute or court order to be published in local newspapers.

The articles and essays published in legal newspapers can be hard to track down, but many newspaper websites now have searchable archives, available free or by subscription. LegalTrac includes indexing coverage of several legal newspapers, including *Chicago Daily Law Bulletin, Los Angeles Daily Journal, National Law Journal,* and *New York Law Journal.* Lexis has full-text coverage of *National Law Journal, New York Law Journal,* and several state *Lawyers Weekly* newspapers.

Legal newspapers across the country are listed by state in *Legal Researcher's Desk Reference* and *Legal Information Buyer's Guide & Reference Manual.* Both lists indicate frequency of publication and provide contact information and URLs. Each includes a few titles omitted by the other.

Two of the leading internet sources for current legal news are law.com (www.law.com), with stories from *National Law Journal* and several regional newspapers, and JURIST (www.jurist.org), supported by the University of Pittsburgh School of Law.

In addition to news sources covering legal developments generally, numerous more specific sources are available in topical areas. Most of these are available online with e-mail or RSS notification of new developments.

Bloomberg is a major publisher of legal news on its Bloomberg Law platform. Its *United States Law Week,* for example, reports weekly not only on the Supreme Court, but also on new court decisions and legislative, regulatory, and professional developments. Bloomberg also publishes online newsletters in over two dozen subject areas, most of which are updated daily.

Law360 (www.law360.com) is another major provider of online legal newsletters, with daily updates in more than sixty subject areas. Law360 claims to report on every major litigation development in the U.S. federal district courts and every major initiative by federal and state legislatures. Its stories are available to subscribers directly and through Lexis.

Numerous additional current awareness newsletters are published online and in print. Specialized newsletters often have a limited circulation and can be hard to find in academic or public law libraries, but they may be the best available sources for information about newly developing areas of law. Newsletters are often the forum through which practitioners in very specialized areas share information and documents. A newsletter may include copies of pleadings or other trial court documents as well as articles on recent developments.

Several newsletter publishers make their products available through Westlaw or Lexis. Westlaw's coverage includes several dozen "Westlaw Journals" and Andrews Publications newsletters, some on specific topics of litigation such as nursing homes or toxic torts and others on broader areas such as antitrust or employment. Lexis has dozens of Mealey's Litigation Reports files on specific litigation topics from antidepressant drugs to welding rods. A general search in either platform will include newsletter results in Secondary Sources/Legal Newspapers & Newsletters (Westlaw) or Legal News (Lexis).

Numerous law firms produce newsletters for their clients and other readers, often with useful information about developing areas of law. They are generally available through law firm websites, and can be identified through topical browsing or keyword searches in resources such as Mondaq (www.mondaq.com), a compendium of information from accountants, law firms, and consulting firms.

You can identify available newsletters in a subject area in the annual *Legal Newsletters: Electronic and Print* (www.infosources pub.com), which describes more than 2,200 newsletters and has information about subscription prices and internet access. A subject index provides topical access to its listings.

Blogs are another major vehicle for timely dissemination of information and opinion. Law blogs (sometimes called "blawgs") are written on a variety of topics, ranging from general ruminations on legal issues such as Balkinization (balkin.blogspot.com) to more focused resources such as Lawfare (www.lawfareblog.com) or IPWatchdog (www.ipwatchdog.com). Some blogs have become leading sources of current information. SCOTUSblog (www. scotusblog.com), for example, often is the first available source with breaking news about the Supreme Court. Others are major sources for the exchange of new ideas in legal scholarship.[6]

Several directories of legal blogs are available. Two of the most extensive, both in blogs covered and in subject categories, are the ABA Journal Blawg Directory (www.abajournal.com/blawgs) and Justia Blawg Search (blawgsearch.justia.com). Both sites have samples of recent postings, links to the blog sites, and search engines for searching blog postings. Other forms of social media such as Twitter can also be used to monitor breaking news in the legal world.[7]

E-mail listservs and discussion groups provide another effective way to keep on top of developments in a particular area and can also be used to seek assistance with difficult research issues. Some lists disseminate information from organizations or government agencies, while others are designed for specialists in an area to share news and ideas. Posing questions to a list often yields results that would otherwise elude most researchers. Chances are that some list subscriber may be able to help with a thorny legal issue or can identify a source for an obscure document. Older messages to a list, if available in a searchable internet archive, may form a valuable repository of information in the area.

§ 14.2 MANUALS, FORMS, AND JURY INSTRUCTIONS

Practice manuals, forms, and jury instructions can be indispensable in the work of an attorney. Because aspects of legal practice are repetitive and some tasks must be done regularly, these kinds of resources have long been mainstays of American law publishing. Practice manuals and handbooks contain short explanations of legal doctrine or processes, often alongside aids like forms and checklists. Some publications and databases specialize in forms, whether for a particular area of practice or jurisdiction. Jury instructions can help at trial, and can also be used to shore up your understanding of the law.

---

[6] *See* Symposium, *Bloggership: How Blogs Are Transforming Legal Scholarship*, 84 WASH. U.L. REV. 1025 (2006).

[7] *See, e.g.*, Tom Gaylord, *Using Twitter to Keep Up with the Law*, 101 ILL. B.J. 590 (2013).

(a) Practice Manuals and Handbooks

Practice manuals can be somewhat difficult to identify for those unused to working with them. A good strategy is to look for the words "manual," "handbook," or "deskbook" in the title. (Deskbooks are so called because they are marketed as being so convenient and so regularly consulted as to occupy a place on a lawyer's desk. Likewise, benchbooks occupy a place on a judge's bench.) These kinds of resources are usually published in a single volume, or in a set of two or three volumes. They tend to be organized by the order in which an attorney might be working through a client's issue. Works on real estate law, for instance, often start with information on purchase-and-sale contracts, proceed to aspects of due diligence, and end with information on closings.

Like many other publications, practitioner-focused works like manuals and handbooks are being adapted into more flexible online formats. Practical Law, a Westlaw resource discussed more fully in Chapter 15, provides guides, checklists, and updates in over a dozen specialized areas such as antitrust, corporate law, and estate planning. Bloomberg Law's Practitioner Tools (also covered in Chapter 15) likewise provide new ways to find, use, and apply content previously distributed in print publications.

Practice manuals can vary greatly between jurisdictions, and a state-specific research guide can provide valuable details and information on sources. Law library websites often have guidance on legal research issues in their home jurisdictions, so browsing these libraries' websites may also yield useful insights. More in-depth guides are published in print for most states, and cover sources of primary law as well as specialized secondary sources like practice manuals. A series of research guides by Carolina Academic Press now covers more than thirty states.[8] Hein publishes guides for several states, and others are published by state continuing legal education entities.[9]

---

[8] States covered in the series include Arizona, Arkansas, California, Colorado, Connecticut, Florida, Georgia, Idaho, Illinois, Iowa, Kansas, Kentucky, Louisiana, Massachusetts, Michigan, Minnesota, Mississippi, Missouri, New York, North Carolina, North Dakota, Ohio, Oklahoma, Oregon, Pennsylvania, Tennessee, Texas, Washington, West Virginia, Wisconsin, and Wyoming. See the publisher's website (www.cap-press.com/p/lrs) for a current listing of authors and titles. Most of these volumes also include brief coverage of federal materials and discuss the process of legal research and analysis more generally.

[9] Hein titles include NEVADA LEGAL RESEARCH GUIDE (Jennifer Larraguibel Gross & Thomas Blake Gross eds., 2d ed. 2012); WILLIAM H. MANZ, GIBSON'S NEW YORK LEGAL RESEARCH GUIDE (4th ed. 2014); SCOTT CHILDS & NICK SEXTON, NORTH CAROLINA LEGAL RESEARCH GUIDE (2d ed. 2009); BRANDON D. QUARLES & MATTHEW C. CORDON, RESEARCHING TEXAS LAW (4th ed. 2019); and JESSICA C. VAN BUREN ET AL., UTAH LEGAL RESEARCH (2011).

One of the most useful sources for identifying state materials is the looseleaf set *State Practice Materials: Annotated Bibliographies* (Frank G. Houdek ed., 2002–date, available on HeinOnline in Spinelli's Law Library Reference Shelf). Its chapters, to date covering almost forty states and the District of Columbia, discuss major state primary sources, treatises, practice guides, and research methods.

(b) Forms and Formbooks

Many basic transactions and court filings occur with regularity in the course of legal practice. Rather than redraft these documents each time, attorneys work from sample versions of standard legal documents and instruments. Model forms are available from a variety of sources, in both printed collections and electronic products. Some sets of forms, like those contained in practice manuals and handbooks, are annotated with discussion of the underlying laws, checklists of steps in completing the forms, and citations to cases in which the forms were at issue.

Several multi-volume compilations of forms are published, and most of these are available online. Some are comprehensive national works containing both procedural forms, such as complaints and motions, and transactional forms, such as contracts and wills. Most, however, focus on particular jurisdictions or particular types of forms. Most resources that include all manner of forms are included in this chapter; those that are particularly useful for transactional practice are also included in Chapter 15.

Two of the major national form sets are published as adjuncts to *American Jurisprudence 2d* and are available on Westlaw. *American Jurisprudence Legal Forms 2d* (1971–date) has forms of instruments such as contracts, leases, and wills, and *American Jurisprudence Pleading and Practice Forms* (rev. ed., 1966–date) focuses on litigation and other practice before courts and administrative agencies. Both sets are divided into several hundred topical chapters mirroring the organization of *Am. Jur. 2d*. Illustration 14-1 shows a sample form from *Am. Jur. Pleading and Practice Forms*, as it appears on Westlaw. The *Am. Jur. Deskbook* has a variety of reference information for lawyers, such as historical documents, government agency information, statistics, and financial tables.

Recent works from other publishers include JOHN K. HANFT, LEGAL RESEARCH IN CALIFORNIA (7th ed. 2011); PAUL AXEL-LUTE, NEW JERSEY LEGAL RESEARCH HANDBOOK (6th ed. 2012); and A GUIDE TO LEGAL RESEARCH IN VIRGINIA (Joyce M. Janto ed., 8th ed. 2017).

Numerous older state guides, still valuable for historical research, can be found in library online catalogs.

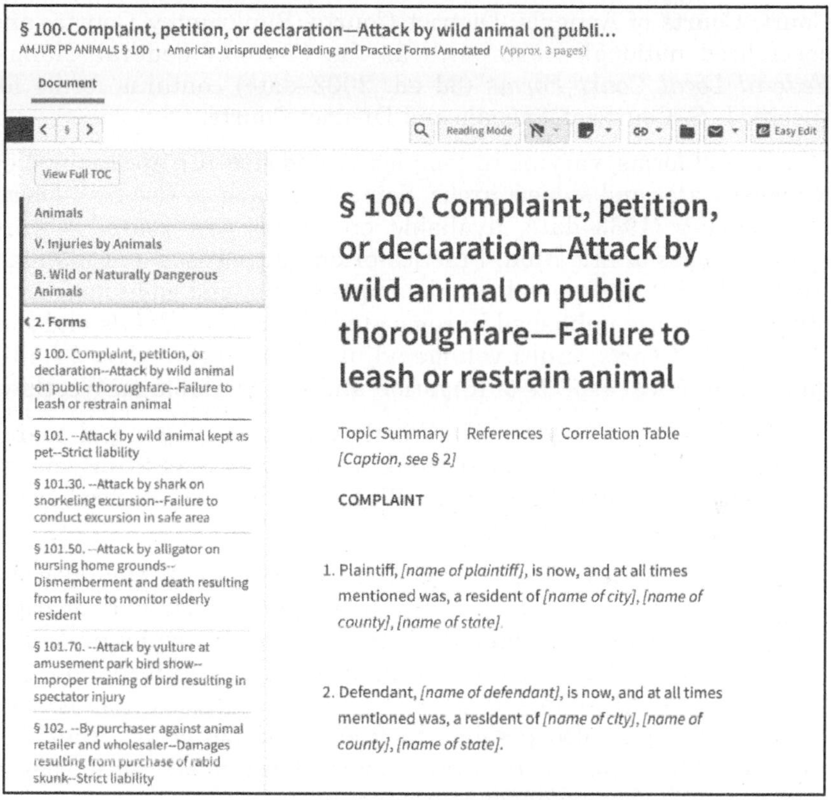

§ 100. Complaint, petition, or declaration—Attack by wild animal on publi...
AMJUR PP ANIMALS § 100 · American Jurisprudence Pleading and Practice Forms Annotated (Approx. 3 pages)

Document

Reading Mode | Easy Edit

View Full TOC

Animals
V. Injuries by Animals
B. Wild or Naturally Dangerous Animals
2. Forms
§ 100. Complaint, petition, or declaration--Attack by wild animal on public thoroughfare--Failure to leash or restrain animal
§ 101. --Attack by wild animal kept as pet--Strict liability
§ 101.30. --Attack by shark on snorkeling excursion--Failure to conduct excursion in safe area
§ 101.50. --Attack by alligator on nursing home grounds--Dismemberment and death resulting from failure to monitor elderly resident
§ 101.70. --Attack by vulture at amusement park bird show--Improper training of bird resulting in spectator injury
§ 102. --By purchaser against animal retailer and wholesaler--Damages resulting from purchase of rabid skunk--Strict liability

§ 100. Complaint, petition, or declaration—Attack by wild animal on public thoroughfare—Failure to leash or restrain animal

Topic Summary | References | Correlation Table
[Caption, see § 2]

COMPLAINT

1. Plaintiff, *[name of plaintiff]*, is now, and at all times mentioned was, a resident of *[name of city]*, *[name of county]*, *[name of state]*.

2. Defendant, *[name of defendant]*, is now, and at all times mentioned was, a resident of *[name of city]*, *[name of county]*, *[name of state]*.

Illustration 14-1. A sample form from *Am. Jur. Pleading and Practice Forms.*

Other comprehensive sets include Jacob Rabkin & Mark H. Johnson, *Current Legal Forms with Tax Analysis* (1948–date, available on Lexis), and *West's Legal Forms* (3d–5th eds. 1996–date, available on Westlaw). Unlike the *Am. Jur.* sets, these are arranged by broad practice area such as estate planning or real estate. This makes them useful for developing an understanding of a wide range of related issues, as well as for finding forms on specific topics.

Three major sets devoted to forms used in federal practice are *Bender's Federal Practice Forms* (1951–date, available on Lexis), *Federal Procedural Forms, Lawyers' Edition* (1975–date, available on Westlaw), and *West's Federal Forms* (1952–date, also on Westlaw). Each of these has a different structure. *Bender's Federal Practice Forms* is arranged by court rule. *Federal Procedural Forms, Lawyers' Edition* is a companion to Thomson Reuters's encyclopedic *Federal Procedure, Lawyers' Edition*, and is organized similarly, with several dozen subject chapters. *West's Federal Forms* is arranged instead by court, with separate volumes covering forms needed in the Supreme

Court, Courts of Appeals, District Courts, Bankruptcy Courts, and specialized national courts such as the Court of Federal Claims. *Federal Local Court Forms* (3d ed. 2002–date) contains forms for specific U.S. Courts of Appeals and District Courts.

Sets of forms, varying in complexity and size, are also published for most states and subject areas. Some sets, such as *Bender's Forms of Discovery* (1963–date, available on Lexis), are geared toward specific stages of litigation. Practice-oriented treatises and manuals frequently include appendices of sample forms, and compilations of official forms are published in some states. *Am. Jur. Trials* and *Am. Jur. Proof of Facts*, multi-volume adjunct sets to *Am. Jur. 2d*, also address practical aspects of litigation and are available on Westlaw.

In an online platform like Westlaw or Lexis, a general search from the main screen can be filtered to see Forms results, or you can use the Form Finder directory on Westlaw to search all forms or to select a more specific source.

A more limited range of forms is available from free internet sites, and some may be sufficient for simple transactions or court filings. The United States Courts website (www.uscourts.gov/services-forms) offers standard forms used in federal litigation, and many forms are available on the websites of state court systems and local courts. It is also possible to find forms online at other free websites, but before using any generic form make sure that it conforms with the law of your jurisdiction.

(c) Jury Instructions

Most jurisdictions have sets of *model* or *pattern jury instructions*, used by judges to explain the applicable law to jurors before they weigh the evidence and reach their decisions. Some of these are produced by state bar associations or judicial committees, while others are unofficial commercial publications. In some states model jury instructions are used by judges only as guides, but in others the instructions must be read verbatim if they are applicable.

Model jury instructions are useful for researchers because they provide a concise summary of a jurisdiction's ruling law often accompanied by notes summarizing the leading cases. In a way, they can serve the same function as a *Restatement* or legal encyclopedia in outlining a state's basic legal doctrines. Illustration 14-2 shows a Florida criminal jury instruction, defining key terms and spelling out the elements that must be proved beyond a reasonable doubt.

29.13 AGGRAVATED ANIMAL CRUELTY
§ 828.12(2), Fla. Stat.

To prove the crime of Aggravated Animal Cruelty, the State must prove the following two elements beyond a reasonable doubt:

1. 1.   (Defendant) [intentionally committed an act to an animal] [or]

    [owned or had custody or control of an animal and failed to act].

1. 2.   (Defendant's) [act] [or] [failure to act] resulted in [excessive or repeated infliction of unnecessary pain or suffering to the animal] [or] [the animal's cruel death].

Give if applicable. Enhancement. § 828.12(2)(a), Fla. Stat.
   If you find (defendant) guilty of Aggravated Animal Cruelty, you must then determine whether the State proved beyond a reasonable doubt that [he] [she] knowingly and intentionally tortured or tormented an animal, and in so doing, [injured] [mutilated] [killed] the animal.

   Definition of "cruelty", if cruel death charged. § 828.02, Fla. Stat. Only read definition for terms "Torture" or "Torment" when State seeks sentencing enhancements pursuant to § 828.12(2)(a), Fla. Stat.
   "Cruelty" ["Torture"] ["Torment"] includes any act, omission, or negligence whereby unnecessary or unjustifiable pain or suffering is caused, permitted, or allowed to continue when there is reasonable remedy or relief, except when done in the interest of medical science.

Lesser Included Offenses

AGGRAVATED ANIMAL CRUELTY — 828.12(2)			
CATEGORY ONE	**CATEGORY TWO**	**FLA. STAT.**	**INS. NO.**
None			
	Attempt	777.04(1)	5.1

Comment

§ 828.12(3) Fla. Stat.
   A person who commits multiple acts of Aggravated Animal Cruelty against an animal may be convicted of multiple counts of Aggravated Animal Cruelty. Also, a person who commits Aggravated Animal Cruelty against more than one animal may be convicted of multiple counts of Aggravated Animal Cruelty.

   This instruction was adopted in 2008 [976 So. 2d 1081] and amended in 2014.

Illustration 14-2. A Florida criminal jury instruction.

Sets of jury instructions are published for every state, for several federal circuits, and for some specialized areas of litigation. Several states provide access to instructions on court or bar websites. Most jurisdictions have separate publications for civil and criminal instructions. Westlaw and Lexis each has publications for about forty states, while Bloomberg Law covers about twenty states. There is considerable overlap, and as with many secondary sources it may pay to check each platform. For Arkansas, for example, Westlaw has the civil instructions while Lexis has the criminal instructions. A few states are covered only by Bloomberg Law, and a few by none of the three.

Some sets of pattern instructions are available for the courts in individual federal circuits, but there is no general set of officially approved jury instructions for the federal courts. There are, however, two sets of commercially published, unofficial instructions covering both criminal and civil cases. Kevin F. O'Malley et al., *Federal Jury Practice and Instructions* (6th ed. 2006–date, available on Westlaw) is a thorough and respected collection with explanatory comments and notes of relevant cases. Leonard B. Sand et al., *Modern Federal Jury Instructions* (1984–date, available on Lexis) is a similar work, consisting of sample instructions, comments, and case notes. Civil and criminal sets are treated separately.

§ 14.3 LEGAL ETHICS RESEARCH

Research in legal ethics is somewhat different from other doctrinal areas because it has its own distinct body of primary sources. In many jurisdictions, courts have delegated the responsibility for governing the professional activities of lawyers to state bar associations or administrative oversight entities. The law of legal ethics is found in codified rules of conduct, disciplinary rules, ethics opinions, and disciplinary decisions. Ethics opinions are advisory documents, usually issued by bar associations, analyzing how lawyers or judges should handle particular or hypothetical problems, while disciplinary decisions punish specific acts of misconduct.[10]

Rules of Conduct. The American Bar Association (ABA) has played a leading role in developing the rules of legal ethics for more than a century. The ABA first adopted a set of Canons of Professional Ethics in 1908, and in 1969 it promulgated a more detailed Model Code of Professional Responsibility consisting of a series of Canons, Ethical Considerations, and Disciplinary Rules. The Model Code was in turn superseded in 1983 by the Model Rules of Professional Conduct, about sixty rules divided into eight broad areas based on lawyers' roles and relationships. The Model Rules have been amended several times since their initial adoption.[11] The ABA Center for Professional Responsibility (www.americanbar.org/groups/professional_responsibility.html) has the text of the Rules and a wide range of other information and documents on legal ethics.

Although provisions and amendments vary from state to state, every jurisdiction has adopted some form of the Model Rules of Professional Conduct.[12] Attorneys in federal courts are subject to

---

[10] For a much more thorough treatment of the issues and resources in this section, see LEE F. PEOPLES, LEGAL ETHICS: A LEGAL RESEARCH GUIDE (2d ed. 2006).

[11] The ABA has published A LEGISLATIVE HISTORY: THE DEVELOPMENT OF THE ABA MODEL RULES OF PROFESSIONAL CONDUCT, 1982–2013 (Art Garwin ed., 4th ed. 2013), a compilation of the various amendments and comments.

[12] California was the last holdout, but its Supreme Court approved new rules modeled on the Model Rules, effective November 1, 2018. *See* STATE BAR OF CALIFORNIA, CALIFORNIA RULES OF PROFESSIONAL CONDUCT (www.calbar.ca.gov/Portals/0/documents/rules/Rules-of-Professional-Conduct.pdf).

professional conduct standards specified in the local rules for the district or circuit in which they are practicing.[13] Each state's rules of professional conduct are available online, from either the state court system or the state bar. Links to these sites are available from the Thomas Woodward Houghton 50 State Ethics Guide at the University of Texas (tarlton.law.utexas.edu/ethics).

Rules of professional conduct are usually included in the volumes containing a state's court rules, although in some states they are part of larger documents such as supreme court rules and can be a bit difficult to find.[14] Westlaw and Lexis include professional conduct rules in their more general state code databases, but typing "[State] rules of professional conduct" into Westlaw's main search bar will take you directly to the rules for most states. For most states the rules are annotated with notes of decisions, and for all states they include citing references.

Annotated Model Rules of Professional Conduct (9th ed. 2019, available on Westlaw) has the text of the ABA rules with comments, legal background, and notes of decisions from various jurisdictions. Although it contains the ABA's rules rather than those adopted in any specific state, this is a useful source for comparative analysis and commentary.

The American Law Institute has also formulated basic rules of legal ethics in its *Restatement of the Law (Third): The Law Governing Lawyers* (2000, available on Westlaw, Lexis, and HeinOnline), employing the standard Restatement format of black-letter provisions, comments, and illustrations. The Model Rules and the *Restatement* have been compared in an ABA publication by Thomas D. Morgan, *Lawyer Law: Comparing the ABA Model Rules of Professional Conduct with the ALI Restatement (Third) of the Law Governing Lawyers* (2005).

In addition to general rules on lawyer ethics, many states have adopted rules specifically governing lawyer discipline. The ABA adopted Model Rules for Lawyer Disciplinary Enforcement in 1989. These rules, most recently amended in 2002, were published in 2007

---

[13] Tonia Lucio, *Regulation of Professional Conduct in Federal Practice*, FED. LAW., July 2017, at 50 (describing the range of ethical conduct and enforcement rules governing attorneys practicing in federal courts). Some courts specify that attorneys follow the state court rules, others have expressly adopted the ABA Model Rules, and some have promulgated their own sets of rules.

[14] This can also make them tricky to cite with consistency as *Bluebook* Rules 12.9.3–12.9.5 provide different formats for court rules and codes (including model codes); if court rules are codified in state statutes, that only adds to the trouble. The citations in Arthur F. Greenbaum, *Lawyer Transfers to Disability Inactive Status—A Comprehensive Guide*, 2017 J. PROF. LAW. 1, illustrate the many ways citations to rules governing attorney ethics could be formatted.

and are available on the ABA's Center for Professional Responsibility website. As with ethics rules, the rules that each jurisdiction has adopted governing attorney discipline can be found in volumes that include state court rules, sometimes as a component of the state's supreme court rules. The rules are supplemented by the ABA's *Annotated Standards for Imposing Lawyer Sanctions* (2d ed. 2019).

Ethics Opinions. Ethics opinions, generally prepared in response to inquiries from attorneys, are issued by the American Bar Association and by state and local bar associations, the latter of which may create new principles of ethical conduct that lawyers can in many instances rely upon. The aim of ethics opinions is to apply professional responsibility rules to specific factual situations.

ABA opinions are available on Westlaw and Lexis, as are opinions from selected state and local bars. Ethics opinions from 1981 to 2011 were published in the *National Reporter on Legal Ethics and Professional Responsibility*, and most state bars have publications either summarizing their opinions or reprinting them in full text. Links to ethics opinions on state bar websites are available from the Houghton 50 State Ethics Guide.[15]

Disciplinary Decisions. States have a variety of agencies to regulate attorney conduct, some part of the state bar association and others a separate agency of the judicial system.[16] In all jurisdictions, the highest court has the ultimate authority to discipline attorneys, with sanctions ranging from reprimands to disbarment. The ABA Center for Professional Responsibility site has a directory of lawyer disciplinary agencies, with contact information and links to websites, and the court decisions can be found through the research methods outlined in Chapter 12. The annotations to state ethics rules are perhaps the easiest way to find relevant disciplinary decisions, and searching the Bar Journals database on Hein can be helpful as well.[17]

---

[15] On the history and purposes of ethics opinions, see Peter A. Joy, *Making Ethics Opinions Meaningful: Toward More Effective Regulation of Lawyers' Conduct*, 15 GEO. J. LEGAL ETHICS 313 (2002). The article includes appendices listing state and local sources of opinions and their precedential value in each state. *Id.* at 384–96.

[16] In Ohio, for example, regulation of attorney conduct is exclusively the domain of the Ohio Supreme Court, and the state bar association is more of a fraternal organization. Ohio's Rules for the Government of the Bar are part of the Ohio Rules of Court, as are the Procedural Regulations of the Board of Professional Conduct of the Supreme Court. In Washington, however, the state bar is the entity governing admission to practice and regulating attorney conduct. Though Washington's Rules for Enforcement of Lawyer Conduct are rules promulgated by the Washington Supreme Court, the Court has delegated regulatory authority to the bar's Office of Disciplinary Counsel.

[17] On the history of lawyer discipline, see Mary M. Devlin, *The Development of Lawyer Disciplinary Procedures in the United States*, 7 GEO. J. LEGAL ETHICS 911 (1994).

Secondary Sources. The leading modern treatise on legal ethics practice under the Model Rules is Geoffrey C. Hazard, Jr. et al., *The Law of Lawyering* (4th ed. 2015–date, available on Cheetah), a two-volume set designed as a workbook "for lawyers faced with immediate practical dilemmas." A shorter work by Ronald D. Rotunda & John S. Dzienkowski, *Legal Ethics: The Lawyer's Deskbook on Professional Responsibility* (annual, available on Westlaw), also provides commentary on the Model Rules.

The *ABA/BNA Lawyers' Manual on Professional Conduct* (1984–date, available on Bloomberg Law) is often a good place to begin research. This resource includes an extensive commentary with background and practical tips, as well as news of developments and abstracts of new decisions.

Judicial Conduct. Judges are governed by a separate set of rules, based in most jurisdictions on the ABA's Model Code of Judicial Conduct. Several states are reviewing their codes or are in the process of adopting the ABA Model Code. The latest edition was promulgated by the ABA in 2007, but some states' rules are still based on its 1990 predecessor. The ABA Center for Professional Responsibility website has both versions of the Model Code, as well as information on state adoptions, background documents, and other judicial ethics resources.

Judicial conduct rules are generally published in state court rules pamphlets and are available in the court rules databases on Westlaw and Lexis. The ABA has published an *Annotated Model Code of Judicial Conduct* (3d ed. 2016), and Charles Gardner Geyh et al., *Judicial Conduct and Ethics* (5th ed. 2013–date, available on Lexis) analyzes issues in this area.

Chapter 15

TRANSACTIONAL LAW RESEARCH

Table of Sections

To this point, we have covered legal research materials without much reference to specific types of legal practice. But as the legal profession has moved toward greater specialization in recent decades, so too has legal information. A wealth of useful tools and resources are now available in many specialized practice areas. One area with a broad array of customized resources is transactional practice.

Transactional practice, as differentiated from litigation practice, primarily involves the handling of legal matters outside of court. A transactional lawyer, sometimes called a business lawyer, may negotiate and draft contracts, prepare wills and create trusts, or structure complex commercial real-estate deals. Transactional lawyers may represent businesses or individuals. And any practicing attorney may also need to research and analyze unfamiliar transactional problems from time to time.

Transactional lawyers represent clients seeking to control risk and avoid litigation. Skills such as researching and reading statutes, regulations, and cases are still of the utmost importance as business lawyers seek to determine the legal issues that will influence their clients' strategies. But business lawyers must also be adept at using specialized research tools in addition to being familiar with the workings of commercial and financial institutions.[1]

First, it is necessary for transactional lawyers to be familiar with business jargon. Newer attorneys without a background in business can be overwhelmed by the unfamiliar vocabulary, and even the most seasoned deal lawyer can find it difficult to keep up. *Dictionary of Finance and Investment Terms* (John Downes & Jordan Elliot Goodman eds., 10th ed. 2018) is an inexpensive single-volume paperback dictionary that covers a variety of stock, bond, and corporate finance terms. There are also several free sources for definitions that can be found online: Investopedia's financial dictionary (www.investopedia.com/dictionary/) in particular will work well in a pinch.

Glossaries of transactional law terms are included in specialized transactional research products like Practical Law (Thomson Reuters) and Lexis Practice Advisor, which we will cover in greater depth as the chapter continues. Another sizeable online glossary is available at Investor.gov, a website maintained by the Securities and Exchange Commission to further that agency's mission of keeping the investing public informed.

Legal resources used in transactional practice can also be confusing to use at first. Traditionally, business lawyers have relied less on standard primary and secondary sources than on specialized looseleaf services and practitioners' manuals. Looseleaf services provide access to primary law, its interpretation, and new developments in its applications. Practitioners' manuals include checklists, forms, and how-to materials. Most of these products are still available in print, but the industry is clearly moving toward online-only publication of these frequently updated resources. These online services combine primary law and practice tools. While the services have improved through the years, they can still be difficult for the uninitiated law student or lawyer to use because of the diversity of material they contain and the idiosyncrasies of different publishers' interfaces.

This chapter covers several different aspects of the specialized online transactional research tools now available on the legal information market. It details the types of documents you can find on

---

[1] For a thorough (and readable) introduction to business, including the basics of accounting, see ROBERT J. RHEE, ESSENTIAL CONCEPTS OF BUSINESS FOR LAWYERS (2d ed. 2016). For those more in need of a refresher, the annual POCKET MBA, a continuing legal education publication from the Practising Law Institute, provides depth and current awareness for specific business concepts.

these platforms, the efficiencies in research and document drafting
you can achieve with them, and how to use them to find digital
versions of essential print sources in a variety of transactional law
practice areas.

§ 15.1 PRACTITIONERS' MATERIALS AND NEWS

Researching topics in transactional law often involves using a
specialized online product or interface offered by one of the major
legal information vendors. These platforms include primary law,
treatises, research guides, practitioners' tools, and news, and are
organized by area or topic of transactional practice.[2]

Thomson Reuters, which owns Westlaw, and LexisNexis have
increased the volume and quality of the materials they provide for
business lawyers, mostly through acquisitions of existing products.
Wolters Kluwer's Cheetah platform incorporates materials from
CCH (Commerce Clearing House), a longtime publisher of business
information. Likewise, Bloomberg Law features current awareness
materials in corporate and other highly regulated areas, including
practice centers for a diverse set of fields, such as antitrust,
environmental law, health, and privacy and data security.

(a) Practitioners' Materials

Specialized online research products marketed to transactional
lawyers tend to be organized by topics that track with the tasks or
problems these lawyers face. These products, expensive but efficient,
are intended to be one-stop-shops for detailed analysis of common,
often-repeated issues in transactional law. While further research is
still often necessary, these specialized tools offer analytical material
alongside sample business documents and checklists. We focus here
on practice notes, checklists, flowcharts, timelines, and other
materials that explain specific elements of transactional law practice,
and we cover sample transactional documents in the next section of
this chapter.

---

[2] There are also specialized research sources available in print or in e-book
format outside of the major legal research services. The Practising Law Institute (PLI)
publishes practitioner materials in specific areas of transactional practice, some of
which are discussed in § 15.4. Other publishers include ALI CLE, formerly ABA-ALI
and primarily a publisher of continuing legal education materials, and the American
Bar Association's Section on Business Law.

For more on smaller, newer online services offering alternatives to Lexis and
Westlaw, see Taryn Marks, *John West and the Future of Legal Subscription Databases*,
107 LAW LIBR. J. 377, 392–95 (2015). Today's startup online service is often tomorrow's
acquisition by one of the major platforms.

Three major online platforms designed specifically for researching transactional practitioners' materials are Practical Law from Thomson Reuters (us.practicallaw.com), Lexis Practice Advisor (www.lexispracticeadvisor.com), and Bloomberg Law's Transactional Intelligence Center (www.bloomberglaw.com/product/btic/). Each of these is available both as a stand-alone product for law firm subscribers and through their publishers' more general websites under law school subscriptions. While each platform has unique content, they are organized by subject area or have options for easily browsing or filtering by the type of document sought. Illustration 15-1 shows the range of topics covered in one Practical Law area.

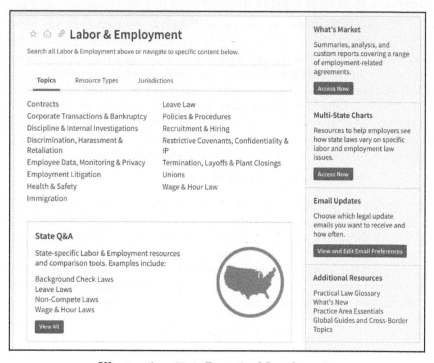

Illustration 15-1. Practical Law's main
Labor & Employment screen.

There are other similarities between the platforms. The first is that each publisher relies on experienced editors to produce and curate much of their material. Marketing materials from Practical Law boast more than 230 "attorney-editors" working on the product, while Lexis Practice Advisor claims to have items from over 850 "attorney-authors" and over 320 contributing law firms. Likewise, Bloomberg Law emphasizes the importance of the experts who contribute to the platform.

Each platform also provides access to relevant primary law materials, generally statutes, regulations, and regulatory documents. Bloomberg Law's Transactional Intelligence Center does this directly from an entry on the main page, while Lexis Practice Advisor and Practical Law make use of connections with databases on Lexis and Westlaw, respectively. Thomson Reuters offers a separate product, Practical Law Connect (formerly Practice Point), that allows users to search across both Westlaw and Practical Law at the same time.[3]

Another similarity between platforms is the ability to conduct research on a large number of narrow, pre-defined transactional law tasks. Within a topical area on each platform, you can select specific events that businesses or individuals are likely to seek representation for. These tasks include, for example, how to register certain types of securities or how to form different business entities.

Each platform allows users to search across all content included. While the browsing functionality works quite well on each platform (dividing materials by subject area, resource type, and jurisdiction), most researchers are expected to search for relevant terms and then filter the results. The search features on each platform are predictive, meaning they suggest resources after the researchers types a word or two. Advanced search, with the ability to select the types of documents being searched, is available on Bloomberg Law's Transactional Intelligence Center, while the other two platforms allow filtering prior to as well as subsequent to searching.

Finally, there are standard types of documents available on each platform. Knowing the general kinds of documents that you will encounter on these platforms will help make your research more efficient.

Practice Notes. Often, attorneys need quick explanations of complicated topics containing leads to other useful sources. Practice notes are a type of secondary source document featuring plain language explanations of topics in transactional law, written by practicing attorneys or other attorney editors. Practice notes can be shorter overviews or longer, in-depth entries on a narrow aspect of business representation. In the practitioners' platforms, practice notes contain hyperlinks to primary law, glossary terms, and to other secondary sources on the platform.

---

[3] An insider account about this product can be found in *Vendor Voice: Practice Point*, AALL SPECTRUM, Jan./Feb. 2017, at 47. For more on the acquisition of Practical Law and its integration into the Thomson Reuters legal product family, see *Practical Law to Join Thomson Reuters Portfolio*, 30 No. 8 LAWYER'S PC 8 (2013).

On Practical Law, practice notes are available for each topic covered, including capital markets, corporate governance, corporate mergers and acquisitions, finance, real estate, and trusts and estates. Notes may be classified in more than one subject area. Practice notes on Lexis Practice Advisor are likewise available on a similar range of topics, and both platforms also provide jurisdiction-specific notes. They also include information about a practice note's currency and its authorship.

Bloomberg Law's Transactional Intelligence Center does not contain a type of document explicitly called a practice note, but Overviews are the equivalent product and are can be found with the practical guidance documents.

Checklists, Flowcharts, and Timelines. Business lawyers have long relied on practitioners' materials that include checklists, flowcharts, timelines, and other similarly detailed, step-by-step materials to assist them in completing transactions successfully.[4] The specialized transactional law platforms have retained these types of materials, which is a testament to their usefulness, and online publication has improved upon some of their features.

Finding these resources is easiest by selecting a topic or task or by searching for appropriate keywords. On Lexis Practice Advisor, checklists are a distinct document type, while flowcharts and timelines can be found with practice notes or sample forms. On Bloomberg Law, checklists, flowcharts, and timelines are separate document types within the Practical Guidance Library. And on Practical Law, all three types of documents are available under a more generic Checklists category.

Transaction Analysis. Business lawyers can be more than mere advisors on the legal aspects of transactions. Indeed, they must also structure deals that will meet a client's needs by steering clear of regulatory or tax problems, thereby maximizing value.[5] It is no surprise, then, that transactional law research platforms contain tools for comparing and analyzing large, complex transactions.

Bloomberg Law's Transactional Intelligence Center includes Deal Analytics, which comprises two digital dashboards—one for mergers and acquisitions (M&A) and one for equity offerings. These products aggregate data from actual past transactions, and researchers can select the elements of the deal they are interested in,

---

[4] To locate print sources for these kinds of practitioners' materials, try searching a law library catalog's title field for keywords like "deskbook," "forms," "practice guide," or "law and practice" combined with the area of law you are interested in. This can be especially helpful when trying to find jurisdiction-specific sources.

[5] A classic article on this topic is Ronald J. Gilson, *Value Creation by Business Lawyers: Legal Skills and Asset Pricing*, 94 YALE L.J. 239 (1984).

such as the parties to the deal, its size, and when it was approved by regulators. Results are displayed in a table, and each deal has a details page listing relevant information.

Bloomberg Law also offers written analysis of trends in different types of transactions beyond M&A and equity offerings in its In Focus: Deal Points collection. Practical Law maintains a similar database of trends and updates across a wider area of transactions in its What's Market tool. What's Market includes written summaries of individual publicly filed deals and prepared comparisons of deals.

Combinations of Sources. Researchers looking for comprehensive coverage of a practice task can find collections or combinations of sources on all three transactional platforms. Generally, these types of resources contain some analytical material but are most useful because they link to a large number of relevant documents on the same platform. They can therefore serve as a good starting or ending point for research, depending on the researcher's level of familiarity with a topic.

On Practical Law, these combinations of sources are known as Toolkits. The Toolkits database can be searched independently from the rest of the content on Practical Law, allowing for more precise results. On Lexis Practice Advisor, these sources are called Resource Kits. The easiest way to locate them is to browse to the Tools & Resources tab on the Practice Advisor platform.

Bloomberg Law's Transactional Intelligence Center contains what it calls Step-by-Step Guidance serving a similar function to the resources on the other platforms. There is less analytical material but more in the way of links to other sources.

(b) Transactional News

Staying up to date with the latest trends in the market and in industry, changes in the law, and in the businesses relevant to clients is essential in transactional practice. There is no shortage of sources for this kind of news, though the cost, quality, and focus can vary widely.

First, each of the three specialized transactional law platforms discussed in the last section contains news sources. Bloomberg Law News provides in-depth coverage of legal, regulatory, and business developments. Many practitioners have relied for years on its predecessors for current awareness.

Lexis Practice Advisor and Practical Law both have databases in which documents are updated or created when significant events occur. Additionally, *Lexis Practice Advisor Journal* is a standalone periodical that can be found on that platform; *Practical Law The*

Journal is the equivalent product on Practical Law. On Bloomberg, there are a limited number of In Focus topic pages that are updated following new developments in regulation or litigation.

Detailed news is also available from other subscription platforms. Wolters Kluwer's Cheetah platform has white papers, news, blogs, and numerous other in-depth current awareness materials, grouped by topical area. The ABI/INFORM Collection (ProQuest) includes articles from business journals and from the trade press, along with reports on market trends. The Deal Pipeline (pipeline.thedeal.com) is a subscription news and data source aimed at lawyers working on complex business transactions.

News articles aimed at transactional lawyers can also be found in online legal newsletter services, like the ones discussed in Chapter 14. A number of sections on the Law360 (LexisNexis) service are particularly relevant to transactional practice, such as commercial contracts, compliance, mergers & acquisitions, and project finance. Corporate Counsel (ALM Law.com) (www.law.com/corpcounsel/, also available on Lexis) is a more targeted source, with a special section for in-house counsel. Practitioners' magazines such as *The Business Lawyer*, published quarterly by the Business Law Section of the American Bar Association, can also be helpful sources on trends in the law important to transactional attorneys.

Any lawyer working closely or regularly with clients in a particular industry should be aware of the trade magazines or newspapers which those clients read and the associations to which they belong. A lawyer representing banks, for example, will learn of new developments affecting the industry by reading the daily *American Banker*, and will learn from the American Bankers Association website (www.aba.com) about the industry's perspective on policy issues and current events. Being knowledgeable about clients' concerns will help you anticipate their legal needs. Finally, business news reporting, often referencing legal issues, can be found in the *Wall Street Journal* and in the *New York Times* sections on business. The *Financial Times* is also an excellent source with a more global perspective. Those newspapers offer daily newsletters to subscribers, such as DealBook (from the *New York Times*), which includes summaries of business and policy stories. Money Stuff, a Bloomberg newsletter available on Bloomberg Law and compiled by Matt Levine, an attorney and former investment banker, discusses finance trends in an often-amusing manner.

§ 15.2 TRANSACTIONAL DRAFTING

Drafting contracts, wills, or other documents is a core transactional lawyering skill. Efficiently locating sample or form documents and clauses is only one component of that skill, but it is an important one. Adapting tried-and-true contract precedents to new and unique situations is especially common in the profession, as is drafting standard corporate documents such as articles of incorporation, bylaws, or board meeting minutes.[6] Some transactional attorneys are also called upon to write third-party legal opinion letters or even specialize in the practice, which involves providing assurances to non-clients who are parties to a business deal.

(a) Precedents and Sample Agreements

Form and sample transactional documents have been a mainstay of the business lawyer's trade for as long as legal publishing has existed.[7] More recently, databases of documents used in actual transactions, known as precedents, have also become available to researchers. Firms have internal collections of precedents, sometimes called "go-bys," for the transactions they have handled for clients, and some have even begun selling their precedents (and the tools for compiling them) on the web.[8] Some forms and sample documents include instructions on how they can be filled out and adopted most advantageously.

While the first stop for locating a sample document or precedent in the firm environment is the firm's internal document management system, it will often be necessary to explore other sources. As mentioned above, there are two main types of databases available for this kind of research: those for precedents and those for forms and sample documents.

Precedents. The largest source for precedents in a major legal research service is Bloomberg Law's DealMaker document collection. DealMaker contains over 800,000 documents (and more than 600 document types) used in actual transactions. These documents are culled from SEC filings on EDGAR, including Exhibit 10 filings containing material contracts.[9] Bloomberg Law offers the ability to search by document type, transaction type, party name, law firm, or

---

[6] A recent ABA task force on business law education put it this way: "Good business lawyers know how to find forms, when to use them (or not), and how to use them. This includes the ability to (i) mark up the form to match the deal . . . , (ii) read provisions critically to determine whether they apply to the lawyer's transaction, and (iii) incorporate provisions from other agreements as needed. Barbara Wagner et al., *Defining Key Competencies for Business Lawyers*, 72 BUS. LAW. 101, 124 (2016).

[7] For more on the history of books of pre-printed forms in the U.S., see ERWIN C. SURRENCY, A HISTORY OF AMERICAN LAW PUBLISHING 138–41 (1990).

[8] Cooley LLP has created a platform, CooleyGo, specifically targeting emerging businesses, with sample documents and guides (www.cooleygo.com/documents/).

[9] See (Item 601) Exhibits, 17 C.F.R. § 229.601 (2019), for the documents that must be attached as exhibits with certain SEC filings.

by governing national or state law. For M&A deals or equity offerings, it is possible to specify the size of the deal in the search criteria as well. Illustration 15-2 shows a sample results screen when searching for precedents on Bloomberg Law.

LawInsider (www.lawinsider.com), a standalone subscription database, also queries the EDGAR system for precedent documents. Information about companies, individuals, and transactions is available, and the company provides contract datasets for education and research purposes.

PRACTICAL GUIDANCE

Results for Transactional Precedents

Result type | Documents

Filters   Clear All Filters

Narrow by Date   ∧

Any   ▼

Topic   ∧

☑ Mergers & Acquisitions (4)

☑ Securities Law (4)

☐ Employment Law (23)

☐ Executive Compensation (18)

☐ Employee Benefits (5)

Show More

Industries   ∧

☐ Pharmaceutical Manufacturing (2)

☐ Computers (1)

☐ Real Estate Investment Trusts (1)

☐ Drug Stores (1)

☐ Semiconductors & Microchips (1)

SIC Industry   ∧

☐ Pharmaceutical Preparations [2834] (2)

☐ Unknown Sic [0000] (1)

☐ Semiconductors & Related Devices [3674] (1)

‹ 1 - 7 of 7 ›   Sort by Date ▼   Details ◖●

☐ Select All   ✎ Edit Search | ⬇ ▾ ⌷ ✉ | Create Alert | Add to ▾

☐ 1. Agreement and Plan of Merger (10/29/2015)

PARTY	Rite Aid Corp, Walgreens Boots Alliance Inc
LAW FIRM	Simpson Thacher & Bartlett LLP, Skadden Arps Slate Meagher & Flom LLP
GOVERNING LAW	Delaware
DOCUMENT TYPES	Merger & Amalgamation Agreements
DOCUMENT SUBTYPES	Merger Agreements
TRANSACTION TYPES	Merger & Acquisition Transactions, Mergers

Notwithstanding anything to the contrary herein, the Parties agree that, for purposes of this Agreement, Parent shall be deemed to have announced plans to enter into any specific Parent Permitted Transaction as a result of having made publicly available a **bear hug** letter, or a tender or exchange, take-over bid or other public offer to acquire all or a controlling interest with respect to a Parent Permitted Transaction.

☐ 2. Prospectus (424B3) (10/30/2013)

PARTY	PHARMATHENE, INC
DOCUMENT TYPES	Prospectuses
DOCUMENT SUBTYPES	Prospectuses (Form 424B3)
TRANSACTION TYPES	SEC Filings & Disclosures

20% or more of the aggregate fair market value of the consolidated assets of PharmAthene and its subsidiaries taken as a whole, (iv) any spin-off, spin-out, split-up, carve-out or similar event pursuant to which assets representing 20% or more of either the aggregate fair market value of the assets of PharmAthene as of the Closing Date or the business of the PharmAthene as of the Closing Date will be transferred in one or more transactions or (v) the public announcement of a third party regarding a **bear hug** letter sent to PharmAthene or the public announcement of a third party regarding a tender offer for shares of PharmAthene Common Stock;

Illustration 15-2. Precedents available from Bloomberg Law.

Form or Sample Documents. Model forms and sample transactional documents can be found in many print and online sources. Online sample documents tend to be easier for the contemporary researcher to work with than print, as they can often be edited in a web interface or downloaded as a Microsoft Word document. But collections of print forms are useful not only for those without access to online databases, but also for those who wish to quickly browse forms to choose the most suitable one for the task at hand.

Practical Law, Lexis Practice Advisor, and Bloomberg Law's Transactional Intelligence Center all have collections of sample documents and clauses in the subject areas covered in those platforms. These sample documents contain different value-added features that take advantage of the digital medium. On Practical Law, the Standard Documents and Standard Clauses documents include notes for each of the document's major portions.[10] On Lexis Practice Advisor, the Forms and Clauses databases function similarly, and some documents come with alternative clauses that can be swapped in at appropriate points. The Transactional Intelligence Center on Bloomberg Law has, in addition to the DealMaker documents discussed above, model forms that can be found in relevant portfolios or practice treatises. Illustration 15-3 shows a sample letter from Lexis Practice Advisor.

Broader collections of forms, including transactional law forms, can be found on Westlaw and Lexis. The Westlaw Form Finder database and the associated Form Builder tool offer coverage across jurisdictions and practice areas. On Lexis, the Forms database is also organized by jurisdiction and practice area and can be searched and filtered. The sources of model forms on these collections are different, but in both databases the forms cover litigation and transactional law documents, so you must narrow your searches in advance to avoid irrelevant results or filter your results post-search.

---

[10] Transactional documents, especially contracts, tend to have standard "building blocks" which go by different names, but typically include: representations and warranties, covenants, rights, conditions precedent, remedial provisions, discretionary authority, definitions, and declarations. *See* Lisa Penland, *What a Transactional Lawyer Needs to Know: Identifying and Implementing Competencies for Transactional Lawyers,* 5 J. ALWD 118, 125 (2008), Tina L. Stark, *Thinking Like a Deal Lawyer,* 54 J. LEGAL EDUC. 223, 225 (2004), and CHARLES M. FOX, WORKING WITH CONTRACTS: WHAT LAW SCHOOL DOESN'T TEACH YOU 7 (2d ed. 2008).

Document: Strategic Investor Bear Hug Letter | Actions⌄
Home / Corporate and M&A / Hostile Takeovers & Shareholder Activism / Hostile Takeovers / **Document**

🗁⌄ 🖨 ✉ ⤓ ⊗ 🗋 | Go to ⌄ | Proposal repres... 1 of 1 ⌄ | ∧ ∨ | Search Document 🔍

Strategic Investor Bear Hug Letter

▶ Summary

+ Expand all Drafting Notes

Board of Directors
[Target Company]
[Target Company Address]
Attention: [Chairman of Board]
Attention: [Chief Executive Office (if different from Chairman)]

Dear Members of the Board:

[I/We] [am/are] writing on behalf of [the Board of Directors] of [Acquiror] to make a proposal for a business combination of [Acquiror] and [Target]. Under our proposal, [Acquiror] would acquire [all/[ ]%] of the outstanding shares of [Target] common stock for per share consideration of $[ ] based on [Acquiror]'s closing share price on [date of letter], payable in the form of [$[ ] in cash [and/or] [0.[ ] of a]/ [ ] share[s] of [Acquiror] common stock. [[Acquiror] would provide each [Target] shareholder with the ability to choose whether to receive the consideration in cash or [Acquiror] common stock, subject to pro-ration so that in the aggregate [ ]% of the [Target] common shares will be exchanged for shares of [Acquiror] common stock and [ ]% of the [Target] common shares will be converted into the right to receive cash.] Our proposal [is/is not] subject to any financing condition.

+ Drafting Note

Our proposal represents a [ ]% premium above the [unaffected] closing price of [Target] common stock of $[ ] [on date of letter][before market speculation of a possible offer [by us] to acquire Target]. By [many] financial measures, our proposal represents a compelling value realization event for your shareholders.

+ Drafting Note

**Illustration 15-3. A form letter available from
Lexis Practice Advisor.**

Print sources with model forms relevant to transactional law include the large, multi-volume *American Jurisprudence Legal Forms 2d* (1971–date, available on Westlaw). Another comprehensive set is Jacob Rabkin & Mark H. Johnson, *Current Legal Forms with Tax Analysis* (1948–date, available on Lexis), containing checklists, forms, and analytical materials. *Nichols Cyclopedia of Legal Forms Annotated* (1936–date, available on Westlaw) is a collection of transactional forms with analysis. For sample corporate documents, see *Fletcher Corporation Forms* (4th ed. 1972–date, available on Westlaw). For legal opinion letter forms, see A. Sidney Holderness, Jr. & Brooke Wunnicke, *Legal Opinion Letters Formbook* (3d ed. 2010–date, available on Cheetah). Specialized treatises, such as

Lindey on Entertainment, Publishing and the Arts (3d ed. 2004–date, available on Westlaw) are also helpful sources for forms and sample agreements.

(b) Drafting Guides and Tools

Transactional attorneys have many tools at their disposal to help improve their documents. On one end of the spectrum are more traditional print or electronic resources that offer instruction and analysis in the drafting of contracts, corporate documents, and legal opinion letters. On the other end are algorithmic tools for comparing transactional drafts to precedents or model forms or for creating new drafts wholesale using expert systems. Legal research databases have expanded to meet the growing demand for tools of this kind.

Drafting Guides. For students, new associates, or attorneys lacking familiarity with writing in the business law context, popular introductory sources include Charles M. Fox, *Working with Contracts: What Law School Doesn't Teach You* (2d ed. 2008, available on PLI PLUS); Tina L. Stark, *Drafting Contracts: How and Why Lawyers Do What They Do* (2d ed. 2013); and Lenné Eidson Espenschied, *Contract Drafting: Powerful Prose in Transactional Practice* (2d ed. 2015). These books, sometimes used in law school drafting classes or to train new transactional associates, present frameworks for analyzing transactional law issues and offer helpful examples.

More in-depth resources on drafting include Robert A. Feldman & Raymond T. Nimmer, *Drafting Effective Contracts: A Practitioner's Guide* (2d ed. 2007, available on Cheetah), and Scott J. Burnham, *Drafting and Analyzing Contracts: A Guide to the Practical Applications of the Principles of Contract Law* (4th ed. 2016). Another helpful resource is Kenneth A. Adams, *A Manual of Style for Contract Drafting* (4th ed. 2017), which includes commentary, tables of contract language, and samples of properly formatted contract sections.

Resources on drafting documents other than contracts can be found in *Legal Opinion Letters: A Comprehensive Guide to Opinion Letter Practice* (M. John Sterba, Jr. ed., 3d ed. 2003–date, available on Cheetah), and Carolyn E.C. Paris, *Drafting for Corporate Finance: Concepts, Deals, and Documents* (2d ed. 2014, available on PLI PLUS).

Drafting Tools. A variety of new, software-driven tools to aid business lawyers have appeared on the market recently. Some tools allow researchers to compare a document they are drafting against a database of precedents or forms. Others, known as document assembly tools, offer question-and-answer prompts to suggest appropriate language to the drafter. Each of the three transactional law research platforms we have discussed throughout this chapter contains drafting tools.

Bloomberg Law's Draft Analyzer tool, available in the Transactional Intelligence Center, works with documents that are uploaded or typed into its interface. These documents are compared to agreements or corporate documents in DealMaker. Researchers can see legal blackline markup showing how similar their phrasing is to what Bloomberg's software has deemed to be consensus language in similar instances. Consensus language is just that—consensus—and does not represent what is best or most correct, but it may still be useful at many stages of the drafting process.[11]

Thomson Reuters's Drafting Assistant, which works with Practical Law data, can be used online or with Microsoft Word. For transactional drafting, the Deal Proof tool is its most salient feature. Deal Proof scans a document entered in its system for problems like inconsistent numbering and missing definitions. Drafting Assistant also allows users to work directly with templates or forms from Practical Law.

Lexis Smart Forms, available in Lexis Practice Advisor, is a document assembly tool. This type of software guides a researcher through a series of questions to determine appropriate language to be used in a document. When the user completes the questions, the tool creates a customized draft. Lexis Smart Forms includes explanatory drafting notes as you work through the question-and-answer interview. There are currently only a handful of Smart Forms available, and they are limited to only a few subject areas, including commercial transactions, corporate M&A, and labor and employment.

§ 15.3 TRANSACTIONAL LAW ACROSS JURISDICTIONS

As discussed in Chapter 5, tools like multistate surveys and chart builders can make locating and comparing laws from several states more efficient. In transactional practice, this tends to be a more common task than in some other areas of legal work due to the nature of business and its reach across jurisdictions. Specialized transactional law platforms, therefore, make this kind of research somewhat easier.

---

[11] Bloomberg Law has a resource describing the potential uses for Draft Analyzer (and other tools) in more depth (help.bloomberglaw.com/docs/blh-050-corporate-and-transactional.html).

Wolters Kluwer's Cheetah platform offers Smart Charts, which allow you to select relevant topics and jurisdictions for comparison. The topics available are more specific given Wolters Kluwer's experience with transactional practice resources. Recent developments in areas of law that change rapidly, like federal tax, can also be tracked through Smart Charts. Results include brief explanations and links to applicable law and to treatises within Cheetah. This information can easily be exported to Microsoft Excel for further analysis.

The Practical Law State Q&A Comparison Tool is more limited in scope than the Cheetah Smart Charts. However, the interface creates comparisons based on a question-and-answer interview, like the expert systems described above. This can be especially helpful in narrowing the range of inquiry, leading to greater precision in the results returned. Information is displayed question-by-question for each jurisdiction selected.

Transactional law practice is notable for the extent to which uniform laws and model acts control policy. The Uniform Commercial Code, enacted in every state, is an obvious example, covering sales of goods, negotiable instruments, bank deposits, and secured transactions, among other things. Other important uniform laws govern trade secrets, agency, and the many varieties of partnerships.

Continuing legal education, or CLE, publications, such as those produced by the Practising Law Institute, are a good way to stay current on multistate transactional law developments. PLI publications are available on its online platform PLI PLUS. Another publisher with significant CLE content related to businesses is the American Law Institute's ALI CLE, formerly ALI-ABA.

§ 15.4 SPECIFIC AREAS OF TRANSACTIONAL PRACTICE

As we have seen, research in transactional law practice areas can be quite different from research in litigation or regulatory practice. However, within transactional practice, legal research sources and methods are quite alike across the different areas of practice. In general, the governing U.S. primary law tends to be statutory and regulatory and exists at both the federal and state levels. There is usually some form of agency oversight. And there are likely specialized online services or platforms as well as print looseleafs from a distinct set of publishers.[12] Finally, if you are lucky,

---

[12] Mary Whisner, *On Specialized Legal Research*, 108 LAW LIBR. J. 483, 486 (2016).

there is a specialized research guide to help you make use of these resources.

This section presents miniature guides, intended to be illustrative starting points for your research in five areas of transactional law practice: securities law, the law governing corporate governance and M&A (mergers and acquisitions), banking and finance law, intellectual property law, and tax law. Each subsection briefly sketches the outline of primary law on the subject. Key treatises, practitioners' materials, and looseleaf services, as well as online tools for research, are also listed and described. Finally, there are references to guides on conducting legal research on each topic. None of these subsections, however, are meant to be comprehensive treatments of research on the topics.

Transactional lawyers may also practice in areas like trusts and estates or real estate, but these topics do not lend themselves to succinct summaries of available research tools. While there are many uniform laws in these areas, such as the widely adopted Uniform Probate Code, relevant resources vary widely from state to state. That said, state formbooks and practice treatises like those described in Chapter 14 tend to be quite useful in these areas, and practitioners must also be aware of the vast federal regulatory landscape.

Several of the subsections below reference chapters in *Specialized Legal Research* (Penny Hazelton ed., new ed. 2014–date), an excellent, in-depth guide to more than a dozen areas of legal practice. Individual chapters are revised on a rotating basis, so some are more current than others. There are also many topical research guides and bibliographies available on law library websites. The appendix to this book lists treatises and services in many transactional law practice areas, as well.

(a) Securities Law

Stocks, bonds, and options are the most well-known and common types of securities. Transactions involving securities are regulated by both federal and state law. At the federal level, there are six essential securities acts as well as numerous regulations and proposed regulations promulgated under their authority by the SEC. At the state level, statutes known as "blue sky laws" regulate conduct in this area. Businesses must follow the applicable law on registration of securities, financial reporting, and disclosure of the purchase or sale of securities by company insiders.

The SEC generates several unique types of primary law documents. Regulatory actions taken by the agency include Interpretive Releases, Concept Releases, Policy Statements, and Exemptive Orders. In response to an enforcement action, the commission's administrative law judges hold hearings and issue decisions on alleged securities law violations. The commission hears appeals to those decisions and issues Commission Opinions which are then appealable to the U.S. Court of Appeals. SEC staff members can also issue No-Action Letters at the request of individuals or entities in response to questions about potential securities law violations. No-Action Letters are issued if staff will not recommend enforcement actions against the requesting party and are binding only in that situation, but they provide guidance as to how the agency will address similar issues.

Several treatises cover securities law. Thomas Lee Hazen, *Treatise on the Law of Securities Regulation* (7th ed. 2016) is available in seven print volumes and on Westlaw. Other treatises are available online in practice centers on Westlaw, Lexis, Bloomberg Law, and Cheetah.

Federal Securities Law Reporter (Wolters Kluwer) is the most respected looseleaf service and is available on the Cheetah platform as well as in print. *Securities Law News* (Bloomberg) is a newsletter good for tracking recent developments and regulatory trends, available on Bloomberg Law. The *Blue Sky Law Reporter* (Wolters Kluwer) covers state securities laws and is available on Cheetah.

Practitioners' materials include Gary M. Brown, *Securities Law and Practice Deskbook* (6th ed. 2012) from the Practising Law Institute and available on PLI PLUS. The Securities Law Handbook Series (annual, available on Westlaw) consists of 27 publications on a variety of narrow topics and includes the more general *Securities Law Handbook*. *Securities Law Techniques* (1985–date, available on Lexis) was edited for nearly twenty years by A.A. Sommer, Jr., a former SEC commissioner, and contains information on securities litigation.

A relatively new online tool is Lexis Securities Mosaic (www.lexissecuritiesmosaic.com), formerly Knowledge Mosaic, which LexisNexis acquired in 2013. The platform is separate from Lexis Practice Advisor and is not part of law school subscriptions. It offers additional materials such as updates from regulatory agencies and a database of law firm commentary and news reports.

For more comprehensive coverage of legal research resources and methods in securities law, see Kay Moller Todd, "Securities Regulation," chapter 1 in *Specialized Legal Research*. The chapter has two helpful appendices: Appendix 1-1 is a concordance of SEC rules, the acts under which they are authorized, the relevant regulations if any, and their location in Title 17 of the *CFR*, and Appendix 1-2 is a concordance of SEC forms and schedules. Both concordances are detailed indexes listing the rules, forms, and schedules alphabetically and pointing to where in the securities law they can be found.

(b) Corporate Governance and M&A

Corporate formation, record-keeping, accounting, decision-making, and combination often involve legal counsel, especially in large corporations. The primary authorities governing these areas of corporate conduct are varied, and can overlap with securities laws, banking and finance law, employment law, intellectual property law, and tax law.

Corporate formation and delegation of responsibility in the U.S. are based in state law. Since so many corporations are organized under Delaware law, Title 8 of the *Delaware Code*, the Delaware General Corporation Law (DGCL), is an essential source. So too is the Model Business Corporation Act, or MBCA, managed by a committee of the ABA's Business Law Section and adopted in whole or in part by over half of the states. Judicial interpretations of statutes in the relevant jurisdiction is also a significant area of the law. Finally, knowing how to access corporate documents like articles of incorporation and bylaws is part of the transactional lawyer's trade.

Several federal statutes are designed to prevent fraud and abuse in accounting and in corporate mergers and acquisitions. A host of statutes and regulations seek to curb the anticompetitive effects of business combination and are enforced by the Federal Trade Commission and the Department of Justice. Corporate accounting oversight has seen a marked increase in complexity due to the Sarbanes-Oxley Act of 2002, which was passed in the wake of several corporate scandals in the early 2000s.[13]

Two preeminent national treatises on corporate governance and combinations are the comprehensive *Fletcher Cyclopedia of the Law of Corporations* (1931–date, available on Westlaw), and James D. Cox & Thomas Lee Hazen, *Treatise on the Law of Corporations* (3d ed. 2010–date, also on Westlaw), which focuses more on jurisdictions following the MBCA. There are also many state-specific treatises. The leading treatises on Delaware corporate law are R. Franklin Balotti & Jesse A. Finkelstein, *The Delaware Law of Corporations and Business Organizations* (3d ed. 1998–date, available on both

---

[13] For an interesting look at how Congress's codified instructions for statutory interpretation relating to text in section or chapter headings of the Sarbanes-Oxley criminal penalties at 18 U.S.C. § 1519 (2006) were ignored by the U.S. Supreme Court, see Tobias A. Dorsey, *Some Reflections on Yates and the Statutes We Threw Away*, 18 GREEN BAG 2d 377 (2015).

Cheetah and Westlaw), and Edward P. Welch et al., *Folk on the Delaware General Corporation Law* (6th ed. 2014–date, available on Cheetah).

The ABA's online M&A Deal Points Studies (www.americanbar.org/groups/business_law/committees/ma/deal_points/) provide in-depth, periodic coverage of mergers and acquisitions, but they are only available to Business Law Section members. Looseleafs in the area are *Corporation Service* (CCH), available on Cheetah, and *Merger & Antitrust News* (Bloomberg), available on Bloomberg Law.

Practitioners' materials tend to deal with one or more specific aspects of corporate law, but there are some more general handbooks on governance. One example is Wolters Kluwer's *Corporate Governance Guide*, available on Cheetah, which provides explanations and updates on relevant topics. In a slightly different vein, the American Law Institute's *Principles of Corporate Governance: Analysis & Recommendations* can be helpful for comparing the law in different states.

(c) Banking and Finance Law

The law governing banking and finance in the U.S. is both state and federal, with states handling bank charters and supervision while federal authorities oversee deposits, currency, and consumer protection. Recent federal legislation passed in the wake of the 2008 financial crisis has added complexity to the area. The main new statute is the Dodd-Frank Wall Street Reform and Consumer Protection Act, Pub. L. No. 111–203, 124 Stat. 1376 (2010) (mostly codified at 12 U.S.C. §§ 5301–5641).

Title 12 of the *CFR* covers federal banking regulations, which are administered by the Federal Reserve Board, the Office of the Comptroller of Currency (OCC), the Federal Deposit Insurance Corporation (FDIC), the Consumer Financial Protection Bureau (CFPB), and now the Federal Stability Oversight Council (FSOC). Regulation at the state level tends to be the purview of banking commissions or departments.

Banking and finance are given treatment in numerous treatises. Burton V. McCullough et al., *Banking Law* (1981–date, available on Lexis) is considered comprehensive, as is Michael P. Malloy, *Banking Law and Regulation* (2d ed. 2011–date, available on Cheetah). Several treatises cover more detailed aspects of financial regulation.

Looseleaf services are also plentiful in this area. *Federal Banking Law Reporter* and *State Banking Law Reporter* (both available on Cheetah) are well-established sources. News and other current awareness tools can be found in *Banking News* (available on

Bloomberg Law) and *The Banker's Letter of the Law* (available on Lexis), which focuses on litigation and case law in the field. *Banking Law Journal* (also on Lexis) is a classic periodical that includes digests of cases from all relevant U.S. jurisdictions.

Print and online practitioners' tools on federal banking law include *Bank Compliance Guide* (available on Cheetah) and Keith R. Fisher, *Banking Law Manual* (2d ed. 2000–date, available on Lexis). Lexis Practice Advisor's Financial Services Regulation section, which covers developing areas in the law, includes analysis and comparison of state law.

For more comprehensive coverage of legal research resources and methods in banking and finance law, see Penny Hazelton, "Banking Law," chapter 10 in *Specialized Legal Research*. Appendices include a glossary of abbreviations and acronyms and lists of banking regulations by subject and by *CFR* section.

(d) Intellectual Property Law

Intellectual property law includes copyright law, patent law, trademark law, and the law protecting trade secrets. It is quite a broad topic, and some even doubt the utility of categorizing these areas as "intellectual property."[14] Each area has its own regulatory structure and specialized resources.

U.S. copyright law protects creative expressions and is almost entirely federal.[15] Article I, section 8, clause 8, of the U.S. Constitution is generally referred to as the patent and copyright clause. Statutes are codified in Title 17 of the *U.S. Code* and regulations, which are made by the U.S. Copyright Office, can be found in Title 37 of the *CFR*.

Patent law protects inventions and is federal, with statutes codified at Title 35 of the *U.S. Code*. The U.S. Patent and Trademark Office (USPTO) reviews patent applications and issues regulations, which can be also be found in Title 37 of the *CFR*.

Trademark law protects businesses and their products, with the federal Lanham Act, codified at 15 U.S.C. §§ 1051–1127. Trademark regulations are also in Title 37 of the *CFR*. There is a significant amount of trademark protection in state statutes and common law, as well.

Law protecting trade secrets was traditionally made entirely at the state level, with many state statutes based on versions of the

---

[14] *See, e.g.*, Mark A. Lemley, *Property, Intellectual Property, and Free Riding*, 83 TEX. L. REV. 1031, 1033–37 (2005).

[15] For a thorough explanation of the history of state and common law copyright, see Zvi S. Rosen, *Common-Law Copyright*, 85 U. CIN. L. REV. 1055 (2018).

Uniform Trade Secrets Act. However, the Defend Trade Secrets Act of 2016, 18 U.S.C. § 1836, now allows, among other things, for private actions in federal court for trade secret misappropriation.

Two copyright law treatises are preeminent: *Nimmer on Copyright* (1963–date, available on Lexis) and *Patry on Copyright* (2006–date, available on Westlaw). *Chisum on Patents* (1978–date, available on Lexis) is an authoritative and widely cited patent law treatise. *McCarthy on Trademarks and Unfair Competition* (5th ed. 2017–date, available on Westlaw) and *Gilson on Trademarks* (1974–date, available on Lexis) are leading treatises in that area. *Milgrim on Trade Secrets* (1967–date, available on Lexis) provides comprehensive coverage including a helpful index.

Topical services cover each of the areas of intellectual property law. *United States Patents Quarterly* (available on Bloomberg Law) reports and digests cases on copyright, patent, and trademark. *Intellectual Property Law News* (also on Bloomberg Law) is a newsletter source. *Copyright Law Reporter* (available on Cheetah) focuses on copyright cases.

There are far too many practitioners' materials in this area to make even a representative selection in this subsection. Deskbooks and manuals from Practising Law Institute such as Ronald B. Hildreth & David Aker, *Patent Law: A Practitioner's Guide* (4th ed. 2012–date, available on PLI PLUS) are popular sources, as are similar works on the Cheetah and Bloomberg Law platforms and those in print from the ABA. Of interest for corporate counsel is John W. Hazard, Jr., *Copyright Law in Business and Practice* (rev. ed. 1998–date, available on Westlaw). Lex Machina (www.lexmachina. com), an online subscription analytics service now owned by LexisNexis, is another excellent source with detailed information about intellectual property litigation.

For more comprehensive coverage of legal research resources and methods in copyright law, see William H. Manz, "Copyright Law," chapter 4, and for patent and trademark, see Harold F. See, "Federal Patent and Trademark Law," chapter 11, in *Specialized Legal Research*.

(e) Tax Law

Taxation in the United States is governed by a complex set of federal and state laws touching every aspect of business and personal affairs. Lawyers specializing in tax law tend to make heavy use of specialized legal resources. Thus, separate research platforms, looseleaf services, and in-depth newsletters are the norm.

The federal tax code, known as the Internal Revenue Code or IRC, makes up Title 26 of the *U.S. Code*, and Internal Revenue Service (IRS) procedures and Department of Treasury regulations are found in Title 26 of the *CFR*. The IRS also generates guidance documents in various forms, each serving a different purpose, including Revenue Rulings, Private Letter Rulings, and other memoranda.

Prominent federal tax treatises include Boris I. Bittker & Lawrence Lokken, *Federal Taxation of Income, Estates, & Gifts* (2d/3d eds. 1989–date, available on Westlaw), and Jacob Rabkin & Mark Johnson, *Federal Income, Gift and Estate Taxation* (1942–date, available on Lexis). *Federal Tax Coordinator 2d* (available on Westlaw) goes into greater depth of analysis on excise and payroll tax in addition to other topics.

Several tax services collect relevant cases and administrative documents and provide annotated versions of the IRC. The *Standard Federal Tax Reporter* (available on Cheetah) and *United States Tax Reporter* (available on Westlaw) are both well-respected and much-used sources in tax practice. *Federal Estate and Gift Tax Reporter* is also available on the Cheetah platform. For state tax practice, see *State Tax Guide* (available on Cheetah) and *All States Tax Guide* (available on Westlaw).

Online platforms are now the main source of everyday tax practice guidance. Thomson Reuters Checkpoint (checkpoint.riag. com) contains vital resources, including news and practice tools; much of its coverage is also available on Westlaw. Lexis Advance Tax collects news and primary law on tax along with secondary sources into one convenient interface. Bloomberg Law: Tax contains the excellent *Tax Management Portfolios*, which contain treatise-like analysis on hundreds of discrete tax topics together with practice tools like checklists and forms.

Staying up to date with changes in the tax code is especially important given the large degree to which the rules change each year. Tax Notes (www.taxnotes.com), from Tax Analysts, is a much sought-after source of daily news and analysis. Articles from tax-related periodicals are also indexed separately from other law journals and publications. CCH's *Federal Tax Articles* contains abstracts of journal articles arranged by Internal Revenue Code section and *Index to Federal Tax Articles* is a subject/author index with retrospective coverage back to 1913.

Finally, tax law research is the focus of several published works, including Joni Larson & Dan Sheaffer, *Federal Tax Research* (2d ed. 2011) and Gail Levin Richmond & Kevin M. Yamamoto, *Federal Tax*

Research: Guide to Materials and Techniques (10th ed. 2018). Mary A. Hotchkiss, "Federal Income Taxation," chapter 3 in *Specialized Legal Research*, is also a helpful source, containing a glossary of tax terms and acronyms as well as lists of tax periodicals, newsletters, and websites.

Chapter 16

FACTUAL INFORMATION

Table of Sections

This chapter looks at resources designed to provide answers to factual questions. These materials generally do not contain primary sources or analyze legal developments, but are instead sources for definitions, telephone numbers, addresses, statistics, financial information, and other related data.

Your first approach to finding factual information may be to run an internet search or check Wikipedia, and in relatively simple instances this may get you just what you need. At times, however, particularly when searching for comprehensive or historical information, more detailed and focused resources can save valuable time and lead to information beyond your initial search results.

§ 16.1 DICTIONARIES AND RELATED WORKS

The law has developed its own means of expression over the centuries. Latin, Law French,[1] and the stylized language of legal documents have produced terminology that can be difficult for the

---

[1] Law French refers to legal terminology derived from the Anglo-Norman language used in legal documents and judicial proceedings beginning in the 13th century. Examples still in use today include attorney, bailiff, felon, plaintiff, and oyez. For an introduction, see Ivona Coghlan, *Law French—When Law and Language Collide*, LAW BOD BLOG (May 31, 2018) (blogs.bodleian.ox.ac.uk/lawbod/2018/05/31/law-french-when-law-and-language-collide) [https://perma.cc/TL8H-2GYQ].

uninitiated to understand. Latin words and phrases are still prevalent in legal practice, from the writs of *certiorari* or *habeas corpus* to doctrines such as *res ipsa loquitur*, and even everyday words such as *infant* or *issue* have specialized meanings in legal documents, necessitating specialized resources to give researchers more information on these terms.

(a) Dictionaries

While a quick online search can find definitions for most terms, the internet may not readily provide the full nuance of legal terminology. A good law dictionary is needed to understand the technical language of the law and to define older terms found in historical documents.

Black's Law Dictionary (Bryan A. Garner ed., 11th ed. 2019, available on Westlaw) is considered by most to be the leading work. It has definitions for more than 55,000 terms, with pronunciations, notes on usage, and quotations from treatises as well as tables of legal abbreviations and legal maxims.[2] Illustration 16-1 shows definitions for *dog* in *Black's*, as they appear in Westlaw.

Wolters Kluwer Bouvier Law Dictionary (Stephen Michael Sheppard ed., compact ed. 2011 and desk ed. 2012) is the only current competitor to *Black's*. Its 8,500 entries are far fewer than *Black's*, but the definitions are generally more thorough. The two-volume desk edition includes notes on derivation and usage, with lengthy excerpts from articles and opinions showing how a term is used in legal writing. The paperback compact edition has the same definitions but omits these notes.

Several other, shorter dictionaries can also be found in law libraries and bookstores. Among the best are Steven H. Gifis, *Law Dictionary* (7th ed. 2016), and Daniel Oran, *Oran's Dictionary of the Law* (4th ed. 2008). Two dictionaries that are available both in print and free online are *Merriam-Webster's Dictionary of Law* (rev. ed. 2016) (earlier edition at dictionary.findlaw.com) and Gerald N. Hill & Kathleen Thompson Hill, *Nolo's Plain English Law Dictionary* (2009) (www.nolo.com/dictionary).

---

[2] For a history of *Black's* since its first edition in 1891, see Sarah Yates, *Black's Law Dictionary: The Making of an American Standard*, 103 LAW LIBR. J. 175 (2011). On the history of law dictionaries more generally, see D. S. Bland, *Some Notes on the Evolution of the Legal Dictionary*, 1 J. LEGAL HIST. 75 (1980), and Gary L. McDowell, *The Politics of Meaning: Law Dictionaries and the Liberal Tradition of Interpretation*, 44 AM. J. LEGAL HIST. 257 (2000).

Black's Law Dictionary (11th ed. 2019), dog

DOG

Bryan A. Garner, Editor in Chief

Preface | Guide | Legal Maxims | Bibliography

dog (bef. 12c) **1.** The common domesticated animal having four legs, fur, and a tail, and frequently kept as a pet or trained to guard people or places; *canis lupus familiaris*, commonly known as the domestic dog (even when feral).

- **arson dog.** (1993) A police dog trained to detect accelerants at the site of a fire.

- **assistance dog.** See *service dog.*

- **attack dog.** (1943) **1.** See *guard dog.* **2.** See WATCHDOG (2).

- **cadaver dog.** (1996) A dog trained to detect the scent of a human corpse, esp. one that is hidden. — Also termed *human-remains detection dog.* Cf. *search dog.*

- **dangerous dog.** (17c) A dog legally classified as one whose behavior poses a threat to the safety of humans and other animals based on its actions, its breed, or the actions of its owner. • The legal definition varies depending on city, county, or state law. See DANGEROUS-DOG LAW; DANGEROUS-DOG REGISTRY; BREED-SPECIFIC LEGISLATION.

- **detection dog.** (1970) A dog trained to use its senses, esp. the sense of smell, to detect particular substances or items such as explosives, illegal drugs, or blood. — Also termed *sniffer dog; sniffing dog; drug-sniffing dog.*

- **guard dog.** (18c) A large, usu. aggressive dog trained to protect property or people by barking loudly when it detects an intruder and to attack or restrain the intruder. — Also termed *attack dog; watchdog.*

- **guide dog.** (1932) See *service dog.*

- **hearing-ear dog.** See *service dog.*

- **human-remains detection dog.** See *cadaver dog.*

- **K-9 dog.** See *police dog.*

Illustration 16-1. Definitions from *Black's Law Dictionary.*

Older editions of dictionaries can also be helpful for determining terms' meanings in an earlier era. A few lawyers swear by Sheppard's ancient but scholarly predecessor, the three-volume *Bouvier's Law Dictionary and Concise Encyclopedia* (Francis Rawle ed., 8th ed. 1914), which is available in HeinOnline's Dictionaries collection in Spinelli's Law Library Reference Shelf.[3] This collection has over 330 other legal dictionaries, including very old editions and those for specialized areas of law and foreign languages. Part of the collection is comprised of Georgetown Law Library's digitized collection of rare legal dictionaries (repository.library.georgetown.edu/handle/10822/559416). *Ballentine's Law Dictionary* (William S. Anderson ed., 3d ed. 1969, available on Lexis) was once the major competitor to *Black's*. Though it has not been updated in decades, it may still be useful for older terms.

Legal maxims sometimes found in court opinions assume a knowledge of Latin and are thus impenetrable to many readers. *Black's* provides translations, definitions, and pronunciation aids for many maxims, and older dictionaries include other phrases that are now obscure. *Latin Words & Phrases for Lawyers* (R. S. Vasan ed., 1980) has extensive coverage of maxims and includes an index by subject. Russ VerSteeg, *Essential Latin for Lawyers* (1990) explains several dozen key phrases still in common use.

Attempts to transform legal writing from legalese jargon into plain English have made some headway in recent years.[4] Bryan A. Garner, *Garner's Dictionary of Legal Usage* (3d ed. 2011) focuses on how words are used in legal contexts, with definitions and essays providing articulate advocacy for clear and simple writing. David Mellinkoff, *Mellinkoff's Dictionary of Legal Usage* (1992) provides examples of usage and distinctions among related terms.

A thesaurus can be a handy (or ready, convenient, or practical) tool when searching for an alternative to an overused or not-quite-correct word. William C. Burton, *Burton's Legal Thesaurus* (5th ed. 2013) focuses on words commonly used in legal writing and argument. It has over 10,000 main entries with related terms, followed by an index of all listed words showing the main entries under which they appear.

---

[3] *See* Mary Whisner, *Bouvier's, Black's, and Tinkerbell*, 92 LAW LIBR. J. 99 (2000).

[4] RICHARD C. WYDICK & AMY E. SLOAN, PLAIN ENGLISH FOR LAWYERS (6th ed. 2019) is the classic work on simplifying legal communication. Several other guides are available, including BRYAN A. GARNER, LEGAL WRITING IN PLAIN ENGLISH (2d ed. 2013). For a broader view of how things got so bad, see DAVID MELLINKOFF, THE LANGUAGE OF THE LAW (1963), and PETER TIERSMA, LEGAL LANGUAGE (1999).

General dictionaries of the English language are used by courts even more frequently than legal dictionaries.[5] Major dictionaries include *Random House Webster's Unabridged Dictionary* (2d ed. 2001), with over 315,000 entries, and *Webster's Third New International Dictionary of the English Language, Unabridged* (1993), with over 450,000 entries. The authoritative reference work on the history and development of the English language is the *Oxford English Dictionary* (www.oed.com), which has representative quotations illustrating usage over the course of a word's lifespan. The current third edition is an online-only version that has been underway since 2000.

Quotations are frequently used in legal writing, but they are not always cited to the volume and page of the sources in which they first appeared. The true origins of many familiar expressions are obscure, and famous politicians and jurists such as Abraham Lincoln and Oliver Wendell Holmes, Jr., are credited with numerous "quotations" they probably never used.[6] Internet searches may turn up only misleading attributions, but a good quotation dictionary provides detailed information so that the original source can be confirmed and the quotation read in context. The leading dictionary of legal quotations is Fred R. Shapiro, *Oxford Dictionary of American Legal Quotations* (1993), with over 3,500 quotations from American judges and legal commentators.

Shapiro has applied the same principled and thorough approach in editing the more general *Yale Book of Quotations* (2006). Other quotation books that may also be of use include *Quote It Completely!: World Reference Guide to More Than 5,500 Memorable Quotations from Law and Literature* (Eugene C. Gerhart ed., 1998, available in HeinOnline's Legal Classics Library); and the general reference works *Bartlett's Familiar Quotations* (Geoffrey O'Brien ed., 18th ed. 2012) and *The Oxford Dictionary of Quotations* (Elizabeth Knowles ed., 8th ed. 2014). Each includes a word index for helping to identify and track down elusive quotations.

---

[5] On the Supreme Court's use of dictionaries, see, e.g., James J. Brudney & Lawrence Baum, *Oasis or Mirage: The Supreme Court's Thirst for Dictionaries in the Rehnquist and Roberts Eras*, 55 WM. & MARY L. REV. 483 (2013), and Jeffrey L. Kirchmeier & Samuel A. Thumma, *Scaling the Lexicon Fortress: The United States Supreme Court's Use of Dictionaries in the Twenty-First Century*, 94 MARQ. L. REV. 77 (2010). Some justices and scholars look to dictionaries from the late 1700s as an aid in interpreting constitutional terms. *See* Gregory E. Maggs, *A Concise Guide to Using Dictionaries from the Founding Era to Determine the Original Meaning of the Constitution*, 82 GEO. WASH. L. REV. 358 (2014).

[6] *See* Fred R. Shapiro, *Quote . . . Misquote*, N.Y. TIMES MAG., July 27, 2008, at 16.

(b) Citation and Abbreviations Guides

One of the first hurdles to understanding legal literature is the telegraphic citation form used in most sources. Legal citations are designed to succinctly communicate the information necessary to find the source and evaluate the scope of its precedential value.[7] Case citations, for example, identify not only where an opinion can be found but also the issuing court and the date of decision.

The format of a legal citation follows strict rules found in manuals and guides. Which set of rules to follow depends on whether you are writing a court document, such as a brief or memorandum, or an academic work, such as a law school paper or law review article.

In legal practice, particularly when submitting documents in court, you must follow the rules of the jurisdiction. New York courts, for example, prescribe citation according to the official *New York Law Reports Style Manual* (www.nycourts.gov/reporter/Styman_Menu. shtml). References to the rules for a specific jurisdiction can be found in practice guides and on court websites.

The standard guide to legal citation in academic writing is *The Bluebook: A Uniform System of Citation* (21st ed. 2020) (www.legal bluebook.com), which is compiled by the editors of the Columbia Law Review, Harvard Law Review, University of Pennsylvania Law Review, and Yale Law Journal.[8] *The Bluebook* is available in both

---

[7] Judge Richard Posner has explained the reasons for standardized citation forms: "Let us consider what purposes are served by having a system of citation forms rather than a free-for-all. There are four. The first is to spare the writer or editor from having to think about citation form; he memorizes the book of forms, or uses its index. . . . The second purpose, which is self-evident, is to economize on space and the reader's time. The third, which is in tension with the second, is to provide information to the reader. The fourth is to minimize distraction." Richard A. Posner, *Goodbye to the Bluebook*, 53 U. CHI. L. REV. 1343, 1344 (1986). Other sources on the history and purpose of legal citation forms include Paul Axel-Lute, *Legal Citation Form: Theory and Practice*, 75 LAW LIBR. J. 148 (1982), and Byron D. Cooper, *Anglo-American Legal Citation: Historical Development and Library Implications*, 75 LAW LIBR. J. 3 (1982). For a discussion of the importance of being able to "read" citations at a glance, see Alexa Z. Chew, *Citation Literacy*, 70 ARK. L. REV. 869 (2018).

[8] *The Bluebook* began life in 1926 as a 26-page pamphlet prepared by Erwin Griswold for his *Harvard Law Review* colleagues, although it was preceded by a similar work from 1921, *Abbreviations and Forms of Citation*, used by *Yale Law Journal* editors. *See* Fred R. Shapiro & Julie Graves Krishnaswami, *The Secret History of the* Bluebook, 100 MINN. L. REV. 1563 (2016). These early *Bluebook* editions are reprinted in THE BLUEBOOK: A SIXTY-FIVE YEAR RETROSPECTIVE (1998). Robert C. Berring's foreword notes that *The Bluebook* "has inflicted more pain on more law students than any other publication in legal history." 1 *id.* at v.

Over the years there has been an extensive law review literature on *The Bluebook*, much of it highly critical. For a review of this history and a recent contribution, see Susie Salmon, *Shedding the Uniform: Beyond a "Uniform System of Citation" to a More Efficient Fit*, 99 MARQ. L. REV. 763 (2016). One particularly intriguing analysis is Aside, *Don't Cry Over Filled Milk: The Neglected Footnote Three to* Carolene Products, 136 U. PA. L. REV. 1553 (1988) (explaining that *The Bluebook*'s rules are so mysterious

print and subscription online versions, and a free restatement of its rules (as of the 20th edition) is available as *The Indigo Book: An Open and Compatible Implementation of a Uniform System of Citation* (2016) (law.resource.org/pub/us/code/blue/IndigoBook.html).

The Association of Legal Writing Directors' *ALWD Guide to Legal Citation* (Coleen M. Barger ed., 6th ed. 2017) is preferred by numerous legal writing programs and a few journals as an alternative to *The Bluebook*. It includes helpful appendices listing local court citation rules and abbreviations for law reviews and other periodicals.[9] Cornell Law School's Legal Information Institute publishes an online Introduction to Basic Legal Citation (www.law. cornell.edu/citation/), a concise guide with examples using both *Bluebook* and *ALWD* rules.

Some state courts use public domain citations that do not require reference to particular volumes and page numbers, but *The Bluebook* and other citation systems generally require citation to printed sources if the material is published in that form. Some electronic resources have page images mirroring the printed version, while others (including Westlaw and Lexis) indicate the printed page numbers in the text of online documents. In some instances, however, for a complete citation it may still be necessary to track down the original printed version in a library.

No matter what citation rules are followed, part of the puzzle is simply deciphering the abbreviations used so that you can identify sources. The online legal research platforms let you enter an unfamiliar citation in the search box, so understanding an abbreviation is not always necessary to obtain a document. This approach frequently works, but at times it may lead to a dead end. Cases and law review articles contain numerous abbreviations and citations that are cryptic even to experienced researchers.

Helpfully, reference works such as *Black's Law Dictionary* and *The Bluebook* contain tables listing the major abbreviations found in legal literature, but these are hardly comprehensive. The most convenient source for deciphering citations is usually the free online Cardiff Index to Legal Abbreviations (www.legalabbrevs.cardiff.ac. uk). It has a British focus but includes many U.S. sources and can be searched by either abbreviation or title keyword. Illustration 16-2 shows the main search page for the Cardiff Index.

---

that they could only have been produced by an advanced extraterrestrial race). For a counterpoint, see David J.S. Ziff, *The Worst System of Citation Except for All the Others*, 66 J. LEGAL EDUC. 668 (2017).

    [9] Another publication listing citation forms for law reviews and other resources is MARY MILES PRINCE, PRINCE'S DICTIONARY OF LEGAL CITATIONS (9th ed. 2017).

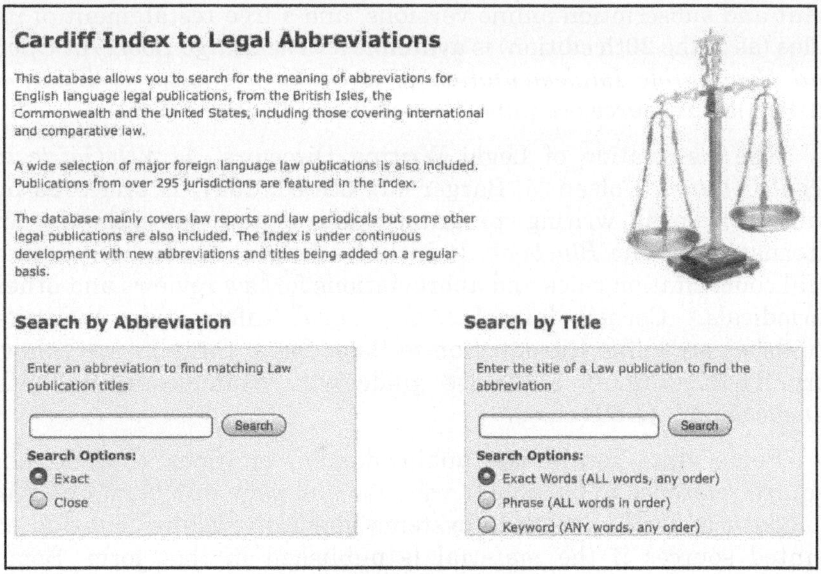

Cardiff Index to Legal Abbreviations

This database allows you to search for the meaning of abbreviations for English language legal publications, from the British Isles, the Commonwealth and the United States, including those covering international and comparative law.

A wide selection of major foreign language law publications is also included. Publications from over 295 jurisdictions are featured in the Index.

The database mainly covers law reports and law periodicals but some other legal publications are also included. The Index is under continuous development with new abbreviations and titles being added on a regular basis.

Search by Abbreviation

Enter an abbreviation to find matching Law publication titles

[   ] (Search)

Search Options:
- ● Exact
- ○ Close

Search by Title

Enter the title of a Law publication to find the abbreviation

[   ] (Search)

Search Options:
- ● Exact Words (ALL words, any order)
- ○ Phrase (ALL words in order)
- ○ Keyword (ANY words, any order)

Illustration 16-2. The Cardiff Index to Legal
Abbreviations search page.

Specialized abbreviation dictionaries are also available. Mary Miles Prince, *Prince's Dictionary of Legal Abbreviations* (7th ed. 2017) and Donald Raistrick, *Index to Legal Citations and Abbreviations* (4th ed. 2013) are the leading U.S. and British resources respectively. Their coverage overlaps, but each includes some sources not found in the other.[10]

§ 16.2   LEGAL DIRECTORIES

Earlier chapters discussed directories covering federal and state legislatures, administrative agencies, and courts. Numerous more general legal directories have contact and biographical information for lawyers. Most of these focus on individual states or particular specialties, but two comprehensive directories of the legal profession are published by divisions of the parent companies of Westlaw and Lexis. Each covers over a million lawyers, but neither includes every lawyer in the country or world.

Martindale-Hubbell Law Directory (www.martindale.com) is the more established source, dating to the 19th century.[11] It is available

---

[10] The still-stymied researcher may consider turning to an internet search engine as a last resort. Sometimes, however, authors or editors may have simply made a citation error.

[11] *Martindale-Hubbell Law Directory* was first published in 1931, and was preceded by *Martindale's American Law Directory* (1868–1930) and *Hubbell's Law*

in an annual printed edition of three volumes, limited to lawyers and law firms who have purchased listings, but its online versions at martindale.com and lawyers.com are far more inclusive. Free listings have only mailing addresses and basic information about education and bar admission dates, but in some instances these are accompanied by ratings and comments from fellow attorneys and clients. Attorneys and law firms can purchase fuller entries with telephone numbers, e-mail addresses, more extensive biographical information, and website links. *Martindale-Hubbell's* listings are available on Lexis as the LexisNexis Law Directory, but without peer or client evaluations.

West Legal Directory, the other nationwide directory of attorneys, is available on Westlaw. For most attorneys listed, in addition to addresses and telephone numbers it has biographical information such as education, professional affiliations, and areas of practice. Entries for some attorneys also include Litigation Analytics statistics on the types of cases handled and links to relevant briefs, motions, and other documents. The FindLaw Lawyer Directory (lawyers.findlaw.com) is a free, stripped-down version of the directory with basic contact information.

Several other national directories of lawyers and law firms are available in print or online, although none is as comprehensive as *Martindale-Hubbell* or the West Legal Directory. *The Best Lawyers in America* (www.bestlawyers.com) is an annual guide to highly respected practicing attorneys, chosen for inclusion by their peers. For each state, lawyers are listed under about seventy specialties and then within each specialty by city. This topical arrangement allows potential clients to browse listings in nearby cities. The online directory Avvo (www.avvo.com) has basic contact information and allows clients to add reviews.[12]

Leadership Connect (www.leadershipconnect.io) has contact and brief biographical information on management and recruiting personnel for over 700 law firms. Vault (www.vault.com) profiles and ranks large and midsize law firms on measures such as salary, diversity, and pro bono participation. Some of its information is available free. The National Association for Law Placement's NALP Directory of Legal Employers (www.nalpdirectory.com) is a free

---

Directory (1870–1930). LLMC has published the volumes from 1868 through 1999 on microfiche, and HeinOnline includes volumes from 1868 to 1963.

[12] Several states and local bar organizations have issued ethics opinions on how lawyers may ethically respond to negative online reviews, and more have been proposed. *See, e.g.,* New York State Bar Ass'n Comm. on Prof'l Ethics, Op. 1032 (2014); Penn. Bar Ass'n Ethics Comm., Op. 2014–200; and Texas Center for Legal Ethics, Op. 662 (2016).

resource designed primarily for job-seeking lawyers, with basic data on more than 1,000 firms and other legal employers.

Other directories focus on attorneys working outside of law firms. *Directory of Corporate Counsel* has biographical information on lawyers working for more than 5,000 corporations and nonprofit organizations and is available on Westlaw. The Association of American Law Schools (www.aals.org) publishes an annual *Directory of Law Teachers*, with biographies of faculty members of all accredited law schools in the United States; older editions from 1922 to 2012 are available on HeinOnline.

State and regional directories often provide more thorough listings of local lawyers than national directories. Many state and local bar associations publish directories or offer attorney search features on their websites. Legal Directories Publishing Co. (www. legaldirectories.com) publishes print and online directories for 22 states (Alabama, Arkansas, Georgia, Illinois, Indiana, Iowa, Kansas, Kentucky, Louisiana, Minnesota, Mississippi, Missouri, North Carolina, Ohio, Oklahoma, Pennsylvania, South Carolina, Tennessee, Texas, Virginia & West Virginia, and Wisconsin). These have alphabetical listings with addresses and telephone numbers, and very few biographical entries, but they are likely to include names missing from the national directories.

Professional and trade organizations can be invaluable sources of information in their areas of interest. Two directories are notable for their broad coverage of both legal and nonlegal organizations. *Encyclopedia of Associations*, available online as Associations Unlimited (www.gale.com), has descriptions and contact information for over 25,000 national organizations. *National Trade and Professional Associations of the United States* (www.associationexecs. com) is less broad in scope but just as useful for basic information on major business-related organizations.

While most directories are somewhat specialized, a few try to answer a wider range of inquiries. *Law and Legal Information Directory*, published by Gale, is a three-volume set with information culled from a number of directories, listing legal organizations, consultants, research centers, law libraries, lawyer referral services, legal aid and defender offices, and a variety of federal and state government agencies. *The Legal Researcher's Desk Reference*, published by Infosources, is a smaller paperback volume with an array of directory information including government offices, courts, and bar associations, and other resources such as state court structure charts.

Both Westlaw and Lexis contain directories of expert witnesses, which can be useful when preparing for litigation. The ALM Expert Witness Directory (1997–date) is available on Lexis, while Westlaw maintains a collection of expert witness curricula vitae and résumés in addition to directories and reports.

As is the case with dictionaries, sometimes you are interested in historical information or need to see how information has changed over time. With most of the directories listed above, the online versions reflect current information and do not provide retrospective data. Thus, researchers should be prepared to seek older print copies via WorldCat (worldcat.org), a process that may become more frustrating as libraries increasingly save space by removing these "outdated" resources from their collections.

§ 16.3 STATISTICS

Legal researchers need demographic and statistical information for many purposes, from supporting a discrimination claim to preparing for the deposition of an expert witness. These statistics are available from an array of printed and online sources.

Statistics on the federal courts, such as the number of cases commenced and terminated by district and by subject, can be found in the Administrative Office of the U.S. Courts' annual *Judicial Business of the United States Courts* and on its website (www.us courts.gov). The National Center for State Courts (NCSC) site has a Court Statistics Project (www.courtstatistics.org) that offers several ways to query its statistical database and examine state court business. It includes the annual publication *State Court Caseload Digest* (successor to *Examining the Work of State Courts*), as well as caseload statistics and court structure charts.

The American Bar Association's Legal Profession Statistics page (www.americanbar.org/about_the_aba/profession_statistics/)   has PDFs of general statistics on lawyer demographics as well as links to various websites with information on the legal profession, including salaries. *The Lawyer Statistical Report*, which was published periodically by the American Bar Foundation, was the leading source on the composition of the U.S. legal profession. The last report was published in 2012 and provides data as of 2005.

Criminal statistics are available from both federal and state governments. The Federal Bureau of Investigation's Uniform Crime Reporting (UCR) Program (www.fbi.gov/about-us/cjis/ucr) provides access to the annual *Crime in the United States*, with information on criminal offenses and persons arrested.[13] The U.S. Sentencing Commission's website (www.ussc.gov), especially its data reports, are invaluable sources of statistics on federal sentencing. The Bureau of Justice Statistics website (www.bjs.gov) has links to a variety of other statistics and publications. The NCSC has resources aggregating state criminal caseloads on its Court Statistics Project website, and crime data may also be available from state agencies.

The U.S. Census Bureau prepares the Census of Population and Housing every ten years, and every census since 1790 is available on its website (www.census.gov/prod/www/decennial.html). The Bureau's American Community Survey provides annual updates to the decennial census data. Information from these and other Census Bureau sources can be found at the Explore Census Data page (data. census.gov/), although locating useful data may be challenging.

The *Statistical Abstract of the United States* was published annually through 2012 by the Census Bureau and has been continued beginning in 2013 by ProQuest (statabs.proquest.com). This essential resource covers a wide range of economic and demographic statistics and is particularly useful because it gives source information for each table. It thus serves as a convenient lead to agencies and publications with more extensive coverage of specific areas. The Census Bureau website includes PDF versions of early editions back to 1878 (www.census.gov/library/publications/time-series/statistical_abstracts.html).[14] *Historical Statistics of the United States* (Susan B. Carter et al. eds., 2006) (hsus.cambridge.org) is a comprehensive, five-volume compendium of statistics from the *Statistical Abstract* and hundreds of other sources.

Illustration 16-3 shows a table from the *Statistical Abstract*, providing information about the number of pets in American households. The table includes a source reference to a publication of the American Veterinary Medical Association, where more detailed information may be available.

---

[13] *Sourcebook of Criminal Justice Statistics* (www.albany.edu/sourcebook/) has a broad survey of the social and economic impacts of crime, but its website was last updated in 2013. Older print editions from 1973 to 2003 are available in HeinOnline's Law Journal Library.

[14] ProQuest's Historical Statistical Abstracts of the United States makes these tables from 1878 to 2012 available in spreadsheet format as well as PDF.

The *Statistical Abstract* was supplemented by two additional publications with more detailed information for specific geographical areas, *State and Metropolitan Area Data Book* and *County and City Data Book*. Like the *Abstract*, these are no longer issued by the government, but updated versions are published by Bernan Press. Bernan has also published COUNTY AND CITY EXTRA: SPECIAL HISTORICAL EDITION, 1790–2010 (Deirdre Gaquin & Mary Meghan Ryan eds., 2015). Older *Data Books* are available on the Census Bureau website (www.census.gov/library/publications/2010/compendia/databooks.html).

Table 1268: Household Pet Ownership: 2011 [Ownership By Household Income And Size; And Veterinary Care And Expenses]

Source: American Veterinary Medical Association. Last Updated: Dec. 2019 Edition: 2020
Note: XLS spreadsheet shows data for selected years beginning in 2006.

Table		Jump to:　Index terms and details　Citation

Table 1268. Household Pet Ownership: 2011

[In percent, except as indicated (69.9 represents 89,900,000). Based on a sample survey of 50,347 households in 2012]

Item	Unit	Dogs	Cats	Birds	Horses
Total companion pet population [1]	Million	69.9	74.1	8.3	4.9
Number of households owning pets	Million	43.3	36.1	3.7	1.8
Percent of households owning companion pets [1]	Percent	36.5	30.4	3.1	1.5
Average number owned per household	Number	1.6	2.1	2.3	2.7
PERCENT OF HOUSEHOLDS OWNING PETS					
Annual household income:					
Under $20,000	Percent	34.5	34.1	4.3	1.4
$20,000 to $34,999	Percent	40.0	36.8	4.0	2.1
$35,000 to $54,999	Percent	42.4	35.8	3.9	1.9
$55,000 to $84,999	Percent	43.8	34.0	3.3	1.9
$85,000 and over	Percent	43.9	31.7	3.1	1.9
Household size: [1]					
One person	Percent	26.8	29.8	2.6	1.3
Two persons	Percent	40.1	34.6	3.2	1.8
Three persons	Percent	50.0	38.3	4.2	2.2
Four persons	Percent	53.7	34.9	4.3	2.0
Five or more persons	Percent	54.2	38.1	6.8	2.6
VETERINARY CARE AND EXPENDITURES					
Households obtaining veterinary care [2]	Percent	81.3	55.1	12.4	53.8
Average visits per household per year	Number	2.6	1.6	0.3	1.9
Expenditures per household per year (mean)	Dollars	378	191	33	373
Expenditures per animal (mean)	Dollars	227	90	14	133

[1] As of December 31, 2011. [2] During the year.

Source: American Veterinary Medical Association, Schaumburg, IL. U.S. Pet Ownership and Demographics Sourcebook, 2012. © See also <http://www.avma.org/reference/marketstats/sourcebook.asp>.

Illustration 16-3. A table from the *Statistical Abstract of the United States*.

Links to statistical sites from over 100 federal government agencies are aggregated on a single USA.gov website (www.usa.gov/statistics). You can also download raw datasets from government agencies at Data.gov (www.data.gov).

Annual reports and other publications of government agencies, trade associations, labor unions, and public interest groups frequently contain statistical data relating to their work. ProQuest's Statistical Insight Collection (statistical.proquest.com) provides access to much of this material, covering nearly 10,000 sources each year. The information is also available in the print indexes *American Statistics Index* (covering U.S. government sources) and *Statistical Reference Index* (covering state government and private sources), and their accompanying microfiche sets.

Index to International Statistics, another component of the Statistical Insight Collection, covers statistics from major intergovernmental organizations. Much of its data comes from the United Nations, which publishes several statistical collections including a general *Statistical Yearbook* and more specific works such as *Demographic Yearbook, Energy Statistics Yearbook, International Trade Statistics Yearbook,* and *National Accounts Statistics.* The three-volume *International Historical Statistics: 1750–2010* (B. R. Mitchell ed., 2013) is a useful compendium of demographic, industrial, and social statistics. For current data, check the U.S. Bureau of Labor Statistics' lengthy list of statistical agency websites around the world (www.bls.gov/bls/other.htm).

Most statistical sources focus on facts rather than opinions, but surveys can be important resources in areas of the law from discrimination to trademark infringement. Polls and other sources of public opinion are available through a number of electronic sources. Gallup, Inc. (www.gallup.com) has recent poll results, and allows keyword searching of questionnaires and poll analyses on major topics such as the Supreme Court and election results. Polling the Nations (www.orspub.com) and the iPoll Databank at the Roper Center for Public Opinion Research (ropercenter.cornell.edu) have polling and survey data from hundreds of organizations, accessible by keyword search or through subject indexes.[15]

§ 16.4 PUBLIC RECORDS

Factual research can be vital in establishing a claim, locating a witness, or negotiating a settlement. News databases and internet searches can provide a great deal of factual background information, and much more is available through public records databases. These are the resources to use for information such as the value of real property or the status of a professional license.

Public records are maintained by federal, state, and local governments. They can often be obtained for free from official websites, but the most convenient starting points for many are extensive national databases available from platforms such as Westlaw and Lexis. "Public Records" is a link on Westlaw's main screen (except for academic subscriptions) and is an option on the menu at the top left of the Lexis display. Both services have real property records, people locators, professional licenses, motor vehicle records, and other information. Professionals doing investigative research also use specialized public record resources such as LexisNexis Accurint (www.accurint.com) or TLOxp (www.tlo.com). Illustration 16-4 shows the range of public records information available in Lexis.

---

[15] These and other electronic polling resources are compared in Stephen Woods, *Public Opinion Poll Question Databases: An Evaluation,* 33 J. ACAD. LIBRARIANSHIP 41 (2007).

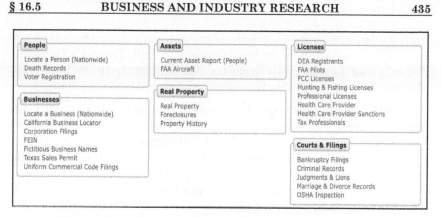

People
Locate a Person (Nationwide)
Death Records
Voter Registration

Businesses
Locate a Business (Nationwide)
California Business Locator
Corporation Filings
FEIN
Fictitious Business Names
Texas Sales Permit
Uniform Commercial Code Filings

Assets
Current Asset Report (People)
FAA Aircraft

Real Property
Real Property
Foreclosures
Property History

Licenses
DEA Registrants
FAA Pilots
FCC Licenses
Hunting & Fishing Licenses
Professional Licenses
Health Care Provider
Health Care Provider Sanctions
Tax Professionals

Courts & Filings
Bankruptcy Filings
Criminal Records
Judgments & Liens
Marriage & Divorce Records
OSHA Inspection

Illustration 16-4. Public records databases on Lexis.

There is considerable variation in the amount of information that jurisdictions make available on their official websites. In some instances, local sites may have more current or more extensive information than that available from Westlaw or Lexis. Many cities and counties have searchable online property databases, and others include information such as birth or marriage records.

Several sites have links to free public record sites in all fifty states. Good places to start include BRB Publications Inc.'s Free Resource Center (www.brbpub.com/free-public-records/) and OnlineSearches' Free Public Records Directory (publicrecords. onlinesearches.com). Even though searches and basic information are free, you may be prompted to pay for more detailed records.

§ 16.5　BUSINESS AND INDUSTRY RESEARCH

There are many sources of information—some free and some quite costly—about businesses and industries. The depth of news and data available varies depending on the type of company or industry being researched.[16]

(a) Public Companies

Publicly held corporations, which sell shares of stock to the general public on the open market, generate a wealth of accessible data. Profiles of public companies aggregate information about the company's structure, leadership, and financials, and are readily available on all the major legal research platforms. These profiles are brief but can be an excellent starting place for researching public companies. Bloomberg Law may offer the easiest access to company

---

[16] For more in-depth coverage see sources such as CELIA ROSS, MAKING SENSE OF BUSINESS REFERENCE: A GUIDE FOR LIBRARIANS AND RESEARCH PROFESSIONALS (2d ed. 2020) and KATHY E. SHIMPOCK, BUSINESS RESEARCH HANDBOOK: METHODS AND SOURCES FOR LAWYERS AND BUSINESS (1996–date).

profiles, because you can simply begin typing a company name into its search box and click on the appropriate link. Hoover's Company Records and LexisNexis Corporate Affiliations, both on Lexis, are also good sources of in-depth records for many larger companies.

Public companies must file a wide range of documents with the Securities and Exchange Commission (SEC). The SEC requires disclosure of company financials and significant events in ongoing business operations. Important forms you should be familiar with include the 10-Q and 10-K, which report financial information at quarterly and annual intervals, respectively, as well as the 8-K, which covers many other more current material disclosures. The periodic filings contain a company's key accounting documents: balance sheets, income statements, and cash flow statements.

These periodic and event-based filings, along with proxy statements and board-related information about insider transactions and mergers and acquisitions, are available through the SEC's EDGAR system (www.sec.gov/edgar.shtml). The EDGAR website includes a quick tutorial of how to use the system as well as a comprehensive list of the types of forms that can be found on the site.

Public company filings are also available through several subscription services, including Westlaw, Lexis, and Bloomberg Law. These services generally combine the data found in filings with the information included on profile pages. Bloomberg Law adds information about litigation a company is involved in and the firms that are handling the representation. Illustration 16-5 shows Bloomberg's display for Caterpillar, Inc.

More generic public company market information is also available from financial news websites and search engines, notably Google's finance search (www.google.com/finance) and Yahoo! Finance (www.finance.yahoo.com), both of which allow users to create watchlists of companies they wish to follow. Company websites are also good sources of documents, and usually include company histories and information about products and services offered as well as documents and other data for investors.

Finally, both public and private companies must register with secretaries of state or similar state offices. Secretary of State Corporate and Business Entity Search (www.secstates.com) has links to searchable corporation registries in each state, most of which provide basic information such as addresses, officers, and registered agents.

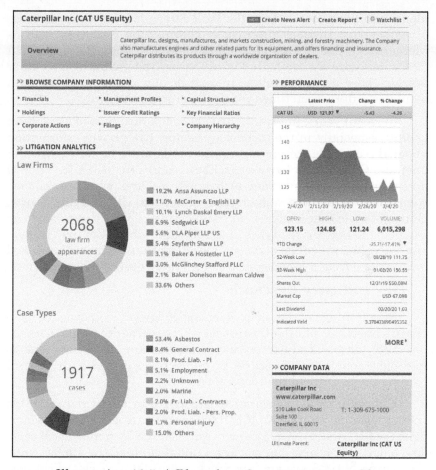

Illustration 16-5. A Bloomberg Law company profile.

(b) Private Companies

Detailed information about private companies, which do not sell stock to members of the general public, is harder to come by and often can be lacking in depth and currency because federal reporting requirements do not apply. Private companies can vary in form and size and include many large corporations such as Koch Industries and Mars, Inc. There are several dedicated online sources for conducting private company research, and the major legal research services have selective coverage as well.

Larger private companies are covered in the resources discussed above, such as Bloomberg Law, Hoover's Company Records, and LexisNexis Corporate Affiliations, although the information available is far less complete than it is for public companies. Factiva (www.factiva.com) provides public and private company profiles along with news stories from the *Wall Street Journal* and numerous other sources. Broader coverage is provided by resources such as Mergent Online (www.mergentonline.com) and ReferenceUSA (www.referenceusa.com). But in all cases, the financial and other data in these services may be inexact or out of date, and the data available differs, sometimes widely, from source to source.

In recent years, interest in private companies funded by venture capital, especially in the technology sector, has grown. Information about the activities of private equity funds more broadly is also in demand. Crunchbase (www.crunchbase.com) provides a free tier of access to information about tech start-ups and more established companies, while the subscription database CB Insights (www. cbinsights.com) specializes in connecting data about start-up financing using various types of graphs and tables. Zephyr (Bureau van Dijk) (www.bvdinfo.com) is a database that tracks mergers and acquisitions from a broader swath of private equity funds.

(c) Industry Research

Researching an industry deepens a lawyer's knowledge of a client's business and the businesses of its competitors, partners, or potential targets. Industry research reports and databases tend to highlight trends and forecasts in addition to providing a general overview of activity in the economic area.

U.S. industries are classified according to two widely adopted coding systems: SIC and NAICS.[17] Companies are placed into a single primary SIC and NAICS category, represented by a numerical code. The older SIC system has not been updated since the 1980s, while the newer NAICS system has much more detailed classifications. "Pet and Pet Supply Stores" are given the code 453910 in the NAICS system, whereas such stores are lumped into SIC code 5999 for "Miscellaneous Retail Stores, Not Elsewhere Classified." Industry research reports and databases, and many government sources of industry information, are organized and searchable by these classification codes. The Census Bureau, for example, uses NAICS codes in its Economic Census (www.census.gov/econ/), which is undertaken every five years and provides a wide range of statistical information on business and industry.

Several commercial databases provide access to industry profiles and reports without relying solely on SIC or NAICS classifications. Hoover's Industry Snapshots, on Lexis, contains basic

---

[17] SIC stands for Standard Industrial Classification and is used by the SEC for its corporate filings. NAICS stands for North American Industry Classification System and is an ongoing collaborative effort among statistical agencies. For more information about NAICS, see www.census.gov/eos/www/naics/.

information about industries and the companies and executives in those industries. Other, costlier commercial databases contain materials written or prepared by market analysts and touch on areas where companies may face risk or opportunity both in the current market and in the future. IBISWorld (www.ibisworld.com) offers specialized industry reports covering new and niche business areas. Frost & Sullivan (ww2.frost.com) has a narrower selection of industries but offers more detailed reports within those industries.

Market research reports tend to focus more on the products and technologies that companies produce. BCC Research (www.bcc research.com) offers a database of reports on the state of markets in life sciences and chemistry, technology and manufacturing, and energy and the environment. The reports are compiled by professional research staff and contain detailed factual reporting and analysis.

§ 16.6 NEWS AND HISTORICAL RESEARCH

For a broader picture of developments in business, politics, and society you'll need to monitor general sources such as major newspapers or news websites. News stories can also be rich resources for factual research or background information on current and historical events. Resources such as archives and manuscripts can be valuable tools in studying the law's development or finding historical information.

Westlaw and Lexis are two of the most convenient news sources for law students. Both have access to hundreds of newspapers, as well as magazines, trade journals, newsletters, and wire services. The two services have considerable overlap in coverage, but each has sources not found in the other; both, for example, have the *Washington Post*, while only Lexis has the full text of the *New York Times* and the *Wall Street Journal*. While it is fairly simple to find a specific newspaper by title on Westlaw and Lexis, it can be challenging to find a complete list of all the newspapers they include.

Other electronic sources of news include websites for individual newspapers, such as the New York Times (www.nytimes.com) and the Washington Post (www.washingtonpost.com), and multisource subscription services such as Factiva (www.factiva.com) and PressReader (www.pressreader.com). Google News (news.google. com) has free, current coverage of a wide range of newspapers, magazines, and wire services.

Back issues of major newspapers are usually available in large libraries on microfilm, and ProQuest Historical Newspapers or ProQuest Digital Microfilm (www.proquest.com) have scanned images from several major newspapers from as far back as 1764, and from as recent as several months ago. More than two dozen titles are covered, including the *Boston Globe, Chicago Tribune, Los Angeles Times, New York Times, Wall Street Journal,* and *Washington Post.*

Numerous other historical newspapers have been digitized in recent years, vastly increasing access to contemporary accounts of legal developments. Major subscription resources include America's Historical Newspapers (www.readex.com), 19th Century U.S. Newspapers (www.gale.com), and NewspaperARCHIVE.com (newspaperarchive.com). Google News Archive (news.google.com/ newspapers) and the Internet Archive's Newspapers collection (archive.org/details/newspapers) also provide access to an assortment of U.S. and foreign historical newspapers for free.

These digitized collections enable you to search in a particular year or era for references to events or people to discover how they were covered contemporaneously. This search functionality has decreased researchers' needs for separate indexes identifying articles by citation, which are essential when scrolling through microfilm is your only option.

While many of the resources discussed throughout this text can be used for historical research, archives and manuscript collections are another valuable resource to consider. These collections may have materials, such as letters and photographs, that are not available in any published sources.

A growing number of manuscript collections have been digitized and are available online. One leading example is *Law and Society since the Civil War: American Legal Manuscripts from the Harvard Law School Library* (www.proquest.com), a collection that includes the papers of Oliver Wendell Holmes, Jr., Louis D. Brandeis, and Felix Frankfurter[18] among those of many other notables.

Much archival research, however, still requires visiting the holding institution, as these materials are not loaned and sometimes cannot even be photocopied or scanned. The Society of American Archivists provides a helpful guide, *Using Archives: A Guide to Effective Research* (www2.archivists.org/usingarchives), that explains archives' function and lists sources for finding archives relevant to your research.

---

[18] An interesting look at the theft of some of Justice Frankfurter's papers from the Library of Congress and an explanation of the differing statuses of some justices' archives can be found in Jill Lepore, *The Great Paper Caper,* NEW YORKER, Dec. 1, 2014, at 32.

Chapter 17

INTERNATIONAL LAW

Table of Sections

Modern legal practice often requires knowledge of international and foreign law. Lawyers representing an American firm investing in another country, for example, must be aware of treaties between the two nations as well as the investment and trade laws of both countries. This chapter focuses on international law, while research in the law of foreign countries is the subject of Chapter 18.

Public international law is the body of rules and procedures intended to govern relations between nation states.[1] Although its primary historical functions have been the preservation of peace and regulation of war, international law now governs an ever-broader range of transnational activities. It regulates matters from copyright

---

[1] *Private* international law (or *conflict of laws*) determines where, and by whose law, controversies involving more than one jurisdiction are resolved, as well as how foreign judgments are enforced. For thorough coverage of this area of law, see *Restatement of the Law Second, Conflict of Laws* (1971). Several chapters of a new draft *Restatement* on the topic may also be useful. For a basic overview, a good but dated online research guide is DON FORD, PRIVATE INTERNATIONAL LAW (2013) (www. asil.org/sites/default/files/ERG_PRIVATE_INT.pdf) [https://perma.cc/VU53-6HLG].

protection to the rights of refugees, and trade conventions have made international law an inherent aspect of commercial activity.

The classic statement of the sources of international law is Article 38 of the Statute of the International Court of Justice, identifying the bases on which it decides disputes:

(a) international conventions, whether general or particular, establishing rules expressly recognized by the contesting States;

(b) international custom, as evidence of a general practice accepted as law;

(c) the general principles of law recognized by civilized nations;

(d) . . . judicial decisions and the teachings of the most highly qualified publicists of the various nations, as subsidiary means for the determination of rules of law.[2]

Treaties and *international custom* are generally considered the two most important sources of international law.[3] If a treaty is relevant to a problem involving its signatories, it is the primary legal authority. International custom is the actual conduct of nations, when it is consistent with the rule of law. Custom is not defined in specific legal sources but is established by evidence of state practices.[4] *General principles of law* are the most amorphous of the sources but are usually considered to be basic principles articulated in the classic texts of international law. *Judicial decisions* and *scholarly writings* are less important than treaties and international custom. Cases are generally not considered binding precedents in subsequent disputes, but they can aid in interpreting treaties and in defining international custom.[5]

---

[2] Statute of the International Court of Justice, art. 38(a), June 26, 1945, 59 Stat. 1055, 1060.

[3] Terms such as *treaty, convention, agreement, protocol, covenant,* and a range of others may be used interchangeably in international practice, though each country may have its own nomenclature. RESTATEMENT (THIRD) OF FOREIGN RELATIONS LAW § 301 (1987).

[4] Even with such evidence, however, a state may disavow being bound by customary law. STEPHEN P. MULLIGAN, CONG. RESEARCH SERV., RL32528, INTERNATIONAL LAW AND AGREEMENTS: THEIR EFFECT UPON U.S. LAW 28 (2018) (crs reports.congress.gov/product/pdf/RL/RL32528). *See also* Curtis A. Bradley & Mitu Gulati, *Withdrawing from International Custom,* 120 YALE L.J. 202 (2010) (exploring states' ability to withdraw from treaties and the application of customary law).

[5] On these sources of law, see, e.g., Wolfgang Friedmann, *The Uses of "General Principles" in the Development of International Law,* 57 AM. J. INT'L L. 279 (1963); J. Patrick Kelly, *The Twilight of Customary International Law,* 40 VA. J. INT'L L. 449 (2000).

The most thorough international law research is not limited to U.S. sources, and a facility with other languages assists greatly in broadening the scope of research. There are, however, many English-language resources available for serious international law study.

§ 17.1   PRELIMINARY RESEARCH

The first step in approaching most research problems in international law is to turn to a reference work, a treatise, or a law review article for general information and for help in analyzing the issues involved.

Encyclopedias and Treatises. The leading reference work, *Max Planck Encyclopedia of Public International Law (MPEPIL)* (Rüdiger Wolfrum ed., 2012) (opil.ouplaw.com/home/mpil), is a ten-volume work providing a comprehensive view of international law issues. Its articles are written by respected authorities, are short but informative, and include brief bibliographies for further research. Illustration 17-1 shows the beginning of *MPEPIL's* article on marine mammals. *Max Planck Encyclopedia of International Procedural Law (MPEIPRO)* (Hélène Ruiz Fabri ed., 2019) addresses procedures in specific courts and organizations and provides a comparative look at procedural issues.

Edmund Jan Osmańczyk, *Encyclopedia of the United Nations and International Agreements* (Anthony Mango ed., 3d ed. 2003) is a four-volume encyclopedia with wide coverage of international law issues, as well as excerpts from treaties and other major documents. Shorter reference works include Anthony Aust, *Handbook of International Law* (2d ed. 2010) and *Routledge Handbook of International Law* (David Armstrong ed., 2008).

Several general treatises provide overviews of international law doctrine. *Oppenheim's International Law* (Robert Jennings & Arthur Watts eds., 9th ed. 1992) is an updated version of a classic work. More recent treatises include James Crawford, *Brownlie's Principles of Public International Law* (9th ed. 2019); Malcolm N. Shaw, *International Law* (8th ed. 2017); and Antonio Cassese, *International Law* (2d ed. 2005). *The Oxford Guide to Treaties* (Duncan B. Hollis ed., 2012) explains issues of treaty formation and interpretation.

The American Law Institute's *Restatement (Third) of the Foreign Relations Law of the United States* (1987) summarizes American law and practice in international law and foreign relations. *Restatement (Fourth) of the Foreign Relations Law of the United States* (2018) is a partial revision that updates sections on treaties, jurisdiction, and sovereign immunity.

Marine Mammals

Alexander Proelß

Content type: Encyclopedia entries
Article last updated: July 2007

Product: Max Planck Encyclopedias of International Law [MPIL]
Module: Max Planck Encyclopedia of Public International Law [MPEPIL]

Subject(s):

Marine living resources

Published under the auspices of the Max Planck Foundation for International Peace and the Rule of Law under the direction of Rüdiger Wolfrum.

A. Notion

1 Marine mammals are mammals, ie warm-blooded animals characterized by the production of milk in the female mammary glands, which spend the majority of their lives in or close to the sea. By definition, all of these animals are air breathers. They include cetaceans, pinnipeds, sirenians, sea otters, and polar bears. Almost all marine mammals are to a greater or lesser extent endangered species (→ *Endangered Species, International Protection*).

2 The term 'cetaceans' encompasses whales, dolphins, and porpoises, thus referring to the oldest, most diverse, and most fully marine adapted group of mammals. Zoologists recognize 90 species of whales and dolphins, all marine except for five species of freshwater dolphins, divided into two subgroups—baleen whales and toothed whales—the latter of which includes both dolphins and porpoises. Among their special characteristics are, inter alia, the cyclic nature of their migration between breeding and feeding grounds, a relatively low reproduction rate, and complex social structures. Cetaceans have been hunted for centuries for their meat, oil, and spermaceti. In his famous novel *Moby-Dick* (1851), Herman Melville created a monument to the mythical struggle between man and whale—a struggle which nearly resulted in the complete extinction of many large whale species following the height of industrial → *whaling* in the late 1960s.

3 Pinnipeds comprise 34 species from the families of walruses, sea lions, eared seals, fur seals, and true seals. In contrast to cetaceans, pinnipeds must come ashore to breed, give birth, and nurse their young. Sirenians include manatees and dugongs, which inhabit rivers, → *estuaries*, coastal marine waters, swamps, and marine → *wetlands*. They are vulnerable to extinction from habitat loss and other negative impacts resulting from human population growth and coastal development (see also → *Marine Living Resources, International Protection*). Their central biological features are extremely low metabolism and zero tolerance for cold water.

Illustration 17-1. An article in the *Max Planck Encyclopedia of Public International Law*.

The historically acknowledged classic texts of international law, originally published between 1557 and 1866, were collected and published by the Carnegie Endowment for International Peace in a set of forty volumes, *The Classics of International Law* (James Brown Scott ed., 1911–50). Texts appear in their original versions and, if needed, in English translation. This series is available in the Legal Classics Library on HeinOnline.

Journal Articles. International law is the focus of numerous scholarly periodicals, including more than eighty specialized journals published at U.S. law schools. Among the more prestigious professional journals are the *American Journal of International Law* and *International and Comparative Law Quarterly. Recueil des Cours,* containing lectures presented at the Hague Academy of

International Law, is a particularly valuable resource of international scope. Many national societies of international law produce annual publications such as the *British Yearbook of International Law* or the *Annuaire Français de Droit International,* which usually contain scholarly articles as well as reprints of selected major documents. *American Society of International Law Proceedings* (1907–date) has shorter discussions of topics of current interest. Most of these sources are available on HeinOnline.

International law topics are also well represented in the standard law review literature discussed in Chapter 3, and articles can be found through any of the full-text and index resources discussed there. *Index to Foreign Legal Periodicals* (1960–date, available on HeinOnline) principally covers journals published in countries outside the common law system, but it also indexes articles on international law in selected American law reviews.

Dictionaries. International law has its own specialized terminology, and a dictionary may be an essential tool in understanding key concepts. The leading work is *Parry & Grant Encyclopaedic Dictionary of International Law* (John P. Grant & J. Craig Barker eds., 3d ed. 2009), which has descriptive entries with citations to major sources. Curtis F. J. Doebbler, *Dictionary of Public International Law* (2018) also features lengthy entries on major topics, while James R. Fox, *Dictionary of International and Comparative Law* (3d ed. 2003) has more concise definitions.

§ 17.2 U.S. PRACTICE IN INTERNATIONAL LAW

The United States enters into a variety of international commitments.[6] American lawyers and law students researching in this field may be trying to determine the extent of U.S. commitments internationally or the domestic impact of these commitments. Materials on United States practice in international law are the most frequently consulted research sources in this field. These include treaties and executive agreements, as well as the materials needed to interpret them and documents dealing with issues in U.S. foreign relations.

(a) Treaties and Executive Agreements

The United States binds itself to international commitments through two mechanisms: *treaties* and *executive agreements.* Treaties are formal agreements between countries, and they have legal significance for both domestic and international purposes. Article VI of the U.S. Constitution provides that treaties are part of the

---

[6] Individual states cannot enter into treaties. U.S. CONST. art. I, § 10, cl. 1.

supreme law of the land, giving them the same legal effect and status as federal statutes. Treaties and statutes can supersede each other as the controlling law within the United States, but a treaty that is no longer valid as U.S. law may still be binding in international law.

The President also makes executive agreements with other countries under the Article II authority to conduct foreign affairs. These are similar in form and effect to treaties, but they do not require Senate approval and hence are often used to streamline the process and avoid controversy. The sources and research procedures discussed in this section generally apply to both treaties and executive agreements.[7]

Treaty and executive agreement research generally involves three steps: (1) finding the treaty or agreement's text in an authoritative source; (2) determining whether it is in force and with what parties and reservations; and (3) interpreting its provisions, with the aid of commentaries, judicial decisions, and legislative history.

Treaty Process. Treaties between two governments are *bilateral*, and those entered into by more than two governments are *multilateral*. Parties' initial signatures to a treaty establish their agreement that its text is authentic and definitive, but nations are not bound until they approve the treaty through ratification or some other procedure. Parties to multilateral treaties may add RUDs: *reservations* excluding certain provisions, or *understandings* or *declarations* providing their own interpretations of treaty terms. The texts of treaties usually identify the point at which they enter into force, often (in the case of multilateral conventions) when a specified number of nations have ratified the document.

Treaties of the United States are negotiated and drafted by the executive branch but require approval by two-thirds of the Senate. After Senate approval, they are ratified and proclaimed by the

---

[7] The classic work on the distinctions between the two forms is Myres S. McDougal & Asher Lans, *Treaties and Congressional-Executive or Presidential Agreements: Interchangeable Instruments of National Policy*, 54 YALE L.J. 181 (1945). See also 2 VED P. NANDA & DAVID K. PANSIUS, LITIGATION OF INTERNATIONAL DISPUTES IN U.S. COURTS §§ 10:4–10:9 (2d ed. 2013). A basic introduction to executive agreements can be found in MULLIGAN, *supra* note 4, at 6–12. Modern scholarship has further explored the distinctions between the two forms of obligation as well as the extent of limitations on executive agreements in particular. *See, e.g.*, Curtis A. Bradley, *Exiting Congressional-Executive Agreements*, 67 DUKE L.J. 1615 (2018); Oona A. Hathaway, *Treaties' End: The Past, Present, and Future of International Lawmaking in the United States*, 117 YALE L.J. 1236 (2008); and Julian Nyarko, *Giving the Treaty a Purpose: Comparing the Durability of Treaties and Executive Agreements*, 13 AM. J. INT'L L. 54 (2019). For more information, see Ryan Harrington, *Understanding the "Other" International Agreements*, 108 LAW LIBR. J. 343 (2016).

President. For domestic purposes, a treaty generally becomes law when it is proclaimed by the President.[8]

Sources. Treaties are published in a variety of forms—official and unofficial, national and international, current and retrospective. The resources available for treaty research depend in large part on whether the United States is a party to the treaty, so answering that question is an important first step in research.

Until 1949, U.S. treaties were published in the *Statutes at Large* for each session of Congress. Compilations of early treaties entered into by the United States between 1778 and 1845 appear in volumes 7 and 8 of the *Statutes at Large*, and volume 64 includes a complete list of all treaties appearing in the set. These treaties were reprinted in *Treaties and Other International Agreements of the United States of America 1776–1949* (Charles I. Bevans comp., 1968–75, available on HeinOnline and through the Library of Congress (www.loc.gov/law/help/us-treaties/bevans.php)), which contains four volumes of multilateral treaties (arranged chronologically), eight volumes of bilateral treaties (arranged alphabetically by country), and indexes by country and subject.[9]

Beginning in 1950, *United States Treaties and Other International Agreements (UST)* became the official, permanent form of publication for treaties and executive agreements to which the United States is a party. Illustration 17-2 shows the first page of a multilateral convention on polar bear conservation, as published in *UST*.

---

[8] Complicating matters is the distinction between self-executing international agreements and non-self-executing international agreements. Self-executing agreements have the force of law when they are entered into. Non-self-executing agreements require Congress to pass legislation for their provisions to become U.S. law.

[9] *Bevans* superseded two predecessors: TREATIES, CONVENTIONS, INTERNATIONAL ACTS, PROTOCOLS, AND AGREEMENTS BETWEEN THE UNITED STATES OF AMERICA AND OTHER POWERS (William M. Malloy comp., 1910–38), and TREATIES AND OTHER INTERNATIONAL ACTS OF THE U.S.A. (Hunter Miller ed., 1931–48). Another source for treaties between the United States and Indian nations is volume two of INDIAN AFFAIRS: LAWS AND TREATIES (C.J. Kappler comp., 1904) (dc.library.okstate.edu/digital/collection/kapplers). All of these sets are available on HeinOnline. Westlaw also includes a database, Native American Law Treaties, containing more than 350 treaties entered into between 1797 and 1870. UNPERFECTED TREATIES OF THE UNITED STATES OF AMERICA (Christian L. Wiktor ed., 1976–74) is a nine-volume set of treaties since 1776 that were concluded but did not enter into force.

THE GOVERNMENTS of Canada, Denmark, Norway, the Union of Soviet Socialist Republics, and the United States of America,

RECOGNIZING the special responsibilities and special interests of the States of the Arctic Region in relation to the protection of the fauna and flora of the Arctic Region,

RECOGNIZING that the polar bear is a significant resource of the Arctic Region which requires additional protection,

HAVING DECIDED that such protection should be achieved through co-ordinated national measures taken by the States of the Arctic Region,

DESIRING to take immediate action to bring further conservation and management measures into effect;

HAVE AGREED AS FOLLOWS:

ARTICLE I

1. The taking of polar bears shall be prohibited except as provided in Article III.

2. For the purpose of this Agreement, the term "taking" includes hunting, killing and capturing.

ARTICLE II

Each Contracting Party shall take appropriate action to protect the ecosystems of which polar bears are a part, with special attention to habitat components such as denning and feeding sites and migration patterns, and shall manage polar bear populations in accordance with sound conservation practices based on the best available scientific data.

ARTICLE III

1. Subject to the provisions of Articles II and IV, any Contracting Party may allow the taking of polar bears when such taking is carried out:

    (a) for bona fide scientific purposes; or

    (b) by that Party for conservation purposes; or

    (c) to prevent serious disturbance of the management of other living resources, subject to forfeiture to that Party of the skins and other items of value resulting from such taking; or

    (d) by local people using traditional methods in the exercise of their traditional rights and in accordance with the laws of that Party; or

    (e) wherever polar bears have or might have been subject to taking by traditional means by its nationals.

2. The skins and other items of value resulting from taking under sub-paragraphs (b) and (c) of paragraph 1 of this Article shall not be available for commercial purposes.

Illustration 17-2. A multilateral treaty in *United States Treaties and Other International Agreements*.

UST, however, was only published through volume 35 (1983–84). The only official source for more recent treaties is a numbered series of separately paginated documents, *Treaties and Other International Acts Series (TIAS)* (www.state.gov/tias/). *TIAS* was issued in pamphlet form through 2006 but is now published only online.

Commercial services are important sources for access to current treaties and retrospective coverage. Both Westlaw and Lexis have comprehensive treaty databases, with coverage from the 1770s through recent months. HeinOnline's U.S. Treaties and Agreements Library and World Treaty Library have PDF versions of treaties in *Statutes at Large*, *UST*, and *TIAS*, as well as very recent treaties not published in these sources.

The American Society of International Law's bimonthly *International Legal Materials (ILM)* (1962–date) contains the texts of treaties of major significance regardless of whether the U.S. is a party, and sometimes has drafts before final agreement. *ILM* is available on Westlaw, Lexis, and HeinOnline.

Some topical government collections of treaties are available online, including trade agreements from the Office of the United States Trade Representative (www.ustr.gov) and tax treaties from the Internal Revenue Service (www.irs.gov/individuals/international-taxpayers/tax-treaties). Treaty collections on particular subjects are also available from commercial publishers, including *U.S. Tax Treaties Reporter* (available on Cheetah) and *Extradition Laws and Treaties* (1979–date, available on HeinOnline).

A citation to a U.S. treaty includes its name, the parties (if bilateral), the signing date, and a reference to one U.S. source (traditionally *Statutes at Large* or *UST*, but more recent treaties are often cited to commercially published compilations and electronic sources). For multilateral treaties, a parallel citation to an official international source (usually the *United Nations Treaty Series*) may be added.[10] The treaty in Illustration 17-2 is cited as: Agreement on the Conservation of Polar Bears, Nov. 15, 1973, 27 U.S.T. 3918.

Guides and Indexes. Treaties are generally published chronologically rather than by subject, so you may need a guide or index to identify agreements with a specific country or on a particular topic and to determine the status of a treaty.

Treaties in Force (www.state.gov/treaties-in-force/), an annual publication of the Department of State, is the official index to current

---

[10] THE BLUEBOOK: A UNIFORM SYSTEM OF CITATION R. 21.4.5(a) (21st ed. 2020); ALWD GUIDE TO LEGAL CITATION R. 19.1(e) (6th ed. 2017).

United States treaties and agreements. It provides citations to all of the major treaty publications, including *UST, TIAS,* and the *United Nations Treaty Series.* The first section of *Treaties in Force* lists bilateral treaties by country and, under each country, by subject; and the second section lists multilateral treaties by subject. Illustration 17-3 shows entries in *Treaties in Force,* including one for the multilateral treaty shown in Illustration 17-2. Westlaw and Lexis have the current *Treaties in Force,* and HeinOnline has current and past editions back to 1929.

Convention for the conservation of Antarctic seals, with annex.
　　Done at London June 1, 1972.
　　Entered into force March 11, 1978.
　　29 UST 441; TIAS 8826
　　Amendment:
　　September 12–16, 1988

　　Depositary: United Kingdom

Agreement on the conservation of polar bears.
　　Done at Oslo November 15, 1973.
　　Entered into force May 26, 1976; for the United States
　　　November 1, 1976.
　　27 UST 3918; TIAS 8409
　　Depositary: Norway

Convention on international trade in endangered species of wild fauna and flora, with appendices.
　　Done at Washington March 3, 1973.
　　Entered into force July 1, 1975.
　　27 UST 1087; TIAS 8249; 993 UNTS 243
　　Amendment:
　　June 22, 1979 (TIAS 11079)

　　Depositary: Switzerland

Illustration 17-3. An entry in *Treaties in Force.*

The commercially published *Kavass's Guide to the United States Treaties in Force* is also issued annually in print and on HeinOnline, and has subject and country indexes to both bilateral and multilateral treaties. These can be useful because the official *Treaties in Force* does not index bilateral treaties broadly by subject nor does it list multilateral conventions by country.

The major collections and series of U.S. treaties and international agreements are indexed by subject, date, and country in *United States Treaty Index Consolidation* (Igor I. Kavass ed.,

2001–date), which is updated semiannually by *Kavass's Current Treaty Index*, available in print and on HeinOnline.

Interpretation. Like statutes or constitutional provisions, most treaties contain ambiguities that can lead to controversies in interpretation and application. Several resources can assist in understanding treaty terms, including court decisions and documents produced during a treaty's drafting and consideration.[11]

Decisions from the Supreme Court or the U.S. Courts of Appeals can be determinative in interpreting a treaty's meaning or effect, and other court decisions can provide useful guidance even if they are not binding. Neither Westlaw Citing References nor Shepard's covers citations to treaties, but you can use a treaty's name or citation in a full-text search to find cases, law review articles, and other secondary sources that discuss it.

The *United States Code Service* includes two volumes that can be useful starting points in finding cases. "International Agreements" contains the texts of about three dozen major conventions and treaties, accompanied by research references and case annotations, and "Annotations to Uncodified Laws and Treaties" has no treaty texts but provides broader coverage of decisions interpreting U.S. treaties. Lexis includes the first volume, under the title USCS— International Conventions.

Anthony Aust, *Modern Treaty Law and Practice* (3d ed. 2013) and *National Treaty Law and Practice* (Duncan B. Hollis et al. eds., 2005) both analyze treaty interpretation and practice, in the United States and generally. The United States has not ratified the Vienna Convention on the Law of Treaties, but its provisions can help explain the interpretation of treaty terms. Two major treatises on the Convention, with very similar titles, are *Vienna Convention on the Law of Treaties: A Commentary* (Oliver Dörr & Kirsten Schmalenbach eds., 2d ed. 2018) and *The Vienna Conventions on the Law of Treaties: A Commentary* (Olivier Corten & Pierre Klein eds., 2011).

For United States treaties, records of Senate deliberation can also be a source of documentation on terms and meaning.[12] Most congressional documents have already been discussed in Chapter 6,

---

[11] For a primer on U.S. treaty interpretation, see David Bederman, *Revivalist Canons and Treaty Interpretation*, 41 UCLA L. REV. 953, 955–75 (1994).

[12] The Senate website has a primer on the treaty process (www.senate.gov/artand history/history/common/briefing/Treaties.htm). For more detail, see CONGRESSIONAL RESEARCH SERVICE, TREATIES AND OTHER INTERNATIONAL AGREEMENTS: THE ROLE OF THE UNITED STATES SENATE, S. PRT. 106–71 (2001). The value of Senate materials in determining the intent of treaty parties, however, has been the subject of dispute. *See United States v. Stuart*, 489 U.S. 353, 367 n.7 (1989).

but two series of Senate documents relate specifically to treaty consideration. *Treaty Documents* (until 1980, called *Senate Executive Documents*) contain the text of treaties as they are transmitted to the Senate for its consideration, and usually include messages from the President and the Secretary of State. The Senate Foreign Relations Committee analyzes treaties and issues *Senate Executive Reports* with its recommendations. Both Treaty Documents and Senate Executive Reports are issued in numbered series identifying the Congress and sequence in which they were issued.

Congress.gov has legislative history summaries of treaty action with links to Treaty Documents (1949–present) and Senate Executive Reports (since the 104th Congress (1995–96)). ProQuest Congressional includes coverage of Senate treaty materials from 1817, with the full text of documents and reports.[13]

The Senate Foreign Relations Committee website lists pending treaties and indicates any actions taken (www.foreign.senate.gov/ treaties). *Congressional Index*, Wolters Kluwer's weekly looseleaf service, also includes a table of treaties pending before the Senate, with references to Treaty Documents, Executive Reports, hearings, and ratifications.

(b) Foreign Relations Documents

State practice is the primary evidence of custom, one of the major sources of international law. To study state practice, it is best to turn to sources that explain how a particular nation has acted in the past.

Detailed discussion of U.S. practice is found in a series of volumes prepared by the Department of State. *Digest of United States Practice in International Law* compiles excerpts from treaties, decisions, diplomatic correspondence, and other documents reflecting the U.S. position on major issues of international law, accompanied by explanatory commentary. The Department of State website (www. state.gov/digest-of-united-states-practice-in-international-law/) has digests since 1989, along with links to the full text of documents excerpted in those volumes. Illustration 17-4 shows a page from the 2018 *Digest* on a new multilateral agreement to regulate fishing in the Arctic Ocean.

---

[13] This information is also available in the printed CIS INDEX TO US SENATE EXECUTIVE DOCUMENTS & REPORTS (1987, for documents before 1970) and CIS/INDEX (1970–date). Like other CIS indexes, these are accompanied by microfiche copies of all indexed documents and reports.

https://www.epa.gov/international-cooperation/commission-environmental-cooperation-cec.

B.   PROTECTION OF MARINE ENVIRONMENT AND MARINE CONSERVATION

1.   Fishing Regulation and Agreements

On October 1, 2018, the State Department announced in a media note, available at https://www.state.gov/u-s-signs-agreement-to-prevent-unregulated-commercial-fishing-on-the-high-seas-of-the-central-arctic-ocean/, that it had signed an agreement to prevent unregulated commercial fishing on the high seas of the central Arctic Ocean. The media note is excerpted below. For background on the agreement, see *Digest 2015* at 582-84.

*   *   *   *

...This is the first multilateral agreement of its kind to take a legally binding, precautionary approach to protect an area from commercial fishing before that fishing has begun. ...
Ice has traditionally covered the high seas of the central Arctic Ocean year-round. Recently, the melting of Arctic sea ice has left large areas of the high seas uncovered for much of the year. As a result, commercial fisheries in the central Arctic Ocean may become viable in areas where such activity was previously not possible. Prior to this agreement, no legally binding international agreement existed to manage potential fishing in the high seas of this region.
In 2009, the United States closed the U.S. Exclusive Economic Zone (EEZ) north of Alaska to commercial fishing until such time as domestic fisheries managers have sufficient information about the ecosystem to allow fishing to proceed on a well-regulated basis. U.S. stakeholders, including the Alaska-based fishing industry, have been concerned foreign fishing vessels could begin fishing here in the foreseeable future. At a time when U.S. vessels cannot fish within the U.S. EEZ, the United States has negotiated this new fisheries agreement for the central Arctic Ocean that reduces the chance that foreign vessels will fish just beyond the U.S. EEZ.
Initial negotiations among the five coastal parties of the central Arctic Ocean—Canada, Denmark (for Greenland and the Faroe Islands), Norway, Russia, and the United States—resulted in the non-legally binding Oslo Declaration signed on July 16, 2015. The Oslo Declaration recognized other governments may have an interest in potential Arctic fisheries. In December 2015 ten parties, including the five Oslo Declaration signatories, as well as China, Iceland, Japan, the Republic of Korea, and the European Union, entered into negotiations towards a legally-binding agreement. The negotiations toward this legally binding agreement concluded November 30, 2017.

*   *   *   *

Illustration 17-4. A page from *Digest of United States Practice in International Law*.

The Department of State also published earlier encyclopedic digests of U.S. practice that may be of value for historical research. The last of these was Marjorie M. Whiteman, *Digest of International Law* (1963–73), focusing largely on the period from the 1940s to the 1960s. Its predecessors were compiled by Francis Wharton (1886; 2d ed. 1887); John Bassett Moore (1906) (covering the period 1776 to 1906 and effectively superseding Wharton); and G.H. Hackworth (1940–44) (covering the period 1906 to 1939). These digests are all available in HeinOnline's Foreign and International Law Resources Database.

More extensive documentation of U.S. practice can be found in *Foreign Relations of the United States* (1861–date, available on HeinOnline), a comprehensive record of material relating to such issues as treaty negotiation and international conflicts. There is a time lag of over thirty years between the original (often confidential) issuance of these documents and their publication in this series. The set from 1861 to 1960 is also available online from the University of Wisconsin (uwdc.library.wisc.edu/collections/frus/), and selected volumes for the Truman through Carter administrations are available from the Department of State (history.state.gov).[14]

§ 17.3   GENERAL TREATY RESEARCH

The United States is not a party to every major multilateral treaty. The International Covenant on Economic, Social and Cultural Rights (ICESCR), the Vienna Convention on the Law of Treaties, and the United Nations Convention on the Law of the Sea are just three of the many agreements that the U.S. has not ratified. Regional agreements in other parts of the world and bilateral treaties between other countries may also be important research sources.[15] In addition to the U.S. treaty resources already discussed, more general resources are frequently needed.

General Sources. The most comprehensive source for modern treaties is the *United Nations Treaty Series* (*UNTS*), containing more than 2,900 volumes and available free online as the United Nations Treaty Collection (treaties.un.org). Since 1946 this series has published virtually all treaties registered with the U.N. by member nations in their original languages, as well as in English and French translations.[16] Illustration 17-5 shows the first page of the 1992 Agreement on the Conservation of Small Cetaceans of the Baltic and North Seas (ASCOBANS), as published in *UNTS*. Footnote 1

---

[14] For more information on the use of foreign relations documents and related sources, see SOURCES OF STATE PRACTICE IN INTERNATIONAL LAW (Ralph Gaebler & Alison Shea eds., 2d rev. ed. 2014), which covers the United States and 29 other countries, and Catherine Deane, *Researching Customary International Law, State Practice and the Pronouncements of States Regarding International Law*, GLOBALEX (Nov./Dec. 2018) (www.nyulawglobal.org/globalex/Customary_International_Law1. html) [https://perma.cc/D7CZ-EYMJ].

[15] The United Nations is the primary source of rules for treaty processes from negotiation to registration, implementation, and withdrawal. THE OXFORD HANDBOOK OF UNITED NATIONS TREATIES (Simon Chesterman et al., 2019) provides an overview of the U.N.'s role in international agreements.

[16] Adopted pursuant to U.N. Charter art. 102, G.A. Res. 97(I) (Dec. 14, 1946) is the initial resolution authorizing creation of the *UNTS*. Though article 1 of the U.N. regulations implementing G.A. Resolution 97 states that every treaty shall be registered and article 12(1) states that every treaty shall be published, articles 12(2)–(3) outline the occasions when publication may be limited.

identifies the ratifications that caused the convention to enter into force in 1994.

---

218   United Nations — Treaty Series • Nations Unies — Recneil des Traités   1994

AGREEMENT[1] ON THE CONSERVATION OF SMALL CETACEANS OF THE BALTIC AND NORTH SEAS

The Parties,

Recalling the general principles of conservation and sustainable use of natural resources, as reflected in the World Conservation Strategy of the International Union for the Conservation of Nature and Natural Resources, the United Nations Environment Programme, and the World Wide Fund for Nature, and in the report of the World Commission on Environment and Development,

Recognizing that small cetaceans are and should remain an integral part of marine ecosystems,

Aware that the population of harbour porpoises of the Baltic Sea has drastically decreased,

Concerned about the status of small cetaceans in the Baltic and North Seas,

Recognizing that by-catches, habitat deterioration and disturbance may adversely affect these populations,

Convinced that their vulnerable and largely unclear status merits immediate attention in order to improve it and to gather information as a basis for sound decisions on management and conservation,

Confident that activities for that purpose are best coordinated between the States concerned in order to increase efficiency and avoid duplicate work,

Aware of the importance of maintaining maritime activities such as fishing,

Recalling that under the Convention on the Conservation of Migratory Species of Wild Animals (Bonn 1979),[2] Parties are encouraged to

---

[1] Came into force on 29 March 1994, i.e., 90 days after six Range States had expressed their consent to be bound by signature, not subject to ratification, acceptance or approval, or by deposit of an instrument of ratification, acceptance or approval with the Secretary-General of the United Nations, in accordance with article 8.5:

Participant	Date of definitive signature (s) or of deposit of the instrument of ratification or approval (AA)	
Belgium	14 May	1993
Denmark	29 December	1993 AA
Germany	6 October	1993
Netherlands	29 December	1992 AA
Sweden	31 March	1992 s
United Kingdom of Great Britain and Northern Ireland	13 July	1993

[2] United Nations, *Treaty Series*, vol. 1651, No. I-28395.

Vol. 1772, I-30865

Illustration 17-5. A multilateral treaty in
United Nations Treaty Series.

The United Nations Treaty Collection website has summaries and information on ratification status as well as treaty texts. Its "Resources" section has reference material, such as *Treaty Handbook* (2012) and *Final Clauses of Multilateral Treaties Handbook* (2003), explaining the treaty process and defining terminology. Search options include popular name, title, and full text, but there is not a simple way to find documents by *UNTS* volume and page number.

The *UNTS* is also available in HeinOnline's United Nations Law Collection and World Treaty Library, which are more convenient sources if you want to retrieve treaties by citation.

Treaties predating the creation of the United Nations can be found in two older series: the *League of Nations Treaty Series* (*LNTS*) (1920–46), similar in scope to the *UNTS*; and a retrospective collection, *Consolidated Treaty Series* (*CTS*) (1969–86), with all treaties between nation states from 1648 to 1919. *CTS* contains treaties in the language of one of the signatories, usually accompanied by an English or French translation. There is no subject index, but the set includes a chronological list and an index to parties. Both *LNTS* and *CTS* are available from HeinOnline, and *CTS* is also online as Oxford Historical Treaties (opil.ouplaw.com/home/oht).

The African Union (au.int/en/treaties), Council of Europe (conventions.coe.int), and Organization of American States (www.oas.org/en/sla/dil/treaties_agreements.asp) all provide online access to treaties among their members. The Hague Conference on Private International Law (www.hcch.net) has the text of several dozen conventions it has drafted on issues such as international civil procedure and recognition of judgments. Many foreign countries publish current treaties in their official gazettes and on government websites, and new treaties are often printed in international law yearbooks and journals.

The United Nations Audiovisual Library of International Law (www.un.org/law/avl/) includes historic archives with entries on instruments grouped by topics like environmental law and international humanitarian law. It also has a research library page with links to sources for treaties, as well as jurisprudence, yearbooks, other official documents, and scholarly writings in international law. In addition to United Nations resources, it also has links to more than two dozen national treaty collections and sites maintained by other organizations.

Subject Collections. Several resources reprint or link to major international treaties and other documents. The University of Minnesota Law School offers two useful online resources: Human Rights Library (www.umn.edu/humanrts/) has the texts of major multilateral conventions and other documents, and "Frequently-Cited Treaties and Other International Instruments" (libguides.law.umn.edu/frequentlycitedtreaties) lists more than 100 major conventions and treaties with official citations and links to sources for their texts.

Several collections reprint a variety of important international law documents, usually in specific subject areas. The most comprehensive of these collections is the online International Law & World Order: Weston's & Carlson's Basic Documents (reference works.brillonline.com). Printed compilations include *Basic Documents in International Law* (Ian Brownlie ed., 6th ed. 2009); *Basic Documents on Human Rights* (Ian Brownlie & Guy S. Goodwin-Gill eds., 6th ed. 2010); *Basic Documents on International Migration Law* (Richard Plender ed., 3d ed. 2007); *Basic Documents on International Trade Law* (Chia-Jui Cheng ed., 4th ed. 2012); *Documents in International Environmental Law* (Philippe Sands & Paolo Galizzi eds., 2d ed. 2004); and *International Criminal Law Deskbook* (John P. Grant & J. Craig Barker eds., 2006).

Indexes and Status Tables. Important early steps in the treaty research process are finding the text of a treaty and determining whether it is in force and what countries are parties. Several resources are available for these purposes.

The most comprehensive collection of treaties, HeinOnline's World Treaty Library, covers over 180,000 agreements back to 1648 and includes almost all of the major treaty series and indexes. Treaties can be searched and retrieved by title, country, subject, keyword, date, or citation.

The Flare Index to Treaties (ials.sas.ac.uk/digital/ials-digital-resources/flare-index-treaties) is one of the broadest current indexes to multilateral conventions dating back to the 1600s, with coverage of significant bilateral treaties up to 1815 as well. It has basic information such as official titles and dates for more than 2,000 multilateral treaties, as well as citations to printed versions and links to online text sources. Illustration 17-6 shows the Flare Index entry for ASCOBANS.[17]

---

[17] Two older indexes to multilateral treaties may also be of use. CHRISTIAN L. WIKTOR, MULTILATERAL TREATY CALENDAR, 1648–1995 (1998) lists more than 6,000 agreements chronologically, identifies sources in more than 100 publications, and provides information on treaty status. M.J. BOWMAN & D.J. HARRIS, MULTILATERAL TREATIES: INDEX AND CURRENT STATUS (1984, with 11th cum. supp. 1995) covers more than 1,000 agreements with information on sources and parties, but it has not been updated in several years.

Other indexes provide broader coverage of both multilateral and bilateral treaties. Retrospective access to *UNTS* treaties by subject and country back to 1946 is provided by a commercial publication, UNITED NATIONS CUMULATIVE TREATY INDEX (1999). The

Agreement on the conservation of small cetaceans of the Baltic and North Seas

Other title:
ASCOBANS

Date concluded :
17/03/1992

Place concluded:
Not known

Web version1:
http://www.official-documents.gov.uk/document/cm21/2119/2119.pdf

Web version2:
http://www.ascobans.org/sites/default/files/basic_page_documents/Ch_XXVI...

Web version3:
http://www.ascobans.org/en/documents/agreement-text

Published in:
1772 UNTS 217; UKTS 52 (1995), Cm 2916

EISIL link:
http://www.eisil.org/index.php?sid=840290245&id=1909&t=link_details&cat=491

Authentic text:
English
French
German
Russian

Depository:
Not known

Illustration 17-6. A Flare Index to Treaties entry.

The source for determining the status of and identifying the parties to major conventions is Multilateral Treaties Deposited with the Secretary-General (MTDSG), now published only online (treaties. un.org). This listing of several hundred treaties is arranged by subject, and has citations, information on status, lists of parties with dates of signature and ratification, and the text of any reservations imposed by individual parties. Illustration 17-7 shows the beginning of the entry for ASCOBANS, including a link to the full text and information on the first two signatory parties.

World Treaty Index (worldtreatyindex.com) is even broader in scope, covering more than 60,000 bilateral and multilateral treaties of the twentieth century. This is an updated version of a five-volume print publication (Peter H. Rohn comp., 2d ed. 1983–84).

> **9. Agreement on the Conservation of Small Cetaceans of the Baltic, North East Atlantic, Irish and North Seas**
>
> New York, 17 March 1992

Entry into force	: 29 March 1994, in accordance with article 8(5). [1]
Registration	: 29 March 1994, No. 30865
Status	: Signatories : 6. Parties : 10
Text	: <u>Certified true copy</u> United Nations, *Treaty Series* , <u>vol. 1772</u>, p. 217; and <u>C.N.338.1995</u>.TREATIES-2 of 22 November 1995 (procès-verbal of rectification of the French authentic text).
Note	: The Agreement was approved at Geneva on 13 September 1991, during the Third Meeting of the Conference of the Parties to the Convention on the Conservation of Migratory Species of Wild Animals pursuant to article IV (4) of the said Convention, which was done at Bonn on 23 June 1979 ("Bonn Convention"). The Agreement was open for signature at United Nations Headquarters in New York on 17 March 1992 and will remain open for signature at United Nations Headquarters until its entry into force. * The Amendment to the Agreement (see Chapter XXVII-9(a) herein), which entered into force on 3 February 2008, changed the name of the Agreement. The Agreement was previously known as "Agreement on the Conservation of Small Cetaceans of the Baltic and North Seas".

Participant	Signature	Definitive signature(s), Ratification, Accession(a), Acceptance(A), Approval(AA)
Belgium	6 Nov 1992	14 May 1993
Denmark	19 Aug 1992	29 Dec 1993 AA

Illustration 17-7. An entry in Multilateral Treaties Deposited with the Secretary-General.

Coverage in MTDSG is limited to treaties concluded under U.N. auspices or for which the Secretary-General acts as depository, so it excludes some major agreements such as the Geneva Conventions of 1949 (ihl-databases.icrc.org/ihl) and the Convention on International Trade in Endangered Species of Wild Flora and Fauna (CITES) (www.cites.org). These organizations' sites have status information, as well as treaty texts and other documents. Even conventions covered by MTDSG may have websites with much more detailed information. The ASCOBANS site, for example, includes not only the text of the treaty but also national reports, information on cetacean species, a newsletter, and other resources.

Interpretation. Scholarly commentary and judicial decisions are the standard sources of treaty interpretation. An additional source available for the interpretation of some multilateral conventions is the *travaux préparatoires* (documents created during the drafting process such as reports and debates). These are recognized under the Vienna Convention as a source for clarifying ambiguous treaty terms.[18] *Travaux* can be difficult to find, but they have been compiled and published for several major conventions. The Yale Law Library website has a guide to collected *travaux* (library. law.yale.edu/collected-travaux-preparatoires), with links to online sources and tables of contents of published works.[19]

§ 17.4   CASES AND ARBITRATIONS

Although most disputes between nations are resolved by direct negotiation between the parties, some are submitted to international tribunals, arbitral bodies, or temporary commissions convened for specific disputes. Courts established by international and regional organizations have developed a growing body of international jurisprudence. Decisions of domestic courts on matters of international law can also be important sources, particularly as evidence of international legal custom.

(a) International Court of Justice

The preeminent international tribunal is the International Court of Justice (ICJ), also known as the World Court, which settles legal disputes between nations. The ICJ was created in 1945 by the Charter of the United Nations as one of the organization's principal organs, succeeding the Permanent Court of International Justice (PCIJ) of the League of Nations. The court meets at the Hague and consists of fifteen judges elected to nine-year terms.

The ICJ issues only a handful of judgments each year. These are published in *Reports of Judgments, Advisory Opinions and Orders* and are available on the ICJ website (www.icj-cij.org). The site has material from every case the court has heard since its inception and from cases heard by the PCIJ, as well as information on the current docket and basic documents such as the Statute of the Court and rules. Illustration 17-8 shows the opening page of the court's decision in *Whaling in the Antarctic (Austl. v. Japan; N.Z. intervening)*, 2014 I.C.J. 226 (Mar. 31).

---

[18] Vienna Convention on the Law of Treaties, May 23, 1969, art. 32, 1155 U.N.T.S. 331, 340 ("Recourse may be had to supplementary means of interpretation, including the preparatory work of the treaty and the circumstances of its conclusion . . . .").

[19] For more information, see Jonathan Pratter, *À la Recherche des Travaux Préparatoires: An Approach to Researching the Drafting History of International Agreements*, GLOBALEX (July/Aug. 2017) (www.nyulawglobal.org/globalex/Travaux_ Preparatoires1.html) [https://perma.cc/4U3E-3659].

INTERNATIONAL COURT OF JUSTICE

2014
31 March
General List
No. 148

YEAR 2014

31 March 2014

WHALING
IN THE ANTARCTIC

(AUSTRALIA *v.* JAPAN: NEW ZEALAND intervening)

Jurisdiction of the Court — Parties' declarations under Article 36, paragraph 2, of the Statute — Australia's reservation — Disputes "concerning or relating to the delimitation of maritime zones" or "arising out of, concerning, or relating to the exploitation of any disputed area of or adjacent to any such maritime zone pending its delimitation" — Dispute concerning maritime delimitation must exist for the reservation to be applicable — No dispute as to maritime delimitation between the Parties — Reservation not applicable — Japan's objection to the Court's jurisdiction cannot be upheld.

*

Alleged violations of the International Convention for the Regulation of Whaling.

Origins of the Convention — Schedule to the Convention — International Whaling Commission — The Scientific Committee and its role — Guidelines issued by the Commission.

Interpretation of Article VIII, paragraph 1, of the Convention — Article VIII to be interpreted in light of the object and purpose of the Convention — Neither a restrictive nor an expansive interpretation of Article VIII justified — Issuance of special permits under Article VIII to kill, take and treat whales for purposes of scientific research — Existence and limits of a State party's discretion under Article VIII — Standard of review to be applied by the Court when reviewing special permits granted under Article VIII — Whether programme involves scientific research — Whether, in the use of lethal methods, the programme's design and implementation are reasonable in relation to achieving its stated objectives — Objective character of the standard of review — The Court not called upon to resolve matters of scientific or whaling policy — The Court's task only to ascertain whether special permits granted in relation to JARPA II fall within scope of Arti-

**Illustration 17-8. The beginning of an International
Court of Justice judgment.**

International Law Reports (1956–date) and its predecessor *Annual Digest and Reports of Public International Law Cases* (1932–55) contain all PCIJ and ICJ decisions, as well as English translations of selected decisions of regional and national courts on international law issues. These cases can be found in several subscription databases. *International Law Reports* are available online from vLex Justis (www.justis.com). HeinOnline has decisions from both PCIJ and ICJ, Westlaw has ICJ decisions, and Lexis has ICJ judgments, filings, and advisory opinions.

Among the most thorough secondary sources on the ICJ are Malcolm N. Shaw, *Rosenne's Law and Practice of the International Court, 1920–2015* (5th ed. 2016) and *The Statute of the International Court of Justice: A Commentary* (Andreas Zimmermann et al. eds., 3d ed. 2019). Shorter works include *La Cour internationale de Justice / International Court of Justice* (2006), an illustrated history published to celebrate the Court's sixtieth anniversary, and Robert Kolb, *The Elgar Companion to the International Court of Justice* (2014).

(b) Other Courts

The ICJ is not the only court of international scope. Various conventions and organizations have established courts to adjudicate disputes among nations or to deal with specific issues such as genocide, human rights, or the law of the sea.

Summaries of courts' organizations and procedures can be found in *Manual on International Courts and Tribunals* (Ruth Mackenzie et al. eds., 2d ed. 2010), and *The Rules, Practice, and Jurisprudence of International Courts and Tribunals* (Chiara Giorgetti ed., 2012).

The World Legal Information Institute's International Courts & Tribunals Collection (www.worldlii.org/int/cases/) allows searching across thousands of decisions from more than thirty of these tribunals. Oxford Reports on International Law (opil.ouplaw.com/home/ORIL) is a major subscription resource with several thousand cases from international and domestic courts, accompanied by commentary and analysis.

International Courts. The International Criminal Court (www.icc-cpi.int) with jurisdiction over war crimes, genocide, and crimes against humanity was created in 1998 and had its first session in March 2003.[20] It has over 120 member countries (and does not include the United States). Cases, documents, court rules, and background information are available on the court's website, and major secondary sources include *Rome Statute of the International Criminal Court: A Commentary* (Otto Triffterer ed., 3d ed. 2016), and two books by William Schabas: *An Introduction to the International Criminal Court* (5th ed. 2017) and *The International Criminal Court: A Commentary on the Rome Statute* (2d ed. 2017).

More focused international criminal courts have been convened to address specific violations of international humanitarian law.

---

[20] Rome Statute of the International Criminal Court, July 17, 1998, 2187 U.N.T.S. 90. The Rome Statute entered into force in 2002.

Some of these are ad hoc criminal tribunals established by the U.N. Security Council, while others are completely separate entities. These courts include the International Criminal Tribunal for the former Yugoslavia (ICTY) (www.icty.org) (1993–2017); the International Criminal Tribunal for Rwanda (ICTR) (www.ictr.org) (1994–2015);[21] the Special Court for Sierra Leone (www.rscsl.org) (2002–13); Extraordinary Chambers in the Courts of Cambodia (www.eccc.gov.kh) (2006–date); and the Special Tribunal for Lebanon (www.stl-tsl.org) (2009–date). Each of these courts has case documents and other information on its website. Procedures and jurisprudence are discussed in William Schabas, *UN International Criminal Tribunals: The Former Yugoslavia, Rwanda, and Sierra Leone* (2006); John D. Ciorciari & Anne Heindel, *Hybrid Justice: The Extraordinary Chambers in the Courts of Cambodia* (2014); and *The Special Tribunal for Lebanon: Law and Practice* (Amal Alamuddin et al. eds., 2014). Major cases can be found in print in *Annotated Leading Cases of International Criminal Tribunals* (1999–date) (www.annotatedleadingcases.com).[22]

Reference works in the area include *The Oxford Companion to International Criminal Justice* (Antonio Cassese ed., 2009) and *Routledge Handbook of International Criminal Law* (William Schabas & Nadia Bernaz eds., 2011). Several more detailed treatises are published, including Kai Ambos, *Treatise on International Criminal Law* (2013–16); Karim A.A. Khan & Rodney Dixon, *Archbold International Criminal Courts: Practice, Procedure, and Evidence* (5th ed. 2018); and *International Criminal Law* (M. Cherif Bassiouni ed., 3d ed. 2008).

The World War II war crimes trials held by the International Military Tribunals in Nuremberg and Tokyo are available in several printed sources including *The Trial of German Major War Criminals* (1946–51) and *The Tokyo War Crimes Trial* (R. John Pritchard & Sonia Magbanua Zaide eds., 1981–87). The U.S. government publication *Nazi Conspiracy and Aggression* (1946–47) is available in HeinOnline's Legal Classics Library and through the Library of Congress's Federal Research Division (www.loc.gov/rr/frd/Military_Law/NT_Nazi-conspiracy.html).

---

[21] The U.N. established the International Residual Mechanism for Criminal Tribunals (www.irmct.org) in 2010 to continue functions of the now-closed ICTY and ICTR, such as prosecuting at-large fugitives and handling post-conviction matters. The Mechanism's website contains cases and documents for all proceedings in its jurisdiction.

[22] For more information on resources about these courts, see Anthony Bestafka-Cruz, *Searching Through Systems: Research Guide for UN Criminal Tribunals*, 40 INT'L J. LEGAL INFO. 516 (2012), and several guides on GlobaLex (www.nyulawglobal.org/globalex/).

Another court of worldwide scope, the International Tribunal for the Law of the Sea (ITLOS) (www.itlos.org), was created by the United Nations Convention on the Law of the Sea and established in 1996.[23] More than 165 countries are parties to the convention. ITLOS rules and cases are available on its website, and P. Chandrasekhara Rao & Philippe Gautier, *The International Tribunal for the Law of the Sea: Law, Practice and Procedure* (2018) is a leading current commentary.

Regional Courts. The decisions of the courts of regional organizations have assumed growing importance in international law as the range of disputes over which they exercise jurisdiction grows. Among the most important of these regional courts are the European Court of Justice, the European Court of Human Rights, and the Inter-American Court of Human Rights.[24]

The European Court of Justice (curia.europa.eu), an organ of the European Union, resolves disputes between EU institutions and member states over the interpretation and application of EU treaties and legislation. A subordinate General Court (formerly the Court of First Instance) handles the initial hearing in most cases. All decisions since the Court of Justice's inception are available on its website, as well as through Westlaw and other online services. The official *Reports of Cases Before the Court of Justice and the General Court* has decisions from both courts, and commercial print sources include *European Union Law Reporter* (1972–date) and *Common Market Law Reports* (1962–date). Secondary sources include K.P.E. Lasok, *Lasok's European Court Practice and Procedure* (3d ed. 2017) and Bertrand Wägenbaur, *Court of Justice of the EU: Commentary on Statute and Rules of Procedure* (2013).

The European Court of Human Rights (www.echr.coe.int) was created under the European Convention of Human Rights of 1950 for the international protection of the rights of individuals.[25] The court's website has basic texts and searchable case law. Decisions are published officially in *Reports of Judgments and Decisions* and are

---

[23] United Nations Convention on the Law of the Sea art. 287, Dec. 10, 1982, 1833 U.N.T.S. 397.

[24] Other regional tribunals include the Court of Justice of the Central American System of Integration, the Tribunal of Mercosur, the Caribbean Court of Justice, the African Commission on Human and Peoples' Rights, the East African Court of Justice, and the Court of the Economic Community of West African States. For more information on these courts including websites and member information, see Katrin Nyman Metcalf & Ioannis F. Papageorgiou, *Regional Courts as Judicial Brakes?*, 10 BALTIC J.L. & POL., no. 2, 2017, at 154.

[25] Convention for the Protection of Human Rights and Fundamental Freedoms art. 19, Nov. 4, 1950, 213 U.N.T.S. 221. The European Commission on Human Rights, which became obsolete in 1998, facilitated the court from 1953 to 1998 in a variety of functions including determining whether petitions to the court could be accepted.

also available in *European Human Rights Reports*. A variety of documents and decisions appear in the annual *Yearbook of the European Convention on Human Rights* (1958–date). *Human Rights Practice* (Jessica Simor ed., 2000–date) is a detailed guide to the Convention and court procedures. Other commentaries include Bernadette Rainey et al., *Jacobs, White & Ovey: The European Convention on Human Rights* (7th ed. 2017) and *Theory and Practice of the European Convention on Human Rights* (Pieter van Dijk et al. eds., 5th ed. 2018).

The Inter-American Commission on Human Rights (www.oas. org/en/iachr/) was created in 1959[26] and hears complaints of individuals and institutions alleging violations of human rights in the American countries. The commission or a member state can refer matters to the Inter-American Court of Human Rights (www. corteidh.or.cr), created in 1978. Twenty-five countries (not including the United States) have accepted its jurisdiction. The court's decisions are reported in two series of judgments (advisory opinions in Series A, *Judgments and Opinions*, and contentious cases in Series C, *Decisions and Judgments*), in its annual report, and on its website. The *Inter-American Yearbook on Human Rights* (1985–date) covers the work of both the commission and the court and includes selected decisions and other documents. The IACHR Project at Loyola Law School, Los Angeles (iachr.lls.edu) has a collection of court decisions that can be searched by case name, country, topic, or specific treaty violation. Laurence Burgorgue-Larsen & Amaya Ubeda de Torres, *The Inter-American Court of Human Rights: Case-Law and Commentary* (2011) and Jo M. Pasqualucci, *The Practice and Procedure of the Inter-American Court of Human Rights* (2d ed. 2013) are major secondary sources.[27]

Another regional human rights court, the African Court on Human and Peoples' Rights (www.african-court.org), was created in 2002[28] and delivered its first judgment in 2009. Its website has basic documents and information on its cases. The African Human Rights Case Law Analyser (caselaw.ihrda.org) covers both the African Court and regional tribunals. The ACtHPR Monitor (www.acthprmonitor. org/) provides commentary, history, procedure, and an atlas that links to the court judgments. For background, see works such as *The*

---

[26] Statute of the Inter-American Commission on Human Rights, G.A. Res. 447, OAS, 9th Sess., art. 18 (1979).

[27] *See also* Víctor Rodríguez Rescia & Marc David Seitles, *The Development of the Inter-American Human Rights System: A Historical Perspective and a Modern-Day Critique*, 16 N.Y. L. Sch. J. Hum. Rts. 593 (2000).

[28] Protocol to the African Charter on Human and Peoples' Rights on the Establishment of an African Court on Human and Peoples' Rights, June 9, 1998, OAU Doc. OAU/LEG/EXP/AFCHPR/PROT (III).

African Regional Human Rights System (Manisuli Ssenyonjo ed., 2012) and Frans Viljoen, *International Human Rights Law in Africa* (2d ed. 2012).

National Courts. Domestic courts often address issues of international law, and their decisions can have international significance. As mentioned earlier, *International Law Reports* contains English translations of decisions of national courts on international law issues. The International Crimes Database (ICD) (www.internationalcrimesdatabase.org) has documents from both international and domestic courts.

ALR International, available on Westlaw, summarizes U.S. and foreign cases on issues such as the construction and application of specific articles of major multilateral conventions. More specific works are also available. Cases from the U.S. and other countries under the Convention on Contracts for the International Sale of Goods are available through UNILEX (www.unilex.info) and Pace Law School's Institute of International Commercial Law (www.iicl. law.pace.edu/cisg/cisg). Case Law on UNCITRAL Texts (CLOUT) (uncitral.un.org/en/case_law) has international trade law cases, and ECOLEX (www.ecolex.org) is a gateway to environmental law decisions by national and international courts as well as treaties, legislation, and other resources. Refworld (www.refworld.org), from the Office of the U.N. High Commissioner for Refugees, has searchable judgments on human rights from domestic and regional courts, as well as thousands of other documents relating to the granting of refugee status.

(c) Arbitrations

Many disputes between nations and between commercial partners are settled by arbitration. Arbitrations between nations are published in the United Nations series, *Reports of International Arbitral Awards* (*RIAA*) (1948–date), which includes agreements reached by mediation or conciliation as well as awards resulting from contested arbitrations. *RIAA* is available online from the U.N. (www. un.org/law/riaa/) and from HeinOnline.[29]

---

[29] For historical arbitrations, see REPERTORY OF INTERNATIONAL ARBITRAL JURISPRUDENCE (1989–91), arranging arbitral decisions from 1794 to 1987 by subject, and SURVEY OF INTERNATIONAL ARBITRATIONS, 1794–1989 (A. M. Stuyt ed., 3d. ed. 1990), digesting these early decisions. The Hague Peace Conferences of 1899 and 1907 created the Permanent Court of Arbitration and the International Commission of Inquiry; their decisions were published in the HAGUE COURT REPORTS (James B. Scott ed., 1916–32, available on HeinOnline). THE PERMANENT COURT OF ARBITRATION: INTERNATIONAL ARBITRATION AND DISPUTE RESOLUTION (P. Hamilton et al. eds., 1999) summarizes its work. HeinOnline has several historical treatises on international arbitration in its Foreign & International Law Resources Database.

Several sources cover international arbitrations between private parties, including *Mealey's International Arbitration Report* (1986–date, available on Lexis), *World Arbitration Reporter* (2d ed. 2010–date), and *Yearbook: Commercial Arbitration* (1975–date). Recent treatises in the area include Margaret L. Moses, *The Principles and Practice of International Commercial Arbitration* (3d ed. 2017) and *Practitioner's Handbook on International Commercial Arbitration* (Frank-Bernd Weigand ed., 3d ed. 2019).

Several subscription platforms are helpful sources of international arbitration cases, awards, treatises, and other material. Kluwer Arbitration (www.kluwerarbitration.com) has a variety of major sources, including conventions, rules, and case law. Westlaw has an international arbitration database. The fastest way to access it is to type International Arbitration Materials in the search bar on the homepage. Material is grouped by cases, awards, rules, institutions, conventions, legislation, model laws and clauses, treatises, and journals. Westlaw's international arbitration collection on Practical Law includes many of these same resources as well as current awareness resources and checklists. Oxford Legal Research Library's *International Commercial Arbitration* (olrl.ouplaw.com/home/ICMA) has over thirty treatises, including coverage on topics like attorney-client privilege, corruption, *res judicata*, and consent in international arbitration.

§ 17.5 INTERNATIONAL ORGANIZATIONS

National governments are the major parties in international law, but worldwide and regional intergovernmental organizations (IGOs) play a vital role by establishing norms, promoting multilateral conventions, and providing mechanisms for the peaceful resolution of conflicts. Several IGOs have established adjudicatory bodies by whose decisions nations agree to be bound. Even when not acting as lawmaking bodies, international organizations compile and publish many of the most important research sources in international law.[30]

(a) United Nations and Related Agencies

The purposes of the United Nations, established in 1945, are (1) to maintain international peace and security; (2) to develop friendly relations among nations based on respect for equal rights and self-determination; (3) to achieve international cooperation in solving

---

[30] Nongovernmental organizations (NGOs) such as Amnesty International are major advocates for causes such as environmental protection, health care, and human rights, and many publish useful resources for the international legal researcher. See Duke University Libraries' Non-Governmental Organizations (NGO) guide (guides.library.duke.edu/ngo_guide) for more information and links to NGO websites.

international problems and in promoting respect for human rights and fundamental freedoms; and (4) to be a center for harmonizing the actions of nations in attaining these goals.[31]

The United Nations' six principal organs are the General Assembly, Security Council, Economic and Social Council, Trusteeship Council,[32] Secretariat, and International Court of Justice (ICJ). Its website (www.un.org) provides a wealth of information on the organization, including news, descriptive overviews of its activities, and access to numerous documents. The best printed source for basic information on the U.N.'s structure and programs is _United Nations Handbook_ (www.mfat.govt.nz), published annually by the New Zealand Ministry of External Relations and Trade.

More extensive commentaries include _The Charter of the United Nations: A Commentary_ (Bruno Simma et al. eds., 3d ed. 2012); Rosalyn Higgins et al., _Oppenheim's International Law: United Nations_ (2017); and _The Oxford Handbook on the United Nations_ (Thomas G. Weiss & Sam Daws eds., 2d ed. 2018). The _Max Planck Yearbook of United Nations Law_ (1997–date) (www.mpfpr.de/) is a major source for current scholarly commentary; most volumes are available free online.

The _Yearbook of the United Nations_ (unyearbook.un.org) is one of the best starting points for historical research on U.N. activities. Although coverage is delayed about five years, this publication summarizes major developments, reprints major documents, and provides references to other sources for the year covered. The website has retrospective coverage from the first volume in 1946.

The _General Assembly Official Records_ (GAOR) are among the most important documents for U.N. research. The records of the meetings of the assembly and its committees are accompanied by _Annexes_ containing the more important documents produced during the session, and by _Supplements_ containing annual reports submitted by the Secretary-General, Security Council, International Court of Justice, and various committees. The final supplement each year is a compilation of the resolutions passed by the General Assembly during the session.

Resolutions are also reprinted in the _Yearbook of the United Nations_ and are available online. The UN Documentation Centre

---

[31] Charter of the United Nations, June 26, 1945, art. 1, 59 Stat. 1031, 1037.

[32] The Trusteeship Council amended its rules in 1994 to eliminate the obligation to meet annually, following the independence of Palau, the last territory under trusteeship. Report of the Trusteeship Council to the Security Council on the Trust Territory of the Pacific Islands, UN Doc. S/1994/1400, Spec. Supp. No. 1.

(www.un.org/documents/) has browsable access to General Assembly and Security Council resolutions since 1946, as well as recent meeting records and other major documents. The United Nations Official Document System (ODS) (documents.un.org) is a search engine with the full text of all resolutions since 1946 and other documents beginning in 1993.

The United Nations also produces several specialized yearbooks. The *Yearbook of the International Law Commission* (legal.un.org/ilc/) reports on efforts to develop and codify selected fields of international law; the *Juridical Yearbook* (legal.un.org/UNJuridicalYearbook/) contains the texts of treaties and other documents relating to legal activities of the U.N. and related organizations. The United Nations Commission on International Trade Law's *UNCITRAL Yearbook* (www.uncitral.org) focuses on the modernization and harmonization of the rules of international business. Each yearbook website has complete retrospective coverage of earlier volumes, which are available as well in HeinOnline's United Nations Law Collection.

The United Nations also coordinates the work of several "specialized agencies" in particular subject fields, such as the Food and Agriculture Organization, the International Labour Organisation, and the World Health Organization, several of which have extensive law-related activities. The United Nations System website (www.unsceb.org) has a directory with links to sites for over eighty specialized organizations.

Nearly a million U.N. publications are available in the United Nations Digital Library (digitallibrary.un.org/). It covers materials since 1979, with older documents gradually being added. A commercial service, Access UN (www.readex.com), has comprehensive retrospective coverage.

The U.N.'s Dag Hammarskjöld Library has published more than three dozen research guides on its website (research.un.org/en), some explaining the major organizational units and others focusing on specific topics such as the environment, health, human rights, or international law. Its Ask DAG (ask.un.org/) page is a regularly updated collection of over 800 frequently asked questions (approximately 600 of which are in English with the remainder in Spanish and French) that covers the General Assembly, Member States, General Debate, U.N. Documents, and more. The library is also a helpful resource if you have a citation but are unable to find a document in ODS or the U.N. Digital Library.[33] Researchers can

---

[33] *See also* Dag Hammarskjöld Library, *I am researching UN documents. When should I use the United Nations Digital Library? When should I use ODS?* (Dec. 10, 2019) (ask.un.org/faq/14557) [https://perma.cc/4AY8-YK7R] (describing the differences among search methodologies and functions for the U.N. Digital Library, ODS,

contact the library for assistance, and if the document is available in print only, it will be quickly added to the U.N. Digital Library and a digital file will be sent to you.

(b) World Trade Organization

The World Trade Organization (www.wto.org) was established in 1995 as the principal international body administering trade agreements among its over 160 member states, succeeding the General Agreement on Tariffs and Trade (GATT). The WTO acts as a forum for negotiations, seeks to resolve disputes, and oversees national trade policies. It is governed by a Ministerial Conference, which meets every two years, while most operations are handled by its General Council. Basic documents governing WTO operations are available on its website, and an *Annual Report* (1996–date) provides trade statistics and a commentary on the organization's work every year.[34]

Disputes are first addressed through consultations. If consultations fail, the dispute is heard by a panel of three to five members whose decision can be reviewed by the Appellate Body. The seven members of the Appellate Body serve four-year terms with the possibility of being reappointed once.[35] WTO panel decisions and appellate body reports are available in the "Trade Topics: Dispute Settlement" section of the WTO website as well as in several commercial series, including *International Trade Law Reports* (1996–date), *World Trade Organization Dispute Settlement Decisions: Bernan's Annotated Reporter* (1998–date), and Westlaw (retrievable by entering WTO & GATT Panel Decisions in the search bar on the home page). WorldTradeLaw.net has summaries and texts of decisions as well as other WTO documents, and *WTO Appellate Body Repertory of Reports and Awards, 1995–2013* (5th ed. 2013) provides subject access to the cases.

Commentaries on the WTO include *Max Planck Commentaries on World Trade Law* (Rüdiger Wolfrum et al. eds., 2006–11), Mitsuo

---

Yearbook, and Index to Proceedings) and Dag Hammarskjöld Library, *What is the Official Document System (ODS)? How can I search ODS?* (Oct. 15, 2019) (ask.un.org/faq/112211) [https://perma.cc/U3S9-UCVN] (providing detailed coverage information for ODS).

[34] Pre-WTO documents are available from the GATT Digital Library: 1947–1994 (exhibits.stanford.edu/gatt) and the WTO GATT Documents site (www.wto.org/english/docs_e/gattdocs_e.htm).

[35] Appointments are made via consensus; thus, members can veto appointments. Since 2016, the United States has vetoed all new appointments, leaving the panel with one panelist. The Appellate Body requires at least three panelists to hear appeals. *See* CATHLEEN D. CIMINO-ISAACS ET AL., CONG. RESEARCH SERV., R45417, WORLD TRADE ORGANIZATION: OVERVIEW AND FUTURE DIRECTION (2019) (crsreports.congress.gov/product/pdf/R/R45417).

Matsushita et al., *The World Trade Organization: Law, Practice, and Policy* (3d ed. 2015), and *The World Trade Organization: Legal, Economic and Political Analysis* (Patrick F. J. Macrory et al. eds., 2005).

(c) European Union and Other Regional Organizations

For American lawyers, the European Union (europa.eu) is probably the most frequently encountered of the world's many regional organizations. The EU was established in 1993 by the Treaty on European Union (the Maastricht Treaty) as the more ambitious successor to the European Communities (European Atomic Energy Community, European Coal and Steel Community, and European Economic Community). As economic and social developments have led to increasing European integration and the Treaty on European Union has been amended by the Treaty of Amsterdam (1997), the Treaty of Nice (2001), and the Treaty of Lisbon (2007), the EU is sometimes seen more as a supranational government than as a regional organization. The United Kingdom's withdrawal from the Union in 2020 has not made EU law any less significant in transnational legal practice.[36]

The major institutions of the EU are the European Commission, which proposes legislation, implements policies, and manages the Union; the European Parliament, a large elected body with legislative and advisory functions; the Council of the European Union, which coordinates economic policies, concludes international agreements, and legislates in conjunction with the European Parliament; and the European Court of Justice (discussed earlier with other regional courts).[37] The EU legislates through *regulations*, which are directly binding and do not require implementing legislation in member states, and *directives*, which must be implemented by member states to become effective.

Official sources of EU legal information include the *Official Journal of the European Union*, consisting of two series, *Legislation* (L) and *Information and Notices* (C). Legislation and major

---

[36] Two significant research guides providing links to the primary sources, commentary, current awareness resources, and other documents chronicling "Brexit" are available from the Middle Temple Library (www.middletemple.org.uk/library-archive/library/electronic-resources/links-lawyers/brexit) and Georgetown Law Library (guides.ll.georgetown.edu/uklegalresearch).

[37] The other three official EU institutions are the European Council, which oversees policy and major initiatives but cannot engage in law-making; the European Central Bank, which implements monetary and economic policies; and the Court of Auditors, which audits use of EU funds. *See* Georgetown Law Library, *European Union Research Guide* (guides.ll.georgetown.edu/EuropeanUnion) for detailed guidance on EU legal research.

documents are published in the EU's 24 official languages: Bulgarian, Croatian, Czech, Danish, Dutch, English, Estonian, Finnish, French, German, Greek, Hungarian, Irish, Italian, Latvian, Lithuanian, Maltese, Polish, Portuguese, Romanian, Slovak, Slovene, Spanish, and Swedish. Thanks to Ireland and Malta, English remains an official language even after the withdrawal of the United Kingdom.

EUR-Lex (eur-lex.europa.eu) has the *Official Journal of the European Union* back to 1998, as well as other major documents and a Directory of European Union Legislation in Force that provides subject access to treaties, regulations, directives, and other legislative actions. Westlaw has extensive coverage of EU resources including cases, legislation, treaties, preparatory acts, information and notices, treatises, and journals. Lexis has the four-volume treatise *Smit & Herzog on the Law of the European Union* (2d ed. 2005–date) as well as EU cases and legislation.

Several other reference sources on EU law are published. *The Oxford Handbook of European Union Law* (Anthony Arnull & Damian Chalmers eds., 2017) provides a broad overview, and *Oxford Principles of European Union Law* (Robert Schütze & Takis Tridimas eds., 2018–date) is a projected three-volume set going into much greater detail. *Encyclopedia of European Union Law: Constitutional Texts* (Neville March Hunnings ed., 1996–date) is a ten-volume work with annotated versions of the treaties and other major texts. Basic one-volume texts include Anthony Arnull et al., *Wyatt and Dashwood's European Union Law* (6th ed. 2011), Ralph H. Folsom, *Principles of European Union Law* (5th ed. 2017), and P.S.R.F. Mathijsen, *A Guide to European Union Law* (11th ed. 2013).[38]

Other important regional organizations include the African Union (www.au.int), Council of Europe (www.coe.int), and Organization of American States (OAS) (www.oas.org), all of which draft and promote multilateral treaties among their member states. As discussed earlier, they also have judicial systems designed to protect human rights in their regions.

Information on more than thirty major intergovernmental organizations can be found in *International Encyclopaedia of Laws: Intergovernmental Organizations* (1997–date) (www.kluwerlaw online.com). *Yearbook of International Organizations* (www.uia.org/yearbook) is a six-volume directory with profiles and contact information for thousands of international groups and associations.

---

[38] Several online guides with more information on EU resources are available, including Alyson Drake, *European Union Legal Materials: An Infrequent User's Guide*, GLOBALEX (Nov./Dec. 2016) (www.nyulawglobal.org/globalex/European_Union1.htm).

§ 17.6 SOURCES FOR FURTHER INFORMATION

International law has a wide range of print and electronic resources beyond those mentioned in this brief survey, and bibliographies and research guides can be invaluable sources of leads and research tips.

GlobaLex (www.nyulawglobal.org/globalex/) is a major source for international law information. It publishes several dozen research guides on specific topics including the expected (such as human trafficking and international commercial law) and the less frequently covered (such as housing and cyberwarfare), each accompanied by numerous links to resources. GlobaLex authors are often practitioners or expert researchers in the topic about which they have written. Several GlobaLex articles have already been cited in this chapter.

Marci Hoffman & Mary Rumsey, *International and Foreign Legal Research: A Coursebook* (2d ed. 2012), Heidi Frostestad Kuehl & Megan A. O'Brien, *International Legal Research in a Global Community* (2018), and Anthony S. Winer et al., *International Law Legal Research* (2013) are thorough examinations of research methods, generally and in several specialized areas. George Washington University Journal of International Law and Economics' annual *Guide to International Legal Research* (available on Lexis) includes chapters on gender, product liability, and maritime law as well as the more prosaic topics such as intellectual property and trade. Each chapter has annotated listings of print and online resources.

Westlaw and Lexis have treatises on specific international practice areas as well. Westlaw's can be found by selecting International Materials on the home page, then selecting treatises. Titles include International Civil Procedure, International Business Transactions, International Family Law Practice, and International Insolvency. Lexis's international treatises can be found by selecting Treatises & Practice Guides (under Secondary Materials) on the homepage, then choosing International Law as the practice area. Titles include International Estate Planning, International Computer Law, and International Agency & Distribution Agreements.

Chapter 18

THE LAW OF OTHER COUNTRIES

Table of Sections

Globalization has made the laws of other countries, known collectively as *foreign law*, increasingly significant to American social, economic, and legal life. The law of a foreign country may be relevant in U.S. court proceedings involving international trade or family law, and scholars and lawmakers can study other legal systems to better understand and improve our own. A serious legal problem involving a foreign legal system requires consultation with a lawyer who is trained and licensed in that jurisdiction, but any American lawyer dealing with a transnational matter must be able to develop a basic understanding of the other country's law.[1]

Foreign law sources are essential to the study of *comparative law*, in which differences among national legal systems are analyzed. The extent to which American courts should cite precedent from other countries is the subject of vigorous debate, involving Supreme Court justices and legislators as well as legal scholars.[2] While the

---

[1]   *Hart v. Carro, Spanbock, Kaster & Cuiffo*, 620 N.Y.S.2d 847, 849 (N.Y. App. Div. 1995) ("When, as here, counsel is retained in a matter involving foreign law, it is counsel's responsibility to conduct the matter properly and to know, or learn, the law of the foreign jurisdiction."). On the increasingly global nature of legal practice, see, e.g., Symposium, *The Globalization of the Legal Profession*, 14 IND. J. GLOBAL LEGAL STUD. 1 (2007), and Scott L. Cummings, *The Internationalization of Public Interest Law*, 57 DUKE L.J. 891 (2008).

[2]   For a recent summary, see Mark C. Rahdert, *Exceptionalism Unbound: Appraising American Resistance to Foreign Law*, 65 CATH. U. L. REV. 537 (2016).

influence accorded to foreign law regarding constitutional issues such as capital punishment is controversial, there is no question that decisions from common law countries have had persuasive value in the development of American tort and contract doctrine. The resources discussed in this chapter provide starting points for the American researcher.

§ 18.1   LEGAL SYSTEMS OF THE WORLD

The legal systems of most countries can be described as belonging to either the *common law* or *civil law* tradition. Each system has its own history, fundamental principles and procedures, and forms of publication for legal sources. As explained in Chapter 1, legal doctrine under the common law is developed over time through specific cases decided by judges rather than from broad, abstract codifications. Judicial decisions are traditionally the most important and vital source of new legal rules in a common law system.

The civil law system is the legal tradition, based on Roman law, that characterizes those systems found in countries of continental Europe, Latin America, and parts of Africa and Asia. Civil law has several distinctive characteristics, including the predominance of comprehensive and systematic codes governing large fields of law (civil, criminal, commercial, civil procedure, and criminal procedure), little weight for judicial decisions as legal authority, and great influence of legal scholars who interpret, criticize, and develop the law through commentaries on the codes.[3]

Some jurisdictions do not fit clearly into either the civil law or common law traditions. A few countries, such as Scotland and South Africa, have aspects of both civil law and common law. Others are strongly influenced by customary law or traditional religious systems, particularly Islamic or Talmudic law. The law of these countries may be a mixture of civil or common law and the customary

---

[3] Major reforms in civil codes in 19th-century France and Germany coincided with the rise of the secular nation-state and account for the structure of civil law systems. For a brief introduction, see JAMES APPLE & ROBERT DEYLING, A PRIMER ON THE CIVIL-LAW SYSTEM (1995) (www.fjc.gov/content/primer-civil-law-system-0). A more detailed explanation can be found in books such as JOHN HENRY MERRYMAN & ROGELIO PÉREZ-PERDORNO, THE CIVIL LAW TRADITION: AN INTRODUCTION TO THE LEGAL SYSTEMS OF EUROPE AND LATIN AMERICA (4th ed. 2019) and ALAN WATSON, THE MAKING OF THE CIVIL LAW (1981). The system of legal education in civil law countries is summarized in Rodrigo Said, *Legal Education and the Civil Law System*, 62 N.Y. L. SCH. L. REV. 165 (2017/18). On codification more generally, see Jean Louis Bergel, *Principal Features and Methods of Codification*, 48 LA. L. REV. 1073 (1988).

or religious legal system. A few countries combine elements of three or more legal systems.[4]

JuriGlobe: World Legal Systems (www.juriglobe.ca), from the University of Ottawa Faculty of Law, is an online guide with maps of world regions, descriptions of the major systems, and lists of countries in each category. Its maps show the world's wide variety of civil law, common law, and other legal systems.

Texts discussing the history and concepts of the world's legal systems include H. Patrick Glenn, *Legal Traditions of the World: Sustainable Diversity in Law* (5th ed. 2014); John W. Head, *Great Legal Traditions: Civil Law, Common Law, and Chinese Law in Historical and Operational Perspective* (2011); and Thomas Lundmark, *Charting the Divide Between Common and Civil Law* (2012).

The differences between the common law and civil law systems have become less marked in recent years, as each system adopts features of the other. American jurisdictions have increasingly enacted comprehensive subject codifications, such as the Uniform Commercial Code, while judicial decisions are being given greater weight in some civil law countries. Nonetheless, basic differences remain in how legal issues are perceived and research is conducted.

§ 18.2 REFERENCE SOURCES IN FOREIGN AND COMPARATIVE LAW

While thorough research on a foreign law issue can be undertaken only in original sources, print and online reference resources can provide a working knowledge of major legal issues. It is usually best to begin with an encyclopedia or treatise for a general introduction to a national legal system or a specific subject, and then to find translations or summaries of the primary sources. Foreign law research guides with descriptions and links for sources can help clarify the range of options.

(a) Encyclopedias and Legal System Guides

Several encyclopedic works provide coverage of national legal systems and specific legal topics within those systems.

Legal Systems of the World: A Political, Social, and Cultural Encyclopedia (Herbert M. Kritzer ed., 2002) is a four-volume work with introductory overviews by jurisdiction and subject. Articles on countries discuss history, major legal concepts, and the structure of

---

[4] See MIXED JURISDICTIONS WORLDWIDE: THE THIRD LEGAL FAMILY (Vernon Valentine Palmer ed., 2d ed. 2012) for an overview and discussion of nine specific jurisdictions.

the legal system, with references for further reading. Subject articles generally compare civil law and common law approaches.

The Oxford International Encyclopedia of Legal History (Stanley N. Katz ed., 2009) is a six-volume set with over 1,000 articles on a wide range of legal topics in ancient, medieval, and modern legal systems. Articles include cross-references and bibliographies.

The United States government publishes several guides to the legal and business environments in foreign countries. The International Trade Administration has Country Commercial Guides for more than 150 countries (www.export.gov/ccg), and the State Department's Bureau of Consular Affairs has a "Legal Resources" page (travel.state.gov/content/travel/en/legal.html), part of which covers International Judicial Assistance topics such as enforcement of judgments and obtaining evidence abroad. The Central Intelligence Agency's *World Factbook* (www.cia.gov) has demographic and economic information about the countries of the world.

Law and Judicial Systems of Nations (4th ed. 2002) has a concise overview of bar organization, legal education, and court systems of 193 countries, with a brief explanation of each legal system. Basic country information, such as economic conditions, political developments, and statistics, can also be found in reference sources such as *The Europa World Year Book* (www.europaworld.com) and *The Statesman's Yearbook*.

Several guides to the legal systems of specific countries are published in English. These generally explain legal institutions, summarize major doctrines, and provide leads to research resources. Examples of recently published titles include *Introduction to Hungarian Law* (Attila Harmathy ed., 2d ed. 2019); Jean-Marie Kamatali, *Introduction to Rwandan Law* (2020); and *The Israeli Legal System: An Introduction* (Christian Walter et al. eds., 2019).

International Encyclopaedia of Laws (IEL) (www.kluwerlaw online.com) consists of more than twenty subject-specific collections of monographic pamphlets for individual countries. The chances of finding a specific subject for a specific country are not always promising, but over 100 countries are covered on at least one topic.[5]

---

[5] The areas of focus of these encyclopedias, and the approximate number of countries each treats (to give some indication of the likelihood that a particular country is covered), are: Civil Procedure (46), Commercial and Economic Law (32), Competition Law (34), Constitutional Law (57), Contracts (50), Corporations and Partnerships (43), Criminal Law (31), Cyber Law (32), Energy Law (41), Environmental Law (62), Family and Succession Law (45), Insurance Law (30), Intellectual Property (72), Media Law (30), Medical Law (42), Migration Law (14), Private International Law (30), Property and Trust Law (29), Religion (19), Social Security Law (41), Sports Law (42), Tort Law

The *International Encyclopedia of Comparative Law* (1971–date) (referenceworks.brillonline.com) is the most comprehensive treatment of its subject, but it is still incomplete after almost fifty years. Individual chapters have been published as pamphlets, but only ten of seventeen planned volumes have been published in their final bound format. Materials are generally not updated upon republication, but original publication dates are noted in parentheses at the ends of chapters.[6] Volume 1 of the set consists of a series of "National Reports" pamphlets on individual countries, but most of these were published in the 1970s and are now of historical interest only.

In addition to encyclopedias, there are discrete publications collecting many countries' laws on a great variety of subjects. One tool for determining whether a given work collects a country's law on the topic it covers is the Global Legal Information Catalog (www.loc.gov/lawweb/servlet/Glic), a free service from the Library of Congress.

Three one-volume reference works have more current coverage of comparative law issues. *The Cambridge Companion to Comparative Law* (Mauro Bussani & Ugo Mattei eds., 2012), *Elgar Encyclopedia of Comparative Law* (Jan Smits ed., 2d ed. 2012), and *The Oxford Handbook of Comparative Law* (Mathias Reimann & Reinhard Zimmermann eds., 2d ed. 2019) all contain chapters by leading scholars analyzing various legal traditions as well as studies of particular topics and subject areas.

(b) Research Guides and Indexes

When starting research in the law of another country, you need a sense of the available publications and the resources with which you can conduct research. Several guides to foreign law research have broad coverage of many subjects and jurisdictions, while others are specialized bibliographic surveys of particular countries, regions, or subjects.

BrillOnline's Foreign Law Guide (referenceworks.brillonline.com) is one of the best starting points. For almost every country in

---

(32), and Transport Law (33). Some topics also cover intergovernmental organizations, and some include documents and case law as well as national monographs.

[6] Volume 16, Civil Procedure, was published in 2014, for example, but it includes a chapter on "State Arbitration in Socialist Countries," completed in 1973 and discussing the law in several countries that no longer exist such as Czechoslovakia, the German Democratic Republic, and the Soviet Union.

Another older resource to use with care is *Modern Legal Systems Cyclopedia* (Kenneth Robert Redden & Linda L. Schlueter eds., 1984–2005, available in HeinOnline's World Constitutions Illustrated Library), which has surveys of the legal systems of more than 170 jurisdictions. The entries range in length from three to more than 100 pages and vary considerably in quality. The publication dates of individual chapters are not indicated, but many are now clearly obsolete.

the world, it has a description of its legal system, notes on the major codifications and gazettes, sources for legislation and court decisions (noting which are available in English or online), and a detailed listing of codes and laws covering specific subject areas with links to online sources.

GlobaLex (www.nyulawglobal.org/globalex/) is a free service with guides prepared by attorneys and librarians on researching the legal systems of more than 160 countries. These guides generally summarize the legal system, describe available documentation, and have extensive links to online resources. Published research guides, such as *Legal Research in New Zealand* (Mary-Rose Russell ed., 2016), and Victoria J. Szymczak, *Charting the Legal Systems of the Western Pacific Islands: A Legal Research Guide* (2017), are also available for some countries.

Articles on foreign legal issues can be found in the periodical databases and indexes discussed in Chapter 3. More specialized resources are also available. *Index to Foreign Legal Periodicals* (1960–date, available through HeinOnline) covers over 600 journals published worldwide, as well as commemorative *festschriften* and other collections of essays. It indexes journals published outside the United States, the United Kingdom, and the Commonwealth, as well as articles in selected American and Commonwealth journals on international law, comparative law, or the domestic law of other countries. *Legal Journals Index* (LJI), a U.K. database available on Westlaw, covers over 800 British and European publications.[7]

(c) Summaries and Translations of Laws

If you are relying on English-language sources in your research, you can find many multinational summaries and digests on specific subjects as well as translations of some actual laws. While summaries and translations cannot substitute for the original sources, they can provide some familiarity with the basic concepts and issues of a foreign law problem.[8]

---

[7] Older sources for literature on foreign legal systems include SZLADITS' BIBLIOGRAPHY ON FOREIGN AND COMPARATIVE LAW (Charles Szladits et al. eds., 1955–2001), covering books and articles in English from 1790 to 1998, and INTRODUCTION BIBLIOGRAPHIQUE À L'HISTOIRE DU DROIT ET À L'ETHNOLOGIE JURIDIQUE/ BIBLIOGRAPHICAL INTRODUCTION TO LEGAL HISTORY AND ETHNOLOGY (John Gilissen ed., 1963–88). A LEGAL BIBLIOGRAPHY OF THE BRITISH COMMONWEALTH OF NATIONS (W. Harold Maxwell & Leslie F. Maxwell eds., 1955–64) lists materials from the United Kingdom, Canada, Australia, and other Commonwealth countries.

[8] *But see* Mary Rumsey, *Basic Guide to Researching Foreign Law*, GLOBALEX (July/Aug. 2016) (www.nyulawglobal.org/globalex/Foreign_Law_Research1.html) [https://perma.cc/2ZZ9-CQ2J] ("Although the web is an increasingly important source of foreign law, it is sometimes impossible to find current foreign law on a topic,

The basic laws of government structure and individual liberties are found in national constitutions. Two works provide introductory overviews. *Encyclopedia of World Constitutions* (Gerhard Robbers ed., 2007) covers almost 200 countries, discussing matters such as constitutional history, lawmaking process, and protected fundamental rights. Robert L. Maddex, *Constitutions of the World* (3d ed. 2008) has summaries of constitutions and brief constitutional histories for about 120 countries. Broader scholarly treatment of major themes is available in *Comparative Constitutional Law* (Tom Ginsburg & Rosalind Dixon eds., 2011) and *The Oxford Handbook of Comparative Constitutional Law* (Michel Rosenfeld & András Sajó eds., 2012), and online in the Max Planck Encyclopedia of Comparative Constitutional Law (oxcon.ouplaw.com/home/MPE CCOL).

Thorough coverage of current national constitutions is available from two online resources, HeinOnline's World Constitutions Illustrated and Oxford Constitutions of the World (oxcon.ouplaw. com). HeinOnline has texts in the original language and, where available, in English, and accompanies each set of constitutional documents with relevant treatises and journal articles as well as bibliographies of other commentaries. The Oxford resource, available in print as *Constitutions of the Countries of the World* (1971–date), has English translations of all documents, and includes bibliographies and constitutional overviews as well.[9]

Constitute (www.constituteproject.org) is a free resource with the text of the world's constitutions. It allows you to search all of its documents by keyword or to filter by topic to compare constitutional provisions on hundreds of specific issues.

Comprehensive collections of historic constitutions have been assembled by Professor Horst Dippel of the University of Kassel. *Constitutions of the World, 1850 to the Present* (2002–07) is a set of modern constitutions on microfiche, and *Constitutions of the World from the Late 18th Century to the Middle of the 19th Century* (2005–14) is a print compilation of historic sources.

Codes and statutes are far less likely than constitutions to be found in translation, but some resources are available. The official

---

particularly in translation. Very few foreign laws, and even fewer cases, are translated into English.").

[9] CONSTITUTIONS OF DEPENDENCIES AND TERRITORIES (Philip Raworth ed., 1998–date) complements this collection and is incorporated into the online version. Amos J. Peaslee & Dorothy Peaslee Xydis, CONSTITUTIONS OF NATIONS (1st–4th eds. 1950–85) may be useful for older constitutions. All four Peaslee editions and several other collections are available in HeinOnline's World Constitutions Illustrated database. For leads to other historical sources, see John Trone, *Print Sources of Historical Constitutions*, 34 INT'L J. LEGAL INFO. 539 (2006).

French site Legifrance (www.legifrance.gouv.fr) has English translations of major French codes, and the German Law Archive (germanlawarchive.iuscomp.org) has numerous statutes and court decisions in English.

Laws affecting international business are the most likely statutes to be available in English. RIA Worldwide Tax & Commercial Law, available on the International Tax tab of Thomson Reuters Checkpoint (checkpoint.riag.com), has English translations of tax and business-related laws from almost 200 countries and territories. The secondary source Getting the Deal Through (getting thedealthrough.com), available on Bloomberg Law, has concise explanations of national laws in more than 100 practice areas for over 150 jurisdictions. *International Labor and Employment Laws* (William L. Keller & Timothy J. Darby eds., 4th & 5th eds. 2013– date), also available on Bloomberg Law, summarizes employment laws in more than forty countries. Several other collections covering specific topics are published, including *Digest of Commercial Laws of the World* (rev. ed. 1998–date), *International Securities Regulation* (1986–date), and *Investment Laws of the World* (1973–date). Alena L. Wolotira & Sherry L. Lysen, *Multinational Sources Compared: A Subject and Jurisdiction Index* (2017, available on HeinOnline) lists books and online resources that compile or summarize laws on nearly 300 subjects.

International organizations also host online collections on national laws, often including translations into English. The Food and Agricultural Organization's FAOLEX (www.fao.org/faolex/) has national laws and regulations on food, agriculture, and natural resources management. The International Labour Organization's NATLEX (natlex.ilo.org) has abstracts of national labor laws in English, French, or Spanish, with links to the full text in many instances. The World Intellectual Property Organization's WipoLex (www.wipo.int/wipolex/) has English-language summaries of national intellectual property legislation.[10]

Relatively few judicial decisions in foreign languages are translated into English, but some case law is available. *International Law Reports* (1919–date) (www.justis.com) contains translations of cases from national courts on international law and human rights topics. Specialized sources include *Bulletin on Constitutional Case- Law* (codices.coe.int) (1993–date) and *International Labour Law Reports* (1978–date, available in HeinOnline's Foreign & International Law Resources Database).

---

[10] Other sites can be found through resources such as Jennifer Allison, *Foreign Law—Subject Law Collections on the Web*, GLOBALEX (Feb. 2017) (www.nyulawglobal. org/globalex/Foreign_Collections1.html) [https://perma.cc/2NF6-MS3F].

While it cannot substitute for professional translation, an automated translation service such as Google Translate (translate. google.com) can give you at least a sense of a document's meaning and help you determine whether a more accurate translation would be needed. Google Translate covers translation to or from more than 100 languages.

(d) Legal Dictionaries

Part of the difficulty of doing legal research in a foreign legal system stems from differences in language. But even legal systems sharing the same language can have different meanings for the same terms.[11] Legal dictionaries can help somewhat, although they usually provide only a superficial sense of the differences in meaning and usage.

Numerous bilingual legal dictionaries translate foreign terms into English, although many of these simply translate words without explaining the underlying legal concepts.[12] Respected works with references to code provisions and other sources to help explain terminology include two by Henry Saint Dahl, *Dahl's Law Dictionary: Spanish-English/English-Spanish* (6th ed. 2015) and *Dahl's Law Dictionary: French to English/English to French* (3d ed. 2007), as well as Jorge A. Vargas, *Mexican Legal Dictionary* (2012 ed.).[13]

Citation forms for foreign legal materials can be confusing for American lawyers. *The Bluebook* includes citation information for more than forty countries, covering statutory, judicial, and other frequently cited sources. Broader coverage is provided by *Guide to Foreign and International Legal Citations* (N.Y.U. Journal of International Law & Politics ed., 2d ed. 2009), which has profiles and citation guides for forty-five countries, and *International Citator and*

---

[11] The major British legal dictionary is JOWITT'S DICTIONARY OF ENGLISH LAW (Daniel Greenberg ed., 4th ed. 2015); two shorter paperback works are J.E. PENNER, THE LAW STUDENT'S DICTIONARY (13th ed. 2008) and OSBORN'S CONCISE LAW DICTIONARY (Mick Woodley ed., 12th ed. 2013). AUSTRALIAN LAW DICTIONARY (Trischa Mann, 3d ed. 2017) and DAPHNE A. DUKELOW, THE DICTIONARY OF CANADIAN LAW (4th ed. 2011) are the most substantial treatment of Australian and Canadian legal definitions.

[12] *See, e.g.,* Gerard-René de Groot & Conrad J.P. van Laer, *Bilingual and Multilingual Legal Dictionaries in the European Union: An Updated Bibliography,* 30 LEGAL REFERENCE SERVICES Q. 149 (2011); and Dennis Kim-Prieto & Conrad J.P. van Laer, *The Possible Dream: Perfecting Bilingual Law Dictionaries by Distinguishing Better Examples from Bad Examples,* 39 INT'L J. LEGAL INFO. 237 (2011).

[13] Several multilingual law dictionaries are also published. ROBERT HERBST & ALAN G. READETT, DICTIONARY OF COMMERCIAL, FINANCIAL AND LEGAL TERMS (3d–6th eds. 1998–2003) provides terminology in English, French, and German, and D.C. VAN HOOF ET AL., ELSEVIER'S LEGAL DICTIONARY (2001) adds Dutch and Spanish as well.

Research Guide: The Greenbook (Joseph Hnylka et al. eds., 2018–date), a work in progress with separate volumes published or planned for Europe, Latin America & Caribbean, Asia, North Africa & Middle East, and Africa (Sub-Saharan). Guides to citation forms in other countries include *OSCOLA: Oxford University Standard for Citation of Legal Authorities* (4th ed. 2012) (www.law.ox.ac.uk/research-subject-groups/publications/oscola) and *Canadian Guide to Uniform Legal Citation* (McGill Law Journal ed., 9th ed. 2018). *World Dictionary of Legal Abbreviations* (Mary Miles Prince ed., 1991–date) is a four-volume work with lengthy lists of foreign abbreviations, in separate sections for some two dozen countries, languages, regions, and subjects.

§ 18.3 ORIGINAL SOURCES

The next step after consulting available reference materials is to investigate primary legal sources from the country itself. Understanding these sources may require knowledge of a foreign language and another legal system, but finding them is often relatively easy thanks to the global reach of the internet. Many countries have extensive official resources online, and some have subscription-based research platforms like those available in the United States.[14] This section focuses on resources available to most American researchers.

(a) Links to Country Websites

Several resources have links to law-related websites in countries around the world. These resources include sites discussed earlier, such as Foreign Law Guide and GlobaLex, both of which combine descriptive summaries with links to sources. The World Bank's Doing Business site (www.doingbusiness.org/law-library/) has links to national laws on business-related topics for over 180 countries.

Other sites with country pages and links to constitutions, legislation, government sites, and other resources include the Library of Congress's Guide to Law Online (www.loc.gov/law/help/guide.php) and the World Legal Information Institute (WorldLII) (www.worldlii.org). Many academic law library websites also feature guides with links to foreign law sources.

---

[14] Some of these subscription platforms may be available in U.S. academic law libraries and law firms. Major platforms include SCC Online (www.scconline.com), covering India and several African and other Asian countries; vLex Global (vlex.com/p/vlex-global/), with primary sources from several Latin American countries; and Westlaw China (www.westlawchina.com), with materials in Chinese and English.

(b) Common Law Jurisdictions

The resources and research methods for other common law countries are similar to those of the United States, making them the most accessible of foreign legal systems. This section looks briefly at two of our most closely related common law jurisdictions: England (which is part of the United Kingdom but has a separate body of law from Northern Ireland and Scotland) and Canada. Similar resources are available for other common law countries such as Australia and New Zealand.

The United Kingdom has an "unwritten" constitution, meaning that its basic constitutional principles are not found in one specific document, but rather across several documents. One major difference between British and U.S. law is that the U.K. Parliament has nearly unlimited power, and most of its acts cannot be held unconstitutional. Canada's Constitution, dating to 1867, is the source of powers for both the federal Parliament and the provincial legislatures. Unlike in the United States, areas such as criminal law and family law are matters of Canadian federal law rather than provincial law, and in general any powers not specifically delegated to the provinces are reserved to the federal government.

Case Law. Judicial decisions from other common law countries are important in their own right, and they can also influence the development of U.S. common law doctrine. Even more significant are English cases predating U.S. independence that were expressly accepted as part of American common law by state reception statutes.

As a unitary jurisdiction, England has one system of trial and appellate courts. Civil actions are tried either in one of the three divisions of the High Court (Queen's Bench, Chancery, or Family) or in lower courts of limited jurisdiction, with review by the Court of Appeal and from there by the Supreme Court, which replaced the House of Lords as the court of last resort in 2009. Criminal trials are conducted in a Crown Court, with the same two-tier appellate system.

The Canadian court system is more like that of the United States, although fundamental differences exist. U.S. state supreme courts, for example, are the final arbiters on issues of state law, while the Supreme Court of Canada is the final court of appeal for both federal and provincial courts. Most matters are first heard in provincial court, but the Federal Court of Canada has trial jurisdiction over matters such as intellectual property, maritime law, and claims against the government.

As in the United States, new British and Canadian decisions are published in official or authorized series of reports and in unofficial commercial reporters and online services. Some U.S. libraries subscribe to ICLR.3 (www.iclr.co.uk), the online service of the Incorporated Council of Law Reporting for England and Wales, and free online access to decisions is provided by the British and Irish Legal Information Institute (BAILII) (www.bailii.org) and the Canadian Legal Information Institute (CanLII) (www.canlii.org).

English decisions before 1865 were discussed as part of the history of case publication in Chapter 10. For decisions since 1865, the standard source is the semi-official *Law Reports*, which now consists of four series: *Appeal Cases* (Supreme Court and the Judicial Committee of the Privy Council), *Queen's Bench Division*, *Chancery Division*, and *Family Division*. Before appearing in these series, new cases are published in *Weekly Law Reports*, which also has some decisions that are unreported in the four *Law Reports* series.

All England Law Reports (1936–date) is a commercially published reporter with some decisions not published in the *Weekly Law Reports*, and numerous specialized subject reporters such as *Criminal Appeal Reports* and *Family Law Reports* are also available. Westlaw has access to the *Law Reports* from 1865, as well as dozens of specialized reporters, and Lexis has the *All England Law Reports*.

Citations for modern English cases have some significant differences from the form usually used in this country. The United Kingdom has adopted a neutral citation policy for decisions after 2001,[15] mandating the use of an official slip opinion numbering system in addition to published reports, such as R (Miller) v. The Prime Minister [2019] UKSC 41. In addition, most published sets of reports are designated by year, and then by volume number for that year, instead of having one series of sequentially numbered volumes as is the U.S. norm. The year is an essential part of the citation because it identifies the volume.

Canada has authorized reports for its federal courts (*Canada Supreme Court Reports* and *Federal Court Reports*), as well as reports for provincial and territorial courts, unofficial series such as *Dominion Law Reports*, and a variety of specialized topical reporters. Westlaw and Lexis have Canada Supreme Court decisions back to 1876, as well as extensive coverage of other Canadian courts. HeinOnline includes *Canada Supreme Court Reports* back to 1876.

While much case research in other common law countries is done online, Britain and Canada also have many of the same types of print

---

[15] Practice Direction (Judgments: Form and Citation), [2001] 1 W.L.R. 194, *superseded in part by* Practice Direction: Citation of Authorities, [2012] 1 W.L.R. 780.

resources found in the United States including treatises, encyclopedias, and digests.

Like *Am. Jur. 2d* and *C.J.S.*, legal encyclopedias in other nations contain concise statements of ruling law and extensive footnote references to primary sources. *Halsbury's Laws of England* (5th ed. 2008–date, available on Lexis in the U.K. but not in the United States) is more definitive than the American legal encyclopedias, in part because it covers just one jurisdiction and can encompass statutes and administrative sources as well as case law. Access to the set is provided by a subject index and by tables of cases and statutes cited. Illustration 18-1 shows a page from *Halsbury's Laws*, on liability for injuries caused by animals. Its notes cite the Animals Act 1971 and cases as far back as 1831.

Two major Canadian legal encyclopedias are published. *Halsbury's Laws of Canada* (2006–date) is available on Lexis in Canada but not in the United States. *Canadian Encyclopedic Digest* (4th ed. 2009–date) is available on Westlaw, along with several dozen Canadian treatises.

Both England and Canada have major national digests, somewhat similar to the West digest system: *The Digest: Annotated British, Commonwealth and European Cases* (3d ed. 1971–date), and the *Canadian Abridgment* (3d ed. 2003–date). Each country also has tools for finding later cases that have considered an earlier decision, such as *Current Law Case Citator* in England and *Canadian Case Citations*.[16] On Westlaw, Canadian cases are accompanied by links to case history and citing references.

---

[16] In the U.K. and Canada, this process of determining the validity of cases or statutes is known as "noting up."

3. LIABILITY OF OWNERS AND KEEPERS OF ANIMALS

(1) INJURIES CAUSED BY ANIMALS

46. **Strict liability for damage.** Where any damage[1] is caused by an animal belonging to a dangerous species[2], any person who is its keeper[3] is strictly liable for the damage, subject to certain exceptions[4].

A dangerous species is one which is not commonly domesticated in the British Islands, and whose fully-grown animals normally have such characteristics that they are likely, unless restrained, to cause severe damage, or that any damage they may cause is likely to be severe[5].

A person is a keeper of an animal if he either owns it or has it in his possession, or if he is the head of a household of which a member under the age of 16 owns the animal or has it in his possession, and if at any time such ownership or possession ceases, then the person who immediately before that time qualified as being the animal's keeper continues as such until replaced by another person[6]. A person does not, however, become a keeper of an animal for this purpose merely by reason of his taking it and keeping it in his possession to prevent its causing damage or to restore it to its owner[7].

1 'Damage' includes the death of, or injury to, any person, including any disease and any impairment of physical or mental condition: Animals Act 1971 s 11.
2 'Species' includes sub-species and variety: Animals Act 1971 s 11.
3 More than one person may qualify as an animal's keeper; thus both the rider and the owner of a horse can be keepers of the horse, and one keeper of an animal is in law capable of suing another: *Flack v Hudson* [2001] QB 698, [2001] 2 WLR 982, [2000] All ER (D) 1701, CA. See also text and notes 5–7. A child could be sued for damage done by a dangerous animal kept by him (see *North v Wood* [1914] 1 KB 629), but it is doubtful whether this is still the case in the light of the Animals Act 1971 ss 1(1)(a), 6(3) (see text and notes 4–5). As to capacity of children generally see CHILDREN AND YOUNG PERSONS.
4 Animals Act 1971 s 2(1). This provision replaces the former common law rules based on the principle of *ferae naturae*: s 1(1)(a). For exceptions from liability see PARA 48.
5 Animals Act 1971 s 6(1), (2). Whether an animal is domesticated or not appears to be a question of law (*McQuaker v Goddard* [1940] 1 KB 687, [1940] 1 All ER 471, CA), but it is submitted that the Act now draws a distinction between 'domesticated' (see *McQuaker v Goddard* [1940] 1 KB 687, [1940] 1 All ER 471, CA) and 'domesticated in these islands'. Clearly an animal may be dangerous under the Act because of its sheer size or its unpredictability (as by becoming frightened and stampeding), regardless of any sort of viciousness in it: cf *Behrens v Bertram Mills Circus Ltd* [1957] 2 QB 1, [1957] 1 All ER 583. Bees appear to be domesticated: see *O'Gorman v O'Gorman* [1903] 2 IR 573 (negligence expressly found). 'British Islands' means the United Kingdom, the Channel Islands, the Isle of Man and the Republic of Ireland; the United Kingdom means Great Britain (ie England, Scotland and Wales) and Northern Ireland: see the Interpretation Act 1978 ss 5, 22, Sch 1.
6 Animals Act 1971 s 6(3). This follows the common law rule that responsibility for an animal's acts depended upon ownership or possession and control: see *M'Kone v Wood* (1831) 5 C & P 1; *Knott v LCC* [1934] 1 KB 126, CA. However, it is submitted that *Smith v Great Eastern Rly Co* (1866) LR 2 CP 4 (stray dog on premises but nothing done to encourage it or exercise control over it: no liability) would still be good law. See also *Flack v Hudson* [2001] QB 698, [2001] 2 WLR 982, [2000] All ER (D) 1701, CA; and note 3.
7 Animals Act 1971 s 6(4).

47. **Necessity for knowledge.** Where damage[1] is caused by an animal which does not belong to a dangerous species[2] its keeper[3] is strictly liable for the damage, subject to certain exceptions[4], if:

    (1)   the damage is of a kind which the animal, unless restrained, was likely to cause or which, if caused by the animal, was likely to be severe[5]; and

Illustration 18-1. A page from *Halsbury's Laws of England*.

Statutes. Legislation in other common law jurisdictions is published both in session laws and in compilations of laws in force, and is available from government and commercial websites. One major difference from the U.S. model is that other common law countries generally compile statutes chronologically or alphabetically by name, rather than by subject as in the *United States Code*. Statutes are not assigned code titles and sections, but instead are usually identified by their original name and date of enactment.

The standard historical collection of English statutes is the *Statutes of the Realm* (1810–28), covering 1235 to 1714. This set is part of HeinOnline's English Reports Library, and is also available from HathiTrust (www.hathitrust.org). Several other chronological collections were published during the 19th century under the titles *Statutes at Large* and *Statutes of the United Kingdom*, extending coverage to the beginning of the modern *Public General Acts* in 1866.[17] Online sources for these later sets include HathiTrust and LLMC Digital (llmc.com).

The first step in identifying and finding an older English statute is deciphering its citation. Acts before 1963 are generally cited not by calendar year but by regnal year (the year of a monarch's rule). The act that changed the citation system, for example, was passed during the session of Parliament that spanned the tenth and eleventh years of the reign of Elizabeth II, and is cited as Acts of Parliament Numbering and Citation Act, 10 & 11 Eliz. 2, ch. 34 (1962). Tables to convert regnal years to calendar years are printed in reference works such as *Black's Law Dictionary*, and several websites offer regnal year calculators to speed the process.

For modern statutes, the most frequently used printed source is the unofficial compilation *Halsbury's Statutes of England and Wales* (4th ed. 1985–date). This is somewhat like U.S. annotated codes, in that sections are followed by footnote annotations to judicial decisions. Current English statutes and regulations (known as *statutory instruments*) are also available from the government website legislation.gov.uk, as well as through services such as Westlaw. Illustration 18-2 shows an excerpt from the Animals Act 1971 in *Halsbury's Statutes*.

---

[17] Acts passed during the Commonwealth are not included in these collections but can be found in *Acts and Ordinances of the Interregnum, 1642–1660* (1911), available on British History Online (www.british-history.ac.uk), HathiTrust, and HeinOnline.

(b) subsections (1) and (2) of section 1 of the Dogs Act 1906 as amended by the Dogs (Amendment) Act 1928 (injury to cattle or poultry); and

(c) the rules of the common law imposing a liability for cattle trespass.

(2) Expressions used in those sections shall be interpreted in accordance with the provisions of section 6 (as well as those of section 11) of this Act.

NOTES

Additional information   See the Introductory Note(s) to this Act.

Dogs Act 1906   See this title. S 1(1), (2) of that Act are repealed by s 13(2) of this Act.

Definitions

"damage": s 11

2 Liability for damage done by dangerous animals   [154]

(1) Where any damage is caused by an animal which belongs to a dangerous species, any person who is a keeper of the animal is liable for the damage, except as otherwise provided by this Act.

(2) Where damage is caused by an animal which does not belong to a dangerous species, a keeper of the animal is liable for the damage, except as otherwise provided by this Act, if—

(a) the damage is of a kind which the animal, unless restrained, was likely to cause or which, if caused by the animal, was likely to be severe; and

(b) the likelihood of the damage or of its being severe was due to characteristics of the animal which are not normally found in animals of the same species or are not normally so found except at particular times or in particular circumstances; and

(c) those characteristics were known to that keeper or were at any time known to a person who at that time had charge of the animal as that keeper's servant or, where that keeper is the head of a household, were known to another keeper of the animal who is a member of that household and under the age of sixteen.

NOTES

Sub-s (1): Person   Unless the contrary intention appears this includes a body of persons corporate or unincorporate; see the Interpretation Act 1978, ss 5, 22(1), Sch 1, Sch 2, Pt I, para 4(5), Vol 41, title Statutes.

Sub-s (1): Liable for the damage, except as otherwise provided, etc   As to exceptions to liability under this section, see s 5(1)–(3).

Sub-s (2): Not normally so found except at particular times or in particular circumstances   Thus the mere fact that a particular animal shares its dangerous characteristics with other animals of its species at particular times or in particular circumstances does not preclude liability where the keeper knows of the presence of those characteristics in his animal. For example if the keeper of a bitch with a litter knows that it is prone to bite strangers, the keeper will be strictly liable under the section, even though proneness to bite is a common characteristic of bitches at such a time (see Law Com No 13, para 18).

Sub-s (2): Age   A person attains a particular age expressed in years at the commencement of the relevant anniversary of the date of his birth; see the Family Law Reform Act 1969, s 9, Vol 6, title Children and Family Law.

Additional information   See the Introductory Note(s) to this Act.

Words and phrases judicially considered

"any person who is a keeper"   There is nothing in this Act limiting the persons who can sue a keeper to third parties and strangers. One keeper can sue another keeper under this section; see Flack v Hudson [2001] QB 698, [2000] All ER (D) 1701, CA.

Illustration 18-2. A page from *Halsbury's Statutes of England and Wales*.

For Canadian statutes there is no annotated, regularly updated publication similar to *Halsbury's Statutes*. Federal statutes and regulations are available from the Department of Justice (laws-lois. justice.gc.ca), and CanLII has links as well to provincial sources. Westlaw also has federal and provincial statutes, accompanied by citing references, and HeinOnline offers a Provincial Statutes of Canada database with current and historical coverage. Illustration 18-3 shows a Canadian federal statute from the Department of Justice website, published in side-by-side English and French.

Illustration 18-3. The beginning of a Canadian federal statute.

Further information on the British and Canadian legal systems and sources is available from their parliaments' websites—(www. parliament.uk) and (www.parl.ca)—and their governments generally—(www.gov.uk) and (www.canada.ca)—as well as from online and print research guides.

(d) Civil Law Jurisdictions

In theory, a code in the civil law tradition is designed to cover all legal situations that might occur. Instead of searching for precedents in factually similar judicial decisions, a civil law researcher looks to the abstract provisions of the code for a logical and appropriate legal principle.[18]

Extensive article-by-article commentaries on the major codes are among the most important legal sources in civil law countries. The most scholarly and reputable of these commentaries have considerable persuasive authority, often greater weight than judicial decisions. Foreign legal encyclopedias, particularly the French *répertoires* published by Dalloz, are often of higher quality and reputation than those in the United States, and contain articles by leading legal scholars. Civil law countries also have a multitude of periodicals covering legal developments and often printing primary sources.

After introductory study in an encyclopedia, treatise, or journal article, your next step is to consult the relevant code (preferably in an edition accompanied by commentary) or other statutes applicable to the problem. Most countries in the civil law system have several separately published codes, often available in unannotated form on government websites. These include the basic general codes (civil, criminal, commercial, civil procedure and criminal procedure), and minor codes compiling statutes on specific subjects such as taxation, labor law, and family law.

After studying the code and commentary, you should then find administrative orders and judicial decisions implementing or interpreting the legislative norms. Legislation, regulations, decrees, and other laws are most often found in official gazettes, comparable to but usually broader in scope than the *Federal Register*.[19] Gazettes

---

[18] "When a true code enthusiast confronts a problem, he reaches first for the code, and later for doctrine and cases. His resort to the code must seem as natural as searching precedents would be for an English barrister. The center of a civilian's private law universe, the civil code must stand out in his intellectual armory." Shael Herman, *The Fate and the Future of Codification in America*, 40 AM. J. LEGAL HIST. 407, 413 (1996) (footnote omitted).

[19] Common law jurisdictions also issue official gazettes, covering the same kinds of material, such as the Australian *Government Notices Gazette*, but the term is generally used in the context of civil law countries.

can contain material not available elsewhere relating to the history of a nation's laws and regulations, as well as some judicial decisions. Foreign Law Guide lists these sources, with links where available.[20]

Court decisions in civil law countries are published, but they are generally of secondary importance. Most jurisdictions have fewer court reports and less developed means for finding cases by subject. In many countries, legal periodicals publish court decisions in addition to articles and other legal news. In France, for example, the leading legal periodicals, *Recueil Dalloz* (1808–date) and *La Semaine Juridique* (1927–date), have legislative texts and judicial decisions as well as scholarly articles.

A last resort in trying to find the law of a jurisdiction may be to contact its embassy. The amount of assistance available from embassies can vary widely, but some provide copies of legal materials or explain where they can be found. *Diplomatic List*, with contact information and key personnel for embassies, is available from the Department of State's Office of the Chief of Protocol (www.state.gov/resources-for-foreign-embassies/diplomatic-list/).

---

[20] GUIDE TO OFFICIAL PUBLICATIONS OF FOREIGN COUNTRIES (2d ed. 1997), an annotated listing of gazettes, statistical yearbooks, court reports, and other publications for more than 170 countries, may be useful for historical research.

Appendix

SELECTED TREATISES AND SERVICES BY SUBJECT

This is a general survey of treatises and topical services in major legal subject areas. Many additional treatises on more specialized topics and areas are published than can be covered here. Every treatise and service listed here is available online, and most are also published in print. Multi-volume and single-volume treatises are listed separately, to provide some sense of each work's scope whether used online or in print. For print users, Library of Congress call numbers for each subject provide leads for browsing for study aids or other works in a library's reserve collection or stacks.

Access to treatises and services via online platforms is noted but may depend on your institution's subscription agreement. Some materials are not available to academic subscribers, and others may require separate subscriptions. Online sources noted are Bloomberg Law (www.bloomberglaw.com), Lexis (advance.lexis.com), Law Journal Press (LJP) (lawjournalpress.com), National Consumer Law Center (NCLC) (library.nclc.org), Practising Law Institute's PLI Plus (plus.pli.edu), Special Ed Connection (www.specialedconnection. com), Thomson Reuters Checkpoint (checkpoint.thomsonreuters. com), West Academic Study Aids (subscription.westacademic.com), Westlaw (www.westlaw.com), Wolters Kluwer Study Aids Subscription (ebooks.aspenlaw.com), and Wolters Kluwer's Cheetah (www.wkcheetah.com).

ADMINISTRATIVE LAW (KF5401–KF5425)

Multi-Volume Treatises

Steven W. Feldman et al., *West's Federal Administrative Practice* (4th ed. 2002–date, Westlaw)

Kristin E. Hickman & Richard J. Pierce, Jr., *Administrative Law Treatise* (6th ed. 2019–date, Cheetah)

Charles H. Koch, Jr., *Administrative Law and Practice* (3d ed. 2010–date, Westlaw)

Jacob A. Stein et al., *Administrative Law* (1977–date, Lexis)

Hornbooks

Alfred C. Aman & William T. Mayton, *Administrative Law* (3d ed. 2014, West Academic)

Keith Werhan, *Principles of Administrative Law* (3d ed. 2019, West Academic)

ADMIRALTY AND MARITIME LAW (KF1096–KF1137)

Multi-Volume Treatises

Benedict on Admiralty (Joshua S. Force ed., 7th ed. 1958–date, Lexis)

Robert Force & Martin J. Norris, *The Law of Maritime Personal Injuries* (5th ed. 2004–date, Westlaw)

Robert Force & Martin J. Norris, *The Law of Seamen* (5th ed. 2003–date, Westlaw)

Thomas J. Schoenbaum, *Admiralty and Maritime Law* (6th ed. 2018–date, Westlaw)

Hornbook

Thomas J. Schoenbaum, *Admiralty and Maritime Law* (6th ed. 2019–date, West Academic)

ADVERTISING (KF1614–KF1617)

Multi-Volume Treatise

James B. Astrachan et al., *The Law of Advertising* (1973–date, Lexis)

One-Volume Treatises

David H. Bernstein & Bruce P. Keller, *The Law of Advertising, Marketing and Promotions* (2011–date, Lexis and LJP)

Steven G. Brody & Bruce E.H. Johnson, *Advertising and Commercial Speech: A First Amendment Guide* (2d ed. 2004–date, PLI Plus)

Service

Advertising Law Guide (Cheetah)

ANTITRUST & TRADE REGULATION (KF1601–KF1668)

Multi-Volume Treatises

Louis Altman & Malla Pollack, *Callmann on Unfair Competition, Trademarks and Monopolies* (4th ed. 1981–date, Westlaw)

Philip Areeda & Herbert Hovenkamp, *Antitrust Law: An Analysis of Antitrust Principles and Their Application* (4th ed. 2013–date, Cheetah)

Herbert Hovenkamp et al., *IP and Antitrust: An Analysis of Antitrust Principles Applied to Intellectual Property Law* (3d ed. 2017–date, Cheetah)

Earl W. Kintner et al., *Federal Antitrust Law* (1st–3d eds., 1980–date, Lexis)

Dee Pridgen et al., *Consumer Protection and the Law* (annual, Westlaw)

Julian O. Von Kalinowski et al., *Antitrust Laws and Trade Regulation* (2d ed. 1996–date, Lexis)

One-Volume Treatises and Hornbooks

Phillip E. Areeda & Herbert Hovenkamp, *Fundamentals of Antitrust Law* (4th ed. 2011–date, Cheetah)

Carolyn L. Carter & Jonathan Sheldon, *Unfair and Deceptive Acts and Practices* (9th ed. 2016–date, NCLC)

William C. Holmes & Melissa Mangiaracina, *Antitrust Law Handbook* (annual, Westlaw)

Herbert Hovenkamp, *Federal Antitrust Policy: The Law of Competition and Its Practice* (5th ed. 2016, West Academic)

Lawrence A. Sullivan et al., *The Law of Antitrust: An Integrated Handbook* (3d ed. 2016, West Academic)

Thomas V. Vakerics, *Antitrust Basics* (1985–date, Lexis and LJP)

Peter C. Ward, *Federal Trade Commission: Law, Practice and Procedure* (1986–date, Lexis and LJP)

Service

Trade Regulation Reporter (Cheetah)

ART, ENTERTAINMENT, AND SPORTS LAW (KF3989, KF4288–KF4305)

Multi-Volume Treatises

Alexandra Darraby, *Art, Artifact, Architecture and Museum Law* (2017 ed., Westlaw)

Leonard D. DuBoff et al., *Art Law Deskbook* (3d ed. 2017–date, Lexis)

James T. Gray, *Sports Law Practice* (3d ed. 2009–date, Lexis)

Ralph E. Lerner & Judith Bresler, *Art Law* (4th ed. 2012, PLI Plus)

Alexander Lindey & Michael Landau, *Lindey on Entertainment, Publishing and the Arts* (3d ed. 2004–date, Westlaw)

Thomas D. Selz et al., *Entertainment Law: Legal Concepts and Business Practices* (3d ed. 2006–date, Westlaw)

One-Volume Treatise

Walter T. Champion, Jr., *Fundamentals of Sports Law* (2d ed. 2004, Westlaw)

BANKING AND CONSUMER FINANCE (KF966–KF1040)

Multi-Volume Treatises

Barkley Clark & Barbara Clark, *The Law of Bank Deposits, Collections, and Credit Cards* (3d ed. 2014–date, Lexis)

Erik Gerding, *Negotiable Instruments Under the Uniform Commercial Code* (1972–date, Lexis)

Richard B. Hagedorn, *Brady on Bank Checks and Funds Transfers* (8th ed. 1997–date, Lexis)

Robert J. Hobbs et al., *Fair Debt Collection* (9th ed. 2018–date, NCLC)

Michael P. Malloy, *Banking Law and Regulation* (2d ed. 2011–date, Cheetah)

Burton V. McCullough, *Letters of Credit* (1987–date, Lexis)

Burton V. McCullough et al., *Banking Law* (1981–date, Lexis)

Dee Pridgen & Richard M. Alderman, *Consumer Credit and the Law* (annual, Westlaw)

Elizabeth Renuart et al., *Truth in Lending* (9th ed. 2019–date, NCLC)

Milton R. Schroeder, *The Law and Regulation of Financial Institutions* (2d ed. 2014–date, Lexis)

Chi Chi Wu et al., *Fair Credit Reporting* (9th ed. 2017–date, NCLC)

One-Volume Treatises and Hornbooks

Sarah Johnson Auchterlonie & Alexandra P. Everhart Sickler, *Consumer Finance Law and Compliance* (2017–date, Bloomberg Law)

Carolyn L. Carter et al., *Consumer Credit Regulation* (2d ed. 2015–date, NCLC)

Keith R. Fisher, *Banking Law Manual* (2d ed. 2000–date, Lexis)

Benjamin Geva, *The Law of Electronic Funds Transfers* (1992–date, Lexis)

Deanne Loonin et al., *Student Loan Law* (6th ed. 2019–date, NCLC)

Michael P. Malloy, *Principles of Bank Regulation* (3d ed. 2011, West Academic)

Fred H. Miller & Alvin C. Harrell, *The Law of Modern Payment Systems* (2d ed. 2017, West Academic)

Andrew G. Pizor et al., *Mortgage Lending: Loan Origination, Preemption and Litigation* (3d ed. 2019–date, NCLC)

John Rao et al., *Mortgage Servicing and Loan Modifications* (2019–date, NCLC)

Lauren K. Saunders et al., *Consumer Banking and Payments Law* (6th ed. 2018–date, NCLC)

Brooke Wunnicke et al., *Standby and Commercial Letters of Credit* (3d ed. 2000–date, Cheetah)

Services

Consumer Credit Guide (Cheetah)

Consumer Financial Protection Bureau Reporter (Cheetah)

Federal Banking Law Reporter (Cheetah)

State Banking Law Reporter (Cheetah)

BANKRUPTCY (KF1501–KF1548)

Multi-Volume Treatises

Bloomberg Law: Bankruptcy Treatise (Samir D. Parikh ed., 2014–date, Bloomberg Law)

Collier on Bankruptcy (Henry J. Sommer & Richard Levin eds., 16th ed. 2009–date, Lexis)

Joan N. Feeney et al., *Bankruptcy Law Manual* (semiannual, Westlaw)

Robert E. Ginsberg et al., *Ginsberg & Martin on Bankruptcy* (5th ed. 2008–date, Cheetah and Westlaw)

Norton Bankruptcy Law & Practice (William L. Norton, III ed., 3d ed. 2008–date, Westlaw)

Thomas J. Salerno & Jordan A. Kroop, *Bankruptcy Litigation and Practice* (4th ed. 2007–date, Cheetah)

Henry J. Sommer et al., *Consumer Bankruptcy Law and Practice* (12th ed. 2020–date, NCLC)

Howard J. Steinberg, *Bankruptcy Litigation* (2d ed. 2007–date, Westlaw)

Hornbooks

David G. Epstein & Steve H. Nickles, *Principles of Bankruptcy Law* (2d ed. 2017, West Academic)

Charles Jordan Tabb, *The Law of Bankruptcy* (4th ed. 2016)

Services

Bankruptcy Law Reporter (Cheetah)

Bankruptcy Service, Lawyers' Edition (Westlaw)

CHILDREN AND THE LAW (KF479, KF9771–9827)

Multi-Volume Treatises

Michael J. Dale, *Representing the Child Client* (1987–date, Lexis)

Thomas A. Jacobs & Natalie C. Jacobs, *Children and the Law: Rights & Obligations* (annual, Westlaw)

Thomas Rob Young, *Legal Rights of Children* (3d ed. 2015–date, Westlaw)

One-Volume Treatise

Samuel M. Davis, *Rights of Juveniles: The Juvenile Justice System* (annual, Westlaw)

CIVIL PROCEDURE (KF8820–KF9050)

Multi-Volume Treatises

Robert C. Casad et al., *Jurisdiction in Civil Actions* (1983–date, Lexis)

Adam I. Cohen & David J. Lender, *Electronic Discovery: Law & Practice* (3d ed. 2019–date, Cheetah)

Joseph M. McLaughlin, *McLaughlin on Class Actions* (annual, Westlaw)

Ved P. Nanda & Bryan Neihart, *Litigation of International Disputes in U.S. Courts* (2d ed. 2005–date, Westlaw)

William Rubenstein et al., *Newberg on Class Actions* (5th ed. 2011–date, Westlaw)

One-Volume Treatises and Hornbooks

David M. Axelrad, *Appellate Practice in Federal and State Courts* (2011–date, Lexis and LJP)

Kevin W. Clermont, *Principles of Civil Procedure* (5th ed. 2018, West Academic)

Richard D. Freer, *Civil Procedure* (4th ed. 2017, WK Study Aids)

Jack H. Friedenthal et al., *Civil Procedure* (5th ed. 2015, West Academic)

Roger S. Haydock & David E. Herr, *Discovery Practice* (8th ed. 2015–date, Cheetah)

Stuart T. Rossman et al., *Consumer Class Actions* (10th ed. 2020–date, NCLC)

CIVIL RIGHTS (KF1307, KF1325, KF4741–KF4786)

Multi-Volume Treatises

Ivan E. Bodensteiner & Rosalie Berger Levinson, *State and Local Government Civil Rights Liability* (1987–date, Westlaw)

Joseph G. Cook & John L. Sobieski, *Civil Rights Actions* (1983–date, Lexis)

Michael B. Mushlin, *Rights of Prisoners* (5th ed. 2017–date, Westlaw)

Sheldon H. Nahmod, *Civil Rights and Civil Liberties Litigation: The Law of Section 1983* (4th ed. 1997–date, Westlaw Next)

Martin A. Schwartz et al., *Section 1983 Litigation* (2d–5th eds. 2003–date, Cheetah and Westlaw)

Sexual Orientation & the Law (Karen Moulding ed., annual, Westlaw)

Isidore Silver, *Police Civil Liability* (1986–date, Lexis)

Rodney A. Smolla, *Federal Civil Rights Acts* (semiannual, Westlaw)

One-Volume Treatises

Michael Avery et al., *Police Misconduct: Law & Litigation* (annual, Westlaw)

Jeremiah Battle, Jr. et al., *Credit Discrimination* (7th ed. 2018–date, NCLC)

John W. Palmer, *Constitutional Rights of Prisoners* (9th ed. 2010–date, Lexis)

Robert G. Schwemm, *Housing Discrimination: Law & Litigation* (1990–date, Westlaw)

COMMERCIAL LAW (KF871–KF890)

Multi-Volume Treatises

Roy Ryden Anderson, *Damages Under the Uniform Commercial Code* (annual, Westlaw)

Barkley Clark & Barbara Clark, *The Law of Secured Transactions Under the Uniform Commercial Code* (3d ed. 2011–date, Lexis)

Debtor-Creditor Law (James M. Lawniczak ed., 1982–date, Lexis)

Equipment Leasing (Barry A. Dubin ed., 1998–date, Lexis)

Ralph H. Folsom, *International Business Transactions* (annual, Westlaw)

Henry Deeb Gabriel & William H. Henning, *Sales & Bulk Transfers Under the Uniform Commercial Code* (1966–date, Lexis)

Hawkland's Uniform Commercial Code Series (Carl S. Bjerre ed., 1982–date, Westlaw)

Lary Lawrence et al., *Lawrence's Anderson on the Uniform Commercial Code* (3d ed. 1981–date, Westlaw)

James P. Nehf & Julian B. McDonnell, *Secured Transactions Under the Uniform Commercial Code* (1963–date, Lexis)

Jeremiah J. Spires et al., *Doing Business in the United States* (1978–date, Lexis)

James J. White et al., *White & Summers' Uniform Commercial Code* (6th ed. 2010–date, Westlaw)

One-Volume Treatises and Hornbooks

Richard F. Duncan et al., *The Law and Practice of Secured Transactions* (1987–date, Lexis and LJP)

Ralph H. Folsom, *Principles of International Trade Law* (2d ed. 2018, West Academic)

Ralph H. Folsom et al., *Principles of International Business Transactions* (4th ed. 2017, West Academic)

Gary M. Lawrence, *Due Diligence in Business Transactions* (1994–date, Lexis and LJP)

Jed S. Rakoff & Howard W. Goldstein, *RICO: Civil and Criminal Law and Strategy* (1989–date, Lexis and LJP)

David B. Smith & Terrance G. Reed, *Civil RICO* (1987–date, Lexis)

James J. White & Robert S. Summers, *Uniform Commercial Code* (6th ed. 2010, West Academic)

James J. White et al., *Principles of Payment Systems* (2d ed. 2019, West Academic)

James J. White et al., *Principles of Sales Law* (2d ed. 2017, West Academic)

James J. White et al., *Principles of Secured Transactions* (2d ed. 2018, West Academic)

Services

RICO Business Disputes Guide (Cheetah)

Secured Transactions Guide (Cheetah)

COMMUNICATIONS LAW (KF2761–KF2849)

Multi-Volume Treatises

Peter W. Huber et al., *Federal Telecommunications Law* (2d ed. 1999–date, Cheetah)

Womble Bond Dickinson LLP, *Telecommunications Regulation: Cable, Broadcasting, Satellite, and the Internet* (1983–date, Lexis)

One-Volume Treatise

Stuart N. Brotman, *Communications Law and Practice* (1995–date, Lexis and LJP)

CONFLICT OF LAWS (KF410–KF418)

Hornbooks

Peter Hay et al., *Conflict of Laws* (6th ed. 2018, West Academic)

Clyde Spillenger, *Principles of Conflict of Laws* (2d ed. 2015, West Academic)

CONSTITUTIONAL LAW (KF4501–KF4558)

Multi-Volume Treatises

William J. Rich, *Modern Constitutional Law* (3d ed. 2011–date, Westlaw)

Ronald D. Rotunda et al., *Treatise on Constitutional Law: Substance and Procedure* (5th ed. 2012–date, Westlaw)

Rodney A. Smolla, *Smolla & Nimmer on Freedom of Speech* (3d ed. 1996–date, Westlaw)

Hornbooks

Erwin Chemerinsky, *Constitutional Law: Principles and Policies* (6th ed. 2019, WK Study Aids)

John E. Nowak & Ronald D. Rotunda, *Constitutional Law* (8th ed. 2010, West Academic)

John E. Nowak & Ronald D. Rotunda, *Principles of Constitutional Law* (5th ed. 2016, West Academic)

CONSTRUCTION LAW (KF901–KF902)

Multi-Volume Treatises

Philip L. Bruner & Patrick J. O'Connor, Jr., *Bruner & O'Connor on Construction Law* (2002–date, Westlaw)

Construction Law (Steven G. M. Stein ed. 1986–date, Lexis)

Construction Law Handbook (Stanley A. Martin & Leah A. Rochwarg eds., 3d ed. 2018–date, Cheetah)

CONTRACTS (KF801–KF839)

Multi-Volume Treatises

E. Allan Farnsworth & Zachary Wolfe, *Farnsworth on Contracts* (4th ed. 2019–date, Cheetah)

Richard A. Lord, *Williston on Contracts* (4th ed. 1990–date, Westlaw)

Timothy Murray et al., *Corbin on Contracts* (rev. ed. 1993–date, Lexis)

One-Volume Treatises and Hornbooks

Robert A. Hillman, *Principles of Contract Law* (4th ed. 2019, West Academic)

Howard O. Hunter, *Modern Law of Contracts* (annual, Westlaw)

John Edward Murray, Jr., *Murray on Contracts* (5th ed. 2011, Lexis)

Joseph M. Perillo, *Contracts* (7th ed. 2014, West Academic)

CORPORATIONS (KF1384–KF1480, KFD213)

Multi-Volume Treatises

R. Franklin Balotti & Jesse A. Finkelstein, *The Delaware Law of Corporations and Business Organizations* (3d ed. 1998–date, Cheetah and Westlaw)

Philip J. Blumberg et al., *Blumberg on Corporate Groups* (2d ed. 2005–date, Cheetah)

Robert E. Buckholz et al., *The Public Company Deskbook: Complying with Federal Governance & Disclosure Requirements* (3d ed. 2014–date, PLI Plus)

Zolman Cavitch et al., *Business Organizations with Tax Planning* (1963–date, Lexis)

Corporate Governance: Law and Practice (Amy L. Goodman & Steven M. Haas eds., 2004–date, Lexis)

James D. Cox & Thomas Lee Hazen, *Treatise on the Law of Corporations* (3d ed. 2010–date, Westlaw)

Clifford R. Ennico, *Advising Small Businesses* (1989–date, Westlaw)

William Meade Fletcher et al., *Fletcher Cyclopedia of the Law of Private Corporations* (1931–date, Westlaw)

Byron E. Fox & Eleanor M. Fox, *Corporate Acquisitions and Mergers* (1968–date, Lexis)

W. Michael Garner, *Franchising and Distribution Law and Practice* (annual, Westlaw)

Martin D. Ginsburg et al., *Mergers, Acquisitions, and Buyouts* (semiannual, Cheetah)

Gladys Glickman et al., *Franchising* (1969–date, Lexis)

Robert J. Haft et al., *Venture Capital & Small Business Financings* (1984–date, Westlaw)

Robert Joe Hull et al., *Representing Start-Up Companies* (1992–date, Westlaw)

William E. Knepper et al., *Liability of Corporate Officers and Directors* (8th ed. 2010–date, Lexis)

Martin Lipton & Erica H. Steinberger, *Takeovers and Freezeouts* (1978–date, Lexis and LJP)

Simon M. Lorne & Joy Marlene Bryan, *Acquisitions & Mergers: Negotiated & Contested Transactions* (1985–date, Westlaw)

Jonathan R. Macey, *Macey on Corporation Laws* (1998–date, Cheetah)

Brent A. Olson, *Publicly Traded Corporations Handbook* (semiannual, Westlaw)

F. Hodge O'Neal & Robert B. Thompson, *O'Neal and Thompson's Close Corporations and LLCs: Law and Practice* (rev. 3d ed. 1997–date, Westlaw)

Samuel C. Thompson, Jr., *Mergers, Acquisitions, and Tender Offers: Law and Strategies* (2010–date, PLI Plus)

Edward P. Welch et al., *Folk on the Delaware General Corporation Law* (6th ed. 2014–date, Cheetah)

One-Volume Treatises and Hornbooks

James D. Cox & Thomas Lee Hazen, *Business Organizations Law* (5th ed. 2020, West Academic)

James A. Fanto, *Directors' and Officers' Liability* (2d ed. 2005–date, PLI Plus)

Richard D. Freer & Douglas K. Moll, *Principles of Business Organizations* (2d ed. 2018, West Academic)

Franklin A. Gevurtz, *Corporation Law* (2d ed. 2010)

Franklin A. Gevurtz & Christina M. Sautter, *Mergers and Acquisitions Law* (2019, West Academic)

Jonathan M. Hoff et al., *Public Companies* (2002–date, Lexis and LJP)

International Corporate Practice: A Practitioner's Guide to Global Success (Carole Basri ed., 2007–date, PLI Plus)

Douglas K. Moll & Robert A. Ragazzo, *Closely Held Corporations* (annual, Lexis)

Aaron Rachelson, *Corporate Acquisitions, Mergers, and Divestitures* (1983–date, Westlaw)

J. Mark Ramseyer, *Business Organizations* (2d ed. 2017, WK Study Aids)

Services

Business Franchise Guide (Cheetah)

Corporate Governance Guide (Cheetah)

Corporation Service (Cheetah)

CRIMINAL LAW AND PROCEDURE (KF9201–KF9479, KF9601–KF9763)

Multi-Volume Treatises

Joel M. Androphy, *White Collar Crime* (2d ed. 2001–date, Westlaw)

Stanley S. Arkin et al., *Business Crime: Criminal Liability of the Business Community* (1981–date, Lexis)

Sara Sun Beale et al., *Grand Jury Law & Practice* (2d ed. 1997–date, Westlaw)

Susan W. Brenner & Lori E. Shaw, *Federal Grand Jury: A Guide to Law and Practice* (2d ed. 2006–date, Westlaw)

James G. Carr & Patricia L. Bellia, *The Law of Electronic Surveillance* (semiannual, Westlaw)

Robert M. Cipes et al., *Criminal Defense Techniques* (1969–date, Lexis)

Neil P. Cohen, *The Law of Probation and Parole* (2d ed. 1999–date, Westlaw)

Joseph G. Cook, *Constitutional Rights of the Accused* (3d ed. 1996–date, Westlaw)

Cybercrime and Security (Pauline C. Reich ed., 1998–date, Westlaw)

Richard E. Erwin et al., *Defense of Drunk Driving Cases: Criminal-Civil* (3d ed. 1978–date, Lexis)

Clifford S. Fishman & Anne T. McKenna, *Wiretapping and Eavesdropping: Surveillance in the Internet Age* (3d ed. 2007–date, Westlaw)

Lissa Griffin et al., *Federal Criminal Appeals* (annual, Westlaw)

John Wesley Hall, Jr., *Search and Seizure* (5th ed. 2013–date, Lexis)

Randy Hertz & James S. Liebman, *Federal Habeas Corpus Practice and Procedure* (7th ed. 2015–date, Lexis)

Mark J. Kadish et al., *Criminal Law Advocacy* (1982–date, Lexis)

Wayne R. LaFave, *Search and Seizure: A Treatise on the Fourth Amendment* (5th ed. 2012–date, Westlaw)

Wayne R. LaFave, *Substantive Criminal Law* (2d ed. 2003–date, Westlaw)

Wayne R. LaFave et al., *Criminal Procedure* (4th ed. 2015–date, Westlaw)

Brian R. Means, *Postconviction Remedies* (annual, Westlaw)

Otto G. Obermaier et al., *White Collar Crime: Business and Regulatory Offenses* (1990–date, Lexis and LJP)

Mark S. Rhodes et al., *Orfield's Criminal Procedure Under the Federal Rules* (2d ed. 1985–date, Westlaw)

William E. Ringel et al., *Searches and Seizures, Arrests and Confessions* (2d ed. 1979–date, Westlaw)

Paul H. Robinson, *Criminal Law Defenses* (1984–date, Westlaw)

David S. Rudstein et al., *Criminal Constitutional Law* (1990–date, Lexis)

Charles E. Torcia, *Wharton's Criminal Law* (15th ed. 1993–date, Westlaw)

One-Volume Treatises and Hornbooks

Arthur W. Campbell, *Law of Sentencing* (3d ed. 2004–date, Westlaw)

William K. Carroll & Michael P. Seng, *Eyewitness Testimony: Strategies and Tactics* (2d ed. 2003–date, Westlaw)

Howard W. Goldstein & Steven M. Witzel, *Grand Jury Practice* (1998–date, Lexis and LJP)

Richard S. Gruner, *Corporate Criminal Liability and Prevention* (2004–date, Lexis)

Thomas W. Hutchison et al., *Federal Sentencing Law & Practice* (annual, Westlaw)

Wayne R. LaFave, *Criminal Law* (6th ed. 2017, West Academic)

Wayne R. LaFave, *Principles of Criminal Law* (3d ed. 2017, West Academic)

Wayne R. LaFave et al., *Criminal Procedure* (6th ed. 2017–date, West Academic)

B. Anthony Morosco, *Prosecution and Defense of Sex Crimes* (1976–date, Lexis)

Ellen S. Podgor et al., *White Collar Crime* (2d ed. 2018, West Academic)

Paul H. Robinson & Michael T. Cahill, *Criminal Law* (2d ed. 2012, WK Study Aids)

Russell L. Weaver et al., *Principles of Criminal Procedure* (6th ed. 2018, West Academic)

Charles H. Whitebread & Christopher Slobogin, *Criminal Procedure: An Analysis of Cases and Concepts* (7th ed. 2020, West Academic)

Zachary J. Wolfe, *Hate Crimes Law* (annual, Westlaw)

DISABILITIES (KF480, KF3469)

Multi-Volume Treatises

Jonathan R. Mook, *Americans with Disabilities Act: Employee Rights & Employer Obligations* (1992–date, Lexis)

Jonathan R. Mook, *Americans with Disabilities Act: Public Accommodations & Commercial Facilities* (1996–date, Lexis)

Michael L. Perlin & Heather Ellis Cucolo, *Mental Disability Law: Civil and Criminal* (3d ed. 2016–date, Lexis)

Henry H. Perritt, Jr., *Americans with Disabilities Act Handbook* (6th ed. 2020–date, Cheetah)

Gary E. Phelan et al., *Disability Discrimination in the Workplace* (1992–date, Westlaw)

One-Volume Treatises

John J. Coleman. III, *Disability Discrimination in Employment* (1991–date, Westlaw)

Laura F. Rothstein & Julia Irzyk, *Disabilities & the Law* (semiannual, Westlaw)

Service

Accommodating Disabilities: Business Management Guide (Cheetah)

DISPUTE RESOLUTION (KF3416–3425, KF9084–9086)

Multi-Volume Treatises

Sarah R. Cole et al., *Mediation: Law, Policy & Practice* (annual, Westlaw)

Martin Domke et al., *Domke on Commercial Arbitration* (3d ed. 2003–date, Westlaw)

Jay E. Grenig, *Alternative Dispute Resolution* (4th ed. 2016–date, Westlaw)

One-Volume Treatise and Hornbook

Elkouri & Elkouri: How Arbitration Works (Kenneth May ed., 8th ed. 2016–date, Bloomberg Law)

Stephen J. Ware, *Principles of Alternative Dispute Resolution* (3d ed. 2016, West Academic)

EDUCATION LAW (KF4101–KF4257)

Multi-Volume Treatises

James A. Rapp, *Education Law* (1984–date, Lexis)

Ronna Greff Schneider, *Education Law: First Amendment, Due Process & Discrimination Litigation* (2004–date, Westlaw)

One-Volume Treatise

Charles J. Russo & Ralph D. Mawdsley, *Education Law* (2002–date, Lexis and LJP)

Service

Individuals with Disabilities Education Law Report (Special Ed Connection)

ELDER LAW (KF390 .A4)

Multi-Volume Treatises

Thomas D. Begley, Jr. & Jo-Anne H. Jeffreys, *Representing the Elderly Client: Law and Practice* (1992–date, Cheetah)

A. Kimberly Dayton et al., *Advising the Elderly Client* (1992–date, Westlaw)

Joan M. Krauskopf et al., *ElderLaw: Advocacy for the Aging* (2d ed. 1992–date, Westlaw)

One-Volume Treatises

Lawrence A. Frolik & Melissa C. Brown, *Advising the Elderly or Disabled Client* (2d ed. 2000–date, Checkpoint and Westlaw)

John J. Regan et al., *Tax, Estate and Financial Planning for the Elderly* (1985–date, Lexis)

EMPLOYMENT AND LABOR LAW (KF3301–KF3580)

Multi-Volume Treatises

David L. Bacon et al., *Employee Benefits Guide* (1991–date, Lexis)

The Developing Labor Law: The Board, the Courts, and the National Labor Relations Act (John E. Higgins, Jr. ed., 7th ed. 2017–date, Bloomberg Law)

Employment Law (Mark A. Rothstein ed., 5th ed. 2014–date, Westlaw)

The Fair Labor Standards Act (Ellen C. Kearns et al. eds., 3d ed. 2015–date, Bloomberg Law)

Guide to Employment Law and Regulation (2d ed. 1998–date, Westlaw)

Bradford T. Hammock & Raymond Perez, II, *Occupational Safety and Health Act* (1977–date, Lexis)

Labor and Employment Arbitration (Tim Bornstein et al. eds., 2d ed. 1997–date, Lexis)

N. Peter Lareau, *National Labor Relations Act: Law and Practice* (2d ed. 1999–date, Lexis)

N. Peter Lareau et al., *Labor and Employment Law* (2003–date, Lexis)

Lex K. Larson & Thomas A. Robinson, *Larson's Workers' Compensation Law* (1952–date, Lexis)

Jeffrey D. Mamorsky, *Employee Benefits Law: ERISA and Beyond* (1980–date, Lexis and LJP)

National Employment Lawyers Association, *Employee Rights Litigation: Pleading and Practice* (1991–date, Lexis)

Les A. Schneider & J. Larry Stine, *Wage and Hour Law: Compliance and Practice* (1995–date, Westlaw)

One-Volume Treatises and Hornbooks

Lisa J. Banks & Jason C. Schwartz, *Whistleblower Law: A Practitioner's Guide* (2016–date, Lexis and LJP)

Mark W. Bennett et al., *Employment Relationships: Law and Practice* (1998–date, Cheetah)

Employee Benefits Law (Ivelisse Berio Lebeau ed., 4th ed. 2018–date, Bloomberg Law)

The Family and Medical Leave Act (William Bush & James M. Paul eds., 2d ed. 2017–date, Bloomberg Law)

Ann C. Hodges & Rafael Gely, *Principles of Employment Law* (2d ed. 2018, West Academic)

Labor Union Law and Regulation (William W. Osborne, Jr. ed., 2017–date, Bloomberg Law)

Laurie E. Leader, *Wages and Hours: Law and Practice* (1990–date, Lexis)

Occupational Safety and Health Law (Gregory N. Dale & Katherine A. Tracy eds., 4th ed. 2018, Bloomberg Law)

Henry H. Perritt, Jr., *Civil Rights in the Workplace* (4th ed. 2018–date, Cheetah)

Henry H. Perritt, Jr., *Employee Dismissal: Law & Practice* (7th ed. 2020–date, Cheetah)

Mark A. Rothstein, *Occupational Safety & Health Law* (annual, Westlaw)

Mark A. Rothstein et al., *Employment Law* (6th ed. 2019, West Academic)

Services

Employment Coordinator (Westlaw)

Employment Practices Guide (Cheetah)

Employment Safety and Health Guide (Cheetah)

Labor Relations (Cheetah)

Pension Plan Guide (Cheetah)

EMPLOYMENT DISCRIMINATION (KF3464)

Multi-Volume Treatises

Alba Conte, *Sexual Harassment in the Workplace: Law and Practice* (5th ed. 2020–date, Cheetah)

Howard C. Eglit, *Age Discrimination* (2d ed. 1994–date)

Lex K. Larson, *Employment Discrimination* (2d ed. 1994–date, Lexis)

Barbara Lindemann et al., *Employment Discrimination Law* (6th ed. 2020–date, Bloomberg Law)

Roger W. Mastair, *Employment Discrimination: Law & Practice* (5th ed. 2020–date, Cheetah)

Susan M. Omilian & Jean P. Kamp, *Sex-Based Employment Discrimination* (1990–date, Westlaw)

Merrick T. Rossein, *Employment Discrimination Law and Litigation* (1990–date, Westlaw)

Andrew J. Ruzicho, Sr. et al., *Litigating Age Discrimination Cases* (1986–date, Westlaw)

One-Volume Treatises and Hornbooks

Age Discrimination in Employment Law (Eric E. Kindler ed., 2018–date, Bloomberg Law)

Martha Chamallas, *Principles of Employment Discrimination Law* (2019, West Academic)

Gender Identity & Sexual Orientation Discrimination in the Workplace (Christine Michelle Duffy ed., 2014, Bloomberg Law)

Lawrence Solotoff & Henry S. Kramer, *Sex Discrimination and Sexual Harassment in the Work Place* (1994–date, Lexis and LJP)

Sandra F. Sperino, *The Law of Employment Discrimination* (2019, West Academic)

Workplace Harassment Law (Gilbert L. Casellas & Diane M. Soubly eds., 2018–date, Bloomberg Law)

Service

Employment Discrimination Coordinator (Westlaw)

ENERGY AND NATURAL RESOURCES (KF1801–KF1873, KF5500–KF5510)

Multi-Volume Treatises

American Law of Mining (Rocky Mountain Mineral Law Foundation ed., 2d ed. 1984–date, Lexis)

George Cameron Coggins & Robert L. Glicksman, *Public Natural Resources Law* (2d ed. 2007–date, Westlaw)

Energy Law and Transactions (David J. Muchow & William A. Mogel eds., 1990–date, Lexis)

Neil E. Harl & Robert P. Achenbach, Jr., *Agricultural Law* (1980–date, Lexis)

Eugene Kuntz et al., *A Treatise on the Law of Oil and Gas* (1962–date, Lexis)

Patrick H. Martin & Bruce M. Kramer, *Williams & Meyers, Oil and Gas Law* (1959–date, Lexis)

Nancy Saint-Paul, *Summers Oil and Gas* (3d ed. 2004–date, Westlaw)

Hornbooks

Owen L. Anderson et al., *Oil and Gas Law and Taxation* (2017, West Academic)

Jan G. Laitos & Sandra B. Zellmer, *Natural Resources Law* (2015, West Academic)

Sandra B. Zellmer & Jan G. Laitos, *Principles of Natural Resources Law* (2d ed. 2020, West Academic)

ENVIRONMENTAL LAW (KF3775–KF3816)

Multi-Volume Treatises

Environmental Law Institute, *Law of Environmental Protection* (semiannual, Westlaw)

Jeffrey M. Gaba & Donald W. Stever, *Law of Solid Waste, Pollution Prevention, & Recycling* (1992–date, Westlaw)

Michael B. Gerrard, *Brownfields Law and Practice* (1999–date, Lexis)

Frank P. Grad et al., *Treatise on Environmental Law* (1973–date, Lexis)

The Law of Hazardous Waste (Susan M. Cooke ed., 1987–date, Lexis)

James T. O'Reilly, *Superfund & Brownfields Cleanup* (annual, Westlaw)

William H. Rodgers, Jr. & Elizabeth Burleson, *Environmental Law* (2d ed. 2016–date, Westlaw)

Donald W. Stever, *Law of Chemical Regulation & Hazardous Waste* (1986–date, Westlaw)

Waters and Water Rights (Amy K. Kelley ed., 3d ed. 2009–date, Lexis)

One-Volume Treatises

Daniel Riesel, *Environmental Enforcement: Civil and Criminal* (1996–date, Lexis)

A. Dan Tarlock & Jason Anthony Robinson, *Law of Water Rights & Resources* (annual, Westlaw)

William L. Want, *Law of Wetlands Regulation* (1989–date, Westlaw)

EVIDENCE (KF8931–KF8969, KF9660–KF9678)

Multi-Volume Treatises

Barbara E. Bergman et al., *Wharton's Criminal Evidence* (15th ed. 1997–date, Westlaw)

David L. Faigman et al., *Modern Scientific Evidence* (annual, Westlaw)

Clifford S. Fischman & Anne T. McKenna, *Jones on Evidence: Civil & Criminal* (7th ed. 1992–date, Westlaw)

Paul C. Giannelli et al., *Scientific Evidence* (5th ed. 2007–date, Lexis)

Michael H. Graham, *Handbook of Federal Evidence* (8th ed. 2016–date, Westlaw)

David M. Greenwald et al., *Testimonial Privileges* (annual, Westlaw)

Edward J. Imwinkelried et al., *Courtroom Criminal Evidence* (6th ed. 2016–date, Lexis)

McCormick on Evidence (Robert P. Mosteller ed., 8th ed. 2020–date, Westlaw)

Christopher B. Mueller & Laird C. Kirkpatrick, *Federal Evidence* (4th ed. 2013–date, Westlaw)

The New Wigmore: A Treatise on Evidence (Richard D. Friedman ed., 1st–3d eds. 2011–date, Westlaw)

Stephen A. Saltzburg et al., *Federal Rules of Evidence Manual* (12th ed. 2019–date, Lexis)

Weinstein's Federal Evidence (Mark S. Brodin et al. eds., 2d ed. 1997–date, Lexis)

John Henry Wigmore et al., *Evidence in Trials at Common Law* (4th ed. 1961–date, Cheetah)

One-Volume Treatises and Hornbooks

Graham C. Lilly et al., *Principles of Evidence* (8th ed. 2019, West Academic)

McCormick on Evidence (Robert P. Mosteller ed., 8th ed. 2020, West Academic)

Christopher B. Mueller et al., *Evidence* (6th ed. 2018, WK Study Aids)

Christopher B. Mueller et al., *Evidence: Practice Under the Rules* (5th ed. 2018, Cheetah)

Roger Park et al., *Evidence Law* (4th ed. 2018, West Academic)

Paul F. Rothstein, *Federal Rules of Evidence 3d* (annual, Westlaw)

Jack B. Weinstein & Margaret A. Berger, *Weinstein's Evidence Manual* (1987–date, Lexis)

FAMILY LAW (KF501–KF553)

Multi-Volume Treatises

Adoption Law and Practice (Joan H. Hollinger ed., 1988–date, Lexis)

Michael Asimow et al., *Valuation and Distribution of Marital Property* (1984–date, Lexis)

Jeff Atkinson, *Modern Child Custody Practice* (2d ed. 2000–date, Lexis)

Family Law and Practice (Arnold H. Rutkin ed., 1985–date, Lexis)

Ann M. Haralambie, *Handling Child Custody, Abuse & Adoption Cases* (3d ed. 2009–date, Westlaw)

Sandra Morgan Little et al., *Child Custody and Visitation Law and Practice* (1983–date, Lexis)

Brett R. Turner, *Equitable Distribution of Property* (4th ed. 2019–date, Westlaw)

One-Volume Treatises and Hornbook

Linda D. Elrod, *Child Custody Practice and Procedure* (annual, Westlaw)

Courtney G. Joslin et al., *Lesbian, Gay, Bisexual and Transgender Family Law* (annual, Westlaw)

Laura W. Morgan, *Child Support Guidelines: Interpretation & Application* (2d ed. 2013–date, Cheetah and Westlaw)

J. Thomas Oldham, *Divorce, Separation and the Distribution of Property* (1987–date, Lexis and LJP)

D. Kelly Weisberg, *Domestic Violence Law* (2019, West Academic)

FEDERAL PRACTICE (KF8820–KF9058, KF9650)

Multi-Volume Treatises

Business & Commercial Litigation in Federal Courts (Robert L. Haig ed., 4th ed. 2011–date, Westlaw)

Steven Alan Childress & Martha S. Davis, *Federal Standards of Review* (4th ed. 2010–date, Lexis)

Lester S. Jayson & Robert C. Longstreth, *Handling Federal Tort Claims: Administrative and Judicial Remedies* (1964–date, Lexis)

James Wm. Moore et al., *Moore's Manual: Federal Practice and Procedure* (1962–date, Lexis)

Moore's Federal Practice (Daniel R. Coquillette et al. eds., 3d ed. 1997–date, Lexis)

Kent Sinclair, *Sinclair on Federal Civil Practice* (5th ed. 2008–date, PLI Plus)

Charles Alan Wright et al., *Federal Practice and Procedure* (1st–4th eds. 1986–date, Westlaw)

One-Volume Treatises and Hornbooks

Erwin Chemerinsky, *Federal Jurisdiction* (7th ed. 2016, WK Study Aids)

Harry T. Edwards & Linda A. Elliott, *Federal Standards of Review* (annual, Westlaw)

Federal Appellate Practice (Philip Allen Lacovara ed., 2d ed. 2013, Bloomberg Law)

Gregory P. Joseph, *Sanctions: The Federal Law of Litigation Abuse* (6th ed. 2020, Lexis)

David G. Knibb, *Federal Court of Appeals Manual* (6th ed. 2007–date, Westlaw)

Eric J. Magnuson & David F. Herr, *Federal Appeals: Jurisdiction & Practice* (annual, Westlaw)

James F. Pfander, *Principles of Federal Jurisdiction* (3d ed. 2017, West Academic)

Stephen M. Shapiro et al., *Supreme Court Practice* (11th ed. 2019, Bloomberg Law)

Charles Alan Wright & Mary Kay Kane, *Law of Federal Courts* (8th ed. 2011, West Academic)

FOOD AND DRUG LAW (KF3861–KF3896)

Multi-Volume Treatises

Iver P. Cooper, *Biotechnology and the Law* (1989–date, Westlaw)

James T. O'Reilly & Katharine A. Van Tassel, *Food & Drug Administration* (semiannual, Westlaw)

Frank C. Woodside, III, *Drug Product Liability* (1974–date, Lexis)

One-Volume Treatises

Arnold & Porter Kaye Scholer, LLP, *Pharmaceutical and Biotech Patent Law* (annual, PLI Plus)

Pharmaceutical and Medical Device Law: Regulation of Research, Development, and Marketing (Michael E. Clark ed., 2d ed. 2015, Bloomberg Law)

John R. Thomas, *Pharmaceutical Patent Law* (3d ed. 2015, Bloomberg Law)

Services

Food Drug and Cosmetic Law Reporter (Cheetah)

Medical Devices Reporter (Cheetah)

GOVERNMENT BENEFITS (KF3600–KF3750)

Multi-Volume Treatises

Dianna Cannon, *Social Security Disability Claims* (annual, Westlaw)

Harvey L. McCormick et al., *Medicare & Medicaid Claims & Procedures* (4th ed. 2005–date, Westlaw)

Harvey L. McCormick et al., *Social Security Claims and Procedures* (6th ed. 2009–date, Westlaw)

National Organization of Social Security Claimants' Representatives, *Social Security Practice Guide* (1984–date, Lexis)

One-Volume Treatise

Barton F. Stichman et al., *Veterans Benefits Manual* (annual, Lexis)

Services

Medicare and Medicaid Guide (Cheetah)

Social Security Reporter (Cheetah)

Unemployment Insurance Reporter (Cheetah)

GOVERNMENT CONTRACTS (KF841–KF869.5)

Multi-Volume Treatises

John T. Boese, *Civil False Claims and Qui Tam Actions* (4th ed. 2011–date, Cheetah and Westlaw)

Steven W. Feldman, *Government Contract Awards: Negotiation and Sealed Bidding* (annual, Westlaw)

Government Contracts: Law, Administration, Procedure (Walter A. I. Wilson ed., 1962–date, Lexis)

One-Volume Treatises

Joel M. Androphy, *Federal False Claims Act and Qui Tam Actions* (2005–date, Lexis and LJP)

John Cibinic, Jr. et al., *Administration of Government Contracts* (5th ed. 2016, Cheetah)

John Cibinic, Jr. et al., *Formation of Government Contracts* (4th ed. 2011, Cheetah)

Steven W. Feldman, *Government Contract Guidebook* (annual, Westlaw)

Harlan Gottlieb et al., *Government Contract Compliance Handbook* (5th ed. 2014–date, Westlaw)

W. Noel Keyes et al., *Government Contracts Under the Federal Acquisition Regulation* (3d ed. 2003–date, Westlaw)

Services

Government Contracts Reporter (Cheetah)

HEALTH CARE (KF3821–KF3838)

Multi-Volume Treatises

American Health Lawyers Association, *Health Law Practice Guide* (2d ed. 2008–date, Westlaw)

Aspen Health Law Center, *Hospital Law Manual* (1974–date, Cheetah)

Mary Ann Chirba et al., *Health Care Reform: Law and Practice* (2013–date, Lexis)

David W. Louisell et al., *Medical Malpractice* (1960–date, Lexis)

Medical Malpractice: Guide to Medical Issues (Lee S. Goldsmith ed., 1986–date, Lexis)

John J. Miles, *Health Care and Antitrust Law* (1992–date, Westlaw)

Steven E. Pegalis, *American Law of Medical Malpractice* (3d ed. 2005–date, Westlaw)

Treatise on Health Care Law (Alexander M. Capron & Irwin M. Birmbaum eds., 1991–date, Lexis)

One-Volume Treatises and Hornbook

Scott Becker, *Health Care Law: A Practical Guide* (2d ed. 1998–date, Lexis)

Barry R. Furrow et al., *Health Law* (3d ed. 2015, West Academic)

Richard M. Patterson, *Harney's Medical Malpractice* (5th ed. 2011–date, Lexis)

Fay A. Rozovsky, *Consent to Treatment: A Practical Guide* (5th ed. 2015–date, Cheetah)

Isabelle Scott & Nancy McKenna, *Domestic Violence: Practice and Procedure* (annual, Westlaw)

Scott Skinner-Thompson, *AIDS and the Law* (6th ed. 2020–date, Cheetah)

Services

Health Care Compliance Reporter (Cheetah)

IMMIGRATION (KF4800–KF4848)

Multi-Volume Treatises

Austin T. Fragomen, Jr. et al., *Immigration Law & Business* (2d ed. 2011–date, Westlaw)

Austin T. Fragomen, Jr. et al., *Immigration Procedures Handbook* (annual, Westlaw)

Charles Gordon et al., *Immigration Law and Procedure* (rev. ed. 1966–date, Lexis)

National Immigration Project of the National Lawyers Guild, *Immigration Law & Defense* (semiannual, Westlaw)

One-Volume Treatises

Austin T. Fragomen et al., *Fragomen on Immigration Fundamentals: A Guide to Law and Practice* (5th ed. 2015–date, PLI Plus)

Sarah B. Ignatius et al., *Immigration Law & the Family* (annual, Westlaw)

Dan Kesselbrenner & Lory D. Rosenberg, *Immigration Law & Crimes* (semiannual, Westlaw)

Charles M. Miller et al. *Immigration Law in the Workplace* (2009–date, Cheetah)

Richard D. Steel, *Steel on Immigration Law* (annual, Westlaw)

Service

Immigration Law Service 2d (Westlaw)

INSURANCE (KF1146–KF1238)

Multi-Volume Treatises

Franklin L. Best, Jr., *Life and Health Insurance Law* (annual, Westlaw)

Benjamin Harnett & Irving I. Lesnick, *The Law of Life and Health Insurance* (1978–date, Lexis)

Mitchell L. Lathrop, *Insurance Coverage for Environmental Claims* (1992–date, Lexis)

David L. Leitner et al., *Law & Practice of Insurance Coverage Litigation* (2000–date, Westlaw)

New Appleman Law of Liability Insurance (2010–date, Lexis)

New Appleman on Insurance Law (Jeffrey E. Thomas ed., 2009–date, Lexis)

Barry R. Ostrager & Thomas R. Newman, *Handbook on Insurance Coverage Disputes* (19th ed. 2019–date, Cheetah)

Steven Plitt et al., *Couch on Insurance 3d* (1995–date, Westlaw)

Responsibilities of Insurance Agents and Brokers (Bertram Harnett ed., 1974–date, Lexis)

Tod I. Zuckerman, *Environmental Insurance Litigation: Law & Practice* (2d ed. 2009–date, Westlaw)

One-Volume Treatises

John H. Mathias, Jr. et al., *Insurance Coverage Disputes* (1996–date, Lexis and LJP)

Graydon S. Staring & Dean Hansell, *Law of Reinsurance* (annual, Westlaw)

INTELLECTUAL PROPERTY (KF2971–KF3193)

Generally

Multi-Volume Treatises

Jay Dratler, Jr. & Stephen M. McJohn, *Intellectual Property Law: Commercial, Creative, and Industrial Property* (1991–date, Lexis and LJP)

Jay Dratler, Jr. & Stephen M. McJohn, *Licensing of Intellectual Property* (1994–date, Lexis and LJP)

Roger M. Milgrim & Eric E. Bensen, *Milgrim on Licensing* (1990–date, Lexis)

One-Volume Treatises and Hornbooks

Jay Dratler, Jr. & Stephen M. McJohn, *Cyberlaw: Intellectual Property in the Digital Millenium* (2000–date, Lexis and LJP)

Michael A. Epstein, *Epstein on Intellectual Property* (5th ed. 2005–date, Cheetah)

Patrick J. Flinn, *Handbook of Intellectual Property Claims and Remedies* (2000–date, Cheetah)

Intellectual Property Law in Cyberspace (G. Peter Albert, Jr. ed., 3d ed. 2017–date, Bloomberg Law)

Gary Myers, *Principles of Intellectual Property Law* (3d ed. 2017, West Academic)

Xuan-Thao N. Nguyen et al., *Intellectual Property, Software, and Information Licensing: Law and Practice* (2d ed. 2018–date, Bloomberg Law)

Roger E. Schechter & John R. Thomas, *Intellectual Property: The Law of Copyrights, Patents and Trademarks* (2003, West Academic)

Copyright

Multi-Volume Treatises

Howard B. Abrams, *The Law of Copyright* (1991–date, Westlaw)

Paul Goldstein, *Goldstein on Copyright* (3d ed. 2005–date, Cheetah)

John W. Hazard, Jr., *Copyright Law in Business and Practice* (rev. ed. 1998–date, Westlaw)

Melville B. Nimmer & David Nimmer, *Nimmer on Copyright* (1963–date, Lexis)

William F. Patry, *Patry on Copyright* (2006–date, Westlaw)

One-Volume Treatises and Hornbook

Bruce P. Keller & Jeffrey P. Cunard, *Copyright Law: A Practitioner's Guide* (2d ed. 2015–date, PLI Plus)

William F. Patry, *Patry on Fair Use* (annual, Westlaw)

Roger E. Schechter & John R. Thomas, *Principles of Copyright Law* (2010, West Academic)

Service

Copyright Law Reporter (Cheetah)

Patents

Multi-Volume Treatises

Donald S. Chisum, *Chisum on Patents* (1978–date, Lexis)

Irah H. Donner, *Patent Prosecution: Law, Practice, and Procedure* (11th ed. 2019–date, Bloomberg Law)

Ethan Horwitz et al., *Horwitz on Patent Litigation* (1971–date, Lexis)

John Gladstone Mills III et al., *Patent Law Fundamentals* (2d ed. 1980–date, Westlaw)

R. Carl Moy, *Moy's Walker on Patents* (4th ed. 2003–date, Westlaw)

One-Volume Treatises and Hornbooks

Robert L. Harmon & Laura A. Lydigsen, *Patents and the Federal Circuit* (14th ed. 2019–date, Bloomberg Law)

Ronald B. Hildreth & David Aker, *Patent Law: A Practitioner's Guide* (4th ed. 2012–date, PLI Plus)

Janice M. Mueller, *Patent Law* (6th ed. 2020, WK Study Aids)

Patent Litigation (Charles S. Barquist ed., 3d ed. 2015–date, PLI Plus)

Roger E. Schechter & John R. Thomas, *Principles of Patent Law* (3d ed. 2019, West Academic)

Lawrence M. Sung & Jeff E. Schwartz, *Patent Law Handbook* (annual, Westlaw)

Trademarks and Trade Secrets

Multi-Volume Treatises

Melvin F. Jager, *Trade Secrets Law* (1985–date, Westlaw)

Anne Gilson LaLonde, *Gilson on Trademarks* (1974–date, Lexis)

J. Thomas McCarthy, *McCarthy on Trademarks and Unfair Competition* (5th ed. 2017–date, Westlaw)

Roger M. Milgrim & Eric E. Bensen, *Milgrim on Trade Secrets* (1967–date, Lexis)

One-Volume Treatises

Adam L. Brookman, *Trademark Law: Protection, Enforcement and Licensing* (2d ed. 2014–date, Cheetah)

Siegrun D. Kane, *Kane on Trademark Law: A Practitioner's Guide* (6th ed. 2013–date, PLI Plus)

Henry H. Perritt, Jr., *Trade Secrets: A Practitioner's Guide* (2d ed. 2005–date, PLI Plus)

James Pooley, *Trade Secrets* (1997–date, Lexis and LJP)

Service

Trademark Law Guide (Cheetah)

INTERNET (KF390.5 .C6)

Multi-Volume Treatises

Ian C. Ballon, *E-Commerce & Internet Law* (2d ed. 2009–date, Westlaw)

Peter N. Barnes-Brown et al., *Internet Law and Practice* (2002–date, Westlaw)

David Bender, *Computer Law: A Guide to Cyberlaw and Data Privacy Law* (1978–date, Lexis)

Megan Costello, *Data Security and Privacy Law* (annual, Westlaw)

George B. Delta & Jeffrey H. Matsuura, *Law of the Internet* (4th ed. 2017–date, Cheetah and Westlaw)

Raymond T. Nimmer et al., *Information Law* (2002–date, Westlaw)

Michael D. Scott, *Scott on Information Technology Law* (3d ed. 2007–date, Cheetah and Westlaw)

One-Volume Treatises and Hornbook

Robert L. Ellis, *Internet and Online Law* (1996–date, Lexis and LJP)

Henry H. Perritt, Jr., *Digital Communications Law* (rev. ed. 2010–date, Cheetah)

Michael L. Rustad, *Global Internet Law* (3d ed. 2020, West Academic)

F. Lawrence Street et al., *Law of the Internet* (3d ed. 2001–date, Lexis)

Kent D. Stuckey & Robert L. Ellis, *Internet and Online Law* (1996–date, Lexis and LJP)

Jane K. Winn & Benjamin Wright, *The Law of Electronic Commerce* (4th ed. 2001–date, Cheetah)

Service

Guide to Computer Law (Cheetah)

LEGAL ETHICS (KF305–KF314)

Multi-Volume Treatises

Geoffrey C. Hazard, Jr. et al., *The Law of Lawyering* (4th ed. 2015–date, Cheetah)

Ronald E. Mallen, *Legal Malpractice* (annual, Westlaw)

One-Volume Treatises and Hornbook

B. Lance Entrekin, *Legal Malpractice Litigation* (2018–date, Bloomberg Law)

Charles Gardner Geyh et al., *Judicial Conduct and Ethics* (5th ed. 2013–date, Lexis)

Robert W. Hillman & Allison Martin Rhodes, *Hillman on Lawyer Mobility: The Law and Ethics of Partner Withdrawals and Law Firm Breakups* (3d ed. 2018–date, Cheetah)

Ronald D. Rotunda & John S. Dzienkowski, *Legal Ethics: The Lawyer's Deskbook on Professional Responsibility* (annual, Westlaw)

Gregory C. Sisk et al., *Legal Ethics, Professional Responsibility, and the Legal Profession* (2018, West Academic)

Jacob A. Stein & Andrew M. Beato, *The Law of Law Firms* (annual, Westlaw)

LOCAL GOVERNMENT (KF5300–KF5332)

Multi-Volume Treatises

John Martinez, *Local Government Law* (2d ed. 2012–date, Westlaw)

McQuillin The Law of Municipal Corporations (3d ed. 1949–date, Westlaw)

Sandra M. Stevenson & Wendy Van Wie, *Antieau on Local Government Law* (2d ed. 1998–date, Lexis)

One-Volume Treatise and Hornbook

Vincent R. Fontana, *Municipal Liability: Law and Practice* (4th ed. 2013–date, Cheetah and Westlaw)

Osborne M. Reynolds, Jr., *Local Government Law* (5th ed. 2019, West Academic)

MEDIA LAW (KF2750, KF3084)

Multi-Volume Treatises

Mark A. Fischer et al., *Perle, Williams & Fischer on Publishing Law* (4th ed. 2013–date, Cheetah)

Lee Levine et al., *Newsgathering and the Law* (5th ed. 2018–date, Lexis)

Michael D. Scott, *Scott on Multimedia Law* (3d ed. 2008–date, Cheetah)

MILITARY AND NATIONAL SECURITY LAW (KF4858, KF7201–KF7695)

Multi-Volume Treatises

Francis A. Gilligan & Frederic I. Lederer, *Court-Martial Procedure* (4th ed. 2015–date, Lexis)

David S. Kris & J. Douglas Wilson, *National Security Investigations & Prosecutions* (3d ed. 2019–date, Westlaw)

Stephen A. Saltzburg et al., *Military Rules of Evidence Manual* (8th ed. 2015–date, Lexis)

One-Volume Treatises and Hornbook

Geoffrey Corn et al., *National Security Law: Principles and Policy* (2d ed. 2019, WK Study Aids)

David A. Schlueter, *Military Criminal Justice: Practice and Procedure* (8th ed. 2012–date, Lexis)

David A. Schleuter et al., *Military Crimes and Defenses* (2d ed. 2018–date, Lexis)

NONPROFIT ORGANIZATIONS (KF1388–1390, KF6449)

Multi-Volume Treatise

William W. Bassett et al., *Religious Organizations and the Law* (2d ed. 2017–date, Westlaw)

Marilyn E. Phelan, *Nonprofit Organizations: Law & Taxation* (semiannual, Westlaw)

Hugh K. Webster, *The Law of Associations* (1975–date, Lexis)

One-Volume Treatise

Marilyn E. Phelan, *Representing Nonprofit Organizations* (1994–date, Westlaw)

PARTNERSHIPS AND LIMITED LIABILITY COMPANIES (KF1371–KF1381)

Multi-Volume Treatises

Carter G. Bishop & Daniel S. Kleinberger, *Limited Liability Companies: Tax and Business Law* (1994–date, Checkpoint and Westlaw)

J. William Callison & Maureen A. Sullivan, *Limited Liability Companies: A State-by-State Guide to Law and Practice* (annual, Westlaw)

Christine Hurt et al., *Bromberg & Ribstein on Partnership* (3d ed. 2020–date, Cheetah)

Nicholas G. Karambelas, *Limited Liability Companies: Law, Practice and Forms* (2d ed. 2004–date, Westlaw)

Larry E. Ribstein & Robert R. Keatinge, *Ribstein & Keatinge on Limited Liability Companies* (semiannual, Westlaw)

One-Volume Treatises

J. William Callison & Maureen A. Sullivan, *Partnership Law & Practice* (annual, Westlaw)

Thomas A. Humphreys, *Limited Liability Companies and Limited Liability Partnerships* (1998–date, Lexis and LJP)

Christine Hurt et al., *Bromberg and Ribstein on Limited Liability Partnerships, the Revised Uniform Partnership Act, and the Uniform Limited Partnership Act* (2d ed. 2018–date, Cheetah)

Robert W. Wood, *Limited Liability Companies: Formation, Operation, and Conversion* (3d ed. 2011–date, Cheetah)

PRODUCTS LIABILITY (KF1296–KF1297)

Multi-Volume Treatises

American Law of Products Liability 3d (1987–date, Westlaw)

Louis R. Frumer et al., *Products Liability* (1960–date, Lexis)

David G. Owen & Mary J. Davis, *Owen & Davis on Products Liability* (4th ed. 2014–date, Westlaw)

Products Liability Practice Guide (John F. Vargo ed., 1988–date, Lexis)

One-Volume Treatise and Hornbooks

Lewis Bass & Thomas Parker Redick, *Products Liability: Design and Manufacturing Defects* (annual, Westlaw)

Michael I. Krauss, *Principles of Products Liability* (3d ed. 2019, West Academic)

David G. Owen, *Products Liability Law* (3d ed. 2015, West Academic)

Services

Consumer Product Safety Guide (Cheetah)

Products Liability Reports (Cheetah)

PROPERTY (KF560–KF720, KF5599)

Multi-Volume Treatises

William G. Baker et al., *Real Estate Financing: Text, Forms, Tax Analysis* (1973–date, Lexis)

Andrew R. Berman, *Friedman on Leases* (6th ed. 2017–date, PLI Plus)

John A. Borron, Jr., *The Law of Future Interests* (3d ed. 2002–date, Westlaw)

David L. Callies et al., *Nichols on Eminent Domain* (3d ed. 1964–date, Lexis)

Milton R. Friedman & James Charles Smith, *Friedman and Smith on Contracts and Conveyances of Real Property* (8th ed. 2017–date, PLI Plus)

Karl B. Holtzschue, *Purchase and Sale of Real Property* (1987–date, Lexis)

Michael T. Madison et al., *The Law of Real Estate Financing* (rev. ed. 1994–date, Westlaw)

Grant S. Nelson et al., *Real Estate Finance Law* (6th ed. 2014, Westlaw)

Joyce D. Palomar, *Patton and Palomar on Land Titles* (3d ed. 2002–date, Westlaw)

Joyce D. Palomar, *Title Insurance Law* (annual, Westlaw)

Patrick J. Rohan et al., *Real Estate Brokerage Law and Practice* (1985–date, Lexis)

Thompson on Real Property (David A. Thomas ed., 2d/3d Thomas eds. 2006–date, Lexis)

Michael Allan Wolf, *Powell on Real Property* (1949–date, Lexis)

One-Volume Treatises and Hornbooks

Brook Boyd, *Real Estate Financing* (1997–date, Lexis)

Jon W. Bruce & James W. Ely, Jr., *The Law of Easements and Licenses in Land* (2001–date, Westlaw)

Barlow Burke, *Law of Real Estate Brokers* (4th ed. 2020–date, Cheetah)

Barlow Burke et al., *Law of Title Insurance* (3d ed. 2000–date, Cheetah and Westlaw)

Carolyn L. Carter et al., *Repossessions* (9th ed. 2017–date, NCLC)

Steven J. Eagle, *Regulatory Takings* (5d ed. 2012–date, Lexis)

Sheldon F. Kurtz et al., *The Law of Property: An Introductory Survey* (7th ed. 2018, West Academic)

National Housing Law Project, *HUD Housing Programs: Tenants' Rights* (5th ed. 2018–date, NCLC)

Grant S. Nelson et al., *Real Estate Finance Law* (6th ed. 2015, Westlaw)

Walter G. Robillard, *Clark on Surveying and Boundaries* (8th ed. 2014–date, Lexis)

Joseph William Singer, *Property* (5th ed. 2017, WK Study Aids)

Geoff Walsh et al., *Home Foreclosures* (2019, NCLC)

Dale A. Whitman et al., *The Law of Property* (4th ed. 2019, West Academic)

REMEDIES (KF9010–KF9039)

Multi-Volume Treatises

John J. Kircher & Christine M. Wiseman, *Punitive Damages: Law and Practice* (annual, Westlaw)

George E. Palmer, *The Law of Restitution* (1978–date, Cheetah)

Linda L. Schlueter, *Punitive Damages* (7th ed. 2015–date, Lexis)

Hornbooks

Dan B. Dobbs & Caprice L. Roberts, *Law of Remedies: Damages, Equity, Restitution* (3d ed. 2018, West Academic)

Russell L. Weaver et al., *Principles of Remedies Law* (3d ed. 2017, West Academic)

SECURITIES (KF1066–KF1084, KF1428–KF1457)

Multi-Volume Treatises

Harold S. Bloomenthal & Samuel Wolff, *Going Public and the Public Corporation* (1986–date, Westlaw)

Harold S. Bloomenthal & Samuel Wolff, *Going Public Handbook* (annual, Westlaw)

Harold S. Bloomenthal & Samuel Wolff, *Securities and Federal Corporate Law* (2d ed. 1998–date, Westlaw)

Harold S. Bloomenthal & Samuel Wolff, *Securities Law Handbook* (annual, Westlaw)

Broker-Dealer Regulation: A Guide to Law and Practice (Clifford E. Kirsch ed., 2d ed. 2011–date, PLI Plus)

Alan R. Bromberg et al., *Bromberg & Lowenfels on Securities Fraud* (2d ed. 1994–date, Westlaw)

James A. Fanto et al., *Broker-Dealer Law and Regulation* (5th ed. 2019–date, Cheetah)

Tamar Frankel & Arthur B. Laby, *The Regulation of Money Managers: Mutual Funds and Advisers* (3d ed. 2015–date, Cheetah)

Howard M. Friedman & Eric C. Chaffee, *Securities Regulation in Cyberspace* (4th ed. 2018–date, Cheetah)

Egon Guttman, *Modern Securities Transfers* (4th ed. 2010–date, Westlaw)

Robert J. Haft & Peter M. Fass, *Tax-Advantaged Securities* (1981–date, Westlaw)

Thomas Lee Hazen, *Treatise on the Law of Securities Regulation* (7th ed. 2016–date, Westlaw)

Thomas Lee Hazen & Jerry W. Markham, *Broker-Dealer Operations Under the Securities and Commodities Laws* (1995–date, Westlaw)

Investment Adviser Regulation: A Step-by-Step Guide to Compliance and the Law (Clifford E. Kirsch ed., 3d ed. 2011–date, PLI Plus)

Arnold S. Jacobs, *Disclosure and Remedies Under the Securities Laws* (1981–date, Westlaw)

Philip McBride Johnson et al., *Derivatives Regulation* (2004–date, Cheetah)

Donald C. Langevoort, *Insider Trading: Regulation, Enforcement, & Prevention* (1991–date, Westlaw)

Scott J. Lederman, *Hedge Fund Regulation* (2d ed. 2012–date, PLI Plus)

Thomas P. Lemke & Gerald T. Lins, *Regulation of Financial Planners* (1985–date, Westlaw)

Thomas P. Lemke et al., *Regulation of Investment Companies* (1995–date, Lexis)

David A. Lipton, *Broker Dealer Regulation* (1988–date, Westlaw)

Joseph C. Long et al., *Blue Sky Law* (1985–date, Westlaw)

Louis Loss et al., *Securities Regulation* (5th/6th eds. 2014–date)

Theodore S. Lynn et al., *Real Estate Investment Trusts* (1987–date, Westlaw)

Roger J. Magnuson, *Shareholder Litigation* (annual, Westlaw)

Jerry W. Markham, *Commodities Regulation: Fraud, Manipulation, and Other Claims* (1987–date, Westlaw)

Mutual Funds and Exchange Traded Funds Regulation (Clifford E. Kirsch ed., 3d ed. 2011–date, PLI Plus)

Marvin G. Pickholz et al., *Securities Crimes* (2d ed. 2013–date, Westlaw)

William M. Prifti, *Securities: Public & Private Offerings* (2d ed. 1995–date, Westlaw)

Robert N. Rapp et al., *Blue Sky Regulation* (2d ed. 2003–date, Lexis)

Marc I. Steinberg, *Securities Regulation: Liabilities and Remedies* (1984–date, Lexis and LJP)

Marc I. Steinberg & Ralph C. Ferrara, *Securities Practice: Federal and State Enforcement* (1985–date, Westlaw)

One-Volume Treatises and Hornbooks

Diane E. Ambler et al., *Sarbanes-Oxley Act: Planning and Compliance* (2006–date, Cheetah)

Harvey E. Bines & Steve Thel, *Investment Management Law and Regulation* (3d ed. 2015–date, Cheetah)

Gary M. Brown, *Securities Law and Practice Deskbook* (6th ed. 2012–date, PLI Plus)

Deborah A. DeMott, *Shareholder Derivative Actions: Law and Practice* (annual, Westlaw)

Peter M. Fass et al., *Real Estate Investment Trusts Handbook* (annual, Westlaw)

Gibson, Dunn & Crutcher LLP, *Securities Litigation: A Practitioner's Guide* (2d ed. 2016–date, PLI Plus)

Jeffrey J. Haas, *Corporate Finance* (2014, West Academic)

Thomas Lee Hazen, *The Law of Securities Regulation* (7th ed. 2017, West Academic)

Thomas Lee Hazen, *Principles of Securities Regulation* (rev. 4th ed. 2017, West Academic)

Charles J. Johnson, Jr. & Joseph McLaughlin, *Corporate Finance and the Securities Laws* (6th ed. 2019–date, Cheetah)

Thomas P. Lemke & Gerald T. Lins, *Regulation of Investment Advisers* (annual, Westlaw)

Louis Loss et al., *Fundamentals of Securities Regulation* (7th ed. 2018–date, Cheetah)

David A. Westerberg, *Initial Public Offerings: A Practical Guide to Going Public* (2d ed. 2012–date, PLI Plus)

Services

Blue Sky Law Reporter (Cheetah)

Commodity Futures Law Reporter (Cheetah)

Federal Securities Law Reporter (Cheetah)

Mutual Funds Guide (Cheetah)

TAXATION (KF6271–KF6645)

Multi-Volume Treatises

Bender's State Taxation: Principles and Practice (Charles W. Swenson ed., 2009–date, Lexis)

Boris I. Bittker & James Eustice, *Federal Income Taxation of Corporations & Shareholders* (7th ed. 2000–date, Checkpoint and Westlaw)

Boris I. Bittker & Lawrence Lokken, *Federal Taxation of Income, Estates, & Gifts* (2d/3d eds. 1989–date, Checkpoint and Westlaw)

Laurence E. Casey & Edward J. Smith, *Federal Tax Practice* (1955–date, Westlaw)

Erin M. Collins & Edward M. Robbins, Jr., *Internal Revenue Service: Practice and Procedure Deskbook* (5th ed. 2019, PLI Plus)

Ian M. Comisky et al., *Tax Fraud & Evasion* (6th ed, 1994–date, Checkpoint and Westlaw)

The Corporate Tax Practice Series (Louis S. Freeman & Eric Solomon eds., 2d ed. 2020–date, PLI Plus)

Andrew M. Eisenberg et al., *Federal Taxation of Corporations and Shareholders* (2016–date, Cheetah)

Walter Hellerstein & John A. Swain, *State Taxation* (3d ed. 1998–date, Checkpoint and Westlaw)

Joseph Isenbergh, *International Taxation: U.S. Taxation of Foreign Persons and Foreign Income* (5th ed. 2019–date, Cheetah)

Joel D. Kuntz & Robert J. Peroni, *U.S. International Taxation* (1991–date, Checkpoint and Westlaw)

Cym H. Lowell & Jack Governale, *U.S. International Taxation: Practice and Procedure* (1997–date, Checkpoint and Westlaw)

William S. McKee et al., *Federal Taxation of Partnerships and Partners* (4th ed. 2007–date, Checkpoint and Westlaw)

The Partnership Tax Practice Series (Louis S. Freeman & Clifford M. Warren eds., 2d ed. 2019–date, PLI Plus)

Jacob Rabkin & Mark Johnson, *Federal Income, Gift and Estate Taxation* (1942–date, Lexis)

Rufus von Thülen Rhoades & Marshall J. Langer, *U.S. International Taxation and Tax Treaties* (1996–date, Lexis)

Edward J. Smith, *Langer on Practical International Tax Planning* (5th ed. 2019–date, PLI Plus)

Arthur B. Willis et al., *Partnership Taxation* (8th ed. 2017–date, Checkpoint and Westlaw)

One-Volume Treatises and Hornbooks

Boris I. Bittker et al., *Federal Income Taxation of Individuals* (3d ed. 2002–date, Checkpoint and Westlaw)

F. Ladson Boyle & Jonathan G. Blattmachr, *Blattmachr on Income Taxation of Estates and Trusts* (17d ed. 2018–date, PLI Plus)

James S. Eustice et al., *Federal Income Taxation of S Corporations* (4th ed. 2001–date, Checkpoint and Westlaw)

Federal Tax Practice and Procedure (Leandra Lederman ed., 2003–date, Lexis)

Douglas A. Kahn & Jeffrey H. Kahn, *Principles of Corporate Taxation* (2d ed. 2019, West Academic)

Stephanie Hunter McMahon, *Principles of Tax Policy* (2018, West Academic)

Joshua D. Rosenberg & Dominic L. Daher, *The Law of Federal Income Taxation* (2008, West Academic)

Michael I. Saltzman & Leslie Book, *IRS Practice and Procedure* (rev. 2d ed. 2002–date, Checkpoint and Westlaw)

Richard B. Stephens et al., *Federal Estate and Gift Taxation* (9th ed. 2013–date, Checkpoint and Westlaw)

Donald B. Tobin & Samuel A. Donaldson, *Principles of Federal Income Taxation* (8th ed. 2017, West Academic)

Services

All States Tax Guide (Checkpoint and Westlaw)

Federal Estate and Gift Tax Reporter (Cheetah)

Federal Tax Coordinator 2d (Westlaw)

Standard Federal Tax Reporter (Cheetah)

State Tax Guide (Cheetah)

Tax Management Portfolios (Bloomberg Law)

United States Tax Reporter (Checkpoint and Westlaw)

TORTS (KF1246–KF1327)

Multi-Volume Treatises

Margie Searcy Alford, *A Guide to Toxic Torts* (1992–date, Lexis)

Business Torts (Joseph D. Zamore et al. eds., 1957–date, Lexis)

Lawrence G. Cetrulo, *Toxic Torts Litigation Guide* (annual, Westlaw)

Dan B. Dobbs et al., *The Law of Torts* (2d ed. 2011–date, Westlaw)

Michael Dore, *The Law of Toxic Torts* (1987–date, Westlaw)

Louis R. Frumer et al., *Personal Injury: Actions, Defenses, Damages* (1957–date, Lexis)

Karen A. Gottlieb, *Toxic Torts Practice Guide* (semiannual, Westlaw)

Fowler V. Harper et al., *Harper, James and Gray on Torts* (3d ed. 2006–date, Cheetah)

Richard E. Kaye et al., *Comparative Negligence Law and Practice* (1984–date, Lexis)

Norman J. Landau & Edward C. Martin, *Premises Liability: Law and Practice* (1987–date, Lexis)

Louis A. Lehr, Jr. & Alfredo J. Marquez-Sterling, *Premises Liability* (3d ed. 2002–date, Westlaw)

Barry A. Lindahl, *Modern Tort Law: Liability and Litigation* (annual, Westlaw)

Litigating Tort Cases (Roxanne Barton Conlin & Gregory S. Cusimano eds., 2003–date, Westlaw)

J. Thomas McCarthy & Roger E. Schechter, *The Rights of Publicity & Privacy* (annual, Westlaw)

Jerome H. Nates et al., *Damages in Tort Actions* (1982–date, Lexis)

Robert D. Sack, *Sack on Defamation: Libel, Slander, and Related Problems* (5th ed. 2017–date, PLI Plus)

Bruce W. Sanford, *Libel and Privacy* (2d ed. 1991–date, Cheetah)

Rodney A. Smolla, *Law of Defamation* (2d ed. 1999–date, Westlaw)

Stuart M. Speiser & James E. Rooks, Jr., *Recovery for Wrongful Death* (4th ed. 2005–date, Westlaw)

Stuart M. Speiser et al., *The American Law of Torts* (1983–date, Westlaw)

Jacob A. Stein, *Stein on Personal Injury Damages* (3d ed. 1997–date, Westlaw)

One-Volume Treatises and Hornbooks

Charlene Brownlee & Blaze D. Waleski, *Privacy Law* (2006–date, Lexis and LJP)

Dan B. Dobbs et al., *Handbook on Torts* (2d ed. 2016, West Academic)

David A. Elder, *Defamation: A Lawyer's Guide* (1993–date, Westlaw)

Richard A. Epstein, *Torts* (1999, WK Study Aids)

Proskauer Rose LLP, *Proskauer on Privacy* (2016–date, PLI Plus)

Victor E. Schwartz & Kathryn Kelly, *Comparative Negligence* (5th ed. 2010–date, Lexis)

Marshall S. Shapo, *Principles of Tort Law* (4th ed. 2016, West Academic)

TRUSTS AND ESTATES (KF726–KF780)

Multi-Volume Treatises

George G. Bogert et al., *The Law of Trusts and Trustees* (2d/3d eds. 1977–date, Westlaw)

A. James Casner & Jeffrey N. Pennell, *Estate Planning* (8th ed. 2012, Cheetah)

McDermott, Will & Emery LLP, *International Estate Planning* (2d ed. 1999–date, Lexis)

William H. Newton, III, *International Income Tax & Estate Planning* (rev. 2d ed. 2014–date, Westlaw)

Jeffrey A. Schoenblum, *Page on the Law of Wills* (1960–date, Lexis)

Austin Wakeman Scott et al., *Scott and Ascher on Trusts* (5th ed. 2006–date)

Robert W. Sheehan & Michael S. Schwartz, *Stocker on Drawing Wills and Trusts* (14th ed. 2015–date, PLI Plus)

One-Volume Treatises and Hornbooks

Jerome A. Manning et al., *Manning on Estate Planning* (7th ed. 2013–date, PLI Plus)

William M. McGovern et al., *Wills, Trusts and Estates* (5th ed. 2017, West Academic)

William M. McGovern et al., *Principles of Wills, Trusts and Estates* (2d ed. 2012, West Academic)

David Westfall et al., *Estate Planning Law & Taxation* (5th ed. 2017–date, Checkpoint and Westlaw)

ZONING AND LAND USE (KF5691–KF5710)

Multi-Volume Treatises

Sara C. Bronin & Dwight H. Merriam, *Rathkopf's The Law of Zoning and Planning* (4th ed. 1975–date, Westlaw)

Douglas Kmiec & Katherine Kmiec Turner, *Zoning and Planning Deskbook* (annual, Westlaw)

Patricia E. Salkin, *American Law of Zoning* (5th ed. 2008–date, Westlaw)

Norman Williams, Jr. & John M. Taylor, *American Land Planning Law* (rev. ed. 2003–date, Westlaw)

E. C. Yokley & Douglas Scott MacGregor, *Zoning Law and Practice* (4th ed. 1978–date, Lexis)

Zoning and Land Use Controls (Eric Damian Kelly ed., 1977–date, Lexis)

One-Volume Treatise and Hornbook

Julian Conrad Juergensmeyer et al., *Land Use Planning and Development Regulation Law* (4th ed. 2018, West Academic)

Daniel R. Mandelker & Michael Allan Wolf, *Land Use Law* (6th ed. 2015–date, Lexis)

Table of Cases

Resource Index

References are to Pages
Boldface references are to Illustrations
See also Subject Index

Journal articles and resources in the appendix
are not indexed

Subject Index

References are to Pages
Boldface references are to Illustrations
See also Resource Index